THIRD EDITION

An Introduction to Theories of Learning

B. R. HERGENHAHN

Hamline University

PRENTICE HALL, Englewood Cliffs, New Jersey 07632

Library of Congress Cataloging-in-Publication Data

HERGENHAHN, B. R. (date)
   An introduction to theories of learning.

   Bibliography.
   Includes indexes.
   1. Learning, Psychology of.   I. Title.
LB1051.H42 1988   370.15′23   87–32691
ISBN   0–13–498569–9

Editorial/production supervision
   and interior design: F. Hubert
Manufacturing buyer: Ray Keating
Cover design: Ben Santora
Cover photo: Slide Graphics
   of New England, Inc.

**Dedicated to my students
from whom I have learned so much.**

Printed in the United States of America

10   9   8   7   6   5

ISBN   0-13-498569-9   01

PRENTICE-HALL INTERNATIONAL (UK) LIMITED, *London*
PRENTICE-HALL OF AUSTRALIA PTY. LIMITED, *Sydney*
PRENTICE-HALL CANADA INC., *Toronto*
PRENTICE-HALL HISPANOAMERICANA, S.A., *Mexico*
PRENTICE-HALL OF INDIA PRIVATE LIMITED, *New Delhi*
PRENTICE-HALL OF JAPAN, INC., *Tokyo*
SIMON & SCHUSTER ASIA PTE. LTD., *Singapore*
EDITORA PRENTICE-HALL DO BRASIL, LTDA., *Rio de Janeiro*

Contents

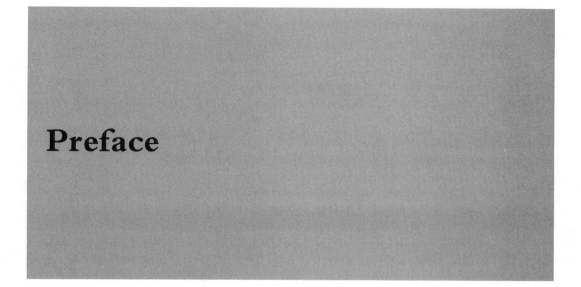

Preface

The four main goals of this edition of *An Introduction to Theories of Learning* remain the same as those of the first two editions. Those goals are (a) to define learning and to show how the learning process is studied (chapters 1 and 2); (b) to place learning theory in historical perspective (chapter 3); (c) to present the essential features of the major theories of learning (chapters 4 through 15); and (d) to examine some of the relationships that exist between learning theory and educational practices (chapter 16).

New developments and old omissions have necessitated several changes in this edition. New topics found in this edition include:

Popper's Philosophy of Science

Animal Research Prior to Thorndike's

Concurrent Schedules of Reinforcement

Herrnstein's Matching Law

Mowrer's Theory of Learning

The Rescorla–Wagner Theory of Classical Conditioning

Mackintosh's, Kamin's, Wagner's, and Bolles's Explanations of Various Classical Conditioning Phenomena

Seligman's Research on Learned Helplessness

A Review of Estes's recent views on Learning and Decision Making

Latent Extinction

Bolles's Theory of Learning

Bandura's Views on How the News and Entertainment Media Influence Behavior

An entirely new chapter on the Information-Processing Approach to the Study of Learning featuring the work of Donald A. Norman

Left-Brain, Right-Brain Functioning and a discussion of what implications that functioning may have for education

Computer-Assisted Instruction

Many individuals were instrumental in the preparation of this edition. Donald Norman, University of California, San Diego, reviewed the newly added chapter summarizing his work on learning and memory. Norman made numerous recommendations, which have resulted in a more accurate reflection of his ideas. Richard C. Sprinthall, American International College, and John Mueller, University of Missouri, have volunteered observations on earlier editions of this text before they became "official" reviewers for this edition. The comments of Sprinthall and Mueller have been extremely helpful through the years, as they were for this edition. For their informed reactions to various parts of the current edition, I would like to express my gratitude to the following individuals: Richard Heck, Hansfield State University; Robert Hamm, Virginia Commonwealth University; Stanley Pliskoff, University of Maine; and Michael Fanselow, Dartmouth College. None of the reviewers are responsible for any discrepancies that remain in the book; I alone am to blame for the final product.

As usual I would like to express my thanks to my colleagues in the Psychology Department at Hamline University. Jerry Greiner, Kim Guenther, Chuck LaBounty, and Matt Olson never complain about the fact that their workload goes up when my time and energy are diverted by projects such as this one. Again I would like to express my appreciation to Madelon Cassavant who miraculously transforms what I give her into something legible and then revises that material again and again as the reviews come in. I would also like to thank Linda Samson who helped solve the many problems that occur as a manuscript evolves.

Finally, I would like to renew my thanks to James J. Jenkins, now at the University of South Florida, who was largely responsible for the form that the first edition of this text took. The Jenkins's influence has continued to manifest itself in the current edition of this text, and it is still appreciated.

B. R. HERGENHAHN
Hamline University

1

What Is Learning?

Learning is one of the most important areas in present day psychology and yet it is an extremely difficult concept to define. The *American Heritage Dictionary* defines learning as follows: "To gain knowledge, comprehension, or mastery through experience or study." Most psychologists, however, would find this definition unacceptable because of the nebulous terms it contains, such as knowledge, comprehension, and mastery. Instead, the trend in recent years is to accept a definition of learning that refers to changes in observable behavior. The most popular of these definitions is the one suggested by Kimble (1961, p. 6), which defines learning *as a relatively permanent change in* **behavioral potentiality** *that occurs as a result of* **reinforced practice.** Although popular, this definition is far from universally accepted. Before reviewing sources of disagreement over Kimble's definition, let us look at it a bit more carefully.

First, learning is indexed by a change in *behavior;* in other words, the results of learning must always be translated into observable behavior. After learning, learners are capable of doing something that they could not do before learning took place. Second, this behavioral change is *relatively permanent;* that is, it is neither transitory nor fixed. Third, the change in behavior need not occur immediately following the learning experience. Although there may be a *potential* to act differently, this potential to act may not be translated into behavior immediately. Fourth, the change in behavior (or behavior potentiality) results from *experience* or practice. Fifth, the experience, or practice, must be reinforced; that is, only those responses that lead to reinforcement will be learned. Although the terms "reward" and "reinforcement" are often used synonymously there are at least two reasons why they should not be. In Pavlov's work, for example, a reinforcer is defined as any unconditioned stimulus, that is, any stimulus that elicits a natural and automatic reaction from an organism. In Pavlovian research it is not uncommon for stimuli such as a mild acid or electric shock to be used as unconditioned stimuli. It is accurate to call such stimuli reinforcers but they can hardly be considered rewards, if rewards are thought of as desirable. The Skinnerians also oppose equating the terms reinforcer and reward. For them, a reinforcer strengthens any behavior that immediately precedes the reinforcers occurrence. In contrast, a reward is usually thought of as something that is given or received only for a worthy accomplishment that required a considerable investment of time and energy or for an act deemed desirable by society. Furthermore, since such desirable behavior typically occurs long before it is acknowledged by reward, reward cannot be said to strengthen it. For the Skinnerians, then, reinforcers strengthen behavior but rewards do not. Skinner (1986) elaborates these points:

> The strengthening effect [of reinforcement] is missed . . . when reinforcers are called *rewards*. People are rewarded, but behavior is reinforced. If, as you walk along the street, you look down and find some money, and if money is reinforcing, you will tend to look down again for some time, but we should not say that you were rewarded for looking down. As the history of the word shows, reward implies compensation, something that offsets a sacrifice or loss, if only the expenditure of effort. We give heroes medals, students degrees, and famous people prizes, but those rewards are not directly contingent on what they have done, and it is generally felt that rewards would not be deserved if they had not been worked for. (p. 569)

In this text we will acknowledge the above concerns and not equate the terms "reward" and "reinforcement." Except where the term "reward" is appropriate as it is defined in Skinner's remarks in the preceding quotation, the terms "reinforcer" or "reinforcement" will be used exclusively.

Kimble's definition of learning provides a convenient frame of reference for discussing a number of important issues that must be confronted when attempting to define learning. We will review these issues in the following sections of this chapter.

MUST LEARNING RESULT IN A BEHAVIORAL CHANGE?

As we shall see in chapter 3, psychology has tended to become a *behavioral* science for good reason. A science requires an observable, measurable subject matter, and within the science of psychology, that subject matter is behavior. Thus, whatever we study in psychology must be expressed through behavior, but this does not mean that the behavior we are studying *is* learning. We study behavior so that we can make inferences concerning the process believed to be the cause of the behavioral changes we are observing. In this case, that process is learning. Most learning theorists covered in this text agree that the learning process cannot be studied directly; instead, its nature can only be inferred from changes in behavior. B. F. Skinner is the only theorist who takes exception to this contention. For Skinner, behavioral changes are learning and no further process needs to be inferred. Other theorists say that behavioral changes *result from* learning. We will have more to say about Skinner's antitheoretical point of view in chapter 5.

Except for Skinner, then, most learning theorists look upon learning as a process that mediates behavior. For them, learning is something that occurs as the result of certain experiences and precedes changes in behavior. In such a definition, learning is given the status of an intervening variable. An intervening variable is a theoretical process that is assumed to take place between the observed stimuli and responses. The independent variables cause a change in the intervening variable (learning), which, in turn, causes a change in the dependent variable (behavior). The situation can be diagrammed as follows:

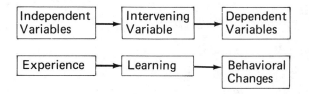

How Permanent Is Relatively Permanent?

Here we run into at least two problems. First, how long must a behavior change last before we say learning has been demonstrated? This was originally inserted into the definition to differentiate between learning and other events that may modify behavior, such as fatigue, illness, and drugs. Clearly, these events and their effects come and go quite rapidly, whereas learning lingers until forgetting takes place over time or until new learning displaces old learning. Thus temporary states as well as learning modify behavior, but with learning the modification is relatively more permanent. However, the duration of the modification that results from either learning or temporary body states cannot be given exactly.

A related problem is more serious. Recently, a number of psychologists have turned their attention to a phenomenon called **short-term memory** (see chapters 14 and 15). Psychologists have found that if unfamiliar information, such as a nonsense syllable, is presented to human subjects who are prevented from rehearsing the information, they will retain the material almost perfectly for about three seconds. In the following fifteen seconds, however, their retention drops to almost zero (Murdock, 1961; Peterson & Peterson, 1959). Despite the fact that the information is lost over such a short period of time, we would hesitate to say that no learning had occurred.

Accepting the qualification of "relatively permanent" in a definition of learning will also determine whether the processes of **sensitization** and **habituation** are accepted as crude examples of learning. Both sensitization and habituation are examples of behavior modification that results from experience, but both are short-lived. Sensitization is the process whereby an organism is made more responsive to certain aspects of its environment. For example, an organism that may not ordinarily respond to a certain light or sound may do so after receiving a shock. The shock, therefore, sensitized the organism, making it more responsive to its environment. Feeling "touchy" or hypersensitive following an upsetting experience is a form of sensitization that we are all familiar with.

Habituation is the process whereby an organism becomes *less* responsive to its environment. For example, there is a tendency for an organism to attend to novel stimuli as they occur in its environment. This tendency is referred to as the orienting reflex, and is exemplified when a dog turns in the direction of a sound that suddenly occurs. After attending to the sound, however, the dog will eventually ignore it (assuming that it poses no threat), and go about its business. We say, in this case, that the dog's response to the sound has habituated. Similarly, Sharpless and Jasper (1956) found that a tone, when first presented, will arouse a sleeping cat. With repeated presentations, however, the tone loses its ability to arouse the cat. Again, we say that habituation has occurred.

Learning and Performance

As mentioned above, what is learned may not be utilized immediately. Football players, for example, may learn how to play their position by watching films and listening to lectures during the week, but may not translate that learning into behavior until Sunday's game. In fact, some may be prevented from actually performing for a prolonged period of time because of an injury or an illness. We say, therefore, that the *potential* to act differently resulted from learning, even though behavior was not immediately affected.

This type of observation has led to the very important distinction between **learning** and **performance,** which will be considered in detail in chapters 6, 12, 13, and 14. Learning refers to a change in behavior potentiality; and performance refers to the translation of this potentiality into behavior.

Why Do We Refer to Practice or Experience?

Obviously not all behavior is learned. Much simple behavior is reflexive. A **reflex** can be defined as an unlearned response in reaction to a specific class of stimuli. Sneezing in response to a tickling in your nose, or producing a sudden knee-jerk when your knee is tapped sharply, or instantly withdrawing your hand when it touches a hot stove are examples of reflexive behavior. Clearly, reflexive behavior is unlearned; it is a genetically determined characteristic of the organism rather than a result of experience.

Complex behavior can also be unlearned. When complex behavior patterns seem to be genetically determined, they are generally referred to as **instinctive.** Instinctive behavior includes such activities as nest building, migration, hibernation, and mating behavior.

For awhile psychologists explained complex behavior patterns by referring to them as instincts. Thus, we said, birds and fish migrate because they possess a migration instinct; birds build nests because of a nest-building instinct. Because the term instinctive was offered as an *explanation* of behavior, we now tend to use the term *species-specific behavior* (Hinde & Tinbergen, 1958) because it is more descriptive. Species-specific behavior refers to complex unlearned, and relatively unmodifiable, behavior patterns engaged in by a certain species of animal under certain circumstances.

Controversy continues, however, over whether species-specific behavior is completely determined by the makeup of the organism or whether some learning is involved. Do birds fly instinctively, or do they learn to fly? Some say that the young bird learns to fly through trial and error while falling to the ground from a tree. Others say that the birds respond reflexively to falling by flapping their wings and therefore fly without learning to do so.

A few examples, however, seem to demonstrate complex behavior that is clearly not influenced by learning. For example, many species of the cuckoo bird lay their eggs in other birds' nests and the young cuckoo is raised by its foster parents. Since each adult cuckoo behaves this way regardless of the foster parents' species, it is very difficult to imagine how such behavior could be learned.

Another example of what appears to be unlearned behavior is the nut-burying behavior of squirrels. Even when an infant squirrel is raised in isolation from other squirrels and sees a nut for the first time, it attempts to bury it. This nut-burying pattern of behavior occurs even if the nut is presented to the squirrel on a bare wooden floor. The squirrel makes scratching motions on the floor as if to dig a hole, tamps the nut with its nose in an apparent effort to push the nut into the floor, and then makes covering movements with its paws (Brown, 1965, p. 23).

Other research supports the contention that species-specific behavior is both learned and unlearned (Hess, 1958; Lorenz, 1952, 1965, 1970; Thorpe, 1963). Lorenz found, for example, that a newly hatched duckling would form an attachment to any kind of moving object and follow it as its mother, provided the object was presented at just the right moment in the duckling's life. Lorenz demonstrated attachments between ducklings and a wooden box on wheels, a human being, and a bird of a different species. The formation of an attachment between an organism and an environmental object is called **imprinting.** Imprinting was found to occur only

Konrad Lorenz and a group of ducklings that have imprinted on him. (Thomas McAvoy/Time-Life Picture Agency, © 1973)

during a **critical period,** after which it was difficult, if not impossible, to imprint the duckling on anything. With imprinting, we have a combination of learned and instinctive behavior. It appears that the animal's genetic endowment causes it to be maximally sensitive to a moving object for a short period of time, during which it can learn the strong habit of following a specific object. If the learning does not occur during that interval, however, it may never occur. Furthermore, the strong habit of following an object does not seem to be built up over time with practice. Rather, the habit seems to be learned at full strength in a single trial. We will have more to say about one-trial learning in chapters 8 and 9.

Studies about imprinting raise a number of questions. The kind of learning, if any, involved in species-specific behavior, and to what extent it is involved must be determined by future research. The main point to emphasize, however, is that to attribute a behavioral change to learning, the change must be relatively permanent and must result from *experience.* If an organism engages in a complex behavior pattern independent of experience, that behavior cannot be referred to as learned behavior.

Does Learning Result from a Specific Kind of Experience?

According to Kimble's definition, learning results from reinforced practice. In other words, only reinforced behavior will be learned. On this point, there is widespread disagreement among learning theorists. Theorists not only disagree over what constitutes reinforcement, but also over whether it is a necessary prerequisite for learning to take place. In a sense, this book is an attempt to review various interpretations

Gregory A. Kimble. (Courtesy of Gregory A. Kimble)

of the nature and importance of reinforcement. This is a question, therefore, to which we will return often.

A Modified Definition of Learning

It is now possible to revise Kimble's definition of learning so that it would be neutral on the matter of reinforcement, thereby making it more widely accepted: *learning is a relatively permanent change in behavior or in behavioral potentiality that results from experience and cannot be attributed to* **temporary body states** *such as those induced by illness, fatigue, or drugs.*

Such a definition still stresses the importance of experience, but leaves it to the theorist to specify the kind of experience he or she feels is necessary for learning to take place, for example, reinforced practice, contiguity between a stimulus and a response, or the acquisition of information. It also reminds us that experience can cause events other than learning that modify behavior. Fatigue is one such event.

ARE THERE DIFFERENT KINDS OF LEARNING?

Learning, as we have seen, is a general term that is used to describe changes in behavior potentiality resulting from experience. **Conditioning,** however, is a more specific term used to describe actual procedures that can modify behavior. Since there are two kinds of conditioning, **instrumental** and **classical,** many theorists conclude that there are at least two kinds of learning, or that learning ultimately can be understood in terms of classical and/or instrumental conditioning. Although both conditioning procedures will be discussed in detail later on in this book, we will summarize both procedures briefly.

Classical Conditioning

We will look at classical conditioning in detail when we discuss Pavlov's views on learning in chapter 7, but for now we can summarize classical conditioning as follows:

1. A stimulus, such as food, is presented to an organism that will cause it to have a natural and automatic reaction, such as salivating. The stimulus causing this natural reaction is called the unconditioned stimulus (UCS). In this case, the food was the UCS. The natural, automatic reaction to the UCS is called the unconditioned response (UCR). In this case, salivation was the UCR.

2. A neutral stimulus (one that does not cause a UCR), such as a tone or a light, is presented to the organism just prior to the presentation of the UCS. This neutral stimulus is called the conditioned stimulus (CS).

3. After the CS and UCS are paired a number of times, with the CS always preceding the UCS, the CS alone can be presented, and the organism will salivate. This salivating response, similar to the organism's response to the UCS, is now given in response to the CS, the tone or the light. We now say that a conditioned response (CR) has been demonstrated.

In classical conditioning, the UCS is called reinforcement, since the entire conditioning procedure depends on it. Note, however, that in classical conditioning, the organism has no control over reinforcement: it occurs when the experimenter wants it to occur. In other words, in classical conditioning, reinforcement is not contingent on any overt response made by the organism.

Instrumental Conditioning

The relationship between reinforcement and the organism's behavior is distinctively different in instrumental conditioning. With instrumental conditioning, the organism must act in a certain way *before* it is reinforced; that is, reinforcement is contingent on the organism's behavior. If the animal does not emit the desired behavior it is not reinforced. Thus in instrumental conditioning, the animal's behavior is "instrumental" in getting it something it wants, that is, a reinforcer.

A small experimental test chamber called the Skinner box is often used to demonstrate instrumental conditioning (or a closely allied form of conditioning called operant conditioning). Such a box is a Plexiglas cage with a grid floor that can be electrified, and a lever that, when pressed, activates a feeder mechanism that delivers food pellets to the animal inside. The experimenter introduces a hungry rat (for example) into the Skinner box. As the rat explores the enclosure, it will eventually activate the lever and receive a pellet of food. Soon the rat will associate lever-pressing with the appearance of food, and its rate of lever-pressing will increase. In this case, the rat must engage in lever-pressing in order to get food. The lever-pressing is the conditioned behavior; the food is the reinforcement. If the Skinner box is programmed so that when a hungry animal presses the lever it is given a pellet of food, the rate at which it presses the lever will increase.

Escape and avoidance conditioning are special kinds of instrumental conditioning. For example, the rat is placed in the Skinner box and the electrified grid is activated, with the lever connected to an off-switch. As the rat leaps around from the shock, it accidentally will hit the lever and terminate the shock. The rat will associate the lever-pressing with the termination of the shock. In this case the lever-pressing is the conditioned behavior, and the termination of shock is the reinforcement. This is an example of **escape conditioning**.

To demonstrate avoidance conditioning, let the Skinner box grid be activated at intervals, with a signal, such as a light, set up to precede the onset of shock by, say, five seconds. The rat will soon learn to associate the light with the onset of shock, and it will press the lever in order to avoid the shock whenever it sees the light go on. The arrangement where an organism can avoid an aversive stimulus by performing some appropriate response is referred to as **avoidance conditioning.**

Recently, learning theorists have become increasingly aware that confining themselves to research involved with just classical and instrumental conditioning leaves out vast areas of human experience. For example, Gagné (1970) feels it is more realistic to assume that there are eight kinds of learning. Gagné believes that the eight kinds of learning are arranged in a hierarchy, with one sort being a prerequisite for the next. Thus, for Gagné, simple conditioning simply provides the basis for the more advanced kinds of learning. As we shall see in chapter 12, Tolman took a similar position much earlier. Although many theorists believed that complex behavior ultimately could be understood in terms of classical or instrumental conditioning, other influential theorists opposed that contention.

LEARNING AND SURVIVAL

Through our long evolutionary past, our bodies have developed the capacity to respond automatically to certain needs. For example, we breathe automatically, and if our body temperature becomes too high or too low, mechanisms are triggered that cause sweating, which cools the body, or shivering, which raises body temperature. Likewise, if blood sugar is too low, the liver secretes sugar into the blood until the concentration of blood sugar is restored to a normal level. These automatic adjustment processes are called **homeostatic mechanisms** because their function is to maintain a physiological equilibrium or *homeostasis*. In addition to the homeostatic mechanisms, we are also born with reflexes which facilitate survival. For example, most living organisms retreat reflexively from a painful stimulus.

Although both homeostatic mechanisms and reflexes are clearly conducive to survival, we would not survive long if we had to depend exclusively on them to meet our needs. For a species to survive it must satisfy its needs for such things as food, water, and sex, and in order to do so it must interact with the environment. No organism would survive long if it did not *learn* which environmental objects could be used to satisfy its basic needs. Nor could an organism survive long if it could not learn which environmental objects were safe and which were dangerous. It is the learning process that allows organisms to do commerce with the environment in a way that allows for the satisfaction of the basic needs that cannot be satisfied by homeostatic mechanisms or reflexes.

It is also the learning process that allows an organism to adjust to a changing environment. Sources of satisfaction and of danger often change and, therefore, if an organism's adjustments to the environment were not dynamic, it could not survive. The learning process provides an organism with the flexibility it needs to survive under a wide variety of environmental conditions. To survive, an organism must learn which environmental objects are positive (conducive to survival), which are negative (detrimental to survival), and which are neutral (irrelevant to survival). In addition to learning whether stimuli are positive, negative, or neutral, the organism must learn to behave in such a way as to obtain or avoid these various stimuli. For example, strawberries may be valued positively because of their ability to reduce the hunger drive, but one may need to get a job and perform specific functions in order to be able to go into a store and buy them. Likewise, a bear may value honey positively, but may need to learn to climb trees in order to obtain it.

In general, it is through classical conditioning that we learn which environmental objects are conducive to survival and which are not; and it is through instrumental or operant conditioning that we learn how to acquire or avoid desirable and undesirable objects. The adaptive value of classical conditioning is further demonstrated by the fact that it typically takes several pairings between a CS and UCS before classical conditioning is established. Schwartz (1984) elaborates this adaptive feature of classical conditioning:

> We can . . . see virtue in the fact that it usually takes numerous CS-US pairings before an association is formed. Suppose we learned after a single pairing of CS and US. If we did, then any stimulus that happened, accidentally, to precede, say, a shock, would produce conditioned fear. Since there is surely always some stimulus around when a shock (or some natural aversive event) occurs, we might end up walking around in fear of almost everything. But if conditioning requires multiple pairings, this possibility is largely eliminated. A tone might precede a shock once, or even twice, by accident. But if the tone precedes the shock 20 or 30 times, it can no longer be an accident. Thus gradual association formation actually enhances our chances of responding only to CSs that are reliable predictors of USs. (p. 92)

Learning, then, should be looked upon as a major tool in adapting to one's environment which supplements innate homeostatic mechanisms, reflexes, and, at least in the case of nonhuman animals, unlearned adaptive behavior.

WHY STUDY LEARNING?

Because most human behavior is learned, investigating the principles of learning will help us understand why we behave as we do. An awareness of the learning process will not only allow greater understanding of normal and adaptive behavior, but will also allow greater understanding of the circumstances that produce maladaptive and abnormal behavior. More effective psychotherapy might result from such an understanding.

Child rearing practices can also utilize the principles of learning. Obviously, individuals differ from one another and these individual differences may be explained in terms of differing learning experiences. One of the most important human attributes is language, and there is little doubt that specific language development results mainly from learning. No doubt many other human attributes are molded in a similar way by the interaction of the environment with the learning process. When parents know more about the learning experiences that create what they would call desirable traits, they may wish to organize the environment of their child so that it encourages these traits. Likewise, learning experiences that tend to produce socially maladaptive behavior can be avoided.

Moreover, there is a close relationship between the principles of learning and educational practices. In many cases, principles that have been uncovered while studying the learning process in the laboratory have eventually been utilized in the classroom. The widespread utilization of programmed learning, teaching machines, and computer-assisted instruction offer three examples of how research on learning influences teaching practices. The current trend in American education toward personalized systems of instruction or individualized instruction can also be considered a spinoff from research on the learning process. We may reasonably conclude that as our knowledge of the learning process increases, educational practices should become more efficient and effective.

DISCUSSION QUESTIONS

1. List the requirements that must be met before a change in behavior can be attributed to learning.
2. Describe the processes of sensitization and habituation as they have occurred in your life.
3. Differentiate between learning and performance.
4. Give a few examples of complex unlearned behavior. Do you feel that complex unlearned behavior exists on the human level? Explain.
5. Why was the term *instinct* replaced with the term *species-specific* behavior?
6. Differentiate between the terms learning and conditioning.
7. How many kinds of learning are there? Explain how you arrived at your answer.

8. What is meant by the statement, "Imprinting seems to result from both learning and instinct"?

9. Describe the relationship between learning and survival.

10. Give a few reasons why it is important to study the learning process.

CHAPTER HIGHLIGHTS

Avoidance conditioning. The experimental arrangement where an organism can avoid experiencing an aversive stimulus by engaging in appropriate behavior.

Behavioral potentiality. The ability to perform some act although the act is not being performed at the present time. Learning may result in a change in behavioral potentiality although the learning may not be translated into behavior until some time after the learning has taken place.

Classical conditioning. An experimental arrangement whereby a stimulus is made to elicit a response that was not previously associated with that stimulus (i.e., the conditioned stimulus, CS, comes to elicit a response similar to the one elicited by the UCS).

Conditioning. An experimental procedure used to modify behavior. Most learning theorists believe that there are two kinds of conditioning—classical and instrumental—and that all learning involves conditioning. To those holding such a belief, learning is a term used to summarize a large number of conditioned responses.

Critical period. A period in an organism's life during which time an important development occurs. If the development does not occur during that time, it may never occur. For example, if imprinting does not occur shortly after a duckling is hatched, it is difficult, if not impossible, to establish it. The period of time immediately following hatching, therefore, is the critical period for imprinting.

Escape conditioning. The experimental arrangement where an organism can terminate an aversive stimulus by engaging in appropriate behavior.

Habituation. The decreased tendency to respond to a stimulus that results from prolonged exposure to that stimulus.

Homeostatic mechanisms. Automatic processes that function to keep the body operating within certain physiological limits, thus maintaining a physiological equilibrium or homeostasis.

Imprinting. The rapid formation, during a critical period, of a close attachment between an organism and an environmental object.

Instinct. The inborn capacity to perform a complex behavioral task. In recent years, the term has been replaced by *species-specific behavior.*

Instrumental conditioning. An experimental procedure whereby the rate or probability of a response is changed from one value before conditioning to another value following conditioning. With instrumental conditioning, the organism must perform an appropriate response in order to be reinforced.

Learning. A relatively permanent change in behavior or behavioral potentiality that comes from experience and cannot be attributed to temporary body states such as illness, fatigue, or drugs.

Performance. The translation of learning into behavior.

Reflex. An unlearned response to a specific class of stimuli.

Reinforced practice. Repeated performance under the conditions where a correct response is followed by reinforcement. Reinforced practice is thought by many learning theorists to be a necessary condition for learning to take place; other theorists do not agree.

Sensitization. The tendency to be more responsive to the environment following an arousing experience.

Short-term memory. The memory of an experience that lasts for only several seconds after the termination of the experience. This is opposed to long-term memory that lasts considerably longer.

Temporary body state. A temporary condition of the body such as fatigue, illness, emotion, the presence of drugs, and sleep loss, that cause a modification in behavior. Such modifications in behavior are differentiated from those caused by learning.

2

Approaches to the Study of Learning

We noted in chapter 1 that most learning theorists contend that learning can be observed only indirectly through changes in behavior. Therefore when we study learning, we observe behavior and based on these observables, we infer that a particular type of learning has or has not occurred. The inaccessibility of learning is one reason why there are so many approaches to its study. Some feel, for example, that the best place to study learning is in the field rather than in the laboratory. This method of studying a phenomenon as it occurs naturally is called **naturalistic observation.** Using this technique, one would make detailed observations and recordings of what is being studied. Such research often results in a grouping or classification of the various elements of the phenomenon being investigated. For example, while using naturalistic observation to study learning in the classroom one might classify learning to read or spell as verbal learning, the learning of athletic prowess as perceptual–motor skill learning, and the learning that requires complex mental processes as problem solving or concept formation.

Two major drawbacks of naturalistic observation become apparent. First, because the classroom situation is extremely complex it is very difficult to observe and record accurately. Second, there is a tendency to classify events into chunks that may be too comprehensive; for example, what is classified as concept formation may in reality consist of many different phenomena whose distinctions get lost in the classifying process. Classifications that seem rather straightforward at first may become extraordinarily complex under closer scrutiny.

Naturalistic observation can be an important first step for a study of learning, but eventually the psychologist must break up the recorded chunks of behavior for closer and more detailed analysis, that is, the psychologist must become more elementistic in order to discover the various laws operating in the learning situation, and discovering laws usually involves experimentation. That is, naturalistic observation may be important in isolating groups of events for further study, but these must then be reduced into smaller components for further analysis. Such an approach is called **elementism.**

THE SYSTEMATIC STUDY OF LEARNING

In recent times, that portion of psychology concerned with the learning process has become more scientific. We will see in the next chapter that using the scientific method in the psychology of learning has been very productive. It is important, therefore, that we look at such a productive method in more detail.

What Is Science?

According to Stevens (1951): "**Science** seeks to generate **confirmable propositions** by fitting a formal system of symbols (language, mathematics, logic) to empirical observations" (p. 22). Stevens's statement points to a number of important characteristics of science. For example, science deals with confirmable propositions. The propositions of science must be capable of having their truth or falsity demonstrated publicly, so that any other interested researcher can replicate the experiment and, hopefully, obtain the same results. This insistence on publicly verifiable propositions is what characterizes a science. Science is not concerned with private or unique events, but only with statements that are empirically verifiable. The statement, "I ate pickles last night and subsequently dreamt of elephants," is scientifically useless because it refers to a personal experience that is unique and undemonstrable. However, the statement, "People who eat pickles tend to dream of elephants," can be thought of as scientific because it is in principle verifiable. If we feed pickles to a large number of people and they subsequently report dreaming of elephants, and if we repeat the procedure a number of times with the same outcome, we have discovered a **scientific law.** A scientific law can be defined as a consistently observed relationship between two or more classes of events. *All sciences seek to discover laws.* The lawful relationship we have discovered in the example above is between the eating of pickles and the *verbal report* of having dreamt of elephants. Again, if there is no way of publicly demonstrating whether a statement is true or false, it is scientifically useless.

Aspects of Theory

Scientific theories have two important aspects. First, a **theory** has a **formal aspect,** which includes the words and symbols the theory contains. Second, a theory has an **empirical aspect,** which consists of the physical events that the theory is attempting to explain. Although the relationship between the formal and empirical aspects of a theory is very complex, it should be noted that the formal part of a theory can make sense by itself even though it may make erroneous predictions about the physical world. The statement, "All learning depends upon drive reduction," makes sense formally, but may not accurately explain learning. The point here is that a theory can sound valid, but it is devoid of scientific meaning unless it withstands the rigors of experimental test. There is always the danger of being overly impressed by the wording of a theory and forgetting to check how accurately it predicts and describes empirical events. Most psychologists would agree that astrology is a highly developed formal system that has little or no relationship to actual empirical events. In other words, astrology sounds good but it adds practically nothing to our understanding of human behavior.

It is important to remember that no matter how abstract and complex a theory becomes, it must ultimately make contact with observable physical events. All scientific theories, no matter how abstract their formal aspects become, begin and end with statements about observable events.

From Research to Theory

As a general example of the use of theory in psychology, we can refer to research examining the relationship between food deprivation and rate of learning, with food as the reinforcer. In this case, learning rate will be indexed by the number of trials it takes for an animal to learn to turn left on every trial in a T-maze. After many separate experiments, a researcher finds that as hours of food deprivation go up, learning occurs more rapidly. That is, animals deprived of food the longest, learn to turn left in a T-maze most rapidly.

These results can be looked upon as the demonstration of a law. Here the observed relationship is between degree of food deprivation and performance on a learning task. The researcher turns next to study water deprivation, and again finds that as hours of water deprivation go up, learning time goes down. Now we have a second law: as hours of water deprivation go up, an animal learns to turn left faster in a T-maze when water is used as a reinforcer.

Next, the researcher turns to the study of sexual behavior. This time the opportunity to copulate is used as a reinforcer for the rat to turn left in the T-maze. Again, it is found that increased hours of sexual deprivation results in faster learning.

Although the goal of science is to discover laws (observed relationships between events), it is seldom enough to simply observe and record hundreds or perhaps thousands of empirical relationships. Scientists usually attempt to make sense out of the laws they discover, that is, they attempt to group them in some coherent fashion. This grouping has at least two functions: (a) to synthesize a large number of observations and (b) to point the way to further research. The latter aspect of grouping or attempting to make sense out of data is called its **heuristic function.**

At this point, therefore, the researcher may wish to go beyond the data. He or she may make statements such as "Hungry animals tend to learn faster than food-satiated ones," or "Thirsty animals tend to learn faster than water-satiated ones." Both statements plunge the researcher into the realm of theory. Although the experiments involved specific situations (e.g., 2, 4, 6, and 8 hr of deprivation) the concept of hunger, which is an abstraction, covers all states of deprivation, even those not involved in the actual research (e.g., 26, 30, 37, 37½, and 50 hr of deprivation). Thus, by postulating the unobservable inner state of hunger, the researcher is at the same time attempting to tie together some of his or her observations and predicting the outcome of future research. The same is true when the concepts of thirst and sexual arousal are used.

The researcher can take an additional step and attempt to synthesize the three theoretical terms into still another theoretical term. He or she can conclude, for example, that deprivation increases drive, and animals with high drive learn faster. Note, in doing this, the researcher is using the two functions of a theory: synthesizing and predicting avenues of future research. By stating that "animals with high drive learn faster than animals with low drive," he or she is suggesting research on oxygen deprivation, heat deprivation, or pain reduction. The relationship among the concepts of hunger, thirst, sexual arousal, and the empirical events from which they stem is shown in Figure 2-1.

The researcher could take still an additional step and postulate the even more general concept of motivation and include psychological factors as well as the physiological ones we have been considering (e.g., the need for achievement or for self-actualization).

Theories as Tools

Because a theory is merely a research tool it cannot be right or wrong; it is either useful or it is not useful. If a theory clarifies the various observations that have been made, and if it generates additional research, the theory is a good one. If it fails in either respect, the researcher is likely to search for a new theory.

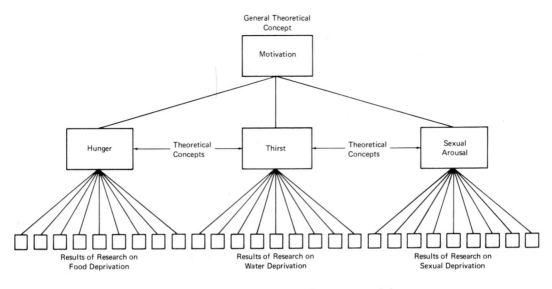

Figure 2–1. The relationship between theoretical concepts and the empirical events from which they stem.

If a hypothesis generated by a theory is confirmed, the theory gains strength. If a hypothesis generated by a theory is rejected, the theory is weakened and must either be revised or abandoned. Again we see how confirmation of a theory depends on empirical observation. Whether a theory is maintained, revised, or abandoned is determined by the outcome of the empirical research generated by the theory. Thus, we see that *theories must continually generate the very hypotheses that may prove they are ineffective.*

The Principle of Parsimony

We noted above that one characteristic of science is that science deals only with statements that are in principle empirically verifiable. Another characteristic of science is that it follows the **principle of parsimony** (sometimes called the principle of economy, Occam's Razor, or Morgan's Canon). This principle states that when two equally effective theories can explain the same phenomenon, but one explanation is simple and the other is complex, we must use the simpler explanation.

Summary of Characteristics of a Scientific Theory

1. A theory synthesizes a number of observations.
2. A good theory is heuristic, that is, it generates new research.
3. A theory must generate hypotheses that can be empirically verified. If such hypotheses are confirmed, the theory gains strength; if not, the theory is weakened and must be revised or abandoned.

4. A theory is a tool and as such cannot be right or wrong; it is either useful or it is not useful.

5. Theories are chosen in accordance with the law of parsimony: of two equally effective theories, the simpler of the two must be chosen.

6. Theories contain abstractions, such as numbers or words, which constitute the formal aspect of a theory.

7. The formal aspect of a theory must be correlated with observable events, which constitute the empirical aspect of a theory.

8. All theories are attempts to explain empirical events and they must, therefore, start and end with empirical observations.

THE LEARNING EXPERIMENT

In the previous section we considered the course from research to theory; here we will look briefly at the course from theory to research. First, we must delineate a subject matter. This usually takes the form of a general definition of learning or a general description of the phenomenon to be studied. Next, we attempt to specify the conditions necessary for the phenomenon to occur. Lastly, we must convert our theoretical statements about the learning process in terms of identifiable and repeatable activities or experimental performances. This way of measurably defining a theoretical term is called an **operational definition.** In other words, an operational definition relates what is being defined (in this case learning), to the operations used to measure it. For example, a common operational definition of learning rate is **trials to criterion,** which is the number of times an experimental subject needs to experience the material to be learned before being able to perform at some specified level; for instance, how many times the subject had to see a list of nonsense syllables before he or she could recite the entire list accurately. Once researchers have operationally defined their theoretical terms, they are ready to experiment.

Every experiment involves something whose changes are measured, the **dependent variable,** and something the experimenter manipulates to see its effect on the dependent variable, the **independent variable.** In the previously mentioned experiment concerning the relationship between the number of hours of food deprivation and rate of learning, rate of learning was measured and was, therefore, the dependent variable. Rate of learning was operationally defined as how many trials it took for the animal to learn to make a left turn in a T-maze a specified number of consecutive times. Thus, trials to criterion was used as the dependent variable. In learning experiments, the operational definition indicates the kind of behavior that will be used to index learning. Hours of food deprivation was systematically manipulated by the researcher and it, therefore, was the independent variable.

Arbitrary Decisions in Setting Up a Learning Experiment

Science is often thought of as a cold, highly objective means for arriving at the "truth." Scientists, however, are often highly emotional, very subjective, and the truth they disclose is dynamic and probabilistic. This can be seen in the number of arbitrary decisions that go into the setting up of any learning experiment. A number of these arbitrary decisions are summarized below.

1. What Aspects of Learning Should Be Investigated? This, of course, will be partially dictated by one's theory concerning learning. One can study learning in the laboratory, or one can observe learning as it occurs in a schoolroom setting via naturalistic observation. In addition, one can study instrumental conditioning, classical conditioning, concept formation, problem solving, or verbal or perceptual-motor learning. Although a theory of learning attempts to specify the conditions under which learning takes place, it is up to the experimenter to choose which of those conditions should be investigated.

2. Idiographic Versus Nomothetic Techniques. Should researchers intensely study the learning process of a single experimental subject under a wide variety of circumstances (**idiographic technique**), or should they use groups of experimental subjects and study their average performance (**nomothetic technique**)? Although quite different, both techniques are respectable and both yield useful information about the learning process. As we shall see later, Skinner uses the idiographic technique, and Hull used the nomothetic technique. As we shall see in chapter 9, the two techniques can result in entirely different conclusions about the nature of learning.

3. Humans Versus "Lower" Animals as Subjects. If researchers choose to use humans as their experimental subjects, they are concerned about how their results generalize from the laboratory situation to the world outside the laboratory. If, however, they use subhuman subjects, such as rats, pigeons, or monkeys, they are concerned about how the learning process generalizes from one species to another in addition to the above concern.

Why, then, use anything but human subjects? There are many reasons why researchers use subhuman subjects instead of humans despite the difficulties involved.

1. Humans are often too sophisticated for certain learning experiments, that is, their previous experience interferes with a clear study of the learning process. The learning history of subhuman subjects can be controlled with relative ease.

2. Often learning experiments are long and boring, and it would be difficult to find humans willing to run in them. Subhuman subjects do not complain.

3. Some experiments are designed to test the effects of genetics on learning ability. By using subhuman subjects, the genetic background of subjects can be systematically manipulated.

4. The relationship between certain drugs and learning can be investigated using subhuman subjects, whereas using human subjects for such research would be difficult, if not impossible.

5. Various surgical techniques can be used on subhuman subjects, not on humans. The surgical removal of certain brain areas and direct brain stimulation

via electrodes implanted in the brain are but two examples. Likewise, human subjects cannot be sacrificed after the experiment to check on such things as neuronal effects of the treatment condition.

6. Last, but not least, human subjects sometimes miss appointments to run in experiments, whereas subhuman subjects almost always show up.

4. Correlation Versus Experimental Techniques. Some researchers may want to correlate learning (operationally defined as a score on an achievement test) with intelligence (operationally defined as a score on an IQ test). Because this involves correlating one response (performance on the achievement test) with another response (performance on the IQ test), the resulting relationship is called an R-R law (response-response law). R-R laws are said to be **correlational** in that they describe how two classes of behavioral events vary together.

Other researchers may want to systematically vary one or more environmental events and note their effect on the dependent variables. Since the relationship examined here is between environmental events (stimuli) and responses (changes on the dependent variable), it is said to be an S-R, or stimulus-response, law.

While one may argue about the relative merits of correlational or **experimental techniques,** the point here is that there are at least these two general approaches available for doing research. Both approaches yield distinctly different information about learning. Which approach is taken depends on the preference of the individual researcher.

5. Which Independent Variables Should Be Studied? Once learning has been operationally defined, the dependent variable in an experiment has been automatically set. If, for example, learning is operationally defined as "trials to criterion," then this is what is measured in the experiment. Next, the researcher must ask, "What variable or variables are likely to have an effect on the behavior being measured?" The answer to that question could involve a long list of possible independent variables to choose from. A sample list follows.

Sex difference	Instructions
Age differences	Intelligence
Size of the stimulus materials used	Drugs
Rate of presentation	Intertrial interval
Meaningfulness of the material used	Interaction with other tasks

An additional function of a theory, by the way, is to give researchers some guidance in choosing their independent variable or variables.

6. What Levels of the Independent Variables Should Be Studied? Once one or more independent variables have been chosen, the researcher must consider how many levels of it should be represented in the experiment. For example, if age is chosen as an experimental variable, how many ages and which ones should be studied is yet to be determined. There are some guidelines that could be used here to assure that the levels of the independent variable chosen will have the greatest effect on the dependent variable (see Anderson, 1971), but this choice is basically arbitrary.

7. Choice of Dependent Variables. Common dependent variables in learning experiments include the following:

Scores on tests	Trials to criterion
Trials to extinction	Latency
Running speed	Probability of response
Rate of responding	Number of errors
Time to solution	Response amplitude

Because each results from an operational definition of learning, it should be clear that there are many acceptable operational definitions of learning available to the researcher. Although which is chosen is arbitrary, the choice may have a profound effect on the conclusions one draws about the outcome of an experiment. In experiments having two dependent variables, it is common for one variable to show an effect due to the independent variable, and for the other to show no effect. For example, when investigating the transfer of training from one hand to the other in our laboratory, we consistently find that practice with one hand increases the speed with which a task can be performed with the other hand (speed of responding being one dependent variable). Using speed as our dependent variable, we find evidence for positive transfer of training from one hand to the other. If, however, we use number of errors as our dependent variable we discover that practice with one hand did not facilitate performance with the other hand. Thus we conclude that no transfer of training took place—two altogether dissimilar conclusions resulting from our choice of the dependent variable.

8. Data Analysis and Interpretation. Once the data (scores on the dependent variable) has been gathered in an experiment, how does one analyze it? Although it is beyond the scope of this book to discuss them, the reader should be aware of the fact that there are many statistical techniques available to the researcher for data analysis. Here again, the choice of a statistical test is somewhat arbitrary and yet may have a significant effect on one's conclusions.

Once the experiment has been designed, run, and analyzed, it must be interpreted. There are usually many interpretations of the data provided by an experiment, and there is really no way of knowing if the one finally decided upon is the most adequate. It is possible that even after following the most rigorous scientific procedures in the gathering of experimental data, the interpretation of those data could be totally inadequate. For example, there is the story of the researcher who trained a flea to jump every time he said "jump." After this preliminary training, the researcher began pulling legs off the flea, and after the removal of each leg, he said "jump" and the flea jumped. The experiment continued in this manner until the flea's last leg had been pulled off. Now when the experimenter said "jump," the flea did not move. The researcher jotted his conclusion in his notebook: "Fleas without legs are deaf." We exaggerate only to stress the point that there are any number of possible conclusions that could be drawn about the same experimental data.

It should be noted that although we refer to the decisions in this section as arbitrary, they are arbitrary only in the sense that there are a number of ways of arranging an experiment in a given area and any one of the ways might be scientifically correct. In a more practical sense, however, the choice of what to study, the kind of subject to use, independent and dependent variables, and approach to data analysis and interpretation will be at least partially determined by such factors as cost, practicality, theoretical orientation, social and educational concerns, and availability of apparatus.

THE USE OF MODELS

The *Random House Dictionary of the English Language* (1968) defines *analogy* as "a partial similarity between like features of two things, on which a comparison may be based." In science, it is often useful to find that two things are analogous, especially when one thing is well known and the other is not. In such cases, we can use what is well known as a *model* in attempting to understand what is less known. At one time, noting the similarity between the functioning of mechanical pumps (about which a great deal was known), and the functioning of human hearts (about which less was known), provided a useful guide for heart research. Also, noting the similarities between lower animals and humans encouraged the intense study of lower animals in order to learn more about human processes.

In recent years, information-processing psychology has tended to use the computer as a model in the study of human intellectual processes. Many information-processing psychologists state that computers and humans are analogous because both receive information (input) from the environment, process that information in one or more ways, and then act upon that information (output). These information-processing psychologists say that the software (programs) placed into computers determine how computers process the information fed into them. Likewise, humans are programmed by experience to process information in certain ways. Because of these similarities, many information-processing psychologists believe that much can be learned about how humans process information by assuming that computers and humans process information in similar ways. In chapter 14, we will see that the computer has proved to be a useful model in the study of human cognitive processes. We will also see, however, that not all information-processing psychologists feel that the computer is a useful model for studying human cognitive processes.

Unlike a theory, a model is typically not used to explain a complicated process; rather, it is used to simplify the process and make it more understandable. The use of models involves showing how something is like something else. A theory, on the other hand, attempts to describe the processes underlying a complex phenomenon. Reinforcement theory, for example, is an attempt to explain why learning occurs. It is not an attempt to show what learning is *like,* as would be the case with a model. In the area of motivation one might say that an organism acts like a mule with a carrot dangling before it, or one might say that the physiological state of hunger is interacting with previously learned habits, causing the organism to run. In the former case, a model is being used to *describe* behavior; in the latter case, a theory is being used in an attempt to *explain* behavior.

LEARNING IN THE LABORATORY
VERSUS NATURALISTIC OBSERVATION

Remember that science deals in statements that are verified through experimentation. Contrasted with naturalistic observation, where the researcher has no control over what is being observed, an experiment can be defined as controlled observation. Information is both gained and lost in laboratory experimentation. On the plus side, the experimenter controls the situation, and therefore is able to systematically examine a number of different conditions and their effect on learning. On the negative side, the laboratory creates an artificial situation that is much different from the circumstances under which learning would ordinarily occur. This always brings into question how information gained in the laboratory is related to learning situations outside the laboratory. Some researchers feel that combining naturalistic observation and laboratory experimentation is best. That is, one could make initial observations in the field, examine them in greater detail in the laboratory, and then observe the phenomenon again in the field with the greater understanding that resulted from the laboratory experimentation.

KUHN'S VIEWS OF HOW SCIENCES CHANGE

To picture science as an activity that gradually evolves toward an increasingly accurate understanding of nature, as we have done above, may be somewhat misleading. In his book *The Structure of Scientific Revolutions* (1973), Thomas Kuhn portrays a much different view of science. According to Kuhn, scientists working in a given area usually accept a certain point of view about what they are studying. For example, at one time most physicists accepted the Newtonian point of view in their study of physics. Kuhn calls a point of view shared by a substantial number of scientists a **paradigm.** A paradigm provides a general framework for empirical research and, as such, is usually more than just a limited theory. A paradigm corresponds more closely to what is called a school of thought or an "ism" such as behaviorism, associationism, or functionalism (these terms will be explained in the next chapter).

The activities of scientists who accept a particular paradigm consist mainly of elaborating and verifying the implications of the framework it superimposes over the subject being studied. In other words, a paradigm is a way of looking at a subject matter which illuminates certain problems and suggests ways of solving those problems. Kuhn calls the problem solving activities of scientists following a paradigm **normal science.** Normal science is what most of this chapter has been about.

The positive result of a community of scientists following a certain paradigm is that a certain range of phenomena, those upon which the paradigm focuses, are explored thoroughly. The negative result is that following a particular paradigm blinds the scientists to other, perhaps more fruitful, ways of dealing with their subject matter. Thus, while research generated by a certain paradigm results in depth, it may inhibit breadth.

According to Kuhn (1973), scientists following a particular paradigm, that is, those engaged in normal science, are providing little more than a "mop-up operation." Kuhn puts the matter as follows:

> Mopping-up operations are what engage most scientists throughout their careers. They constitute what I am here calling normal science. Closely examined, whether historically or in the contemporary laboratory, that enterprise seems an attempt to force nature into the preformed and relatively inflexible box that the paradigm supplies. No part of the aim of normal science is to call forth new sorts of phenomena; indeed those that will not fit the box are often not seen at all. Nor do scientists normally aim to invent new theories, and they are often intolerant of those invented by others. Instead, normal-scientific research is directed to the articulation of those phenomena and theories that the paradigm already supplies. (p. 24)

How then do new paradigms emerge? According to Kuhn, innovations in science come when scientists following a particular paradigm are consistently confronted with events that are inconsistent with the point of view they are holding. Eventually, as the anomalies persist, an alternative paradigm will emerge that will be able to explain the anomalies as well as the events supporting the previous paradigm. The new paradigm will usually be associated with one individual or a small group of individuals who attempt to convince their colleagues that their paradigm is more effective than its predecessor. Typically, the new paradigm meets with great resistance and converts are won very slowly. Kuhn says this resistance comes from the fact that a particular paradigm has implications for every aspect of one's scientific life and, therefore, changing from one paradigm to another involves an enormous change in how one does science; for this reason, there is emotional involvement in the decision. Kuhn says: "Like the choice between competing political institutions, that between competing paradigms proves to be a choice between incompatible modes of community life" (p. 94). Because of this emotional involvement, scientists will usually do everything possible to make their accepted paradigm work before pondering a change. At some point, however, the older paradigm will be "overthrown" and the new one will replace it. The displacement of Newton's theory by Einstein's theory would be one example, and the displacement of religious notions concerning the creation of man by Darwin's theory of evolution would be another.

According to Kuhn, then, a science changes (although it does not necessarily advance) through a series of **scientific revolutions,** which are similar to political revolutions, rather than through a continuous evolutionary process within a single theoretical framework. To Kuhn, the evolution of a science is at least as much a sociological phenomenon as it is a scientific phenomenon. We might add that because of the emotional involvement it also appears to be a psychological phenomenon.

As valid as Kuhn's argument appears to be, it seems most forceful when applied to the physical sciences rather than the behavioral sciences. Within the more mature physical sciences, it is the rule that most scientists accept some prevailing paradigm and, therefore, a change in paradigm tends to be revolutionary. In the younger behavioral sciences, however, a variety of paradigms exist simultaneously. The book you are now reading provides a good example since it offers various ways of looking at the learning process. Every theory in this book is accepted to some extent by a substantial number of researchers of the learning process. Although followers of one theory tend to form a camp, they still communicate and influence members of other camps. It would be difficult to find an area in physics for which this would be true. For example, one could not find a book on theories of gravity, since there are not as many paradigms that exist simultaneously in that area.

Thus, it seems that under the conditions that exist in the behavioral sciences, the revolutionary change of paradigms is less possible and/or necessary. One possible exception to this contention would be the widespread acceptance of associationism, one of psychology's oldest and most widely accepted doctrines. In fact, most theories in this book assume some aspect of associationism. At the present time, there is growing dissatisfaction with the assumptions underlying associationism; thus we have the necessary condition for the kind of scientific revolution that Kuhn so eloquently elaborates in his book.

POPPER'S VIEW OF SCIENCE

As we have seen, science has traditionally been viewed as involving empirical observation, theory formation, theory testing, theory revision, and the search for lawful relationships. Like Kuhn, Karl Popper has been critical of this traditional view of science. According to Popper, scientific activity does not start with empirical observation, as is so often claimed. Rather, it starts with the existence of a problem. For Popper, the idea that scientists wander around making empirical observations and then attempting to explain those observations is just plain silly. Popper (1963) says:

> Twenty-five years ago I tried to bring home the same point to a group of physics students in Vienna by beginning a lecture with the following instructions: "Take pencil and paper: carefully observe, and write down what you have observed!" They asked, of course, *what* I wanted them to observe. Clearly the instruction, "Observe!" is absurd . . . observation is always selective. It needs a chosen object, a definite task, an interest, a point of view, a problem. (p. 46)

For Popper, then, problems determine which observations are made by scientists. The next step in scientific activity, according to Popper, is to propose a solution to the problem. A scientific theory is a proposed solution to a problem.

What distinguishes a scientific theory from a nonscientific theory is the **principle of refutability** (sometimes called the principle of falsification). According to this principle, a scientific theory must make specific predictions about what will happen under certain circumstances. Furthermore, the predictions must be risky in the sense that there is a real possibility that the predictions will be erroneous and thus refute the theory upon which they were based. Einstein's theory of relativity made the risky predictions that as objects approached the speed of light, they would diminish in size and increase in mass. If these predictions were found to be false, Einstein's theory would have needed to be revised or abandoned. It turns out, however, that his predictions were accurate.

Popper criticizes a number of theories in psychology because they do not pass the test of refutability. Freud's theory, for example, makes no risky predictions. Everything that a person does can be "explained" by Freud's theory. If, for example, Freud's theory predicts that on the basis of early experience a man should hate women, but is found to love them, the Freudian can say that he is displaying a "reaction formation." That is, he really does hate women on the unconscious level, and he is simply going overboard in the opposite direction in order to reduce the anxiety that his recognition of his true hatred of women would cause. Astrology suffers the same fate, since there is no conceivable observation that could be made that would refute its claims. Contrary to common belief, if every conceivable observation agrees with a theory, the theory is weak, not strong.

Berkson and Wettersten (1984) suggest that there is a theory of learning contained within Popper's philosophy of science. We will discuss that theory and its implications for education in chapter 16.

Kuhn Versus Popper

According to Popper, what Kuhn calls normal science is not science at all. For Popper, the subjective beliefs that Kuhn claims bind scientists to a paradigm, inhibit effective problem solving. In his analysis of scientific activity, Kuhn stresses sociological and psychological factors; whereas Popper's analysis stresses the logical refutation of proposed solutions to problems. For Popper, either proposed solutions (theories) to problems pass the rigorous attempts to refute them or they do not; there is no room for subjectivity. Can the analyses of both Kuhn and Popper be correct? Robinson (1981) suggests that they can be, and we agree: "In a conciliatory spirit, we might suggest that the major disagreement between Kuhn and Popper vanishes when we picture Kuhn as describing what science has been historically, and Popper asserting what it ought to be" (p. 24).

DISCUSSION QUESTIONS

1. In what way(s) do you feel science differs from other fields of inquiry, such as philosophy and theology?

2. What is a scientific law? How does the scientific concept of law differ from how the term is used in a legal or a religious sense?

3. Discuss the strengths and weaknesses of naturalistic observation.
4. Briefly discuss the characteristics of a scientific theory.
5. Discuss the steps involved in going from experimentation to theory.
6. Discuss the steps involved in going from a theory to experimentation.
7. What is a scientific model? Give an example of how a model has been used in psychology.
8. Differentiate between a theory and a model.
9. List and briefly describe the arbitrary decisions that are involved in setting up, running, and analyzing a learning experiment.
10. What does Kuhn mean when he says normal science is a "mop-up" operation?
11. Describe the process of scientific revolution as it is viewed by Kuhn.
12. Discuss Popper's criticisms of the traditional views of science.
13. How can the analyses of science offered by Kuhn and Popper be reconciled?

CHAPTER HIGHLIGHTS

Analogy. A partial correspondence or similarity between things otherwise dissimilar.

Confirmable propositions. Propositions whose truth or falsity can be publicly demonstrated. Such propositions are also called verifiable.

Correlational techniques. Research where two response measures are related. Such research is usually interested in detecting how two kinds of behavior vary together. For example, how is performance on an IQ test related to performance on a creativity test? Correlational techniques generate R-R laws, since two response measures are being related.

Dependent variable. The variable that is measured in an experiment, usually some kind of behavior (e.g., trials to criterion).

Elementism. The belief that the best way to study a complex phenomenon is to divide it up into smaller components.

Empirical aspect of a theory. The empirical events that the theory purports to explain.

Experimental techniques. Research where one or more independent variables are systematically manipulated in order to detect their effects on one or more dependent variables. Since an experiment attempts to relate stimuli (independent variables) to responses (dependent variables), it is said to generate S-R laws. This is contrasted with correlational techniques which demonstrate R-R laws.

Formal aspect of a theory. The signs, symbols, or words that a theory contains.

Heuristic function of a theory. A theory's ability to generate research.

Idiographic technique. The intense study of a single experimental subject.

Independent variable. The variable that is systematically manipulated in an experiment. Typical independent variables would include hours of deprivation, sex of subject, age, rate of presentation, or degree of meaningfulness.

Model. When a fairly well known situation is used to describe a relatively less known situation. Models are used to show that the two situations are alike in some respects.

Naturalistic observation. Studying a phenomenon as it occurs naturally in the environment.

Nomothetic technique. The study of a group of experimental subjects, the interest being in the *average* performance of the group.

Normal science. Those activities of scientists as they are guided by a particular paradigm.

Operational definition of learning. A definition that states the procedures to be followed in determining whether, and to what extent, learning has taken place. Operational definitions of learning can range from grades on achievement tests to some behavioral measure in a learning experiment, such as trials to criterion or the number of errors in maze-running.

Paradigm. A point of view shared by a substantial number of scientists that provides a general framework for empirical research. A paradigm is usually more than just one theory and corresponds more closely to what is called a "school of thought" or an "ism."

Principle of parsimony. When researchers have a choice between two equally effective theories, they are obliged to choose the simpler of the two.

Principle of refutability (sometimes called the principle of falsification). Popper's contention that in order for a theory to be scientific, it must make risky predictions which, if not confirmed, would refute the theory.

Science. A method of inquiry that involves the use of experimentation to test theories about various aspects of nature.

Scientific law. A consistently observed relationship between two or more empirical events.

Scientific revolution. According to Kuhn, the displacement of one paradigm with another. Such a displacement usually occurs over a fairly long period of time and after great resistance. A paradigm is associated with the scientist's total view of science—what counts as a good problem, what counts as a good answer, what a good experiment is like, and so on. Thus, a change in paradigm is a widespread change for scientists which invalidates almost every aspect of their previous scientific life. There is, therefore, emotional involvement in such a change.

Theory. An attempted explanation that makes sense out of a large number of observations and indicates to the researcher where to look for additional information. Or, according to Popper, a proposed solution to a problem.

Trials to criterion. The number of trials an experimental subject requires to reach the criterion that the experimenter sets as a definition of learning. For example, if perfect recall of a list of nonsense syllables is defined as learning the list, then trials to criterion is the number of times the subject had to go through the list before he or she could recall the items without error.

3

Early Notions About Learning

EPISTEMOLOGY AND LEARNING THEORY

Epistemology is a branch of philosophy that is concerned with the nature of knowledge. The epistemologist asks questions such as, What is knowledge? What can we know? What are the limits of knowledge? What does it mean to know? What are the origins of knowledge? Questions of this kind go back at least as far as the early Greeks. In fact, the views of Plato and Aristotle concerning the nature of knowledge have set philosophical trends that have persisted until this day. Plato believed that knowledge was inherited and was, therefore, a natural component of the human mind. According to Plato, one gained knowledge by reflecting on the contents of one's mind. Aristotle, on the other hand, believed that knowledge was the result of sensory experience and was not inherited.

The position taken by Plato is an example of **rationalism,** since it stresses the activities of the mind in explaining the nature of knowledge. The rationalist believes that the mind must somehow become involved before knowledge is obtainable. Plato's particular brand of rationalism is also called **nativism,** since he stressed the fact that knowledge was innate.

The position taken by Aristotle has come to be called **empiricism,** since it stresses the importance of sensory experience as the basis of all knowledge. The nativist and empiricist explanations of knowledge that started with Plato and Aristotle over 2000 years ago are still very much alive in the area of learning theory, as we shall see throughout this book.

Since the views of Plato and Aristotle concerning the nature of knowledge have played such an important role in the history of learning theory, we will look at them in greater detail below.

PLATO

Plato (427–347 B.C.) was Socrates's most famous student. In fact, Socrates never wrote a word about his philosophy—it was all written by Plato. This is a most significant fact, since the early dialogues were designed primarily to show the Socratic approach to knowledge and were memories of the great teacher at work. The later dialogues, however, seem to represent Plato's own philosophy and have little to do with Socrates. Plato was so upset by the execution of Socrates for impiety that he went on a self-imposed exile to southern Italy, where he came under the influence of the **Pythagoreans.** This fact has profound implications for western man and is directly related to all approaches to epistemology, including learning theory, that have occurred since.

The Pythagoreans believed that the universe was governed by numerical relationships that influenced the physical world. In fact, numbers and their various combinations *caused* events in the physical world. And both events, the number and the empirical event that it caused, were real. Thus, to the Pythagoreans, the abstract had an independent existence and was capable of influencing physical objects. Furthermore, physical events were thought to be but manifestations of the abstract. Although number and matter interact, it is matter that we experience with our senses, not number. This results in a dualistic view of the universe, where one aspect can be experienced through the senses and the other cannot. Following this notion, the Pythagoreans made great strides in mathematics, medicine, and music. Through time, however, they developed into a mystical cult, allowing only a few individuals to become members and share their wisdom. Plato was one such individual.

Plato's later dialogues reflect complete acceptance of the dualistic universe that the Pythagoreans believed in. He developed a theory of knowledge based on the Pythagorean notion that the abstract has an independent and influential existence. This theory has greatly influenced epistemology in general, and psychology in particular. Because all approaches to explaining human knowledge or learning refer back to Plato's ideas it is important for us to look at his theory of knowledge in some detail.

Plato's Theory of Knowledge

Every object in the physical world has a corresponding abstract "idea" or "form" that causes it. For example, the abstract idea of *chair* interacts with matter to produce what we call a chair. The idea of *tree* interacts with matter to form what we see as a tree. All physical objects have such an origin. Thus, what we experience through our senses is a chair, a tree, or a house, but not chairness, treeness, or houseness. The pure idea of these things exists independent of matter, and something is lost when the idea is translated into matter. Therefore, if we attempt to gain knowledge by examining things that we experience through the senses, we will be misled. Sensory information provides only opinion; the abstract ideas themselves are the only bases of true knowledge.

But how do we obtain information about the ideas if we cannot experience them through the senses? Plato said we experience them through the "mind's eye." We turn our thoughts inward and ponder what is innately available to us. All human beings have in their mind complete knowledge of all the ideas that make up the world; thus true knowledge comes from introspection or self-analysis. We must learn to divorce ourselves from sensory information that can only deceive or, at best, remind us of what we already know.

How does one come to have knowledge of the ideas? Here Plato becomes extremely mystical. All humans possess a soul. Before being placed in the body at birth, the soul dwells in pure and complete knowledge. Thus, all human souls know everything before entering the body. Upon entering the body, the knowledge of the soul begins to be "contaminated" by sensory information. According to Plato if humans accept what they experience through the senses as truth, they are doomed to live a life of opinion and ignorance. Only by turning away from the physical impure world to the world of ideas, pondered by the mind's eye, can we hope to gain true knowledge. Thus, all knowledge is **reminiscence** or recollection of the experience our soul had in the "heaven which is beyond the heavens." Plato advises the astronomer to "let the heavens alone" and use "the natural gift of reason" (*Republic* VII, p. 296).

As we have already seen, Plato was a nativist because he felt knowledge was inborn. He was also a rationalist, because he felt this knowledge could only be made available through reasoning. As we shall see later, other rationalists were not as extreme as Plato in their negative attitude toward sensory information. However, it was Plato's philosophy that dominated Europe for the first twelve centuries of the Christian Era. It is through this early influence on Christianity that we still have remnants of Platonism in western culture today. Time and time again, Plato's nativism has appeared in psychology. We will see one example of it when we discuss Gestalt psychology in chapter 10.

ARISTOTLE

Aristotle (384–322 B.C.) was one of Plato's students who first followed Plato's teachings quite closely and later broke away from them almost completely. A basic difference between the two thinkers was in their attitude toward empirical information. To Plato, it was a hindrance and something to be distrusted, but to Aristotle, sensory information was the basis of all knowledge. With his favorable attitude toward empirical observation, Aristotle compiled an extraordinarily large number of facts about physical and biological phenomena.

Reason, however, was in no way abandoned by Aristotle. He felt sense impressions were only the beginning of knowledge—the mind must then ponder these impressions to discover the lawfulness that runs through them. The laws that govern the empirical world are not knowable through sensory information alone, but must be discovered by active reason. Thus, Aristotle believed that knowledge was gained from sense experience *and* thinking.

There are two major differences here between Aristotle's and Plato's theory of knowledge. First, the laws, or forms, or universals that Aristotle was looking for did not have an existence independent of their empirical manifestation, as they did for Plato. They were simply observed relationships in nature. Second, for Aristotle, all knowledge is based on sensory experience. This, of course, was not the case with Plato. Because Aristotle contended that the source of all knowledge was sensory experience he is labeled an empiricist.

In elaborating his empiricistic view of knowledge, Aristotle formulated his **laws of association.** He said the experience or recall of one object will elicit the recall of things similar to that object (law of similarity), or recall of opposite things (law of contrast), or recall of things that were originally experienced along with that object (law of contiguity). Aristotle also noted that the more frequently two things are experienced together, the more likely it will be that the experience or recall of one will stimulate the recall of the second. Later in history, this came to be known as the law of frequency. Thus, according to Aristotle, sensory experience gives rise to ideas. The ideas stimulated by sensory experience will stimulate other ideas in accordance with the laws of similarity, contrast, contiguity, and frequency. Within philosophy, the attempt to explain the relationship between ideas using these or other laws has come to be called **associationism.** An example of how ideas become associated through contiguity is shown in Figure 3–1.

Besides making empirical investigation respectable, Aristotle made several other contributions to psychology. He wrote the first history of psychology, which was entitled *De Anima*. He wrote extensively on the human sensory apparatus, which he listed as consisting of sight, hearing, smell, taste, and touch. He contributed greatly to later conceptions of memory, thinking, and learning. As we saw

Figure 3–1.   An example of how seeing and touching a chair and hearing the word "chair" become associated through contiguity. (From *Introduction to Modern Behaviorism*, 2nd ed., by Howard Rachlin. Copyright © 1970, 1976 W.H. Freeman and Company. Reprinted with permission)

above, his associative principles of similarity, contrast, contiguity, and frequency later became the bases for the doctrine of associationism, which is still very much part of modern psychology. In view of his immense contributions, we can forgive him for locating the mind in the heart and treating the brain as a system for cooling the blood. About Aristotle's great influence on learning theory, Weimer has recently said the following (1973):

> A moment's recollection . . . shows that Aristotle's doctrines are at the heart of contemporary thought in epistemology and the psychology of learning. The centrality of associationism as the mechanism of the mind is so well known as to require only the observation that *not one single learning theory* propounded in this century *has failed to base its account on associative principles.* (p. 18)

With Aristotle's death died the hope for the development of empirical science. In the centuries following Aristotle there was no follow-up to the scientific study that Aristotelian thinking had promoted. The collapse of the Greek city-states, barbarian invasions throughout Europe, and the rapid spread of Christianity stunted the growth of scientific inquiry. Early medieval thinkers depended on the teachings of past authorities instead of seeking new information.

Plato was by far the most important influence on early Christianity. The conception of man that prevailed during these times is described by Marx and Hillix as follows (1963):

> He [man] was regarded as a creature with a soul, possessed of a free will which set him apart from ordinary natural laws, subject only to his own willfulness and perhaps to the rule of God. Such a creature, being freewilled, could not be an object of scientific investigation. Even the body of man was regarded as sacrosanct, and dissection was dangerous for the dissector. These strictures against observation hindered the development of anatomy and medicine for centuries, and misconceptions that are today considered incredible persisted for over a thousand years. A science of man could not flourish in such an atmosphere. (p. 24)

Religion has been defined as philosophy in the absence of dialogue; when Plato's views concerning the nature of knowledge were incorporated into Christian dogma, they could not be challenged. Some 1500 years elapsed before the rediscovery of Aristotle's writings challenged the antiempiricism of the Church. When inquiry into the nature of man did begin, it spread like wildfire. For psychology, the writings of René Descartes is one of the most important examples of this renaissance.

THE BEGINNING OF MODERN PSYCHOLOGY

René Descartes (1596–1650) tried to approach all philosophical inquiry with an attitude of complete doubt. "I can doubt everything," he argued, "except one thing, and that is the very fact that I doubt. But when I doubt I think; and when I think I must exist." He thus arrived at his celebrated conclusion, "I think, therefore I am."

He went on from that point to prove the existence of God and from there he inferred that our sensory experiences must be a reflection of an objective reality, since God would not deceive us.

Descartes went on to postulate a separation between the mind and the body. He viewed the human body as a machine that moves in predictable ways; in this respect we were the same as any other animal. The mind, however, is a uniquely human attribute. The mind was free and could decide the actions of the body. Descartes believed the pineal gland to be the point of contact between the mind and body. The mind could move the gland from side to side and could thus open or close the pores of the brain. Through these pores, the "animal spirits" flowed down tiny tubes to the muscles, filling and swelling them and making them become short and thick, thus moving the parts of the body to which they were connected. Although that is what happens when the mind causes behavior, sensory experience can also cause behavior. Motion outside the body exerts a pull on the "taut strings" that lead to the brain; the pull opens the pores of the brain, releasing the "animal spirits" which flow into the muscles and cause behavior. Therefore, the mind or the physical environment can initiate behavior. This description of *reflex action* was to have a long-lasting influence on psychology. Descartes can be considered a predecessor of the stimulus-response psychologists.

By comparing the human body to a machine, Descartes helped to make it accessible to scientific study. He urged physiologists to use the method of dissection in order to better understand the machinery of the body. Because Descartes believed that humans and animals were physiologically similar, the study of animals to learn about man was given greater respectability. Descartes, therefore, did much to pave the way for physiological and comparative psychology.

The mind, however, was free and possessed by humans alone. In explaining the working of the mind, Descartes relied heavily on **innate ideas,** thus showing Plato's influence on his philosophy. Innate ideas were not derivable from experience but were integral to the mind. Examples of innate ideas included the concepts of God and the self; the axioms of geometry; and the ideas of space, time, and motion. The question of innate ideas caused much philosophical discussion following Descartes, and it is still very much an issue in psychology today.

Thomas Hobbes (1588–1679) opposed the notion that innate ideas are a source of knowledge. He maintained that sense impressions are the source of all knowledge. With this belief, Hobbes reopened the philosophical school of empiricism and its related school of associationism. As we have seen, rationalism looks upon the mind as the source of knowledge. Empiricism, on the other hand, maintains that sensation is the source of knowledge and explains memory, thinking, and imagination as combinations of persistent sense impressions held together by association.

Hobbes also believed that stimuli either help or hinder the vital functions of the body. A stimulus that aids in the vital functioning of the body causes a feeling of pleasure; therefore, the person seeks to experience this pleasure again. Stimuli that hinder the vital functioning of the body cause an aversive feeling, and the person seeks to retreat from it. According to Hobbes, human behavior is controlled by these "appetites" and "aversions." Those events approached by a person are called "good," and those avoided are called "evil." Thus, the values of good and evil are individually determined; they are not absolute. Later, Jeremy Bentham (1748–1832) said human behavior was governed by the "pleasure principle," an idea that was picked up by Freud and later by the reinforcement theorists.

[handwritten margin note: Wrong Answer →]

Hobbes was mainly interested in the political and societal conditions under which humans live. He felt that humans were basically selfish and aggressive and if allowed to live in accordance with their nature, life would be characterized by self-satisfaction and war. Humans form political systems and societies because it is to our advantage to do so, not because we are by nature gregarious. In other words, Hobbes believed that forming human societies was the lesser of two evils since it reduced the likelihood of constant struggle with other humans. This view of the function of society comes very close to the one held by Freud many years later.

John Locke (1632–1704) also strongly opposed the notion of innate ideas. For him, the mind is made up of ideas, and ideas come from experience. He indicated that children have no awareness of most universally accepted truths and that different cultural groups differ markedly in what they believe. Thus, the infant mind at birth is a *tabula rasa,* a blank tablet, and experience writes upon it. The mind becomes what it experiences; *there is nothing in the mind that is not first in the senses.* Simple ideas come directly from sense experience, complex ideas come from combining simple ideas.

Locke also distinguished between "primary" and "secondary" qualities. Primary qualities are characteristics of physical objects, such as size, weight, solidity, shape, and mobility. The secondary qualities are in the mind of the perceiver and include such things as colors, odors, and tastes. This distinction between primary and secondary qualities, made earlier by Galileo, is often cited as the reason that psychology can never become a true science. It is claimed that since secondary qualities are purely cognitive, they cannot be objectively analyzed in the same way that primary qualities can be. For many it is this inaccessibility of secondary qualities to direct objective study that causes them to be beyond the reach of scientific scrutiny. Many years later, it was this very concern that caused many behaviorists to place the study of mental events off-limits in their analysis of human behavior.

For Locke, ideas are elements that constitute the mind, and therefore, the mind can be understood by analyzing its elements. The laws of association explain how the ideas come to be combined. To postulate a separate faculty of willing or understanding, Locke said, is as ridiculous as postulating a faculty of singing or dancing.

George Berkeley (1685–1753) claimed Locke did not go far enough. There was still a kind of dualism in Locke's view that physical objects cause ideas about them. While Locke contended that there is an empirical world (primary qualities) about which we have ideas (secondary qualities), Berkeley claimed that we can experience only secondary qualities. *The only reality is the mind.* What we call primary qualities, such as shape and size, are really only secondary qualities or ideas. Ideas are the only things we experience directly and are therefore the only things we can be sure of. Despite such beliefs, however, Berkeley is still considered an empiricist because he believed the contents of the mind were derived from experience.

David Hume (1711–1776) carried the argument one step further. Although he agreed with Berkeley that we could know nothing for sure about the physical environment, he added that we could know nothing for sure about ideas. *We can be sure of nothing.* Mind, for Hume, was no more than a stream of ideas, memories, imaginings, and feelings.

This is not to deny Hume's empiricist and associationist leanings. He believed strongly that human knowledge consists of ideas which somehow come from experience and which come to be associated through the principles of similarity and contiguity. Hume was saying, however, that we only experience the empirical world indirectly through our ideas. Even the laws of nature are constructs of the imagination; the "lawfulness" of nature is in our heads, not necessarily in nature. General concepts such as causation, for example, come from what Hume referred to as the "habitual order of ideas."

Needless to say, Hume upset everyone. To accept Hume was to question the foundation of rational thought, science, psychology, and religion. All dogma, whether religious or scientific, now became suspect. Hergenhahn (1986) summarizes Hume's philosophy:

> Hume had argued that all conclusions we reached about anything were based on subjective experience, since that was the only thing we ever encountered directly. According to Hume, all statements about the nature of the physical world or about morality were derived from ideas and the feelings that ideas aroused, as well as from the way ideas were organized by the laws of association. Even causation, which was so important to many rationalists, was reduced to a habit of the mind in Hume's philosophy. For example, even if B always follows A, and the interval between the two is always the same, we cannot ever conclude that A causes B, since there is no way for us to verify an actual causal relationship between the two events. For Hume, rational philosophy, physical science, and moral philosophy were all reducible to subjective psychology. Therefore, nothing could be known with certainty, since all knowledge was based on the interpretation of subjective experience. (p. 113)

Immanuel Kant (1724–1804) claimed that Hume awoke him from his "dogmatic slumbers" and caused him to attempt to rescue philosophy from Hume's skepticism. Kant attempted to correct the impractical features of both rationalism and empiricism. Rationalism can only involve the manipulation of concepts, and empiricism confines knowledge to sensory experience and its derivatives. Kant attempted to reconcile both points of view.

Kant felt that careful analysis of our experience revealed certain categories of thought. For example, Kant indicated that we do have such ideas as causality, unity, and totality, but we never, as Hume had said, experience any of these things empirically. These categories of thought, or "faculties," are neither part of our sensory experience, nor derived from it. If these thoughts are not the result of sensory experience, Kant reasoned, they must be **innate categories of thought.** These innate mental faculties are superimposed over our sensory experiences, thereby providing them with structure and meaning. Kant believed that there were twelve of these innate faculties that give meaning to our experiences of the physical world; examples included unity, totality, reality, existence, necessity, reciprocity, and causality.

What we consciously experience, according to Kant, is influenced by both sensory experience, caused by the empirical world, and by the faculties of the mind, which are innate. The faculties of the mind transform sensory experience, thereby giving it greater organization and meaning. Any attempt to determine the nature of knowledge must, according to Kant, also take into consideration the active contribution of the mind. We will see a current example of this point of view when we review Gestalt psychology in chapter 10 and Jean Piaget's theory in chapter 11.

Thus, Kant kept rationalism alive by showing that the mind is the source of knowledge. In other words he kept alive an approach to explaining knowledge in terms other than its reduction to sensory experience. By taking a nativistic point of view—that much knowledge is inborn—Kant revived the Platonist point of view that had been losing ground since the time of Descartes.

John Stuart Mill (1806–1873) was disturbed by the contention of the early associationists, such as Hobbes and Locke, that complex ideas are nothing more than combinations of simple ideas. Although he remained an empiricist and an associationist, he made a very important revision in the position taken by other associationists. Accepting the notion that complex ideas are made up of simpler ideas, Mill added the notion that simple ideas combine into a new totality that may bear little resemblance to its parts. For example, if we combine blue, red, and green lights, we get white. In other words, Mill believed that *the whole is more than the sum of its parts*. We will encounter this idea again when we discuss Gestalt psychology in chapter 10.

OTHER HISTORICAL INFLUENCES ON LEARNING THEORY

Thomas Reid (1710–1796) also opposed the extreme elementism of the empiricists, but his opposition took a different form than that of John Stuart Mill. Like Kant, Reid believed that the mind has powers of its own which strongly influence how we perceive the world. Unlike Kant, however, Reid believed these powers or faculties correspond to specific areas of the brain. He hypothesized twenty-seven discrete areas of the brain, each corresponding to a specific faculty. These faculties were believed to be innate and not the product of experience. The belief in the existence of such faculties in the mind was later called **faculty psychology.** The faculty psychologist is a strange mixture of nativism, rationalism, and empiricism. Kant, for example, explored sensory experience (empiricism) in order to discover categories of thought (rationalism) that were innate (nativism).

Reid argued that Hume's contention that we cannot know anything directly about the physical world was ridiculous. Hergenhahn (1986) summarizes Reid's position:

Reid said that since all humans were convinced of the existence of physical reality, it must exist. "All mankind," he said, "could not be wrong and go against the wisdom of the ages." If Hume's logic caused him [Hume] to conclude that we could never know the physical world, then, said Reid, something was wrong with Hume's logic. We can trust our impressions of the physical world because it makes *common sense* to do so. We are naturally endowed with the abilities to deal with and make sense out of the world. If reasoning denies either these human abilities or the physical world, it must be faulty. (p. 111)

Reid gives examples of what life would be like if we denied the fact that our senses accurately represent physical reality: "I resolve not to believe my senses. I break my nose against a post. . . . I step into a dirty kennel; and after twenty such wise and rational actions, I am taken up and clapped into a madhouse" (Lehrer & Beanblossom, 1975, p. 86).

Franz Joseph Gall (1758–1828) carried faculty psychology one step further. He believed that the faculties of the mind did not exist to the same extent in every individual. Furthermore, he believed that if a faculty was well developed, there would be a bump or protrusion on the part of the skull corresponding to the place in the brain that houses that faculty. Likewise, if a faculty was poorly developed, a hollow or depression would be found on the skull. Armed with these assumptions, Gall set out to examine the shape of people's skulls. He developed an elaborate chart showing what faculties the various parts of the skull correspond to. Using this chart and analyzing the bumps and hollows of a person's skull, Gall and his followers believed they could tell which of the person's faculties were the most highly developed, and which were underdeveloped. This analysis of mental attributes by examining the characteristics of the skull is called **phrenology.** A typical phrenology chart is shown in Figure 3-2.

Phrenology had two lasting effects on psychology, one good and one questionable. First, it led to research designed to discover the function of various parts of the brain. It was this very research, however, that disproved the assumptions upon which phrenology was based. Second, many faculty psychologists believed that the

Figure 3–2. A typical phrenology chart.

faculties became stronger with practice just like the biceps become stronger with practice. For this reason the faculty psychologists were said to have taken a "mental muscle" approach to learning. Learning, to them, meant strengthening faculties by practicing those traits associated with them. One could improve one's reasoning abilities, for example, by formally studying such topics as mathematics or Latin. The belief that a particular course of training would strengthen certain faculties was called **formal discipline,** a concept that provides one answer to the question of how learning transfers from one situation to another. We will have more to say about the transfer of training when we discuss E. L. Thorndike in chapter 4. It should be noted here, however, that the idea of formal discipline, based on faculty psychology, dominated school curricula for many years and was used to justify requiring students to study intensely the most difficult topics available, such as mathematics and Latin, regardless of their vocational aspirations. One suspects that many present day educators still believe in the benefits of formal discipline.

Charles Darwin (1809–1882) supported the notion of biological evolution with so much evidence that it had to finally be taken seriously. The Church bitterly opposed Darwin's notions. In fact, Darwin himself was so worried about the impact his findings would have upon religious thought that he wished to have his research published only after his death.

The final acceptance of evolutionary theory by the scientific community marked a blow to the collective ego of humans equal only to the one dealt by Copernicus and the future one dealt by Freud. Evolution restored the continuity between humans and other animals that had been denied for centuries. No longer was there the clear-cut distinction between man and other animals that had been the cornerstone of so many systems of thought, such as those of Plato, Aristotle, Descartes, and Kant. If we are biologically related to the "lower" animals, do they also have minds, souls, and innate categories of thought, and if so, to what extent? Obviously, animal research was now to take on a much greater respectability. Descartes's thinking tolerated animal research as a way of finding out how the human body works, but from his point of view, it could not disclose anything concerning the human mind. Until Darwin, man's behavior was thought to be rational and animal behavior thought to be instinctive. With Darwin, that handy dichotomy was lost. Many questions arose such as "Can an animal's behavior also be rational, at least in part?" "Can man's behavior be instinctive, at least in part?" A mind resulting from a long evolutionary process is looked at differently than a mind which is divinely implanted into the body by God.

Darwin changed all thoughts about human nature. Human beings were now looked upon as a combination of their biological heritage and their life's experiences. The pure associationism of the empiricists was now coupled with physiology in a search for the underlying mechanisms of thought, and the function of behavior as a way of adjusting to the environment was studied intensely. Individuality was appreciated as never before and its study became popular. This new attitude was exemplified by Darwin's cousin, *Francis Galton* (1822–1911), who devised a number of methods, such as the questionnaire, psychological scales, and the method of correlation, specifically designed to measure individual differences. Probably the most famous person directly influenced by Darwin was *Sigmund Freud* (1856–1939), who explored the problems of the human animal living in a civilized world.

Such philosophic questions as "How do humans think?" and "What can humans know?" changed to "How do humans adjust to their environment?" and "Given certain circumstances, what do humans *do?*" Thus, the mood was set for a science of behavior. If human behavior was now to be studied like any other aspect of the environment, then the experimental approach that had been so successful in the physical sciences could be applied to the study of the human being.

Hermann Ebbinghaus (1850–1909) is said to have emancipated psychology from philosophy by demonstrating that the "higher mental processes" of learning and memory could be studied experimentally. Rather than assuming that associations had already been formed, and studying them through reflection, as had been the case for many centuries, Ebbinghaus studied the associative process as it was taking place. This way, he could systematically study the conditions that influenced the development of associations. He was an extremely careful researcher and repeated his experiments over a period of many years before he finally published his results in 1885. Many of his findings concerning the nature of learning and memory are still valid.

An important principle of association was the law of frequency, which Ebbinghaus focused on in his research. The law of frequency stated that the more frequently an experience occurred, the more easily the experience was recalled. In other words, memory gains strength through repetition. In order to test this notion, Ebbinghaus needed material that was not contaminated by the subject's previous experience. In order to control for the effects of previous experience, he invented his now famous **nonsense syllable,** which consisted of a vowel between two consonants (e.g., *qaw, jiq, xuw, cew,* or *tib*). The nonsense syllables were usually arranged in groups of twelve, although he varied group size to measure rate of learning as a function of the amount of material to be learned. He found that as the number of nonsense syllables to be learned became larger, it took a greater amount of time to learn them. Ebbinghaus was the first to demonstrate this fact that sounds so obvious to us today.

Using himself as a subject, Ebbinghaus would look at each syllable in the group for a fraction of a second, and he would pause fifteen seconds before starting through the group again. He continued in this manner until "complete mastery" had occurred, which meant he could recite each syllable in the group without making a mistake. At that point, he noted how many exposures to the group of syllables it took before mastery was reached. Also, he plotted the number of errors made as a function of successive exposures to the group of syllables, thus creating psychology's first learning curve.

At various intervals following original "mastery," Ebbinghaus went back and relearned a group of nonsense syllables. He noted the number of trials it took to relearn a group of syllables and subtracted that number from the number of exposures it took to originally learn the list. The difference was called **savings.** He plotted savings as a function of time elapsed since original learning, thus creating psychology's first retention curve. His graph indicated that the rate of forgetting is

Hermann Ebbinghaus. (From *Great Experiments in Psychology*, p. 102a, by H. E. Garrett, 1930, New York: The Century Company)

very fast for the first few hours following a learning experience, and very slow thereafter. He also found that *overlearning* reduces the rate of forgetting considerably. That is, if he continued to expose himself attentively to a group of nonsense syllables even after they had been mastered, they would be retained much better than if his learning stopped with only one perfect recitation of the syllables.

Ebbinghaus also studied the effects of what is now called meaningfulness on learning and retention. He found, for example, that it took nine readings to memorize eighty syllables of material from Byron's *Don Juan,* but about nine times as many exposures to learn eighty nonsense syllables. Not only was learning rate much faster for the more meaningful material, but retention was far superior also.

Ebbinghaus's research revolutionized the study of the associative process. Instead of hypothesizing about the law of frequency, he demonstrated how it functioned. Ebbinghaus brought the "higher mental processes" into the laboratory, where they have been ever since.

PSYCHOLOGY'S EARLY SCHOOLS

Structuralism

As far as learning theory is concerned, associationism has been one of the most important developments in psychology's long philosophical history. As we have seen, philosophers over the centuries studied the problems of how ideas were associated with other ideas and how simple ideas combined to form complex ones. As the scientific technique was being successfully applied to investigate physics and chemistry, it was to be only a matter of time before it would be applied to study psychology as well. Thus the first school of psychology, called **structuralism,** developed out of the philosophical school of associationism combined with the scientific method. Although the structuralists had good intentions, their subject matter was unreliable, thus making their scientific effort a dubious one.

Within the structuralist school, which was headed by **Wilhelm Wundt** (1832–1920), and later by his student *Edward Titchener* (1867–1927), psychology was the systematic study of human consciousness. The structuralists believed that human consciousness could be studied the same way as chemical substances, that is, complex entities could be broken down into simpler elements. Thus, the structuralist, like all associationists, believed that the mind is made up of various combinations of ideas, and that the smallest element of consciousness was the idea.

The structuralists set out to discover the structure of the mind. In analyzing the elements of thought, the major tool of the structuralist was **introspection,** or self-analysis. Experimental subjects had to be carefully trained not to misuse the introspective technique. They were trained to report their **immediate experience** as they perceived an object, and not to report their interpretations of that object. In other words, Wundt and Titchener were interested in the subject's "raw" experiences, but not in what they had learned about those experiences. In that sense, learning was looked upon as more of a hindrance than a topic worthy of study for itself. When shown an apple, for example, the subject was supposed to report hues, brightnesses, and spatial characteristics, rather than labeling the object as an apple. Naming the object of experience during an introspective report was called a **stimulus error.** An example of a stimulus error would be calling an apple an apple. In other words, the subject is reporting a compound idea rather than simple ones, and therefore the building blocks of the mind remain obscure. Clearly, the structuralists were more interested in the contents of the mind than with the origins of those contents.

As a school of psychology, structuralism was short-lived and died within Titchener's own lifetime. There were many reasons for the death of structuralism,

Wilhelm Wundt. (Courtesy of Archives of the History of American Psychology, University of Akron, Ohio)

but the most important one was probably the rising popularity of functionalism, which we will consider below. The structuralists made a rather sterile attempt to use the methods of science to substantiate an ancient philosophical belief. It failed to take into consideration one of the most important developments in human history—the doctrine of evolution. As the importance of the evolutionary process became more apparent, there was increased attention given to the organism's adaptation to its environment. Also, the doctrine of evolution made the study of "lower" animals a legitimate way of learning about people. Structuralism ignored both of these trends. It also ignored the growing evidence for the existence of unconscious processes that was being provided by researchers such as Sigmund Freud. For these and other reasons, structuralism came and went. It has been said that perhaps the most important thing about structuralism was that it appeared, it was tried, and it failed. Psychology was able, therefore, to get such an approach out of its system.

Functionalism

Structuralism, psychology's first scientific school of thought, originated in Germany when Wundt founded his laboratory in 1879 in Leipzig. **Functionalism,** however, originated in this country and was America's first school of psychology. Although functionalist beliefs diverged, their emphasis was always the same—*the utility of consciousness and behavior in adjusting to the environment.* Clearly, the functionalists were strongly influenced by Darwin's doctrine of evolution.

The founder of the functionalist movement is usually thought to be **William James** (1842–1910). In his highly influential book, *The Principles of Psychology* (1890), James took the structuralists to task. Consciousness, he said, cannot be reduced into elements. Rather, consciousness functions as a unity whose purpose is

William James. (Courtesy of Archives of the History of American Psychology, University of Akron, Ohio)

to allow the organism to adjust to its environment. The "stream of consciousness" changes as total experience changes. Such a process cannot be reduced to elements because a person's conscious processes as a whole are involved with adaptation to his or her environment. The most important thing about consciousness, as far as James was concerned, was that it had a purpose. James also wrote about the importance of studying psychology scientifically. He emphasized that humans were both rational and irrational (emotional). He pointed out the importance of understanding the biological foundations of mental events, and urged the study of lower animals to learn more about humans. Many of James's ideas are still current. It should be noted that James had a significant influence on psychology, both through his writings and through his ability as a teacher to inspire. Many consider James as one of the greatest psychologists of all times.

In addition to James, two of the most influential members of the functionalist movement were John Dewey (1859–1952) and James R. Angell (1869–1949). In Dewey's famous article, "The Reflex Arc Concept in Psychology" (1896), he attacked the growing tendency in psychology to isolate a stimulus-response relationship for study. He argued that isolating such a unit for study was a total waste of time since the purpose of behavior is overlooked. The goal for psychology should be to study the significance of behavior in adapting to the environment. The main contribution of Angell was that he built up a department of psychology at the University of Chicago around the functionalistic point of view. Under his leadership, the department trained many functionalistic psychologists.

The main contribution the functionalists made to learning theory, is that they studied the relationship of consciousness to the environment, rather than studying it as an isolated phenomenon. They opposed the introspective technique of the structuralists because it was elementistic, not because it studied consciousness. The functionalists were not opposed to studying mental processes, but they insisted that they always be studied in relationship to survival.

Behaviorism

The founder of **behaviorism** was **John B. Watson** (1878–1958), who noted that consciousness could only be studied through the process of introspection, a notoriously unreliable research tool. Because consciousness could not be reliably studied, he said, it should not be studied at all. To be scientific, psychology needed a subject matter that was stable enough to be reliably measured, and that subject matter was behavior. Watson felt that the main concern for the psychologist should be with behavior and how it varies with experience. Leave the study of consciousness to the philosophers, he said. Thus, what was the focal point of epistemological inquiry for thousands of years was looked upon by the behaviorist as only a hindrance in the study of human behavior.

No more introspection, no more talk of instinctive behavior, and no more attempts to study the human conscious or unconscious mind. Behavior is what we can see and therefore behavior is what we study. According to Watson (1913):

John Broadus Watson. (From *Psychologies of 1925*, 1926, Worcester, MA: Clark University Press)

Psychology as the behaviorist views it is a purely objective experimental branch of natural science. Its theoretical goal is the prediction and control of behavior. Introspection forms no essential part of its methods, nor is the scientific value of its data dependent upon the readiness with which they lend themselves to interpretation in terms of consciousness. The behaviorist, in his efforts to get a unitary scheme of animal response, recognizes no dividing line between man and brute. The behavior of man, with all its refinement and complexity, forms only a part of the behaviorist's total scheme of investigation. . . . (p. 158)

Elsewhere Watson said (1929):

The behaviorist cannot find consciousness in the test tube of his science. He finds no evidence anywhere for a stream of consciousness, not even for one so convincing as that described by William James. He does, however, find convincing proof of an ever-widening stream of behavior. (p. 26)

Watson was enthusiastic about his work and its implications. He saw behaviorism as a means of stripping ignorance and superstition from human existence, thereby paving the way for a more rational, meaningful life. Understanding the principles of behavior, he thought, was the first step toward that kind of life. He said (1925):

I think behaviorism does lay a foundation for saner living. It ought to be a science that prepares men and women for understanding the first principles of their own behavior. It ought to make men and women eager to rearrange their own lives, and especially eager to prepare themselves to bring up their own children in a healthy way. I wish I had time more fully to describe this, to picture to you the kind of rich and wonderful individual we should make of every healthy child; if only we could let it shape itself properly and then provide for it a universe unshackled by legendary folk lore of happenings thousands of years ago; unhampered by disgraceful political history; free of foolish customs and conventions which have no significance in themselves, yet which hem the individual in like taut steel bands. (p. 248)

Clearly, Watson was a rebel. He took the various objective approaches to the study of psychology that were appearing here and there, and through his forceful writing and speaking, organized them into a new school of psychology. Unfortunately, Watson's career as a professional psychologist was cut short when he was asked to leave Johns Hopkins University because of marital troubles leading to divorce. The same year he left the university he married Rosalie Rayner, with whom he did the famous study with the infant named Albert (we will discuss this study in chapter 7), and went into the advertising business. From that point on, instead of writing in professional journals, Watson published his ideas in *McCall's, Harper's,* and *Collier's* magazines.

Watson never wavered from his behaviorist outlook, and in 1936 he had the following to say about the position he took in 1912:

I still believe as firmly as ever in the general behavioristic position I took overtly in 1912. I think it has influenced psychology. Strangely enough, I think it has temporarily slowed down psychology because the older instructors would not accept it wholeheartedly, and consequently they failed to present it convincingly to their classes. The youngsters did not get a fair presentation, hence they are not embarking wholeheartedly upon a behavioristic career, and yet they will no longer accept the teachings of James, Titchener, and Angell. I honestly think that psychology has been sterile for several years. We need younger instructors who will teach objective psychology with no reference to the mythology most of us present-day psychologists have been brought up upon. When this day comes, psychology will have a renaissance greater than that which occurred in science in the Middle Ages. I believe as firmly as ever in the future of behaviorism—behaviorism as a companion of zoology, physiology, psychiatry, and physical chemistry. (p. 231)

Of course, the behaviorist's main point was that behavior should be studied because it could be dealt with directly. Mental events should be ignored because they could not be dealt with directly. Behaviorism had a profound effect on American learning theory. In fact, most of the theories of learning in this book can be thought of as behavioristic. It is possible, however, to make subdivisions within the behavioristic camp. Some theories concentrate on behavior related to an organism's survival. Such behavioristic theories can be called functional theories. Other behavioristic theories are less concerned with adaptive behavior, and explain all learned behavior in terms of the laws of association. Such theories tend to treat functional and nonfunctional behavior in the same way. Thus, under the general heading of behaviorism we can list both functionalistic and associationistic theories. Whether a behavioristic theory is labeled as functionalistic or associationistic depends on the kind of behavior the theory concentrates on and how the theory explains the origins of that behavior.

SUMMARY AND AN OVERVIEW

From the brief history presented in this chapter, it can be seen that learning theory has a rich and diverse heritage. As a result of this heritage, numerous viewpoints concerning the learning process exist today. In chapter 2, we referred to a point of view shared by a substantial number of scientists as a paradigm. At least four such points of view can be identified among modern theories of learning.

One paradigm we will refer to as *functionalistic*. This paradigm reflects the influence of Darwinism in that it stresses the relationship between learning and adjustment to the environment. A second paradigm we will refer to as *associationistic*, since it studies the learning process in terms of the laws of association. This paradigm originated with Aristotle and was perpetuated and elaborated on by Locke, Berkeley, and Hume. As mentioned before, both the functionalistic and associationistic paradigms are considered behavioristic. The third paradigm we shall label *cognitive,* since it stresses the cognitive nature of learning. This paradigm originated with Plato and came to us through Descartes, Kant, and the faculty psychologists. The fourth paradigm is referred to as *neurophysiological,* since it attempts to isolate the neurophysiological correlates of such things as learning, perception, thinking, and intelligence. This paradigm represents a current manifestation of a line of investigation which started with Descartes's separation of the mind and the body. The current goal of most neurophysiological psychologists, however, is to reunite mental and physiological processes.

These paradigms should be viewed as only very crude categories, since it is difficult to find any theory of learning that fits unambiguously into any one of them. We will place a theory in a particular paradigm because of its major emphasis. However, within almost every theory, certain aspects of other paradigms can be identified. For example, even though Hull's theory is listed under the functionalistic paradigm below, it relies heavily on associationistic ideas. Similarly, Piaget's theory is listed under the cognitive paradigm only because of its major emphasis. Piaget's theory, as much influenced by Darwinism as any other, has a great deal in common with the theories listed under the functionalistic paradigm. Tolman's theory is also difficult to categorize since it has both functionalistic and cognitive elements. We list it as a cognitive theory only because the main emphasis of the theory is cognitive. Likewise, Hebb's theory, although its major emphasis is neurophysiological, also stresses cognitive events. In fact, Hebb's theory can be looked upon as an effort to describe the neurophysiological correlates of cognitive experiences.

With these reservations in mind, the major theories of learning covered in this book are organized as follows:

Functionalistic Paradigm	**Cognitive Paradigm**
Thorndike	Gestalt theory
Skinner	Piaget
Hull	Tolman
	Bandura
	Norman

Associationistic Paradigm	**Neurophysiological Paradigm**
Pavlov	Hebb
Guthrie	
Estes	

Which paradigm is correct? Probably all of them. No doubt they all emphasize certain truths about the learning process and ignore others. At this point in history, it appears that in order to obtain the most accurate picture of the learning process, one must be willing to view it from a number of different angles. It is hoped that this book will allow the student to do just that.

DISCUSSION QUESTIONS

1. Compare Plato's theory of knowledge with that of Aristotle. Include a definition of the terms *rationalism, nativism,* and *empiricism* in your answer.
2. Summarize Descartes's influence on psychology.
3. Briefly describe what Kant meant by an "innate category of thought."
4. What important departure from traditional associationistic thinking did John Stuart Mill suggest?
5. Summarize Reid's argument against Hume's skepticism.
6. Discuss phrenology and the theory of the mind upon which it is based.
7. Discuss Darwin's influence on learning theory.
8. What was the significance of the work of Ebbinghaus as far as the history of learning theory is concerned?
9. Summarize the important features of the schools of structuralism, functionalism, and behaviorism.
10. What caused the downfall of structuralism?
11. List each individual discussed in this chapter and indicate which of them can be labelled a rationalist, a nativist and/or an empiricist.

CHAPTER HIGHLIGHTS

Aristotle (384–322 B.C.). Because he believed sensory experience to be the basis of all knowledge, he was the first major empiricist. He also proposed the laws of similarity, contrast, contiguity, and frequency to explain how ideas became associated with other ideas. Therefore, he was the first associationist.

Associationism. The philosophical belief that the relationship between ideas can be explained by the laws of association.

Behaviorism. A school of psychology, founded by J. B. Watson, that completely rejected the study of consciousness. In order to be scientific, psychology needed a subject matter that could be reliably measured, and according to the behaviorist, that subject matter was behavior.

Berkeley, George (1685–1753). He said we have no direct knowledge concerning the empirical world; we only have ideas caused by the empirical world. The only reality we can ever know is the ideas contained in the mind.

Darwin, Charles (1809–1882). He demonstrated the utility of behavior in adjusting to the environment, and that human development is biologically continuous with that of lower animals. Both observations had a profound and lasting effect on psychology, especially on learning theory.

Descartes, René (1596–1650). He postulated that the mind and the body were governed by different laws. The mind was free and possessed only by humans, whereas the body was mechanical and its functions were the same for both humans and other animals. He is responsible for creating the duality of mind and body, stimulating interest in physiological and comparative psychology, and for updating Plato's belief in innate ideas.

Ebbinghaus, Hermann (1850–1909). He was the first to study learning and memory experimentally. Demonstrating how the law of frequency worked in the forming of new associations, he invented the nonsense syllable to control for previous experience in a learning situation.

Empiricism. The philosophical belief that sensory experience is the basis of all knowledge.

Epistemology. The study of the nature of knowledge.

Faculty psychology. The belief that the mind contains certain powers or faculties.

Formal discipline. The belief held by many faculty psychologists that specific training can strengthen a specific faculty. For example, practicing being friendly would strengthen the friendliness faculty, thereby making the person more friendly.

Functionalism. America's first school of psychology. The primary goal of the functionalist was to discover how mental and behavioral processes are related to an organism's adaptation to its environment. Members of this school were strongly influenced by Darwin's writings.

Gall, Joseph Franz (1758–1828). He believed that a person's strong and weak faculties could be detected by analyzing the bumps and depressions on the person's skull. This system of analysis is called phrenology.

Hobbes, Thomas (1588–1679). He reasserted Aristotle's doctrine of associationism and also suggested that experiences of pleasure and pain influence how associations are formed.

Hume, David (1711–1776). He said we can know nothing with certainty. All ideas are products of the mind and do not necessarily relate to a reality outside of the mind.

Therefore, the so-called natural laws are more the result of "habits of thought" than of any lawfulness in nature.

Immediate experience. The raw psychological experience that was the object of introspective analysis; experience that was not contaminated by interpretation of any kind.

Innate category of thought. According to Kant, a genetically determined faculty of the mind that molds our cognitive experiences by giving them greater structure and meaning than they otherwise would have.

Innate ideas. Ideas that are not derived from experience, but rather are thought to be inherited as part of the mind.

Introspection. The reporting of one's own mental events while experiencing a certain object or situation; the technique employed by the structuralists to study the structure of the mind.

James, William (1842–1910). The founder of the functionalist movement. He attacked the way that the structuralists used the introspective method to search for the elements of thought. Consciousness, he felt, could not be subdivided since it acted as a functional unit that was constantly changing. The most important thing about consciousness is that it aids human survival. He also encouraged psychology to embrace the scientific method, to search for the physiological correlates of mental processes, and to investigate human emotions as well as the intellect.

Kant, Immanuel (1724–1804). He believed that the mind was active and not passive, as the empiricist-associationists had assumed. The mind has innate powers or faculties which act upon sense impressions and give them meaning.

Laws of association. Principles such as similarity, contrast, contiguity, and frequency that are supposed to explain how one idea is related to another or how one experience elicits ideas related to it.

Locke, John (1632–1704). He strongly opposed the notion of innate ideas and suggested that at birth the mind was a *tabula rasa,* or a blank tablet. He said "there is nothing in the mind that is not first in the senses." He distinguished between primary qualities, the physical characteristics of an object, and secondary qualities, the psychological experience caused by a physical object, such as the experience of color or taste.

Mill, John Stuart (1806–1873). An associationist who disagreed with his fellow associationists' contention that complex ideas are nothing more than a compound of simpler ones. He felt that ideas could fuse together and the fusion could create an idea distinctly different from the simple ideas that made it up.

Nativism. The philosophical belief that a mental attribute is inherited and therefore is independent of experience.

Nonsense syllable. A meaningless consonant-vowel-consonant combination invented by Ebbinghaus to control for previous experience in a learning situation.

Phrenology. The study of the location of bumps and depressions on a person's skull in order to determine his or her strong and weak faculties.

Plato (427–347 B.C.). He proposed a reminiscence theory of knowledge where knowing was explained as remembering the pure knowledge that the soul had experienced before entering the body. Plato was the first major rationalist and the first nativist.

Pythagoreans. Followers of Pythagoras who believed abstractions, such as numbers, were just as real as physical objects and that these abstractions could influence the physical world. Such beliefs had a strong influence on the development of Plato's theory of knowledge.

Rationalism. The philosophical belief that the mind must become actively involved before knowledge can be attained.

Reid, Thomas (1710–1796). He believed that the faculties of the mind corresponded to certain areas of the brain. Later individuals, such as Kant and Reid who attributed certain powers or faculties to the mind, were called faculty psychologists. Reid believed that any philosophical position that denied that we can reliably experience the physical world was ridiculous. Reid argued that we can believe that our sense impressions, and the ideas that they give rise to, accurately reflect the physical world because it makes common sense to do so.

Reminiscence theory of knowledge. The belief held by Plato that all knowledge is present in the human soul at birth; thus to know was to remember the contents of the soul.

Savings. The difference in the time it takes to relearn something as compared to the amount of time it took to learn it originally; a measure of retention used by Ebbinghaus.

Stimulus error. The error of naming an object while introspecting about it instead of reporting one's immediate experience.

Structuralism. The first school of thought in psychology. The goal of structuralism was to discover the basic elements of thought by using the technique of introspection.

Watson, J. B. (1878–1958). Founder of the school of behaviorism. According to Watson, the only reliable, observable, and measurable subject matter available to psychologists is behavior and, therefore, behavior is all that psychologists should study.

Wundt, Wilhelm (1832–1920). Founder of the structuralist school; also founded psychology's first psychological laboratory in Leipzig, Germany, in 1879.

4

Edward Lee Thorndike

Revised Law of Effect

Belongingness

Spread of Effect

Thorndike on Education

Science and Human Values

It is fitting that we begin our discussion of the major learning theorists with Edward L. Thorndike (1874–1949), perhaps the greatest learning theorist of all time. He did pioneer work not only in learning theory but also in the areas of educational practices, verbal behavior, comparative psychology, intelligence testing, the nature-nurture problem, transfer of training, and the application of quantitative measures to sociopsychological problems (e.g., he developed scales with which to compare the quality of life in different cities). It may be of interest to note that Thorndike began this latter project, as well as many others, when he was more than 60 years old.

His research started with the study of mental telepathy in young children (which he explained as the unconscious detection on the part of the child of minute movements made by the experimenter). His later experiments involved chicks, cats, rats, dogs, fish, monkeys, and finally adult humans. He wanted to use apes also but could not afford to buy and maintain them.

Thorndike's scientific productivity was almost unbelievable. At his death in 1949 his bibliography comprised 507 books, monographs, and journal articles. Always attempting to measure everything, Thorndike reports in his autobiography that up to the age of 60 he had spent well over 20,000 hr reading and studying scientific books and journals—this in spite of the fact that he was primarily a researcher rather than a scholar.

Thorndike was born in Williamsburg, Massachusetts, in 1874, and was the second son of a Methodist minister. He claims never to have seen or heard the word psychology until he was a junior at Wesleyan University. At that time he read William James's *Principles of Psychology* (1890) and was deeply impressed. Later, when he went to Harvard and took a course from James they became good friends. When Thorndike's landlady forbade him to go on hatching chicks in his bedroom, James tried to get him laboratory space on the Harvard campus. When this failed, James allowed Thorndike to continue his studies in the basement of his home—much to the dismay of James's wife and to the delight of his children.

After two years at Harvard, where he earned a living by tutoring students, he accepted a fellowship at Columbia working under James McKeen Cattell. Although Thorndike carried two of his "most educated" chicks with him to New York, he soon switched from chicks to cats upon arrival at Columbia. His years of animal

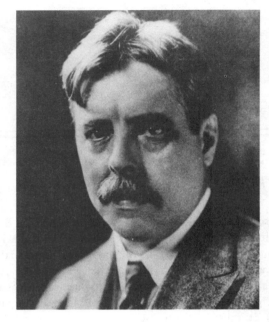

Edward L. Thorndike. (From *The Sane Positivist: A Biography of Edward L. Thorndike*, p. 22a, by G. Joncich, 1968, Middletown, CT: Wesleyan University Press)

research were summarized in his doctoral dissertation entitled, *Animal Intelligence: An Experimental Study of the Associative Processes in Animals* which was published in 1898 and expanded and republished in 1911 as *Animal Intelligence*. The fundamental ideas put forth in these documents permeate all of Thorndike's writings and, in fact, all of learning theory. The extent of Thorndike's influence is indicated by the following quotation from Tolman (1938):

> The psychology of animal learning—not to mention that of child learning—has been and still is primarily a matter of agreeing or disagreeing with Thorndike, or trying in minor ways to improve upon him. Gestalt psychologists, conditioned-reflex psychologists, sign-Gestalt psychologists—all of us here in America seem to have taken Thorndike, overtly or covertly, as our starting point. And we have felt very smart and pleased with ourselves if we could show that we have, even in some very minor way, developed new little wrinkles of our own. (p. 11)

ANIMAL RESEARCH BEFORE THORNDIKE

Descartes's contention that the bodies of both humans and non-human animals functioned according to the same mechanical principles did much to stimulate the anatomical investigations of nonhuman animals. It was Darwin, however, who suggested that humans and nonhumans were similar in all respects: anatomically, emotionally, and cognitively. Darwin's *The Expression of Emotions in Man and Animals* (1872) is generally considered the first text on comparative psychology. Not long after Darwin published the aforementioned book, his friend **George John Romanes** (1848–1894) published *Animal Intelligence* (1882), *Mental Evolution in Animals* (1884), and *Mental Evolution in Man* (1885). The evidence that Romanes offered to support the continuity of intelligent and emotional behavior from lower animals to humans was largely anecdotal and was often characterized by **anthropomorphizing,** or attributing human thought processes to nonhuman animals. For example, Romanes attributed the emotions of anger, fear, and jealousy to fish; affection, sympathy, and pride to birds; and slyness and reasoning to dogs. Sargent and Stafford (1965) report one of Romanes's anecdotes.

> One day the cat and the parrot had a quarrel. I think the cat had upset Polly's food, or something of that kind; however, they seemed all right again. An hour or so after, Polly was standing on the edge of the table; she called out in a tone of extreme affection, "Puss, Puss, come then—come then, Pussy." Pussy went and looked up innocently enough. Polly with her beak seized a basin of milk standing by, and tipped the basin and all its contents over the cat, then chuckled diabolically, of course broke the basin, and half drowned the cat. (p. 149)

In an effort to describe animal behavior more objectively, **Conway Lloyd Morgan** (1842–1936) gave the following advice to animal researchers in his book *Introduction to Comparative Psychology* (1891). The advice became known as **Morgan's canon:** "In no case may we interpret an action as the outcome of the exercise of a higher psychical faculty, if it can be interpreted as the outcome of the exercise of one which stands lower in the psychological scale" (p. 53).

Instead of attributing higher mental processes to nonhuman animals, as Romanes had done, Morgan attempted to explain their behavior in terms of instinct, habit, and association. Although Morgan's research was much more objective than that of Romanes, it was still naturalistic. That is, Morgan was still describing the behavior of animals as it occurred in the natural environment. For example, he described in great detail how his dog had learned to lift the latch of his garden gate thereby escaping confinement. Although Morgan's research was an improvement over what had preceded it, an additional step was needed; animal behavior needed to be studied systematically under controlled laboratory conditions. In other words, animal behavior had to be studied scientifically. It was E. L. Thorndike who took this important next step.

MAJOR THEORETICAL NOTIONS

Connectionism

Thorndike called the association between sense impressions and impulses to action a bond or a connection. This marked the first formal attempt to link sensory events to behavior. Earlier brands of associationism attempted to show how *ideas* became linked together; thus Thorndike's approach is quite different and can be regarded as the first modern theory of learning. Thorndike's emphasis on the functional aspects of behavior is due mainly to the influence of Darwin. In fact, Thorndike's theory can be understood as a combination of associationism, Darwinism, and the methods of science.

Thorndike's concern was not only for stimulus conditions and tendencies to action, but for what held the stimulus and response together. He believed they were connected by a neural bond. His theory is called **connectionism,** with the connection referred to being the neural connection between stimuli (S) and responses (R).

Selecting and Connecting

To Thorndike the most basic form of learning was **trial-and-error learning,** or what he originally called **selecting and connecting.** He reached this basic notion of trial-and-error learning through his early experimentation, which involved putting an animal in an apparatus that was arranged so that when the animal made a certain kind of response it escaped. The apparatus shown in Figure 4-1 was a small confining box with a pole sticking up in the middle of it, or a chain hanging from its top. Pushing against the pole or pulling on the chain enabled the animal to escape. Some arrangements, however, required the animal to engage in a complex series of responses before it could escape. Different responses were called for at different times in Thorndike's experiments but the idea was always the same—the animal had to perform in a certain way before it was allowed to leave the box. The following quotation from *Animal Intelligence* (1911) exemplifies his work with the puzzle box.

Figure 4-1.   One kind of puzzle box that Thorndike used in his research on learning.

The behavior of all but 11 and 13 was practically the same. When put into the box the cat would show evident signs of discomfort and of an impulse to escape from confinement. It tries to squeeze through any opening; it claws and bites at the bars or wire; it thrusts its paws out through any opening and claws at everything it reaches; it continues its efforts when it strikes anything loose and shaky; it may claw at things within the box. It does not pay very much attention to the food outside, but seems simply to strive instinctively to escape from confinement. The vigor with which it struggles is extraordinary. For eight or ten minutes it will claw and bite and squeeze incessantly. With 13, an old cat, and 11, an uncommonly sluggish cat, the behavior was different. They did not struggle vigorously or continually. On some occasions they did not even struggle at all. It was therefore necessary to let them out of the box a few times, feeding them each time. After they thus associate climbing out of the box with getting food, they will try to get out whenever put in. They do not, even then, struggle so vigorously or get so excited as the rest. In either case, whether the impulse to struggle be due to instinctive reaction to confinement or to an association, it is likely to succeed in letting the cat out of the box. The cat that is clawing all over the box in her impulsive struggle will probably claw the string or loop or button so as to open the door. And gradually all the other non-successful impulses will be stamped out and the particular impulse leading to the successful act will be stamped in by the resulting pleasure, until after many trials, the cat will, when put in the box, immediately claw the button or loop in a definite way. (pp. 35–40)

Thus, whether working for a piece of fish or for release from confinement, all his animals learned to do whatever was necessary to escape from the box.

Figure 4–2. The figure exemplifies both the incremental improvement in performance observed by Thorndike and the nonincremental (insightful) improvement which Thorndike did not observe.

Thorndike plotted the time it took the animal to solve the problem as a function of the number of opportunities the animal had to solve the problem. Every opportunity was a trial and the trial terminated when the animal hit upon the correct solution. A typical graph generated under these circumstances is shown in Figure 4–2. In this basic experimental arrangement Thorndike consistently noted that the time it took to solve the problem (his dependent variable) systematically decreased as the number of trials increased, that is, the more opportunities the animal had, the faster it solved the problem.

Learning Is Incremental, Not Insightful

Noting the slow decrease in time to solution as a function of successive trials, Thorndike concluded that learning was **incremental** rather than **insightful.** In other words, learning occurs in very small systematic steps rather than in huge jumps. He noted that if learning was insightful the graph would show that the time to solution would remain relatively stable and high while the animal was in the unlearned state. At the point where the animal would gain insight into the solution, the graph would drop very rapidly and would remain at that point for the duration of the experiment. Figure 4–2 also shows how the graph would look if the learning that took place was insightful.

Learning Is Not Mediated by Ideas

Based on his research, Thorndike also concluded emphatically that learning was direct and was not mediated by thinking or reasoning. He said in 1895:

> The cat does not look over the situation, much less *think* it over, and then decide what to do. It bursts out at once into the activities which instinct and experience have settled on as suitable reactions to the situation *"confinement when hungry with food outside."* It does not ever in the course of its success realize that such an act brings food and therefore decide to do it and thenceforth do it immediately from decision instead of from impulse. (p. 45)

Elsewhere (1911) Thorndike made the same point with regard to monkeys:

> In discussing these facts we may first of all clear our way of one popular explanation, that this learning was due to "reasoning." If we use the word reasoning in its technical psychological meaning as the function of reaching conclusions by the perception of relations, comparison and inference, if we think of the mental content involved as feelings of relation, perceptions of similarity, general and abstract notions and judgments, we find no evidence of reasoning in the behavior of the monkeys toward the mechanisms used. And this fact nullifies the arguments for reasoning in their case as it did in the case of the dogs and cats. The argument that successful dealings with mechanical contrivances imply that the animal reasoned out the properties of the mechanisms, is destroyed when we find mere selection from their general instinctive

activities sufficient to cause success with bars, hooks, loops, etc. There is also positive evidence of the absence of any general function of reasoning. (pp. 184–186)

Thus, following the principle of parsimony, Thorndike rejected reason in favor of direct selection and connection in learning. The demotion of reasoning and of the importance of ideas in learning was the beginning of what was to become the behavioristic movement in America.

All Mammals Learn in the Same Manner

Many were disturbed by Thorndike's insistence that all learning is direct and not mediated by ideas especially because he also insisted that the learning of all mammals including humans followed the same laws. According to Thorndike, no special processes need to be postulated when one is attempting to explain human learning. The following quotation (1913a) serves both to point out Thorndike's belief that the laws of learning were the same for all animals, and to introduce other aspects of Thorndike's theory to which we will turn next:

These simple, semi-mechanical phenomena . . . which animal learning discloses, are the fundamentals of human learning also. They are, of course, much complicated in the more advanced states of human learning, such as the acquisition of skill with the violin, or of knowledge of the calculus, or of inventiveness in engineering. But it is impossible to understand the subtler and more planful learning of cultural men without clear ideas of the forces which make learning possible in its first form of directly connecting some gross bodily response with a situation immediately present to the senses. Moreover, no matter how subtle, complicated and advanced a form of learning one has to explain, these simple facts—the selection of connections by use and satisfaction and their elimination by disuse and annoyance, multiple reaction, the mind's set as a condition, piecemeal activity of a situation, with prepotency of certain elements in determining the response, response by analogy, and shifting of bonds—will as a matter of fact, still be the main, and perhaps the only, facts needed to explain it. (p. 16)

THORNDIKE BEFORE 1930

Thorndike's thinking about the learning process can be conveniently divided into two parts: one part consisting of his thoughts prior to 1930, and the second part consisting of his views after 1930 when some of his earlier views changed considerably.

The Law of Readiness

The **law of readiness,** proposed in his book *The Original Nature of Man* (Thorndike, 1913a), had three parts, abbreviated as follows:

1. When a conduction unit is ready to conduct, conduction by it is satisfying.
2. For a conduction unit ready to conduct, not to conduct is annoying.
3. When a conduction unit is not ready for conduction and is forced to conduct, conduction by it is annoying.

We notice some terms here whose subjectivity might worry the modern learning theorist. We must remember, however, that Thorndike was writing before the behavioristic movement and that many of the things that he discussed had never been systematically analyzed before. It is also important to note that what appears to be subjective terms in Thorndike's writing, may not be. For example, what he meant here by a conduction unit ready to conduct is merely a preparedness for action or goal directedness. Using current terminology we can restate Thorndike's law of readiness as follows:

1. When someone is ready to perform some act, to do so is satisfying.
2. When someone is ready to perform some act, not to do so is annoying.
3. When someone is not ready to perform some act and is forced to do so, it is annoying.

Generally, we can say that interfering with goal-directed behavior causes frustration and causing someone to do something they do not want to do is also frustrating.

Even terms such as "satisfying" and "annoying" were defined in such a way as to be acceptable to most modern behaviorists (1911): "By a satisfying state of affairs is meant one which the animal does nothing to avoid, often doing such things as attain and preserve it. By a discomforting or annoying state of affairs is meant one which the animal commonly avoids and abandons" (p. 245). These definitions of satisfiers and annoyers should be kept in mind throughout our discussion of Thorndike.

The Law of Exercise

Before 1930, Thorndike's theory included the **law of exercise,** which had two parts.

1. Connections between a stimulus and a response are strengthened as they are used. In other words, merely exercising the connection between a stimulating situation and a response strengthens the connection between the two. This is the part of the law of exercise called the **law of use.**
2. Connections between situations and responses are weakened when practice is discontinued or if the neural bond is not used. This is the portion of the law of exercise called the **law of disuse.**

What did Thorndike mean by the strengthening or weakening of a connection? Here again he was ahead of his time and on this issue he could be speaking today. He defined strengthening as an increase in the probability that a response will be made when the stimulus recurs. If the bond between a stimulus and a response is strengthened, the next time the stimulus occurs, there is an increased probability that the response will occur. If the bond is weakened, there is a decreased probability that the next time the stimulus occurs, the response will occur. In brief, the law of exercise says we learn by doing and forget by not doing.

The Law of Effect

The law of effect, before 1930, refers to the strengthening or weakening of a connection between a stimulus and a response as a result of the consequences of the response. For example, if a response is followed by a **satisfying state of affairs,** the strength of the connection is increased. If a response is followed by an **annoying state of affairs,** the strength of the connection is decreased. In modern terminology, if a stimulus leads to a response, which in turn leads to reinforcement, the S-R connection is strengthened. If, on the other hand, a stimulus leads to a response which leads to punishment, the S-R connection is weakened.

The law of effect was a historical break from traditional associationistic theory that claimed frequency of occurrence or mere contiguity to be the determiners of the strength of an association. Although Thorndike accepted both the law of frequency and the law of contiguity, he went further by saying that the consequences of a response are important in determining the strength of association between the situation and the response to it. The importance of the consequences of an act in forming associations was only hinted at previously by philosophers such as Hobbes and Bentham. Here we see Thorndike's concern with the utility of behavior in helping the organism adjust to its environment, a concern which he shared with all the functionalists.

Thorndike's law of effect was attacked on several grounds. Critics said his argument was circular: If the response probability went up, it was said to be due to the presence of a satisfying state of affairs; if it did not go up, it was claimed none was present. It was believed that such a situation did not allow for a test of the theory, since the same event (increased or decreased probability of a response) was used to detect both learning and a satisfying state of affairs. Later defenders of Thorndike have shown this criticism to be invalid since once something has been shown to be a satisfier, it can be used to modify behavior in other situations (Meehl, 1950). In other words, it is the "transituational" nature of satisfiers that saves the law of effects from circularity.

A second criticism has been concerned with the fact that the effect of a response appears to work back in time on the neural bond that caused it. First, there is a stimulus which causes a certain response to occur, since there is a neural connection between that stimulus and that response. If a response results in a satisfying state of affairs the S-R connection is strengthened. How can this happen, since the conduction unit has already fired before the satisfying state of affairs had occurred? Thorndike attempted to answer this question by postulating the existence of a **confirming reaction** which was triggered in the nervous system if a response resulted in a satisfying state of affairs. Thorndike felt that this confirming reaction was neurophysiological in nature and the organism was not conscious of it. Although Thorndike did not elaborate on the characteristics of this reaction, he did suspect that such a neurophysiological reaction was the true strengthener of neural bonds. We will have more to say about the confirming reaction when we consider Thorndike's concept of belongingness.

More recently, some learning theorists have attempted to answer the question of how reinforcement can strengthen the response that produced it by postulating the existence of a neural trace that is still active when the satisfaction occurs. In other words, for these theorists, the conduction unit is still active at the time the organism experiences the satisfying state of affairs. Although the neural trace notion became a popular answer to the question, the problem of how reinforcement strengthens a response is still essentially unsolved.

A third criticism of Thorndike's law of effect concerned the automatic way that the connections were strengthened or weakened. Even with the law of effect, Thorndike believed learning to be direct and not the result of any conscious mechanism such as thinking or reasoning. Clearly, Thorndike felt that an organism need not be aware of various satisfiers for them to have their effect. The debate over whether or not a learner must be aware of reinforcement contingencies before they can influence behavior continues today and, therefore, we will return to it often throughout this book.

SECONDARY CONCEPTS BEFORE 1930

Before 1930, Thorndike's theory included a number of ideas that were less important than the laws of readiness, effect, and exercise. These secondary concepts included multiple response, set or attitude, prepotency of elements, response by analogy, and associative shifting.

Multiple Response

Multiple response, or varied reaction, was, for Thorndike, the first step in all learning. It refers to the fact that if our first response does not solve the problem we try other responses. Trial-and-error learning, of course, depends upon the animal trying first one response and then another until a response that works is hit upon. When this happens the probability of that response being made again goes up. In other words, for Thorndike, much learning depends on the fact that organisms tend to remain active until a response that solves an existing problem is made.

Set or Attitude

What Thorndike called "attitudes," "dispositions," "preadjustments," or "sets" was his recognition of the importance of what the learner brings to the learning situation. He said (1913b):

It is a general law of behavior that the response to any external situation is dependent upon the condition of the man, as well as upon the nature of the situation; and that, if certain conditions in the man are rated as part of the situation, the response to it depends upon the remaining conditions in the man. Consequently, it is a general law of learning that the change made in a man by the action of any agent depends upon the condition of the man when the agent is acting. The condition of the man may be considered under the two heads of the more permanent or fixed and the more temporary or shifting, attitudes, or "sets." (p. 24)

Thus, individual differences in learning can be explained by the basic differences among people: their cultural and genetic heritage or by temporary states such as deprivation, fatigue, or various emotional conditions. What can act as a satisfier or an annoyer depends on both the organism's background and its temporary bodily state at the time of learning. For example, animals with considerable experience in a puzzle box will probably solve new puzzle box problems faster than animals with no prior puzzle box training. Furthermore, animals who have been deprived of food for a considerable length of time will probably find food more satisfying than food-satiated animals. It is with his concept of set or attitude that Thorndike recognized that an animal's drive state will, to a large extent, determine what is satisfying and/or annoying to it.

Prepotency of Elements

This is what Thorndike called "the partial or piecemeal activity of a situation." It refers to the fact that only some elements of any situation will govern behavior. He said (1913a):

One of the commonest ways in which conditions within the man determine variations in his responses to one same external situation is by letting one or another element of the situation be prepotent in effect. Such partial or piecemeal activity on the part of a situation is, in human learning, the rule. Only rarely does man form connections, as the lower animals so often do, with a situation as a gross total—unanalyzed, undefined, and, as it were, without relief. He does so occasionally, as when a baby, to show off his little trick, requires the same room, the same persons present, the same tone of voice and the like. Save in early infancy and amongst the feeble-minded, however, any situation will most probably act unevenly. Some of its elements will produce only the response of neglect; others will be bound to only a mild awareness of them; others will connect with some energetic response of thought, feeling or action, and become positive determiners of the man's future. (pp. 26–27)

With the notion of **prepotency of elements,** Thorndike recognized the complexity of the environment and concludes that we respond selectively to aspects of it. In other words, we typically respond to some of the elements in a situation and not to others. Therefore, how we respond to a situation depends on both what we attend to and what responses are attached to what we attend to.

Response by Analogy

What determines how we respond to a situation we have never encountered before? Thorndike's answer was that we respond to it as we would to a related situation that we had encountered before. The amount of **transfer** between the familiar situation and the unfamiliar one is determined by the number of elements that the two situations have in common. This is Thorndike's famous **identical elements theory of transfer** of training.

With his theory of transfer, Thorndike opposed the long-held view of transfer based on the doctrine of **formal discipline.** As we saw in chapter 3, formal discipline was based on faculty psychology which contended that the human mind was made up of several powers or faculties such as reasoning, attention, judgment, and memory. It was believed that these faculties could be strengthened with practice, for example, practicing reasoning made one a better reasoner. Thus, the study of mathematics and Latin were justified because they strengthened the reasoning and memory faculties. It should be obvious why this position was referred to as the "mental muscle" approach to education, since it claims that faculties of the mind are strengthened with practice just as people would strengthen their biceps. This position also maintained that if students were forced to solve a number of difficult problems in school they would be able problem solvers outside of school. Thorndike felt that there was little evidence that education generalized so readily. In fact, he believed that education resulted in highly specific skills rather than general ones. He said (1906):

> A man may be a tip-top musician but in other respects an imbecile: he may be a gifted poet, but an ignoramus in music; he may have a wonderful memory for figures and only a mediocre memory for localities, poetry or human faces: school children may reason admirably in science and be below the average in grammar: those very good in drawing may be very poor in dancing. (p. 238)

Thorndike and Woodworth (1901) critically examined the formal discipline theory of transfer and found no support for it. Instead they found transfer from one situation to the next only occurred to the extent that both situations had elements in common. These elements, according to Thorndike, may be actual stimulus conditions or they may be procedures. For example, looking up words in a dictionary in school may transfer to a variety of situations outside of school that have nothing to do with the exact words you were looking up in the classroom, but the ability to look things up may transfer. This would be the transfer of procedure rather than of stimulus elements. Learning to pay attention for long periods and learning to be punctual would be further examples of the transfer of procedures rather than stimulus elements.

Why is it, then, that the more difficult courses seem to produce brighter students? Because, said Thorndike, the brighter students went into these courses to begin with. Thorndike summarized his elaborate study with Woodworth on the transfer of training involving 8,564 high school students as follows (1924):

By any reasonable interpretation of the results, the intellectual values of studies should be determined largely by the special information, habits, interests, attitudes, and ideals which they demonstrably produce. The expectation of any large differences in general improvement of the mind from one study rather than another seems doomed to disappointment. The chief reason why good thinkers seem superficially to have been made such by having taken certain school studies, is that good thinkers have taken such studies, becoming better by the inherent tendency of the good to gain more than the poor from any study. When the good thinkers studied Greek and Latin, these studies *seemed* to make good thinking. Now that the good thinkers study Physics and Trigonometry, these seem to make good thinkers. If the abler pupils should all study Physical Education and Dramatic Art, these subjects would seem to make good thinkers. . . . After positive correlation of gain with initial ability is allowed for, the balance in favor of any study is certainly not large. Disciplinary values may be real and deserve weight in the curriculum, but the weights should be reasonable. (p. 98)

Concerning the question of how many elements two situations must have in common before the same behavior occurs in both, Thorndike said (1905): "The case may be likened roughly to that of the direction taken by a four horse team at a fork in the roads, when the team has never traveled either road *as a team* but some one horse or a pair *has*. Their previous habit of taking, say, the left turn, will cause the whole team to go that way" (pp. 212–213).

Because all schools are attempting to influence the way students behave outside of school, the problem of the transfer of training should be a central one for educators. Thorndike urged that the school curriculum be designed to include tasks that would be similar to those students will be asked to perform when they leave school. Thus, the study of mathematics should not be included because it strengthens the mind but because students will actually be using mathematics when they leave school. *For Thorndike, schools should emphasize the direct training of those skills thought to be important beyond the school.*

The transfer of identical elements theory was Thorndike's solution to the problem of how we respond to a novel situation and to the problem of the transfer of training in general. Thorndike offered what some thought was a weakness in his theory, namely, the fact that we respond smoothly to new situations, as supportive evidence for his theory (1913b): "There is no arbitrary *hocus pocus* whereby man's nature acts in an unpredictable spasm when he is confronted with a new situation. His habits do not then retire to some convenient distance while some new and mysterious entities direct his behavior. On the contrary, nowhere are the bonds acquired with old situations more surely revealed in action than when a new situation appears" (pp. 28–29).

When attempting to explain how what was learned transfers from one situation to another, it is Thorndike's theory of identical elements that many modern learning theorists still accept.

Associative Shifting

Associative shifting is closely related to Thorndike's identical elements theory of the transfer of training. The procedure for demonstrating associative shifting is to begin with a connection between a certain situation and a certain response. Then one gradually drops out stimulus elements that were part of the original situation, and adds stimulus elements that were not part of the original situation. According to Thorndike's identical elements theory, as long as there are enough elements from the original situation in the new situation, the same response will be given. In this way the same response can be carried through a number of stimulus changes and finally be made to stimulating conditions totally dissimilar to those associated with the original response. Thorndike said (1913b):

> Starting with response X made to *abcde,* we may successively drop certain elements and add others, until the response is bound to *fghij,* to which perhaps it could never otherwise have become connected. Theoretically the formula of progress, from *abcde* to *abcfg* to *abfgh* to *afghi* to *fghij,* might result in attaching any response whatever to any situation whatever, provided only that we arrange affairs so that at every step the response X was more satisfying in its consequences than balking or doing anything else that the person could do. (pp. 30–31)

An example of associative shifting is found in the work of Terrace (1963) on discrimination learning. Terrace first taught pigeons to make a red–green discrimination by reinforcing them with grain when they pecked at a red key but not when they pecked at a green key. Next Terrace superimposed a vertical bar over the red key and a horizontal bar over the green key. Gradually the red and green colors were faded out leaving only the vertical and horizontal bars on the keys. It was found that the discrimination previously associated with red and green was transferred without the pigeons making any errors to the vertical and horizontal bar discrimination. Now the pigeons pecked at the vertical bar and ignored the horizontal bar. The shifting process is shown in Figure 4-3.

The association shifts from one stimulus (red) to another (vertical bar) because the procedure allows enough elements from the preceding situation to guarantee that the same response is made to the new stimulus. This, of course, demonstrates transfer of training according to Thorndike's identical elements theory.

In a more general way much advertising is based on the principle of associative shifting. The advertiser need only find a stimulus object that elicits positive feelings, such as a picture of a beautiful female or handsome male, a respected personality, a medical doctor, a mother, or a romantic outdoor scene. Then the advertiser pairs this stimulus object with the product—a brand of cigarettes, an automobile, or a deodorant—as often as possible so that the product will elicit the same positive feelings elicited by the original stimulus object.

In reading Thorndike, we should note that associative shifting is really quite different from trial-and-error learning, which is governed by the law of effect.

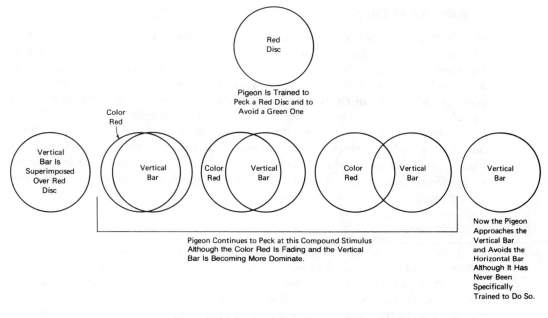

Figure 4–3.   The process that Terrace used to shift a discriminatory
response from one stimulus (the color red) to another stimulus
(a vertical bar).

Unlike learning that depends on the law of effect, associative shifting depends only on contiguity. Associative shifting represents, therefore, a second kind of learning that is similar to the theories of Pavlov and Guthrie, which we consider in chapters 7 and 8.

THORNDIKE AFTER 1930

In September 1929, Thorndike stood before the International Congress of Psychology in New Haven and started his address by saying "I was wrong." This points out an important aspect of good scientific practice: Good scientists are obliged to change their conclusions if the data require it.

Revised Law of Exercise

Thorndike essentially renounced the entire law of exercise. The law of use that stated that mere repetition strengthened a connection was found to be inaccurate. By the same token, simple disuse did not weaken a connection to any large extent. Although Thorndike still maintained that practice led to minor improvement and that lack of practice led to slight forgetting, for all practical purposes he discarded the entire law of exercise after 1930.

Revised Law of Effect

After 1930, the earlier law of effect was found to be only half true. The salvaged half was the half stating that a response followed by a satisfying state of affairs was strengthened. For the other half, Thorndike found that punishing a response had no effect on the strength of the connection. His revised law of effect stated that *reinforcement increases the* **strength of a connection,** *whereas punishment does nothing to the strength of a connection.* This finding still has profound implications today. Thorndike's conclusion concerning the effectiveness of punishment ran contrary to thousands of years of common sense and has numerous implications for education, child rearing, and behavior modification in general. We will often return to the question of the effectiveness of punishment as a means of modifying behavior in the following chapters.

Belongingness

Thorndike observed that in the learning of associations a factor in addition to contiguity and the law of effect was often involved. He noted that if the elements of an association somehow belonged together the association between them was learned and retained more readily than if the elements did not belong together. In one experiment designed to investigate this phenomenon Thorndike read his subjects the following sentences ten times (1932):

> Alfred Dukes and his sister worked sadly. Edward Davis and his brother argued rarely. Francis Bragg and his cousin played hard. Barney Croft and his father watched earnestly. Lincoln Blake and his uncle listened gladly. Jackson Craig and his son struggle often. Charlotte Dean and her friend studied easily. Mary Borah and her companion complained dully. Norman Foster and his mother bought much. Alice Hanson and her teacher came yesterday. (p. 66)

Afterwards his subjects were asked the following questions:

1. What word came next after rarely?
2. What word came next after Lincoln?
3. What word came next after gladly?
4. What word came next after dully?
5. What word came next after Mary?
6. What word came next after earnestly?
7. What word came next after Norman Foster and his mother?
8. What word came next after and his son struggle often?

If contiguity was the only influential factor, all sequences of words should be learned and remembered equally well. This, however, was not the case. The average number of correct associations from the end of one sentence to the beginning of the next was 2.75, whereas the average number of correct associations between the first and second word combinations was 21.50. Clearly, something is operating here beyond mere contiguity and that something is what Thorndike called **belonging-ness,** that is, subjects and verbs belong together more than the last word in one sentence and the first in another.

Thorndike also related his notion of a confirming reaction, discussed earlier, to his concept of belongingness. He felt that if there was a natural relationship between the need state of the organism and the effect caused by a response, learning would be more effective than if the relationship was unnatural. We can say, for example, that a hungry animal would find food satisfying and a thirsty animal would find water satisfying. However, this is not to say that a hungry or thirsty animal would not find other things satisfying. Both would still find escape from confinement and freedom from pain satisfying, but the existence of a powerful drive creates a class of events that would be most satisfying at the moment. It was Thorndike's contention that an effect that belongs to the existing needs of the organism elicits a stronger confirming reaction than effects that do not belong to those needs, even though the latter effects may be powerful satisfiers under different circumstances.

We see, then, that Thorndike used the concept of belongingness in two ways. First, he used it to explain why, when learning verbal material, a person tends to organize what is learned into units that are perceived as belonging together. Second, he said that if the effects produced by a response are related to the needs of the organism, learning will be more effective than it would be if the effects produced by a response were not related to the organism's needs.

Many believed that with his concept of belongingness Thorndike was making concessions to the Gestalt psychologists who said organisms learn general principles and not specific S-R connections (see chapter 10). Thorndike responded with his **principle of polarity** which stated that a learned response is most easily given in the direction in which it was formed. For example, almost everyone can recite the alphabet forward but rarely can a person recite it backward. Likewise, most any school child can recite the pledge of allegiance forward, but it would be uncommon to find a child able to recite it backward. Thorndike's point was that if general principles and/or understandings were learned instead of specific S-R connections, a person should be able to perform what had been learned in either direction with almost equal ease. Thus, even with his concept of belongingness, Thorndike maintained his mechanistic, nonmental view concerning the learning process.

Spread of Effect

After 1930, Thorndike added another major theoretical concept, which he called the **spread of effect.** During one of his experiments Thorndike accidentally found that a satisfying state of affairs not only increased the probability of recurrence of the response that led to the satisfying state of affairs, but also increased the probability of recurrence of the responses surrounding the reinforced one.

One typical experiment demonstrating this effect involved presenting ten words, including *catnip, debate,* and *dazzle,* to subjects to which they were instructed to respond with a number from 1 to 10. If the subject responded to a word with a number that the experimenter had previously chosen to go with that word, the experimenter said "right." If the subject responded with any other number the experimenter said "wrong." The experiment proceeded in this fashion for several trials. Two important observations were made from this research. First, it was found that reinforcement (the experimenter saying "right") strongly increased the probability of the same number being repeated the next time the stimulus word was given, but punishment (the experimenter saying "wrong") did not reduce the probability of an incorrect number being repeated again. It was partially on the basis of this research that Thorndike revised his earlier law of effect. Second, it was found that the numbers that preceded and followed a reinforced number also increased in probability of recurring, even though they were not themselves reinforced, and even if these surrounding numbers had themselves been punished. Thus, what Thorndike called a satisfying state of affairs apparently "spread" from the reinforced response to neighboring responses. He called this phenomenon the spread of effect. Thorndike also found that this effect diminishes with distance. In other words, the reinforced response has the greatest probability of recurring, then the responses next to the reinforced one, then the responses next to those, and so on.

In discovering the spread of effect, Thorndike felt that he had found additional confirmation for his revised law of effect, since reinforcement not only increased the probability of a reinforced response, but also increased the probability of neighboring responses even though these may have been punished. He also felt that the spread of effect further demonstrated the automatic, direct nature of learning.

Thorndike on Education

Thorndike believed strongly that educational practices should be studied scientifically. It was obvious to him that there should be a close relationship between the knowledge of the learning process and teaching practices. Thus, he expected that as more was discovered about the nature of learning, more could be applied to improve teaching practices. Thorndike said (1906):

> Of course present knowledge of psychology is nearer to zero than to complete perfection, and its applications to teaching must therefore be often incomplete, indefinite and insecure. The application of psychology to teaching is more like that of botany and chemistry to farming than like that of physiology and pathology to medicine. Anyone of good sense can farm fairly well without science, and anyone of good sense can teach fairly well without knowing and applying psychology. Still, as the farmer with the knowledge of the applications of botany and chemistry to farming is, other things being equal, more successful than the farmer without it, so the teacher will, other things being equal, be the more successful who can apply psychology, the science of human nature, to the problems of the school. (pp. 9–10)

At many points Thorndike's thinking ran contrary to traditional notions about education; we saw one clear example of this with his identical elements theory of transfer. He also had a low opinion of the lecture technique of teaching that was so popular then (and now). He said (1912):

> The lecture and demonstration methods represent an approach to a limiting extreme in which the teacher lets the pupil find out nothing which he could possibly be told or shown. They frankly present the student with conclusions, trusting that he will use them to learn more. They ask of him only that he attend to, and do his best to understand, questions which he did not himself frame and answers which he did not himself work out. They try to give him an educational fortune as one bequeaths property by will. (p. 188)

Elsewhere he said (1912): "The commonest error of the gifted scholar, inexperienced in teaching, is to expect pupils to know what they have been told. But telling is not teaching. The expression of the facts that are in one's mind is a natural impulse when one wishes others to know these facts, just as to cuddle and pat a sick child is a natural impulse. But telling a fact to a child may not cure his ignorance of it any more than patting him will cure his scarlet fever" (p. 61).

What then is good teaching? Good teaching involves first of all knowing what you want to teach. If you do not know exactly what it is you want to teach you will not know what material to present, what responses to look for, and when to apply satisfiers. This principle is not as obvious as it sounds. Only recently have we realized the importance of behaviorally defining educational objectives. Although Thorndike's seven rules that follow were formulated for the teaching of arithmetic, they represent his advice for teaching in general (1922):

1. Consider the situation the pupil faces.
2. Consider the response you wish to connect with it.
3. Form the bond; do not expect it to come by a miracle.
4. Other things being equal, form no bond that will have to be broken.
5. Other things being equal, do not form two or three bonds when one will serve.
6. Other things being equal, form bonds in the way that they are required later to act.
7. Favor, therefore, the situations which life itself will offer, and the responses which life itself will demand. (p. 101)

One can see here the seeds of B. F. Skinner's attitude toward educational practices which we will consider in chapter 5.

Science and Human Values

Thorndike was also criticized for assuming determinism in the study of human behavior. Reducing human behavior to automatic reactions to the environment destroys human values, the critics said. Thorndike answered that on the contrary, the human sciences offered people their greatest hope for the future (1940):

The welfare of mankind now depends upon the sciences of man. The sciences of things will, unless civilization collapses, progress, extend man's control over nature, and guide technology, agriculture, medicine, and other arts effectively. They will protect man against dangers and disasters except such as he himself causes. He is now his own worst enemy. Knowledge of psychology and of its applications to welfare should prevent, or at least diminish, some of the errors and calamities for which the well-intentioned have been and are responsible. It should reduce greatly the harm done by the stupid and vicious. (p. v)

Elsewhere Thorndike stated (1949):

Thus, at last, man may become ruler of himself as well as of the rest of nature. For strange as it may sound man is free only in a world whose every event he can understand and foresee. Only so can he guide it. We are captains of our own souls only in so far as they act in perfect law so that we can understand and foresee every response which we will make to every situation. Only so can we control our own selves. It is only because our intellects and morals—the mind and spirit of man—are a part of nature, that we can be in any significant sense responsible for them, proud of their progress, or trustful of their future. (p. 362)

Obviously, Thorndike was a very colorful person who expressed opinions on a wide variety of topics. In this chapter we have concentrated on outlining his thoughts on the learning process, and his views concerning the relationship between the learning process and educational practices. The student who is interested in knowing more about Thorndike is urged to read *The Sane Positivist: A Biography of Edward L. Thorndike,* by Geraldine Joncich (1968).

DISCUSSION QUESTIONS

1. Summarize the nature of animal research prior to Thorndike's efforts. In what way was Thorndike's research different from that which preceded it? Include in your answer a discussion of Morgan's canon.

2. Do you agree with Thorndike's contention that the same laws of learning apply to both human and subhuman animals? Explain.

3. Assuming Thorndike's revised law of effect to be valid, do you feel classroom practice in this country is in accordance with it? Child rearing practices? Explain.

4. How would you arrange schoolroom practices so that they take into consideration Thorndike's theory concerning the transfer of training?

5. Summarize Thorndike's theory before 1930. Include in your answer the law of readiness, the law of exercise, and the law of effect.

6. Discuss Thorndike's concept of the confirming reaction.

7. Discuss the importance of sets or attitudes in Thorndike's theory.

8. According to Thorndike, what determines what will transfer from one learning situation to another?

9. Summarize Thorndike's criticisms of the formal discipline approach to education.

10. Describe how you would reduce the probability of a child being fearful of a new situation, such as a new babysitter, using the procedure of associative shifting.

11. Discuss Thorndike's principles of belongingness and polarity.

12. Summarize what Thorndike learned from his research on the spread of effect.

13. What, according to Thorndike, provides humans with their greatest hope for the future?

CHAPTER HIGHLIGHTS

Annoying state of affairs. A condition that an organism actively avoids. If such a condition occurs the organism attempts to abandon it as soon as possible.

Anthropomorphizing. Attributing human characteristics to nonhuman animals.

Associative shifting. The process whereby a response is "carried" from one set of stimulating conditions to another by gradually adding new stimulus elements and subtracting old ones. The result is that a response that was originally given to one set of circumstances is now given to an entirely new set of circumstances. Associative shifting is based on the principle of contiguity.

Belongingness. Material is learned more readily when it is structured in certain ways. Contiguity alone does not determine how well something will be learned. How the material "fits together" must also be taken into consideration. Also, Thorndike maintained that learning is most effective when there is a natural relationship between the needs of an organism and the effects produced by a response.

Confirming reaction. A neurophysiological reaction which is stimulated when a response produces a satisfying state of affairs. The confirming reaction was thought by Thorndike to be the true strengthener of a neural bond.

Connectionism. A term often used to describe Thorndike's explanation of learning since he assumed learning involved the strengthening of neural bonds (connections) between stimulating conditions and the responses to them.

Formal discipline. See chapter highlights for chapter 3.

Identical elements theory of transfer. The theory which states that the likelihood of something which was learned in one situation being applied in a different situation is determined by the number of common elements in the two situations. As the number of common elements goes up the amount of transfer between the two situations goes up. The elements can be either stimuli or procedures.

Incremental learning. Learning that occurs a little bit at a time rather than all at once.

Insightful learning. Learning that occurs all at once rather than a little bit at a time (see also chapter highlights for chapter 10).

Law of disuse. That portion of the law of exercise which states that the strength of a connection diminishes when the connection is not used. The law of disuse was discarded by Thorndike after 1930.

Law of effect. The law which states that the strength of a connection is influenced by the consequences of a response. Before 1930, Thorndike believed that pleasurable consequences strengthened a connection and annoying consequences weakened a connection. After 1930, however, he believed that only pleasurable consequences had an effect on the strength of a connection.

Law of exercise. The law which states that the strength of a connection is determined by how often the connection is used. The law of exercise has two components—the law of use and the law of disuse.

Law of readiness. The law which states that when an organism is ready to act it is reinforcing for it to do so, and annoying for it not to do so. Also, when an organism is not ready to act, forcing it to act will be annoying to it.

Law of use. That portion of the law of exercise which states that the strength of a connection increases with its use. The law of use was discarded by Thorndike after 1930.

Morgan, Lloyd Conway (1842–1936). An early comparative psychologist who attempted to be objective in his descriptions of animal behavior by carefully avoiding anthropomorphizing.

Morgan's canon. Morgan's rule that animal researchers should never explain animal behavior as resulting from a higher mental process, such as reasoning or thinking, if that behavior could be explained by a lower process, such as instinct, habit, or association.

Multiple response. Refers to the fact that if one response does not solve the problem the organism continues to try other responses until it hits upon one that is effective in solving the problem; a prerequisite to trial-and-error learning.

Principle of polarity. The observation that learned material is most easily performed in the same direction in which it was originally learned.

Prepotency of elements. Refers to the fact that different aspects of the environment have different responses connected to them; similar to what we now refer to as selective perception.

Response by analogy. Refers to the fact that our response to an unfamiliar situation is determined by its degree of similarity to a familiar situation. Insofar as two situations are similar they will tend to be similarly responded to. Thorndike describes similarity in terms of the number of elements that the two situations have in common. This is related to his identical elements theory of transfer of training.

Romanes, John George (1848–1894). An early comparative psychologist whose evidence for the continuity between nonhuman and human mental processes was anecdotal and replete with anthropomorphizing.

Satisfying state of affairs. A condition that an organism seeks out and attempts to preserve. Once such a condition exists, the organism does nothing to avoid it.

Selecting and connecting. See **Trial-and-error learning.**

Sets (Attitudes). Temporary conditions, such as food deprivation, fatigue, or emotion, that determine what will be annoying or pleasurable to a given organism.

Spread of effect. The observation that reinforcement not only strengthens the response that produced it, but that it strengthens neighboring responses as well.

Strength of a connection. Determined by how likely a certain response is in a given set of circumstances. In other words, the strength of a connection is equated with response probability.

Transfer of training. When something learned in one situation is applied in another situation.

Trial-and-error learning. The trying of different responses in a problem-solving situation until a response which is effective in solving the problem is hit upon. Thorndike originally called this phenomenon selecting and connecting.

5

Burrhus Frederic Skinner

Skinner was born in Susquehanna, Pennsylvania, in 1904 and is considered by many to be the most famous, influential psychologist alive today. He received his Masters degree in 1930 and his PhD in 1931 from Harvard University. His BA degree was obtained from Hamilton College in New York where he majored in English.

While at Hamilton, Skinner had lunch with Robert Frost, the great American poet, who encouraged Skinner to send him a sample of his writing. Frost reviewed favorably the three short stories that Skinner sent and Skinner decided definitely to become a writer. This decision was a great disappointment to his father who was a lawyer and who wanted his son to become a lawyer.

Skinner's early efforts to write were so frustrating that he thought of seeing a psychiatrist. He eventually went to work for the coal industry summarizing legal documents. In fact, his first book, coauthored by his father, concerned those legal documents and was entitled *A Digest of Decisions of the Anthracite Board of Conciliation*. After finishing this book, Skinner moved to Greenwich Village in New York City where he lived like a Bohemian for six months before going to Harvard to study psychology. By that time he had developed a distaste for most literary pursuits. In his autobiography, he says (1967): "I had failed as a writer because I had had nothing important to say, but I could not accept that explanation. It was literature which must be at fault" (p. 395).

When he failed in describing human behavior through literature, Skinner attempted to describe human behavior through science. Clearly, he was much more successful at the latter pursuit.

Skinner taught psychology at the University of Minnesota between 1936 and 1945, during which time he wrote his highly influential text, *The Behavior of Organisms* (1938). One of Skinner's students at the University of Minnesota was W. K. Estes, whose work has had a considerable impact on psychology (see chapter 9). In 1945 Skinner went to the University of Indiana as chairman of the psychology department, and in 1948 he returned to Harvard where he has been ever since.

As we shall see, Skinner's position is similar to Thorndike's position after 1930 in that it emphasizes the effects of a response on the response itself. Moreover, like Thorndike, Skinner concludes that the effects of reinforcement and punishment are not symmetrical, that is, reinforcement changes the probability of a response's recurring, but punishment does not.

Through the years, Skinner has been a highly prolific writer. One of his main concerns has been to relate his laboratory findings to the solution of human problems. His work has led to the development of programmed learning and teaching machines. Two representative articles in this area are "The Science of Learning and the Art of Teaching" (1954), and "Teaching Machines" (1958). Following his own ideas on this topic, he and his coauthor, Holland, produced a programmed text on his theoretical notions entitled *The Analysis of Behavior* (1961). In 1948 he wrote a Utopian novel called *Walden Two.* The title paid tribute to Thoreau's *Walden.* In *Walden Two,* which Skinner wrote in only seven weeks, he attempted to utilize his principles of learning in the building of a model society. Skinner has recently written *Beyond Freedom and Dignity* (1971) where he shows how a technology of behavior can be used in designing a culture. In *Beyond Freedom and Dignity* he discusses many reasons why the idea of cultural engineering is met with so much opposition. Skinner's writings have been extended into the area of child development through the efforts of Bijou and Baer (1961, 1965). His thoughts have been related to the area of personality through the writings of Lundin, who wrote *Personality: A Behavioral Analysis* (1974), and to child rearing by Hergenhahn, who wrote *Shaping Your Child's Personality* (1972).

Most students of psychology are well aware of the widespread utilization of Skinnerian notions in the area of psychotherapy. For example, Lovaas's early work with autistic children relied heavily on Skinner's ideas. Today the behavior modification approach, based on Skinner's ideas, has become the most widely used and most effective way of working with autistic or retarded children. Behavioral engineering, however, is by no means limited to children. The technique has been successfully applied to the alleviation of a number of adult problems such as stuttering, phobias, eating disorders, and psychotic behavior.

During the Second World War, while at the University of Minnesota, Skinner attempted to apply his theory to the problem of national defense. He trained pigeons to peck at discs upon which moving pictures of enemy targets were being shown. The discs and the motion pictures were ultimately to be contained in a glider loaded with high explosives. The glider was called the *Pelican,* thus, the name of the article describing these events, "Pigeons in a Pelican" (1960). The pecking of the pigeons closed various electronic circuits and thereby kept the vehicle on target. This American version of kamikaze fighter planes would involve no losses of human lives. Although Skinner demonstrated to a group of America's top scientists that he and his coworkers had perfected a homing device that was practically immune to electronic jamming, was capable of reacting to a wide variety of enemy targets, and was simple to build, their proposed project was turned down. Skinner speculates that the whole idea was simply too fantastic for the committee to cope with.

MAJOR THEORETICAL NOTIONS

Respondent and Operant Behavior

Skinner distinguishes two kinds of behavior: **respondent behavior,** which is elicited by a known stimulus, and **operant behavior,** which is not elicited by a known stimulus but is simply emitted by the organism. Unconditioned responses would be examples of respondent behavior since they are elicited by unconditioned stimuli. Examples of respondent behavior would include all reflexes, such as jerking one's hand when jabbed with a pin, the constriction of the pupil of the eye when it is exposed to bright light, and salivation in the presence of food. Because operant behavior is *not* initially correlated with known stimuli it seems to appear spontaneously. Examples include beginning to whistle, standing up and walking about, a child abandoning one toy in favor of another, and moving one's hands, arms, or legs arbitrarily. Most of our everyday activities would be operant behaviors. Note that Skinner does not say that operant behavior occurs independently of stimulation; rather, he says that the stimulus causing such behavior is unknown and that it is not important to know its cause. Unlike respondent behavior which is dependent on the stimulus that preceded it, operant behavior is controlled by its consequences. We will say more about how consequences influence operant behavior.

Type S and Type R Conditioning

Along with the two kinds of behavior described above, there are two kinds of conditioning. Type S conditioning is also called **respondent conditioning** and it is identical to classical conditioning. It is called Type S conditioning to emphasize the

Burrhus Frederic Skinner. (Courtesy of B. F. Skinner)

importance of the stimulus in eliciting the desired response. The type of conditioning that involves operant behavior is called Type R because of the emphasis on the response. Type R conditioning is also called **operant conditioning.**

It is important to note that in Type R conditioning the strength of conditioning is shown by *response rate,* whereas in Type S conditioning, strength of conditioning is usually determined by the *magnitude* of the conditioned response. We see, then, that Skinner's Type R conditioning very closely resembles Thorndike's instrumental conditioning, and Skinner's Type S conditioning is identical to Pavlov's classical conditioning. After making the distinction between Type S and Type R conditioning, Skinner's research has been concerned almost entirely with Type R, or operant conditioning.

Although Skinner and Thorndike are in close agreement on a number of important issues, there are still important differences between them. For example, the dependent variable in Thorndike's learning experiments (his measure of the extent to which learning took place) was *time to solution.* Thorndike was interested in measuring how long it took an animal to perform whatever task was necessary to release it from confinement. Skinner, on the other hand, uses *rate of responding* as his dependent variable. Although Skinner sometimes talks about how reinforcement affects the probability of a response's recurring, his main concern is with how reinforcement affects the rate with which an operant response occurs. In other words, Thorndike was mainly interested in noting how long it took an animal to make a certain response, whereas Skinner is interested mainly in what variables affect rate or pattern of responding.

Operant Conditioning Principles

Two general principles are associated with Type R conditioning: (a) any response that is followed by a reinforcing stimulus tends to be repeated; and (b) a reinforcing stimulus is anything that increases the rate with which an operant response occurs. Or, as we saw above, we can say that a reinforcer is anything that increases the probability of a response's recurring.

Skinner does not provide a rule that one would follow in discovering what would be an effective reinforcer. Rather, he says that whether or not something is reinforcing can only be ascertained by its effect on behavior. He says (1953):

> In dealing with our fellow men in everyday life and in the clinic and laboratory, we may need to know just how reinforcing a specific event is. We often begin by noting the extent to which our own behavior is reinforced by the same event. This practice frequently miscarries; yet it is still commonly believed that reinforcers can be identified apart from their effects upon a particular organism. As the term is used here, however, the only defining characteristic of a reinforcing stimulus is that it reinforces. (p. 72)

In operant conditioning, the emphasis is on behavior and its consequences; with operant conditioning, the organism must respond in such a way as to produce the reinforcing stimulus. This process also exemplifies contingent reinforcement, because getting the reinforcer is contingent (dependent) upon the organism's emitting a certain response. We will have more to say about contingent reinforcement in our subsequent discussion of superstitious behavior.

The principles of operant conditioning can apply to a variety of situations. To modify behavior, one merely has to find something that is reinforcing for the organism whose behavior one wishes to modify, wait until the desired behavior occurs, and then immediately reinforce the organism. When this is done, the rate with which the desired response occurs goes up. When the behavior next occurs, it is again reinforced, and the rate of responding goes up even more. Any behavior that the organism is capable of performing can be manipulated in this manner.

The same principles are thought to apply to the development of human personality. According to Skinner, we are what we have been reinforced for being. What we call personality is nothing more than consistent behavior patterns that summarize our reinforcement history. We learn to speak English, for example, because we have been reinforced for approximating the sounds of the English language in our early home environment. If we happened to be brought up in a Japanese or Russian home, we would learn to speak Japanese or Russian because when we approximated sounds in that language, we would have been attended to or reinforced in some other way. Skinner (1971) says:

> The evidence for a crude environmentalism is clear enough. People are extraordinarily different in different places, and possibly just because of the places. The nomad on horseback in Outer Mongolia and the astronaut in outer space are different people, but, as far as we know, if they had been exchanged at birth, they would have taken each other's place. (The expression "change places" shows how closely we identify a person's behavior with the environment in which it occurs.) But we need to know a great deal more before that fact becomes useful. What is it about the environment that produces a Hottentot? And what would need to be changed to produce an English conservative instead? (p. 185)

Skinner defines culture as a set of reinforcement contingencies. His answers to the above questions would be that a particular set of reinforcement contingencies produce a Hottentot and another set produces the English conservative. Different cultures reinforce different behavior patterns. This fact must be clearly understood before an adequate technology of behavior can be developed. Skinner (1971) says:

> The environment is obviously important, but its role has remained obscure. It does not push or pull, it *selects,* and this function is difficult to discover and analyze. The role of natural selection in evolution was formulated only a little more than a hundred years ago, and the selective role of the environment in shaping and maintaining the behavior of the individual is only beginning to be recognized and studied. As the interaction between organism and environment has come to be understood, however, effects once assigned to states of mind,

feelings, and traits are beginning to be traced to accessible conditions, and a technology of behavior may therefore become available. It will not solve our problems, however, until it replaces traditional prescientific views, and these are strongly entrenched. (p. 25)

If one controls reinforcement, one can also control behavior. However, this need not be looked upon as a negative statement, since behavior is constantly being influenced by reinforcement whether we are aware of that fact or not. It is never a question of *whether* behavior is going to be controlled, but who or what is going to control it. Parents, for example, can decide to give direction to their child's emerging personality by reinforcing certain behavior, or they can let society rear their child by letting TV, peers, school, books, and babysitters reinforce him or her. Giving direction to a child's life is difficult, however, and any parents wishing to do so must take at least the following steps (Hergenhahn, 1972):

1. Decide the major personality characteristics you want your child to possess as an adult. Let's say, for example, you want the child to grow up to be a creative adult.

2. Define these goals in behavioral terms. In this case you ask, "What is a child doing when he is being creative?"

3. Reward behavior that is in accordance with these goals. With this example, you would reward instances of creativity as they occurred.

4. Provide consistency by arranging the major aspects of the child's environment so that they too reward the behavior you have deemed important. (pp. 152–153)

Without a knowledge of these principles, a parent could easily misapply them without knowing it. Skinner says (1951):

The mother may unwillingly promote the very behavior she does not want. For example, when she is busy she is likely not to respond to a call or request made in a quiet tone of voice. She may answer the child only when it raises its voice. The average intensity of the child's vocal behavior therefore moves up to another level. . . . Eventually the mother gets used to this level and again reinforces only louder instances. This vicious circle brings about louder and louder behavior. . . . The mother behaves, in fact, as if she has been given the assignment of teaching the child to be annoying. (p. 29)

According to Skinner, living organisms are constantly being conditioned by their environment. We can either allow the principles of learning to operate capriciously on our children, or by systematically applying those principles, we can give some direction to their development.

The Skinner Box

Most of Skinner's early animal work was done in a small test chamber which has come to be called the **Skinner box.** It is a direct descendant of the puzzle box used by Thorndike. The Skinner box usually has a grid floor, a light, a lever, and a food

Figure 5–1.   A typical Skinner box. (Courtesy of the Gerbrands Company, Inc.)

cup. It is arranged so that when the animal depresses the lever, the feeder mechanism is activated and a small pellet of food is released into the food cup. A typical Skinner box is shown in Figure 5-1.

The Cumulative Recording

Skinner uses a **cumulative recording** to keep track of an animal's behavior in the Skinner box. A cumulative recording is quite different from other ways of graphing data in learning experiments. Time is recorded on the X-axis and total number of responses is recorded on the Y-axis. The cumulative recording never goes down—the line either climbs or remains parallel to the X-axis. Let's say we are interested in how often the animal presses the lever. When the cumulative recording shows a line parallel to the X-axis, it indicates no responding, that is, the animal is not pressing the lever. When the animal makes a lever-pressing response, the pen goes up a notch and remains at that level until the animal makes another response. If, for example, the animal presses the lever when it is first placed in the Skinner box, the pen will go up a notch and remain there until the animal responds again, at which time the pen will go up another notch, and so on. If the animal responds very rapidly, the line will rise very rapidly. The rate with which the line ascends indicates rate of responding; a very steep line indicates very rapid responding, and a line parallel to the X-axis indicates no responding. If at any time you want to know the total number of responses made by the animal, you just measure the distance between the line of the graph and the X-axis, and this can easily be transformed into total number of responses. Sample cumulative recordings are shown in Figure 5-2.

Conditioning the Lever Press Response

Typically, conditioning the lever press response involves the following steps:

   1. Deprivation. The experimental animal is put on a deprivation schedule. If food is to be used as the reinforcer, then the animal is deprived of food for a 23-hr period for a number of days prior to the experiment, or it is maintained at 80% of its

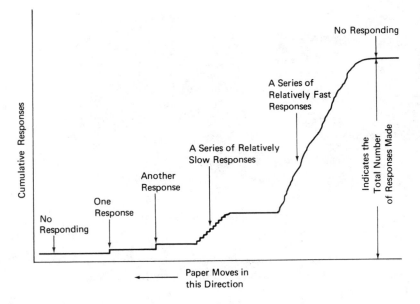

Figure 5-2. A cumulative recording. Note that the steeper the line, the faster is the rate of responding. A line parallel to the baseline indicates no responding.

free-feeding body weight. If water is to be used as the reinforcer, the animal is deprived of water for a 23-hr period for a number of days prior to the experiment. (Some Skinner boxes are designed to deliver small pellets of food and others small drops of water.) Skinner does not say that these procedures "motivate" the animal; he even hesitates to say that they produce a drive state. Deprivation is simply a set of procedures that is related to how an organism performs on a certain task; nothing more needs to be said.

2. Magazine Training. After being on a deprivation schedule for a number of days, the animal is placed into the Skinner box. Using an external hand switch, the experimenter periodically triggers the feeder mechanism (also called the magazine), making sure the animal is not in the vicinity of the food cup when he or she does so (otherwise the animal would learn to remain near the food cup). When the feeder mechanism is activated by the hand switch, it produces a fairly loud clicking sound prior to delivering a pellet of food into the food cup. Gradually the animal associates the click of the magazine with the presence of a food pellet. At that point, the click has become a secondary reinforcer through its association with a primary reinforcement (food). (We will discuss secondary reinforcement in a later section.) The click also acts as a cue or signal indicating to the animal that if it responds by going to the food cup, it will be reinforced.

3. Lever Pressing. Now the animal can be left in the Skinner box on its own. Eventually, it will press the lever, which will fire the food magazine, producing a click that reinforces the bar press, and also signals the animal to go to the food cup

Figure 5–3. A typical cumulative recording which reflects the acquisition of a lever press response.

where it is reinforced by food. According to operant conditioning principles, the lever press response, having been reinforced, will tend to be repeated and when it is, it is again reinforced, which further increases the probability that the lever press response will be repeated, and so on. A typical cumulative recording generated by an animal placed in a Skinner box after magazine training is shown in Figure 5-3.

Shaping

The process of operant conditioning we have described so far takes considerable time. As we saw above, one way to train the lever press response is to place the deprived animal in the Skinner box and simply leave it there. The experimenter merely checks the cumulative recording periodically to see if the lever press response has been learned. Under these conditions the animal either learns or it dies.

There is another approach to operant conditioning that does not take as long as the procedure described above. Again, the animal is placed on a deprivation schedule and is magazine trained, and again, the experimenter uses the hand switch to trigger the feeder mechanism externally. This time, however, the experimenter decides to fire the feeder mechanism only when the animal is in the half of the Skinner box containing the lever. When the animal is reinforced for being near the lever, it will tend to remain in that part of the test chamber. Now that the animal remains in the vicinity of the lever, the experimenter begins to reinforce it only when it is still closer to the lever. Next it is reinforced only when it touches the lever, then only when it is putting pressure on it, and finally, only when it is pressing it by itself.

The process is similar to a childhood game called "You're Hot, You're Cold," where a child hides something and her or his playmates try to find it. As they get closer to the hidden object, the child who hid the object says, "You're getting warm, you're warmer, you're boiling hot, you're on fire." As they get farther from the object the child says, "You're getting cold, colder, very cold, you're freezing." When this game is played in the laboratory, it is called **shaping.** In the shaping procedure described above, the lever press response was shaped rather than waiting for it to happen.

Shaping has two components: **differential reinforcement,** which simply means some responses are reinforced and others are not; and **successive approximation,** which refers to the fact that only those responses are reinforced that become increasingly similar to the one the experimenter wants. In our example, only those responses which successively approximated the lever press response were differentially reinforced.

Recently it has been found that under certain circumstances some organisms seem to be able to shape their own behavior. This phenomenon is called autoshaping, which we will have more to say about later in this chapter.

Extinction

As with classical conditioning, when we remove the reinforcer from the operant conditioning situation, we produce **extinction.** During acquisition, the animal gets a pellet of food whenever it presses the lever. Under these circumstances, the animal learns to press the lever and persists in doing so until it is satiated with food. If the feeder mechanism was suddenly disconnected, thus preventing a lever press from producing a pellet of food, we would note that the cumulative recording would gradually become shallower and would eventually become parallel to the X-axis, indicating that no lever press responses are being made. At that point, we say that extinction has occurred.

We are being somewhat inaccurate when we say that after extinction a response is no longer made; it is more accurate to say that after extinction, the response rate goes back to where it was before reinforcement was introduced. This baseline rate is the frequency with which the response occurs naturally in the life of the animal without the introduction of reinforcement. This is called the **operant level** for that response. When we remove reinforcement from the experimental arrangement, as in extinction, the response tends to go back to its operant level.

Spontaneous Recovery

After extinction, if the animal is returned to its home cage for a period of time and then brought back into the experimental situation, it will again begin to press the lever for a short period of time without any additional training. This is referred to as spontaneous recovery. A cumulative recording showing both extinction and **spontaneous recovery** is shown in Figure 5-4.

Superstitious Behavior

In our earlier discussion of operant conditioning, we briefly mentioned **contingent reinforcement.** Reinforcement following the lever press response is an example of contingent reinforcement since the reinforcer is dependent on the response. What would happen, however, if the situation was arranged so that the feeder mechanism would fire every now and then, independently of the animal's behavior? In other

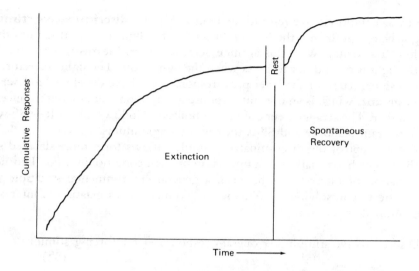

Figure 5-4. A cumulative recording which depicts the extinction and spontaneous recovery of a lever press response.

words, we are now going to arrange the situation so that the feeder mechanism delivers a pellet of food periodically *regardless of what the animal is doing.*

According to the principles of operant conditioning, we can predict that whatever the animal is doing when the feeder mechanism is activated will be reinforced, and the animal will tend to repeat the reinforced behavior. At some time the reinforced behavior will be repeated when the feeder mechanism randomly fires again, and the response will be strengthened. Thus the animal is apt to develop strange ritualistic responses; it may bob its head, turn in a circle, stand up on its back legs, or perform a series of actions according to what it was doing when the feeder mechanism fired. This ritualistic behavior is referred to as superstitious because the animal looks as if it believes that what it is doing is causing a pellet of food to appear. Because the reinforcer in this situation is independent of the animal's behavior, it is referred to as **noncontingent reinforcement.**

One can think of numerous examples of **superstitious behavior** on the part of humans. Organized sports, for example, are filled with many examples. Imagine what happens to the baseball player who, after stepping to the plate, adjusts his hat in a certain way, and hits the very next pitch out of the ball park. There will be a strong tendency on his part to adjust his hat in a similar way the next time he is at bat.

Discriminative Operant

Now we return to the Skinner box and discuss the light that we referred to earlier. After we have conditioned the animal to press the lever, we can make the situation more complex. We can arrange the situation so that the animal receives a pellet of food only when the light in the Skinner box is on, but not when the light is off.

Under these conditions, we refer to the light as S^D or a **discriminative stimulus.** The light being on defines the S^D condition and the light being off defines the S^Δ condition (Δ = delta). With this arrangement, the animal learns to press the lever when the light is on and not to press when the light is off. The light, therefore, has become a signal (cue) for the lever press response. We have developed a **discriminative operant,** which is an operant response given to one set of circumstances but not to another. The arrangement can be symbolized as follows: $S^D \rightarrow R \rightarrow S^R$ where R is the operant response and S^R is the reinforcing stimulus.

The concept of the discriminative stimulus allows for a more detailed statement about which association is of interest in operant conditioning. For Thorndike, the association of interest was between a general environmental situation and a response effective in solving a problem. For Skinner, the association of interest can be diagrammed as follows:

Discriminative stimulus $\rightarrow$ operant response $\rightarrow$ reinforcing stimulus
(S^D) (R) (S^R)

association of interest

Except for slight differences in terminology, Skinner's views of learning are quite similar to those of Thorndike after 1930. In fact, except for the way each researcher measured the dependent variable, which was pointed out earlier in this chapter, instrumental conditioning and operant conditioning can be considered the same procedure.

There is some slight similarity between the discriminative operant and respondent conditioning. You will recall that respondent behavior is elicited by a known stimulus. The behavior occurs because of its association with the stimulus. Such behavior, as we have seen, is not under the control of its consequences. In the case of the discriminative operant, the light becomes a signal associated with a certain response that the organism has learned will be followed by reinforcement. Operant behavior is emitted behavior, but Skinner (1953) says:

Most operant behavior . . . acquires important connections with the surrounding world. We may show how it does so in our pigeon experiment by reinforcing neck-stretching when a signal light is on and allowing it to be extinguished when the light is off. Eventually stretching occurs only when the light is on. We can then demonstrate a stimulus-response connection which is roughly comparable to a conditioned or unconditioned reflex: the appearance of the light will be quickly followed by an upward movement of the head. But the relation is fundamentally quite different. It has a different history and different current properties. We describe the contingency by saying that a *stimulus* (the light) is the occasion upon which a *response* (stretching the neck) is followed by *reinforcement* (with food). We must specify all three terms. The effect upon the pigeon is that eventually the response is more likely to occur when the light is on. The process through which this comes about is called *discrimination*. Its importance in a theoretical analysis, as well as in the practical control of behavior, is obvious: when a discrimination has been established, we may alter the probability of a response instantly by presenting or removing the discriminative stimulus. (pp. 107–108)

Thus, the discriminative operant involves a signal which leads to a response which, in turn, leads to reinforcement.

There are numerous examples of discriminative operants in everyday life. A certain time of the day (S^D) indicates that you must be in a certain place (R) in order to transact some business (S^R). As you're driving down the street, you encounter a red light (S^D), which causes you to stop (R), thereby avoiding a ticket or an accident (S^R). You see someone you don't care for (S^D), causing you to change the direction you are walking in (R), thereby avoiding the person (S^R).

Secondary Reinforcement

Any neutral stimulus paired with a primary reinforcer (e.g., food or water) takes on reinforcing properties of its own; this is the principle of secondary reinforcement. It follows then that every S^D must be a secondary reinforcer since it consistently precedes primary reinforcement.

One way to demonstrate the reinforcing properties of a previously neutral stimulus is to wire the Skinner box so that a light comes on prior to the animal's receiving food for making a lever press response. According to the principle of secondary reinforcement, the pairing of the light with food should cause the light to take on reinforcing properties of its own. One way to test this notion is to extinguish the lever press response so that the animal presses the lever and neither light nor food is produced. When the response rate decreases to its operant level, we arrange for the lever press to turn on the light but not deliver a pellet of food. We note that the response rate goes way up. Since the light alone has increased the response rate and thereby prolonged extinction, we say it has developed secondary reinforcing characteristics through its association with food during acquisition (training). A light not associated with a primary reinforcer will not produce a similar effect during extinction.

In addition to maintaining the lever press response, we can now use the light to condition other responses. Once a previously neutral stimulus takes on reinforcing properties through its association with primary reinforcement, it can be used to reinforce any number of responses.

Keller and Schoenfeld (1950) provide an excellent summary of secondary reinforcement:

1. A stimulus that occasions or accompanies a reinforcement acquires thereby reinforcing value of its own, and may be called a conditioned, secondary, or derived reinforcement. A secondary reinforcement may be extinguished when repeatedly applied to a response for which there is no ultimate primary reinforcement.

2. A secondary reinforcement is positive when the reinforcement with which it is correlated is positive, and negative when the latter is negative.

3. Once established, a secondary reinforcement is independent and nonspecific; it will not only strengthen the same response which produced the original reinforcement, but it will also condition a new and unrelated response. Moreover, it will do so even in the presence of a different motive.

4. Through generalization, many stimuli besides the one correlated with reinforcement acquire reinforcing value—positive or negative. (p. 260)

Generalized Reinforcers

A **generalized reinforcer** is a secondary reinforcer that has been paired with more than one primary reinforcer. Money is a generalized reinforcer because it is ultimately associated with any number of primary reinforcers. The main advantage of the generalized reinforcer is that it does not depend upon a certain condition of deprivation to be effective. Food, for example, is only reinforcing for an organism deprived of food, but money can be used as a reinforcer whether or not someone is deprived of food. Grades, trophies, medals, and awards would also classify as generalized reinforcers.

Moreover, the very activities that once led to reinforcement may themselves become reinforcing. Skinner (1953) says:

> Eventually generalized reinforcers are effective even though the primary reinforcers upon which they are based no longer accompany them. We play games of skill for their own sake. We get attention or approval for its own sake. Affection is not always followed by a more explicit sexual reinforcement. The submissiveness of others is reinforcing even though we make no use of it. A miser may be so reinforced by money that he will starve rather than give it up. (p. 81)

With these comments, Skinner comes very close to Gordon Allport's concept of **functional autonomy.** Allport (1961) maintains that although an activity may once have been engaged in because it led to reinforcement, after awhile the activity itself may become reinforcing. In other words, the activity may become independent of the reinforcer upon which it was originally dependent. For example, a person might originally join the merchant marines in order to make a living, but later in life go sailing because it is enjoyable to do so even though sailing no longer provides an income. In the latter case, we say that sailing has become functionally autonomous, that is, it continues in the absence of the original motive. Skinner would say that such an activity must ultimately result in primary reinforcement or it would extinguish. Allport, on the other hand, would say that the activity no longer depends on primary reinforcement.

Chaining

One response can bring the organism into contact with stimuli that act as an S^D for another response, which in turn causes it to experience stimuli that cause a third response, and so on. This process is referred to as **chaining.** In fact, most behavior can be shown to involve some form of chaining. For example, even the lever press in the Skinner box is not an isolated response. The stimuli in the Skinner box act as S^Ds, causing the animal to turn toward the lever. The sight of the lever causes the animal to approach it and press it. The firing of the feeder mechanism acts as an additional S^D which elicits the response of going to the food cup. Consuming the food pellet acts as an S^D causing the animal to return to the lever and again press it. This sequence of events (chain) is held together by the food pellet, which, of course, is a primary positive reinforcer. It can be said that various elements of a behavioral chain are held together by secondary reinforcers, but that the entire chain depends upon a primary reinforcer.

In order to explain how chaining comes about from Skinner's point of view, one must utilize the concepts of secondary reinforcement and associative shifting. Because of their association with the primary reinforcer, the events prior to the delivery of the food pellet take on secondary reinforcing properties. Thus, the sight of the lever itself becomes a secondary reinforcer, and the response of looking at the lever is reinforced by the sight of the lever. Now, through a process similar to associative shifting (or higher order conditioning which we will discuss in chapter 7), other stimuli more remote from the lever develop reinforcing properties. Thus, after considerable training, when the animal is placed in the Skinner box, the initial stimuli it encounters will act as an S^D, causing the animal to orient toward the lever. The sight of the lever at this point acts both as a reinforcer and an S^D eliciting the next response in the chain. The situation is diagrammed in Figure 5-5.

It is important to note that the development of a chained response always acts from the primary reinforcer backward. As more and more related stimuli take on reinforcing properties, the chain is extended. It is possible, for example, for the chain to gradually extend all the way back to the animal's home cage.

Occasionally rats have been trained to perform complex chained responses such as climbing a staircase, riding in a cart, crossing a bridge, playing a note on a toy piano, entering a small elevator, pulling a chain, riding the elevator down, and receiving a small pellet of food. This chain, too, is developed backward so that the events that precede the primary reinforcer gradually become secondary reinforcers.

S^D	→	R	→	S^D S^R	→	R	→	S^D S^R	→	R	→	S^R
General Stimuli in the Test Chamber		Orient Toward Lever		Sight of Lever Reinforces Response of Turning Toward It and Acts as a Cue for the Next Response		Approach Lever		Contact With Lever Reinforces Approaching and Acts as Cue to Press		Press Lever		Food Pellet

Figure 5-5. An example of chained behavior.

When they do, they reinforce the responses prior to them, and so on along the chain of behaviors.

Chained responses can also occur between two people. For example, seeing someone you know acts as an S^D to say "hello." Your hello acts as an S^D for your friend to say "hi." The response of "hi" acts not only as a reinforcer for your "hello" but also acts as an S^D for you to say "How are you?" This two-person chain can be diagrammed as follows:

$$
\begin{array}{llcccccc}
 & & & & S^D & & S^D & \\
You: & S^D & \rightarrow & R & \rightarrow S^R \rightarrow & R & \rightarrow S^R & \rightarrow R \rightarrow \text{etc.} \\
 & \text{Seeing} & & & \uparrow & \text{How are} & \uparrow & \\
 & \text{friend} & & \text{Hello} & & \text{you?} & & \\
 & & & & & \downarrow & & \\
 & & & \downarrow & & S^D & & \\
Your\ friend: & & & S^D & \rightarrow R \rightarrow & S^R & \rightarrow & R \\
 & & & & \text{Hi} & & & \text{Fine}
\end{array}
$$

Not only do the consequences of certain responses act as cues for other responses, but certain thoughts can act as S^Ds for other thoughts. Skinner (1953) says:

> A response may produce or alter some of the variables which control another response. The result is a "chain." It may have little or no organization. When we go for a walk, roaming the countryside or wandering idly through a museum or store, one episode in our behavior generates conditions responsible for another. We look to one side and are stimulated by an object which causes us to move in its direction. In the course of this movement, we receive aversive stimulation from which we beat a hasty retreat. This generates a condition of satiation or fatigue in which, once free of aversive stimulation, we sit down to rest. And so on. Chaining need not be the result of movement in space. We wander or roam verbally, for example, in a casual conversation or when we "speak our thoughts" in free association. (p. 224)

Positive and Negative Reinforcers

To summarize Skinner's position on reinforcement, we have first of all **primary positive reinforcement.** This is something that is naturally reinforcing to the organism and is related to survival, such as food or water. Any neutral stimulus associated with primary positive reinforcement takes on positive secondary reinforcing characteristics. *A positive reinforcer, either primary or secondary, is something which, when added to the situation by a certain response, increases the probability of that response's recurring.*

A **primary negative reinforcer** is something naturally harmful to the organism, such as an aversive high-pitched tone or an electric shock. Any neutral stimulus associated with a primary negative reinforcer takes on negative secondary reinforcing characteristics. *A negative reinforcer, either primary or secondary, is something* *which, when removed from the situation by a certain response, increases the probability of that response's recurring.* For example, if a Skinner box is arranged so that an aversive tone is discontinued when the lever is pressed, the lever press response will soon be learned. In this case, by pressing the lever, the animal avoids experiencing an aversive stimulus. Thus, reinforcement occurs when either a response adds something positive to the situation or removes something negative. Each one increases the probability of a response's recurring. Negative reinforcement, however, should not be confused with punishment. Skinner (1953) says:

> Events which are found to be reinforcing are of two sorts. Some reinforcements consist of *presenting* stimuli, of adding something—for example, food, water, or sexual contact—to the situation. These we call *positive* reinforcers. Others consist of *removing* something—for example, a loud noise, a very bright light, extreme cold or heat, or electric shock—from the situation. These we call *negative* reinforcers. In both cases the effect of reinforcement is the same—the probability of response is increased. We cannot avoid this distinction by arguing that what is reinforcing in the negative case is the *absence* of the bright light, loud noise, and so on; for it is absence after presence which is effective, and this is only another way of saying that the stimulus is removed. The difference between the two cases will be clearer when we consider the *presentation* of a *negative* reinforcer or the *removal* of a *positive*. These are the consequences which we call punishment. (p. 73)

Punishment

Punishment occurs when a response removes something positive from the situation or adds something negative. In everyday language we can say that punishment is either taking away something an organism wants, or giving it something it does not want. Skinner and Thorndike agree on the effectiveness of punishment: it does not decrease the probability of a response. Although punishment suppresses a response as long as it is applied, it does not weaken the habit. Skinner (1971) says:

> Punishment is designed to remove awkward, dangerous, or otherwise unwanted behavior from a repertoire on the assumption that a person who has been punished is less likely to behave in the same way again. Unfortunately, the matter is not that simple. Reward and punishment do not differ merely in the direction of the changes they induce. A child who has been severely punished for sex play is not necessarily less inclined to continue; and a man who has been imprisoned for violent assault is not necessarily less inclined toward violence. Punished behavior is likely to reappear after the punitive contingencies are withdrawn. (pp. 61–62)

A typical experiment which led Skinner to this conclusion was done by one of his students, Estes (1944). Two groups of eight rats each were trained to press the lever in a Skinner box. After training, both groups were placed on extinction. One group was extinguished in the regular way, that is, food was withheld following a lever press. Rats in the second group, in addition to not receiving food, received a shock when they pressed the lever. Rats in this group were shocked an average of nine times. There were three extinction sessions and the rats were only shocked during the first of the three sessions. The second and third sessions were the same for both groups. The results indicated that the punished group made fewer responses during the first extinction session than did the nonpunished group. The number of responses made during the second extinction session was about the same for both groups, with the nonpunished group making slightly more responses. From the data of the first two sessions, one can conclude that punishment was effective since the number of responses to extinction was much lower for the punished group. During the third extinction session, however, the previously punished group made many more responses than did the nonpunished group. Thus, in the long run, the originally punished group caught up in the total number of responses to extinction to the nonpunished group. The conclusion was that simple nonreinforcement (extinction) is as effective in extinguishing a habit as nonreinforcement plus punishment. The results of the Estes study are summarized in Figure 5-6.

Skinner's main argument against the use of punishment is that it is ineffective in the long run. It appears that punishment simply suppresses behavior and when the threat of punishment is removed, the rate with which the behavior occurs returns to its original level. Thus, punishment often appears to be very successful when, in fact, it has produced only a temporary effect. Other arguments against the use of punishment follow.

Figure 5-6. The results of Estes's research showing that the effect of punishment is to suppress rate of responding only temporarily. (From Estes, 1944, p. 5)

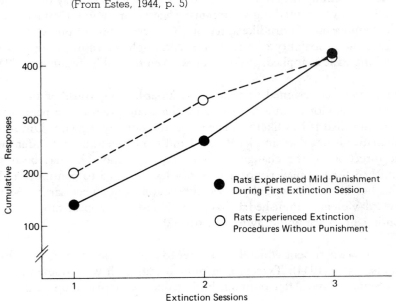

1. **It causes unfortunate emotional by-products.** The punished organism becomes fearful and this fear generalizes to a number of stimuli related to those present as the punishment was occurring.

2. **It indicates what the organism should not do, not what it should do.** Compared to reinforcement, punishment conveys practically no information to the organism. Reinforcement indicates that what was done is effective in the situation; therefore, no additional learning is required. Very often punishment informs the organism only that the punished response is one that will not work to bring reinforcement in a given situation, and additional learning is required to hit upon a response that will work.

3. **It justifies inflicting pain on others.** This, of course, applies to the use of punishment in child rearing. When children are spanked, the only thing they may be learning is that under some circumstances it is justifiable to inflict pain on others.

4. **Being in a situation where previously punished behavior could be engaged in without being punished may excuse a child to do so.** Thus, in the absence of a punishing agent, children may swear, break windows, be disrespectful to elderly people, push smaller children around, etc. These children have learned to suppress these behaviors when they could lead to punishment, but in the absence of a punishing agent, there is no reason to avoid engaging in these activities.

5. **Punishment elicits aggression toward the punishing agent and others.** Punishment causes the punished organism to become aggressive and this aggression may cause additional problems. For example, our penal institutions which use punishment as their major means of control, are filled with highly aggressive individuals who will continue to be aggressive as long as punishment or the threat of punishment is used to control their behavior.

6. **Punishment often replaces one undesirable response with another undesirable response.** For example, a child who is spanked for making a mess may now cry instead, just as a person punished for stealing may now become aggressive and commit even more crimes when he or she has the opportunity.

In their study of how 379 New England suburban mothers brought up their children from birth to kindergarten age, Sears, Maccoby, and Levin (1957) concluded the following concerning the relative effects of emphasizing reinforcement as opposed to punishment in child rearing:

> In our discussion of the training process, we have contrasted punishment with reward. Both are techniques used for changing the child's habitual ways of acting. Do they work equally well? The answer is unequivocally "no"; but to be truly unequivocal, the answer must be understood as referring to the kind of punishment we were able to measure by our interview method. We could not, as one can with laboratory experiments on white rats or pigeons, examine the effects of punishment on isolated bits of behavior. Our measures of

punishment whether of the object-oriented or love-oriented variety, referred to *Levels of Punitiveness* in the mothers. Punitiveness, in contrast with reward-ingness, was a quite ineffectual quality for a mother to inject into her child training.

The evidence for this conclusion is overwhelming. The unhappy effects of punishment have run like a dismal thread through our findings. Mothers who punished toilet accidents severely ended up with bedwetting children. Mothers who punished dependency to get rid of it had more dependent children than mothers who did not punish. Mothers who punished aggressive behavior severely had more aggressive children than mothers who punished lightly. They also had more dependent children. Harsh physical punishment was associated with high childhood aggressiveness and with the development of feeding problems.

Our evaluation of punishment is that *it is ineffectual over the long term as a technique for eliminating the kind of behavior toward which it is directed.* (p. 484)

Why, then, is punishment so widely used? Because, says Skinner, it is reinforcing to the punisher (1953).

Severe punishment unquestionably has an immediate effect in reducing a tendency to act in a given way. This result is no doubt responsible for its widespread use. We "instinctively" attack anyone whose behavior displeases us—perhaps not in physical assault, but with criticism, disapproval, blame, or ridicule. Whether or not there is an inherited tendency to do this, the immediate effect of the practice is reinforcing enough to explain its currency. In the long run, however, punishment does not actually eliminate behavior from a repertoire, and its temporary achievement is obtained at tremendous cost in reducing the over-all efficiency and happiness of the group. (p. 190)

It is interesting to note that Skinner himself was never physically punished by his father and only once by his mother, who washed his mouth out with soap for swearing (Skinner, 1967, p. 390).

Alternatives to Punishment

Skinner lists a number of alternatives to the use of punishment. The circumstances causing the undesirable behavior can be changed, thereby changing the behavior. For example, removing fine china from the living room will eliminate the problem of a child's breaking fine china. The undesirable response can be satiated by letting the organism perform the undesired response until it is sick of it, such as letting a child continue to light matches or eat candy (advice similar to that given by Guthrie as we shall see in chapter 8). If the undesirable behavior is a function of the child's developmental stage, it can be eliminated by simply waiting for the child to outgrow it. Skinner says about the latter approach (1953): "It is not always easy to put up with the behavior until this happens, especially under the conditions of the average household, but there is some consolation if we know that by carrying the child through a socially unacceptable stage we spare him the later complications arising from punishment" (p. 192).

Another method is simply to let time pass, but this approach may take too long. Habits are not soon forgotten. For example, in his "Pigeons in a Pelican" project, mentioned earlier, Skinner found that his trained animals "immediately and correctly" performed their task after six years of inactivity.

Still another alternative to punishment is to reinforce behavior incompatible with the undesirable behavior (e.g., a child is reinforced for reading in the presence of matches rather than striking them). The best way to discourage an undesirable habit, however, is to ignore it. Skinner says (1953):

> The most effective alternative process [to punishment] is probably *extinction.* This takes time but is much more rapid than allowing the response to be forgotten. The technique seems to be relatively free of objectionable by-prod-ucts. We recommend it, for example, when we suggest that a parent "pay no attention" to objectionable behavior on the part of his child. If the child's behavior is strong only because it has been reinforced by "getting a rise out of" the parent, it will disappear when this consequence is no longer forthcom-ing. (p. 192)

Generally speaking, behavior persists because it is being reinforced; this is true of undesirable as well as desirable behavior. To eliminate objectionable behavior one needs to find the source of reinforcement and remove it. Behavior that does not lead to reinforcement extinguishes.

Schedules of Reinforcement

Although Pavlov had done some work with partial reinforcement, using classical conditioning (1927, pp. 384–386), it was Skinner who has thoroughly investigated the topic. Skinner had already published data on the effects of partial reinforcement when Humphreys (1939a, 1939b) startled the psychological world by showing that the extinction process was more rapid following 100% reinforcement than after partial reinforcement. That is, if an organism receives a reinforcer every time it makes an appropriate response during learning, and then is placed on extinction, it will extinguish faster than an organism who had only a certain percent of its correct responses reinforced during acquisition. In other words, partial reinforcement leads to greater resistance to extinction than continuous, or 100% reinforcement, and this fact is called the **partial reinforcement effect (PRE).**

Skinner studied the partial reinforcement effect extensively and eventually wrote a book with Ferster called *Schedules of Reinforcement* (1957). This book sum-marized years of research on various types of partial reinforcement. Five schedules of reinforcement have become the most common and they are described below.

1. Continuous Reinforcement Schedule (CRF). Using a continuous rein-forcement schedule, every correct response during acquisition is reinforced. Usually in a partial reinforcement study, the animal is first trained on a 100% reinforcement schedule and then switched to a partial reinforcement schedule. It is difficult to bring about the acquisition of any response when partial reinforcement is used during the initial training period.

2. **Fixed Interval Reinforcement Schedule (FI).** Using a fixed interval reinforcement schedule, the animal is reinforced for a response made only after a set interval of time. For example, only a response following a 3-min interval is reinforced. At the beginning of the fixed time interval the animal responds slowly, or not at all. As the end of the time interval approaches the animal gradually increases its speed of responding, apparently anticipating the moment of reinforcement. This kind of responding produces a pattern on the cumulative recording referred to as the *fixed-interval scallop*. Such a pattern is shown in Figure 5-7.

The behavior of an animal under this schedule is somewhat similar to the way a person behaves as a deadline approaches. After putting off a certain task as long as possible, the due date is rapidly approaching and activity increases accordingly. Often a student preparing a term paper will act in this manner.

3. **Fixed Ratio Reinforcement Schedule (FR).** An FR schedule of reinforcement occurs when every *n*th response that the animal makes is reinforced. FR5, for example, means that the animal will get reinforced at every fifth response. Here the important factor in determining when a response is reinforced is the number of responses made. Theoretically, an animal on a fixed interval schedule could make just one response at the end of the interval and be reinforced each time it responds. With a fixed ratio schedule, this is not possible; the animal *must* respond a fixed number of times before it is reinforced.

For both the FI and FR reinforcement schedules, a reinforced response is followed by a depression in the rate of responding. This is called the *post-reinforce-*

Figure 5-7. Typical cumulative recordings generated by fixed ratio, variable ratio, fixed interval, and variable interval reinforcement schedules. The slash marks in the recordings indicate a reinforced response.

ment pause. There is considerable speculation as to why such a pause exists. Perhaps the animal learns that the responses immediately following a reinforced response are never reinforced. However, the scallop on the cumulative recording of an FI schedule is usually not found on that of an FR schedule. The FR schedule usually generates a steplike cumulative recording, indicating that the animal temporarily stops responding after a reinforced response and then, at some point, resumes responding at a rapid rate. Such behavior has been characterized as "break and run." A cumulative recording generated by an animal under an FR schedule is shown in Figure 5-7.

4. Variable Interval Reinforcement Schedule (VI). With the VI schedule, the animal is reinforced for responses made at the end of time intervals of variable durations. That is, rather than having a fixed time interval, as with FI schedules, the animal is reinforced on the *average* of say, every three minutes, but it may be reinforced immediately after a prior reinforcement, or it may be reinforced after thirty seconds or after seven minutes. This schedule eliminates the scalloping effect found in FI schedules and produces a steady, moderately high response rate. A typical cumulative recording generated by an animal on a VI schedule is shown in Figure 5-7.

5. Variable Ratio Reinforcement Schedule (VR). With the FR schedule, an animal is reinforced after making a specific number of responses, say five. With the VR5 schedule, the animal is reinforced on the *average* of every five responses; thus it might receive two reinforcers in a row or may make ten or fifteen responses without being reinforced. The VR schedules eliminate the steplike cumulative recording found with the FR schedule and produce the highest response rate of the five schedules we are considering. A cumulative recording produced by an animal under a VR schedule is shown in Figure 5-7.

The VR reinforcement schedule is the one governing the behavior of gamblers at a place like Las Vegas. The faster one pulls the handle of a slot machine, for example, the more frequently one is reinforced.

To summarize, continuous reinforcement yields the least resistance to extinction and the lowest response rate during training. All partial reinforcement schedules produce greater resistance to extinction and higher response rates during training than continuous reinforcement. Generally speaking, the VR schedule produces the highest response rate, FR produces the next highest rate, then VI, followed by FI, and finally CRF.

6. Concurrent Reinforcement Schedule. Thus far we have discussed how various schedules of reinforcement influence the rate with which a single response is made. With a concurrent schedule, two responses are involved and each is reinforced according to an independent schedule of reinforcement. For example, a Skinner box can be arranged so that pressing lever A is reinforced according to a FR 10 schedule, whereas pressing lever B is reinforced according to a FI 10 schedule. Using concurrent schedules, a wide variety of preferences (choices) can be investigated. Preference is measured by the number of times the animal makes one of the two available responses relative to the other. That is, if lever A is responded to 50 times in an hour and lever B is responded to 25 times, it is assumed that the schedule of reinforcement governing lever A is preferred twice as much as the one governing lever B.

With concurrent schedules, the animal is allowed to freely switch back and forth between response alternatives, and it is the animal's relative response rate that is of interest, that is, how often it responds to alternative A as compared to alternative B.

Perhaps the most interesting finding that has emerged from research on concurrent schedules is that there appears to be a law governing animals' choices. Herrnstein (1961) has made a strong case that the relative rate of responding when concurrent schedules are involved is governed by what he calls the **matching law.** The matching law states that the relative rate of responding to each alternative matches the relative rate of reinforcement generated by the alternatives. The matching law is symbolized as follows:

$$\frac{R_A}{R_A + R_B} = \frac{r_A}{r_A + r_B}$$

Where:

R_A = rate of responding to alternative A
R_B = rate of responding to alternative B
r_A = rate of reinforcement for alternative A
r_B = rate of reinforcement for alternative B

Herrnstein (1961) divided 40 reinforcements per hour between two response alternatives. Variable interval (VI) schedules were manipulated so that for a time, response A generated most of the 40 reinforcers and response B generated almost none. This would be the case when response A is on a VI 1 min schedule and response B is on a VI 60 min schedule. At different points during the experiment, the two alternatives were governed by different VI schedules. At one point, to give but one more example, alternative A was on a VI 6 min schedule (about 10 reinforcers per hr) and alternative B was on a VI 2 min schedule (about 30 reinforcers per hr). Figure 5-8 shows how well Herrnstein's matching law described the behavior of two pigeons pecking discs according to various combinations of VI schedules.

Although some experimenters have found undermatching and some overmatching, Herrnstein's matching law has been found to be generally valid for rats, pigeons, monkeys, and humans. Moreover, it has been found to be valid not only for frequency of reinforcement but for amount and delay of reinforcement as well. In general, organisms will prefer schedules that produce frequent, large, and immediate reinforcers over infrequent, small, and delayed reinforcers.

7. Concurrent-Chain Reinforcement Schedule. Whereas concurrent schedules of reinforcement are used to investigate simple choice behavior, concurrent-chain schedules are used to investigate complex choice behavior. With concur-

Relative rate of responding on key A

Relative rate of reinforcement on key A

● — ● Pigeon #055
● – – ● Pigeon #231

Figure 5–8. Results of two pigeons pecking on concurrent VI VI schedules. The pecking of key A is plotted relative to the pecking of key B. The total possible number of reinforcers from pecking both keys is 40 per hr; therefore, if pecking key A generated 10% of the reinforcers (4), pecking key B generated 90% (36). Notice that the relative rate of responding very nearly equaled the relative rate of reinforcement. (From R. J. Herrnstein, "Relative and Absolute Strength of Response as a Function of Frequency of Reinforcement." *Journal of the Experimental Analysis of Behavior*, 1961, *4*, 267–272. Copyright 1961 by the Society for the Experimental Analysis of Behavior, Inc.)

rent-chain schedules an animal's behavior during the initial phase of the experiment determines what schedule of reinforcement it experiences during the second, or terminal, phase.

One interesting finding using concurrent-chain schedules is in the area of self-control. Under ordinary circumstances, organisms will clearly prefer small, immediate reinforcers over large, delayed reinforcers. Using concurrent schedules, if response A is reinforced by small, immediate reinforcers and response B is reinforced by large reinforcers following a delay, response A will be overwhelmingly preferred. Likewise, using a concurrent-chain schedule, if responding to alternative A switches in a schedule providing small, immediate reinforcers and responding to alternative B switches in a schedule producing large, delayed reinforcers, animals will show a strong preference for alternative A. Rachlin and Green (1972), however, showed that under certain circumstances, large, delayed reinforcers are preferred over small, immediate reinforcers. Rachlin and Green (1972) used a concurrent-chain reinforcement schedule where pigeons initially had a choice of pecking one of two white discs. Pecking the white disc on the left 15 times (FR 15) was followed by a 10-sec blackout and then a choice between a red and a green disc. Pecking the red disc produced 2 sec of food (a relatively small reinforcer) immediately, and pecking the green disc produced 4 sec of food (a relatively larger reinforcer) following a delay of 4 sec. In the original choice phase of the experiment, if the white disc on the right was responded to 15 times (FR 15), there was also a 10-sec blackout and then the opportunity to peck a green disc. Pecking the green disc produced a 4-sec delay followed by 4 sec of food. Under these experimental conditions, it was found that

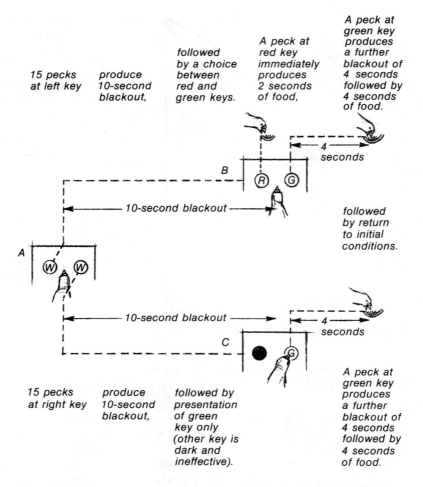

15 pecks at left key · produce 10-second blackout, · followed by a choice between red and green keys. · A peck at red key immediately produces 2 seconds of food, · A peck at green key produces a further blackout of 4 seconds followed by 4 seconds of food.

4 seconds

B

10-second blackout

followed by return to initial conditions.

A

10-second blackout

4 seconds

C

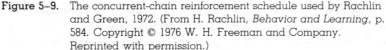

15 pecks at right key · produce 10-second blackout, · followed by presentation of green key only (other key is dark and ineffective). · A peck at green key produces a further blackout of 4 seconds followed by 4 seconds of food.

Figure 5–9. The concurrent-chain reinforcement schedule used by Rachlin and Green, 1972. (From H. Rachlin, *Behavior and Learning*, p. 584. Copyright © 1976 W. H. Freeman and Company. Reprinted with permission.)

pigeons chose the white disc on the right 65% of the time, thus reversing the preference for small, immediate reinforcers. The experimental arrangement used by Rachlin and Green is shown in Figure 5-9.

What is it that changed the preference for small, immediate reinforcers to large, delayed reinforcers? The answer seems to be time. It has been shown that reinforcers lose their reinforcement value over time. Thus, an organism may opt for a small reinforcer if it is immediately available but will not plan to have one sometime in the future. If a delay is involved, organisms tend to choose larger reinforcers over smaller ones. Schwartz (1984) generalizes these findings to humans:

One can imagine many human choices between immediate small reinforcement and delayed large reinforcement. Consider, for example, the choice between going to the movies and studying on a particular evening. We could imagine that going to the movies involves a small but immediate reinforcement (an evening's entertainment) while studying involves a large delayed reinforcement (a good exam grade). Given the choice between studying and an 8 p.m. movie at 7:45 p.m., the student, like the pigeon, might choose the small immediate reinforcement. But if the choice were required at 9 a.m., so that both reinforcers were going to be delayed, the student might choose to study. If we arranged contingencies so that people had to commit themselves to one or the other outcome well in advance, the chances of commitment to studying rather than going to the movies might increase. It is possible that many problems in "self-discipline" or "self-control" might be ameliorated if contingencies involving early commitment were instituted. (pp. 307–308)

Although it is beyond the scope of this text to explain how, it is interesting to note that the switchover in preference from small, immediate to large, delayed reinforcers found by Rachlin and Green (1972) is predicted by Herrnstein's matching law (see Rachlin, 1976, pp. 585–586, for an explanation).

Verbal Behavior

Skinner believes that verbal behavior (language) can be explained within the context of reinforcement theory. Talking and listening are responses that are influenced by reinforcement just as any other response. Any utterance, therefore, will tend to be repeated if it is reinforced.

Skinner classified verbal responses in terms of how they were related to reinforcement, that is, in terms of what was being done in order to be reinforced. These classifications are discussed briefly below.

1. Mand. About the mand, Skinner says (1957):

A mand is characterized by the unique relationship between the form of the response and the reinforcement characteristically received in a given verbal community. It is sometimes convenient to refer to this relation by saying that a mand "specifies" its reinforcement. *Listen!, Look!, Run!, Stop!*, and *Say yes!* specify the behavior of a listener; but when a hungry diner calls *Bread!*, or *More soup!*, he is specifying the ultimate reinforcement. Frequently both the behavior of the listener and the ultimate reinforcement are specified. The mand *pass the salt!* specifies an action (pass) and an ultimate reinforcement (the salt). (p. 37)

The word *mand* comes from the fact that a demand is being made. When the demand is met, the utterance (mand) is reinforced and next time the need arises, the person is likely to repeat the mand.

2. Tact. About the tact, Skinner says (1957):

this type of operant is exemplified when, in the presence of a doll, a child frequently achieves some sort of generalized reinforcement by saying *doll;* or when a teleost fish, or picture thereof, is the occasion upon which the student of zoology is reinforced when he says *teleost fish.* There is no suitable term for this type of operant. "Sign," "symbol," and more technical terms from logic and semantics commit us to special schemes of reference and stress the verbal response itself rather than the controlling relationship. The invented term "tact" will be used here. The term carries a mnemonic suggestion of behavior which "makes contact with" the physical world. A tact may be defined as a verbal operant in which a response of given form is evoked (or at least strengthened) by a particular object or event or property of an object or event. We account for the strength by showing that in the presence of the object or event, a response of that form is characteristically reinforced in a given verbal community. (pp. 81–82)

Generally speaking the tact involves naming objects or events in the environment appropriately, and its reinforcement comes from other people's reinforcing the match between the environment and the verbal behavior.

3. Echoic Behavior. This is verbal behavior that is reinforced when someone else's verbal response is repeated verbatim. Echoic behavior is often a prerequisite to a more complicated verbal behavior; for example, first a child must imitate a word before he or she can learn how that word is related to other words or other events. Thus, repeating something someone else has said is reinforced, and when this response is learned, it permits the speaker to learn more complex verbal relationships.

4. Autoclitic Behavior. According to Skinner (1957), "the term 'autoclitic' is intended to suggest behavior which is based upon or depends upon other verbal behavior" (p. 315). The main function of autoclitic behavior is to qualify responses, express relations, and provide a grammatical framework for verbal behavior.

The most severe critic of Skinner's explanation of verbal behavior has been Noam Chomsky (1959). Chomsky contends that language is too complex for a child to have learned. Some process other than learning must explain all the verbal utterances that, say, a 3-year-old is capable of making. Miller (1965) in fact, points out that there are 10^{20} possible 20-word sentences in the English language, and it would take 1,000 times the estimated age of the earth just to listen to them all. Obviously, says Chomsky, operant conditioning just does not explain the complexity of our language capabilities. Chomsky's explanation of language development is that our brain is structured to generate language. The underlying grammatical structure of all human languages reflects an underlying brain structure. That is, we are "wired" to produce grammatical utterances just as a computer can be wired to produce moves in a chess game. Chomsky and Skinner seem to be continuing the nature-nurture debate launched by Plato and Aristotle: Chomsky's deep brain structures theory of language acquisition represents the nature, or Platonic, side and Skinner's view that verbal behavior is shaped by environment represents the nurture, or Aristotelian, side.

Programmed Learning

Skinner, like Thorndike, was very interested in applying his theory of learning to the process of education. To Skinner, learning proceeds most effectively if (a) the information to be learned is presented in small steps; (b) the learners are given rapid feedback concerning the accuracy of their learning (i.e., they are shown immediately after a learning experience whether they have learned the information correctly or incorrectly); and (c) the learners are able to learn at their own pace.

Skinner learned firsthand that these principles were not being used in the classroom. He reflects upon a visit he made in 1953 to one of his daughter's classes (1967): "On November 11, as a visiting father, I was sitting in the back of the room in an arithmetic class. Suddenly the situation seemed perfectly absurd. Here were twenty extremely valuable organisms. Through no fault of her own, the teacher was violating almost everything we knew about the learning process" (p. 406).

It is interesting to note that the most common teaching technique is the lecture, and the lecture technique violates all three of the above principles. Skinner proposes an alternative teaching technique, **programmed learning,** which does incorporate all three principles. A device invented to present programmed material has been called a **teaching machine.** The advantages of using a teaching machine are outlined by Skinner as follows (1958):

> The machine itself, of course, does not teach. It simply brings the student into contact with the person who composed the material it presents. It is a labor-saving device because it can bring one programmer into contact with an indefinite number of students. They may suggest mass production, but the effect upon each student is surprisingly like that of a private tutor. The comparison holds in several respects. (i) There is a constant interchange between program and student. Unlike lectures, textbooks, and the usual audio-visual aids, the machine induces sustained activity. The student is always alert and busy. (ii) Like a good tutor, the machine insists that a given point be thoroughly understood, either frame-by-frame or set-by-set, before the student moves on. Lectures, textbooks, and their mechanized equivalents, on the other hand, proceed without making sure that the student understands and easily leave him behind (iii) Like a good tutor, the machine presents just that material for which the student is ready. It asks him to take only that step which he is at the moment best equipped and most likely to take (iv) Like a skillful tutor, the machine helps the student to come up with the right answer. It does this in part through the orderly construction of the program and in part with techniques of hinting, prompting, suggesting, and so on, derived from an analysis of verbal behavior . . . (v) Lastly, of course, the machine, like the private tutor,

reinforces the student for every correct response, using this immediate feed-back not only to shape his behavior most efficiently but to maintain it in strength in a manner which the laymen would describe as "holding the student's interest." (p. 971)

We will have more to say about programmed learning in chapter 16.

Contingency Contracting

Contingency contracting is a fairly recent extension of Skinnerian thinking. Briefly, it involves making arrangements so that a person gets something he or she wants when he or she acts in a certain way. Some arrangements can be simple and cover simple behavior, such as when a teacher says to a child, "If you sit quietly for five minutes, you can go out and play." Other arrangements can extend over a much longer period of time. For example, if a person has a weight problem, and has difficulty losing weight on his own, he may wish to arrange the environment so that he is reinforced for losing weight. One may, for example, sign over to another person something personally important such as money, a record collection, a stamp collection, or favorite clothes. Taking money as an example, the person trying to lose weight may put up, say, 100 dollars and draw up an agreement whereby the other person gives back 10 dollars each week if three pounds are lost. Each week that one does not lose at least three pounds, one loses 10 dollars. The same kind of arrangement can be made utilizing anything important to the person, and the behavior involved could as easily be smoking as losing weight.

The term "contingency contracting" comes from the fact that an agreement (contract) is made that certain activities will be reinforced that otherwise may not have been. In other words, the contract rearranges the reinforcement contingencies in the environment causing them to be responsive to behavior patterns that one hopes to modify in some way.

Many behavior problems occur because our behavior is influenced more by immediate reinforcers than by distant ones. For example, for some the taste of food in the present is more reinforcing than the distant promise of a longer life if one eats in moderation. Likewise, the immediate effect of nicotine is more reinforcing than the promise of a longer life without smoking. Contingency contracting is a way of modifying behavior through current reinforcing contingencies rather than distant ones. It is hoped that as desirable behavior is shaped using this procedure, the desirable behavior itself will be functional in obtaining reinforcers from the social environment. Not being overweight and not smoking both can be very reinforcing, but the problem is switching the overweight person and the smoker to another class of reinforcing experiences. Contingency contracting can be a very effective tool in accomplishing this switchover. Once the switch in reinforcement systems has been made, however, the desired behavior is usually sustained by the social environment and, therefore, the artificial reinforcement contingencies are no longer needed.

Contingency contracting need not involve a second person; one can follow these procedures alone by giving oneself a "treat" of some kind each day one goes without smoking, or drinking, or overeating. For a more detailed discussion of contingency contracting see Homme, Csanyi, Gonzales, and Rechs (1970).

Skinner's Attitude Toward Learning Theory

Skinner believes that it is unnecessary to formulate complicated theories to study human behavior, and he believes it is unnecessary to know the physiological correlates of behavior. He believes that behavioral events must be described in terms of things that directly affect behavior, and that it is logically inconsistent to attempt to explain behavior in terms of physiological events. For this reason, Skinner's method of research has been called "the empty organism approach."

Skinner also thinks that complex theories of learning, such as Hull's (chapter 6), are time-consuming and wasteful. Some day such theories may be useful in psychology, but not until we have collected much more basic data. Our main concern at this time should be, Skinner believes, to discover basic relationships between classes of stimuli and classes of responses. Therefore, the use of theory in studying the learning process cannot be justified. Skinner says (1950):

> Research designed with respect to theory is also likely to be wasteful. That a theory generates research does not prove its value unless the research is valuable. Much useless experimentation results from theories, and much energy and skill are absorbed by them. Most theories are eventually overthrown, and the greater part of the associated research is discarded. This could be justified if it were true that productive research requires a theory—as is, of course, often claimed. It is argued that research would be aimless and disorganized without a theory to guide it. The view is supported by psychological texts which take their cue from the logicians rather than empirical science and describe thinking as necessarily involving stages of hypothesis, deduction, experimental test, and confirmation. But this is not the way most scientists actually work. It is possible to design significant experiments for other reasons, and the possibility to be examined is that such research will lead more directly to the kind of information which a science usually accumulates. (pp. 194–195)

Skinner's approach to research is to do a **functional analysis** between stimulating events and measurable behavior. Skinner says (1953):

> The external variables of which behavior is a function provide for what may be called a causal or functional analysis. We undertake to predict and control the behavior of the individual organism. This is our "dependent variable"—the effect for which we are to find the cause. Our "independent variables"—the causes of behavior—are the external conditions of which behavior is a function. Relations between the two—the "cause-and-effect relationships" in behavior—are the laws of a science. A synthesis of these laws expressed in quantitative terms yields a comprehensive picture of the organism as a behaving system. (p. 35)

Thus, Skinner manipulates hours of food or water deprivation and notes the effect on the rate with which the lever press response is learned; or he observes the effect of schedules of reinforcement on response rate or resistance to extinction. In interpreting the results of his research, Skinner stays very close to the data, that is, if partial reinforcement produces greater resistance to extinction than does 100% reinforcement, that is a fact and that is all that can be said. In other words, Skinner does not attempt to explain why this is the case.

Even in deciding *what* to investigate, Skinner claims he is not guided by theoretical notions, but rather uses a hit-and-miss process. He tries first one thing and then another. If he sees one line of research is not producing anything worthwhile, he will shift to something that looks more fruitful and will continue in this trial-and-error fashion until he hits upon something of value. This rather liberal attitude toward scientific investigation is summarized in Skinner's article, "A Case Study in Scientific Method" (1956).

The Need for a Technology of Behavior

Skinner feels very strongly that a carefully worked out behavior technology could solve many human problems; yet many people would oppose such a technology because it seems to challenge a number of our cherished beliefs about ourselves, especially that human beings are rational, free, and dignified. Skinner believes that these beliefs are now interfering with the solution of our major problems and also preventing the development of the very tool that could solve them. Skinner says (1971):

> What we need is a technology of behavior. We could solve our problems quickly enough if we could adjust the growth of the world's population as precisely as we adjust the course of a spaceship, or improve agriculture and industry with some of the confidence with which we accelerate high-energy particles, or move toward a peaceful world with something like the steady progress with which physics has approached absolute zero (even though both remain presumably out of reach). But a behavioral technology comparable in power and precision to physical and biological technology is lacking, and those who do not find the very possibility ridiculous are more likely to be frightened by it than reassured. That is how far we are from "understanding human issues" in the sense in which physics and biology understand their fields, and how far we are from preventing the catastrophe toward which the world seems to be inexorably moving. (p. 5)

Elsewhere, Skinner says (1953):

> the traditional view of human nature in Western culture is well known. The conception of a free, responsible individual is embedded in our language and pervades our practices, codes, and beliefs. Given an example of human behavior, most people can describe it immediately in terms of such a conception.

The practice is so natural that it is seldom examined. A scientific formulation, on the other hand, is new and strange. Very few people have any notion of the extent to which a science of human behavior is indeed possible. In what way can the behavior of the individual or of groups of individuals be predicted and controlled? What are laws of behavior like? What over-all conception of the human organism as a behaving system emerges? It is only when we have answered these questions, at least in a preliminary fashion, that we may consider the implications of a science of human behavior with respect to either a theory of human nature or the management of human affairs. (pp. 9–10)

In an article entitled "What Is Wrong with Daily Life in the Western World?" (1986), Skinner has renewed his plea for the utilization of behavior technology in solving human problems. In this article, Skinner argues that five cultural practices are eroding the strengthening effects of reinforcement contingencies. These cultural practices are: "(a) Alienating workers from the consequences of their work; (b) helping those who could help themselves; (c) guiding behavior with rules rather than supplying reinforcing consequences; (d) maintaining aversive sanctions of government and religions with long-deferred benefits for the individual; and (e) reinforcing looking, listening, reading, gambling, and so on, while strengthening few other behaviors" (p. 568).

According to Skinner, the many problems caused by these cultural practices could be solved by strengthening desirable behavior using the principles derived from an experimental analysis of behavior, that is, by using the principles described in this chapter.

Skinner's theory of learning has had, and is having, a profound influence on psychology. No matter what area of psychology one studies, one is apt to find reference to some aspect of Skinner's work. As we noted in chapter 2, a characteristic of any good theory is that it generates research, and Skinner's theory has certainly done that. In the next section we shall review the work of an important researcher who has been influenced by Skinner's work.

THE RELATIVITY OF REINFORCEMENT

David Premack

Traditionally, reinforcers have been thought of as stimuli. A primary reinforcer is usually thought of as being related to an organism's survival, and a secondary reinforcer is a stimulus that has been consistently paired with a primary reinforcer. Premack, however, has suggested that all *responses* be thought of as potential reinforcers. Specifically, he suggests that any response that occurs with a fairly high frequency can be used to reinforce a response that occurs with a relatively lower frequency. Using Premack's notion of reinforcement, one would allow an organism to engage freely in whatever activities it wanted to and carefully record what activities were engaged in, and with what frequency. Afterward, the various activities that the organism engaged in would be arranged in a hierarchy. The activity that

David Premack. (Courtesy of David Premack)

was engaged in most frequently would be listed first, the next frequently engaged in activity would be listed next, and so on. By referring to this list, the experimenter would know exactly what could and could not be used to reinforce that particular organism. Say, for example, it was found that in a 24-hr period, the activity engaged in most frequently by a rat was eating, then drinking, then running in an activity wheel, then grooming, and finally, gazing out of the cage. According to Premack, allowing the animal to eat could be used to reinforce any of the other activities. For example, if the animal was allowed to eat each time it groomed itself, grooming would increase in frequency. Likewise, allowing the animal to groom itself could be used to reinforce the animal for looking outside the cage. The opportunity to look outside the cage, however, could not be used to reinforce any of the other activities, because they all occurred with a greater frequency than the response of looking outside the cage.

According to Premack, the way to find out what can be used as a reinforcer is to observe the organism's behavior while it has the opportunity to engage in any number of activities, and the activities that it engages in most often can be used to reinforce the activities that it engages in less often.

In summary we can say that if one activity occurs more often than another, it can be used to reinforce the activity that occurs less often. This is called the **Premack principle** and it seems to hold for humans as well as for lower organisms.

In order to test his theory, Premack (1959) allowed 31 first-grade children to either play a pinball machine or to operate a candy dispenser as often as they wanted. Some of the children played mainly with the pinball machine, and they were called "manipulators." The children who were primarily interested in the candy dispenser were called "eaters." The first phase of the study merely determined the children's preferences for these two events.

In the second phase of the study, the groups of "manipulators" and "eaters" were each subdivided into two groups. One group was placed on "manipulate-eat" contingencies, where the children had to play the pinball machine before they were allowed to operate the candy dispenser. The other group was placed on "eat-manipulate" contingencies, where they had to operate the candy dispenser before they could play the pinball machine. It was found that for the "manipulators" the "manipulate-eat" arrangement made little difference in their behavior. They simply went right on playing the pinball machine as before. Under the "eat-manipulate" conditions, however, the frequency of eating went way up for the manipulators, since they now had to eat in order to play the pinball machine. Likewise, for the "eaters" the "eat-manipulate" condition made little difference. They simply went on eating candy as before. But under the "manipulate-eat" conditions, their frequency of playing the pinball machine went way up. Thus, Premack found support for his contention that a less frequently engaged in activity can be reinforced by the opportunity to engage in a more frequently engaged in activity.

When preferences change, the reinforcers also change. For example, as long as an animal is hungry, it will eat frequently, and therefore the opportunity to eat can be used to reinforce any number of activities. When the animal is satiated, however, the frequency of its eating will decrease and the opportunity to eat will become ineffective as a reinforcer. Premack demonstrated the reversibility of reinforcement in a study involving a running response and a drinking response (1962). It was found that if animals were deprived of water for a considerable length of time, they will turn an activity wheel in order to gain access to water. But they would not increase their drinking in order to run in the activity wheel. That is, drinking reinforces running, but running did not reinforce drinking. This is what one would predict from traditional reinforcement theory. Premack also found that if an animal was allowed to drink all the water it wanted but was prevented from running in the activity wheel, the situation was reversed. Under these circumstances, drinking activity increased if it resulted in the animal having the opportunity to run, but running did not increase if it allowed the animal to drink. That is, now running could reinforce drinking, but not vice versa.

The implications of Premack's research are far-reaching. For one thing, what can act as a reinforcer becomes a very personal and continuously changing thing. The teacher can apply this knowledge by noticing individual children's preferences in a free choice situation and determining their reinforcers accordingly. For one child, the opportunity to run and play may be a reinforcer; for another child, playing with clay may be a reinforcer. The idea of recess as a way to improve the performance of the class as a whole will need to be looked at more carefully. For examples of how the Premack principle can be used to control the behavior of school children, see Homme, deBaca, Divine, Steinhorst, and Rickert (1963).

There is no doubt that Skinnerian notions have had, and are having, far-reaching theoretical and practical implications. Recently, however, there has been a growing recognition of the limitations of operant principles in modifying behavior. In the next section we will examine a few of the reasons why operant principles seem to have limited applicability.

THE MISBEHAVIOR OF ORGANISMS

We saw in the last chapter that Thorndike concluded that the same laws of learning apply to all mammals, including humans. Skinner, like many other learning theorists, agrees with Thorndike's conclusion. After observing how different species of animals performed under a certain schedule of reinforcement, Skinner commented (1956): "Pigeon, rat, monkey, which is which? It doesn't matter. Of course, these species have behavioral repertories which are as different as their anatomies. But once you have allowed for differences in the ways in which they make contact with the environment, and in the ways in which they act upon the environment, what remains of their behavior shows astonishingly similar properties" (pp. 230–231). Skinner goes on to say that one can also add the performance of mice, cats, dogs, and human children and the curves would still have more or less the same characteristics.

The alternative to believing that the same laws of learning apply to all mammals seems to necessitate going back to the concept of instinct, which the behaviorists attempted to bury forever. Those believing in the existence of instincts say that different species have different inborn behavior tendencies which interact or even negate the laws of learning. In other words, because of their innate behavior tendencies, certain species can be conditioned to do some things but not others. According to this point of view, some responses should be easier to condition for some species than for others, because the responses of interest may occur more naturally for some species than for others.

Current interest in how innate behavior tendencies interact with learning principles has been stimulated by two of Skinner's ex-associates, Marian Breland (now Marian Bailey) and Keller Breland. Armed with a knowledge of operant principles, the Brelands moved from Minnesota, where they had worked with Skinner, to Arkansas, where they started a business called Animal Behavior Enterprises. By using operant techniques the Brelands were able to train a wide variety of animals to perform many different tricks, and their trained animals were put on display at fairs, conventions, amusement parks, and on television. As of 1961, the Brelands reported having conditioned 38 species (totaling over 6,000 animals), including chickens, pigs, raccoons, reindeer, cockatoos, porpoises, and whales.

Everything seemed to be going fine for the Brelands until they began to experience breakdowns of conditioned behavior. Their problems became so pronounced that they were moved to report them in an article whose title, "**The Misbehavior of Organisms**" (1961), was a parody of the title of Skinner's first major work, *The Behavior of Organisms* (1938).

The Brelands found that although their animals were initially highly conditionable, eventually instinctive behavior would appear and interfere with what had been learned. For example, an attempt was made to train raccoons to pick up coins and deposit them into a 5-in metal box. Conditioning a raccoon to pick up a single coin was no problem. Next, the metal box was introduced and that is when the problem began. The raccoon seemed to have trouble letting the coin fall into the box. The animal would rub the coin inside of the container, take it back out, and

Marian Bailey. (Courtesy of Marian Bailey)

hold it firmly for several seconds. Eventually, however, the raccoon released the coin into the box and received its food reinforcement. The next phase in training required that the raccoon place *two* coins into the metal box before receiving reinforcement. It was found that the raccoon could not let go of the two coins. Instead, it would rub them together, dip them into the container, and then remove them. The rubbing behavior became more and more pronounced even though such behavior delayed or even prevented reinforcement. The Brelands concluded that conditioning a raccoon to place two coins into a metal box was not feasible. It seemed that the innate behaviors associated with eating were too powerful to be overcome by operant conditioning principles. In other words, in this case, a raccoon's innate tendency to wash and manipulate its food competed successfully with the learned response of placing one or more coins into a container.

Another example involved the training of pigs to pick up large wooden coins and deposit them in a large "piggy bank." The coins were placed several feet from the bank and the pig had to transport them to the bank before receiving reinforcement. Early conditioning was very effective and the pigs seemed eager to perform the task. As time went on, however, the animals performed more slowly, and on their way to the "piggy bank" they would repeatedly drop the coin, root it (push it along the ground with their snouts), pick it up, drop it, root it, toss it in the air, and so on. The Brelands first believed that such behavior may have been the result of low drive so they intensified the deprivation schedule that the animals were on, which only intensified the animals' misbehavior. Eventually it took the pigs about 10 minutes to transport the coins a distance of about six feet, even when such delays postponed or eliminated reinforcement. Again, it appeared that the animal's instinctive behavior associated with eating became more powerful than the behavior it had learned.

From these and other similar observations, the Brelands concluded (1961): "It seems obvious that these animals are trapped by strong instinctive behaviors, and clearly we have here a demonstration of the prepotency of such behavior patterns over those which have been conditioned" (p. 185).

The Brelands called the tendency for innate behavior patterns to gradually displace learned behavior **instinctual drift,** which they elaborate as follows (1961):

> The general principle seems to be that wherever an animal has strong instinctive behaviors in the area of the conditioned response, after continued running the organism will drift toward the instinctive behavior to the detriment of the conditioned behavior and even to the delay or preclusion of the reinforcement. In a very boiled-down, simplified form it might be stated as "Learned behavior drifts toward instinctive behavior." (p. 185)

The Brelands feel that their work challenges three assumptions made by the behaviorists, namely, (1) that animals come to the learning situation as a *tabula rasa* (blank tablet); (2) that differences among various species are unimportant; and (3) that any response can be conditioned to any stimulus. Rather than making these assumptions, the Brelands conclude (1961): "After 14 years of continuous conditioning and observation of thousands of animals, it is our reluctant conclusion that the behavior of any species cannot be adequately understood, predicted, or controlled without knowledge of its instinctive patterns, evolutionary history, and ecological niche" (p. 126).

Thus, we are once again confronted with the age-old empiricism/nativism controversy, that is, is behavior learned or is it genetically determined? The phenomenon of instinctual drift seems to indicate that, at least for some species, behavior can be nudged only a limited amount from its instinctual basis before instinctual tendencies override learned tendencies as the most powerful determiners of behavior. What about humans? Do we have within us the remnants of our evolutionary past toward which we periodically drift? Can culture, society, or circumstances push us only so far before we resort to more primitive forms of behavior? The answer depends on who is being asked. Many learning theorists such as Skinner would say no. Others such as Freud and the sociobiologists would say yes.

Autoshaping. Another phenomenon that seems to show the importance of instinctive behavior in a learning situation is autoshaping. We saw earlier in this chapter that the shaping process can be used to encourage an animal to make a response that it ordinarily would not make in a situation. To do so, the experimenter reinforces increasingly closer approximations to the desired behavior until the desired behavior is performed by the animal. In the case of autoshaping, however, the animal seems to shape its own behavior. For example, Brown and Jenkins (1968) found that if a pigeon was reinforced at certain intervals, regardless of what it was doing (noncontingent reinforcement), and if a disc was illuminated just prior to the presentation of the reinforcer (in this case, food), the pigeon learned to peck at the disc. The question is, why did the pigeon learn to peck the disc when it had never been reinforced for doing so?

One attempt to account for autoshaping has likened it to superstitious behavior, saying that the pigeon may have been pecking at the disc just prior to when food was delivered and therefore pecking the disc would be maintained as a superstitious response. One problem with this explanation is that almost all pigeons peck the disc under these circumstances. It seems that if superstitious behavior were involved, some pigeons would peck the disc, others would turn in circles, others would peck other parts of the test chamber, and so on. A second explanation of autoshaping has been based on classical conditioning principles. According to this explanation, the illuminated disc becomes a secondary reinforcer because of its proximity to food, a primary reinforcer. Under the circumstances described thus far, this explanation is reasonable, except it does not explain why the pigeon would peck at the disc. Earlier in this chapter we saw that, indeed, discriminative stimuli (S^Ds) become secondary reinforcers, and thus can be used to maintain behavior, but why the animal should respond overtly to the secondary reinforcer as if it were the primary reinforcer is not clear.

An experiment by Williams and Williams (1969) casts further doubt on explanations of autoshaping as either a superstitious or a classical conditioning phenomenon. In their experiment, Williams and Williams arranged the situation so that pecking at the lighted disc actually *prevented* reinforcement from occurring. Food was presented to the pigeons every 15 sec, unless the pigeon pecked the illuminated disc, in which case food was withheld on that trial. In this study pecking the illuminated disc was *never* followed by reinforcement. In fact, the more the pigeon pecked the disc, the less food it received. According to the explanations of autoshaping in terms of both superstitious behavior and of classical conditioning, the experimental arrangement in this study should have eliminated or, at least, drastically reduced disc pecking. It did not, however. The pigeons went right on pecking the disc at a high rate. In fact, for some pigeons disc pecking occurred so frequently that it virtually eliminated all reinforcement.

A study by Jenkins and Moore (1973) further complicates the situation. In their study it was found that if food was used as a reinforcer, pigeons responded to the disc with an eating posture and if water was used as a reinforcer, pigeons responded to the disc with a drinking posture. In other words, when food was used as a reinforcer the pigeons seemed to be eating the disc, and when water was used as a reinforcer they seemed to be drinking the disc.

By the process of elimination, one is forced to view the autoshaping phenomenon as involving instinctive behavior patterns. It can be assumed, for example, that a hungry organism in a situation where eating is possible will most likely give responses related to eating. In the case of pigeons, pecking is such a response. Furthermore, it may be assumed that while in a high drive state, such behaviors can be easily elicited by any stimulus in the animal's environment which is vivid and on which an eating-related response could be easily released. A lighted disc in the environment of a hungry pigeon could be such a stimulus. According to this explanation, the lighted disc is simply eliciting instinctive behavior which has a high probability of occurring under the circumstances. Because disc pecking in autoshaping experiments is typically what the experimenter is looking for, it is not referred to as misbehavior as were certain instinctive responses in the Brelands' work.

If one accepts the instinctive explanation of autoshaping, one needs to conclude that no learning takes place at all. The animal simply becomes hypersensitive in the situation and releases innate responses which are appropriate under the circumstances to the most vivid stimuli in its environment. This is the position taken by Robert Bolles (see e.g., Bolles, 1979, pp. 179–184).

The work of the Brelands and the work on autoshaping are but two examples of a growing recognition in psychology that the innate response tendencies of an organism interact with the laws of learning. In other words, what may hold true for one type of organism may not hold true for another type of organism. Furthermore, what may hold true for a given organism at one developmental level may not hold true for that organism at another developmental level. For a more detailed elaboration of these points see Seligman and Hager (Eds.), *Biological Boundaries of Learning* (1972).

DISCUSSION QUESTIONS

1. Outline the procedure you would use while following Skinner's theory to increase the probability of a child's becoming a creative adult.

2. Would you use the same reinforcers to manipulate the behavior of both children and adults? If not, what would make the difference?

3. Are there some forms of adult human behavior for which you feel Skinner's theory is not applicable? Explain.

4. What would characterize the classroom procedures suggested by Skinner's theory of learning? List a few differences between these procedures and those now being followed in our schools.

5. Assuming the conclusions Skinner reached concerning the effectiveness of punishment are valid, what major change would they suggest in the area of child rearing? Criminal behavior? Education?

6. What is the partial reinforcement effect? Briefly describe the basic reinforcement schedules that Skinner studied.

7. Propose an explanation for the partial reinforcement effect.

8. Describe concurrent and concurrent-chain schedules of reinforcement and give an example of each.

9. What is Herrnstein's matching law? What aspects of reinforcement has the law been found to hold true for? What are the implications of the law for dealing with human behavior problems?

10. What is contingency contracting? Give an example of how it could be used.

11. From Skinner's point of view, what are the advantages of programmed learning and teaching machines over the traditional lecture technique of teaching?

12. According to Skinner, why have we not developed a more adequate technology of behavior in this country? What would need to be done before we would be willing to utilize such a technology in solving our problems?

13. Give an example of how the Premack Principle can be used to modify the behavior of a primary school child.

14. Discuss chaining from Skinner's point of view.

15. Explain language development from Skinner's point of view. Explain Chomsky's opposition to Skinner's explanation of language development.

16. Distinguish among positive reinforcement, negative reinforcement, and punishment.

17. Describe the phenomenon of instinctual drift.

18. Describe autoshaping and attempt to account for it.

CHAPTER HIGHLIGHTS

Autoclitic behavior. Provides a grammatical framework for verbal behavior.

Autoshaping. The observation that under certain circumstances the behavior of some organisms seems to be shaped automatically.

Chaining. According to Skinner, chaining occurs when one response brings the organism into proximity with stimuli that both reinforce the last response and cause the next response. That response in turn causes the organism to experience stimuli that both reinforce the response and cause the next response, and so on.

Concurrent reinforcement schedule. A schedule involving two alternative responses each of which is maintained by an independent schedule of reinforcement.

Concurrent-chain reinforcement schedule. On such a schedule the responses made during an initial phase determine what response alternatives and what reinforcement schedules are available during the terminal phase.

Contingency contracting. Making arrangements, sometimes with another person, so that certain behavior will be reinforced. For example, each time the person goes a week without smoking he or she receives 10 dollars.

Contingent reinforcement. Reinforcement that only occurs if a specific response is made. If the response is not made, the organism is not reinforced.

Continuous reinforcement schedule (CRF). The condition where the organism is reinforced each time it makes an appropriate response.

Cumulative recording. A special kind of graphing technique used by Skinner. Each time a response is made, the cumulative recording rises one notch and remains at that level until another response is made. The steepness of the line, therefore, indicates rate of responding.

Differential reinforcement. The condition where some responses made by the organism are reinforced and others are not.

Discriminative operant. An operant response that is made selectively to one set of circumstances but not to another set of circumstances.

Discriminative stimulus (S^D). A cue or signal indicating that if a certain operant response is made it will be reinforced.

Echoic behavior. Repeating someone else's verbal utterances.

Extinction of an operant response. In operant conditioning, extinction involves the gradual decrease in the *frequency* with which a conditioned response occurs after it is no longer reinforced, whereas in classical conditioning, the extinction of a conditioned response involves the gradual decrease in *amplitude* of the conditioned response following the removal of reinforcement. When the frequency of an operant response returns to its operant level, it is said to be extinguished.

Fixed interval reinforcement schedule (FI). The condition where only the response made after a certain interval of time has passed is reinforced.

Fixed ratio reinforcement schedule (FR). The condition where only the *n*th response made is reinforced.

Functional analysis. The investigation of how certain stimuli and certain responses vary together. Skinner's approach to research was to avoid theorizing and to deal only with the manipulation of observable stimuli and note how their manipulation affected behavior; sometimes called the "empty organism" approach to research.

Functional autonomy. A term introduced by Gordon Allport to explain behavior that apparently occurs independently of external reinforcement. Such behavior, according to Allport, was originally dependent upon reinforcement, but eventually becomes autonomous or self-reinforcing.

Generalized reinforcers. Stimuli that derive their reinforcement properties from being paired with more than one primary reinforcer. Generalized reinforcers have wide application since their effectiveness does not depend on any particular need of the organism.

Instinctual drift. The tendency for the behavior of some organisms, after prolonged conditioning, to revert back to instinctual patterns of behavior.

Magazine training. Training the animal to approach the food cup when it hears the feeder mechanism operate. This way, the click of the feeder mechanism is associated with food and thereby becomes a secondary reinforcer.

Mand. A verbal command that is reinforced when the listener carries out the command. For example, the mand "pass the salt" is reinforced when the person receives the salt.

Matching law. Herrnstein's observation that when two alternative responses are governed by two independent schedules of reinforcement, relative rate of responding to the alternatives approximately matches the relative rate at which the alternatives are reinforced. The matching law holds not only for rate (frequency) of reinforcement but for amount and delay of reinforcement as well. All other things being equal, organisms will prefer schedules of reinforcement that produce frequent, large, and immediate reinforcers as compared to infrequent, small, and delayed reinforcers.

Misbehavior of organisms. The term used by the Brelands to describe the tendency that some organisms have to behave instinctually instead of in a way that they had been conditioned to behave.

Noncontingent reinforcement. Reinforcement that occurs independently of the organism's behavior.

Operant behavior. Behavior that is simply emitted by the organism rather than elicited by a known stimulus. Operant behavior may come under the control of its consequences.

Operant conditioning. Increasing the rate with which a response occurs or the probability of a response by arranging the situation so that the occurrence of that response is followed by reinforcement. Also called type R conditioning.

Operant level. The frequency with which an operant response occurs before it is systematically reinforced.

Partial reinforcement effect (PRE). The fact that a response that has been reinforced only sometimes takes longer to extinguish than a response that had been reinforced each time it occurred.

Premack principle. The opportunity to engage in a frequently occurring activity can be used to reinforce a less frequently occurring activity.

Primary negative reinforcer. An aversive stimulus which, when removed from the situation following a response, increases the probability of the response's recurring.

Primary positive reinforcer. A stimulus related to an organism's survival which, when added to the situation following a response, increases the probability of the response's recurring.

Programmed learning. A procedure that provides information to the learner in small steps, guarantees immediate feedback concerning whether or not the material was learned properly, and allows the learner to determine the pace with which he or she goes through the material.

Punishment. The arrangement whereby either a response produces an aversive stimulus or removes a positive one.

Resistance to extinction. The number of nonreinforced responses that occur before an operant response returns to its operant level.

Respondent behavior. Behavior elicited by a known stimulus.

Respondent conditioning. The same as classical conditioning; also called type S conditioning.

Secondary negative reinforcer. A previously neutral stimulus that has taken on reinforcing properties through its pairing with a primary negative reinforcer.

Secondary positive reinforcer. A previously neutral stimulus that has taken on reinforcing properties through its pairing with a primary positive reinforcer.

Shaping. The process whereby a desired response is encouraged through the use of differential reinforcement and successive approximation rather than simply waiting for it to occur.

Skinner box. An experimental test chamber usually consisting of a grid floor, a lever, a light, and a food cup.

Spontaneous recovery of an operant response. The increased frequency with which a conditioned operant response occurs following a delay after extinction and with no further training.

Successive approximation. Reinforcing only those responses that become increasingly similar to the response that is finally desired; a component of the process of shaping.

Superstitious behavior. Behavior that looks as if it is governed by the belief that it must be engaged in before reinforcement can be obtained, whereas, in reality, the behavior has nothing to do with the presence or absence of reinforcement. Superstitious behavior results from noncontingent reinforcement.

Tact. The verbal behavior of naming things. Such behavior results in reinforcement when objects or events are named correctly.

Teaching machine. A device used to present programmed material.

Variable interval reinforcement schedule (VI). The condition where only the response made after the passage of some *average* interval of time is reinforced.

Variable ratio reinforcement schedule (VR). The condition where a certain *average* number of responses need to be made before the organism is reinforced.

6

Clark Leonard Hull

Clark L. Hull (1884–1952) received his PhD from the University of Wisconsin in 1918 where he also taught from 1916 to 1929. In 1929 he moved to Yale where he stayed until his death.

Hull's career can be divided into three separate parts. His first major concern was with the testing of aptitudes. He gathered material on aptitude testing while teaching a course on the topic at the University of Wisconsin, and published a book entitled *Aptitude Testing* in 1928. Hull's second major concern was with hypnosis and after a long study of the hypnotic process, he wrote a book entitled *Hypnosis and Suggestibility* (1933b). His third concern, and the work for which he is most famous, was the study of the learning process. Hull's first major book on learning, *Principles of Behavior* (1943), radically changed the study of learning. It was the first attempt to apply comprehensive scientific theory to the study of a complex psychological phenomenon. We saw in chapter 3 that Ebbinghaus was the first to use an experiment to investigate learning. But it was Hull who first utilized a rigorous theory to study and attempt to explain learning. Hull's theory, as presented in 1943, was extended in 1952 in *A Behavior System*. He intended to write a third book on learning, but never did.

For his efforts, Hull received the Warren Medal in 1945 from the Society of Experimental Psychology. The award read:

> To Clark L. Hull: For his careful development of a systematic theory of behavior. This theory has stimulated much research and it has been developed in a precise and quantitative form so as to permit predictions which can be tested empirically. The theory thus contains within itself the seeds of its own ultimate verification and of its own possible final disproof. A truly unique achievement in the history of psychology to date.

Hull was a cripple most of his life. He suffered partial paralysis from polio which he had as a child. In 1948, he had a coronary attack and four years later he died. In the last book he wrote (*A Behavior System*), he expressed regret that the third book that he intended to write on learning would never be written.

Even though Hull felt that his theory was incomplete, it has had a profound influence on learning theory throughout the world. Kenneth Spence, one of Hull's many famous students, indicates that 40% of all experiments in the *Journal of Experimental Psychology* and in the *Journal of Comparative and Physiological Psychology* during the period between 1941 and 1950 refer to some aspect of Hull's work, and when one looks only at the areas of learning and motivation, this figure rises to 70% (Spence, 1952). Ruja (1956) reports that in the *Journal of Abnormal and Social Psychology* between 1949 and 1952 there are 105 references to Hull's *Principles of Behavior*, and the next most popular reference was listed only 25 times. In fact, it is still quite common for the student of learning to come across numerous references to Hull's work while going through the psychological journals. By any measure, Clark Hull was a major contributor to our knowledge of the learning process.

Hull, like most functionalistic learning theorists, was significantly influenced by Darwin's writings. The purpose of Hull's theory was to explain the adaptive behavior and to understand the variables affecting it. In fact, it can be said that Hull was interested in developing a theory that explained how bodily needs, the environment, and behavior interact so as to increase the probability of the organism's surviving.

Clark Leonard Hull. (From *A History of Psychology in Autobiography*, Vol. 4, p. x, by C. A. Murchison, ed., 1952, Worcester, MA: Clark University Press)

Hull's Approach to Theorizing

As a first step in developing his theory, Hull reviewed the research on learning up to that time. Next, he attempted to summarize those findings. Finally, he attempted to deduce testable consequences from those summary principles. We will look at this approach to theory construction in somewhat more detail below.

Hull's approach to theory construction has been called **hypothetical–deductive** or **logical deductive.** His theory has a logical structure of postulates and theorems much like Euclid's geometry. The postulates are general statements about behavior which cannot be directly verified. From the postulates, theorems are generated. The theorems follow logically—that is, they are *deduced*—from the postulates. Although the postulates are not testable, the theorems that they generate can be tested. An experiment is designed to test the theorem and if the results of the experiment are as predicted, the theorem is said to be correct and the postulate from which it is deduced gains in strength. If the experiment does not come out in the predicted direction, the theorem is said to be incorrect, and the postulate from which it is deduced must either be revised or abandoned.

It can be seen that this type of theorizing creates a dynamic, open-ended system. Hypotheses are constantly being generated; some of them are supported by experimental outcomes, some are not. When experiments come out in a predicted direction, the whole theory, including postulates and theorems, is strengthened. When the experiments do not come out as predicted, the theory is weakened and must be revised. A theory such as the one suggested by Hull must continually be updated in accordance with the outcome of empirical investigation.

Hull (1943) said:

Empirical observation, supplemented by shrewd conjecture, is the main source of the primary principles or postulates of a science. Such formulations, when taken in various combinations together with relevant antecedent conditions, yield inferences or theorems, of which some may agree with the empirical outcome of the conditions in question, and some may not. Primary propositions yielding logical deductions which consistently agree with the observed empirical outcome are retained, whereas those which disagree are rejected or modified. As the sifting of this trial-and-error process continues, there gradually emerges a limited series of primary principles whose joint implications are progressively more likely to agree with relevant observations. Deductions made from these surviving postulates, while never absolutely certain, do at length become highly trustworthy. This is in fact the present status of the primary principles of the major physical sciences. (p. 382)

As was mentioned in chapter 2, any scientific theory is merely a tool that aids the researcher in synthesizing facts and in knowing where to look for new information. The ultimate value of a theory is determined by how well it agrees with observed facts, or in this case, with the outcome of experiments. The ultimate authority in science is the empirical world. Although a theory such as Hull's can become very abstract, still it must make statements concerning observable events. No matter how elaborate and abstract a theory becomes, it must ultimately generate propositions that are empirically verifiable; Hull's theory does exactly that.

MAJOR THEORETICAL CONCEPTS

Although Hull's 1952 version of his theory is highly complex, it is still an extension of his 1943 theory; therefore the best way to summarize Hull's thoughts on learning is to outline the 1943 version of his theory and then to point out the major changes that were made in 1952. Following that plan, we will first discuss Hull's sixteen major postulates as they appeared in 1943 and then, later in the chapter, we will turn to the major revisions Hull made in his theory in 1952.

Postulate 1: Sensing the External Environment and the Stimulus Trace. External stimulation triggers an afferent (sensory) neural impulse that outlasts the environmental stimulation. Thus, Hull postulates the existence of a **stimulus trace** that continues for a few seconds after the stimulus event has terminated. Because this afferent neural impulse becomes associated with a response, Hull changes the traditional S-R formula to S-s-R, where s is the stimulus trace. For Hull, the association of interest is between s and R. The stimulus trace ultimately causes an efferent (motor) neural reaction (r) that results in an overt response. Thus we have S-s-r-R, where S is external stimulation, s is the stimulus trace, r is the firing of motor neurons, and R is an overt response.

Postulate 2: The Interaction of Sensory Impulses. This postulate indicates the complexity of stimulation and, therefore, the difficulties in predicting behavior. Behavior is seldom a function of only one stimulus. Rather, it is a function of many stimuli converging upon the organism at any given time. These many stimuli and their related traces interact with one another and their synthesis determines behavior. We can now refine the S–R formula further as follows:

$$S_1 \rightarrow s_1$$
$$S_2 \rightarrow s_2$$
$$S_3 \rightarrow s_3 \rightarrow \bar{s} \rightarrow r \rightarrow R$$
$$S_4 \rightarrow s_4$$
$$S_5 \rightarrow s_5$$

where $\bar{s}$ represents the combined effects of the five stimuli acting upon the organism at the moment.

Postulate 3: Unlearned Behavior. Hull believed that the organism is born with a hierarchy of responses that is triggered when a need arises. For example, if a foreign object enters the eye, considerable blinking and tear secretion may follow automatically. If the temperature varies from that which is optimal for normal bodily functioning, the organism may sweat or shiver. Likewise, experiencing pain, hunger, or thirst will trigger certain innate response patterns that have a high probability of reducing the effects of those conditions.

The term hierarchy is used in reference to these responses because more than one reaction may occur. If the first innate response pattern does not alleviate a need, another pattern will occur. If the second response pattern does not reduce the need, still another will occur, and so on. If none of the innate behavior patterns is effective in reducing the need, the organism will have to *learn* new response patterns. Thus, according to Hull, learning is required only when innate neural mechanisms and their related responses fail to reduce an organism's need. Generally, as long as either innate responses or previously learned responses are effective in satisfying needs, there is no reason to learn new responses.

Postulate 4: Contiguity and Drive Reduction as Necessary Conditions for Learning. This postulate states that if a stimulus leads to a response, and if the response results in the satisfaction of a biological need, then the association between the stimulus and the response is strengthened. The more often the stimulus and the response that leads to need satisfaction are paired, the stronger the relationship between the stimulus and the response becomes. On this basic point, Hull is in complete agreement with Thorndike's revised law of effect. Hull, however, is more specific about what constitutes a "satisfying state of affairs." Primary reinforcement, according to Hull, must involve need satisfaction, or what Hull called **drive reduction.**

Postulate 4 also describes a secondary reinforcer as "a stimulus which has been closely and consistently associated with the diminution of a need" (Hull, 1943, p. 178). Secondary reinforcement following a response will also increase the strength of the association between that response and the stimulus with which it was contiguous. To summarize, we can say that if a stimulus is followed by a response, which in turn is followed by reinforcement (either primary or secondary), the association between that stimulus and that response is strengthened. It can also be said that the "habit" of giving that response to that stimulus gets stronger. Hull's term, **habit strength,** will be explained below.

Although Hull, like Thorndike and Skinner, was very much a reinforcement theorist, he was more specific about his definition of reinforcement. Skinner simply said that a reinforcer was anything that increased the rate with which a response occurred, and Thorndike talked about a nebulous "satisfying" or "annoying" state of affairs. For Hull, reinforcement was drive reduction, and reinforcers were stimuli that were capable of reducing a drive.

Habit Strength ($_sH_R$). Habit strength is one of Hull's most important concepts, and as stated above, it refers to the strength of the association between a stimulus and a response. As the number of reinforced pairings between a stimulus and a response goes up, the habit strength of that association goes up. The mathematical formula that describes the relationship between $_sH_R$ and number of reinforced pairings between S and R is as follows:

$$_sH_R = 1 - 10^{-0.0305\ N}$$

N is the number of reinforced pairings between S and R. This formula generates a negatively accelerated learning curve, which means early reinforced pairings have more of an effect on learning than do later ones. In fact, a point is reached where additional reinforced pairings have no effect on learning. Figure 6-1 shows that early reinforcements have more of an effect on learning than do later ones.

Postulate 5: Stimulus Generalization. Here Hull is saying that the ability of a stimulus (other than the one used during conditioning) to elicit a conditioned response is determined by its similarity to the stimulus used during training. Thus,

Figure 6–1. The relationship between gains in habit strength $_sH_R$ and successive reinforcements. (From *Principles of Behavior*, p. 116, by C. L. Hull, 1943, Englewood Cliffs, NJ: Prentice Hall)

$_sH_R$ will generalize from one stimulus to another to the extent that the two stimuli are similar. This postulate also indicates that prior experience will effect current learning, that is, learning that took place under similar conditions will transfer to the new learning situation. Hull called this **generalized habit strength** which he symbolized $_sH_R$. This postulate essentially described Thorndike's identical elements theory of the transfer of training.

Postulate 6: Stimuli Associated with Drives. Biological deficiency in the organism produces a drive state (D) and each drive has specific stimuli associated with it. Hunger pangs that accompany the hunger drive and dry mouth, lips, and throat that accompany the thirst drive are examples. The existence of specific drive stimuli make it possible to teach an animal to behave in one way under one drive and another way under another drive. For example, an animal can be taught to turn right in a T-maze when it is hungry, and to turn left when it is thirsty. As we will see later in the chapter, the concept of drive stimuli became very important in Hull's 1952 revision of his theory.

Postulate 7: Reaction Potential as a Function of Drive and Habit Strength. The likelihood of a learned response's being made at any given moment is called **reaction potential** and is symbolized $_sE_R$. Reaction potential is a function of both habit strength ($_sH_R$) and drive (D). In order for a learned response to occur, $_sH_R$ has to be activated by D. Drive does not direct behavior; it simply arouses it and intensifies it. Without drive, the animal would not emit a learned response even though there had been a large number of reinforced pairings between a stimulus and a response. Thus, if an animal has learned to press a bar in a Skinner box in order to obtain food, it would press the bar only when it was hungry, no matter how well it was trained. The basic components of Hull's theory that we have covered thus far can be combined into the following formula:

$$\text{Reaction potential} = {}_sE_R = {}_sH_R \times D$$

Thus, reaction potential is a function of how often the response was reinforced in that situation and the extent to which a drive is present. By looking at the above formula, it can be seen that if either $_sH_R$ or D were zero, $_sE_R$ would necessarily be zero. As we shall see in postulates 13 to 15, in addition to being related to response probability, $_sE_R$ is also related to resistance to extinction, latency, and amplitude of response.

Postulate 8: Responding Causes Fatigue Which Operates Against the Elicitation of a Conditioned Response. Responding requires work, and work results in fatigue. Fatigue eventually acts to inhibit responding. **Reactive inhibition (I_R)** is caused by the fatigue associated with muscular activity and is related to the amount of work involved in performing a task. Since this form of inhibition is related to fatigue, it automatically dissipates when the organism stops performing. This concept has been used to explain the spontaneous recovery of a conditioned response after extinction. That is, the animal may stop responding because of the buildup of I_R. After a rest, the I_R dissipates and the animal commences to respond once again. For Hull, extinction is not only a function of nonreinforcement, but it is also influenced by the buildup of reactive inhibition.

I_R has also been used to explain the **reminiscence effect,** which is the improvement of performance following the cessation of practice. For example, if experimental subjects are trained to track a rotating disc with a stylus, their performances will gradually improve until some asymptotic (maximal) level is reached. If the subjects are allowed to rest for a few minutes after this asymptotic level is reached, and then are asked to track the disc again, their performances will tend to exceed their previous asymptotic levels. This is called the reminiscence effect and it is explained by assuming that I_R builds up during training and operates against tracking performance. After a rest, I_R dissipates and performance improves. Figure 6-2 presents an example of the reminiscence effect.

Additional support for Hull's notion of I_R comes from research on the difference between **massed** and **distributed practice.** It is consistently found that when practice trials are spaced far apart (distributed practice), performance is superior to what it is when practice trials are close together (massed practice). On a tracking task, for example, subjects resting between practice trials reach higher asymptotic levels of performance than subjects who go immediately from one practice trial to the next. Figure 6-2 shows the difference in performance under massed and distributed practice conditions.

Figure 6–2. There were three groups of subjects in this experiment which measured ability to track a rotating disc with a stylus. One group received distributed practice; another received massed practice; and a third group was first given massed practice, then a rest period, and then massed practice again. Clearly, the group receiving distributed practice performed much better than the other two groups. The vast improvement of the massed practice-rest group following the rest is an example of the reminiscence effect. (From *Principles of General Psychology,* 3rd ed., p. 290, by G. A. Kimble & N. Garmezy, 1968, New York: The Ronald Press Co. Copyright © 1968)

Postulate 9: The Learned Response of Not Responding. Fatigue being a negative drive state, it follows that not responding would be reinforcing. Not responding allows I_R to dissipate, thereby reducing the negative drive of fatigue. The learned response of not responding is called **conditioned inhibition,** which is symbolized $_sI_R$. Both I_R and $_sI_R$ operate *against* the elicitation of a learned response and are therefore subtracted from reaction potential ($_sE_R$). When I_R and $_sI_R$ are subtracted from $_sE_R$, **effective reaction potential** is the result. Effective reaction potential is symbolized $_s\bar{E}_R$.

$$\text{Effective reaction potential} = {}_s\bar{E}_R = {}_sH_R \times D - (I_R + {}_sI_R).$$

Postulate 10: Factors Tending to Inhibit a Learned Response Change from Moment to Moment. According to Hull, there is an "inhibitory potentiality," which varies from moment to moment and operates against the elicitation of a learned response. This "inhibitory potentiality" is called the **oscillation effect** and is symbolized $_sO_R$.

The oscillation effect was the "wild card" in Hull's theory—it is his way of taking into consideration the probabilistic nature of predictions concerning behavior. There is, he says, a factor operating against the elicitation of a learned response, whose effect varies from moment to moment but always operates within a certain range of values, that is, although the range of the inhibitory factor is set, the value that may be manifested at any time could vary within that range. The values of this inhibitory factor are assumed to be normally distributed with middle values most likely to occur. If, by chance, a large inhibitory value does occur, it considerably reduces the chances of a learned response's being made. This oscillation effect ($_sO_R$) explains why a learned response may be elicited on one trial but not on the next. Predictions concerning behavior based upon the value of $_s\bar{E}_R$ will always be influenced by the fluctuating values of $_sO_R$ and will thus always be probabilistic in nature. $_sO_R$ must be subtracted from effective reaction potential ($_s\bar{E}_R$) which creates **momentary effective reaction potential,** symbolized $_s\dot{\bar{E}}_R$. Thus we have

$$\text{Momentary effective reaction potential} = {}_s\dot{\bar{E}}_R = [{}_sH_R \times D - (I_R + {}_sI_R)] - {}_sO_R.$$

Postulate 11: Momentary Effective Reaction Potential Must Exceed a Certain Value Before a Learned Response Can Occur. The value that $_s\dot{\bar{E}}_R$ must exceed before a conditioned response can occur is called the **reaction threshold,** symbolized $_sL_R$. Therefore, a learned response will be emitted only if $_s\dot{\bar{E}}_R$ is greater than $_sL_R$.

Postulate 12: The Probability of a Learned Response's Being Made is a Combined Function of $_s\bar{E}_R$, $_sO_R$, and $_sL_R$. In the early stages of training, that is, after only a few reinforced trials, $_s\bar{E}_R$ will be very close to $_sL_R$ and, therefore, due to the effects of $_sO_R$, a conditioned response will be elicited on some trials but not on others. This is because on some trials the value of $_sO_R$ subtracted from $_s\bar{E}_R$ will be large enough to reduce $_s\bar{E}_R$ to a value below $_sL_R$. As training continues, subtracting $_sO_R$ from $_s\bar{E}_R$ will have less and less of an effect since the value of $_s\bar{E}_R$ will become much larger than the value of $_sL_R$. Even after considerable training, however, it is still possible for $_sO_R$ to assume a large value, thereby preventing the occurrence of a conditioned response.

Postulate 13: The Greater the Value of $_s\dot{E}_R$ the Shorter Will Be the Latency Between S and R. Latency is the time between when a stimulus is presented to the organism and a learned response is made. Latency is symbolized $_st_R$. This postulate simply states that the reaction time between the onset of a stimulus and the elicitation of a learned response goes down as the value of $_s\dot{E}_R$ goes up.

Postulate 14: The Value of $_s\dot{E}_R$ Will Determine Resistance to Extinction. The value of $_s\dot{E}_R$ at the end of training determines how many nonreinforced responses will need to be made before extinction occurs. The greater the value of $_s\dot{E}_R$, the greater the number of nonreinforced responses that have to be made before extinction takes place. Hull used n to symbolize the number of nonreinforced trials that occurred before extinction resulted.

Postulate 15: The Amplitude of a Conditioned Response Varies Directly with $_s\dot{E}_R$. This postulate deals with the situation where the learned response occurs in degrees, for example, salivation or the galvanic skin response (GSR). When the conditioned response is one that can occur in degrees, the magnitude of the conditioned response will be directly related to the size of $_s\dot{E}_R$, the momentary effective reaction potential. Hull used A to symbolize response amplitude.

Postulate 16: When Two or More Incompatible Responses Tend to Be Elicited in the Same Situation, the One with the Greatest $_s\dot{E}_R$ Will Occur. This postulate seems self-explanatory.

Summary of the Symbols Used in Hull's Theory

D = drive
$_sH_R$ = habit strength
$_sE_R$ = reaction potential = $_sH_R \times D$
I_R = reactive inhibition
$_sI_R$ = conditioned inhibition
$_s\bar{E}_R$ = effective reaction potential = $_sH_R \times D - (I_R + _sI_R)$
$_sO_R$ = oscillation effect
$_s\dot{E}_R$ = momentary effective reaction potential = $_s\bar{E}_R - _sO_R$
     = $[_sH_R \times D - (I_R + _sI_R)] - _sO_R$
$_sL_R$ = the value that $_s\dot{E}_R$ must exceed before a learned response can occur
$_st_R$ = reaction time
p = response probability
n = trials to extinction
A = response amplitude

MAJOR DIFFERENCES BETWEEN HULL'S
1943 AND 1952 THEORIES

Incentive Motivation (K)

In the 1943 version of his theory, Hull treated magnitude of reinforcement as a learning variable: the greater the amount of reinforcement the greater the amount of drive reduction, and thus the greater the increase in $_sH_R$. Research showed this notion to be unsatisfactory. Experiments showed that performance was dramatically altered as size of reinforcement was varied *after* learning was complete. For example, when an animal trained to run a straight runway for a small reinforcer was switched to a larger reinforcer, its running speed suddenly went up. When an animal trained on a large reinforcer was shifted to a smaller reinforcer, its running speed went down. Crespi (1942, 1944) and Zeaman (1949) were two early experimenters who found that performance changed radically when the magnitude of reinforcement was changed. The results of Crespi's (1942) experiment are shown in Figure 6–3.

The changes in performance following a change in magnitude of reinforcement could not be explained in terms of changes in $_sH_R$ since they were too rapid. Moreover, $_sH_R$ was thought to be fairly permanent. Unless one or more factors operated against $_sH_R$, it would not decrease in value. Results like those found by

Figure 6–3. The results show that when animals are trained on a large reinforcer (256 pellets of food) and are then switched to a relatively small reinforcer (16 pellets of food), performance drops off rapidly. Likewise, when animals are trained on a small reinforcer (1 pellet of food) and then are switched to a relatively large reinforcer (16 pellets of food), performance improves rapidly. (From *Theories of Motivation*, p. 293, after Crespi, 1942, by R. C. Bolles, 1975, New York: Harper & Row. Copyright © 1967, 1975 by R. C. Bolles. Reprinted by permission of Harper & Row, Publishers, Inc.)

Crespi and Zeaman led Hull to reach the conclusion that organisms learn as rapidly for a small incentive as they do for a large one, but they *perform* differently as the size of the incentive varies. The rapid change in performance following a change in reinforcement size is referred to as the **Crespi effect,** after Crespi who first observed it.

Stimulus–Intensity Dynamism (V)

According to Hull, this was an intervening variable that varied along with the intensity of the external stimulus (S). Stated simply, the stimulus–intensity dynamism indicates that the greater the intensity of a stimulus, the greater the probability that a learned response will be elicited. Thus, we must revise Hull's earlier formula for momentary reaction potential as follows:

$$_s\dot{E}_R = [_sH_R \times D \times V \times K - (I_R + _sI_R)] - _sO_R.$$

It is interesting to note that since $_sH_R$, D, V, and K are multiplied together, if any one had a value of zero, reaction potential would be zero. For example, there could have been many reinforced pairings between S and R ($_sH_R$) but if drive is zero, reinforcement absent, or if the organism cannot detect the stimulus, a learned response will not occur.

Change from Drive Reduction to Drive Stimulus Reduction

Originally, Hull had a drive reduction theory of learning, but later he revised it to a **drive stimulus reduction** theory of learning. One reason for the change was the realization that if a thirsty animal is given water as a reinforcer for performing some act, it takes a considerable amount of time for the thirst drive to be satisfied by the water. The water goes into the mouth, the throat, the stomach, and eventually into the blood. The effects of ingesting water must ultimately reach the brain, and finally the thirst drive will be reduced. Hull concluded that the drive reduction was too far removed from the presentation of the reinforcer to explain how learning could take place. What was needed to explain learning was something that occurred soon after the presentation of a reinforcer, and that something was the reduction of **drive stimuli** (S_D). As mentioned earlier in this chapter, drive stimuli for the thirst drive include dryness in the mouth and parched lips. Water almost immediately reduces such stimulation, and thus Hull had the mechanism he needed for explaining learning.

A second reason for changing from a drive reduction theory to a drive stimulus reduction theory was provided by Sheffield and Roby (1950), who found that hungry rats were reinforced by nonnutritive saccharine that could not possibly have reduced the hunger drive. About this research Hull (1952) said:

> Sheffield and Roby appear to have presented a critical case in point. . . . They showed that hungry albino rats are reinforced by water sweetened by saccharine which presumably is not at all nourishing (i.e., it does not reduce the

need in the least). It may very well be that the ingestion of saccharine-sweetened water reduces hunger tension S_D for a brief period sufficient for a mild reinforcement, much as the tightening of the belt is said to do in hungry men, thus reinforcing that act. (p. 153)

S_D symbolizes drive stimulus or drive stimuli.

Fractional Antedating Goal Response (r_G)

You will recall that when a neutral stimulus is consistently paired with primary reinforcement, it takes on reinforcing properties of its own, that is, it becomes a secondary reinforcer. The concept of secondary reinforcement is vital in understanding the operations of the **fractional antedating goal response** (r_G), which is clearly one of Hull's most important concepts.

Let us suppose we are training a rat to solve a multiple component maze. We place the animal in the start box and eventually it reaches the goal box where it is reinforced with food, a primary reinforcer. All the stimuli in the goal box that were experienced just prior to the animal's receiving primary reinforcement (food) will, therefore, through the process of classical conditioning, become secondary reinforcers. Moreover, following classical conditioning principles, the rat will develop a conditioned response that closely resembles the unconditioned response. In our present example, the unconditioned response would be that of salivation, chewing, and licking caused by presenting food to a hungry animal. The conditioned response, also involving salivation, chewing, or licking, would be elicited by the various stimuli in the goal box as the rat approaches the food. It is the conditioned response to stimuli, experienced prior to the ingestion of food, that is called the fractional antedating goal response (r_G). The development of r_G is shown in Figure 6-4.

In the chapter on Pavlov we will learn that neutral stimuli paired with secondary reinforcers come to have reinforcing properties of their own through the process of higher order conditioning (a process similar to associative shifting). When applied to maze learning, this process would cause stimuli prior to those occurring in the goal box to also become reinforcers, and then the stimuli before them, and so on. Gradually the process works backward until even the stimuli in the start box come to have reinforcing properties. When these previously neutral stimuli become secondary reinforcers, they perform two very important functions: (a) they reinforce the overt responses that bring the organism into contact with them; and (b) they elicit r_Gs.

Now as the animal leaves the start box, it comes into contact with a variety of stimuli, some with reinforcing properties, others without reinforcing properties. Those responses that bring the animal into close proximity to reinforcing stimuli will tend to be repeated while other responses will extinguish. In this manner the animal learns to make the correct turns in the maze. *Thus, maze learning is thought to involve both classical and instrumental conditioning.* Classical conditioning produces the secondary reinforcers and r_Gs; instrumental conditioning produces the appropriate motor responses that bring the animal into proximity with both the primary and

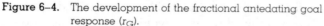

Figure 6-4.   The development of the fractional antedating goal response (r_G).

secondary reinforcers. Thus far, the explanation for maze learning is essentially the same as Skinner's explanation of chaining (see chapter 5); but as we shall see below, Hull assigns the r_G a prominent role in the learning of chained responses.

Two characteristics of the r_G must be noted. First, r_G must always be some fraction of the goal response (R_G). If the goal response involves eating, then r_G will be minute chewing movements and perhaps salivation. Secondly, and more important, *the r_G produces stimulation.* Overt responding causes the kinesthetic receptors in the muscles, tendons, and joints to fire, causing what Guthrie (see chapter 8) called movement-produced stimuli. More technically, the firing of these kinesthetic receptors causes **proprioceptive stimuli.** Like any other response, the r_G has stimulation associated with it. The proprioceptive stimulation caused by the r_G is symbolized s_G. The r_G and s_G are inseparable since whenever r_G occurs, so does s_G. Perhaps the most important aspect of r_G is the fact that it produces s_G.

After a considerable amount of maze learning has taken place the situation that emerges is as follows: the stimuli in the start box will become signals or S^Ds for leaving the start box, since leaving it brings the animal into proximity with secondary reinforcers. A secondary reinforcer in this situation does three things: it reinforces the response the animal just made; it acts as an S^D for the next overt response; and it elicits an r_G. When the r_G is elicited, it automatically produces an s_G. The main function of the s_G is to elicit the next overt response. Thus, both the secondary reinforcers, which are external, and the s_Gs, which are internal, tend to elicit overt responses. The response that exposes the animal to the next secondary reinforcer

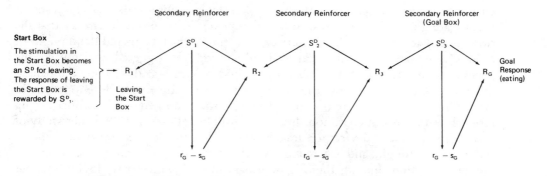

Figure 6–5. How S^D's, overt responses (R), and the r_G–s_G mechanism combine to produce a chained response.

most rapidly will be the one that finally becomes associated with the s_G. When the next secondary reinforcer is experienced, it reinforces the overt response made prior to it, it elicits the next overt response, and it elicits the next r_G. When the r_G is elicited, it triggers the next s_G, which triggers the next overt response, and so on. The process continues in this manner all the way to the goal box. The chaining process, as Hull saw it, is diagrammed in Figure 6-5. An example of chaining on the human level is shown in Figure 6-6.

It should be clear that Hull really had two explanations for chaining that he used simultaneously. One explanation, which emphasized external stimuli, was very much like Skinner's explanation of chaining. The other, which emphasized internal events, was very much like Guthrie's explanation of chaining as we shall see in chapter 8. Hull, then, combined the notions of Skinner and Guthrie, and said that chained behavior is a function of either internal or external cues or, more probably, of both internal and external cues.

One might ask why it is important to postulate the r_G-s_G mechanism if Skinner's explanation of chaining is adequate. The answer is that the r_G-s_G mechanism is thought to be important because of the other things that it may be related to. For example, the r_G-s_G mechanism can be thought of as the "mental" component of

Figure 6–6. An example of chaining on the human level.

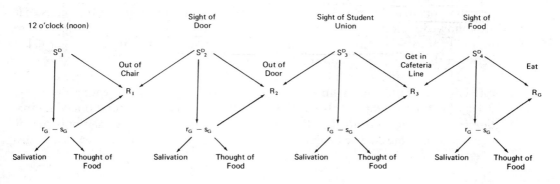

chaining. Generally speaking, the r_G-s_G concept provides an objective means of investigating thought processes. In the example in Figure 6-6, one can say that the time (noon) acted as an S^D, which triggered an r_G, which triggered the thought of food. Or one can say that the "expectation" of food was triggered, which keeps the person moving toward his or her goal of food. Clearly, at this point, the behavioristic point of view and the cognitive point of view come very close together. In fact, it might be said that the main value of the proposed r_G-s_G is opening up research in the area of cognition. In this regard Hull (1952) said: "Further study of this major automatic device presumably will lead to the detailed behavioral understanding of thought and reasoning, which constitute the highest attainment of organic evolution. Indeed, the r_G-s_G mechanism leads in a strictly logical manner into what was formally regarded as the very heart of the psychic: interest, planning, foresight, foreknowledge, expectancy, purpose, and so on" (p. 350).

Thus Hull, in the tradition of Watson, Pavlov, and Guthrie, concluded that thinking consists of a minute internal representation of things that happen overtly. The "thought" of eating is nothing more than an s_G elicited by an r_G. We will review one of the many theoretical extensions of the r_G-s_G mechanism when we consider Abram Amsel's theory later on in this chapter. Also, we will see that Spence, who worked with Hull on the development of the r_G-s_G mechanism, later tied it closely to the concept of incentive motivation (K).

The Habit Family Hierarchy

Because there are any number of overt responses possible to any particular s_G, there are many alternative ways of reaching a goal. However, the route that is most likely is the one that brings the animal into proximity of reinforcement most rapidly. This fact was originally referred to as the "goal-gradient hypothesis" in Hull's early writings, but appeared as a corollary to one of his postulates in 1952. The corollary concerned the delay of reinforcement (J) and read: "The greater the delay in reinforcement of a link within a given behavior chain, the weaker will be the resulting reaction potential of the link in question to the stimulus traces present at the time" (1952, p. 126).

Here Hull is talking about a single link in a behavioral chain but the same idea can be generalized to whole behavioral chains. Whether one is talking about a single response, or a series of responses, delay of reinforcement has a deleterious effect on reaction potential. Likewise, either individual responses or chains of responses that are followed rapidly by reinforcement have relatively higher values of $_sE_R$ and are more likely to occur than those responses or behavioral chains with a longer delay between their occurrence and reinforcement.

The most direct route through a maze, whether a T-maze or a more complicated maze, has the greatest amount of $_sE_R$ associated with it because it results in less delay of reinforcement and also because there is less reactive and conditioned inhibition to be subtracted from $_sE_R$. But the shortest route through a maze is only one of many possible routes. The habit family hierarchy simply refers to the fact that in any learning situation, any number of responses are possible and the one that is most likely is the one that brings about reinforcement most rapidly and with the least amount of effort. If that particular way is blocked, the animal will prefer the next shortest route, and if that is blocked, it will go to the third route, etc.

There is a close relationship between the habit family hierarchy and how the fractional antedating goal response (r_G) and the stimulus it gives rise to (s_G) operate in chaining. We noted earlier that any number of overt responses can follow the occurrence of an s_G. Some of these responses will result immediately in exposure to a secondary reinforcer, and others will not. Eventually the responses that bring the animal into contact with the secondary reinforcers most rapidly will be the ones made, since they will have the highest values of $_sE_R$ associated with them. Remember, the greater the delay of reinforcement (J), the lower the value of $_sE_R$. Thus, there is a hierarchy of possible responses associated with every s_G and, therefore, there is a large number of routes through a maze. If the route consisting of the responses with the highest values of $_sE_R$ is blocked, the next one in the hierarchy will be chosen, etc. The situation can be diagrammed as follows:

Hull's Final System Summarized

There are three kinds of variables in Hull's theory:

1. **Independent variables**, which are stimulus events systematically manipulated by the experimenter.

2. **Intervening variables**, which are processes thought to be taking place within the organism but are not directly observable. All the intervening variables in Hull's system are operationally defined (see chapter 2).

3. **Dependent variables**, which are some aspect of behavior that is measured by the experimenter in order to determine whether the independent variables had any effect.

Figure 6-7 summarizes Hull's theory as it appeared in 1952. It should be noted that Hull's 1952 theory comprised 17 postulates and 133 theorems. Therefore the review of Hull in this chapter should be regarded as a brief introduction to a theory known for its thoroughness and complexity.

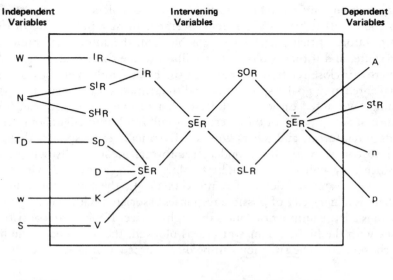

Independent Variables	Intervening Variables	Dependent Variables

W = Work
N = Number of Prior Reinforcements
T_D = Total Drive
w = Amount of Reinforcement
S = Stimulus Intensity
I_R = Reactive Inhibition
S^I_R = Conditioned Inhibition
i_R = Combined Inhibitory Potential
S^H_R = Habit Strength
S_D = Drive Stimulus
D = Drive
K = Incentive Motivation

V = Stimulus Strength
S$\bar{E}$R = Reaction Potential
S$\bar{E}$R = Effective Reaction Potential
S^O_R = Behavioral Oscillation
S^L_R = Response Threshold
S$\dot{\bar{E}}$R = Momentary Effective Reaction Potential
A = Response Amplitude
S^t_R = Response Latency
n = Trials to Extinction
p = Probability of a Response

Figure 6–7. Summary of Hull's theory of learning after 1952.

EVALUATION OF HULL'S THEORY

As mentioned earlier, Hull's learning theory had an enormous impact on psychology. Marx and Hillix (1987) put the matter aptly:

> Hull's most important contribution to psychology was his demonstration of the value of setting one's sights upon the ultimate goal of a thoroughly scientific and systematic behavior theory. He lived his own scientific life in pursuit of that goal, and thereby influenced even those who disagreed most vehemently with the details of his work. Few psychologists have had so great an effect on the professional motivation of so many researchers. He popularized the strictly objective behavioristic approach as it had never been popularized previously. (p. 326)

In spite of its overwhelming influence, Hull's theory did have its problems. Hull's theory was criticized for being of little value in explaining behavior beyond the laboratory, for insisting too much that all concepts of interest be operationally defined and, most importantly, for making inconsistent predictions. In his review of the final (1952) version of Hull's theory, Hill (1985) says:

> Suppose you want to know how many successive nonreinforced trials it will take to produce complete extinction. One approach would be to use Postulate 16, which translates excitatory potential directly into trials to extinction. A second approach would be to use Postulate 9 to calculate the amounts of reactive and conditioned inhibition and subtract them from excitatory potential. A third would be to note (Postulate 7) that when the amount of reward is zero, the value of K is also zero, which makes excitatory potential zero regardless of the values of the other intervening variables. It turns out that these three approaches, to the extent that they give precise answers at all, give conflicting ones . . . When a theory makes incorrect predictions, it can be modified, as Hull intended that his theory should be. When a theory does not deal with a given issue at all, we can accept this limitation in its scope and hope that some day it may be expanded to include the neglected topic. However, when a theory is internally inconsistent, so that it makes conflicting predictions about a given issue, its worth as a rigorous theory is seriously compromised. (pp. 61–62)

Yet, with all its faults, Hull's theory was among the most heuristic in psychology's history. In addition to stimulating an unprecedented number of experiments, Hull's explanations of reinforcement, drive, extinction, and generalization have become standard frames of reference in discussions of these concepts today.

After Hull's death the main spokesman for the Hullian point of view was Kenneth W. Spence who both expanded and significantly modified Hull's theory (see Spence, 1956, 1960). We will encounter some of Spence's ideas later in this chapter. Other important followers of Hull include Neal E. Miller, who extended Hull's theory into the areas of personality, conflict, social behavior, and psychotherapy (e.g., Dollard & Miller, 1950; Miller & Dollard, 1941); Robert R. Sears, who translated a number of Freudian concepts into Hullian terms and who also worked extensively in the area of experimental child psychology (e.g., Sears, 1944; and Sears, Whiting, Nowlis, & Sears, 1953); and O. Hobart Mowrer, who followed many of Hull's ideas while studying such areas as personality dynamics and the special characteristics of learning where fear or anxiety are involved. It is to Mowrer's work that we turn next.

O. HOBART MOWRER

O. Hobart Mowrer (1907–1982) was born in Unionville, Missouri, and received his PhD from Johns Hopkins in 1932. During most of the 1930s, Mowrer was at Yale University, first as a postdoctoral fellow and then as an instructor of psychology. While at Yale, Mowrer was strongly influenced by Hull. In 1940, Mowrer joined the Harvard School of Education and remained there until 1948 when he moved to the

O. Hobart Mowrer. (Courtesy of Archives of
the History of American Psychology,
University of Akron, Ohio)

University of Illinois (Urbana) where he stayed for the rest of his professional
career.

The Problem of Avoidance Conditioning. Mowrer's career as a learning
theorist began with his efforts to solve the problem that avoidance learning posed
for Hullian theory. If an apparatus is arranged so that an organism receives an
electric shock until it performs a specified response, it will quickly learn to make that
response when it is shocked. Such a procedure is called **escape conditioning** and it
is diagrammed below:

$$\text{pain} \longrightarrow \text{R} \longrightarrow \text{escape from pain}$$
$$\text{(electric shock)} \quad \text{(response)} \quad \text{(reinforcement)}$$

Escape conditioning is easily handled by Hullian theory by assuming that the
response is learned because it is followed by drive (pain) reduction. However,
avoidance conditioning is not so easily explained by Hullian theory. With avoidance conditioning, a signal, such as a light, reliably precedes the onset of an aversive
stimulus, such as an electric shock. Other than the presence of the signal which
precedes the shock, the procedure is the same as for escape conditioning. The
procedure used in avoidance conditioning is as follows:

$$\text{signal} \longrightarrow \text{pain} \longrightarrow \text{R} \longrightarrow \text{escape from pain}$$
$$\text{(light)} \quad \text{(electric shock)} \quad \text{(response)} \quad \text{(reinforcement)}$$

With avoidance conditioning, the organism gradually learns to make the appropriate response when the signal light comes on, thus *avoiding* the shock. Furthermore, this avoidance response is maintained almost indefinitely even though the shock itself is no longer experienced. Avoidance conditioning posed a problem for the Hullians because it was not clear what was reinforcing the avoidance response. In other words, what drive does such a response reduce? In his effort to solve this problem, Mowrer proposed a two-factor theory of learning.

Mowrer's Two-Factor Theory of Learning. Mowrer noted that the early stages of avoidance conditioning were arranged so that Pavlovian or classical conditioning would occur. The signal acted as a conditioned stimulus (CS) and the electric shock acted as an unconditioned stimulus (UCS) which elicited, among other things, fear. Eventually, the CS, through its pairings with the UCS, would by itself elicit a response similar to the UCR, that is, fear. Now when the light comes on, the organism experiences fear. Thus the first factor in Mowrer's two-factor theory is simply classical or Pavlovian conditioning. Mowrer called such conditioning **sign learning** because it explained how previously neutral stimuli, through their association with certain UCSs, could become signs of danger and, thus, elicit fear.

Mowrer called the second factor in his two-factor theory, **solution learning**, and it is what Thorndike and Hull called instrumental conditioning or what Skinner called operant conditioning. Solution learning involves learning to perform those activities that will either terminate aversive stimuli or those negative emotions, such as fear, elicited by stimuli that have become signs of danger through classical conditioning.

Others, such as Skinner, had recognized two kinds of learning (respondent and operant conditioning), but Mowrer's contribution was in showing how the two are interrelated. Mowrer summarized his position as follows:

> Basically the two-factor, or two-process, hypothesis holds that *habits* are learned on the basis of the reinforcement provided by reward, or drive reduction, and that *fears* are learned (conditioned) on the basis of contiguous occurrence of a signal and punishment, in the sense of drive induction. Pavlov had held that *all* learning is a matter of conditioning or stimulus contiguity, while Thorndike and Hull had stressed habit formation on the basis of reward. Two-factor theorists, by contrast, have held that it is not here a matter of either-or but of *both*: both sign learning (conditioning) and solution learning (habit formation). (1956, p. 114)

Thus Mowrer found the drive that the Hullians were looking for in order to explain avoidance conditioning, and that drive was conditioned fear. Mowrer believed that the onset of a CS that had been associated with pain motivated an avoidance response which was reinforced by the termination of the CS.

Decremental and Incremental Reinforcement. In 1960, Mowrer extended his theory to show how emotions other than fear become associated with various CSs. Which emotion becomes associated with a CS depends on the kind of UCS

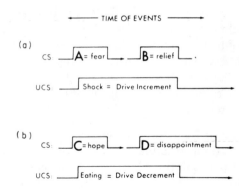

Figure 6–8. The emotion that becomes associated with a CS depends on which kind of UCS the CS is associated with and whether the CS is associated with the onset or termination of the UCS. Under the contingencies depicted, CS A will come to elicit fear, CS B will come to elicit relief, CS C will come to elicit hope, and CS D will come to elicit disappointment. (From G. H. Bower & E. R. Hilgard, *Theories of Learning,* 5th ed., p. 111, © 1981. Reprinted by permission of Prentice-Hall, Inc., Englewood Cliffs, NJ)

that was involved and at what point in time the CS is presented. In his analysis, Mowrer first distinguishes between UCSs that produce an increment in drive, for example, shock, and those that produce a decrement in drive, for example, food. UCSs such as food are called decremental reinforcers because they reduce a drive, in this case hunger. UCSs such as shock are called incremental reinforcers because they produce or increase drive. For each of the two kinds of UCSs, it is possible to present a CS at its onset or at its termination. If a CS is presented prior to the onset of shock, it will come to elicit the emotion of fear. If a CS is presented prior to the termination of shock, it will come to elicit the emotion of relief. If a CS is presented prior to the presentation of food, it will come to elicit the emotion of hope. If a CS is presented prior to the removal of food, it will come to elicit the emotion of disappointment. The two kinds of UCSs and the emotions conditioned by various CS-UCS relationships are shown in Figure 6-8.

By suggesting that important learning can occur as the result of both drive induction (onset) as well as drive reduction (termination), Mowrer moved away from the Hullian tradition which stressed drive reduction. As we shall see below in Mowrer's final position, he moved even farther away from Hullian theory.

All Learning Is Sign Learning. In the final version of his theory (1960), all learning was considered sign learning. Mowrer had already shown that external stimuli associated with positive UCSs such as the termination of pain or the presentation of food come to elicit the emotions of relief and hope respectively. Likewise, external stimuli associated with negative UCSs such as the onset of pain or the removal of food come to elicit the emotions of fear and disappointment respectively. Why, Mowrer asked, should not the same principles hold true for internal stimuli?

Internal bodily reactions, for example proprioceptive stimuli caused by the firing of the kinesthetic receptors, always precede overt responses. When an organism is attempting to solve a problem such as learning to escape from an aversive stimulus, learning to ride a bicycle, learning to speak a language, or learning to play tennis, certain overt responses will lead to success while others will lead to failure. The bodily sensations that precede successful overt responses will come to elicit hope for the same reasons that external stimuli come to elicit hope. The bodily sensations that precede unsuccessful or punished overt responses will come to elicit fear, again, for the same reasons that external stimuli come to elicit fear. In this way, bodily sensations provide an internal guidance system in the sense that certain sensations will signal impending failure, thus necessitating a behavioral correction, while other bodily sensations will provide information that things are being done correctly and success is imminent. Thus, in Mowrer's final position, even solution learning, previously thought to be learned via drive reduction, was seen as governed by signs learned because of their association with positive and negative outcomes. In other words, all learning was considered sign learning. Another way of phrasing Mowrer's final position is to say that organisms learn expectancies. That is, some signs, both external and internal, elicit the expectation of such things as pain or failure while others elicit the expectation of such things as pleasure or success.

In the final version of Mowrer's theory, emotions were of central importance. It was the emotions elicited by both internal and external stimuli that provided the primary guidance system for behavior. This emphasis on emotions was a major departure from traditional learning theory, but Mowrer felt no need to apologize for this departure.

> There has been a widespread tendency in Western civilization to look upon "the emotions" with a certain distrust and contempt and to elevate "the intellect" (reason, logic) high above them. If the present analysis is sound, the emotions are of quite extraordinary importance in the total economy of living organisms and do not at all deserve being put into opposition with "intelligence." The emotions are, it seems, themselves a high order of intelligence. (Mowrer, 1960, p. 308)

With his contention that all learning is sign learning, Mowrer created an essentially cognitive theory of learning. In particular, there is great similarity between Mowrer's final theory and that of Edward Tolman's cognitive theory which we will review in chapter 12.

KENNETH W. SPENCE

Although Hull had many ardent disciples, it was Kenneth W. Spence who became the major spokesman for Hullian theory after Hull's death. For many years Hull and Spence had a reciprocal influence on each other. It is clear that Hull had a profound influence on Spence, but it is also clear that Spence influenced Hull's evolving theory in several important ways. The two worked so closely together that it is not uncommon for their combined efforts to be referred to as the Hull-Spence theory of learning. In the end, however, Spence made several radical changes in traditional Hullian theory, and in so doing he created a learning theory that was essentially his own.

Spence was born in Chicago on May 6, 1907 and died in Austin, Texas, in 1967. At the age of four Spence moved to Montreal, Canada, where he remained until obtaining his BA degree in 1929 and his MA degree in 1930 from McGill

Kenneth W. Spence. (Reprinted by
permission of University of Iowa, Office of
Public Information)

University. Spence then moved to Yale where he obtained his PhD in 1933. After
obtaining his doctorate, he remained at Yale as a research assistant and instructor
until 1937. It was during his time at Yale that Spence came under the influence of
Hull. Spence served on the faculty of the University of Virginia from 1937 to 1942,
at which point he moved to the University of Iowa. He remained there for 26 years
until 1964 when he moved to the University of Texas (Austin) where he remained
until his premature death in 1967.

Spence made several contributions to learning theory, but we can only summarize what seem to be his more important ones here.

Discrimination Learning. In discrimination learning an animal is typically
presented with two stimuli and is reinforced for responding to one and not reinforced for responding to the other. It was within the area of discrimination learning
that Spence defended Hull's theory against an attack by a group of cognitively
oriented psychologists. This group contended that during discrimination learning
animals learn principles (subjective strategies) rather than S-R associations as Hull
had maintained. We will give more details of both the attack of the cognitive
psychologists and Spence's reaction to it in chapter 10, but, in general, here are the
assumptions that Spence made about learning in a situation where an organism must
choose between two objects (Spence, 1936, 1937):

1. Habit strength ($_sH_R$) toward the stimulus that is reinforced increases with each
   reinforcement.

2. Inhibition (I_R and $_SI_R$) toward the stimulus that is not reinforced builds on each nonreinforced trial.

3. Both habit strength and inhibition generalize to stimuli that are similar to those that are reinforced and to those that are not reinforced.

4. The magnitude of generalized habit strength is greater than the magnitude of generalized inhibition.

5. Generalized habit strength and generalized inhibition combine algebraically.

6. Which stimulus is approached is determined by the algebraic summation of approach (habit strength) and avoidance (inhibition) tendencies.

7. When two stimuli are presented, the stimulus with the greatest net habit strength will be approached and responded to.

With these assumptions, Spence was able to use Hullian theory to explain phenomena that cognitive theorists were offering as evidence against it. Not only did Spence's assumptions and the research they generated prevail against the arguments of the cognitive theorists, but they also became the cornerstone of research on discrimination learning for many years.

Rejection of Reinforcement as a Necessary Condition for Instrumental Conditioning. The Hullians were having difficulties accounting for the results of latent learning experiments which seemed to be indicating that animals could learn without being reinforced. The term **latent learning** refers to learning that appears to take place in the absence of reinforcement. For example, Tolman and Honzik (1930) found that if rats were initially run through a maze without being reinforced in the goal box and were later reinforced for responding correctly, their performance rapidly matched (or exceeded) that of rats that had been reinforced on every trial (see chapter 12 for the details of this experiment). Tolman and his followers argued that such results indicated that learning occurred independent of reinforcement.

Spence replicated a number of these so-called latent learning experiments and confirmed Tolman's findings. For example, Spence and Lippitt (1940) ran rats that were neither hungry nor thirsty through a Y-maze where water was consistently found in one arm of the Y and food in the other. After reaching one of the two goals the rat was removed from the apparatus. The rats were run for several trials while satiated with both food and water. During the second phase of the experiment, half of the original group was deprived of food and the other half was deprived of water. It was found that on the initial trial the hungry rat went directly to the arm of the Y-maze where they had previously experienced food and the thirsty rats went directly to the arm of the Y-maze where they had previously experienced water. The rats had obviously learned where the reinforcer appropriate to their drive state was located during the first phase of the experiment, but such learning could not have involved drive reduction since the animals were satiated at the time. Hull's explanation of these findings was that removing the animal from the apparatus following a goal response provided enough of a reinforcer for the animal to learn under the circumstances. The reader may recall that Hull believed that learning occurred at the same rate whether the size of the reinforcer (K) was large or small. Thus, according to Hull, even though the reinforcer in this situation was small, it was sufficient to cause the animals to learn where things were in the maze.

Spence agonized over Hull's interpretation of the latent learning experiments and eventually came up with his own explanation. Spence was not comfortable with Hull's assumption that in learning there is no difference between a very small reinforcer and a very large reinforcer, but there is a very important difference between a very small reinforcer and no reinforcer at all. Remember, for Hull, reinforcement was a necessary condition for learning, but *how much* reinforcement occurred was irrelevant.

In one sense, Spence's solution to the problem placed him in essential agreement with Guthrie's theory of learning (see chapter 8), and in another sense, in agreement with Tolman's theory (see chapter 12). Spence concluded that *instrumental conditioning occurs independent of reinforcement*. The animal learns a response simply by making it. Thus, as far as instrumental conditioning was concerned, Spence was not a reinforcement theorist (as Hull was), rather, he was a contiguity theorist (as Guthrie was). The law of contiguity is one of Aristotle's laws of association which states that events become associated simply because they occur together. Spence (1960) summarized his position on instrumental conditioning as follows:

> The habit strength (H) of the instrumental response, it is important to note, is assumed to be a function of the number of occurrences of the response (N_R) in the situation and to be quite independent of the occurrence or non–occurrence of a reinforcer. Thus, if the response occurs there will be an increment in H regardless of whether a reinforcer does or does not result. This assumption, it is apparent, makes this formulation a contiguity and not a reinforcement theory. (p. 96)

It should be clear that Spence also accepted Aristotle's **law of frequency** which states that the more often two events are experienced together the stronger the association between them will become. We will see in chapter 8 that although Guthrie accepted Aristotle's **law of contiguity,** he did not accept his law of frequency.

Incentive Motivation. So, what function did reinforcement play in Spence's theory? According to Spence, reinforcement had an influence only through **incentive motivation (K).** Spence was largely responsible for Hull adding the concept of incentive motivation to his theory. In fact, it is widely believed that K was chosen as a symbol because it is the first letter in Spence's first name. It turns out, however, that Spence gave K a much more prominent role in his own theory than Hull gave it in his theory. In fact, Hull seemed to have problems with K because it was not clear to what physiological processes it was related. Most of Hull's concepts were thought to have some physiological basis. For example, habit strength was tied directly to drive or drive stimulus reduction and inhibition was tied to fatigue. However, it was not clear to Hull what physiological process K was related to and that was troublesome.

Spence solved the problem by relating K direction to the r_G-s_G mechanism. As we saw earlier in the chapter, the r_G-s_G mechanism works back through a maze and eventually guides the animal's behavior from the start box to the goal box. Spence added the concept of incentive to this automatic guiding process. According to Spence, the strength of r_G-s_G is determined by K, and the stronger the r_G-s_G the greater the incentive to traverse the maze. Simply restated, the r_G-s_G mechanism creates in the animal the expectation of reinforcement which motivates it to run, and the greater the expectation the faster the animal will run. By discussing the r_G-s_G mechanism as a means of providing the animal with expectations, Spence moved Hull's behavioristic theory closer to Tolman's cognitive theory. However, it should be noted that although Spence discussed expectations, he did so in mechanistic and not in mentalistic terms. In fact, Spence believed that the same laws that apply to overt S-R associations apply to the r_G-s_G mechanism.

For Spence then, K was the energizer of learned behavior. The habit strength of an instrumental response developed in accordance with the laws of contiguity and frequency but independent of reinforcement. However, according to Spence, the r_G-s_G mechanism requires reinforcement for its development and it is this mechanism that determines whether an organism will perform a learned response and, if so, with what degree of enthusiasm it will perform it. Thus, Spence, like Mowrer before him, ended up with a two-factor theory. As we have seen, a two-factor theory postulates two different kinds of learning, each governed by a different set of principles. As far as instrumental conditioning was concerned, Spence was a contiguity theorist and not a reinforcement theorist. As far as classical conditioning was concerned (the process by which the r_G-s_G mechanism develops), he was a reinforcement theorist. In other words, Spence believed that instrumental behavior is learned without reinforcement, but reinforcement provides the incentive to perform what has been learned.

A Change in Hull's Basic Equation. As the reader may remember, Hull combined the major components of his theory as follows:

$$_sE_R = D \times K \times {}_sH_R - (I_R + {}_sI_R)$$

As we saw earlier in the chapter this means that if either D or K equals 0, a learned response will not be emitted no matter how high the value of $_sH_R$ is. In other words, for Hull, no matter how many times an animal has been reinforced for performing a response in a given situation, it will not perform the response if the animal is not in a drive state. Likewise, even if the animal is in a high drive state, it will not perform a learned response if there is no reinforcement for doing so. Again, Spence felt that Hull's assumptions were untenable and revised Hull's equation to read:

$$_sE_R = (D + K) \times {}_sH_R - I_N$$

Note that Spence added D and K together rather than multiplying them as Hull did. The major implication of Spence's revision is that a learned response may be given in a situation even if no drive is present. For example, if one has eaten frequently at 6 p.m. in a certain location and one is in that location at 6 p.m., one may have the urge to eat even if one is not hungry. According to Spence's equation, as long as K and $_sH_R$ have a value greater than 0, a learned response will be emitted even if no drive is present. Thus, organisms sometimes eat when they are not hungry, drink when they are not thirsty, and perhaps even engage in sexual activities when they are not sexually aroused, simply because they have developed strong tendencies to perform these acts under certain circumstances. Likewise, animals, including humans, may go on working for reinforcers that are no longer needed to satisfy basic drives, such as when a person continues to work to accumulate money even though he or she has more than enough to satisfy his or her basic needs.

Another implication of Spence's revised equation is that as long as D and $_sH_R$ have a value above 0, an organism should go on making a learned response even if K = 0. In other words, an organism should go on making a learned response even if there is no reinforcement for doing so. How then does Spence explain extinction? It is to the problem of extinction that we turn next.

The Frustration-Competition Theory of Extinction. The astute reader may have noticed in the above equations that Hull's symbols for inhibition were I_R and $_sI_R$ and Spence's symbol was I_N. This apparently minor difference in symbols reflects a major theoretical difference between Hull and Spence concerning the nature of inhibition. For Hull, responding causes fatigue (I_R) which operates against the emission of a learned response. Likewise, when fatigue builds up it is reinforcing the animal not to respond. Therefore, there is a learned tendency not to respond ($_sI_R$) which also operates against the emission of a learned response. Hull explains extinction by saying that when reinforcement is removed from the situation (K = 0), I_R and $_sI_R$ become the dominant influences of behavior and the animal stops emitting the learned response.

Spence disagreed with Hull's explanation of extinction. For Spence, nonreinforcement causes *frustration* which elicits responses that are incompatible with the learned response and therefore compete with it. The frustration that occurs in the goal box when the animal finds the reinforcer missing is called primary frustration (R_F). With continued nonreinforced trials the animal learns to anticipate frustration (r_F) just as it has learned to anticipate reinforcement during acquisition (r_G). As nonreinforced trials continue, r_F generalizes (just as r_G did) and occurs earlier and earlier in the behavioral chain that previously led to reinforcement. Just as r_Gs give rise to s_Gs which stimulate behavior compatible with reaching the goal box, r_Fs give rise to s_Fs which stimulate behavior that is incompatible with reaching the goal box. Eventually, the behavior stimulated by frustration and by the anticipation of frustration becomes dominant and we say the learned response has extinguished.

Thus, Hull has explained extinction in terms of the fatigue that results from responding in the absence of reinforcement, whereas Spence has explained extinction as due to the active interference of learned behavior by the responses caused by frustration. Deductions from both of these positions have been tested experimentally and Spence's explanation appears to fare best. For example, it has been found that during acquisition using large reinforcers produces more rapid extinction than does using small reinforcers (Hulse, 1968; Wagner, 1961). According to Spence's theory, this is because removing a large reinforcer produces more frustration than removing a smaller reinforcer, thus, more competing behavior is stimulated. Since the magnitude of the competing behavior is greater than it would be if a smaller reinforcer was removed, it generalizes more rapidly through the chain of behavior that has been previously learned; therefore, extinction occurs more rapidly. According to Hull, magnitude of reinforcement during acquisition should have little or no effect on the speed with which extinction occurs.

Most, if not all, of Spence's modifications made Hullian theory much more capable of dealing with the higher mental processes with which the cognitive theorists are concerned. Spence has made it possible to deal effectively with concepts such as expectation and frustration without sacrificing scientific rigor. Spence's theory can be considered behavioristic, but it is a behavioristic theory that is much more compatible with cognitive theory than was Hull's.

Next we turn to the work of Abram Amsel, who was a student of Spence's at the University of Iowa. Amsel's relationship to Spence was much like Spence's relationship to Hull, that is, Amsel and Spence had a reciprocal influence on each other. Although Spence was equating inhibition and frustration as early as 1936, it was Amsel who worked out many of the details of Spence's frustration theory of extinction and who used the theory to explain the partial reinforcement effect (PRE).

ABRAM AMSEL

Amsel's work can be looked upon as an elaboration of Spence's contention that extinction is caused by the competing responses caused by frustration. In general, Amsel (1958, 1962) assumes that after an organism is reinforced a number of times in a given situation, it learns to expect reinforcement in that situation. An organism experiences frustration when its expectation of reinforcement is unfulfilled. This frustration has motivational properties similar to those of punishment. For example, it has been found that animals will learn to perform a response that terminates a stimulus which was present when the animal experienced frustration (Daly, 1969; Wagner, 1963).

Further evidence for the motivational properties of frustration is provided by an experiment run by Amsel and Roussel (1952). In this experiment two straight alley runways were linked together. For the first 84 trials, the animals were reinforced at the end of each runway. After this preliminary training, however, the animals were run under conditions where they were reinforced at the end of runway 1 on only 50% of the trials, while they continued to be reinforced at the end of runway 2 on each trial. It was found that running speed in runway 2 was significantly faster following nonreinforcement in runway 1 than it was following reinforcement in runway 1. This increased vigor following nonreinforcement is called

Abram Amsel. (Courtesy of Abram Amsel)

the **frustration effect** (**FE**). This finding supports the contention that nonreinforce-ment causes frustration and that frustration is motivating or drive inducing.

Further support for the above contention was provided by a study by Bower (1962). Bower reasoned that amount of frustration should be related to amount of reinforcement reduction. To test his assumption, he used a two-runway apparatus similar to that used by Amsel and Roussel. In Bower's experiment, however, the rats were given four pellets of food at the end of each runway. The training phase of the experiment consisted of 6 trials a day for 24 days, or a total of 144 trials. After training, the conditions were changed so that the number of food pellets found at the end of the first runway was either 4, 3, 2, 1, or zero. The 4 food pellets found at the end of the second runway remained constant throughout the experiment. Bower found that running speed in runway 2 was inversely related to the number of food pellets present in runway 1 (fewer food pellets, faster running). That is, the animals ran fastest in runway 2 when they received no reinforcement in runway 1; next fastest when they received only 1 pellet, then 2, then 3, and slowest after receiving 4 food pellets in runway 1. This experiment supports Bower's hypothesis that amount of frustration is related to the amount of reinforcement reduction, and this, of course, is in accordance with Spence's and Amsel's view of frustration.

Next we turn to the relationship between frustration and the Hull-Spence $r_G\text{-}s_G$ mechanism. First, Amsel assumes, as Spence assumed, that when nonrein-forcement occurs after a prolonged period of reinforcement, the organism experi-ences **primary frustration** ($\mathbf{R_F}$). Thus, if an animal is reinforced a number of times for running down a straight alley and then is not reinforced after running down that same alley, it will experience primary frustration in the goal box where it had been previously reinforced.

We learned earlier in this chapter that when the animal experiences primary reinforcement in a goal box, the stimuli in the goal box take on secondary reinforcing properties, that is, they develop the capacity to elicit r_Gs, which in turn elicit s_Gs. We also saw that through stimulus generalization and/or higher order conditioning, these r_Gs slowly develop associations all the way back to the start box. After this happens, when the animal leaves the start box, its behavior is guided to the goal box by these r_Gs and the s_Gs which they elicit. According to Amsel, the same process is associated with primary frustration. That is, stimuli associated with primary frustration will develop the capacity to elicit a fractional anticipatory frustration reaction, or r_F, which is associated with an s_F, just as r_G necessarily is associated with an s_G. The r_G-s_G and the r_F-s_F mechanisms have different behavior patterns associated with them, however. Whereas the r_G-s_G mechanism causes locomotion toward the goal box, r_F-s_F tends to cause avoidance of the goal box. In general, we can say that r_G is related to the expectancy of reinforcement, while r_F is related to the expectancy of frustration.

During extinction, the animal experiences nothing but frustration, which gradually generalizes backward to the start box, through the r_F-s_F mechanism. When this happens, the animal experiences stimuli that elicit r_Fs either in the start box, or shortly after leaving the start box, and they cause it to stop running. At that point we say extinction has occurred. This is the theory of extinction that Amsel and Spence worked out together. Remember we said they had a reciprocal influence on each other.

Now we come to what is perhaps the most important aspect of Amsel's theory: its proposed explanation of the **partial reinforcement effect** (**PRE**). The PRE refers to the fact that it takes longer to extinguish a response that was intermittently reinforced during training than if it was continuously reinforced. In other words, PRE means that partial reinforcement yields greater resistance to extinction than does 100% reinforcement. A number of theories have been offered to explain the PRE and Amsel's is one of the most widely accepted.

Amsel explains PRE as follows. First, the animal is trained to make a response, such as running down a straight alley. During this training, the animal usually experiences primary reinforcement (R_G) in the goal box on 100% of the trials. Under these circumstances, all the stimuli in the runway will eventually become associated with R_G through the r_G-s_G mechanism. Next, the animal is placed on a partial reinforcement schedule where it is reinforced on, say, only 50% of the trials. Since the animal had developed a strong expectancy for reinforcement, it will experience primary frustration (R_F) on those trials when it does not receive reinforcement. As we saw above, the stimuli just prior to the experience of primary frustration will come to elicit r_Fs which give rise to s_Fs. After several nonreinforced trials, a conflict develops, because the same stimuli tend to elicit conflicting habits. When an r_G-s_G is elicited, the animal tends to run toward the goal box, but when an r_F-s_F is elicited, the animal tends to avoid the goal box. Since the animal had already developed a strong habit of running toward the goal during training prior to being switched to a partial reinforcement schedule and perhaps because positive reinforcement is more influential than frustration, the animal continues to approach the goal box while under the partial reinforcement schedule. In other words, although there is an approach-avoidance conflict associated with the goal box, the approach tendency wins out.

Since the animal continues to approach the goal box even though it is not reinforced on some trials, eventually all the stimuli in the apparatus become associated with the running response, even those stimuli associated with frustration. Perhaps you have already anticipated Amsel's next step in his explanation of the PRE. When subjects trained on a continuous or 100% reinforcement schedule are switched to extinction, they experience frustration for the first time. For them, the effects of this frustration associate backward to the start box and normal extinction occurs. Subjects trained on a partial reinforcement schedule, however, have already experienced frustration during training and have learned to run in the presence of the stimuli associated with frustration. The partial reinforcement subjects will therefore take much longer to extinguish, thus the PRE.

One could deduce from Amsel's proposed explanation of the PRE that great variation in behavior would accompany the conflict stage of partial reinforcement training. That is, when the same stimuli in the apparatus are eliciting both approach and avoidance tendencies, running speed should vary from trial to trial. At the same time, when the stimuli become associated with the running response later in training, the running response should stabilize. Amsel (1958) found support for both deductions. One could also deduce from Amsel's theory that the PRE will occur only when there are a substantial number of preliminary training trials. This is because his explanation depends on frustration and the animal will not experience frustration unless it has learned to expect a reinforcer. Evidence supporting this contention was also found by Amsel (1958). It was found that the PRE resulted if animals had 84 preliminary training trials before being switched to a partial reinforcement schedule, but did not if they had only 24 preliminary training trials.

Amsel's theory of frustrative nonreinforcement is but one of the many creative extensions of the Hull-Spence r_G-s_G mechanism. The student of psychology or education will experience a number of others in advanced courses. In fact, a review of the many uses of the r_G-s_G mechanism to explain various psychological phenomena would make an excellent independent study project.

DISCUSSION QUESTIONS

1. How would one overcome or minimize the negative contribution of work (I_R and $_sI_R$) in a learning situation?
2. According to Hull's theory, what effect would increasing the size of the reinforcer have on learning? Explain.
3. Describe a situation that would allow one to differentiate between learning and performance.

4. What would characterize classroom procedures designed in accordance with Hull's principles of learning? Give a few specific examples.

5. According to Hull's theory, who do you think would learn faster: high anxious students or low anxious students? Explain.

6. On what basic points would Skinner disagree with Hull? Where would the two most closely agree?

7. In your opinion, what do you think Hull means when he says "psychic phenomena" will someday be explained in terms of the r_G-s_G mechanism?

8. Explain chaining from Hull's point of view.

9. What is a habit family hierarchy?

10. Describe Hull's approach to theory construction. What is meant by the statement that Hull's theory is "open-ended"?

11. Diagram Hull's final version of his theory as it was presented in this chapter.

12. You drive around a corner and see the house of the good friend you are about to visit and you begin to smile. How would Hull explain this smiling behavior?

13. Describe the procedure used in avoidance conditioning.

14. Describe the two-factor theory that Mowrer developed in order to explain avoidance conditioning. In your answer be sure to define sign learning and solution learning.

15. Discuss Mowrer's distinction between incremental and decremental reinforcement. Also discuss the ways that CSs can be made contingent upon the two kinds of reinforcement and what emotions result from each contingency.

16. Summarize the final version of Mowrer's theory and explain why it is considered basically cognitive in nature.

17. Summarize the evidence that caused Spence to change from a reinforcement theorist to a contiguity theorist with regard to instrumental conditioning.

18. In what sense did Spence remain a reinforcement theorist?

19. Describe the implications of $D \times K \times {_sH_R}$ versus $(D + K) \times {_sH_R}$.

20. Summarize the Spence-Amsel frustration-competition theory of extinction.

21. Summarize Amsel's explanation of the partial reinforcement effect.

CHAPTER HIGHLIGHTS

Avoidance conditioning. See Chapter Highlights for chapter 1.

Conditioned inhibition ($_sI_R$). A learned response of not responding. Since responding produces fatigue (I_R) and fatigue is a negative drive state, not responding is reinforcing; hence conditioned inhibition.

Crespi effect. The rapid change in performance level as size of reinforcement is varied.

Decremental reinforcement. According to Mowrer, an unconditioned stimulus that causes a reduction in drive, such as when food is given to a hungry animal.

Distributed practice. Learning a skill under the conditions where practice trials are separated by a considerable length of time.

Drive (D). The condition that exists when there is a biological deficiency in the body. For all practical purposes, the terms *drive* and *need* mean the same thing.

Drive reduction. The satisfaction of a biological deficiency. Originally Hull thought it to be a necessary condition for learning. Hull later turned to a drive stimulus reduction theory of learning.

Drive stimuli (S_D). The stimuli that characteristically accompany a certain drive, such as the dryness of the mouth, lips, and throat that accompany the thirst drive.

Drive stimulus reduction. The reduction or removal of the stimuli that accompany a drive. This usually occurs before the drive itself is actually reduced; for example, the dryness of the mouth, lips, and throat are eliminated before the effects of drinking water can reach the brain and thereby reduce the thirst drive.

Effective reaction potential ($_s\bar{E}_R$). Reaction potential ($_sE_R$) minus the effects of I_R and $_sI_R$.

Escape conditioning. See Chapter Highlights for chapter 1.

Fractional antedating goal response (r_G). A response that is conditioned to the stimuli present prior to the ingestion of a primary reinforcer. The conditioned response (r_G) is always some fraction of the goal response (R_G). For example, if the goal response is eating then r_G would consist of minute chewing responses. Each r_G automatically produces a stimulus, which is symbolized s_G. The r_G-s_G mechanism plays an important role in Hull's explanation of chained behavior.

Fractional anticipatory frustration reaction (r_F). Stimuli that precede primary frustration will develop the capacity to elicit some portion of the primary frustration response. These fractions of the primary frustration response that occur prior to the goal are called fractional anticipatory frustration reactions or r_Fs.

Frustration-competition theory of extinction. Spence's and Amsel's contention that extinction is caused by responses stimulated by frustration which interfere with the performance of a previously learned response.

Frustration effect (FE). The increased vigor of responses following nonreinforcement. For example, it has been found that rats will run faster following nonreinforcement than following reinforcement.

Generalized habit strength ($_s\bar{H}_R$). Habit strength from previous learning experiences that generalizes to a new learning experience because of the similarity between the new learning experience and older ones.

Habit family hierarchy. A hierarchy of responses arranged according to their values of $_sE_R$. When a particular response is thwarted, the animal makes the next response available in its response repertoire. Responses that result in an organism's being reinforced most rapidly have the greatest value of $_sE_R$ associated with them and are, therefore, most likely to occur. If a response with the highest value of $_sE_R$ is blocked, however, the response with the next highest value of $_sE_R$ will occur, etc.

Habit strength ($_sH_R$). A measure of the strength of association between a stimulus and a response. The magnitude of the $_sH_R$ depends on the number of reinforced pairings between the stimulus and the response. In the final version of Hull's theory, $_sH_R$ was the only learning variable; the other factors were performance variables. In other words, Hull believed that the only thing that affected learning directly was the number of reinforced trials.

Hypothetical–deductive theory (also called logical–deductive). A theory consisting of postulates and theorems. Postulates are assumptions that cannot be verified directly; theorems are deduced from the postulates and they can be verified experimentally. If an experiment designed to test a theorem comes out in the predicted direction, its postulate is indirectly verified and the theory gains strength. If the experiment does not come out in the predicted direction, the theory loses strength. A hypothetical–deductive theory is constantly changing in light of experimental evidence.

Incentive motivation (K). Size of reinforcement. Originally (1943), Hull felt that K affected learning, but he later (1952) concluded that it only affected performance. For Spence, incentive motivation was extremely important. It worked through the r_G-s_G mechanism and was the energizer of learned behavior.

Incremental reinforcement. According to Mowrer, an unconditioned stimulus that causes an increase in drive, such as electric shock.

Interaction of sensory impulses (s̄). Behavior is usually the result of many stimuli impinging on sensory receptors at any given time. The afferent (sensory) neural impulses caused by these stimuli interact with each other and it is their combined effect that causes an efferent (motor) neural impulse and finally an overt response (R).

Latency ($_s t_R$). The time between the presentation of a stimulus and the occurrence of a learned response.

Latent learning. Learning that appears to take place independent of reinforcement and which remains dormant until the organism is given an incentive for translating what had been learned into behavior.

Law of contiguity. When two or more events occur together they become associated with each other.

Law of frequency. The more often two events or more occur together the stronger will be the association between them.

Massed practice. Learning a skill under the conditions where practice trials are separated by only a very short interval of time.

Momentary effective reaction potential ($_s\dot{E}_R$). Reaction potential ($_s E_R$) minus the effects of I_R, $_s I_R$, and $_s O_R$.

Oscillation effect ($_s O_R$). An "inhibitory potentiality" that opposes the emission of a conditioned response and whose value changes from moment to moment. The values of $_s O_R$ are normally distributed and therefore the value that manifests itself at any given moment can be large or small, but will most likely be a value that is neither very large nor very small.

Partial reinforcement effect (PRE). The fact that a response that has been reinforced only sometimes takes longer to extinguish than a response that has been reinforced each time it occurred.

Primary frustration (R_F). The response that occurs when an organism experiences nonreinforcement after it had learned to expect reinforcement.

Primary need. A deviation from the optimal conditions of air, water, food, temperature, or sex which are necessary for survival.

Proprioceptive stimuli. The stimuli that result from the firing of the kinesthetic receptors in the muscles, joints, and tendons of the body. Also called movement-produced stimuli.

Reaction potential ($_sE_R$). Directly influences four response measures. As reaction potential goes up, the probability of a learned response being elicited by a stimulus goes up, resistance to extinction goes up, the amplitude of a conditioned response goes up, and latency goes down.

Reaction threshold ($_sL_R$). The minimal value that the momentary effective reaction potential ($_s\dot{E}_R$) must exceed before a learned response can occur.

Reactive inhibition (I_R). The fatigue caused by responding, which operates against the emission of a conditioned response.

Reinforcer. Anything that causes either drive reduction or drive stimulus reduction.

Reinforcement. Drive reduction or drive stimulus reduction.

Reminiscence effect. The improvement of performance on a skill following a rest after cessation of practice.

Resistance to extinction. See Chapter Highlights for chapter 5.

Sign learning. The kind of learning, in Mowrer's two-factor theory, whereby stimuli become signs of fear, hope, relief or disappointment because of their proximity to various unconditioned stimuli.

Solution learning. The kind of learning, in Mowrer's two-factor theory, whereby an organism learns the behavioral skills necessary to avoid aversive situations and to embrace positive ones.

Stimulus generalization (see Generalization in Chapter Highlights for chapter 7).

Stimulus–intensity dynamism (V). The internal result of varying the magnitude of an external stimulus. A larger external stimulus will result in a larger stimulus trace, thereby increasing the probability of a learned response's being elicited.

Stimulus trace (s). The afferent (sensory) neural impulse that is caused by an external stimulus and continues for a short while after the external stimulus has ceased.

Two-factor theory. A theory that postulates one set of principles to explain one kind of learning and a different set of principles to explain another kind of learning.

Unlearned behavior. Associations between stimuli and responses that are genetically determined and therefore do not depend upon experience for their development.

7

Ivan Petrovich Pavlov

THE BIOLOGICAL BOUNDARIES OF LEARNING

JOHN B. WATSON'S EXPERIMENT WITH LITTLE ALBERT

FURTHER APPLICATIONS OF CLASSICAL CONDITIONING TO CLINICAL PSYCHOLOGY

Pavlov was born in Russia in 1849 and died there in 1936. His father was a priest and originally Pavlov himself studied to become a priest. He changed his mind, however, and spent most of his life studying physiology. In 1904 he won a Nobel Prize for his work on the physiology of digestion. He did not begin his study of the conditioned reflex until he was 50 years of age.

With Thorndike we saw that scientists are obliged to change their views when the data require it, an important characteristic of the scientific enterprise. With Pavlov, we see the importance of serendipity, or accidental discovery, in science. Pavlov's method of studying digestion involved a surgical arrangement on a dog that allowed gastric juices to flow through a fistula to the outside of the body where it was collected. This arrangement is shown in Figure 7-1.

Pavlov was measuring stomach secretions as the dog's response to such things as meat powder when he noticed that the mere sight of the food caused the dog to salivate. In addition, the mere sight of the experimenter or the sound of his or her footsteps would cause salivation. Originally Pavlov called such responses "psychic" reflexes. Being an extremely objective scientist and at heart a physiologist, Pavlov originally resisted investigating the "psychic" reflex. After a long personal struggle, however, and contrary to the advice of some of his colleagues, he finally decided to delve into the issue. He decided to study it, however, as a purely physiological problem to guard against any subjective element entering into his research. In fact, Pavlov's coworkers were fined if they used subjective, nonphysiological language in

Figure 7-1. Dog with esophageal and gastric fistulae. Such an arrangement allowed the dog to be fed, but prevented the food from reaching the stomach. Also, gastric juices flowing from the stomach could be measured. (From *Principles of General Psychology*, p. 208, by G. A. Kimble, N. Garmezy, & E. Zigler, 1974, New York: John Wiley & Sons, Inc.)

Figure 7-2. Dog with a tube entering its cheek. When the dog salivates, the saliva is gathered in the test tube and its quantity is recorded on the rotating drum to the left. (From *Great Experiments in Psychology*, p. 5, by H. E. Garrett, 1951, New York: Appleton-Century-Crofts)

describing their research (Watson, 1978, p. 441). The apparatus used by Pavlov to study the "psychic" reflex is shown in Figure 7-2.

Just as Pavlov started a second career at age 50 when he turned to the study of the psychic reflex, he started a third career at age 80 when he turned to the application of his work on conditioning to mental illness. This work resulted in a book entitled *Conditioned Reflexes and Psychiatry* (1941), which many consider a monumental contribution to psychiatry.

At the time Thorndike was developing his theory, American psychology was struggling to be objective. Structuralism, with its introspective method, was losing influence. In fact, consciousness per se was becoming a highly questionable subject matter. With his blending of associationism, Darwinism, and experimental science, Thorndike represented the best in American objective psychology. He was an important part of the functionalist movement which, as we have seen, was the first major psychological movement in America. Under the influence of Darwin, the functionalist's main concern was survival which, of course, involved adapting to the environment. The functionalists tried to discover how human actions as well as thought processes contribute to adaptation and survival.

At the time Thorndike was doing his major research, Pavlov was also investigating the learning process. He, too, was impatient with subjective psychology, and in fact, had almost decided not to study the conditioned reflex because of its "psychic" nature. Although Pavlov did not have a high opinion of psychologists, he had considerable respect for Thorndike and acknowledged him as the first to do systematic research on the learning process in animals (Pavlov, 1928):

> Some years after the beginning of the work with our new method I learned that somewhat similar experiments on animals had been performed in America, and indeed not by physiologists but by psychologists. Thereupon I studied in more detail the American publications, and now I must acknowledge that the honour of having made the first steps along this path belongs to E. L. Thorndike. By two or three years his experiments preceded ours, and his book must be considered as a classic, both for its bold outlook on an immense task and for the accuracy of its results. (pp. 38–40)

Thorndike and Pavlov, although traveling two different paths in many respects, shared an enthusiasm toward science and a belief in its ultimate ability to solve major human problems (Pavlov, 1928): "Only science, exact science about human nature itself, and the most sincere approach to it by the aid of the omnipotent scientific method, will deliver man from his present gloom, and will purge him from his contemporary shame in the sphere of interhuman relations" (p. 28).

Pavlov never wavered from his scientific outlook and in 1936 at the age of 87 he wrote the following letter to the young scientists of his country (Babkin, 1949):

This is the message I would like to give to the youth of my country. First of all, be systematic. I repeat—be systematic. Train yourself to be strictly systematic in the acquisition of knowledge. First study the rudiments of science before attempting to reach its heights. Never pass on to the next stage until you have thoroughly mastered the one on hand. Never try to conceal the defects in your knowledge even by the most daring conjectures and hypotheses. Practice self-restraint and patience. Learn to do the drudgery of scientific work. Although a bird's wing is perfect, the bird could never soar if it did not lean upon the air. Facts are the air on which the scientist leans. Without them you will never fly upward. Without them your theories will be mere empty efforts. However, when studying, experimenting or observing, try not to remain on the surface of things. Do not become a mere collector of facts but try to penetrate into the mystery of their origin. Search persistently for the laws which govern them.

The second important requisite is modesty. Never at any time imagine

Ivan Petrovich Pavlov. (From *Experimental Psychology and Other Essays*, p. 4, by I. P. Pavlov, 1957, New York: Philosophical Library)

that you know everything. No matter how highly you are appreciated by others, have the courage to say to yourself, "I am ignorant." Do not let pride possess you.

The third thing that is necessary is passion. Remember that science demands of a man his whole life. And even if you could have two lives, they would not be sufficient. Science calls for tremendous effort and great passion. Be passionate in your work and in your search for truth. (p. 110)

MAJOR THEORETICAL NOTIONS

Development of a Conditioned Reflex

Exactly what is meant by a psychic or conditioned reflex is indicated by the following statement by Pavlov (1955):

> I shall mention two simple experiments that can be successfully performed by all. We introduce into the mouth of a dog a moderate solution of some acid; the acid produces a usual defensive reaction in the animal: by vigorous movements of the mouth it ejects the solution, and at the same time an abundant quantity of saliva begins to flow first into the mouth and then overflows, diluting the acid and cleaning the mucous membrane of the oral cavity. Now let us turn to the second experiment. Just prior to introducing the same solution into the dog's mouth we repeatedly act on the animal by a certain external agent, say, a definite sound. What happens then? It suffices simply to repeat the sound, and the same reaction is fully reproduced—the same movements of the mouth and the same secretion of saliva. (p. 247)

The ingredients necessary to bring about conditioning include (a) an **unconditioned stimulus (UCS),** which elicits a natural and automatic response from the organism; (b) an **unconditioned response (UCR),** which is the natural and automatic response elicited by the UCS; (c) a **conditioned stimulus (CS),** which is a neutral stimulus in that it does not elicit a natural and automatic response from the organism. When these ingredients are mixed in a certain way, a **conditioned response (CR)** occurs. In order to produce a CR, the CS and the UCS must be paired a number of times. First the CS is presented and then the UCS. The order of presentation is very important. Each time the UCS occurs, a UCR occurs. Eventually the CS can be presented alone and it will elicit a response similar to the UCR. When this happens, a CR has been demonstrated. The procedure can be diagrammed as follows:

Training procedure: CS → UCS → UCR
Demonstration of conditioning: CS → CR

In Pavlov's example above, the UCS was acid, the UCR was salivation (caused by the acid), and the CS was a sound. The sound, of course, would not ordinarily cause the dog to salivate, but by being paired with the acid, the sound developed the capability to elicit salivation. Salivation as the result of hearing the sound was the CR.

Pavlov believed that the UCR and the CR were always the same kind of response; if the UCR is salivation, then the CR must also be salivation. The magnitude of the CR, however, is always less than that of the UCR. For example, Pavlov, who measured the magnitude of a response by counting drops of saliva, found that the UCS elicited more drops of saliva than did the CS. When we consider recent research on classical conditioning later in this chapter, we will see that Pavlov's contention that CRs are smaller versions of UCRs has been found, at least in some cases, to be incorrect.

Experimental Extinction

A CR depends upon a UCS for its existence and that is precisely why Pavlov referred to the UCS as a *reinforcer*. Obviously, without the UCS, a CS would never develop the capability of eliciting a CR. Likewise, if after a CR has been developed, the CS is continually presented without the UCS following the CS, the CR gradually disappears. When the CS no longer elicits a CR, experimental **extinction** is said to have occurred. Again, extinction results when the CS is presented to the organism and is not followed by reinforcement. In classical conditioning studies, reinforcement is the UCS. The terms Pavlovian conditioning and classical conditioning are synonymous.

Spontaneous Recovery

After a period of time following extinction, if the CS is again presented to the animal, the CR will temporarily reappear. The CR has "spontaneously recovered" even though there had been no further pairings between the CS and the UCS. Again, if there is a delay following extinction and the CS is presented to the organism, it will tend to elicit a CR. The extinction and **spontaneous recovery** of a CR are shown in Figure 7-3.

Higher Order Conditioning

After a CS has been paired with a UCS a number of times, it can be used much like a UCS. That is, through its pairing with the UCS, the CS develops reinforcing properties of its own and it can be paired with a second CS to bring about a CR. Let us pair, for example, a blinking light (CS) with the presentation of food powder (UCS). Food powder will cause the animal to salivate and after a number of pairings between the CS and the UCS, the blinking light presented alone will cause the animal to salivate. That the animal salivates to the blinking light is, of course, a conditioned response.

Now that the blinking light can elicit salivation, it can be paired with a second CS, say, a buzzer. The direction of the pairing is the same as in the original conditioning: first the new CS (buzzer) is presented and then the old one (blinking light).

Figure 7–3. Typical curves showing the extinction and spontaneous recovery of a conditioned response.

Note that food is no longer involved. After a number of such pairings, the buzzer, when presented alone, causes the animal to salivate. In this example, the first CS was used much like a UCS is used to bring about a conditioned response. This is called *second order conditioning*. We also say that the first CS developed *secondary reinforcing properties* since it was used to condition a response to a new stimulus. Therefore the CS is called a **secondary reinforcer.** Since secondary reinforcement cannot develop without the UCS, the UCS is called a **primary reinforcer.**

This procedure can be carried one more step. The second CS (buzzer) can be paired with one more CS, such as a 2,000 cps tone. The direction of the pairing is the same as before: first the tone, then the buzzer. Eventually, the tone presented alone will cause the animal to salivate. Thus, through its pairing with the blinking light, the buzzer too became a secondary reinforcer and therefore could be used to condition a response to another new stimulus, the 2,000 cps tone. This is *third order conditioning*. Both second and third order conditioning come under the general heading of higher order conditioning.

Since higher order conditioning must be studied during the extinction process, it is very difficult, if not impossible, to go beyond third order conditioning. In fact, such studies are quite rare. As one goes from first to third order conditioning, the magnitude of the CR becomes smaller and the CR lasts only for a few trials. In this example, the tone would only elicit a few drops of saliva and do so only the first few times it was presented to the animal.

Generalization

To illustrate **generalization,** we return to the basic conditioning procedure. We will use a 2,000 cps tone for our CS and meat powder for our UCS. After a number of pairings, the tone alone causes the animal to salivate; thus we have developed a CR. Once this has been accomplished, we enter the extinction phase of the experiment, only this time we will expose the animal to tones other than the one it was trained on. Some of the new tones will have a frequency higher than 2,000 cps and some will have a lower frequency. Using the number of drops of saliva as our measure of the magnitude of the CR, we find the CR has its greatest magnitude when the 2,000 cps tone is presented, but CRs are also given to other tones. The magnitude of the CR given to the other tones depends on their similarity to the tone the animal was actually trained on; in this case, the greater the similarity to the 2,000 cps tone, the greater the magnitude of the CR. An example of generalization is shown in Figure 7-4.

There is a relationship between Pavlov's concept of generalization and Thorndike's explanation of the transfer of training. With generalization, as the training and testing situations have more in common, there is a greater probability that the same response will be made to both. This could easily be subsumed under Thorndike's "identical elements" theory of transfer. Likewise, both generalization and transfer explain how we can have a learned reaction to a situation we have never encountered before; that is, we respond to a new situation as we would respond to a similar situation that we are familiar with.

It is important to note the distinction between Thorndike's spread of effect and Pavlov's generalization. The spread of effect refers to the influence of reinforcement on responses neighboring the reinforced response, regardless of their similarity to the reinforced response. With the spread of effect, proximity is the important thing.

Figure 7-4. Idealized stimulus generalization curve showing that as stimuli become increasingly dissimilar to the one used as the CS during training the magnitude of the CR goes down.

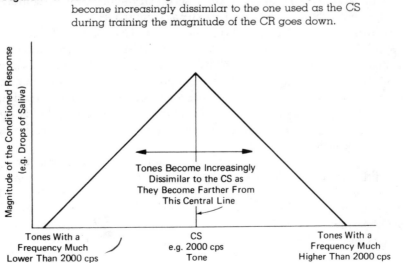

Generalization describes the increased capability of producing a CR of stimuli related to the stimulus which actually preceded reinforcement. With generalization, similarity and not proximity is the important thing.

Discrimination

The opposite of generalization is **discrimination.** As we saw above, generalization refers to the tendency to respond to a number of stimuli that are related to the one actually used during training. Discrimination, on the other hand, refers to the tendency to respond to a very restricted range of stimuli or to only the one used during training.

Discrimination can be brought about in two ways: prolonged training, and differential reinforcement. If a CS is paired with a UCS many times, the tendency to respond to stimuli related to the CS, but not identical to it, goes down. In other words, if the minimum number of pairings between the CS and UCS necessary to develop a CR is used, there is a relatively strong tendency to respond to stimuli related to the CS during extinction; that is, there is considerable generalization. However, if training is prolonged, there is a reduced tendency to respond to stimuli related to the CS during extinction. Thus, it is possible to control generalization by controlling training level: the greater the amount of training, the less generalization.

The second way of bringing about discrimination is through differential reinforcement. This procedure involves, using the above example, presenting the 2,000 cps tone along with a number of other tones that will occur during extinction. Only the 2,000 cps tone is followed by reinforcement. After such training, when the animal is presented with tones other than the 2,000 cps tone during extinction, it tends not to respond to them. Thus, discrimination is demonstrated. Pavlov's attempt at providing a physiological explanation for generalization and discrimination will be considered later in this chapter.

Relationship Between the CS and the UCS

Two general considerations about classical conditioning must be mentioned. First, there appears to be an optimal interval of presentation between the CS and UCS for conditioning to take place most rapidly. A number of investigators have found that if the CS comes on a half-second before the UCS, conditioning proceeds most efficiently. The most common procedure is to have the CS come on and stay on until the UCS comes on. If the time between these two events is greater or less than 0.5 sec, conditioning is relatively more difficult to establish. This should be looked upon as an oversimplification, however, since the optimal interval of time between the onset of the CS and the onset of the UCS for conditioning to occur depends upon many factors, and it is the subject of a considerable amount of research. For example, when we consider research on taste aversion later in this chapter we will see that a phenomenon like classical conditioning occurs even when the delay between the CS and the UCS is several hours. Also, as we shall see below, and again later in this chapter, there are circumstances where a CS precedes a UCS at the optimal interval and yet no conditioning occurs.

The second matter is related to the first. Using traditional classical conditioning procedures, it was typically found that if the CS comes on *after* the UCS is presented, conditioning is extremely difficult, if not impossible, to establish. This is referred to as **backward conditioning.** One explanation for the apparent lack of backward conditioning was that a CS must be "informative" to the organism before conditioning will occur. Clearly, a CS that comes on after the UCS has already been presented cannot be used by the organism to predict the occurrence of the UCS. This would be true not only of the backward conditioning situation but would also be true if CSs are redundant or unreliable. Evidence for this point of view is supplied by Egger and Miller (1962, 1963) who found that (a) if two CSs reliably predict a UCS, the first one presented will become conditioned, and the second one, which is redundant, will not; and (b) if two signals precede a UCS but one is always followed by the UCS and the other is only sometimes followed by the UCS, the more reliable signal becomes conditioned much more than the unreliable signal. It appeared that stimuli that occurred after the UCS or stimuli that were either redundant or unreliably correlated with the UCS could not be used by the organism to predict the occurrence of primary reinforcements, that is, they had no **information value.** In general, Egger and Miller concluded that for classical conditioning to take place, the organism must be able to use the CS to predict whether or not reinforcement will occur. Egger and Miller's general conclusion is still widely accepted, but recent research on classical conditioning has necessitated a change in the beliefs about both backward conditioning and the circumstances under which a CS is informative. Later in this chapter we will discuss current research that shows that CSs presented *after* the UCS are as informative as CSs that are presented *before* the UCS, and therefore backward conditioning is not only possible, it is, under certain circumstances, as easy to establish as forward conditioning.

PAVLOV'S PHYSIOLOGICAL EXPLANATIONS OF CONDITIONING PHENOMENA

Pavlov considered himself to be an experimental physiologist and he therefore sought to explain his observations in physiological terms. Many of his physiological explanations were highly speculative and most have since been found erroneous, but correcting for the time and conditions under which they were made, his explanations were quite remarkable. It was obvious to Pavlov that a CS and UCS became associated through the consistent pairings of the two. The question was, "What is the physiological basis for this association?" Pavlov answered this question as follows: The unconditional stimulus sets up a dominant activity in some area of the cerebral cortex. All other stimuli present at the time also cause cerebral activity, but this activity is weaker and is drawn toward the area of dominant activity caused by the UCS. The weaker activity is drawn toward the stronger activity and a temporary connection is formed between these various centers in the brain. In this way, all the stimuli preceding the onset of the UCS become associated with it. Thus, when one of the stimuli that accompanied the UCS is presented to the organism, it causes activity in the area of the brain associated with it. If it is a visual stimulus, it will cause activity in the visual part of the brain. The activity in this area in turn causes activity in the area corresponding to the unconditioned stimulus because of the temporary connection between the two. The result is that the organism emits a response to the visual stimulus that is associated naturally with the UCS; that is, we have a conditioned response. To summarize, Pavlov simply said that brain centers that are repeatedly active together form temporary connections, and the arousal of one will cause the arousal of the others. Thus, if a tone is consistently presented to a dog just before it gets fed, the area of the brain aroused by the tone will form a temporary connection with the area of the brain which responds to food. When this connection is formed, the presentation of the tone will cause the animal to act as if food was present. At that point, we say a conditioned reflex has been developed.

Excitation and Inhibition

According to Pavlov, the two basic processes governing all central nervous system activity were **excitation** and **inhibition.** Babkin said (1949):

> The fundamental theoretical conception of Pavlov concerning the functional properties of the nervous system, and of the cerebral cortex in particular, was that they were based on two equally important processes: the process of excitation and the process of inhibition. Very often he compared the nervous system with the ancient Greek god Janus, who had two faces looking in opposite directions. The excitation and the inhibition are only sides of one and the same process; they always exist simultaneously, but their proportion varies in each moment, at times the one prevailing, at times the other. Functionally the cerebral cortex is, according to Pavlov, a mosaic, consisting of continuously changing points of excitation and inhibition. (p. 313)

Pavlov believed that each environmental event corresponded to some point on the cortex and that as these events were experienced they tended to either excite or inhibit cortical activity. Thus, the cortex is constantly being excited or inhibited depending on what the organism is experiencing. This pattern of excitation and inhibition that characterizes the brain at any given moment is what Pavlov called the **cortical mosaic.** The momentary cortical mosaic determines how an organism will respond to its environment. As either the external environment or the internal environment changes, the cortical mosaic changes and behavior changes accordingly.

The Dynamic Stereotype

When events consistently occur in the environment, they come to have neurological representation and they become increasingly easy to respond to. Thus, responses to a familiar environment become rapid and automatic. When this happens, a **dynamic stereotype** is said to have been developed. Roughly, the dynamic stereotype is a cortical mosaic that has become stable because the organism has been in a highly predictable environment for a considerable length of time. As long as this cortical mapping accurately reflects the environment and produces appropriate responses, everything is fine. If, however, the environment is radically changed, the organism may find it difficult to change a dynamic stereotype. Pavlov (1955) put the matter as follows:

> The entire establishment and distribution in the cortex of excitatory and inhibitory states, taking place in a certain period under the action of external and internal stimuli, become more and more fixed under uniform, recurring conditions and are effected with ever-increasing ease and automatism. Thus, there appears a dynamic stereotype (systematization) in the cortex, the maintenance of which becomes an increasingly less difficult nervous task; but the stereotype becomes inert, little susceptible to change and resistant to new conditions and new stimulations. Any initial elaboration of a stereotype is, depending on the complexity of the system of stimuli, a difficult and often an extraordinary task. (p. 259)

To summarize, certain environmental events tend to be followed by certain other environmental events, and as long as this continues to be true, the association between the two on the neural level continues to grow stronger. (Note the similarity here to Thorndike's early thinking concerning the effect of exercise on a neural bond.) If the environment abruptly changes, new neural paths must be formed, and that is no easy matter.

Irradiation and Concentration

Pavlov used the term "analyser" to describe the path from a sense receptor to a certain area of the brain. An analyser consists of sense receptors, the sensory tract in the spinal cord, and the area of the brain onto which the sensory activity is projected. Sensory information projected onto some area of the brain causes excitation in that area. Initially, this excitation spills over into neighboring brain areas; in other words, there is an **irradiation of excitation.** It is this process that Pavlov used to explain generalization. In our example of generalization described above, we noted that when an animal was conditioned to respond to a 2,000 cps tone, it responded not only to that tone but to other related tones. The magnitude of the response was determined by the similarity between the tone being presented and the actual CS used during training. As the similarity increased, the CR's magnitude increased.

Pavlov's explanation for generalization was that neural impulses travelled from the sense receptors—in this case from the ears—to a specific area of the cortex that reacted to a 2,000 cps tone. The activity caused by the 2,000 cps tone irradiates from this location out into the neighboring regions. Pavlov assumed that tones closest to the 2,000 cps tone would be represented in brain regions close to the area corresponding to the one for the 2,000 cps tone. As tones become dissimilar, the brain regions representing them will be farther away from the area representing the 2,000 cps tone. In addition, Pavlov assumed that excitation diminished with distance: it was strongest at the point corresponding to the CS and weaker farther away. Therefore an association was made not only between the CS and the UCS but with a number of stimuli related to the CS that had representation in neighboring brain regions. In addition to his hypothesis that excitation irradiated or spread to neighboring regions of the cortex, Pavlov found that inhibition also irradiated.

Pavlov also found that concentration, a process opposite to irradiation, can govern both excitation and inhibition. He found that under certain circumstances both excitation and inhibition can be concentrated at specific areas of the brain. As the process of irradiation is used to explain generalization, so is the process of concentration used to explain discrimination.

At first the organism has a generalized tendency to respond to a CS during conditioning. For example, if a signal is followed by a reinforcer, there is a learned tendency to respond to that and related signals. Likewise, if a signal is presented and is not followed by a reinforcer, there is a learned tendency not to respond to that and related signals. We say, therefore, that both excitation and inhibition have irradiated. With prolonged training, however, the tendencies to respond and not to respond become less general and increasingly specific to a narrow range of stimuli. In the latter case, we say the excitation and inhibition have been concentrated.

As we noted earlier in this chapter, discrimination, or the ability to respond differentially to related stimuli, can be brought about by prolonged training or differential reinforcement. If a large number of pairings are made between the CS and the UCS the excitation begins to concentrate. After such training, one would find that the organism tends to respond only to the CS or to stimuli very similar to the CS. In other words, because excitation has been concentrated, very little generalization would take place.

Summary of Pavlov's Views on Brain Functioning

Pavlov saw the brain as a mosaic of points of excitation and inhibition. Each point on the brain corresponded to an environmental event. Depending on what was being experienced at the moment, a different pattern of excitation and inhibition would occur in the brain and that pattern would determine behavior. Some connections in the brain are between unconditioned stimuli and their associated responses, and some are between conditioned stimuli and their associated responses. The former are permanent and the latter are temporary and change with varied environmental conditions.

When a temporary connection is first being formed in the brain, there is a tendency for a conditioned stimulus to have a very general effect in the brain. That is, the excitation caused by a conditioned stimulus irradiates over a relatively larger portion of the cortex. The same thing is true when an organism is learning not to respond to, or to avoid, a stimulus. The inhibitory effects of such a stimulus also irradiates over a fairly large portion of the brain in the early stages of learning. As learning proceeds, however, the excitation caused by a positive stimulus and the inhibition caused by a negative stimulus become concentrated in specific areas of the cortex. As the organism develops the connections between environmental events and brain processes that allow it to survive, a dynamic stereotype develops, which is a kind of neural mapping of the environment. The dynamic stereotype makes it easier to respond to a highly predictable environment but makes it difficult to adjust to a new environment.

Pavlov never explained how all these processes interact to produce the smooth, coordinated behavior we see from organisms, but he did express amazement that systematic behavior did result from such a large number of influences. Pavlov put the matter as follows (1955):

> Countless stimuli, different in nature and intensity, reach the cerebral hemi-spheres both from the external world and the internal medium of the organism itself. Whereas some of them are merely investigated (the orienting reflex), others evoke highly diverse conditioned and unconditioned effects. They all meet, come together, interact, and they must, finally, become systematized, equilibrated, and form, so to speak, a dynamic stereotype. What truly grandiose work! (p. 454)

The "orienting reflex" to which Pavlov refers is the tendency for organisms to attend to and explore novel stimuli that occur in their environment. The orienting reflex has been the topic of considerable research in recent years.

First and Second Signal Systems

Pavlov believed that human behavior was much more complex than that of other animals because humans utilize language, which Pavlov called a **second signal system.** The **first signal system** consists of the organism's reactions—both learned and unlearned—to environmental stimuli. Our discussion of learning up to this point has been concerned with the first signal system. Even though words are only symbols of reality, they too can have responses conditioned to them and, therefore, words can govern our behavior. For example, actual objects associated with previous pain or anxiety will be avoided but so will things labeled dangerous or harmful.

One example of how language complicates classical conditioning is found in the area of **semantic generalization** (sometimes called mediated generalization). Semantic generalization studies have shown that a response can be conditioned to the *meaning* of a stimulus rather than to the concrete stimulus itself. For example, if a response is conditioned to the number 4, human subjects will emit a conditioned response when they are confronted with such stimuli as $\sqrt{16}$; $2\overline{|8}$; 2×2; $10\overline{|40}$; and so forth. In other words, the number 4 elicits a conditioned response, but so will a variety of other stimuli that result in 4 after mental operations have been performed. The conclusion to be drawn is that for human subjects the true CS is the concept of "fourness" (see Razran, 1961, for additional examples of semantic conditioning).

Semantic generalization also seems to vary as a function of age. In his work with children of different ages, Reiss (1946) found that after initial training which involved visually presenting a word such as "right" as a CS, children generalized by giving conditioned responses according to their level of language development. He found that 8-year-olds generalized to visually presented homophones (e.g., *rite*); 11-

year-olds generalized to antonyms (e.g., *wrong*); and 14-year-olds generalized to synonyms (e.g., *correct*).

Although the second signal system is clearly more complex than the first signal system, Pavlov felt that the same laws of conditioning govern both and therefore they both could be studied objectively. In other words, the process by which we develop a reaction to an environmental event is the same process by which we develop a reaction to a word or a thought.

A COMPARISON BETWEEN CLASSICAL AND INSTRUMENTAL CONDITIONING

The kind of conditioning that Thorndike studied is now called instrumental conditioning because the response being observed was instrumental in getting the animal something it wanted (reinforcement). In the case of the cat in the puzzle box, the cat had to learn to perform a certain response which released it from the box and reinforced it with a piece of fish. If the appropriate response did not occur, the animal was not reinforced. To summarize, we can say that in instrumental conditioning, any response that leads to reinforcement tends to be repeated, and a reinforcer is something the animal wants.

Classical conditioning elicits a response from the animal, and instrumental conditioning depends on the animal's emitting the response. The former can be said to be involuntary and automatic; the latter to be voluntary and under the animal's control.

The function of reinforcement is also quite different for classical and instrumental conditioning. With instrumental conditioning reinforcement is presented to the animal *after* the response of interest has been made. With classical conditioning, however, the reinforcer (UCS) is presented in order to *elicit* the response of interest. The two situations can be diagrammed as follows:

Instrumental Conditioning

Environmental situation →   Effective behavior   →   Reinforcement
  (e.g., puzzle box)   (e.g., behavior which   (e.g., being released
                         releases the animal   from confinement
                         from confinement)   and/or receiving a
                                                  piece of fish)
       Association of interest

Classical Conditioning

Conditioned Stimulus →   Reinforcement   → Unconditioned response
   (e.g., a tone)   (Unconditioned   (e.g., salivation)
                       stimulus, e.g., food)
                                          → Conditioned response
       Association of interest   (salivation)

Pavlov felt that he had discovered the physiological bases for the associations that philosophers and psychologists had been talking about for so many years. To him, conditioned reflexes could explain how the mind works. Pavlov placed himself squarely among the associationists with the following statement (1955):

> Are there any grounds . . . for distinguishing between that which the physiologist calls the temporary connection and that which the psychologist terms association? They are fully identical; they merge and absorb each other. Psychologists themselves seem to recognize this, since they (at least, some of them) have stated that the experiments with conditioned reflexes provide a solid foundation for associative psychology, i.e., psychology which regards association as the base of psychical activity. (p. 251)

The two kinds of conditioning reflect basic differences in outlook between Pavlov and Thorndike. Pavlov was basically an experimental physiologist who was interested in learning how the brain functioned. Thorndike was an early functionalist who was strongly influenced by Darwin. Thorndike's main concern was how learning was involved in adapting to one's environment. He was more concerned with the *function* of learned behavior than was Pavlov. This may be why Thorndike did little more than acknowledge associative shifting, a kind of learning based strictly on contiguity between stimuli and response, whereas Pavlov developed a physiological model to explain this phenomenon in detail.

Despite basic differences between the classical and instrumental conditioning paradigms, they have many similarities. Most importantly, both kinds of conditioning are dependent upon reinforcement. In classical conditioning the UCS is the reinforcer and if it is removed from the experimental arrangement, extinction occurs. In instrumental conditioning the reinforcer is the "satisfying state of affairs" that *follows* an appropriate response. If reinforcement no longer follows a certain response, the probability of that response goes back to the point where it was before reinforcement was introduced. Classical and instrumental conditioning not only have in common the necessity of reinforcement (extinction follows when it is removed), but also the phenomena of spontaneous recovery, generalization, discrimination, and secondary reinforcement.

It should also be pointed out that it is impossible to separate instrumental and classical conditioning completely. For example, every instrumental conditioning study that utilizes a primary reinforcer (such as food or water) will necessarily produce classical conditioning. That is, all of the stimuli that consistently occur prior to the primary reinforcer will, through the process of classical conditioning, become secondary reinforcers.

RECENT RESEARCH ON CLASSICAL CONDITIONING

In his analysis of conditioning Pavlov emphasized contiguity. That is, if a CS precedes a UCS eventually a CS will elicit a CR. We saw earlier that the work of Egger and Miller (1962, 1963) cast doubt on this analysis by showing that CSs that are unreliable or redundant do not become conditioned to a UCS. Recently several other researchers have also shown that factors other than simple contiguity are involved in classical conditioning. We will review the work of these researchers in this section, but first we will discuss another possible inaccuracy in Pavlov's theory, the fact that he viewed CRs as smaller versions of UCRs.

CRs Are Not Necessarily Little UCRs. Pavlov believed that in the course of conditioning the CS comes to substitute for the UCS. This is why classical conditioning has sometimes been referred to as stimulus substitute learning. It was assumed that, since the CS acts as a substitute for the UCS, CRs were smaller versions of UCRs. Indeed, there are times when the CR and UCR have much in common, as when the UCR caused by food (UCS) is, among other things, salivation and so is the CR. Also when the UCS is a puff of air to the eye, the UCR is, among other things, an eye-blink, and a CS consistently paired with the UCS, will eventually, when presented alone, cause an eye-blink. Often a CR does look like a smaller version of the UCR. However, careful study of the nature of CRs have shown them to often be quite different from UCRs. For example, Zener (1937) carefully photographed a classical conditioning experiment and made the following observations:

> Except for the component of salivary secretion the conditioned and unconditioned behavior is not identical. (a) During most of the time in which the bell is reinforced by the presence of food, chewing generally occurs with the head raised out of the food-pan but not directed either at the bell or into the food-pan, or at any definite environmental object. Yet this posture practically never, even chewing only occasionally, occurs to the conditioned stimulus alone. Despite Pavlov's assertions, the dog does not appear to be eating an imaginary food. (b) Nor is the behavior that does appear an arrested or partially unconditioned reaction consisting of those response elements not conflicting with other actions. It is a different reaction, anthropomorphically describable as a looking for, expecting, the fall of food with a readiness to perform the eating behavior which will occur when the food falls. The effector pattern is not identical with the unconditioned. (c) Movements frequently occur which do not appear as part of the unconditioned response to food: All the restless behavior of stamping, yawning, panting. (p. 393)

Not only has it been found that CRs and UCRs are often different in nature, but some researchers have found them to be antagonistic. Obrist, Sutterer, and Howard (1972) verified the fact that the typical UCR when shock is used as the UCS is heart rate acceleration. And, as Pavlov would have predicted, with minimal pairings of the CS and UCS the CR is heart rate acceleration. With prolonged training, however, the CR became heart rate *deceleration*.

Another example of CR and UCR being antagonistic is found when drugs are used as UCSs. Shepard Siegel (1979) describes a series of experiments in which morphine was used as a UCS. One reaction to morphine is analgesia—or a reduction in the sensitivity to pain. Under the influence of morphine a rat will take significantly longer to remove its paw from a hot plate than a rat not under the influence of morphine. Since the injection itself precedes the experience of morphine (the UCS) it (the injection) can be viewed as a CS. Thus, after several injections of morphine, injecting the rat with plain water should reduce its sensitivity to pain. It turns out, however, the opposite is true. Under the circumstances described above, rats become *more* sensitive to pain. That is, animals that were previously injected with morphine and are then injected with water remove their paw from a hot plate significantly *faster* than control animals that had never been injected with morphine. The CR (increased sensitivity to pain) appears to be opposite to the UCR (decreased sensitivity to pain). Essentially the same results have been attained when lights or tones were used as CSs instead of the injection itself.

It has also been found (e.g., Holland, 1977) that even when the same UCS is used, CRs will take different forms when different CSs are paired with that UCS. Clearly the relationship between CRs and UCRs is much more complex than Pavlov had assumed. It turns out that sometimes CRs do mimic UCRs, sometimes CRs seem to prepare the organism for the UCS, and sometimes CRs are antagonistic to the UCR. For a discussion of the different kinds of CR–UCR relationships and the conditions that produce them see Hilgard and Marquis (1940) and Hollis (1982).

Overshadowing and Blocking. Pavlov (1927) observed that if he used a compound stimulus as a CS and one component of the stimulus was more salient than the other, only the more salient component would be conditioned. This phenomenon is called **overshadowing.** If, for example, a compound CS consisted of a light and a loud noise (presented together), all of the conditioning would occur to the loud noise because it was the stronger or more salient element of the compound. When a compound stimulus is used as a CS, overshadowing is demonstrated when conditioning occurs to the dominant component of the stimulus but not to the weaker component. The phenomenon of overshadowing is of theoretical interest because both elements of the compound stimulus are presented to the organism in accordance with Pavlovian principles, and yet, conditioning only occurs in the case of one element. Much of the current research on classical conditioning has been designed to explain the phenomenon of overshadowing and the related phenomenon of blocking which we will consider next.

In 1969, Leon Kamin reported an influential series of experiments on a phenomenon that he calls **blocking** (also called the blocking effect). Before discussing Kamin's work on blocking we need to describe the **conditioned emotional response** (CER) which he used to demonstrate the blocking phenomenon. The CER was first described by Estes and Skinner (1941) as a method of measuring the strength of a CS-UCS association. The procedure involves first placing a rat in a Skinner box and shaping it to press a lever for food reinforcement. The rat is then switched to a fixed interval schedule of reinforcement (e.g., an FI-4-min schedule) to produce a steady rate of responding. Next, the rat experiences 1-hr experimental sessions during which a tone is sounded for 3 min at a time and upon the termination of the tone, the rat receives a brief, unavoidable shock. Throughout the tone-shock sequences, the fixed interval reinforcement schedule remains in effect. After several sessions, the rats greatly reduced their rate of lever-pressing each time the tone came on. The reduction in rate of responding during the time that the CS (tone) was on is called **conditioned suppression.** It was found that the suppression lasted until the end of the shock that terminated each tone-shock sequence. After the shock was terminated, response rate increased to its normal rate and continued at that rate until the tone came on again. During the time that the tone was on, Estes and Skinner noted emotional responses such as defecation, squealing, and freezing. It was these conditioned emotional responses that were thought responsible for suppressing response rate. Using this procedure, the extent of classical conditioning (tone-shock relationship) could be indexed by changes in the rate with which an operant response is made.

Kamin (1969) used a variation in the CER procedure to demonstrate blocking. First, rats were trained to press a lever for food reinforcement. Next, the rats were exposed to 16 trials in which a tone was followed by an electric shock. The result of this training was response suppression when the tone came on. The next phase of the study involved pairing the tone from the previous phase with a light, thus creating a compound stimulus. The light-tone compound stimulus was presented to the rat on 8 trials and was always followed by shock. The final phase of the study involved

Figure 7–5. Kamin's blocking experiment. In Phase 1, a tone is paired with shock, and after several pairings, when presented alone, the tone causes response suppression. In Phase 2, the tone is paired with a light and both precede a shock. Phase 3 shows that the tone continues to cause response suppression, but the light does not. In spite of the fact that the light was reliably paired with the shock in Phase 2, such pairing did not result in conditioning.

presenting only the light to the rat to see if it would produce response suppression, and it did not. A control group indicated that if both the light and the tone are paired with shock independently, both produce response suppression. If, however, the tone is first paired with shock and then is presented to the rat along with the light, little or no conditioning will occur to the light. Under these conditions, conditioning to the tone *blocked* conditioning to the light. The blocking effect is also found if the light is used first and is then paired with the tone in which case no conditioning occurs to the tone. Kamin's procedure and results are summarized in Figure 7-5.

We will examine possible explanations for blocking shortly, but it should be noted here that blocking, like overshadowing, exemplifies a situation where stimuli are paired in accordance with classical conditioning principles, and yet no conditioning occurs. Once again it is suggested that something more than mere stimulus contiguity is involved in classical conditioning.

Overshadowing occurs when one component of a compound stimulus is intrinsically stronger than the other and therefore dominates the other, weaker component, thus preventing the weaker component from becoming conditioned. Blocking, on the other hand, occurs because prior conditioning somehow prevents the formation of an association between a newly inserted stimulus and a UCS.

The Rescorla–Wagner Theory of Classical Conditioning

Robert Rescorla and Allan Wagner have devised a theory of classical conditioning that not only accounts for blocking but for many other classical conditioning phenomena as well (see, e.g., Rescorla & Wagner, 1972; Wagner & Rescorla, 1972). In a sense, the Rescorla–Wagner theory of classical conditioning builds upon the work of Egger and Miller (1962, 1963) discussed earlier in this chapter. Both Egger and Miller and Rescorla and Wagner claim that in order for a stimulus to become an effective CS, it must be informative. That is, it must provide the organism with reliable, nonredundant information about the onset of the UCS.

Although the Rescorla–Wagner theory is usually summarized in a mathematical equation, we will attempt to present the theory verbally. The major assumptions made by the theory are:

1. A given UCS can support only so much conditioning, and stronger UCSs can support more conditioning than weaker ones.

2. The amount of conditioning that can occur on any given trial to a given CS is limited by the amount of conditioning that has already taken place to that CS.

3. The amount of conditioning that can occur on any given trial to a CS is not only limited by the amount of conditioning already associated with that CS, but also by the amount of conditioning associated with other CSs present in the situation. In other words, there is only so much conditioning that can take place in a given conditioning situation, and that total amount is divided up among the various CSs involved in the situation.

4. Conditioning will occur faster for strong, salient CSs than for weak, less salient CSs.

Robert A. Rescorla. (Courtesy of Robert A. Rescorla)

Blocking is easily accounted for by the Rescorla–Wagner theory. It is simply assumed that during Phase 1 of Kamin's blocking experiment when, say, a tone is paired with shock, conditioning occurred to the maximal level possible. Then, in Phase 2 when the tone was paired with a light to form a compound stimulus, there was little, or no, potential for additional conditioning to take place so none occurred to the light. Thus, according to Rescorla and Wagner, the tone "blocked" conditioning to the light, by "using up" all of the available conditioning before the light was introduced.

Contingency Not Contiguity. In 1966, Rescorla dramatically demonstrated that stimulus contiguity is not enough to establish classical conditioning. Rescorla trained dogs to jump over a hurdle in a shuttle-box in order to avoid an electric shock that was delivered at regular intervals of 30 sec. The situation was arranged so that the shock could be avoided if the dog jumped the hurdle before the end of the time interval. Each time the dog jumped over the hurdle, the clock was reset to zero and started running again. There was no external signal indicating when a shock would be delivered; the only signal was the animal's internal sense of the passage of time. All of the dogs in the experiment learned to jump often enough to avoid most of the shocks. It was this rate of jumping that was used as a frame of reference to judge the effects of other variables introduced into the experiment.

After the preliminary training described above, the dogs were removed from the hurdle-jumping apparatus and were subjected to tones followed by electric shock. The dogs were divided into three groups. Group 1 received standard conditioning where a CS (a 5-sec tone) was always followed by a UCS (an electric shock). This procedure is generally referred to as **forward conditioning** and was called a positive contingency in Rescorla's study. Group 2 first experienced the UCS *and then* the CS. The situation for this group was arranged so that the CS was never paired with shock, nor was the CS ever followed within 30 sec by the shock. The arrangement by which a CS *follows* a UCS generally referred to as backward conditioning, was referred to as a negative contingency in Rescorla's study. This was an especially interesting experimental condition since it has been widely believed that when the CS follows the UCS, no conditioning occurs. Group 3 experienced the CS preceding the UCS and following it an equal number of times. By randomizing the occurrence of the CS relative to the UCS, a situation is created whereby there is no correlation between the two. That is, the UCS is as likely to occur following the presentation of the CS as it is when the CS does not occur. Therefore, for subjects in Group 3, the CS had no predictive value.

In the final phase of the experiment, the dogs were placed back in the shuttle-box and were again given avoidance training until the rate of their avoidance responses stabilized. At this point, the CS (tone) from the classical conditioning phase of the study was presented for 5 sec a number of times. It was observed that when the CS was introduced to animals in Group 1 (forward conditioning or positive contingency), they *increased* their rate of responding relative to what it was in the initial stage of the experiment. In fact, subjects in this group almost doubled their response rate when the tone came on. When the CS was introduced to animals in Group 2 (backward conditioning or negative contingency), they *decreased* their rate of responding by about one third. When the CS was introduced to animals in Group 3 (no correlation), their rate of responding remained essentially the same as what it was in the initial phase of the experiment.

One crucial point to remember while interpreting the results of the above experiment is that all animals received the same number of shocks during the classical conditioning phase of the experiment. What was varied was the relationship between the CS and the UCS. As we have seen, Rescorla (1966, 1967) calls a relationship between a CS and a UCS a *contingency,* and he says that it is contingencies that determine whether conditioning takes place and if so, what kind of conditioning. In Group 1, there was a positive contingency between the CS and the UCS and therefore the CS accurately predicted the occurrence of the UCS. This, according to Rescorla, is why the animals in this group jumped the hurdle more rapidly when the CS was presented. In Group 2, there was a negative contingency between the CS and the UCS. That is, the CS was never paired with or followed by the UCS within 30 sec. Thus, for subjects in this group, the CS became a signal for safety. Contrary to the common belief that no classical conditioning occurs under these conditions (backward conditioning), Rescorla found that the animals in this group indeed learned a contingency. They learned that the CS predicted the absence of the shock and therefore when the CS was introduced to these animals, they inhibited their rate of jumping. Rescorla says that it is important to realize that the procedure followed in Group 2 is the most common "control" condition in classical conditioning studies. It has been commonly believed that because no facilitative conditioning occurs under these circumstances, no conditioning of any kind occurs, but this is clearly not the case. Since inhibitory conditioning does take place, this procedure cannot be used as a control group in classical conditioning studies. It is only the procedures followed by Group 3 that provide a **truly random control group** for classical conditioning studies. In this group the appearance of the CS and of the UCS were independent of each other, and therefore, animals in this group could not use the CS to predict either the subsequent presence or absence of the UCS. It is only under these conditions that there is no contingency between the CS and UCS, and this is why, according to Rescorla, no classical conditioning occurs.

Again, Rescorla's explanation of his results is similar to the one offered earlier by Egger and Miller (1962, 1963). Both claim that in order for conditioning to take place, a CS must be informative; that is, it must provide the organism with useful information about the UCS. Rescorla expanded upon Egger and Miller's work, however, by showing that negative contingencies are as informative as positive ones. According to Rescorla, it is only the truly random control procedure that creates an uninformative relationship between the CS and UCS, and, thus, produces no conditioning.

LEARNED HELPLESSNESS

As we have just seen, Rescorla claimed that his truly random control group created a situation where there was no predictive relationship between the CS and the UCS, and therefore, no conditioning should occur. Indeed, Rescorla and others have demonstrated that no conditioning does occur in the truly random control condition, but perhaps they are looking at the wrong kind of behavior.

Martin Seligman (1969, 1975) has provided convincing evidence that animals do indeed learn something very important under what Rescorla calls the truly random control condition. In his analysis, Seligman first points out that in a classical conditioning experiment, the organism is helpless, and it learns that it is helpless. To demonstrate that animals learn to be helpless as the result of classical conditioning, Seligman and his colleagues reversed the experimental procedures followed by Kamin and Rescorla and Wagner. Instead of first teaching animals an instrumental response and then exposing them to classical conditioning, Seligman gave his animals classical conditioning first and *then* attempted to teach them an instrumental response. It turns out that reversing the experimental procedures has a profound effect on the animals' behavior. Maier, Seligman, and Solomon (1969) report the results of a number of studies in which classical conditioning (using a shock as a UCS) preceded an attempt to teach animals an instrumental response. The consistent finding is that exposing animals to a series of brief, intense, and unavoidable electric shocks rendered animals unable to subsequently learn a simple instrumental response, like jumping a hurdle to escape from or avoid an electric shock. Furthermore, it did not matter how the CS was paired with the UCS. It was found that the animals were unable to learn a simple instrumental response in the second phase of the experiment, regardless of whether they had experienced what Rescorla referred to as a positive contingency, a negative contingency, or a truly random condition. Maier, Seligman, and Solomon (1969) contrast the ability of dogs that had received classical conditioning to learn a simple escape or avoidance response with that of

Martin Seligman. (Courtesy of Martin Seligman)

naive animals that did not experience classical conditioning:

> In a dramatic contrast to a naive dog, a dog which has experienced inescapable shocks prior to avoidance training soon stops running and howling and remains silent until shock terminates. The dog does not cross the barrier and escape the shock. Rather it seems to give up and passively accept the shock. On succeeding trials, the dog continues to fail to make escape movements and will take as much shock as the experimenter chooses to give.
>
> . . . Such dogs occasionally jump the barrier and escape or avoid, but then revert to taking the shock; they fail to profit from exposure to the barrier-jumping-shock-termination contingency. In naive dogs a successful escape response is a reliable predictor of future, short-latency escape responses. (pp. 311–312)

According to Seligman, an animal learns that it is helpless in a classical conditioning situation precisely because it *is* helpless. Furthermore, the helplessness that is learned has nothing to do with the shock that is experienced per se; rather, it has to do with the animal's inability to control the shock. To demonstrate the importance of control, or lack of it, Seligman and Maier (1967) performed a two-phase experiment using dogs as subjects. During Phase 1 of the experiment, subjects in Group 1 were shocked while constrained in a hammock. Subjects in this group could terminate the shock by pressing a panel with their snouts. Subjects in Group 2 were shocked whenever subjects in Group 1 were shocked, but subjects in Group 2 could do nothing to terminate the shocks. A third control group was placed in the hammock but was given no shock. Seligman and Maier (1967) hypothesized that during Phase 1 of the experiment, subjects in Group 1 were learning that shock was potentially controllable through their behavior, whereas subjects in Group 2 were learning that their behavior could have no influence on the shock. For them, shock was inescapable.

To test their hypothesis, Seligman and Maier employed escape-avoidance training using a shuttle-box in Phase 2 of their study. Prompt responding to a tone by jumping the hurdle between compartments was followed by the termination of the tone and the shock. Subjects in Group 1 (escapable shock) and Group 3 (no shock) quickly learned to avoid shock by jumping the hurdle. In vivid contrast, subjects in Group 2 (inescapable shock) learned neither to avoid nor to escape the shock. When the shock came on in the shuttle-box, they just took the shock and whined. Even when a member of this group occasionally blundered over the hurdle, thus escaping the shock, the response was not repeated when the shock next occurred. According to Seligman and Maier, these animals had learned in Phase 1 of the study that there was nothing that they could do to avoid shock so in Phase 2 of the study they tried nothing. When the belief that one can do nothing to terminate or avoid an aversive situation generalizes to other situations, it is called **learned helplessness.** Thus, learned helplessness is not caused by traumatic experience per se, but by the inability, or perceived inability, to do anything about it. Animals who learned that they could not control an aversive situation became generally passive.

The phenomenon of learned helplessness has been found in many species of animals, including humans using both appetitive and aversive UCSs. The symptoms of learned helplessness include a reluctance to initiate any action to attain reinforcement or to escape punishment, general passivity, withdrawal, fearfulness, depression, and a general willingness to accept whatever happens. Seligman (1975) has suggested that learned helplessness in humans may be experienced as depression and may characterize individuals who have been so thwarted in their attempts in life that they become hopeless, withdrawn, and finally just give up.

We see, then, that even in what Rescorla called a truly random control condition, organisms learn that they are helpless to avoid or escape an aversive situation so they no longer try to do so. This feeling of helplessness generalizes beyond the experimental situation and results in general passivity.

OTHER THEORETICAL ACCOUNTS OF CLASSICAL CONDITIONING

The Importance of Attention. Nicholas Mackintosh (1975) theorizes that organisms seek information that allows them to predict biologically significant events (e.g., UCSs). Once such relevant information is attained, the organism ignores other information. Thus, Mackintosh's position relies on the active processing of information. Attention is paid to stimuli in the environment until a cue that predicts a significant event is found and, at that point, the search for predictive cues stops. A major difference between the position of Rescorla–Wagner and that of Mackintosh is that the Rescorla–Wagner position views the organism as passively receiving and recording information from the environment and Mackintosh does not. The Rescorla–Wagner position represents a modern example of the older view of learning, which sees the learning process as mechanical, automatic, and associative in nature. Schwartz (1984) says of the Rescorla–Wagner theory:

> It provides a way of describing seemingly complex processes, involving the evaluation of probabilities and the selection of best predictors, in a mechanical, trial-by-trial fashion. The organism does not need to be able to consider its various experiences with CSs and USs [same as UCSs] over time, and combine them in some complex fashion, to be able to respond as though it was making these considerations. The Rescorla-Wagner theory gives the animal a simple solution to the complex problem of forming selective, informative associations. (p. 112)

Contrary to the Rescorla–Wagner position, Mackintosh emphasizes the active processing of information by the organism. Mackintosh's explanation of blocking is straightforward. When one CS (say a light) reliably predicts the occurrence of a biologically significant event (say a shock), the organism becomes aware of this predictive relationship. When the light is paired with a second predictive CS (say a tone), the second CS is not attended to because the first predictive relationship (light → shock) provides all of the information that the organism requires. It may be remembered that the Rescorla–Wagner theory explained the lack of conditioning to the newly inserted CS by saying that all of the conditioning that the UCS could support was "used up" by the first CS. So both the Rescorla–Wagner theory and Mackintosh's theory explain blocking, but they do so making quite different assumptions about the nature of the learning process.

There is at least one phenomenon that Mackintosh's theory explains that presents a problem for the Rescorla–Wagner theory, and that is the effects of preexposure to the CS before conditioning. Many studies have shown that preexposing an organism to a CS before it is paired with a UCS, retards conditioning when the CS and UCS are paired (e.g., Baker & Mackintosh, 1977; Best & Gemberling, 1977; Fenwick, Mikulka, & Klein, 1975). Adverse effects of preexposure are a problem for the Rescorla–Wagner theory because according to it, preexposure to the CS should have no effect on conditioning. According to the Rescorla–Wagner theory, only the salience and the intensity of the CS will influence its subsequent association with the UCS. Neither the salience nor the intensity of a CS are changed as the result of preexposure and, therefore, preexposure should not interfere with subsequent conditioning. Mackintosh explains the adverse effects of preexposure by saying that during the time that the CS is presented alone, the organism attends to it and learns that it is irrelevant, that is, that it is not correlated with any significant event. Once the CS is found to be irrelevant, it is ignored and it continues to be ignored when it is first presented along with the UCS, thus retarding the formation of a predictive relationship between the two. Both blocking and the effects of preexposure to CSs are explained by Mackintosh as the learning by the organism to ignore irrelevant or redundant information.

Surprisingness. In an effort to explain blocking, Kamin (1969) argued that when the UCS first comes on, the animal is surprised by it. If a CS reliably precedes the UCS, the animal gradually learns to expect the UCS shortly after the CS is presented. Eventually the animal is no longer surprised by the UCS, and no additional conditioning takes place. According to Kamin, when the CS elicits a memory of the UCS, the occurrence of the UCS is no longer surprising and there is no reason to learn anything else under the circumstances. Thus, for Kamin, the mechanism that explains classical conditioning is surprisingness. When the onset of the UCS is a complete surprise, the animal searches its memory for an event that anticipated the UCS. When such an event is found, surprisingness diminishes, and so does so-called conditioning. If the CS was such an event, it will become associated with the UCS in the sense that when the CS comes on, it will elicit a memory of the UCS. The elicited memory of the UCS will at first be weak but will become stronger with increased pairings of the CS and UCS. As the memory of the UCS elicited by the CS becomes more vivid, surprisingness diminishes and so does so-called conditioning.

Blocking is easily explained using the concept of surprisingness. Since stimulus A reliably predicts the UCS, the occurrence of the UCS is no longer surprising at the time stimulus B is introduced, and therefore, no conditioning occurs to stimulus B. According to Kamin, no surprise means no conditioning. Wagner (1969, 1971, 1978) has elaborated and substantiated Kamin's contention that surprisingness is reduced or eliminated to the extent that the CS elicits a memory of the UCS. Schwartz (1984) summarizes the Kamin–Wagner theory as follows:

1. We only learn about things to the extent that we process them actively.
2. We only process things actively to the extent that they are surprising, that is, to the extent that we do not yet understand them.
3. As conditioning proceeds, CS and US become less surprising. As a result they get processed less. And therefore we learn less about them. (p. 118)

It is possible to relate the positions of Rescorla–Wagner with that of Kamin–Wagner by assuming that the difference between the maximum amount of conditioning possible and the amount of conditioning that has already taken place, reflects the extent to which an organism is surprised by the onset of the UCS. When the amount of possible conditioning matches the amount of conditioning that has taken place, there is no longer any surprise.

Also, because the amount of conditioning possible is directly proportional to the amount of surprise, it should be clear how the Kamin–Wagner theory accounts for the negatively accelerated curve that typically characterizes the learning process.

Conditioning as the Formation of Expectancies. Bolles (1972, 1979) suggests that organisms do not learn any new responses during conditioning. Rather, they learn to execute species-specific reactions that are appropriate to the situation. According to Bolles, what organisms do learn are *expectancies* that guide their unlearned behavior. A *stimulus expectancy* is formed when a CS is correlated with an important outcome such as the presence or absence of a UCS. In other words, the typical classical conditioning experiment creates a stimulus expectancy. A stimulus expectancy involves predicting the presence of one stimulus (UCS) from the presence of another stimulus (CS). Organisms also learn *response expectancies* which are predictive relationships between responses and outcomes. According to Bolles, reinforcement does not strengthen behavior, rather it strengthens the expectancy that a certain response will be followed by a reinforcer.

Bolles (1979) feels that recent findings call into question the traditional mechanist-associationistic explanation of classical conditioning and proposes that his cognitive explanation be accepted instead:

> The unpredictability of the CR, the difficulty of not really knowing what kind of behavior to expect from a conditioned animal, suggests that what is learned in a Pavlovian situation is not a response at all. Perhaps what is learned is something else, perhaps something about the . . . CS-US relationship. Maybe what the animal learns then when the CS comes on is not to respond to it in some fixed manner but rather to expect the US. Whether or not we finally accept such a cognitive conclusion, it is clear that one of the oldest and most basic assumptions about the conditioning process is open to question. We can no longer take for granted that conditioning produces an automatic connection of some response to the CS. (p. 155)

In his explanation of conditioning, Bolles follows rather closely the theory of Edward Tolman. We will have more to say about Bolles's theory after our presentation of Tolman's theory in chapter 12.

In the last few sections, we have learned that the principles governing classical conditioning are still being disputed. Basic questions such as, "What is learned during classical conditioning?" and, "Under what circumstances is it learned?" are the focus of much current research, theory, and discussion, and it looks like this will be true for some time. In any case, it is now clear that classical conditioning is much more complex than was realized before. Rather than attempting to determine which account of classical conditioning is the correct one, it seems that it would be more accurate to conclude that all accounts accurately explain some aspect of classical conditioning. It seems reasonable to conclude that when the entire story is told, aspects of classical conditioning will be found to depend upon predictability of cues, memory processes, the formation of expectancies, attentional processes, and the automatic formation of associations when there is a contingent relationship between CSs and UCSs.

THE BIOLOGICAL BOUNDARIES OF LEARNING

Originally, it was believed that any stimulus that an organism could detect would become a CS if it was presented shortly before the onset of a UCS. As we have seen, this belief has been challenged by such individuals as Egger and Miller, Kamin,

Rescorla, Mackintosh, Bolles, and Seligman. In this section, we will review evidence that casts further doubt on the contention that classical conditioning will occur automatically if any stimulus is paired with a UCS. As we saw in chapter 5, there is growing recognition that the genetic endowment of an organism must be taken into consideration in any learning experiment. The Brelands' concept of instinctual drift demonstrated the importance of instinctive response tendencies in the operant conditioning situation. The importance of genetically determined tendencies has also been found in the classical conditioning situation. For example, Seligman (1970) maintains that some species learn associations more easily than other species do because they are biologically prepared to do so. Likewise, for some species an association may be difficult to learn because they are biologically **contraprepared** to learn them. Thus, where an association falls on the **prepared–contraprepared continuum** will determine how easily it will be learned.

A study by Wilcoxon, Dragoin, and Kral (1971) exemplifies Seligman's concept of **preparedness.** In their study, rats and quail were given blue, salty water which was treated to make them sick. After the experience of drinking the water and becoming ill, both species were offered a choice between blue water or salty water. The rats avoided the salty water whereas the quail avoided the blue water. This finding reflects the fact that rats rely on taste in an eating (or drinking) situation and quail rely on visual cues. Thus each species formed an association in accordance with its genetic makeup. In other words, although the UCS (treated blue, salty water) and the UCR (illness) were the same for both species, each species selected a CS in accordance with its genetic endowment. For the rats, the taste of salt became the CS, whereas for the quail, the color blue was the CS. In Seligman's terms, the rats were more biologically prepared to make the salt-illness association than were the quail, but the quail were more prepared to make the blue-illness association.

A series of experiments run by Garcia and his colleagues also give credence to the contention that genetic endowment influences what associations are made by an organism. Whereas the research of Wilcoxon, Dragoin, and Kral (1971) demonstrates that different associations will be optimal for different species, Garcia's research indicates that within a species certain associations will be easier to form than others because of the genetic endowment of that species. For example, Garcia and Koelling (1966) offered thirsty rats the opportunity to drink under four conditions. One group was offered bright, noisy water, and drinking it was immediately followed by an electric shock to the feet. The bright, noisy water was created by attaching an electrode to the drinking tube in a way that set off flashing lights and loud clicking sounds when the organism touched the water. A second group was offered the bright, noisy water, but instead of being shocked for drinking they were injected with lithium chloride, which induces nausea. A third group was given water without the flashing lights and clicking sounds but with the taste of saccharin; these animals, like those in the first group, were shocked through the feet immediately after drinking the saccharin solution. A fourth group was given the saccharin solution and then was made ill by an injection of lithium chloride.

Garcia and Koelling (1966) found that animals in Group 1 developed an aversion to bright, noisy water, whereas animals in Group 2 did not. In addition, animals in Group 3 did not develop an aversion to saccharin flavored water, whereas animals in Group 4 did develop an aversion to the water. The experimental design and the results of the experiment can be summarized as follows:

Group 1: Bright, noisy water → shock: Developed an aversion to the water

Group 2: Bright, noisy water → nausea: No aversion to the water

Group 3: Saccharin Solution → shock: No aversion to saccharin

Group 4: Saccharin Solution → nausea: Developed an aversion to saccharin

It can be seen that bright, noisy water became an effective CS when paired with shock, but not when it was paired with nausea. Likewise, the taste of saccharin was an effective CS when paired with nausea, but not when it was paired with shock. Garcia and Koelling (1966) explained their results by saying that there was a natural relationship between external events and the pain that the animals experienced. In other words, the pain was coming from "out there" and therefore the animals searched for an external predictor of that pain, which in this case was the lights and noise associated with drinking. On the other hand, nausea comes from something which is ingested and not experienced externally. Therefore, the animals associated the taste of saccharin (which is internal) and not the bright, noisy water (which is external) with nausea. To use Seligman's terminology, we can say that the rats were biologically prepared to form an association between bright, noisy water and pain, but not prepared to form an association between bright, noisy water and nausea. Likewise, the animals were biologically prepared to form an association between the taste of saccharin and nausea, but they were not biologically prepared to form an association between the taste of saccharin and pain.

Although the Garcia and Koelling experiment seems to follow classical conditioning procedures, it presents a few problems when the results are interpreted as classical conditioning phenomena. First, the time delay between the CS (the taste of saccharin) and the UCS (nausea) greatly exceeds the time interval considered necessary for classical conditioning. The interval between the time an animal tastes a substance and then experiences illness can be several hours. Second, it is repeatedly found that a strong taste aversion can develop after only a few (sometimes only one) pairings of a substance and nausea. Ordinarily it takes many pairings between a CS and a UCS to produce a conditioned response (CR). Sometimes when strong punishment is used, conditioning has been found to take place in one trial, but never when the interval between the CS and the UCS is as long as it typically is in taste aversion studies. Third, although taste aversions develop after long time delays and, in some cases in just one trial, they are extremely resistant to extinction. Usually, resistance to extinction goes up as the number of pairings between the CS and the UCS goes up, but taste aversions seem to violate this principle.

Thus, taste aversions are formed rapidly and they last a long time, and these facts seem directly related to an organism's survival. It seems that if an organism is biologically prepared to form any associations, they would be those conducive to survival and that appears to be the case with the development of taste aversions. The formation of taste aversions has so many unique features that the phenomenon has been given a name (Bolles, 1979): "The remarkable facility with which rats (and a number of other animals) learn about the relationship between the taste of a particular food substance and a subsequent illness we shall call the 'Garcia effect'" (p. 167).

Does the **Garcia effect** have any practical implications? The answer seems to be yes. Wild coyotes have long been a problem in the western United States because they prey on lambs and other livestock. This has led to a debate between farmers and ranchers who often want to kill the coyotes and environmentalists who want to save the coyotes for ecological reasons. Gustavson, Garcia, Hankins, and Rusiniak (1974) have shown that the Garcia effect can be used to control the eating habits of coyotes. In their study, three coyotes were fed lamb flesh treated with lithium chloride and three were fed rabbit flesh treated with the same substance. After only one or two experiences with the treated flesh the coyotes avoided attacking the kind of animals whose flesh had made them ill but showed no avoidance of the other type of flesh. That is, those coyotes that ate treated lamb flesh avoided sheep but ate rabbits, and those coyotes that ate treated rabbit flesh avoided rabbits but ate sheep. Thus, it appears that we have a straightforward way of controlling the eating habits of predators that satisfies the wishes of both ranchers and farmers and the environmentalists.

The findings of instinctual drift, autoshaping, and the preparedness continuum are currently causing learning theorists to recognize that genetically determined response tendencies are powerful determinants of behavior and, therefore, must be taken into consideration when attempting to modify behavior using either instrumental or classical conditioning principles. We will have more to say about how innate behavior patterns can influence the outcome of learning experiments when we discuss Bolles's theory of learning in chapter 12.

JOHN B. WATSON'S EXPERIMENT WITH LITTLE ALBERT

Before discussing the clinical applications of classical conditioning in the next section, we will review **J. B. Watson's** famous experiment with an infant named Albert. We saw in chapter 3 that Watson, the founder of the school of **behaviorism,** felt that psychology should be purged of all mentalistic concepts and explanations of human behavior based on instinct.

Personality was, to Watson, a collection of conditioned reflexes. Human emotion was a product of both heredity and experience. According to Watson, we inherit three emotions—fear, rage, and love. Through the conditioning process, these three basic emotions become attached to different things for different people. Speech was behavior that resulted from the movement of the muscles in the throat. Thinking was implicit or subvocal speech. During overt speech, the vocal apparatus responded with vigor; during thinking, the same apparatus is involved but its movements are minute. Speech could indeed be studied but it had to be studied as behavior and not as a tool used to investigate "inner experience."

Watson was an extreme environmental determinist. He held the position that all we come equipped with at birth is a few reflexes and a few basic emotions, and through classical conditioning, these reflexes become paired with a variety of stimuli. He emphatically denied that we are born with any mental abilities or predispositions. In this, Watson's thinking followed that of John Locke, who said that the mind was a blank slate at birth. The extreme to which Watson was willing to carry this position is exemplified by his following famous (or infamous) statement (1926): "Give me a dozen healthy infants, well-formed, and my own specified world to bring them up in and I'll guarantee to take any one at random and train him to become any type of specialist I might select—doctor, lawyer, artist, merchant, chief, and yes, even beggarman and thief, regardless of his talents, penchants, tendencies, abilities, vocations, and race of his ancestors" (p. 10).

To demonstrate how inborn emotional reflexes become conditioned to neutral stimuli, Watson and Rosalie Rayner (1920) performed an experiment on an 11-month-old infant named Albert. In addition to Albert, the other ingredients in the experiment were a white rat, a steel bar, and a hammer. At the onset of the study, Albert showed no fear of the rat. In fact, he reached out and tried to touch it. During the initial part of the experiment, when Albert saw the rat and reached for it, the experimenter took the hammer and struck the steel bar behind the infant, making a loud noise. In response to the noise, Albert "jumped violently and fell forward." Again Albert saw the rat and reached for it, and again, just as his hand touched the rat, the bar was struck making a loud noise. Again Albert jumped violently and began to whimper. Because of Albert's emotional state, the experiment was suspended for one week so Albert would not become too disturbed.

After a week, the rat was again presented to Albert. This time Albert was very cautious of the animal and watched it very carefully. At one point, when the rat came into contact with his hand, Albert withdrew his hand immediately. There were several more pairings between the rat and the sound and eventually Albert developed a strong fear of the rat. Now when the rat was presented to Albert again, he began to cry and "almost instantly he turned sharply to the left, fell over, raised himself on all fours and began to crawl away . . . rapidly" (1920, p. 5).

It was also shown that Albert's fear generalized to a variety of objects that were not feared at the onset of the experiment: a rabbit, a dog, a fur coat, cotton, and a Santa Claus mask. Thus, Watson showed that our emotional reactions can be rearranged through classical conditioning. In the experiment above, the loud noise was the UCS, fear produced by the noise was the UCR, the rat was the CS, and the fear of the rat was the CR. Albert's fear of all white and furry objects showed that generalization also took place.

Bregman's Replication of Watson's Experiment. In 1934, O. E. Bregman replicated Watson's experiment and found that a child's fear could indeed be conditioned to a CS, but that such conditioning took place only under certain circumstances. Bregman found that conditioning took place only if the CS was a live animal (as it was in Watson's experiment), but *no conditioning occurred if the CS was an inanimate object,* such as a block, a bottle, or even a wooden animal. Bregman's findings were inconsistent with Pavlov's and Watson's claim that the nature of a CS should be irrelevant to the conditioning process. On the other hand, her findings were consistent with Seligman's contention that some associations are easier to form than others because of the biological preparedness of the organism. In this case, Seligman (1972) says that since animals have the potential to do harm, humans are biologically prepared to suspect them and therefore learn with relative ease to fear or avoid them.

Eliminating Conditioned Fears. Watson had demonstrated that an innate emotion, such as fear, could be "transferred" to stimuli that did not originally elicit that emotion, and that the mechanism for the transfer was classical conditioning. This was an extremely important finding even if it would be demonstrated later that conditioning was easier with some stimuli than with others. If fears are learned, it should be possible to unlearn or extinguish them. Unfortunately, Watson and Rayner never removed Albert's fears because his mother removed him from the hospital where the experiment was being conducted shortly after fear was instilled (Harris, 1979, p. 152). Watson felt that his research had shown how learned fears develop and no further research of that kind was necessary. Instead, his strategy was to find a child who had already developed a fear, and then attempt to eliminate it. Watson, now working with Mary Cover Jones, found such a child—a 3-year-old named Peter who was intensively frightened of, among other things, rats, rabbits, fur coats, frogs, and fish. Hergenhahn (1986) summarizes the efforts of Watson and Jones to eliminate Peter's fears:

> Watson and Jones first tried showing Peter other children playing fearlessly with objects that he was frightened of, and there was some improvement. (This is a technique called modeling, which Bandura and his colleagues employ today.) [See chapter 13 of this text.] At this point, Peter came down with scarlet fever and had to go to the hospital. Following recovery, he and his nurse were attacked by a dog on their way home from the hospital, and all of Peter's fears returned in magnified form. Watson and Jones decided to try to uncondition Peter. Peter ate lunch in a room 40 feet long. One day as Peter was eating lunch, a rabbit in a wire cage was displayed far enough away from him so that Peter was not disturbed. The researchers made a mark on the floor at that point. Each day they moved the rabbit a bit closer to Peter, until one day it was sitting beside Peter as Peter ate. Finally, Peter was able to eat with one hand and play with the rabbit with the other. The results generalized, and most of Peter's other fears were also eliminated or reduced. This is one of the first examples of what we now call *behavior therapy*. In 1924 Jones published the results of the research with Peter, and in 1974 she published more of the details surrounding the research. (pp. 251–252)

The procedure used by Watson and Jones to eliminate Peter's fear is quite similar to a procedure called systematic desensitization that was developed much later. We will consider systematic desensitization in the next section.

Watson's Theory of Learning. It is interesting to note that although Watson did as much as anyone to introduce Pavlovian psychology to the United States, he never fully accepted Pavlovian principles. For example, Watson did not believe that conditioning depended upon reinforcement. For Watson, learning occurred simply because events followed each other closely in time. Classical conditioning occurs, not because the UCS reinforces the CS, but because the CS and the UCS follow each other in close succession. Also, the more often events occur together, the stronger will be the association between them. Watson, then, accepted *only* the ancient laws of contiguity and frequency. For him, other learning principles were either mentalistic, like Thorndike's law of effect, or unnecessary, like Pavlov's notion of reinforcement. In the next chapter we will review Guthrie's theory of learning and see that it is very similar to Watson's theory.

FURTHER APPLICATIONS OF CLASSICAL CONDITIONING TO CLINICAL PSYCHOLOGY

Extinction. Clinical practices based on classical conditioning assume that since behavior disorders or bad habits are learned, they can be unlearned or can be replaced by more positive behaviors. Let us assume that smoking and the excessive drinking of alcohol are behavior disorders, or at least bad habits. In such cases, the taste of alcohol or cigarettes can be considered CSs and the physiological effects of alcohol or nicotine are the UCSs. After many CS-UCS pairings, experiencing the CSs alone produce immediate pleasure (CR). One possible way to eliminate these habits is to present the CSs without presenting the UCSs, thus causing extinction. Schwartz (1984) points out the problems with this procedure:

> While in principle this procedure should work there are a few practical problems with it. First, extinction takes time; a number of trials are required before conditioned responding stops. Second, it is not easy to produce substances that taste just like cigarettes or liquor but contain no nicotine or alcohol. Third, if after treatment the person should happen to smoke or drink, the original taste —US pairing will be reintroduced and conditioning will quickly redevelop. For practical effectiveness, a procedure more powerful than simple extinction is necessary. (p. 132)

Counterconditioning. A procedure more powerful than simple extinction is **counterconditioning.** In counterconditioning the CS is paired with a UCS other than the original one. For example, a person is allowed to smoke or drink and then is given a drug which produces nausea. With repeated pairings, the taste of cigarettes or alcohol will produce conditioned nausea which in turn will create an aversion to smoking or drinking. For example, Mount, Payton, Ellis, and Barnes (1976) injected anectine into the arm of alcoholic clients immediately after they drank a glass of their favorite alcoholic beverage. Anectine produces a paralyzing effect on the respiratory system which most people report as a frightening experience. After such treatment, only one of the nine individuals involved in this study started drinking again. Although counterconditioning has been found to be successful in a number of cases, the benefits from the procedure are often only temporary. Schwartz (1984) says:

> This is not entirely surprising. As we indicated in discussing a possible extinction procedure, the problem with counterconditioning is that in the person's natural environment liquor or cigarette tastes will again be paired with their usual physiological effects. So unless the treatment effectively eliminates any tendency to reingest the target substance, we can see how the original conditioned responses will eventually be reestablished. Moreover if the person continues to inhabit the very same environment in which the addiction arose in the first place, it would be no surprise if whatever influences initially contributed to the addiction reasserted themselves, making readdiction likely. (p. 134)

Flooding. A major problem in treating phobias is the fact that individuals avoid or escape from frightening experiences. Since extinction is an active process (the CS must be presented and *not* followed by the UCS), avoiding fear-producing stimuli prevents extinction from occurring. If, for example, a person has a dog phobia, he or she never experiences a dog long enough to learn whether it is safe or not. Any CS that elicits fear will cause the organism to escape or avoid it, and such behavior prevents the organism from learning that the CS may no longer be associated with an aversive UCS. So how can such a phobia be extinguished? In the natural environment it probably never would be. The only possible way of extinguishing a phobia is to force the organism to remain in the presence of the CS long enough to learn that nothing negative will follow. When such forced extinction is used to eliminate phobias, it is called **flooding.** Rimm and Masters (1979) report that flooding is a relatively fast way of eliminating phobias but the technique produces results that are variable. Using the flooding procedure, some individuals improve but some get worse. That some individuals become worse is not surprising in light of the fact that they are forced to experience something that they had spent a good deal of their lives fearing and thus avoiding. Also not surprising is the fact that client dropout rates are higher when flooding is used compared to the dropout rates for systematic desensitization, the therapeutic technique that we shall consider next.

Systematic Desensitization. One of the most thorough attempts to apply classical conditioning principles to psychotherapy was undertaken by Joseph Wolpe (1958) who developed a therapeutic technique referred to as **systematic desensitization.** Wolpe's technique, which is used primarily for treating clients with phobias, involves three phases. The first phase consists of developing an **anxiety hierarchy,** which is done by taking a sequence of related anxiety-provoking events and ordering them from those that produce the greatest amount of anxiety to those that produce the least amount. Let us say that a person has an extreme fear of flying in an airplane. Such a person's anxiety hierarchy may look something like this:

1. Flying in an airplane
2. Sitting in an airplane while it is on the ground with its engines running
3. Sitting in an airplane while it is on the ground with its engines turned off

4. Being in close proximity of an airplane

5. Seeing an airplane at a distance

6. Being in an airport

7. Hearing the sound of airplane engines

8. Talking about being on an airplane

9. Planning a trip without airplanes involved

10. Hearing others plan a trip without airplanes involved

In the second phase of his procedure, Wolpe teaches his clients to relax. He teaches them how to reduce muscle tension and, in general, how it feels when one is not experiencing anxiety. In the third phase, the client first experiences deep relaxation and then is asked to imagine the weakest item on the anxiety hierarchy. While experiencing this item the client is again asked to induce relaxation. When this is accomplished, the client is asked to ponder the next item on the list, and so forth through the entire list. It is assumed by Wolpe that if each time an item on the list is experienced along with relaxation (the absence of anxiety) a little bit of the phobic response associated with the terminal item on the list extinguishes. This procedure allows the client to gradually approximate the situation that he or she was too frightened to ponder previously. Such an anxiety-provoking experience must be approached gradually and with a great deal of care; otherwise the client will be unable to ponder the feared item, and therefore fear of it will never extinguish. As we have seen, one problem that a person with a phobia has is that he or she avoids the very experiences that will eliminate the phobia. In other words a person with a flying phobia typically avoids flying and all related experiences; the person with sex phobia avoids sexual and related experiences; and so on. If a phobia is ever going to extinguish, the feared item must be experienced in the absence of anxiety.

After this cognitive extinction has occurred it is hoped that the person will be able to repeat the steps in the real world. After systematic desensitization, the client should be able to deal with his or her fear (or previous fear) more rationally, and hopefully, in this case, fly in an airplane without experiencing dishabilitating anxiety.

Whereas Wolpe had his clients move slowly closer to feared objects psychologically, Watson and Jones slowly moved a feared object physically closer to a child. Except for this difference the two approaches to extinguishing fears have much in common.

We will compare the effectiveness of Wolpe's technique of systematic desensitization with that of other techniques used to treat phobias in chapter 13.

DISCUSSION QUESTIONS

1. Design a cigarette commercial utilizing the principles of classical conditioning. How would this commercial differ from one based upon the principles of instrumental conditioning?

 2. Differentiate between classical conditioning and Thorndike's notion of associative shifting.

 3. Give a few examples of your own conditioned reflexes.

 4. Briefly describe the following: acquisition of a conditioned response, extinction, spontaneous recovery, generalization, discrimination, and higher order conditioning.

 5. Briefly describe Pavlov's physiological explanation of conditioning, generalization, and discrimination.

 6. What observations did Egger and Miller make that were contrary to Pavlov's explanation of classical conditioning?

 7. According to Pavlov, what determines how we respond to the environment at any given time?

 8. Discuss the major differences and similarities between instrumental and classical conditioning.

 9. Provide evidence that CRs are not necessarily small versions of UCRs.

10. First define overshadowing and blocking and then discuss how the phenomena are contrary to what the law of contiguity would predict.

11. Describe how conditioned emotional responses (CERs) are used to index the strength of CS-UCS associations.

12. What assumptions about conditioning does the Rescorla–Wagner theory make about the nature of classical conditioning?

13. How does the Rescorla–Wagner theory explain blocking?

14. Explain the distinction that Rescorla makes between contingency and contiguity as a necessary condition for classical conditioning to occur.

15. What experimental arrangement produces what Rescorla calls a truly random control condition? Why, according to Rescorla, is a truly random control group necessary in classical conditioning studies?

16. Describe what kind of conditioned behavior is produced by positive and negative contingencies.

17. What, according to Seligman, is learned helplessness? Describe the circumstances under which learned helplessness develops.

18. How, according to Seligman, can learned helplessness be avoided?

19. Discuss Mackintosh's theory of classical conditioning based on attention. Include in your answer Mackintosh's explanation of blocking.

20. Discuss Kamin and Wagner's theory of classical conditioning based on surprisingness. Include in your answer Kamin and Wagner's explanation of blocking.

21. Discuss Bolles's theory of classical conditioning based on expectancy formation. Why does Bolles feel that his theory is opposed to those theories of classical conditioning in the associationistic tradition?

22. What is the Garcia effect?

23. Summarize the problems involved in trying to explain the development of taste aversions as a classical conditioning phenomenon.

24. How can the Garcia effect be used to change the eating habits of predators?

25. If the Garcia effect exists on the human level, why do you suppose so many individuals continue to smoke or consume alcohol even though their initial experience with smoking or drinking alcohol made them extremely ill?

26. Explain Seligman's concepts of preparedness and contrapreparedness.

27. Explain emotional development from J. B. Watson's point of view.

28. Describe the procedure used by Watson and Jones to extinguish Peter's fear of rabbits.

29. Explain how extinction and counterconditioning could be used as therapeutic techniques and then explain why these techniques have limited usefulness.

30. Discuss flooding as a therapeutic technique. Include in your answer the problems associated with flooding.

31. Summarize Wolpe's therapeutic technique of systematic desensitization.

CHAPTER HIGHLIGHTS

Anxiety hierarchy. The initial stage of Wolpe's therapeutic technique of systematic desensitization which involves taking a series of related anxiety experiences and ordering them from the experience that causes the greatest amount of anxiety to the experience that causes the least amount of anxiety.

Backward conditioning. An experimental arrangement in which the conditioned stimulus is presented to the organism after the unconditioned stimulus is presented.

Behaviorism. The school of psychology started by J. B. Watson. The behaviorist believes that the proper subject matter for psychology is behavior, not mental events.

Blocking (also called the blocking effect). When one CS (A) is paired with UCS, it will become conditioned to that UCS. If, after initial conditioning, CS (A) is paired with a second CS (B) and presented to the organism as a compound stimulus CS (AB), it is found that little or no conditioning occurs to CS (B). It is as if the initial conditioning to CS (A), somehow blocked any conditioning to CS (B).

Conditioned emotional response (CER). A procedure used to determine the strength of a relationship between a CS and a UCS which combines operant or instrumental conditioning and classical conditioning. In Phase 1, animals learn an instrumental or operant response to the point that it is emitted at a steady rate. In Phase 2, the classical conditioning phase, a CS is paired with a UCS a number of times. In Phase 3, as animals are again performing the instrumental or operant response, the CS from Phase 2 is presented and its effect on rate of responding is noted. Depending upon how the CS and UCS were paired in Phase 2, it is found that presenting the CS in Phase 3 facilitates, inhibits, or has no effect on the rate with which the instrumental or operant behavior is emitted.

Conditioned response (CR) (also called conditioned reflex). A response that is made to a stimulus not originally associated with the response. For example, salivation to the sound of a tone is a conditioned response because an organism would not ordinarily salivate to the sound of a tone.

Conditioned stimulus (CS). A stimulus that before conditioning does not cause an organism to respond in any particular way. Before conditioning, the stimulus is a neutral stimulus. After conditioning, however, the conditioned stimulus elicits a conditioned response.

Conditioned suppression. The inhibition of a conditioned response caused by conditioned emotional responses (CERs).

Contrapreparedness. The fact that an organism's genetic endowment makes it difficult for certain associations to be formed.

Cortical mosaic. The pattern of excitation and inhibition that constitutes the activity of the cortex at any given moment.

Counterconditioning. The technique used to eliminate undesirable behavior by which a CS is paired with a UCS other than the one that originally reinforced the undesirable behavior. For example, if a CS was originally followed by shock, thus producing fear, the CS could not be paired with food, thus producing a response incompatible with fear.

Discrimination. Learning to respond to one stimulus but not to other stimuli although they may be related to the first. For example, through discrimination training a tone of 500 cps elicits a conditioned response, whereas a tone of 490 cps does not.

Dynamic stereotype. A cortical mapping of events consistently occurring in the environment. A stable environment comes to have neurological representation on the cortex.

Excitation. An increase in brain activity. A stimulus that causes excitation is called a positive stimulus.

Extinction. The procedure whereby a conditioned stimulus is presented but is not followed by reinforcement. Under these circumstances, the magnitude of the conditioned response gradually becomes smaller. When a conditioned response is no longer elicited by a conditioned stimulus, the conditioned response is said to have been extinguished.

First signal system. Physical events in the environment and the responses that they produce.

Flooding. Since organisms typically avoid experiencing those things that frighten them, it is unlikely that unjustified fears would ever extinguish naturally. Using the technique of flooding, the organism is forced to experience feared CSs long enough to learn that an aversive experience will not follow, thus creating the conditions necessary for extinction.

Forward conditioning. An experimental arrangement in which the conditioned stimulus is presented before the unconditioned stimulus.

Garcia effect. The name given to the observation that animals form taste aversions easily and in apparent contradiction to several principles of classical conditioning.

Generalization. The tendency for an organism to respond not only to the specific stimulus it was trained on, but also to other related stimuli. For example, if an organism was trained with a 500 cps tone as a conditioned stimulus, such tones as 600, 550, and 490 cps will also tend to elicit conditioned responses.

Higher order conditioning. After classical conditioning has taken place, a second conditioned stimulus is paired with the first conditioned stimulus. After a number of such pairings, the second conditioned stimulus can also elicit a conditioned response. This is called second order conditioning. Once the second conditioned stimulus has the power to elicit a conditioned response, it can be paired with a third conditioned stimulus to produce third order conditioning.

Information value of a stimulus. The ability of a stimulus to act as a signal to an organism that a significant event is about to occur. For example, a stimulus that signals the occurrence of food for a hungry animal has information value.

Inhibition. A decrease in brain activity. A stimulus that causes inhibition is called a negative stimulus.

Irradiation. The tendency for excitation or inhibition in a specific area of the brain to spill over into neighboring brain regions.

Learned helplessness. When organisms learn that their behavior is independent of outcomes, they sometimes give up trying. Such animals become passive, withdrawn, and seem to accept whatever happens to them. With humans, learned helplessness is often associated with the emotional state of depression.

Orienting reflex. The tendency for an organism to attend to and explore a novel stimulus as it occurs in its environment.

Overshadowing. The observation that the most salient component of a compound stimulus will become conditioned to a UCS and the weaker component will not. It is as if a dominant component of a compound CS overshadows the weaker component.

Preparedness. The fact that an organism's genetic endowment makes it easy for certain associations to be formed.

Preparedness–contrapreparedness continuum. Seligman's observation that each CS falls somewhere on a biologically determined continuum, and where it falls on that continuum determines how easily it can be conditioned to a UCS.

Primary reinforcer. Something related to survival such as food, water, or sex. Pavlov believed that all conditioning ultimately depends upon primary reinforcement. In classical conditioning, the primary reinforcer is the unconditioned stimulus.

Secondary reinforcer. A previously neutral stimulus that takes on reinforcing properties through its close association with primary reinforcement. After conditioning has taken place, a conditioned stimulus must necessarily be a secondary reinforcer.

Second signal system. Language. The symbols humans use in communication. Since responses can be conditioned to symbols, they can influence human behavior. The second signal system, which is peculiarly human, makes human behavior much more complex than the behavior of other animals.

Semantic generalization. Generalization to symbols that have a meaning similar to the meaning of the conditioned stimulus used during training, although the physical characteristics of symbols may be totally dissimilar to those of the conditioned stimulus. For example, if human subjects are taught to salivate when they see the number 10, they will also salivate when they see $8|\overline{80}$ or $\sqrt{100}$. In semantic generalization, it is meaning that determines how much generalization occurs rather than the physical similarity between stimuli.

Spontaneous recovery. When a conditioned response is no longer elicited by a conditioned stimulus, extinction is said to have taken place. Following a delay after extinction, the conditioned stimulus again elicits conditioned responses, although there were no further pairings between the conditioned stimulus and the unconditioned stimulus. The reappearance of the conditioned response after extinction has taken place is called spontaneous recovery.

Systematic desensitization. A therapeutic technique developed by Wolpe whereby a phobia is extinguished by having a client approach the feared experience one small step at a time while relaxing after each step.

Truly random control group. Rescorla has shown that the only true control condition for classical conditioning studies is one where there is no predictive relationship between a CS and a UCS. In other words, in a truly random control condition, a UCS precedes and follows a CS an equal number of times. Rescorla says that in such a condition there is no contingency between the CS and the UCS.

Unconditioned response (UCR). The natural and automatic response that is elicited when an unconditioned stimulus is presented to an organism. Withdrawing when stuck by a pin, salivating when food or acid is placed in the mouth, and the constriction of the pupil of the eye when light is shone into it, are all examples of unconditioned responses.

Unconditioned stimulus (UCS). A stimulus that causes a natural and automatic response from the organism. An object that causes pain to a certain part of the body will cause the organism to automatically withdraw from the source of pain. Pain, therefore, is an unconditioned stimulus. Shining a light into the pupil of the eye will cause the pupil to automatically constrict; the light, therefore, is an unconditioned stimulus.

Watson, J. B. The founder of the school of behaviorism. Watson relied heavily on Pavlov's theory of learning in his explanation of human behavior. Watson believed that, except for a few basic emotions, human behavior was learned. Therefore, he believed that by controlling the learning process it is possible to control human personality. For this reason, Watson was considered an extreme environmental determinist.

8

Edwin Ray Guthrie

Guthrie was born in 1886 and died in 1959. He was professor of psychology at the University of Washington from 1914 until his retirement in 1956. His most basic work was *The Psychology of Learning,* published in 1935 and revised in 1952. His style of writing is easy to follow, humorous, and involves many homespun anecdotes to exemplify his ideas. There are no technical terms or mathematical equations, and he firmly believed that his theory—or any scientific theory for that matter—should be stated so that it would be understandable to college freshmen. He placed a great emphasis on practical application of his ideas and in this regard was very much like Thorndike and Skinner. He was not really an experimentalist himself, although he certainly had an experimental outlook and orientation. He, along with Horton, performed only one experiment related to his theory of learning, and we will discuss that experiment later on. He was, however, clearly a behaviorist. As a matter of fact, he felt theorists like Thorndike, Skinner, Hull, Pavlov, and Watson were too subjective, and that by carefully applying the law of parsimony, it was possible to explain all learning phenomena by using only one principle. As we shall see below, this one principle was one of Aristotle's laws of association. It is for this reason that we place Guthrie's behavioristic theory within the associationistic paradigm.

MAJOR THEORETICAL NOTIONS

The One Law of Learning

In general, most learning theories can be thought of as attempts to determine the rules by which stimuli and responses become associated. Guthrie felt that the rules that had been generated by theorists like Thorndike and Pavlov were unnecessarily complicated and in their place he proposed one law of learning, the **law of contiguity,** which he stated as follows (1952): "A combination of stimuli which has accompanied a movement will on its recurrence tend to be followed by that movement. Note that nothing is here said about 'confirmatory waves' or reinforcement or pleasant effects" (p. 23).

There is nothing new about the law of contiguity as a principle of learning. In fact, as we noted in chapter 3, it goes all the way back to Aristotle's laws of association. Guthrie, however, made the law of contiguity the cornerstone of his unique theory of learning.

Another way of stating the law of contiguity is to say that if you did something in a given situation, the next time that you are in that situation, you will tend to do the same thing. In his last publication before he died, Guthrie (1959) revised his law of contiguity to read, "What is being noticed becomes a signal for what is being done" (p. 186). This was Guthrie's way of recognizing the enormous number of stimuli that confront an organism at any given time and the fact that the organism cannot possibly form associations with all of them. Rather, the organism responds selectively to only a small proportion of the stimuli confronting it and it is that proportion that becomes associated with whatever response is being made. One can note the similarity between Guthrie's thinking and Thorndike's concept of "prepo-

Edwin Ray Guthrie. (Courtesy of Peter M. Guthrie)

tency of elements" which also stated that organisms respond selectively to different aspects of the environment.

Guthrie explained why, although the law of contiguity may be true, prediction of behavior will always be probabilistic, as follows (1952):

> Although the principle as it has just been stated is short and simple, it will not be clear without a considerable amount of elaboration. The word "tend" is used because behavior is at any time subject to a great variety of conditions. Conflicting "tendencies" or incompatible "tendencies" are always present. The outcome of any one stimulus or stimulus pattern cannot be predicted with certainty because there are other stimulus patterns present. We may express this by saying that the final behavior is caused by the total situation, but we may not, in making this statement, flatter ourselves that we have done more than offer an excuse for a failure to predict. No one has recorded and no one ever will record any stimulus situation in its totality, or observed any total situation, so that to speak of it as a "cause" or even as the occasion of a bit of behavior is misleading. (p. 23)

One-Trial Learning

Another of Aristotle's laws of association was the law of frequency which stated that the strength of an association depends upon the frequency with which it has occurred. If the law of frequency is modified to refer to the association between a response which leads to a "satisfying state of affairs" and the stimulating conditions preceding the response, Thorndike, Skinner, and Hull would accept it. The more often a response is reinforced in a given situation the greater the probability of that response's being made when that situation recurs. If the association is between a CS and a UCS, Pavlov would accept the law of frequency. The greater the number of pairings between the CS and the UCS the greater is the magnitude of the conditioned response elicited by the CS.

Guthrie completely rejected the law of frequency as a learning principle. He said (1942): "*A stimulus pattern gains its full associative strength on the occasion of its first pairing with a response*" (p. 30). Thus, to Guthrie learning is the result of contiguity between a pattern of stimulation and a response, and learning is complete (the association is at full strength) after only one pairing between the stimuli and the response.

The Recency Principle

The principles of contiguity and **one-trial learning** necessitate the **recency principle,** which states: that which was done last in the presence of a set of stimuli will be that which will tend to be done when that stimulus combination next recurs. In other words, whatever we did *last* under a given set of circumstances will be what we will tend to do again if those circumstances are reencountered.

Movement-Produced Stimuli

Although Guthrie reasserted his belief in the law of contiguity throughout his career, he felt it would be misleading to think of the learned association to be exclusively between environmental stimuli and overt behavior. For example, an environmental event and the response that it produces sometimes are separated by a fairly large interval of time, and it would be difficult, therefore, to think of the two as contiguous. Guthrie solves this problem by postulating the existence of **movement-produced stimuli,** which, as the name implies, are caused by the movements of the body. If we hear a sound and turn toward it, for example, the muscles, tendons, and joints produce stimuli that are distinctly different from the external stimulation that caused us to move. The important fact about movement-produced stimuli is that they can have responses conditioned to them. That is, after a response has been initiated by an external stimulus, the body itself can produce the stimulus for the next response and that response can furnish the stimulus for the next one, and so on. Thus, the interval between the occurrence of an external stimulus and the response finally made to it is filled with movement-produced stimuli. Conditioning is still between contiguous events, but in some cases the contiguity is between movement-produced stimuli and behavior rather than between external stimuli and behavior. Guthrie gave the following example of how he believed movement-produced stimuli function (1935):

> Such a movement as listening or looking is not over like a flash or an explosion. It takes time. The movement, once started, maintains itself by the stimuli it furnishes. When the telephone bell rings we rise and make our way to the instrument. Long before we have reached the telephone the sound has ceased to act as a stimulus. We are kept in action by the stimuli from our own

movements toward the telephone. One movement starts another, that a third, the third a fourth, and so on. Our movements form series, very often stereotyped in the form of habit. *These movements and their movement-produced stimuli make possible a far-reaching extension of association or conditioning.* (p. 54)

A simplified version of the situation described in Guthrie's example could be diagrammed as follows:

External stimulation ⟶ Overt response ⟶ Movement-produced stimuli ⟶
(telephone ringing)   (e.g., turning
                        toward
                        telephone)

Overt response ⟶ Movement-produced stimuli ⟶ Overt response ⟶
(e.g., rising   (e.g., walking
from chair)   toward
                                                telephone)

Movement-produced stimuli ⟶ Overt response
                            (e.g., picking up
                             telephone)

Guthrie's contention that a response can provide stimulation for the next response is very popular among learning theorists today and is usually involved in an explanation of **chaining.**

As we have seen in chapter 5, Skinner's explanation of chaining emphasized external stimuli and their secondary reinforcing properties. In this chapter we have seen that Guthrie's explanation of chaining emphasized internal stimuli. Hull and Spence's explanation of chaining, covered in chapter 6, can be looked upon as a combination of Skinner's and Guthrie's views because it maintains that both internal and external stimulation are involved in chaining.

Why Does Practice Improve Performance?

To answer this question Guthrie differentiated between **acts** and **movements.** Movements are simple muscle contractions; acts are made up of a large number of movements. Acts are usually defined in terms of what they accomplish, that is, what change they make in the environment. As examples of acts, Guthrie lists such things as typing a letter, eating a meal, throwing a ball, reading a book, or selling a car. Guthrie and Horton explained improvement as the result of practice as follows (1946):

> We have taken the position that acts are made up of movements that result from muscular contraction, and that *it is these muscular contractions that are directly predicted by the principle of association.* We are assuming that such movements are subject to conditioning or associative learning and that this condi-

tioning is in itself an "all or none" affair, and its degree is not dependent on practice. One experience is sufficient to establish an association.

But the learning of an act does take practice. We assume that the reason for this is that the act names an end result that is attained under varied circumstances and by movements varied to suit the circumstances. Learning an act as distinguished from a movement does require practice because it requires that the proper movement has been associated with its own cues. Even so simple an act as grasping a rattle requires different movements according to the distance and direction and position of the object. One successful experience is not sufficient to equip the infant with an act because the one movement acquired on that occasion might never again be successful. (pp. 7–8)

Just as an act is made up of many movements, a skill is made up of many acts. Thus, learning a skill such as playing golf or driving a car consists of learning thousands of associations between specific stimuli and specific movements. For example, learning to putt a golf ball into the cup from 10 ft away from a certain angle under specific conditions (wind coming from a certain direction at a certain velocity, temperature is 85°, and so on) is only one of thousands of responses that constitute the game of golf. Practice allows more and more of these specific associations to be made. The same is true of driving, typing, and all other skills. Elsewhere Guthrie said (1942): "Learning occurs normally in one associative episode. The reason that long practice and many repetitions are required to establish certain skills is that these really require many specific movements to be attached to many different stimulus situations. A skill is not simple habit, but a large collection of habits that achieve a certain result in many and varied circumstances" (p. 59).

To summarize, a skill is made up of many acts, and acts are made up of many movements. The relationship between one set of stimuli and one movement is learned at full strength in one trial, but this does not bring about proficiency at a skill. For example, driving a car, typewriting, or playing baseball are all very complicated skills consisting of a large number of stimulus-response associations, and any one of these bonds or associations is learned at full strength in one trial. But it takes time and practice for all the necessary associations to be made. Learning to type the letter A while looking at an A on a written sheet of paper alongside the typewriter might be considered a specific stimulus-response (S-R) association. Looking at the letter B and typing the letter B is another specific association, as is looking at and typing the letter C. These specific associations must be built up for the entire alphabet, and then for the numbers, and then for the capital letters, and finally for the various symbols that occur on the typewriter. Also, the typist must learn to make these responses under a wide variety of circumstances, such as under varying lighting and temperature conditions, from different angles of seeing the material, and on different kinds of paper. When all these responses have been learned, we say the person has become a proficient typist. Thus, a skill such as typing involves an enormously large number of specific S-R connections each of which is learned in a single trial.

According to Guthrie, the reason Thorndike found systematic improvement through successive trials was that he was studying the learning of a skill, not the learning of individual movements. Guthrie and Horton said (1946):

> We believe that when the puzzle-box situation varies indefinitely, as it did in the Thorndike box with the hanging loop, it is necessary for the cat to establish a large repertoire of specific escape movements adjusted to the specific differences in the situation. In other words, the cat establishes a skill, rather than a stereotyped habit. But the skill is made up of many specific habits. The gradual reduction of time reported by Thorndike is a consequence of the varied situation confronting the cat. (p. 41)

Whether or not learning occurs after one experience, as Guthrie believed, or in small increments, as Thorndike believed, is still a controversial issue and one which we will discuss in more detail in the next chapter.

Nature of Reinforcement

What is the place of reinforcement in Guthrie's theory? On this point Guthrie took issue with Thorndike, who, as you remember, made the revised law of effect the cornerstone of his theory. According to Thorndike, when a response led to a satisfying state of affairs, its probability of recurring increased. Guthrie felt the law of effect was completely unnecessary. For Guthrie, reinforcement was merely a mechanical arrangement which he felt could be explained by his one law of learning. According to Guthrie, *reinforcement changes the stimulating conditions and thereby prevents unlearning*. For example, in a puzzle box, the last thing the animal does before receiving a reinforcer is to move a pole or pull on a ring, which allows it to escape from the box. Therefore, the response that allowed the animal to escape—moving the pole, in this case—changed the entire pattern of stimuli that the animal experienced. According to the recency principle, when the animal is placed back into the puzzle box, it will tend to move the pole again. In other words, being released from the puzzle box after moving the pole preserves the association between being in the puzzle box and moving the pole. In fact, the last response that was made in the puzzle box will be the response the animal makes when it is again placed into the box, *regardless of what that response was*. Guthrie and Horton (1946) said:

> In our opinion the second occasion tends to repeat the behavior of the first, errors and all, except in so far as remaining in the puzzle box for a long time tends to establish new responses to the puzzle-box situation. *The reason for the remarkable preservation of the end action leading to escape is that this action removes the cat from the situation and hence allows no new responses to become attached to the puzzle-box situation.* Escape protects the end action from relearning. (p. 39)

Elsewhere (1940) Guthrie said:

> The position taken in this paper is that the animal learns to escape with its first escape. This learning is protected from forgetting because the escape removes

the animal from the situation which has then no chance to acquire new associations.

. . . what encountering the food does is not to intensify a previous item of behavior but to protect that item from being unlearned. The whole situation and action of the animal is so changed by the food that the pre-food situation is shielded from new associations. These new associations can not be established in the absence of the box interior, and in the absence of the behavior that preceded latch-opening. (pp. 144–145)

The Guthrie–Horton Experiment

Guthrie and Horton carefully observed approximately 800 escapes by cats from a puzzle box. Their observations were reported in a small book entitled *Cats in a Puzzle Box* (1946). The puzzle box they used was very similar to the apparatus that Thorndike used in his selecting and connecting experiments. Guthrie and Horton used a large number of cats as subjects but they noted that each cat learned to escape from the puzzle box in its own peculiar way. The particular response learned by a particular animal was the one the animal had hit upon just prior to being released from the box. Since that exact response tended to be repeated the next time the animal was placed into the puzzle box, it was referred to as **stereotyped behavior.** For example, Cat A would hit the pole by backing into it, Cat B would push it with its head, or Cat C would move it with its paw. Guthrie would say that in each case the door's flying open was an abrupt change in the stimulating conditions. By changing the stimulating conditions, the response of backing into the pole, for example, is protected from unlearning. The last thing that the animal did before the chamber was opened was to back into that pole, and because it backed into the pole the stimulating conditions changed. Thus, applying the law of recency, the next time we put that animal into the puzzle box, it should respond by backing into the pole, and this is exactly what Guthrie and Horton observed. A pictorial record of a typical cat's performance is shown in Figure 8-1.

Guthrie and Horton observed that very often the animal, after escaping from the puzzle box, would ignore a piece of fish that was offered to it. Even though the animal ignored the so-called reinforcement, it was just as proficient at leaving the box the next time it was placed in it. This observation, according to Guthrie, added further support to his contention that reinforcement is merely a mechanical arrangement that prevents unlearning. Guthrie concluded that any event following the desired response from an animal would change the stimulating conditions and thereby preserve that response under the preceding stimulating conditions.

Forgetting

Not only does learning occur in one trial, but so does **forgetting.** All forgetting occurs, according to Guthrie, by merely causing an alternative response to occur in the presence of a stimulus pattern. After a stimulus pattern results in the alternative response, that stimulus pattern will thereafter tend to bring about the new response. Thus for Guthrie, *all forgetting must involve new learning.* This is an extreme form of

Figure 8–1. A pictorial record of a series of escape responses made by one of Guthrie's cats. The pictures were taken automatically when the cat moved the pole. Note that the cat tended to move the pole in the same way on each trial. (From *Cats in a Puzzle Box*, pp. 53–55, by E. R. Guthrie & G. P. Horton, 1946, New York: Holt, Rinehart & Winston. Reprinted by permission.)

retroactive inhibition, which refers to the fact that old learning is interfered with by new learning. To demonstrate retroactive inhibition, let us suppose someone learns task A and then learns task B and then is tested for retention on task A. Another person learns task A, does *not* learn task B, and is tested on task A. It is generally found that the first person remembers less of task A than does the second person. Thus, it is demonstrated that learning something new (task B) has interfered with the retention of what was learned previously (task A).

Guthrie accepted an extreme form of retroactive inhibition. His position was that whenever something new is learned it must completely "knock out" something old. In other words, all forgetting is due to interference. *No interference, no forgetting.*

About forgetting, Guthrie said (1942):

The child who has left school at the end of the seventh grade will recall many of the details of his last year for the rest of his life. The child who has continued on in school has these associations of the schoolroom and school life overlaid by others, and by the time he is in college may be very vague about the names and events of his seventh-grade experience.

When we are somehow protected from established cues we are well aware that these may retain their connection with a response indefinitely. A university faculty member's wife recently visited Norway, the original home of her parents. She had not spoken Norwegian since the death of her grandmother when she was five and believed that she had forgotten the language. But during her stay in Norway, she astonished herself by joining in the conversation. The language and atmosphere of her childhood revived words and phrases she could not remember in her American home. But her conversation caused much amusement among her relatives because she was speaking with a facile Norwegian "baby talk." If her family in America had continued to use Norwegian, this "baby talk" would have been forgotten, its association with the language destroyed by other phrases.

Forgetting is not a passive fading of stimulus-response associations contingent upon the lapse of time, but requires active unlearning, which consists in learning to do something else under the circumstances. (pp. 29–30)

Summary of Guthrie's Theory as Presented Thus Far

Associations between stimulating conditions and movements are constantly being made. An association between a stimulus and a response is made simply because the two occur together. The association can be between either external stimuli and overt responses, or between movement-produced stimuli and overt responses. This association will continue until the same response occurs in the presence of other stimuli or until the same stimuli occur and the response is prevented from occurring. In a structured learning situation, such as a puzzle box, the environment is arranged so that there is an abrupt change in stimulation after a certain response is made. For example, if the cat hits the pole, the door opens and it is allowed to escape. Guthrie would say that after the cat hit the pole the stimulus situation abruptly changed and whatever association existed before that time will be preserved. The most recent association before the abrupt change was between the stimulation in the puzzle box and the response that allowed the animal to escape. According to the recency principle, when the animal is again placed in the puzzle box, it will tend to repeat that same response (it will tend to hit the pole again) and we say that the cat has learned how to escape from the box.

Unlike Thorndike, Skinner, Hull, and Pavlov, Guthrie was not a reinforcement theorist. Thorndike did, of course, discuss associative shifting, which he felt occurred independent of reinforcement. However, since Thorndike's main focus was on the kind of learning governed by the law of effect, he is generally considered a reinforcement theorist.

Of the theorists that we have covered thus far, Guthrie's theory is most similar to Watson's theory. Neither Watson nor Guthrie were reinforcement theorists. Watson believed that all learning could be explained by employing the laws of contiguity and frequency. The main difference between Watson's theory and Guthrie's is the fact that Watson accepted the law of frequency whereas Guthrie did not.

How to Break Habits

A habit is a response that has become associated with a large number of stimuli. The more stimuli that elicit the response, the stronger the habit. Smoking, for example, can be a strong habit because the response of smoking has taken place in the presence of so many cues. Each cue present as a person smokes will tend to elicit smoking when next it is encountered. Guthrie indicated the complexities of a habit in the following quotation (1952):

> The chief difficulty in the way of avoiding a bad habit is that the responsible cues are often hard to find, and that in many bad habit systems, they are extremely numerous. Each rehearsal is responsible for a possible addition of one or more new cues which tend to set off the undesired action. Drinking and smoking after years of practice are action systems which can be started by thousands of reminders, and which become imperative because the absence of the object of the habit, the drink or the smoke, results in a block to action and so in restlessness and tension. The desire, which includes tension in the muscles used in drinking or smoking, disrupts other action. The writer who "wants a smoke" is disturbed in his writing and the disturbed state will continue until the aroused action tendency is allowed to go through. The original wakening of the desire may be caused by any of the chance accompaniments of previous smoking—the smell of smoke, the sight of another person smoking, or of a cigar, the act of sitting back in the office chair, sitting down to a desk, finishing a meal, leaving the theater, and a thousand other stimulus patterns. Most smokers, while busily engaged in activities not associated with smoking, can go for long periods with no craving. Others find that the craving is strictly associated with such things as the end of a meal, if it has been their practice to smoke at that time. I once had a caller to whom I was explaining that the apple I had just finished was a splendid device for avoiding a smoke. The caller pointed out that I was smoking at that moment. The habit of lighting a cigarette was so attached to the finish of eating that smoking had been started automatically. (p. 116)

Threshold Method. To break a habit, the rule is always the same: find the cues that initiate the bad habit and practice another response in the presence of those cues. Guthrie lists three ways in which an organism can be made to make a response, other than an undesirable one, to a certain pattern of stimuli. The first technique is referred to as the **threshold method.** According to Guthrie (1938), this method involves:

> introducing the stimulus at such weak strengths that it will not cause the response and then gradually increasing the intensity of the stimulus, always taking care that it is below the "threshold" of the response. A gradual introduction to the motion of a ship which, unfortunately, cannot be controlled by human means, but depends on the gradualness of change in the weather, can bring about tolerance of a considerable storm. Most children react to the taste

of green olives by spitting them out. But if they begin with small nibbles, not enough to cause rejection, whole olives will eventually be taken with pleasure.

. . . members of families learn to make use of this type of associative inhibition in dealing with their housemates. The proposal to send the daughter to an expensive school is "broken gently" to the father. Casual mention of the school's advantages without directly submitting the issue, criticism of the present school, at first so mild that it will not stir defense, prepare the father so that when the question is at last put squarely before him he does not make a scene over the expense. He is by this time used to the idea and there will be no violent reaction. (pp. 60–61)

The threshold method can also be exemplified by what is ordinarily done when a horse is being broken. If you walk up to a horse that has never worn a saddle and attempt to throw a saddle on its back, it will no doubt start kicking and run away. The horse will do whatever it can to prevent you from putting that saddle on its back. If, instead of the saddle, you put a very light blanket on its back, chances are that it will not react violently. If the horse remains calm, you can gradually increase the weight on its back by using heavier and heavier blankets. You can then go from blankets to a light saddle and finally to the regular saddle itself. There is a process akin to this in psychotherapy. If the therapist is trying to help a patient overcome a phobia of some kind, he or she may use the method of approximation described above. If the patient has a terrible fear of a relative, for example his or her mother, the therapist may first start out talking about people in general, then women, and then women who are related to the patient, and in this way, gradually build up to the point where they are talking about the mother without the patient being fearful. This method of treating a phobia is very much like Wolpe's technique of systematic desensitization which was discussed in the last chapter.

Fatigue Method. The second method proposed by Guthrie is referred to as the **fatigue method.** Again, to take horse-training as an example, the fatigue method would correspond to bronco-busting where a saddle is thrown on the horse, the rider climbs on, and the horse is ridden until it gives up. That is, the horse is ridden until its fatigue causes it to do something other than buck while the saddle and the rider are on its back. Then, according to Guthrie, the response of riding calmly will replace the bucking response to the stimulus provided by the saddle and the rider. Once you get the animal to act calmly in the presence of the saddle and rider, then forevermore it will act calmly in their presence.

To break a dog of the habit of chasing chickens, all you have to do is to tie a chicken around the dog's neck and let it run around and try to get rid of it. When the dog eventually becomes fatigued it will be doing something other than chasing in the presence of the chicken. The chicken has then become a cue for doing something other than chasing.

Another example that Guthrie uses in describing the fatigue method involves a little girl who upsets her parents by lighting matches. Guthrie's advice is to allow the girl (or perhaps force her) to continue to light matches to the point where it is no longer fun. Under these conditions matches become a cue for avoidance rather than for lighting.

Incompatible Response Method. The third method of breaking a habit is called the incompatible response method. With this method, the stimuli for the undesired response are presented along with other stimuli that produce a response which is incompatible with the undesired response. For example, a young child receives a panda bear as a gift, and her first reaction is fear and avoidance. On the other hand, the child's mother elicits a warm relaxed feeling in the child. Using the incompatible response method, you would pair the mother and the panda bear; hopefully the mother will be the dominant stimulus. If she is the dominant stimulus, the child's reaction to the mother-panda bear combination will be one of relaxation. Once this reaction has been elicited in the presence of the bear, the bear can be presented alone, and it will produce relaxation in the child. With the incompatible response method, both stimuli are presented to the learner: the one that causes the undesired response, and a stronger stimulus that causes a response incompatible with the undesired response. The learner then tends to make a response other than the undesired one in the presence of the stimuli that previously elicited the undesired response. Because of this pairing, the stimuli that used to elicit the undesired response will now elicit the response associated with the stronger stimulus.

All three of these methods for breaking a habit are effective for the same reason. Guthrie (1938) said: "All three of these methods are, of course, only one method. All of them consist in presenting the cues of an undesirable action and seeing to it that the action is not performed. Since there is always other behavior going on when we are awake, the cues we present become stimuli for this other behavior and are alienated from the obnoxious response" (p. 62).

The three examples we gave of breaking a habit can be summarized as follows:

Threshold Method

1. Regular saddle ⟶ kicking
2. Light blanket ⟶ calm
3. Heavier blanket ⟶ calm
4. A still heavier blanket ⟶ calm
5. Light saddle ⟶ calm
6. Regular saddle ⟶ calm

Fatigue Method

1. Saddle ⟶ kicking
2. Passage of time
3. Saddle ⟶ calm

Incompatible Response Method

1. Panda bear ⟶ fear
2. Mother ⟶ relaxation

3. Panda bear and mother ⟶ relaxation
4. Panda bear ⟶ relaxation

We noted in our discussion of Thorndike's theory (chapter 4) that he believed associative shifting to be a second kind of learning, one based on contiguity alone and not governed by the law of effect. Since Guthrie believed learning is dependent on contiguity alone, one would expect to find a great deal of similarity between Thorndike's concept of associative shifting and Guthrie's views about learning. In fact, Guthrie's entire theory can be looked upon as an effort to describe how a response that is associated with one stimulus shifts over and becomes associated with another stimulus.

The incompatible response method of breaking a habit seems to represent one kind of associative shifting. Stimulus 1, the mother, elicits relaxation. Stimulus 2, the panda bear, elicits fear. When Stimulus 1 is presented along with Stimulus 2, the response previously associated with Stimulus 1 now is elicited by Stimulus 2, simply because the two stimuli are contiguous. Now the panda bear elicits the response that was previously associated with the mother.

The threshold method of breaking a habit also appears to represent a kind of associative shifting. Using the threshold method to eliminate the child's fear of the panda bear would involve *gradually* associating the bear with the mother. To begin with something only indirectly related to the bear, perhaps another of the child's toys, would be paired with the mother. Then the objects paired with the mother would become increasingly similar to the panda bear on successive pairings, and finally, the panda bear itself is presented with the mother. Again, the end result is that the response once associated with the mother "shifts over" to the panda bear.

Sidetracking a Habit

There is a difference between breaking a habit and sidetracking a habit. Sidetracking a habit can be accomplished by avoiding the cues that elicit the undesirable behavior. If you have accumulated a large number of behavior patterns that are not effective or for other reasons cause concern and anxiety, probably the best thing to do would be to leave the situation altogether. Guthrie would advise going to an environment that would give you a fresh start, since you would not have as many associations built up in a new environment. Going to a new environment would release you to develop new behavior patterns. This would only be a partial escape, however, since many of the stimuli causing your undesired behavior are internal and you would, therefore, be taking them with you to the new environment. Also, as we shall see, stimuli in the new environment identical or similar to stimuli in the old environment will tend to elicit the responses previously attached to them.

Punishment

Guthrie said the effectiveness of **punishment** is determined by what it causes the punished organism to do. Punishment works, not because of the pain experienced by the individual, but because it changes the way the individual responds to certain stimuli. Punishment is effective only when it results in a new response to the same stimuli. Punishment succeeds in changing the undesired habit because it elicits behavior incompatible with the punished behavior. Punishment fails because the behavior caused by the punishment is not incompatible with the punished behavior.

Let's say that you have a dog that chases cars and you want it to stop. Guthrie would say, get in your car and allow the dog to chase it. As it is running along the side of the car, reach down and slap its nose. This is likely to be effective. On the other hand, slapping its rear as it is chasing the car is not likely to be effective, although it can be assumed that a slap on the nose and a slap on the rear are equally painful to the dog. The difference is that the slap on the nose tends to make it stop and jump backward in the presence of the car, whereas the slap on the rear tends to make it continue forward, perhaps even a little more energetically. Thus one form of punishment causes incompatible behavior and is effective, and the other does not and is ineffective.

Guthrie (1952) said:

> what is learned will be what is done—and what is done in intense feeling is usually something different from what was being done. Sitting on tacks does not discourage learning. It encourages one in learning to do something else than sit. It is not the feeling caused by punishment, but the specific action caused by punishment that determines what will be learned. In training a dog to jump through a hoop, the effectiveness of punishment depends on where it is applied, front or rear. It is what the punishment makes the dog *do* that counts, or what it makes a man do, not what it makes him feel. The mistaken notion that it is the feeling that determines learning derives from the fact that often we do not care what is done as a result of punishment, just as long as what is done breaks up or inhibits the unwanted habit.
>
> . . . as the outcome of this discussion punishment and reward are not summarily to be ejected from the place they hold in public favor. No doubt whatever has been thrown on their general effectiveness. Children may still be spanked or caressed. But we shall have a much better insight into the uses of punishment and reward if we analyze their effects in terms of association and realize that punishment is effective only through its associations. Punishment achieves its effects not by taking away strength from the physiological basis of the connection . . . but by forcing the animal or the child to do something different and thus establishing inhibitory conditioning of unwanted habit. Punishment is effective *only in the presence of cues for the bad habit.*
>
> Furthermore, when the effect of punishment is only emotional excitement, punishment facilitates the stereotyping of the undesired habit. Punishment and reward are essentially moral terms, not psychological terms. They are defined not in terms of their effects on the recipient, but in terms of the purposes of the individual who administers them. Theory stated in their terms is bound to be ambiguous. (pp. 132–133)

Guthrie talked about a 10-year-old girl who threw her hat and coat on the floor whenever she came home (1935, p. 21). Each time she did so, her mother scolded her and made her hang her hat and coat up. The situation continued until the mother guessed that her nagging had become the cue for the child to hang her clothes up. Realizing this, the next time the child threw her hat and coat on the floor, the mother made her pick them up and go back outside. Now as the girl came in the door, the mother insisted that she hang her coat and hat up immediately. This procedure was repeated a few times and soon the girl learned to hang up her hat and coat upon entering the house. Now the response of hanging up her clothes was attached to the stimuli present as she entered the house rather than to her mother's nagging. In this case, punishing the girl after her hat and coat were already on the floor could have no effect on the habit, except perhaps to strengthen it.

Guthrie and Powers also advise that a command never be given if it could be disobeyed. They said (1950): "The skilled animal trainer never gives a command that he does not expect to be obeyed. In this he is like the army officer and the experienced teacher. If a teacher makes a request for silence in the room and it is disregarded, the request actually becomes a signal for disturbance" (p. 129).

Summary of Guthrie's Views on Punishment

Everything that Guthrie said about punishment is directly in accordance with his one law of learning—the law of contiguity. When stimuli and responses are paired, they become associated and remain associated unless the stimuli occur in the presence of another response, at which time they will become associated with the new response. While discussing ways of breaking a habit, we saw three mechanical arrangements that could be used to rearrange the associations between stimuli and responses. Punishment is another such arrangement. Punishment, when used effectively, causes stimuli that previously elicited an undesired response to elicit an acceptable response. Guthrie's views about punishment can be summarized as follows:

1. The important thing about punishment is not the pain it may cause, but what it makes the organism do.
2. In order to be effective, punishment must cause behavior that is incompatible with the punished behavior.
3. In order to be effective, punishment must be applied in the presence of the stimuli that elicited the punished behavior.
4. If the conditions specified in 2 and 3 are not met, punishment will be ineffective or may even strengthen the undesired response.

Thus, when punishment is effective, it causes the organism to do something other than what it was punished for doing while the stimuli that elicited the punished behavior are still present. This, of course, causes a new association to be formed and the next time those stimuli appear, they will tend to elicit a favorable response instead of an unfavorable one.

Is there anything other than the anecdotal evidence that Guthrie offers to support his views on punishment? The answer is yes. Fowler and Miller (1963) trained rats to traverse a runway for food reinforcement. Subjects in the control group simply ran the runway and obtained food. Subjects in one experimental group were given a mild electric shock to the *front paws* just as they reached the food cup. Subjects in a second experimental group received a mild electric shock to the *hind paws* just as they reached the food cup. Relative to the running speed of the control subjects, subjects that had their front paws shocked as they reached the food cup ran slower on subsequent trials, whereas the subjects that had their hind paws shocked ran *faster*. Just as Guthrie predicted, shocking the rats on their hind paws actually facilitated running rather than inhibiting it. Since members of both experimental groups received the same intensity of shock, it was not the shock itself that facilitated or inhibited running speed. Rather, it was what the shock caused the animals to do. Shocking the front paws caused behavior incompatible with running while shocking the hind paws caused faster running.

Not all research on punishment has been supportive of Guthrie's theory, and it is now realized that Guthrie's account was at best incomplete. For a review of the complex topic of punishment see, for example, Walters and Grusec (1977).

Drives

Physiological **drives** provide what Guthrie called **maintaining stimuli** that keep the organism active until a goal is reached. For example, being hungry produces internal stimulation that continues until food is consumed. When food is obtained, the maintaining stimuli are terminated and therefore the stimulating conditions have changed, thus preserving the response that led to the food. It should be emphasized, however, that physiological drives are only one source of maintaining stimuli. Any persistent source of stimulation, whether it be internal or external, can provide maintaining stimuli. Guthrie (1938) said:

> To explain this requires that we first understand what a problem is. What makes the puzzle box or an unyielding parent a problem? The answer to this is that problems are persistent stimulus situations of such a nature that they keep the animal or the person disturbed and excited until some act is hit upon which removes the "maintaining stimuli" and allows the excitement to subside.
>
> Such persistent and disturbing stimuli are sometimes called "drives." In a hungry animal, the recurring spasms of the stomach serve to make the animal disturbed and to produce excitement. . . .
>
> The same behavior could be produced by some artificial and external stimulation. A paper bag fastened to the cat's foot with a rubber band will similarly activate the cat, and it will become disturbed and excited and this state will continue until some one of its movements eventually removes the bag. (p. 96)

Guthrie went on to say (1938):

> And here is a point very apt to be overlooked. The next time that the disturbers are present, they will tend to call out, by virtue of their last association, the act that removed them. Other acts associated with them have been dissoci-

ated or unconditioned each by the next act. But after successful removal of the disturber, it is no longer there to be associated with a new act. The drive remains faithful to the act that removed it because that was its last association. After that no new associations could be established because the drive is gone. (p. 98)

Guthrie explains the habitual use of alcohol and other drugs in a similar way. Let's say, for example, a person feels tense or anxious. In this case, tension or anxiety provides maintaining stimuli. If under these circumstances, the person takes a drink or two, his or her tension may be reduced. According to Guthrie, this assures the relationship between tension and drinking. Therefore, the next time the person feels tense, he or she will tend to have a drink. Gradually tension will tend to elicit drinking (or drug taking) under a wider range of circumstances, with the result that the person becomes a habitual drinker or a drug addict.

Intentions

Responses that are conditioned to maintaining stimuli are called **intentions.** They are called intentions because maintaining stimulation from a drive usually lasts for a period of time (until the drive is reduced). Thus the *sequence of behavior* preceding the drive reducing response is repeated next time the drive with its related stimuli occurs. The sequence of behavior associated with maintaining stimuli seems to be interrelated and logical and is, therefore, referred to as intentional. If an animal is hungry and is allowed to eat, it will do so. If, however, the direct satisfaction of the hunger drive is not possible, it will tend to perform whatever behaviors led to food last time it was hungry: it may turn in a certain direction in a maze, press a lever, or move a pole. If a person is hungry and has a sandwich in her office, she will eat it; if, however, she forgot her lunch, she will get up, put on her coat, get into her car, find a restaurant, enter the restaurant, place an order, and so on. Different reaction patterns have been associated with the maintaining stimuli from hunger plus the stimuli from environmental circumstances, that is, having one's lunch or not. Behavior triggered by maintaining stimuli may look purposive or intentional but Guthrie felt it too could be explained by the law of contiguity.

Transfer of Training

It should be clear that Guthrie would expect very little transfer of training. He would say that if a child learns to add 2 and 2 at the blackboard, there is no guarantee that that child is going to know how to add 2 and 2 when she returns to her seat. The stimulating conditions under which that association was made is much different than those prevailing at her seat. So the child really must learn the response of adding 2 and 2 at the blackboard, at her seat, at home, and wherever she hopes to practice that response.

Guthrie would say to the college student, if you want to get the most from your studies, you should practice in exactly the same situation in which you're going to be tested. The best place to study, according to Guthrie, is in the room where you're going to be tested because all the stimuli in that room will be associated with the information that you're studying. If you learn something in your dorm room, there is no guarantee that this knowledge will transfer into the classroom. This is how Guthrie would explain why a student may say after taking a test, "I don't know what happened to me; I went over that material a hundred times; I knew it quite well, and yet, it didn't come to me during the test." Guthrie would say that there simply was not enough similarity between the conditions under which the student studied and the conditions under which he or she was tested.

Guthrie's advice is to always practice the exact behaviors that are going to be demanded of us; in addition we should practice them in the exact conditions under which we are going to be tested or evaluated. If you want to utilize this information beyond the testing situation, you must go beyond the classroom and associate other stimuli with the behavior that the book or the class or the lecture caused you to do. Guthrie's advice to the student preparing for an essay examination is the same: in preparing for an essay test, write essay questions. Guess what the questions will be and answer them. Force yourself to respond to the questions under the time conditions that you are going to be exposed to during the test. Guthrie would give the same advice to the automobile mechanic, or the electrician. If you want to learn how to fix engines, work on engines, and work on them under conditions similar to those that will prevail in real life situations. This will maximize transfer.

Essentially, Guthrie accepted Thorndike's identical elements theory concerning the transfer of training. The probability of making the same response to two different situations is determined by the similarity between the two situations. Like Thorndike, Guthrie rejected the formal discipline theory of transfer and felt that acceptance of such a position would generate unfortunate classroom practices. Guthrie and Powers said (1950):

> The teacher's acceptance or rejection of the formal discipline theory of transfer, the identical elements or generalization explanation, will be reflected in numerous day-to-day teaching practices. *The subject-matter* teacher no doubt would give evidence of an actual, if not verbal, acceptance of the formal discipline doctrine. Exposure to the content of certain courses becomes in itself, then, the objective of education; methods of teaching and the attempt to link content and the needs of the learner are of relatively secondary importance. The student must conform to subject matter requirements and must develop a docile, submissive role.
>
> A challenging or questioning attitude on the part of the teacher as regards the validity of the formal discipline doctrine paves the way for educational experimentation. The teacher will ask what values, direct and indirect, are being served by pupil participation in given curricular areas. He will be willing to revise content and method as facts regarding transfer are uncovered. The child will be viewed as a growing and developing organism constantly organizing and reorganizing experience into more or less efficient patterns of behavior. The discovery of the child's interests and wise use of effective incentives in order to motivate participation become primary tasks of instruction. (p. 256)

Elsewhere Guthrie said (1942): "it is essential that the student be led to do what is to be learned . . . a student does not learn what was in a lecture or in a book. He learns only what the lecture or book caused him to do" (p. 55). According to Guthrie, *we learn what we do.* The notions of insight, understanding, and thinking had little or no meaning to Guthrie. The only law of learning is the law of contiguity which states that when two events occur together, they are learned. All learning, whether it be subhuman or human, simple or abstract, is subsumed under the law of contiguity and its related principles. There is no reference to conscious events in Guthrie's theory, nor is there any special interest in the survival value of learned behavior. According to Guthrie, incorrect responses are learned just as readily as correct ones, and the acquisition of both is explained by the same law of learning.

VOEKS'S FORMALIZATION OF GUTHRIE'S THEORY

As mentioned earlier, Guthrie did little research to test the validity of his own theory. Three explanations for Guthrie's lack of experimentation have been offered. First, Bolles (1979) suggests that it was because Guthrie's theory minimized the roles of motivation and reinforcement. These two components of most other learning theories in the 1930s and 1940s stimulated most of the research associated with them. Second, Carlson (1980) suggests it was because psychology, at the time that Guthrie was at the University of Washington, was offered only on the undergraduate level, and therefore the theses and dissertations of graduate students which were often used to experimentally test other theories, were not available to Guthrie. Third, as Guthrie himself realized, his principles of learning were stated in terms that were too general to be tested easily.

Virginia W. Voeks, who was a student at the University of Washington when Guthrie was influential there, attempted to restate Guthrie's theory in terms that were precise enough to be empirically verifiable. Voeks obtained her BA in 1943 from the University of Washington where she was influenced by Guthrie, and obtained her PhD in 1947 from Yale where she was apparently influenced by Hull. In fact, the outcome of Voeks's work was a theory whose structure was very Hullian but whose content was very Guthrian. After obtaining her PhD, Voeks returned to the University of Washington where she remained until 1949. In 1949, she moved to San Diego State College where she has been ever since.

In Voeks's restatement of Guthrie's theory there are four basic postulates, eight definitions, and eight theorems. The postulates attempt to summarize many of Guthrie's general principles of learning, the definitions attempt to clarify several Guthrian concepts (such as stimulus, cue, response and learning), and the theorems were deductions from the postulates and definitions that are experimentally testable. Voeks tested a number of her deductions and found considerable support for Guthrie's theory.

Most of Voeks's formalization of Guthrie's theory, and the research that it stimulated, is too complex to be presented here. Voeks's four postulates, however, act both as a convenient summary of Guthrie's theory and as a sample of her thoughtful formalization of Guthrie's theory.

Postulate I: Principle of Association. (*a*) Any stimulus-pattern which once accompanies a response, and/or immediately precedes it by one-half second or less, becomes a full-strength direct cue for that response. (*b*) This is the only way in which stimulus-patterns not now cues for a particular response can become direct cues for that response (Voeks, 1950, p. 342).

Postulate II: Principle of Postremity. (*a*) A stimulus which has accompanied or immediately preceded two or more incompatible responses is a conditioned stimulus for only the last response made while that stimulus was present. (*b*) This is the only way in which a stimulus now a cue for a particular response can cease being a cue for that response (Voeks, 1950, p. 344).

Postulate III: Principle of Response Probability. The probability of any particular response's occurring . . . at some specified time is a . . . function . . . of the proportion . . . of the stimuli present which are at the time cues for that response. . . . (Voeks, 1950, p. 348).

Postulate IV: Principle of Dynamic Situations. The stimulus-pattern of a situation is not static but from time to time is modified, due to such changes as result from the subject's making a response, accumulation of fatigue products, visceral changes and other internal processes of the subject, introduction of controlled or uncontrolled variations in the stimuli present (Voeks, 1950, p. 350).

The reader should not conclude that Guthrie's theory of learning is of historical interest only. As we shall see in the next chapter when we consider the work of William K. Estes, one trend in modern learning theory is toward the greater use of mathematical models in explaining the learning process. It was Guthrie's theory of learning that formed the bases for the early mathematical models of learning and continues to be at the heart of most of them. Indeed, Guthrie's theory of learning is, to many, the most viable learning theory available today.

DISCUSSION QUESTIONS

1. What law of association did Guthrie build his theory around? Describe this law and explain how the recency principle is deduced from it.
2. Given Guthrie's belief in one-trial learning, how did he explain the improvement in performance that results from practice? Include in your answer a distinction between movements and acts.
3. Is Guthrie's theory a reinforcement theory or not? Justify your answer.
4. How did Guthrie explain forgetting?
5. For Guthrie, what was the relationship between drives and "intentions"?
6. Explain how, according to Guthrie, the transfer of skills from where they are learned to where they are applied could be facilitated.

7. What suggestions did Guthrie offer for breaking a bad habit? Choose one of the suggestions and show how it could be used to break the smoking habit.

8. How would Guthrie explain the phenomenon of regression, such as the tendency to act as you did at a younger age under certain conditions, like when you visit the house or room you grew up in?

9. How would Guthrie explain the tendency for someone to act like a "different person" under various conditions?

10. How would you revise your study habits so that they are in accordance with Guthrie's theory?

11. How might Guthrie explain the development of drug addiction?

12. Describe Guthrie's use of the term "reinforcement."

13. According to Guthrie, under what circumstances would punishment be an effective technique in modifying behavior? Do you feel punishment is usually used as Guthrie says it should be? Explain.

14. What was Guthrie's purpose in introducing the notion of "movement-produced stimuli"?

15. Design an experiment to test Guthrie's contention that anything that disrupts a stimulus pattern will preserve the last response made to that stimulus pattern.

16. What are three reasons why Guthrie's theory did not initially generate much research?

17. Discuss the key points of Voeks's restatement of Guthrie's theory.

CHAPTER HIGHLIGHTS

Acts. Complicated behavior patterns usually involving some goal accomplishment. Acts are made up of many individual movements.

Chaining. The process whereby the stimulation caused by one response acts as a stimulus for another response and that response in turn triggers another, and so on. Chaining, according to Guthrie, depends on movement-produced stimuli.

Drives. Maintaining stimuli usually caused by some physiological need, such as hunger or thirst.

Fatigue method of breaking a habit. Forcing an organism to continue to respond to a source of stimulation until it is fatigued. When it is fatigued it will respond to the source of stimulation in a way different from the way it originally responded to it.

Forgetting. All forgetting, according to Guthrie, involves the blocking out of old associations by the formation of new ones. This is an extreme form of retroactive inhibition.

Incompatible response method of breaking a habit. The stimulus for an undesired response is presented along with another stimulus that will cause a response incompatible with the undesired one. Because of this pairing, the stimulus that originally elicited the undesired response will no longer do so.

Intentions. Behavior patterns that are conditioned to maintaining stimuli.

Law of contiguity. Guthrie's one law of learning, which states that when a pattern of stimuli is experienced along with a response, the two will become associated so that when that pattern of stimuli next recurs, it will tend to elicit that response. In 1959, Guthrie revised the law of contiguity to read, "What is being noticed becomes a signal for what is being done."

Maintaining stimuli. Any source of stimulation that persists until some specific act is performed. For example, putting a rubber band around an animal's nose provides maintaining stimuli until it is removed, and the hunger drive provides maintaining stimuli until the animal eats.

Movement-produced stimuli. Stimulation caused by the receptors found in the muscles, tendons, and joints of the body. As the body moves, these receptors fire, thereby providing a source of stimulation, or what Guthrie called movement-produced stimuli.

Movements. Specific responses to specific stimuli. Acts are made up of many specific movements.

One-trial learning. The contention that the association between a pattern of stimuli and a response develops at full strength as a result of just one pairing between the two.

Principle of association. Voeks's first postulate which states that when a stimulus and response occur together they become associated, and that it is only through such contiguity that S-R associations are formed.

Principle of dynamic situations. Voeks's fourth postulate which states that stimulus patterns are dynamic since they can be changed by such things as an organism's response, fatigue, or by the systematic control of an experimenter.

Principle of postremity. Voeks's second postulate which states that only the last response made in a situation is the response that will be made when the situation recurs and that other responses previously made in the situation will no longer be associated with it.

Principle of response probability. Voeks's third postulate which states that the probability of a response being made in a given situation is a function of the number of cues in that situation associated with the response.

Punishment. The presentation of an aversive stimulus in order to modify behavior. According to Guthrie, two conditions must be met before punishment will be effective: (1) the punishment must produce behavior that is incompatible with the undesired response; and (2) the punishment must be applied in the presence of the stimuli that elicit the undesired response.

Recency principle. The principle that states that the response that was last made in a situation is the response that will be made when that situation next recurs.

Reinforcement. According to Guthrie, one of many events that can change a stimulus pattern, thus allowing the association between the previous stimulus pattern and the last response made to it to remain intact. Reinforcement, to Guthrie, is nothing more than a mechanical arrangement that prevents unlearning.

Retroactive inhibition. The interference of old learning by new learning.

Stereotyped behavior. The tendency to repeat exactly the behavior patterns that were previously made to a situation.

Threshold method of breaking a habit. A change in stimulating conditions is introduced so slowly that the organism does not notice it. Finally, the organism is reacting to the changed conditions in a manner other than it would have if the change had not occurred so slowly.

9

William Kaye Estes

One current trend in learning theory today is to move away from the broad, comprehensive theory and toward miniature systems. Researchers are marking off an area of interest and exploring it thoroughly. Breadth is sacrificed for depth. Exemplifying this trend are the so-called statistical learning theorists who attempt to build a rigorous minisystem from which a restricted range of learning phenomena can be deduced. The most influential of these, and one of the earliest, was developed by Estes (1950). Estes, born in 1919, is now at Rockefeller University in New York. In chapter 5, we encountered some of the research on punishment that Estes performed while he was a student of Skinner at the University of Minnesota. It is for his development of statistical learning theory, however, that Estes is best known. Estes's theory can be thought of as an attempt to quantify Guthrie's theory of learning. Guthrie's theory appears deceptively simple, but when one asks about the nature of a stimulus in more detail, for example, one soon realizes that his theory is much more complex than it appeared to be at first. Estes investigates this complexity and offers a model that effectively deals with it.

ESTES'S STIMULUS SAMPLING THEORY (SST)

Before giving a concrete example of how his theory works, we will first look at a number of assumptions made by Estes. First, he looks upon the learning situation as being comprised of a large but finite number of stimulus elements. These elements consist of the many things that the experimental subject experiences at the onset of a learning trial. They include the experimental conditions themselves, such as a light, a buzzer, verbal material presented in a memory drum, the sight of a bar in a Skinner box, or the runway in a T-maze. They also include the experimenter, the room temperature, extraneous noises inside and outside the room, and conditions within the experimental subject, such as fatigue, or a headache. All these stimulus elements taken collectively are symbolized S. S, therefore, is the total number of stimuli that accompany a trial in a learning situation.

Further, all responses made in the experimental situation fall into one of two categories. If the response is one that the experimenter is looking for (such as salivation, an eye blink, a bar press, turning right in a T-maze, or reciting a nonsense syllable correctly), it is called an A_1 response. If the response is anything other than what the experimenter wants, it is wrong and is labeled A_2. Thus, Estes divides all

William Kaye Estes. (Courtesy of W. K. Estes)

responses that may occur in a learning experiment into two classes: correct (A_1) or incorrect (A_2). There are no gradations in between: either an animal makes a conditioned response or it does not; either students recite a nonsense syllable correctly or they do not.

Next, Estes assumes that all elements in S are attached to either A_1 or A_2. Again this is an all-or-nothing situation: all stimulus elements in the experimental situation are either conditioned to (attached to) A_1 or to A_2. As we will see below, elements conditioned to A_1 tend to elicit A_1 responses, and elements conditioned to A_2 tend to elicit A_2 responses. It can be seen that in certain experiments, such as those involving the bar press, almost all the stimulus elements will be conditioned to A_2 responses (not pressing the bar) at the beginning of the experiment. Therefore, in the early stages of such an experiment, the animal will tend not to press the bar.

The next assumption that Estes makes is that the experimental subject does not experience all of the elements in S on any given trial, but only a small proportion of them. The proportion of elements experienced, or sampled, on any given trial remains constant throughout the experiment, and is symbolized θ (theta). **Theta** *is a proportion of stimulus elements from S that the subject experiences at the onset of a learning trial.* After the trial, the sample of elements θ is returned to S.

Next, Estes assumes that if an A_1 response terminates a trial, then θ proportion of S will become conditioned to the A_1 response. Following Guthrie, Estes accepts a contiguity explanation of learning. Since an A_1 response occurs, an association is formed between that response and the stimuli that preceded it. In other words, since θ proportion of the stimulus elements in S were sampled at the beginning of the trial, those elements will become conditioned to A_1 through the principle of contiguity. Thus, when an A_1 response terminates a learning trial, the number of stimulus elements conditioned to A_1 goes up. As the number of elements in S that are conditioned to A_1 goes up, the tendency for an A_1 response to be elicited at the onset of a learning trial also goes up. In this manner, the attachment of stimulus elements to A_1 and A_2 responses gradually changes, and this is what Estes calls learning. The **state of the system** at any given moment is the proportion of elements attached to A_1 and A_2 responses.

What determines which response will occur on any given trial? The answer to this question indicates why Estes's theory is called a statistical learning theory. The probability of an A_1 response occurring is equal to the proportion of stimulus elements in θ conditioned to A_1 at the beginning of a learning trial. If all the stimulus elements in θ are conditioned to A_1, then an A_1 response has a 100% chance of occurring. If, however, only 75% of the stimulus elements in θ are conditioned to A_1, then we would expect to get an A_2 response about 25% of the time. The proportion of elements in θ conditioned to A_1 reflects the proportion of elements in S that are conditioned to A_1 since θ is a random sample of elements from S. It can be seen that the probability of getting an A_1 response on any given trial changes as the state of the system changes.

The following formula summarizes the learning process as it is seen by Estes:

$$P_n = 1 - (1 - P_1)(1 - \theta)^{n-1}$$

where:

n = any particular trial in a learning experiment.
P_n = the probability of an A_1 response occurring on Trial n.
$(1 - P_1)$ = the probability of an A_1 response *not* occurring on Trial 1 (i.e., the proportion of elements *not* conditioned to A_1 at the beginning of the experiment).
$(1 - \theta)$ = the proportion of stimulus elements in S that are not sampled on Trial n.

Since the expression $(1 - P_1)(1 - \theta)^{n-1}$ must necessarily get smaller as n increases (that is, as the number of successive learning trials goes up), this formula generates a negatively accelerated learning curve with an asymptote of 1. The learning curve generated by Estes's formula is essentially the same as the one generated by Hull's formula which was described in chapter 6 (see Figure 6-1). Both Estes and Hull assume that more learning takes place in the early stages of a learning experiment than in the later stages.

The negatively accelerated curve occurs, according to Estes, because trials in a learning experiment usually end with an A_1 response, and as a result, an increasing number of elements become conditioned to A_1. But there are diminishing returns. Taking as an example the situation where, at the onset of an experiment, an A_1 response is highly unlikely (e.g., with eye-blink conditioning), we see that almost all elements in S would be conditioned to A_2 (not blinking when a light is presented). Suppose, however, that blinking occurs at the end of Trial 1. This results in all the elements sampled on that trial (θ) switching from A_2 to A_1, since they were all conditioned to A_2 to begin with. On the next trial, a few elements will be conditioned to A_1, but most will still be conditioned to A_2. Therefore, it is now possible that some elements conditioned to A_1 will be sampled along with those conditioned to A_2. This means the rate of changeover (from A_2 to A_1) will not be as great on Trial 2 as it was on Trial 1, since only those elements conditioned to A_2 can be transferred to A_1. As we saw earlier, this changeover from A_2 to A_1 is what constitutes learning. In the later trials, more and more elements are already conditioned to A_1 and therefore, the number of elements conditioned to A_2 responses contained in θ on any given trial is small. It can be seen then that as learning trials progress, the rate of learning goes down. When all the elements in S are conditioned to A_1, no further learning can occur and the probability of an A_1 response occurring is 1. Thus, we have a negatively accelerated learning curve which again simply indicates that learning progresses more rapidly in the early stages of learning than it does in the later stages. This negatively accelerated rate of changeover of the stimulus elements is diagrammed in Figure 9-1.

Generalization

Generalization from the original learning situation to other situations is easily taken care of by stimulus sampling theory. Estes takes the same position on transfer as did Thorndike. That is, transfer takes place to the extent that two situations have stimulus

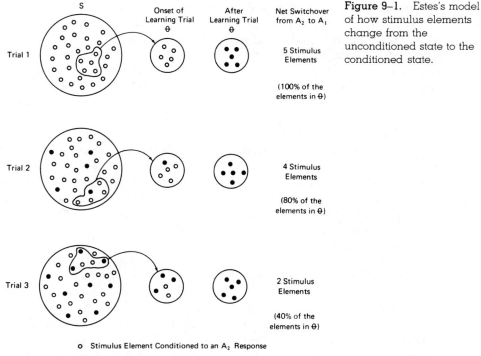

Figure 9-1. Estes's model of how stimulus elements change from the unconditioned state to the conditioned state.

elements in common. If many of the elements previously conditioned to an A_1 response are present in a new learning situation, the probability is high that an A_1 response will be elicited in the new situation. If no elements are conditioned to A_1 at the onset of new learning situations, then the probability of an A_1 response being given is zero. In a new situation, as with original learning, the probability of an A_1 response occurring is equal to the proportion of stimulus elements in S conditioned to it.

Extinction

Estes handles the problem of extinction essentially the same way as Guthrie did. Since in extinction, a trial usually ends with the subject doing something other than A_1, the stimulus elements previously conditioned to A_1 gradually switch back to A_2. The laws for acquisition and for extinction are the same. In fact, in Estes's system, it doesn't make sense to speak of extinction. What is called extinction results whenever conditions are arranged so that stimulus elements are switched from an A_1 response to an A_2 response.

Spontaneous Recovery

As you may remember from chapter 7, spontaneous recovery refers to the reappearance of a conditioned response after that response has undergone extinction. In order to explain spontaneous recovery, Estes expands slightly on his notion of S.

Earlier in this chapter, S was defined as the total number of stimulus elements present at the beginning of a trial in a learning experiment. We also noted that these stimulus elements included transitory events such as extraneous noises from the outside (e.g., a car backfiring, thunder, loud voices), and temporary body states of the experimental subject (e.g., indigestion, headache, anxiety). Since these and many other events are transitory, they may be part of S on one occasion but not on others. Likewise, when they are part of S, they are available to be sampled by the subject; when they are not part of S, they cannot be sampled. In other words, only those elements present in S can be sampled as part of θ.

Under the above conditions, it is possible that during training, A_1 responses become conditioned to many of these transitory elements. If it turns out that these elements are not available during extinction, then the A_1 response conditioned to them cannot be switched to A_2 responses. Switching can only occur for stimulus elements actually sampled; thus if certain elements had been conditioned to A_1 responses during training and are subsequently not available during extinction, their status remains the same, that is, attached to A_1.

Now the importance of these transitory elements for spontaneous recovery becomes evident. It is entirely possible that many elements that were conditioned to A_1 during acquisition are not available during extinction, but may reappear some time after extinction has taken place. Thus, if the subject is placed back into the experimental situation some time after extinction, a portion of these elements may now be present and would therefore tend to elicit an A_1 response. Spontaneous recovery is explained then by assuming the extinction process (switching elements from A_1 to A_2) was never complete in the first place.

Probability Matching

For years, behaviorists puzzled over the phenomenon of **probability matching.** The traditional probability matching experiment involves a signal light that is followed by one of two other lights. When the signal light comes on, the subject is to guess which of the other two lights will come on. The experimenter arranges the situation so that the lights come on in any pattern he or she wishes, such as left light 75% of the time, right light 25% of the time; left light 100% of the time, or right light 0% of the time. The results of such an arrangement are usually that the subject ends up guessing the frequencies at which the lights come on almost exactly as the experimenter had arranged them, for example, if the right light comes on 80% of the time, the subject will predict that light will come on about 80% of the trials. This is referred to as probability matching.

To handle these results, we need to add symbols for the two new stimulus events to Estes's theory:

E_1 = left light going on
E_2 = right light going on

In this case, an A_1 response is predicting E_1, and A_2 is predicting E_2. In Estes's analysis of probability matching, the subject's actual guess is irrelevant. It is assumed that when E_1 occurs, it evokes in the subject an implicit A_1 response, and when E_2 occurs, it evokes an implicit A_2 response. Thus, for Estes, the event itself acts as a "reinforcer" (see Estes & Straughan, 1954, for greater detail). The experimental situation can be diagrammed as follows:

Two additional symbols are necessary for Estes's analysis of probability matching:

$$\pi = \text{the probability of } E_1 \text{ occurring}$$
$$1 - \pi = \text{the probability of } E_2 \text{ occurring}$$

On a trial in which E_1 occurs, all elements sampled from S on that trial become conditioned to A_1, and on a trial on which E_2 occurs, the sample of elements will become conditioned to A_2.

As before, the probability of an A_1 response on any given trial is equal to the proportion of elements in S that are conditioned to A_1 (P_n) and the probability of an A_2 response is equal to the proportion of those elements not conditioned to A_1 or $(1 - P_n)$. As before, θ equals the proportion of elements sampled on each trial, and again, this value remains the same throughout the experiment.

The probability of an A_1 response after n trials is given by the following formula:

$$P_n = \pi - (\pi - P_1)(1 - \theta)^{n-1}$$

Because $(1 - \theta)$ is less than 1, with n getting larger, this equation yields a negatively accelerated curve with an asymptote of π. Thus, whatever the value of π, this formula predicts that the proportion of A_1 responses made by the subject will eventually match the proportion of E_1 occurrences set by the experimenter. In other words, Estes predicts probability matching by the subject, and this is what occurs. For more detail concerning the application of Estes's theory to probability matching, see Estes and Straughan (1954) or Estes (1964b).

ESTES'S MARKOV MODEL OF LEARNING

All statistical learning theories are probabilistic, that is, the dependent variable that they study is response probability. There is, however, a difference in opinion over what these changing response probabilities tell us about the nature of learning. The classic argument is over whether learning is gradual or complete in one trial. Thorndike concluded that learning was gradual, that it increased in small increments from trial to trial. Hull and Skinner went along with Thorndike on this matter. Guthrie differed by saying that learning occurred in an all-or-none fashion and only looked gradual because of the complexity of the task being learned. We shall see in chapter 10 that Gestalt theorists, with their insight studies, also felt they demonstrated that the learner went from the unlearned state to the learned state very rapidly and not bit by bit.

Estes's early stimulus sampling theory accepted both an incremental (gradual) and an all-or-none point of view concerning the learning process. You will remember that only a small proportion of the total number of stimulus elements present during an experiment is sampled on any given trial. The sampled elements were conditioned in an all-or-none fashion to whatever response terminated the trial. However, since only a small portion of elements is conditioned on any given trial, learning proceeds bit by bit and this is how the characteristic negatively accelerated learning curve is generated. To repeat, Estes's early position was that those stimulus elements that were sampled on a given trial were conditioned in an all-or-none manner; but since only a small number of them were sampled on a trial, learning proceeded in an incremental or gradual fashion. The probability of making an A_1 response changed gradually from one trial to the next, and if the total number of stimulus elements present in the experiment was large enough, the all-or-none nature of learning could not be detected. That is, with a large number of stimulus elements present in an experiment, there would be very small changes in response probabilities from one learning trial to the next, and when those probabilities were plotted, it would look *as if* learning was incremental rather than all-or-none in nature.

Later, Estes designed a number of studies that allowed the learning process to be observed in more detail (e.g., Estes, 1960, 1964a; Estes, Hopkins, & Crothers, 1960). These studies showed that when the number of elements to be sampled is very small, learning clearly occurs in an all-or-none fashion; in fact, it can be said that learning occurs completely on one trial or it does not occur at all—there appears to be no in-between. This rapid change from the unlearned state to the learned state is said to correspond to a **Markov process,** which is characterized by an abrupt, stepwise change in response probabilities rather than a relatively slow, gradual change from trial to trial.

In his 1964a study, Estes used *paired associates* to show the stepwise nature of learning. In **paired associate learning,** subjects learn pairs of items so that when they are shown the first member of the pair, they can respond with the other. Estes used a variation of paired associate learning where, when subjects were shown the first member of the pair, they had four responses to choose from and only one of the four was correct. Thus, after subjects see the first member of the pair, the probability of their choosing the correct response by chance alone was .25 (1 in 4). Estes found that if a subject guessed correctly on one trial, the probability of that subject guessing correctly on the next trial went to 1 and stayed there. In other words, after guessing correctly, the subject would be correct on 100% of the subsequent trials.

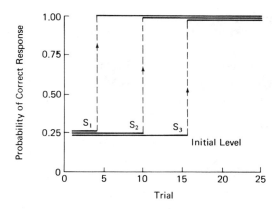

Figure 9–2. Subjects go from chance level performance to perfect performance in just one trial, but this process occurs at different times for different subjects. (From "All-or-None Processes in Learning and Retention," by W. K. Estes, 1964, *American Psychologist, 19*, pp. 16–25. Copyright by the American Psychological Association. Reprinted by permission of the publisher and author.)

Subjects who did not guess correctly went on guessing at chance level until they guessed correctly, at which time their subsequent probability of being correct jumped to 1. The most important fact here is that different subjects learned the correct response at different points in the experiment; that is, when subjects learned, they learned completely, but this occurred on different trials for different subjects. This fact is shown in Figure 9-2.

What happens when the individual instances of going from the unlearned to the learned state are overlooked and the data from all subjects are pooled together? Under these circumstances, the probabilities of making a correct response for the subjects in the unlearned state would be combined with those in the learned state and *average* probabilities would be plotted. For example, if there were five subjects in an experiment and three were in the unlearned state (probability of making a correct response = .25), and two were in the learned state (probability of making a correct response = 1), the average probability of making a correct response for the group would be .55. As more learning trials occur, more subjects will enter the learned state, and the average probability for the group would increase. This is demonstrated in Figure 9-3.

Figure 9–3. Even though individual subjects learned completely in one trial, when the data from a number of individual subjects are pooled, a negatively accelerated learning curve is generated. This gives the erroneous impression that learning is continuous and does not occur in an all-or-none fashion. (From "All-or-None Processes in Learning and Retention," by W. K. Estes, 1964, *American Psychologist, 19*, pp. 16–25. Copyright by the American Psychological Association. Reprinted by permission of the publisher and author.)

$P(C_{n+1}|N_n)$ is read "the probability that subjects will be correct on trial $n + 1$, given that they were incorrect on trial n." $P(C_n)$ is the probability that subjects will be correct on trial n.

It is important to note that because the data were combined, one gets the impression that learning is gradual and improves slightly from trial to trial. When one looks at individual performance, however, the illusion of gradual learning disappears.

In an earlier study, Estes (1960) used another paired associate situation involving a nonsense syllable and a number. He ran 48 subjects on an 8-item paired associate list; that is, there were 8 pairs of nonsense syllables and numbers. Each subject was presented with each of the 8 syllable-number pairs once, and then tested by seeing the syllable alone and guessing the number that was associated with it. This time there was not a multiple choice as there was in the other paired associate study mentioned above.

To differentiate between the point of view that says learning is gradual and the one that says it is all-or-none, Estes hypothesizes four subjects who start the experiment with zero probability of being correct. These four hypothetical subjects see a syllable and a number paired once. When tested, one of the four anticipates the number correctly after seeing the nonsense syllable. Estes supposes that the probability of being correct on subsequent tests is raised from 0 to .25 for the group. But this increase in the probability of being correct can occur in two ways: (a) those who believe in the gradual nature of learning would say that the "associative strength" is increased in all four subjects and therefore on subsequent tests all members of the group have a probability of being correct of .25 and a probability of being wrong

Figure 9–4. The diagram shows what the effects of a single reinforcement is thought to be according to the "associative strength" (upper part of diagram) and all-or-none (lower part of diagram) points of view. N = an incorrect response; C = a correct response; R = the response made on a test trial following one reinforcement. For example, R = N means the subject made an incorrect response on the test trial. (From "Learning Theory and the 'New Mental Chemistry'," by W. K. Estes, 1960, *Psychological Review*, 67, pp. 207–223. Copyright 1960 by the American Psychological Association. Reprinted by permission of the publisher and author.)

R₁   T₁   Rest   T₂

Figure 9–5. Results of paired associated learning experiment. See text for explanation. (From "Learning Theory and the 'New Mental Chemistry'," by W. K. Estes, 1960, *Psychological Review*, 67, pp. 207–223. Copyright 1960 by the American Psychological Association. Reprinted by permission of the publisher and author.)

of .75; (b) the alternative explanation is that one member of the group formed the correct association while the other three did not. According to the principle of all-or-none learning, one person will always be correct on subsequent tests and the other three will always be wrong. The difference between the associative strength point of view and the all-or-none point of view is diagrammed in Figure 9-4.

Now we return to the real experiment involving 48 subjects. Estes indicates that according to the associative strength point of view, how subjects perform on a second test, in the situation described above, should have little to do with whether or not they were correct on the first test. In other words, if the performance of subjects who were wrong on the first test is compared with the performance of subjects who were correct on the first test, it should show that they do about as well on the second test. The all-or-none point of view, on the other hand, would say that all or most of the subjects who were correct on the first test should also be correct on the second test, and the subjects who were wrong on the first test should also be wrong on the second test. Estes ran such a test and the results are summarized in Figure 9-5.

It can be seen in Figure 9-5 that of the 384 possibilities of being correct (48 subjects × 8 paired associates), 49% of the responses on Test 1 were correct and 51% were incorrect. Seventy-one percent of the items that were responded to correctly on Test 1 were also responded to correctly on Test 2, whereas only 9% of the items that were responded to incorrectly on Test 1 were responded to correctly on Test 2. This lends support to the notion that when something is learned, it is learned completely; if it is not learned completely, it is not learned at all. Estes ran some trials with control groups which showed that the 51% of the items missed were just as difficult as the 49% not missed, and that the subjects missing the 51% had the same average learning ability as the other subjects.

As with most notions in learning theory today, Estes's work has not gone uncriticized. Underwood and Keppel (1962), for example, find fault with many aspects of the experiment we have just discussed. Among other things, they wonder, if the all-or-none point of view is correct, why *all* the items that were correct on the first test were not also correct on the second test instead of only 71% of them? Underwood and Keppel feel that Hull's incremental learning theory is better able to handle the data than Estes's all-or-none theory. They say (1962):

> it could be said that if an item were incorrect on the first test trial then it was below the performance threshold; there is no reason why it should be correct on the second test with no intervening study. Likewise, an item above threshold on the first test trial has a high probability of being correct on the second. Items which were correct on the first test trial but not on the second, and those which were not correct on the first but correct on the second, would be handled by some incremental theories via the notion of *oscillation*. (pp. 3–4)

As you may recall, the oscillation effect ($_sO_R$) was part of Hull's theory of learning (see chapter 6). According to Hull, the oscillation effect operated against a learned response in varying amounts from trial to trial and in a random fashion. When the value of $_sO_R$ happened to be high, the probability of a learned response being made on that particular trial was low. When the value of $_sO_R$ was low, it had little effect on the elicitation of a learned response. Hull used the oscillation effect to explain why a learned response may occur on one trial but not on a subsequent trial.

ESTES AND COGNITIVE PSYCHOLOGY

Although Estes remains a contiguity theorist, in recent years, he has been emphasizing cognitive mechanisms in his analysis of learning (see, e.g., Estes 1969a, 1969b, 1971, 1972, 1973, 1978). As we have seen, his earlier analysis followed Guthrie by assuming that whatever stimuli were present at the termination of a learning trial became associated with whatever response terminated the trial. Both Guthrie and Estes viewed learning as the mechanical, automatic association of contiguous events. Essentially, organisms, including humans, were viewed as machines that could sense, record, and respond. Although still mechanistic, Estes's current analysis of learning is much more complex because it considers the influence of cognitive events.

The Importance of Memory. Earlier, Estes maintained that stimuli and responses become associated by contiguity and, once associated, when the stimuli recur, they will elicit the responses associated with them. Now, Estes adds a third element to his analysis, namely, memory (see, e.g., Estes, 1969b, 1972, 1973, 1978). In Estes's current analysis, rather than stimuli leading directly to responses, stimuli elicit memories of previous experiences, and it is the interaction of current stimulation with memories of previous experiences that produces behavior.

Estes (1976) describes what he believes occurs in a decision-making situation where different responses are associated with different outcomes. For example, making an A_1 response will yield 5 points and making an A_2 response will yield 3 points. First, according to Estes, the subject learns the value of each response, and this information is stored in memory. Subsequently, when given the opportunity to respond, the subject will scan the situation to determine what responses are possible and recall what their outcomes are. Given this information, the subject will choose to make the response that yields the most valuable outcome. Estes (1976) calls this the **scanning model of decision-making.** In general, the model claims that in any decision-making situation, an organism will utilize whatever information it has stored in memory concerning response–outcome relationships and will respond in such a way as to produce the most beneficial outcome. It is this scanning model that Estes now uses to explain probability matching (see Estes, 1976).

Memory also plays a prominent role in Estes's analysis of higher order cognitive operations such as those involving language. Following in the tradition of the British empiricists, Estes assumes that simple memories are combined to form complex memories. In learning a language, for example, first individual letters of the alphabet are learned and retained, then words, then sentences, and then other principles of organization. Language utilization, then, requires memories arranged in a hierarchy ranging from the memory of simple elements (e.g., letters) to the memory of complex grammatical rules and principles. Estes (1971) says that complex human behavior such as that involving language: "is better understood in terms of the operation of rules, principles, strategies, and the like than in terms of successions of responses to particular stimuli" (p. 23). According to Estes, it is the interaction of such complex cognitive processes with sensory stimulation that determines how a situation is responded to.

Clearly, with his current analysis, Estes has embraced cognitive psychology in general and information-processing psychology in particular. Information-processing psychology will be discussed in chapter 14.

Estes's Current View of the Role of Reinforcement. Estes's current view of reinforcement is also cognitive in nature. Estes has never been a reinforcement theorist, and he is not one now. His earlier position rejected the law of effect which stated that reinforcement strengthened the bond or connection between a stimulus and a response. Following Guthrie, Estes believed that "reinforcement" prevented the unlearning of an association by preserving the association between certain stimuli and certain responses. Estes's current view of the role of reinforcement stresses the *information* that it provides to the organism (see, e.g., Estes, 1969a, 1971, 1978).

According to Estes, organisms not only learn S-R relationships but R-O (Response-Outcome) relationships as well. That is, organisms learn, and remember, which responses lead to which consequences. In a given situation, some responses lead to reinforcement, some lead to punishment, and others lead to neither reinforcement nor punishment. Reinforcement and punishment do not strengthen or weaken behavior since R-O relationships leading to neither reinforcement nor punishment are learned as readily as those that do (Estes, 1969a). The organism simply learns what leads to what, and this information determines which response is preferred over others that are possible.

In his analysis of reinforcement, Estes makes the extremely important distinction between learning and performance. For him, reinforcement and punishment are not learning variables since learning occurs in their absence. Rather, reinforcement and punishment are performance variables, since they determine how material already learned will manifest itself in behavior.

Although Estes's current position emphasizes cognitive mechanisms (e.g., memory) and views reinforcement and punishment as providing information to the organism, his position still views humans as machinelike. In this regard the major difference between his earlier position and current one is that the machine has become much more complex. Hulse, Egeth, and Deese (1980) nicely summarize Estes's views on how reinforcement and punishment automatically guide behavior:

> The function of reinforcement, in Estes's theory, is not to strengthen directly the formation of new associations; simple contiguity suffices for that. In this regard he is in close harmony with Guthrie. Instead, reinforcing events have their effects on *performance,* which, in Guthrie's terms, means the tendency for a given sequence of learned responses to run to some final conclusion. The function of reinforcement is to provide feedback based on the anticipation . . . of impending reward or punishment which *summates* with current stimuli (or stimuli recalled from memory) in the learning situation and so *guides* behavior preferentially along one path as opposed to another. In essence, in other words, Estes's theory emphasizes a cybernetic model for the influence of reinforcement upon performance: behavior is guided toward goals and away from aversive situations through positive or negative feedback from the reinforcing event. (pp. 73–74)

The term cybernetic in the above quotation refers to a system that is automatically guided by feedback from the environment. Examples of cybernetic systems include the automatic pilot on an aircraft or a thermostat that regulates the temperature of a home. We will have more to say about cybernetic models in chapter 14.

With his informational interpretation of reinforcement, and with distinction between learning and performance, Estes aligns himself with the theories of Edward Tolman (see chapter 12) and Albert Bandura (see chapter 13). Estes, Tolman, and Bandura all believe that we learn what we observe and that how this information is translated into behavior depends upon the goals of the organism. There is also a kinship between Estes's current position and the information-processing approach to psychology. Information-processing psychology maintains that input from the environment (stimuli) interacts with one or more mental processes before it results in output (behavior). Like Estes, many information-processing psychologists accept a cybernetic model in explaining human behavior. In this text, information-processing psychology will be represented by the work of Donald Norman in chapter 14.

LEARNING TO LEARN

The controversy over the incremental versus the all-or-none position of learning (sometimes called the continuity–noncontinuity controversy) is still very much alive and promises to be for some time to come. As with most extreme positions, howev-

Harry F. Harlow. (Courtesy of Harry F. Harlow, University of Wisconsin Primate Laboratory)

er, the truth will probably be found somewhere between the two. An example that seems to be satisfactory to both sides of the debate is Estes's earlier position that, with a complex learning environment, learning proceeds in an all-or-none fashion, only it does so a little bit at a time. In fact, logically, all incremental theories of learning can be reduced to all-or-none theories. What the theorists are really arguing over is the size of the "chunk" of material that is learned on any given trial.

Indeed, there is considerable evidence showing that the incremental and all-or-none positions are both correct. One example comes from the famous work of Harry Harlow. Harlow (1905–1981) received both his undergraduate and graduate education at Stanford University and then went to the University of Wisconsin where he remained until his recent death. Harlow was president of the American Psychological Association (APA) in 1957 and was given the Distinguished Scientific Contribution Award by the APA in 1960. Through the years, Harlow has used his creative research on monkeys to shed light on a variety of topics relevant to human behavior. It is his work on the learning process that concerns us here.

Using the Wisconsin General Test Apparatus shown in Figure 9-6, Harlow presented monkeys with a large number of discrimination problems to solve. In an early study, Harlow (1949) confronted monkeys with a total of 344 discrimination problems, including 32 practice problems. On each problem, they were to pick the one of two objects that had a reinforcer placed underneath it. Each of the 344 problems involved a different set of objects. Harlow's remarkable finding was that the more discrimination problems the monkeys solved, the better they became at solving them. It appeared that the animals were **learning to learn,** or forming what Harlow called a **learning set.** In the early discrimination problems, the monkeys tended to make a large number of errors and improvement from problem to problem was fairly slow. The later problems, however, tended to be solved either with only one error or with none. On the last block of 56 problems, the monkeys chose the correct object 95% of the time by the second trial. It was as if they had developed

Figure 9-6. The Wisconsin General Test Apparatus. (From "The Formation
of Learning Sets," by H. F. Harlow, 1949, *Psychological
Review, 56*, p. 52. Copyright 1949 by the American
Psychological Association. Reprinted by permission.)

the strategy of "win-stay, lose-shift." That is, if they picked the correct object on
the first trial, they stayed with it on the next; if their first choice was incorrect,
however, they switched to the other object on the next trial. The percentage of
correct responses for the first six trials of each of the discrimination problems is
shown in Figure 9-7.

The gains from the early learning trials were slow and incremental in nature.
Later learning, however, was very rapid and more like the all-or-none variety.
Harlow (1949) said: "Before the formation of a discrimination learning set, a single
training trial produces negligible gain; after the formation of a discrimination learning set, *a single training trial constitutes problem solution.* These data clearly show that
animals can gradually learn insight" (p. 56).

To explain his results, Harlow used the concept of **error factors** (Harlow,
1950, 1959). Error factors were erroneous strategies that had to be extinguished
before a discrimination problem could be solved. In other words, error factors are
response tendencies that lead to incorrect responses. One error factor could be the
tendency to always choose the object on the left (position preference); another might
be the tendency to continue to choose the same object although it is incorrect
(stimulus preservation). For Harlow, learning is more a matter of eliminating incorrect strategies (error factors) than it is a matter of strengthening a correct response.
Thus, early learning is slow, since it involves the elimination of error factors; later
learning is rapid since it is based upon a strategy that can be effectively applied to all
two-choice discrimination problems.

Figure 9–7. Harlow found a gradual improvement in the ability to solve discrimination problems. Although performance is relatively poor on early discrimination problems, later problems tend to be solved in just one trial. (From "The Formation of Learning Sets," by H. F. Harlow, 1949, *Psychological Review*, 56, pp. 51–65. Copyright 1949 by the American Psychological Association. Reprinted by permission.)

Another theorist who accepts both the slow incremental and rapid all–or–none interpretations of learning is Donald Hebb. According to Hebb, learning that occurs very early in life is of the incremental variety, whereas later learning is cognitive, insightful, and more all–or–none in nature. We will have more to say about Hebb's views of learning in chapter 15.

THE CURRENT STATUS OF MATHEMATICAL MODELS OF LEARNING

Although we have minimized the mathematics in our coverage of Estes in this chapter, his approach is often referred to as a mathematical model of learning because he attempts to show how the learning process can be described in terms of various mathematical formulations. Mathematical models of learning are relatively new in psychology, and their newness is evident. Psychologists have always wanted to be scientific, and the language of science is mathematics. Therefore, when an opportunity came along to use mathematics in a new way in psychology, it was met with considerable enthusiasm and optimism. Since then, however, it has been found that one of the main contributions of the mathematical study of learning has been to allow a precise description of phenomena that have been studied for years without being described in terms of mathematical models. Outside of this cleanup operation, mathematical models have provided little new information concerning the nature of the learning process. Currently, there are a large number of mathematical formulations to describe different learning phenomena without any unifying theme running through the various formulations. To say that there is a lack of synthesis is not a criticism of mathematical models of learning; rather, it characterizes any new approach to the field.

DISCUSSION QUESTIONS

1. Categorize each of the following theories as accepting either an incremental explanation of learning or an all-or-none explanation: Thorndike, Pavlov, Watson, Guthrie, Skinner, and Hull. Briefly explain your reason(s) for categorizing each theorist as you did.

2. Design an experiment that would allow one to clearly determine whether learning is incremental or all-or-none.

3. Discuss the importance of memory in the current version of Estes's learning theory.

4. Describe Estes's scanning model of decision-making.

5. Why is Estes's explanation of behavior referred to as a cybernetic model?

6. List some advantages and disadvantages of statistical learning theory.

7. From your everyday experience do you feel that learning is incremental or all-or-none? What place do personal feelings of this kind have in science? Explain.

8. Do you feel that a process similar to "learning to learn" occurs in the life of the student? Explain becoming "testwise" in terms of learning to learn.

9. How does Harlow's error factor theory of learning compare to most of the other theories of learning you have covered in this book? For example, does his theory emphasize the "stamping in" of correct responses?

10. Regarding the learning process, briefly describe the incremental (continuity) position, the all-or-none (noncontinuity) position, and the compromise position that would accept both at different times or for different reasons.

11. Do you feel the size of θ would influence the learning process as Estes views it? List some factors you feel might influence the size of θ.

CHAPTER HIGHLIGHTS

Continuity–noncontinuity controversy. Another label for the debate over whether learning occurs gradually and in small increments, or in large steps in an all-or-none fashion.

Error factors. False strategies that operate against the solution of a problem. According to Harlow, learning is more a matter of eliminating error factors than it is a matter of strengthening correct responses.

Learning to learn. The tendency to become increasingly effective at solving problems as more problems are solved. Also called learning set.

Learning set. See Learning to learn.

Markov process. The situation where probabilities of response increase and decrease in a stepwise fashion rather than in small, steady amounts.

Negatively accelerated learning curve. A learning curve that shows the rate of learning to be more rapid during the early trials in a learning situation than it is in the later trials. In other words, as the number of successive learning trials increases, the rate of learning decreases.

Paired associate learning. The learning of pairs of stimuli so that when subjects see the first member of the pair, they can respond by reporting the second member.

Probability matching. In a situation where subjects are asked to guess whether or not an event will occur, the proportion of the trials where they predict the event will occur comes to approximately match the proportion of the trials that it does actually occur. For example, if a light is illuminated on 60% of the trials, subjects will come to predict that it will be illuminated on about 60% of the trials.

Scanning model of decision-making. Estes's description of the decision-making process as involving first learning which responses lead to which outcomes. Given this knowledge of response-outcome relationships, when the person is in a choice situation, he or she will scan the response possibilities and then choose the response that will result in the most valuable outcome.

State of the system. The proportion of stimulus elements in S that are conditioned to A_1 and A_2 responses at any given point in a learning experiment.

Stimulus sampling theory (SST). A theory such as the one developed by Estes that attempts to show how stimuli are sampled and attached to responses.

Theta (θ). The proportion of stimulus elements sampled from S at the onset of a trial in a learning experiment.

10

Gestalt Theory

After J. B. Watson, behaviorism became the rage among American psychologists, and since his time most eminent learning theorists, such as Guthrie, Skinner, and Hull, have been behaviorists. The behavioristic attack on the introspective method of Wundt and Titchener resulted in introspectionism's almost completely being abandoned. At about the same time the behaviorists were attacking introspection in America, a group of psychologists began attacking its use in Germany. This small group of German psychologists called themselves Gestalt psychologists. While the behavioristic movement is thought to have been launched by Watson's article "Psychology as the Behaviorist Views It" which appeared in 1913, the Gestalt movement is thought to have been launched by Wertheimer's article on apparent motion which appeared in 1912.

Although Max Wertheimer (1880–1943) is considered the founder of Gestalt psychology, from its very inception he worked closely with two men who can be considered cofounders of the movement, Wolfgang Köhler (1887–1967) and Kurt Koffka (1886–1941). Köhler and Koffka acted as subjects in the first experiments performed by Wertheimer. Although all three men made significant and unique contributions to Gestalt psychology, their ideas were always in close agreement.

Apparently the entire Gestalt movement started as the result of an insight Wertheimer had while riding a train heading for the Rhineland for a vacation. It occurred to him that if two lights blink on and off at a certain rate, they give the

Max Wertheimer. (From "Max Wertheimer," by W. Köhler, 1944, *Psychological Review*, *51*, pp. 142–146.)

observer the impression that one light was moving back and forth. He left the train and bought a toy stroboscope (a device that is used to present visual stimuli at various rates) with which he conducted numerous simple experiments in his hotel room. He substantiated the notion he had on the train that if the eye sees stimuli in a certain way, they give the illusion of motion. Wertheimer called this apparent motion the **phi phenomenon.** Wertheimer's discovery was to have a profound influence on the history of psychology.

The importance of the phi phenomenon was that it was different from the elements that caused it. The sensation of motion could not be explained by analyzing each of the two lights flashing on and off; somehow the experience of motion emerged from the combination of the elements. For this reason, the members of the Gestalt school believed that although psychological experiences resulted from sensory elements they were different from the sensory elements themselves. In other words, they believed that phenomenological experience (e.g., apparent motion) resulted from sensory experience (e.g., flashing lights) but could not be understood by analyzing the phenomenal experience into its components. That is, *the phenomenological experience is different from the parts that make it up.* This, of course, is what John Stuart Mill had said many years before.

Thus, the Gestaltists believed that the organism added something to experience that is not contained in sensory data, and that something is organization. **Gestalt** is the German word for *configuration* or *organization.* The members of this school believed that we experience the world in meaningful wholes. We do not see isolated stimuli but stimuli gathered together into meaningful configurations or *Gestalten* (plural of *Gestalt*). We see people, chairs, cars, trees, and flowers. We do not see lines and patches of color. Our perceptual field is broken up into organized wholes or Gestalten, and these are the basic subject matter of psychology.

The battle cry of the Gestaltists became "the whole is more than the sum of its parts" or "to dissect is to distort." You cannot really get the full impact of the "Mona Lisa" by looking at first one arm and then another, then the nose, then the mouth, and then trying to put all these experiences together. You cannot understand the experience of listening to a symphony orchestra by analyzing the separate contributions of each of the musicians. The music emanating from the orchestra is more than the sum of the various notes being played by the various musicians. The melody has an *emergent quality* which is something different from the sum of the parts.

Opposition to Both Behaviorism and Structuralism

The structuralists had used the introspective method in order to discover the chemistry of the mind. Influenced by the success of physical chemistry, they attempted to isolate the elements of thought that they believed were combined to produce our complex mental experiences. Since they were interested in studying the mental analog to sensation, they instructed their experimental subjects to avoid naming things and otherwise reading things into their experience. Instead, they were instructed to describe their raw experiences. The structuralists were associationists in that they believed complex ideas were made up of simpler ideas which were combined in some way. Their main concern was to discover these simpler ideas that supposedly were the building blocks of more complicated thoughts.

The functionalist movement, under the influence of Darwinian thought, was gaining momentum in America and began to challenge structuralism. The functionalist was primarily concerned with how human behavior or thought processes were related to survival, and attacked the structuralists for the irrelevance of their approach. Thus, the structuralists were suspect even before the behaviorists came along.

The behaviorists attempted to make psychology completely scientific, and being scientific necessarily involved measurement. They concluded that the only psychological subject matter that could be reliably and publicly measured was overt behavior. The description of conscious elements, as in structuralism, was unreliable because it was influenced by, among other factors, the verbal ability of the reporter. Because it can only be studied indirectly, the behaviorists found consciousness a dubious subject matter for a science.

The Gestalt psychologists maintained that both the structuralists and the behaviorists were making the same basic error in using an elementistic approach. Both attempted to divide up their subject matter into elements in order to understand it; the structuralists sought the elemental ideas that combine to form complex thoughts, and the behaviorists attempted to understand complex behavior in terms of habits, conditioned responses, or stimulus–response combinations.

The Gestaltists saw nothing wrong with the introspective method in general, but they felt the structuralists had misused it. Rather than using the introspective method to divide experiences, it should be used to investigate whole, meaningful experiences. It should be used to investigate how people perceive the world. When the technique is used in this way, it is found that a person's perceptual field consists of events that are organized and meaningful. It is these organized and meaningful events that the Gestaltists believed should be the subject matter of psychology. When these Gestalten are divided up in any way, they lose their meaning. Therefore, perceptual phenomena are to be studied directly and without further analysis. Because of this approach of studying perceptual phenomena directly, the Gestalt psychologist has sometimes been called a phenomenologist. A phenomenologist studies meaningful, intact mental events without dividing them up for further analysis. Following is a list of terms that have been used to describe both the Gestalt and the behavioristic approaches:

Gestalt	Behavioristic
holistic	atomistic, reductionistic, elementistic
molar	molecular
subjective	objective
nativistic	empiricistic
cognitive, phenomenological	behavioral

The only terms on the list whose meaning may not be obvious are **molar** and molecular. In general, *molar* means large and *molecular* means small; when describing behavior, however, molar means a large segment of behavior that is goal directed and purposive, and **molecular behavior** is a small segment of behavior, such as a conditioned reflex, that is isolated for analysis. Obviously, the former would be of more interest to the Gestalt psychologist than the latter. We will have more to say about molar behavior in our discussion of Tolman in chapter 12.

MAJOR THEORETICAL CONCEPTS

Field Theory

Gestalt psychology can be thought of as an attempt to apply **field theory** from physics to the problems of psychology. Roughly speaking, a *field* can be defined as a dynamic interrelated system, any part of which influences every other part. The important thing about a field is that nothing in it exists in isolation. Gestalt psychologists utilize the concept of field on many levels. Gestalten themselves, for instance, can be thought of as a small field; the perceived environment can be looked upon as a field; and people themselves can be thought of as a dynamic interrelated system. Gestalt psychologists believe that whatever happens to a person influences everything else about him or her; for example, the world simply does not look the same if one has a sore toe or an upset stomach. For the Gestalt psychologist, the emphasis is always on a totality or whole and not on individual parts.

Kurt Lewin (1890–1947), another early Gestalt psychologist, used field theory and developed a theory of human motivation around it. He said that human behavior

Kurt Lewin. (From "Kurt Lewin," by E. C. Tolman, 1948, *Psychological Review*, 55, pp. 1–4.)

at any given time is determined by the total number of psychological facts being experienced at the time. A psychological fact, according to Lewin, is anything that has an effect on behavior, including being hungry, a memory of a past event, being in a certain physical location, the presence of certain other people, or having a certain amount of money. All of these psychological facts make up the person's **life space.** Some of these facts will exert a positive influence on the person's behavior and some a negative influence. It is the totality of these events that determines behavior at any given time. For Lewin, only those things consciously experienced could influence behavior; therefore, before anything experienced in the past can influence current behavior, the person must be conscious of it. A change in any psychological fact rearranges the entire life space. Thus, the causes of behavior are continually changing; they are dynamic. The person exists in a continually changing field of influences, and a change in any one of them affects all the others. This is what is meant by a psychological field theory.

Nature Versus Nurture

The behaviorists tended to look upon the brain as the passive receiver of sensations that, in turn, produced responses. The brain to them was a complex switchboard. Human nature, said the behaviorists, is determined by what we experience. The content of the "mind" is therefore looked upon as the synthesis of our experiences, and little else. The Gestaltists assigned a more active role to the brain. The brain, to them, was not a passive receiver and storer of information from the environment. The brain acted upon incoming sensory information in such a way as to make it more meaningful and organized. This is not a learned function but is the result of the brain's structure. The organizational abilities of the brain are genetically determined and occur in every normal, healthy, human brain. Thus, like Plato, Descartes, and Kant, the Gestalt psychologists can be considered nativists, since they all believed important attributes of the mind exist independently of experience. This belief, of course, is diametrically opposed to the behaviorist's notion of the passive mind.

We can say, therefore, that according to the Gestalt psychologists, the tendency to divide our perceptual field into meaningful units is inherited. Note that the Gestalt psychologists are not saying that *ideas* are inherited, but only the tendency to organize incoming sensory information in certain lawful ways. In summary, we can say that the Gestaltists, stressing the importance of genetic influences on perception, are nativistic; that is, they stress the importance of abilities that the organism comes equipped with at birth. The behaviorists, on the other hand, say that even the tendency to organize experience comes from experience, thus stressing nurture rather than nature in explaining perception and learning. As we shall see later in this chapter, however, the Gestaltists did not neglect the role of experience altogether.

Law of Prägnanz

The Gestalt psychologists' main concern has always been with perceptual phenomena. Through the years, well over 100 perceptual principles have been studied by Gestalt theorists. However, one overriding principle applies to all mental events, including the principles of perception, and that is the **law of Prägnanz** (*Prägnanz* is the German word for precision). Koffka (1935/1963) defined the law of Prägnanz as follows: "Psychological organization will always be as good as the controlling circumstances allow" (p. 110). By "good," Koffka meant such qualities as simple, concise, symmetrical, or harmonious. In other words, there is a tendency for every psychological event to be meaningful, complete, and simple. A good figure, or a good perception, or a good memory, cannot be made simpler or more orderly through any kind of perceptual shift; that is, there is nothing more we can do mentally that would make the conscious experience any more organized. The law of Prägnanz was used by the Gestaltists as their guiding principle while studying perception, learning, and memory. Later the law of Prägnanz was also applied to the areas of personality and psychotherapy.

Of the many principles of perception studied by the Gestalt theorists we will discuss only the **principle of closure** because it relates directly to the topics of learning and memory. The principle of closure states that we have a tendency to complete incomplete experiences. For example, if a person looks at a line that is almost circular except for a small gap in it, the person will tend to fill in the gap perceptually and respond to the figure as if it were a complete circle. This principle, like all the others, follows the general law of Prägnanz which says that we respond to the world so as to make it maximally meaningful under existing conditions. Because responding to a complete geometric form is more meaningful than responding to what is really physically present (an incomplete circle), we tend to fill in

Figure 10–1. Examples of how incomplete figures are perceived as complete ones, thus exemplifying the principle of closure. (The cat example is from *Psychology: Understanding Human Behavior*, 4th ed., p. 229, by Q. A. Sartain, J. A. North, R. J. Strange, & M. H. Chapman, 1973, New York: McGraw-Hill. Reprinted by permission.)

the gap perceptually. Examples of closure are shown in Figure 10-1. We will discuss a possible explanation for closure later in this chapter and again when we discuss Hebb's theory in chapter 15.

THE PERCEPTUAL CONSTANCIES

Perceptual constancy refers to the fact that we see an object as the same object under a variety of circumstances. We say a door is a door regardless of what position the door is in. We identify a person as the same person whether he or she is standing in front of us or a block away. The Gestaltists point out that in each case, the actual stimulation has changed radically; what has remained constant is the *meaning* of the object. Thus, the meaning an object conveys is much more important than the actual physical stimulation involved. Köhler (1929) said:

> The man approaching us on the street does not grow larger, as for simple optical reasons he should. The circle observed on the oblique plane does not become an eclipse; it seems to remain a circle after its retinal image has become a very flat eclipse. The white object in the shadow remains white, the black paper remains black in full light, though the first may reflect much less light than the second. These three examples have one common property: the physical object *as such* remaining constant, while actual stimulation varies according to more or less accidental conditions (of distance, of position, of illumination), our experience agrees with the constancy of the physical object much better than with the varying stimulation produced by it. (p. 80)

The elementistic approach of the behaviorist which emphasizes either basic sensations or the nature of the stimulating environment would probably, according to the Gestaltists, miss the most important point involved in perceptual constancies—the object's *meaning* remains constant. Once again we have an example of how the brain organizes sensory information to make it more meaningful. The fact that the brain recognizes the same object under a wide variety of circumstances makes our conscious experiences much more harmonious than if we had to learn to recognize an object anew each time it was presented to us in a slightly different way. The behaviorist would say, however, that the notion of stimulus generalization could handle this problem quite easily.

THE BRAIN AND CONSCIOUS EXPERIENCE

Every major psychological theory must in some way deal with the mind-body problem. The problem can be stated in many ways, for example, "How can something purely physical cause something purely mental?" or "What is the relationship between the body and consciousness?" No matter how elementistic one's answer becomes—even studying how individual brain cells respond to various forms of stimulation—the question as to how the external world is translated into conscious experience still remains.

The behaviorists solved the mind-body problem by ignoring it. In fact, they concentrated their investigations on behavior in order to avoid the mind-body problem. The structuralist's view of the mind-body was that bodily sensations gave rise to, or caused, mental images. The belief that the contents of the mind vary as a function of sensory experience is referred to as **epiphenomenalism.** Thus, for the structuralists, there was a direct relationship between the body (sensation) and the mind (the ideas caused by sensations).

The Gestaltists took a much different approach to solving the mind-body problem than did the structuralists or the behaviorists. They assumed an **isomorphism** between psychological experience and the processes that exist in the brain. External stimulation causes reactions in the brain and we experience those reactions *as they occur in the brain.* The main difference between this point of view and the one held by the structuralists is that the Gestaltists believed *the brain actively transformed sensory stimulation.* The brain, they thought, organized, simplified, and made meaningful incoming sensory information. We experience the information only after it has been transformed by the brain in accordance with the law of Prägnanz. Köhler said (1947): "Experienced order in space is always structurally identical with a functional order in the distribution of underlying brain processes" (p. 61). Koffka said (1935/1963): "Thus, isomorphism, a term implying equality of form, makes the bold assumption that the 'motion of the atoms and molecules of the brain' are not 'fundamentally different from thoughts and feelings' but in their molar aspects, considered as processes in extension, identical" (p. 62). Over and over, the Gestalt psychologists stated their belief that the phenomenal world (consciousness) is an accurate expression of the circumstances that exist in the brain.

With their concept of psychophysical isomorphism, the Gestaltists felt they solved a major problem that the more mechanistic theories had not solved, that is, "How does the *mind* organize sensory information and make it meaningful?" The Gestalt psychologist answered this question by saying that the content of thought (consciousness) comes to us already organized; it is organized by the brain before we experience it or as we are experiencing it. Therefore, to the Gestaltists, *the activities of the brain correspond dynamically with the content of thought.* It should be made clear that from this point of view the brain is much more than a complex switchboard. According to the Gestaltists, the brain actively transforms incoming sensory information according to the law of Prägnanz and this transformed information is what we are "conscious" of. The relationship among external stimulation, the brain, and conscious experience can be diagrammed as follows:

Because of their strong belief in an "active mind," the Gestaltists are clearly rationalists, and because they believe the "powers of the mind" are genetically determined, they are clearly nativists. These beliefs place them in the tradition of Plato, Descartes, and Kant.

SUBJECTIVE AND OBJECTIVE REALITY

Since we can only experience impulses from the physical world after they have been transformed by the brain, what is it that determines behavior? It cannot be the physical environment because, in a sense, we never experience the physical environment directly. For the Gestalt theorists, it is consciousness or subjective reality that determines behavior, and that fact has profound implications. According to the Gestalt theorists, the law of Prägnanz is not the only thing that transforms and gives meaning to what we experience physically. Things such as beliefs, values, needs, and attitudes also embellish what we experience consciously. This means, of course, that people in exactly the same physical environment will vary in their interpretation of that environment and, therefore, in how they react to it. To make this point, Koffka distinguished between the **geographical environment** (objective or physical reality) and the **behavioral environment** (psychological or subjective reality). Koffka believed that in order to understand why people act as they do, it is more important to know their behavioral environments than it is to know their geographical environment. Koffka (1935/1963) uses an old German legend to show the importance of subjective reality in determining behavior:

> On a winter evening amidst a driving snowstorm a man on horseback arrived at an inn, happy to have reached a shelter after hours of riding over the wind-swept plain on which the blanket of snow had covered all paths and landmarks. The landlord who came to the door viewed the stranger with surprise and asked him whence he came. The man pointed in the direction straight away from the inn, whereupon the landlord, in a tone of awe and wonder, said: "Do you know that you have ridden across the Lake of Constance?" At which the rider dropped stone dead at his feet.
>
> In what environment, then, did the behavior of the stranger take place? The Lake of Constance? Certainly, because it is a true proposition that he rode across it. And yet, this is not the whole truth, for the fact that there was a frozen lake and not ordinary solid ground did not affect his behavior in the slightest. It is interesting for the geographer that this behavior took place in this particular locality, but not for the psychologist as the student of behavior; because the behavior would have been just the same had the man ridden across a barren plain. But the psychologist knows something more: since the man died from sheer fright after having learned what he had "really" done, the psychologist must conclude that had the stranger known before, his riding behavior would have been very different from what it actually was. Therefore the psychologist will have to say: There is a second sense to the word environment according to which our horseman did not ride across the lake at all, but

across an ordinary snow-swept plain. His behavior was a riding-over-a-plain, but not a riding-over-a-lake.

What is true of the man who rode across the Lake of Constance is true of every behavior. Does the rat run in the maze *the experimenter* has set up? According to the meaning of the word "in," yes and no. Let us therefore distinguish between a *geographical* and a *behavioral* environment. Do we all live in the same town? Yes, when we mean the geographical, no, when we mean the behavioral "in." (pp. 27–28)

Thus, according to Koffka, beliefs are powerful determinants of behavior. In this regard, he was in close agreement with the theories of Tolman and Bandura, which will be covered in chapters 12 and 13.

GESTALT PRINCIPLES OF LEARNING

The most famous work on learning by a member of the Gestalt school was done by Köhler at the University of Berlin Anthropoid Station on Tenerife, one of the Canary Islands. Köhler did his work between 1913 and 1917 and summarized his findings in *The Mentality of Apes* (1925). While on Tenerife, Köhler also studied the problem-solving ability of chickens, although this work is rarely mentioned.

Since Gestalt psychologists were primarily field theorists interested in perceptual phenomena, it is no surprise to find them looking at learning as a special problem in perception. They assumed that when an organism is confronted with a problem, a state of cognitive disequilibrium is set up and continues until the problem is solved. Therefore, to the Gestalt psychologist, cognitive disequilibrium had motivational properties that caused the organism to attempt to regain the balance in its mental system. According to the law of Prägnanz, cognitive balance is more satisfying than cognitive disbalance. On this point the Gestaltists are in close agreement with both Guthrie and Hull. It can be said that problems provide maintaining stimuli (or drive, to use Hull's term) which persist until the problem is solved, at which point the maintaining stimuli terminate (the drive is reduced). Support for this point of view was provided by the work of Bluma Zeigarnik who found that incompleted tasks were remembered longer and in greater detail than completed ones. She explained this phenomenon in terms of the motivational properties of a problem that persist until the problem is solved. The tendency to remember incompleted tasks better than completed ones has come to be called the **Zeigarnik effect.**

Learning, to the Gestaltist, is a cognitive phenomenon. The organism "comes to see" the solution after pondering a problem. The learner thinks about all the ingredients necessary to solve a problem and puts them together (cognitively) first one way and then another until the problem is solved. When the solution comes, it comes suddenly, that is, the organism gains an *insight* into the solution of a problem. The problem can exist in only two states: (a) unsolved and (b) solved; there is no state of partial solution in between. As we saw in chapter 4, Thorndike believed that learning was continuous in that it increased systematically in small amounts as a

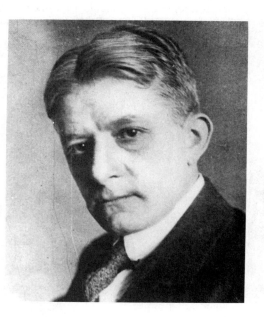

Wolfgang Köhler. (From *Psychologies of 1925*, p. 144, by C. Murchison, ed., 1926, Worcester, MA: Clark University Press.)

function of reinforced trials. The Gestaltists believed that either a solution is reached or it is not; learning to them was discontinuous. As we saw in chapter 9 the continuity–noncontinuity controversy is still very much alive today.

In order to test his notions about learning, Köhler used a number of creative experimental arrangements. One arrangement involved detour problems. In a detour problem, the animal can clearly see its goal but is unable to reach it directly. The animal must turn away from the sight of the object it wants and take an indirect route to reach it. A typical detour problem is diagrammed in Figure 10-2. With this type of problem, Köhler found that chickens had great difficulty in reaching a solution, but apes did so with relative ease.

A second kind of arrangement utilized by Köhler necessitated the animal's using an implement of some kind in reaching a goal. For example, a banana was placed just out of the reach of an ape so that it must either use a stick to reach it or put two sticks together so that they were long enough for the animal to reach it. In either case, the animal had all the ingredients necessary to solve the problem available to it; it was just a matter of putting them together in an appropriate manner.

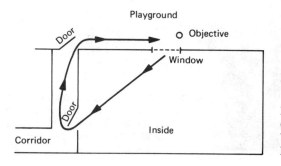

Figure 10-2. A typical detour problem. (From *The Mentality of Apes*, p. 21, by W. Köhler, 1925, London: Routledge and Kegan Paul Ltd.)

Figure 10–3. An ape named Chica using a pole to obtain food. (From *The Mentality of Apes*, p. 72a, by W. Köhler, 1925, London: Routledge and Kegan Paul Ltd.)

Figure 10–4. An ape named Grande using a stack of boxes to obtain food as Sultan watches. (From *The Mentality of Apes*, p. 138a, by W. Köhler, 1925, London: Routledge and Kegan Paul Ltd.)

Figure 10–5. Grande creating an even more elaborate structure. (From *The Mentality of Apes*, p. 142a, by W. Köhler, 1925, London: Routledge and Kegan Paul Ltd.)

Figure 10–6. Chica beating down her objective with a pole. (From *The Mentality of Apes*, p. 146a, by W. Köhler, 1925, London: Routledge and Kegan Paul Ltd.)

Figure 10–7. Sultan putting two sticks together. (From *The Mentality of Apes*, p. 128a, by W. Köhler, 1925, London: Routledge and Kegan Paul Ltd.)

Figure 10-3 shows the ape named Chica using a pole to obtain fruit. Figure 10-4 shows the ape named Grande using a stack of boxes that it arranged in order to reach some bananas. Figure 10-5 shows Grande putting together an even more complex structure. Figure 10-6 shows Chica using both boxes and a pole to obtain the fruit. Figure 10-7 shows Sultan, Köhler's most intelligent ape, putting together two sticks in order to reach fruit that otherwise would be inaccessible.

The Presolution Period

Usually a rather lengthy period of time transpires before an insightful solution to a problem is reached. Describing what happens during this period, the Gestalt psychologist comes fairly close to the concept of trial-and-error learning, but the trial-and-error learning they refer to is cognitive rather than behavioral. The organism, they say, runs through a number of "hypotheses" concerning an effective way to solve the problem. The animal *thinks* about different possible solutions until it hits upon one that works and then it acts upon that solution behaviorally. When the correct strategy is discovered, insight is said to have occurred. Of course, for insightful learning to occur, the organism must be exposed to all elements of the problem; if it is not, its behavior will seem to be blind and groping. This, say the Gestaltists, was the problem with Thorndike's research. Thorndike found what appeared to be incremental learning because important elements of the problem were hidden from the animal, thus preventing insightful learning. The reader can experience the "aha" experience that usually accompanies insightful learning by trying to find the hidden bear in Figure 10-8.

Typically one searches through a good portion of the picture before the hidden shape is found. The problem creates a cognitive disequilibrium whose mild tension lasts until the problem is solved. In this case, discovering the bear restores cognitive equilibrium, relaxes the tension, and may make one feel like saying "aha."

Figure 10–8.   Can you find the hidden bear? (From *Introduction to Psychology*, p. 164, by N. L. Munn, D. L. Fernald, Jr., & P. S. Fernald, 1972, Boston: Houghton Mifflin.)

Insightful Learning Summarized

Insightful learning is usually regarded as having four characteristics: (a) the transition from presolution to solution is sudden and complete; (b) performance based upon a solution gained by insight is usually smooth and free of errors; (c) a solution to a problem gained by insight is retained for a considerable length of time; and (d) a principle gained by insight is easily applied to other problems. We shall see an example of this last characteristic of insightful learning in our discussion of transposition below.

Transposition

When a principle learned in one problem solving situation is applied to the solution of another problem, the process is referred to as **transposition.** Köhler's early work on transposition was done with chickens and apes. The typical experiment involved training an animal to approach one of two shades of gray paper; for example, chickens were fed on a dark shade of gray paper, but not on a lighter shade. After such training, when the animal was given a choice between the two shades of gray, it approached the darker one. If the experiment was to end at this point, the behaviorists would be delighted, since that is exactly how the animal should react according to their point of view. It is the second part of the experiment, however, that the Gestaltists felt was most revealing.

After the preliminary training, the animal was given a choice between the dark

Stimuli: Used During Preliminary Training

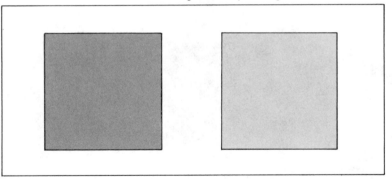

Stimuli: Used During the Transposition Test

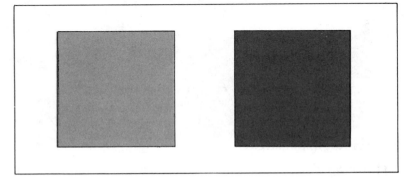

Figure 10–9. First the animal is taught to approach a dark gray stimulus and then is offered a choice between the dark gray stimulus and a still darker gray stimulus. If the animal chooses the darker of the two, transposition is said to have been demonstrated.

paper on which it was trained and a still darker sheet of gray paper. The situation is diagrammed in Figure 10-9.

How will the animal respond to the new situation? The answer to that question depends on how one views the learning process. The Gestaltists felt that the behaviorists would have to predict that the animal would approach the lighter of the two shades of gray in the new situation since it is the exact one that had been reinforced in the first phase of the experiment. The Gestaltists, however, did not view learning as the development of specific habits or S-R connections. To them what was learned in this kind of a situation was a relational principle, that is, they felt the animal learned the principle of approaching *the darker of the two objects* in the first phase of the experiment and that same principle would be applied in the second phase of the experiment. The Gestaltists would predict, therefore, that the animal would choose the darker of the two objects in Phase 2, although they had been reinforced for choosing the other object in Phase 1. Generally speaking, the prediction made by the Gestalt psychologists in this situation is an accurate one.

The Behaviorists' Explanation of Transposition

In the kind of learning situation described above, the behaviorists tend to talk about the learning of specific S-R connections. As a result, their views on learning have been referred to as an **absolute theory.** On the other hand, since the Gestalt view of learning emphasizes the comparison between the two stimuli, it has been referred to as a **relational theory.** Köhler's research created some problems for the absolute position until Spence came up with his now famous explanation of the transposition phenomenon based on S-R concepts (Spence, 1937).

Suppose, said Spence, that an animal is reinforced for approaching a box whose lid measures 160 sq cm, and not reinforced for approaching a box whose lid measures 100 sq cm. Soon the animal will learn to approach the larger box exclusively.

In Phase 2 of this experiment, the animal chooses between the 160 sq cm and a box whose lid is 256 sq cm. The animal will usually choose the larger box (256 sq cm) even though it had been reinforced specifically for choosing the other one (160 sq cm) during Phase 1. Again, this finding seems to support the relational learning point of view.

Spence's behavioristic explanation of transposition is based on generalization. As was mentioned in chapter 6, Spence assumed that the tendency to approach the positive stimulus (160 sq cm) generalizes to other related stimuli. Second, he assumed that the tendency to approach the positive stimulus (and the generalization of this tendency) is stronger than the tendency to avoid the negative stimulus (and the generalization of this tendency). What behavior occurs will be determined by the algebraic summation of the positive and negative tendencies. Spence's explanation is diagrammed in Figure 10-10.

Figure 10-10.   According to Spence's explanation of transposition, the tendency to avoid a stimulus (dashed curve) must be subtracted from the tendency to approach a stimulus (solid curve). It is the net value that results when these positive and negative influences are added algebraically that determines which of the two stimuli will be approached. (From "The Basis of Solution by Chimpanzees of the Intermediate Size Problem," by K. W. Spence, 1942, *Journal of Experimental Psychology, 31,* p. 259.)

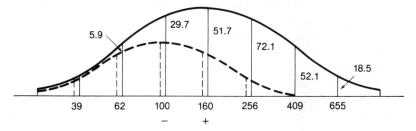

Whenever there is a choice between two stimuli, the one eliciting the greatest net approach tendency will be chosen. In the first phase of Spence's experiment, the animal chose the 160 sq cm box over the 100 sq cm box because the net positive tendency was 51.7 for the former and 29.7 for the latter. In Phase 2, the 256 sq cm box was chosen over the 160 sq cm box because the net positive tendency was 72.1 for the former and still 51.7 for the latter.

Spence's explanation has the advantage of making some unexpected predictions of transpositional phenomena. For example, his theory would predict that transposition should break down at some point and, in the example above, the animal would choose the smaller object in a pair of test stimuli. This would happen if the animal were presented with a choice between a 256 sq cm box and any box larger than 409 sq cm. In all choices involving a 256 sq cm box and a box 409 sq cm or larger, the animal will choose the *smaller of the two,* thereby reversing the principle the animal was supposed to have learned. Likewise, if given a choice between a 160 sq cm box and one slightly larger than 409 sq cm, choices will be about equally divided, since the net positive tendency for each box is about the same.

Since Spence's theory could predict both the successes and failures of the transposition phenomenon, his point of view became more popular than the Gestalt point of view. Research on various aspects of transposition, however, has demonstrated that both S-R and Gestalt predictions fail under certain circumstances, and the matter is still very much unsettled.

PRODUCTIVE THINKING

During the later years of his life, Max Wertheimer was especially interested in applying Gestalt principles to education. His book **Productive Thinking,** which addressed educational issues, was published in 1945, two years after his death, and was expanded and republished in 1959 under the editorship of his son Michael. In *Productive Thinking,* Wertheimer explored the nature of problem solving and the techniques that could be used to teach it. The conclusions reached were based on personal experience, experimentation, and personal interviews with individuals such as Albert Einstein. For example, chapter 10 in his book is entitled "Einstein: The Thinking That Led to the Theory of Relativity."

Wertheimer contrasts rote memorization with problem solving based on Gestalt principles. With the former, the learner has learned facts or rules without truly understanding them. Such learning is rigid, forgotten easily, and can be applied only to limited circumstances. Learning in accordance with Gestalt principles, however, is based on an understanding of the underlying nature of the problem. Such learning comes from within the individual and is not imposed by someone else; it is easily generalizable and it is remembered for a long time.

When one acts upon memorized facts or rules without understanding them one can often make stupid mistakes, such as when a nurse, while making her rounds on the night shift, wakes up patients to give them their sleeping pills (Michael Wertheimer, 1980). As a further example of what can result if basic principles are not understood, Wertheimer (1945/1959, pp. 269–270) gives the example of a school inspector who was impressed by the children that he had observed but wanted to ask one more question before departing. "How many hairs does a horse have?" he asked. Much to the amazement of both the inspector and the teacher, a 9-year-old boy raised his hand and answered "3,571,962." "How do you know that your answer is correct?" asked the inspector. "If you do not believe me," answered the boy, "count them yourself." The inspector broke into laughter and vowed to tell the story to his colleagues when he returned to Vienna. When the inspector returned the following year for his annual visit, the teacher asked him how his colleagues responded to the story. Disappointedly, the inspector said, "I wanted very much to tell the story but I couldn't. For the life of me, I couldn't remember how many hairs the boy had said the horse had." Although the story was admittedly hypothetical, Wertheimer used it to demonstrate what can happen if a person depends on memorized facts instead of on the understanding of principles.

Wertheimer insisted that two traditional approaches to teaching actually inhibit the development of understanding. The first is teaching which emphasizes the importance of logic. Both inductive and deductive logic prescribe rules that must be followed in arriving at conclusions. Although such rules may have relevance for a narrow range of problems, they do not, according to Wertheimer, facilitate problem-solving ability. Wertheimer (1945/1959) said: "Traditional logic is concerned with the criteria that guarantee exactness, validity, consistency of general concepts, propositions, inferences and syllogisms. The main chapters of classical logic refer to these topics. To be sure, sometimes the rules of traditional logic remind one of an efficient police manual for regulating traffic" (p. 6).

According to Wertheimer, reaching an understanding involves many aspects of learners, such as their emotions, attitudes, and perceptions, as well as their intellects. In gaining insight into the solution to a problem, a student need not—in fact should not—be logical. Rather, the student should cognitively arrange and rearrange the components of the problem until a solution based on understanding is reached. Exactly how this is done will vary from student to student.

The second teaching strategy believed by Wertheimer to inhibit understanding is based on the doctrine of associationism. This approach to teaching typically emphasizes the learning of correct S-R connections through drill, memorization, and external reinforcement. Although Wertheimer believed that learning does occur under these circumstances, he believed it to be trivial compared to insightful learning. Wertheimer (1945/1959) made the following comment about teaching based on associationism: "Basically the items are connected in the way in which my friend's telephone number is connected with his name, in which nonsense syllables become reproducible when learned in a series of such syllables, or in which a dog is conditioned to respond with salivation to a certain musical sound" (p. 8).

Wertheimer believed that any teaching strategy based either on associationism or on logic could do little to enhance understanding, but could do a great deal to inhibit it.

As an example of the difference between rote memorization of facts and/or rules and understanding based on insight, Wertheimer (1945/1959) gave the example of students learning to determine the area of a parallelogram. The standard way of teaching children to find the area of a parallelogram is as follows:

1. First students are taught how to find the area of a rectangle by multiplying its altitude by its base.

2. Next a parallelogram is introduced and the teacher demonstrates how it is converted into a rectangle by drawing three lines as follows:

3. Once converted into a rectangle the area can be found by multiplying altitude times base.

Wertheimer discovered that following such training students could find the areas of parallelograms presented in a standard way, but many were confused when figures were presented in a nonstandard way or when they were asked to find the areas of geometric forms other than parallelograms. An example of a figure that caused confusion in some students is shown in Figure 10-11.

Other students, however, seemed to grasp the principle behind the formula. They saw that a rectangle was a balanced figure that could be subdivided into columns and rows of small squares which when multiplied together gave the number of squares in the entire rectangle, or its area. For example:

It was this conceptualization that was behind the formula altitude × base. Students with this insight knew that the manipulations done on the parallelogram merely rearranged the configuration so that the squares could be easily counted. Students understanding the "squares solution" were able to solve a wide variety of problems that other students without such an understanding were unable to solve. The students who had gained insight into the nature of the problem knew that their task was to take whatever form was presented to them and rearrange it so that its area was represented as a rectangle.

Figure 10-12 shows three figures presented to students and how those students with an understanding of the principle involved found their areas as compared to the students who blindly attempted to apply the rule they had been taught to reach their

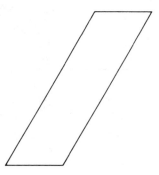

Figure 10–11. An example of a figure that caused confusion in students who attempted to find its area by dropping perpendicular lines from the two upper corners to the base line. (From *Productive Thinking*, p. 15, by M. Wertheimer, 1959, New York: Harper & Row. Copyright © 1945, 1959 by Valentin Wertheimer. Reprinted by permission of Harper & Row, Publishers, Inc.)

solutions. Note that when students attempted to apply the formula that they had memorized in finding the areas of these figures their results were incorrect.

When the insight of rearranging a geometric form so that its area is represented as a rectangle is reached, students know which kinds of problems can be solved using this principle and which cannot be. Students with this insight know that the

Figure 10–12. The portion of the figure labeled A indicates the forms presented to students. The portion of the figure labeled B shows how students with an understanding of the problem found the areas of the forms. The portion of the figure labeled C indicates how students without an understanding of the problem attempted to find the area of the forms. (From *Productive Thinking*, p. 18, by M. Wertheimer, 1959, New York: Harper & Row. Copyright © 1945, 1959 by Valentin Wertheimer. Reprinted by permission of Harper & Row, Publishers, Inc.)

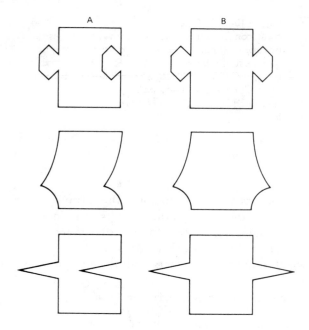

Figure 10–13.   The areas of the forms in Column A can be found using the strategy of balancing excesses and discrepancies, whereas the areas of the forms in Column B cannot be. (From *Productive Thinking*, p. 19, by M. Wertheimer, 1959, New York: Harper & Row. Copyright © 1945, 1959 by Valentin Wertheimer. Reprinted by permission of Harper & Row, Publishers, Inc.)

"excesses" in the forms on the left in Figure 10-13 equal the indentations and therefore they can be solved using this principle; the figures on the right cannot be.

The students solving the problems with an understanding seem to see the various figures as having "too much here" and "not enough there." Their goal, then, becomes one of balancing the figures so that the part that is "too much" is placed in the part of the figure where there is "not enough." In this way the "strange" figures are converted into ones they are familiar with and therefore can be dealt with. This rearrangement can be cognitive or physical. For example, one of the students that Wertheimer worked with asked for a scissors and cut one end of the parallelogram and placed it on the other end, thus creating a rectangle. Another student asked for a scissors and cut the parallelogram in the middle and fastened the two pieces together, creating a rectangle. These operations are shown in Figure 10-14.

Wertheimer emphasized the same point over and over. That is, learning based on understanding is deeper and more generalizable than learning involving rote memorization. To truly learn students must come to see the nature or the structure of the problem and this they must do themselves. It is true that a teacher can guide students to such insights, but ultimately they must occur within the students themselves.

In closing this section, one additional example of the difference between rote memorization and understanding will be offered. Michael Wertheimer (1980) describes an experiment performed by Katona in 1940. In this experiment, a slip with the following 15 digits was handed to a group of subjects with the instruction that they study the digits for 15 sec:

1 4 9 1 6 2 5 3 6 4 9 6 4 8 1

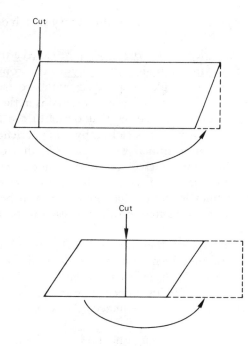

Figure 10–14. Two methods used by students to convert a parallelogram into a rectangle. (From *Productive Thinking*, p. 48, by M. Wertheimer, 1959, New York: Harper & Row. Copyright © 1945, 1959 by Valentin Wertheimer. Reprinted by permission of Harper & Row, Publishers, Inc.)

After the subjects observed the list of digits, they were asked to reproduce the sequence of numbers in the order that they appeared. Most subjects were able to reproduce only a few of the numbers. After a week most of the subjects remembered none of the digits. Another group of subjects was asked, prior to seeing the series of digits, to look for a pattern among the digits. Upon seeing the series some of these subjects declared, "Those are the squares of the digits from 1 to 9." The subjects that saw the pattern were able to reproduce the series perfectly not only during the experiment but weeks and months afterward. Thus we see again that learning based on an understanding of the principles involved in a problem-solving situation is very thorough and is retained almost perfectly for long periods of time. Also note that no external reinforcement was involved in this experiment. The only reinforcement was intrinsic and came when the learner gained an insight into the solution of the problem. The emphasis on intrinsic reinforcement as opposed to extrinsic reinforcement has characterized most of the cognitive theories since the early work of the Gestalt psychologists.

THE MEMORY TRACE

We mentioned earlier that Gestalt psychologists tended to be nativists in that they stressed inherited abilities in their explanation of learning and perception. Although they mainly stressed genetic factors, they also took into account the effects of experience. There was too much substantial evidence for the effects of prior experience on present experience to be ignored. Koffka (1935/1963) attempted to link the past with the present through his concept of the **memory trace.** Koffka's treatment of the memory trace is long and complicated and only a rudimentary sketch of it can be presented here.

Koffka assumed that a current experience gave rise to what he called a **memory process.** The process is the activity in the brain caused by an environmental experience. This process could be simple or complex, depending on the experience it was based on. When a process is terminated, a trace of its effect remains in the brain. This trace, in turn, will influence all similar processes that occur in the future. According to this point of view, a process, which is caused by an experience, can occur only once in "pure" form; thereafter similar experiences result from the interaction between the process and the memory trace. Thus, each time a process is aroused, it modifies the organism and that modification influences future experiences. In fact, Koffka says, if one defines learning as a modification in behavior potential that results from experience, each elicitation of a process can be looked upon as a learning experience.

What is the nature of the influence of the trace on the process? Koffka (1935/1963) answers that a trace "exerts an influence on the process in the direction of *making it similar to the process which originally produced the trace*" (p. 553). The stronger the memory trace, the stronger will be its influence on the process; therefore, one's conscious experience will tend to be more in accordance with the trace than with the process.

According to this point of view, if the last thing one did in a problem-solving situation was to solve the problem, the solution becomes "etched" in one's mind. The next time one is in a similar problem-solving situation, a process will occur that will "communicate" with the trace from the previous problem-solving situation. The trace then will influence the ongoing process in the direction stated above,

Kurt Koffka. (From *Psychologies of 1925*, by C. Murchison, ed., 1926, Worcester, MA: Clark University Press.)

making the problem easier to solve. With repetition the trace becomes more and more influential over the process. In other words, as the animal solves more problems that are similar, it becomes a better problem-solver. Koffka explains improvement in a skill as the result of the increasing influence of the trace on the process.

At this point in Gestalt theorizing, we see considerable agreement with Guthrie. It seems, for example, that Koffka accepts the recency principle, which states that what an organism did last in a situation is what it will do if the situation recurs. Likewise, as we shall see below, the Gestaltists are in essential agreement with Guthrie's explanation as to how repetition results in improvement of a skill.

Individual Trace Versus Trace System

Solving an individual problem is but a specific occurrence of problem-solving behavior, and learning to type the letters *A, B,* and *C* are but specific occurrences of the more general behavior we call typing. Every complex skill can be looked upon as consisting of many processes and their corresponding traces, and yet each of the individual traces have in common that they are related to the same skill. Numerous interrelated individual traces are referred to as a **trace system.** Koffka assumes that through repetition the trace system becomes more important than the individual traces that make it up. The "wholeness" quality of the skill comes to dominate the individual traces, thereby causing them to lose their individuality. This phenomenon may at first seem paradoxical; that is, repetition can benefit learning although it tends to destroy the traces of individual experiences. Koffka (1935/1963) said:

> There is loss of consolidation of the *single individual* traces which we are apt to overlook because it is accompanied by a gain in the stability of the *trace system.* When we learn to type, the individual lessons will soon be forgotten, and the clumsy movements which we originally executed will at a later stage be impossible; i.e., the traces of the first lessons have become changed by the aggregate of traces which has been produced by the many repetitions and is responsible for the improvement of the skill. Similarly, when we stay in a room for any length of time, we get a great number of impressions of it by moving about or merely letting our eyes roam. But only a few of them can be recalled. (p. 545)

Just as the individual trace exerts a greater influence on future processes as it becomes more fixed, so does the trace system exert greater influence on related processes as it becomes more fixed. This contention has very interesting implications. For example, it is assumed that through the years we develop trace systems that correspond to similar experiences. Thus we develop trace systems that correspond to chairs, dogs, trees, males, females, or pencils. These trace systems will be a kind of neurological summation of all our experiences with objects in a certain class, such as cows, or clowns. Since these trace systems become firmly established, they will have a profound effect on any individual experience we may have. For example, if we look at an individual elephant, the process aroused by that elephant will be influenced by the trace system that resulted from all our other experiences with elephants. The resulting experience will be a combination of the two influences, with the trace system being the most important. Our memory of that event, then, will be one of "elephantness" that has little to do with any particular elephant but has more to do with what they have in common. This also serves to explain the phenomenon of closure. The individual experience of a partial circle is dominated by the trace system of "circleness" and the resulting experience is one of a complete circle.

Memory, like perception and learning, follows the law of Prägnanz. Memories tend to be complete and meaningful, even when the original experience was not. Irregular experiences tend to be remembered as regular, unique events are remembered in terms of something familiar (e.g., a catlike object will be remembered as a cat), and minor flaws or discrepancies in a figure will tend to be forgotten. It is the enduring features of past experience, rather than uncommon occurrences, that guide our behavior. Again, the emphasis is on the pattern, the Gestalt, the wholeness of experience and the recollection of experience. This is contrasted with the association theory of memory accepted by the behaviorists. The associationists accept the "bundle hypothesis" which states that complex thoughts are made up of simple ideas bound together by contiguity, similarity, or contrast. Memory occurs when one element in the bundle causes the recall of the other elements. The Gestaltists rejected association theory in favor of the law of Prägnanz in explaining all aspects of human experience, including perception, learning, and memory.

Behaviorism had nothing to say about perception and early Gestalt theory had little or nothing to say about learning. But when the Gestaltists fled to America from Nazi Germany, they began to address the problem of learning because it was a major interest of American psychologists. Gestalt theory was clearly better able to handle problems in perception, mostly because behaviorism, in excluding mental events from its domain of study, ignored the topic of perception. So on the one hand we had the Gestalt theorists attempting to expand their perceptual theory to cover learning, and on the other hand, we had the behaviorists ignoring perceptual learning. As usual, accepting a paradigm as an ideology blinded both the Gestaltists and the behaviorists to important aspects of the learning process. Fortunately, later thinkers have attempted to utilize the best of both paradigms. The best example of an effort to combine the two paradigms is Tolman's theory of learning, to which we turn in chapter 12.

The healthy debate between the Gestalt psychologists and the behaviorists resulted in each point of view's being modified because of criticism from the other. Both positions were extreme and both have left an indelible mark on psychology. Thanks to the Gestalt psychologists the study of cognitive processes is no longer taboo. However, cognitive processes currently are being studied under rigorous laboratory conditions under such headings as risk-taking, problem solving, and concept formation. For the insistence on operationally defining these concepts and on empirically verifying any statement made about them, we can thank the behavioristic influence.

DISCUSSION QUESTIONS

1. What was it about the approaches to the study of psychology used by the structuralists and the behaviorists that the Gestalt theorists disagreed with?

2. What is meant by the statement, "The law of *Prägnanz* was used by the Gestalt psychologists as an overriding principle in their explanation of perception, learning, memory, personality, and psychotherapy"?

3. Discuss the term *isomorphism* as it is used in Gestalt theory.

4. Distinguish between geographical and behavioral environments. Which of the two did the Gestalt theorists believe was the more important determinant of behavior? Explain why you do or do not agree with the Gestalt theorists on this matter.

5. Discuss the topic of memory from the point of view of a Gestalt psychologist. Include in your answer the concepts of process, individual trace, and trace system.

6. Explain transposition from both a Gestalt and a behavioristic point of view.

7. Summarize the characteristics of insightful learning.

8. What is meant by the statement, "For the Gestalt psychologist, learning is basically a perceptual phenomenon"?

9. List some differences between classroom procedures developed according to Gestalt principles and those developed according to S-R principles. In general, do you feel American public schools are based on a Gestalt model or a behavioristic model? Explain.

10. How might a behaviorist explain the "perceptual constancies"?

11. Summarize Wertheimer's thoughts on productive thinking. Include in your answer some of the differences between solutions to problems that are based on rote memorization and those based on an understanding of the principles involved in the problem.

CHAPTER HIGHLIGHTS

Absolute theory. The contention of the behaviorists that what an organism learns are specific responses to specific stimuli.

Behavioral environment. According to Koffka, the environment as it is consciously experienced. Also referred to as subjective reality.

Epiphenomenalism. The belief that bodily sensations cause mental images. In other words, mental images are seen as the byproducts of bodily experiences.

Field theory. The belief that the environment consists of interdependent events. In psychology, field theory assumes that behavior and/or cognitive processes are a function of many variables that exist simultaneously, and a change in any one of them changes the effect of all the others.

Geographical environment. According to Koffka, the physical or objective environment. Also referred to as objective reality.

Gestalt. A German word meaning pattern or configuration.

Individual memory trace. The memory trace left by a specific experience.

Insightful learning. Learning that occurs very rapidly, is remembered for a considerable length of time, and transfers readily to situations related to the one in which the insightful learning took place.

Isomorphism. As the term is used by the Gestalt psychologists, it means the relationship that exists between brain activity and consciousness.

Law of Prägnanz. The overriding principle in Gestalt psychology which states that all mental events tend toward completeness, simplicity, and meaningfulness.

Life space. A concept employed by Kurt Lewin to describe the simultaneous influences on a person at a given time. Anything that can affect behavior was called a "psychological fact" and the total number of "psychological facts" influencing a person at any given moment was his or her life space.

Memory process. The brain activity that is caused by environmental stimulation.

Memory trace. The remnants of an environmental experience after the experience is terminated.

Molar behavior. A large segment of behavior that is goal-directed and therefore purposive.

Molecular behavior. A small segment of behavior, such as a conditioned reflex, that is isolated for detailed study.

Nativist. See Chapter Highlights, chapter 3.

Nature-versus-nurture controversy. The debate as to whether genetics or experience is more important in determining the characteristics of such cognitive processes as perception and reasoning.

Perceptual constancy. The tendency to respond to an object as the same object although it is experienced under varying circumstances.

Phenomenology. The study of intact, meaningful mental events. These intact, meaningful mental events are called phenomenological experiences. It is these phenomenological experiences that the structuralists wanted their subjects to actively avoid and that the Gestalt psychologists felt were the basic subject matter of psychology.

Phi phenomenon. The experience of apparent motion that is caused by lights flashing on and off at a certain frequency. Wertheimer's discovery of apparent motion launched the Gestalt school of psychology.

Principle of closure. Tendency to complete incomplete experiences, thereby making them more meaningful.

Productive thinking. Wertheimer's term for thinking that is based on the understanding of the principles involved in a problem rather than on logic and/or the rote memorization of facts and/or rules.

Relational theory. The contention of the Gestalt psychologists that the organism learns in terms of a principle or relationship and not in terms of specific responses to specific stimuli.

Trace system. A number of interrelated individual memory traces.

Transposition. The Gestalt version of transfer of training which states that a principle that works in solving a problem will tend to be applied to the solution of similar problems.

Zeigarnik effect. The tendency to remember uncompleted tasks longer than completed ones.

11

Jean Piaget

Jean Piaget was born on August 9, 1896 in Neuchâtel, Switzerland. His father was a historian whose specialty was medieval literature. Piaget showed early interest in biology and when only 11 years old he published a one-page article on a partially albino sparrow he had seen in a park. Between 15 and 18, he published a number of articles on mollusks. Piaget noted that because of his many publications, he was accidentally offered the position of curator of the mollusk collection in the Geneva Museum while he was still a secondary school student.

As an adolescent, Piaget vacationed with his godfather who was a Swiss scholar. It was through this visit with his godfather that Piaget developed an interest in philosophy in general and in **epistemology** in particular. (Epistemology is a branch of philosophy that is concerned with the nature of knowledge.) Piaget's interests in biology and epistemology continued throughout his life and were clearly evident almost everywhere in his theoretical writings.

Piaget received his PhD in biology at the age of 21 and by the time he was 30, he had published over 20 papers, mainly on mollusks, but on other topics as well. For example, at the age of 23, he published an article on the relationship between psychoanalysis and child psychology. After receiving his doctorate, Piaget held a variety of jobs, among them a position with the Binet Testing Laboratory in Paris where he helped to standardize intelligence tests. The Binet Laboratory's approach to testing was to develop a number of test questions which were then presented to children of different ages. It was found, in general, that older children could answer more questions correctly than younger children, and that some children could answer more questions correctly than other children of the same age. The former children were considered to be more intelligent than the latter children. Thus, the child's intelligence quotient was derived from the number of questions a child of a certain age could answer correctly. It was during his employment at the Binet Laboratory that Piaget developed his interest in the intellectual abilities of children. This interest in the intellectual abilities of children, as well as his interests in biology and epistemology, permeated all of Piaget's work.

Jean Piaget. (Courtesy of the Université de Genève.)

While working on the standardization of intelligence tests, Piaget noted something that was to have a major influence on his later theory of intellectual development. He discovered that a child's *incorrect* answers to test questions were more informative than the child's correct answers. He observed that the same kind of mistakes were made by children of approximately the same age, and that the kind of mistakes generally made by children of one age was *qualitatively* different from the kind of mistakes made by children of different ages. Piaget observed further that the nature of these mistakes could not be explored adequately in a highly structured testing situation where children either answered questions correctly or they did not. Instead, Piaget employed the **clinical method,** which was an open-ended form of questioning. Using the clinical method, Piaget's questions were determined by the child's answers. If the child would say something of interest, Piaget would formulate a number of questions designed to explore further that item of interest. This method of gathering data is used by Piaget's followers to this day.

It was during his employment at the Binet Laboratory that Piaget began to realize that "intelligence" could not be equated with the number of test items that a child answered correctly. To Piaget, the more basic question was *why* some children were able to answer some questions correctly and other children were not, or why a child could answer some items correctly but miss other items. Piaget began his search for the variables influencing the test performance of children. His search was to result in a view of intelligence which was as revolutionary as Freud's view of human motivation.

Piaget left Binet's laboratory to become director of research at the Jean-Jacques Rousseau Institute in Geneva, Switzerland, where he was able to pursue his own interests using his own methods. Soon after his affiliation with the institute, his first major works on developmental psychology began to appear. Piaget, who never had a course in psychology, soon became an internationally known authority on child psychology. He continued his work using his own three children as subjects. He and his wife (a former student of his at the Rousseau Institute) made careful observations about their children over a long period of time and summarized their findings in several books. The fact that Piaget's own children were used as sources of information in the development of his theory has often been criticized. The fact that more elaborate observations, involving large numbers of other children, have been in agreement with Piaget's earlier observations has tended, however, to still this criticism.

Piaget published about 30 books and over 200 articles, and continued doing productive research at the University of Geneva until his death in 1980. His theory of intellectual development in the child was extensive and complicated and in this chapter we merely will summarize its essential features. It will also become apparent that Piaget's approach to the learning process is different from all the other approaches covered in this text.

The information in this chapter was compiled from several sources. The secondary sources utilized were Beard, 1969; Flavell, 1963; Furth, 1969; Phillips, 1975, 1981; and Ginsberg and Opper, 1979. The primary sources utilized were Inhelder and Piaget, 1958; Piaget, 1966, 1970a, 1970b; and Piaget and Inhelder, 1969.

MAJOR THEORETICAL NOTIONS

Intelligence

We noted earlier that Piaget was opposed to defining **intelligence** in terms of the number of items answered correctly on a so-called intelligence test. To Piaget, an intelligent act is one that causes an approximation to the conditions optimal for an organism's survival. In other words, intelligence allows an organism to deal effectively with its environment. Since both the environment and the organism are changing constantly, an "intelligent" interaction between the two must also change constantly. An intelligent act always tends to create optimal conditions for the organism's survival *under the existing circumstances*. Thus, for Piaget, intelligence is a dynamic trait since what is available as an intelligent act will change as the organism matures biologically and as it gains experience. Intelligence, according to Piaget, is an integral part of any living organism since all living organisms seek those conditions conducive to their survival, but how intelligence manifests itself at any given time will necessarily vary as conditions vary. Piaget's theory has often been referred to as **genetic epistemology** since it attempts to trace the development of intellectual capabilities. It should be clear that the term *genetic* refers to developmental growth rather than biological inheritance. Piaget's views on how intellectual potential develops will be summarized in the remainder of this chapter.

Schemata

A child is born with a few highly organized reflexes such as sucking, looking, reaching, and grasping. Rather than discussing individual occurrences of any one of these reflexes, Piaget chose to talk about the general potential to do such things as suck, look, reach, or grasp. The potential to act in a certain way was labeled **schema** (plural, schemata). For example, the grasping schema refers to the general ability to grasp things. The schema is more than a single manifestation of the grasping reflex. The grasping schema can be thought of as the cognitive structure that makes all acts of grasping possible.

When any particular instance of grasping is being observed or described, one must talk in terms of a specific response to specific stimuli. These aspects of any particular manifestation of a schema are called **content.** Again, schema refers to a general potential to perform a class of behaviors and content describes the conditions that prevail during any particular manifestation of that general potential.

Schema was an extremely important term in Piaget's theory. A schema can be thought of as an element in the organism's cognitive structure. The schemata available to an organism will determine how it can respond to the physical environment. Schemata can manifest themselves in overt behavior, as in the case of the grasping reflex, or they can manifest themselves covertly. Covert manifestations of a schema can be equated roughly with thinking. We will have more to say about covert manifestations of a schema later in this chapter. In both the case of overt behavior and of thinking, the term content refers to the specifics of a particular manifestation of a schema.

Obviously, the way a child is able to deal with its environment changes as he or she grows older. In order for new organism-environment interactions to occur, the schemata available to the child must change. We will examine next the circumstances under which schemata change.

Assimilation and Accommodation

As we saw above, the number of schemata available to an organism at any given time constitutes that organism's **cognitive structure.** How an organism interacts with its environment will depend on the kind of cognitive structures it has available. In fact, how much of the environment can be understood, or even responded to, is determined by the various schemata available to the organism. In other words, the cognitive structures determine what aspects of the physical environment can even "exist" for the organism.

The process of responding to the environment in accordance with one's cognitive structures is called **assimilation.** Assimilation refers to a kind of matching between the cognitive structures and the physical environment. The cognitive structures that exist at any given moment set bounds on what can be assimilated by the organism. For example, if only the sucking, looking, reaching, and grasping schemata are available to a child, then everything she or he experiences will be assimilated into those schemata. As cognitive structures change it becomes possible for the child to assimilate different aspects of the physical environment.

Clearly, if assimilation were the only cognitive process, there would be no intellectual growth since an organism would simply go on assimilating its experiences into its existing cognitive structures. However, a second equally important process provides a mechanism for intellectual growth. The second process is called **accommodation.** Accommodation is the process by which cognitive structures are modified.

Every experience a person has involves both assimilation and accommodation. Events for which the organism has corresponding cognitive structures are readily assimilated, but events for which the organism has no existing cognitive structures necessitate accommodation. Thus, all experiences involve two equally important processes: recognition, or knowing, which corresponds to the process of assimilation, and accommodation which results in the modification of cognitive structures. Such modification can be roughly equated with learning. To put the matter still another way, we respond to the world according to our previous experience (assimilation) but each experience contains aspects unlike anything we had experienced before. These unique aspects of experience cause changes in our cognitive structures (accommodation). Accommodation, then, provides a major vehicle for intellectual development. Ginsburg and Opper (1979) give an example of how assimilation and accommodation are related:

Suppose an infant of 4 months is presented with a rattle. He has never before had the opportunity to play with rattles or similar toys. The rattle, then, is a feature of the environment to which he needs to adapt. His subsequent behavior reveals the tendencies of assimilation and accommodation. The infant tries to grasp the rattle. In order to do this successfully he must accommodate in more ways than are immediately apparent. First, he must accommodate his visual activities to perceive the rattle correctly, for example by locating it in space. Then he must reach out, adjusting his arm movements to the distance between himself and the rattle. In grasping the rattle, he must mold his fingers to its shape; in lifting the rattle he must accommodate his muscular exertion to its weight. In sum, the grasping of the rattle involves a series of acts of accommodation, or modifications of the infant's behavioral structures to suit the demands of the environment.

At the same time, grasping the rattle also involves assimilation. In the past the infant has already grasped things; for him, grasping is a well-formed structure of behavior. When he sees the rattle for the first time he tries to deal with the novel object by incorporating it into a habitual pattern of behavior. In a sense he tries to transform the novel object to something that he is familiar with—namely, a thing to be grasped. We can say, therefore, that he assimilates the objects into his framework and thereby assigns the object a "meaning." (p. 19)

Assimilation and accommodation are referred to as **functional invariants** because they occur at all levels of intellectual development. It should be clear, however, that early experiences tend to involve more accommodation than later experiences, because more and more of what is experienced will correspond to existing cognitive structures making substantial accommodation less necessary as the individual matures.

Equilibration

One might ask what the driving force behind intellectual growth is. For Piaget, the answer would be found in his concept of **equilibration.** Piaget assumed that all organisms have an innate tendency to create a harmonious relationship between themselves and their environment. In other words, all aspects of the organism are geared toward optimal adaptation. Equilibration is this innate tendency to organize one's experiences so as to assure maximal adaptation. Roughly, equilibration can be defined as the continuous drive toward equilibrium or balance.

The concept of equilibration is for Piaget what the concept of hedonism was for Freud or self-actualization was for Maslow or Jung. It is his major motivational concept which, along with assimilation and accommodation, is used to explain the steady intellectual growth observed in children. Next we will describe how these three processes interact.

As we have seen, assimilation permits the organism to respond to a present situation in accordance with previous knowledge. Because the unique aspects of the situation cannot be responded to on the basis of previous knowledge, these novel or unique aspects of an experience cause a slight cognitive disbalance. Since there is an innate need for harmony (equilibrium), the organism's mental structures change in order to incorporate these unique aspects of the experience, thus causing the sought-after cognitive balance. As with the Gestalt psychologists, lack of cognitive balance has motivational properties that keep the organism active until a balance is attained. In addition to restoring the balance, however, this adjustment paves the way for new and different interactions with the environment. The accommodation described causes a change in mental structures so that if those previously unique aspects of the environment were again encountered they would not cause a disbalance, that is, they would be readily assimilated into the organism's existing cognitive structure. In addition, this new cognitive arrangement forms the basis for new accommodations, since accommodation always results from a disbalance and what causes a disbalance must always be related to the organism's current cognitive structures. Gradually, through this adaptive process, information that could not at one time be assimilated eventually can be. It is the dual mechanisms of assimilation and accommodation, along with the driving force of equilibration, that provides for slow, but steady intellectual growth. The process can be diagrammed as follows:

Interiorization

Children's early interactions with the environment are strictly sensorimotor, that is, they respond directly to environmental stimuli with reflex motor reactions. Children's early experiences, then, involve the use and elaboration of their innate schemata such as grasping, sucking, looking, and reaching. The results of these early experiences are registered in the cognitive structures and gradually transform them. With increasing experience, children expand their cognitive structures, thereby making it possible for them to adapt more readily to an ever increasing number of situations.

As more elaborate cognitive structures develop, children are capable of responding to more complex situations. Also, they are less dependent on the here and now. For example, they are capable of "thinking" of objects that are not before them. Now, what children experience are functions of both the physical environment and their cognitive structures which reflect their cumulative prior experiences. This gradual decreasing dependence on the physical environment and the increased utilization of cognitive structures is called **interiorization**.

As the cognitive structures develop, they become increasingly important in the adaptive process. For example, elaborate cognitive structures make more complex problem solving possible. As more experiences are interiorized, thinking becomes a tool in adapting to the environment. Early in development a child's adaptive responses are direct and simple and without thought. The child's early adaptive responses are mainly overt. As the process of interiorization continues, however, the child's adaptive responses become more covert; they involve internal actions rather than external ones. Piaget called these internal covert actions **operations** and the term operation can be roughly equated with "thinking." Now, rather than manipulating the environment directly, the child can do so mentally through the use of operations.

The most important characteristic of any operation is that it is reversible. **Reversibility** means that once something is thought, it can be "unthought"; that is, an operation, once performed, can be mentally undone. For example, one can first mentally add 3 and 5 making a total of 8 and then mentally subtract 3 from 8 making a total of 5.

As we have seen, first the child's adjustment to the environment is direct and involves no thinking (operations). Next, as the child develops more complex cognitive structures, thinking becomes more important. The early use of operations depends upon those events the child can experience directly; that is, the child can think about those things that he or she can see. Piaget called these **concrete operations** since they are applied to concrete environmental events. Later operations, however, are completely independent of physical experience and they therefore allow the child to solve purely hypothetical questions. Piaget called the latter **formal operations.** Unlike the concrete operation, the formal operation is not bound to the environment.

Interiorization, then, is the process by which adaptive actions become increasingly covert rather than overt. In fact, operations can be thought of as interiorized actions. Adaptive behavior, which first involves only sensorimotor schemata and overt behavior, evolves to the point where formal operations are utilized in the adaptive process. The use of formal operations characterizes the highest form of intellectual development.

Although intellectual growth is continuous, Piaget found that certain mental abilities tend to appear at certain stages of development. It is important to note the word *tend*. Piaget and his colleagues found that although mental abilities appear around a certain age level, some children will show the ability earlier and some later than other children. Although the actual age at which an ability appears may vary from child to child or from culture to culture, the order in which mental abilities appears does not vary since mental development is always an extension of what has already preceded. Thus, although children of the same age may have different mental abilities available to them, the order with which the abilities emerge is constant. Below we will summarize the various stages of intellectual development suggested by Piaget.

STAGES OF DEVELOPMENT

(1) **Sensorimotor stage (birth to 2 years).** This stage is characterized by the absence of language. Because the children have no words for things, objects cease to exist when children are not dealing directly with them. Interactions with the en-

vironment are strictly sensorimotor and deal only with the here and now. Children at this stage are egocentric. Everything is seen with themselves as a frame of reference and their psychological world is the only one that exists. Toward the end of this stage, children develop the concept of object permanence. In other words, they come to realize that objects go on existing even when they are not experiencing them.

(2) **Preoperational thinking (2 to 7 years).** This stage has two subdivisions:

a. Preconceptual thinking (about 2 to 4 years). During this part of preoperational thinking, children begin rudimentary concept formation. They begin to classify things in certain classes because of their similarity, but they make a number of mistakes because of their concepts; thus, all men are "Daddy," and all women are "Mommy," and all toys they see are "mine." Rather than their logic being either inductive or deductive, it is *transductive.* An example of transductive reasoning would be "cows are big animals with four legs. That animal is big and has four legs; therefore, it is a cow."

b. Period of intuitive thought (4 to 7 years). During this part of preoperational thinking, the child solves problems intuitively, instead of in accordance with some logical rule. The most striking characteristic of the child's thinking during this stage is his or her failure to develop **conservation.** Conservation is defined as the ability to realize that number, length, substance, or area remains constant even though these things may be presented to the child in a number of different ways. For example, a child is shown two containers filled to some level with some liquid.

Next, the contents of one container are poured into a taller, thinner container.

At this stage of development, the child, who observed that the first containers contained an equal amount of liquid, will now tend to say that the taller container has more liquid because the liquid is higher in the container. The child at this stage cannot mentally reverse cognitive operations, which means he or she cannot mentally pour the liquid from the tall container back into the shorter one and see that the amount of liquid is the same in both.

For Piaget, conservation is an ability that comes about as a result of the child's cumulative experiences with the environment and it is not an ability that can be taught until the child has had these preliminary experiences. As with all stage theories, teachability is a central issue. Do various capabilities come about because of certain experiences (e.g., learning), or do they unfold as a function of maturation along some genetically determined path? For Piaget it is both. Maturation provides the necessary sensory apparatus and brain structures but it takes experience to develop the ability. The question as to whether conservation can be taught before "its time has come" is still open; some say yes (e.g., LeFrançois, 1968), and some say no, thus agreeing with Piaget (e.g., Smedslund, 1961).

(3) **Concrete operations (about 7 to 11 or 12 years).** Children now develop the ability to conserve, along with the abilities to deal adequately with classes, with seriation (i.e., they can arrange things from smallest to largest, and vice versa), and with number concepts. During this stage, however, the thought processes are directed to real events observed by the child. The child can perform rather complex operations on problems as long as the problems are concrete and not abstract.

The following diagram represents a typical problem given to children who are about 11 years old in order to study their thought processes. Their task is to determine what letter should go into the empty section of the circle. Perhaps you would like to try to solve the problem yourself.

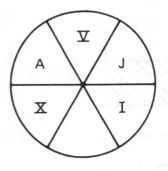

In order to solve the problem, one must realize that the letter of the alphabet opposite the Roman numeral I is A, the first letter of the alphabet. Also, the letter across from Roman numeral X is J, the tenth letter of the alphabet. Thus, the letter across from Roman numeral V must be the fifth letter of the alphabet, or E. At least two concepts must be utilized in solving such a problem: "one-to-one correspondence" and "opposite to." That is, it must be realized that Roman numerals and letters of the alphabet can be placed so that they correspond and it must also be realized that the corresponding numerals and letters are placed opposite one another. If children do not have these concepts available, they cannot solve the problem. Likewise, if they can solve the problem, they must have the concepts available.

4. Formal operations (about 11 or 12 to 14 or 15 years). Children can now deal with hypothetical situations and their thought processes are not tied down exclusively to what is immediate and real. Thinking at this stage is as logical as it will ever become. This means that the mental apparatus that a person has is as sophisticated as it will ever be, but this apparatus can be directed toward the solution of a never ending array of problems throughout one's life.

OPTIMAL CONDITIONS FOR LEARNING

It should be clear that if something cannot be at least partially assimilated into an organism's cognitive structure, it cannot act as a biological stimulus. It is in this sense that the cognitive structures create the physical environment. As the cognitive structures become more elaborate, the physical environment becomes better articulated. Likewise, if something is so far from an organism's cognitive structure that it cannot be accommodated, no learning will take place. For optimal learning to take place, information must be presented that can be assimilated into present cognitive structures, but at the same time, be different enough to necessitate a change in those structures. If the information cannot be assimilated, it simply cannot be understood. If it is completely understood, however, no learning is necessary. In fact, in Piaget's theory, assimilation and understanding mean about the same thing. This is about what Dollard and Miller meant by their term **learning dilemma,** which points out that all learning depends upon failure. According to Piaget, failure of previous knowledge to allow for assimilation of an experience causes accommodation, or new learning. Experiences should be moderately challenging in order to stimulate cognitive growth. Again, no such growth will occur if only assimilation occurs.

One must determine for each individual learner what kind of cognitive structures they have available and slowly change these structures one small step at a time. It is for this reason that Piaget would favor a one-to-one relationship between teacher and pupil. It should be obvious, however, that he would favor such a relationship for much different reasons than a theorist like Skinner, who also favors such a relationship.

Often Piaget is thought of as a pure nativist who believes intellectual development occurs as the result of biological maturation. Clearly this is not the case. Piaget believed that maturation provides only the framework for intellectual development, but in addition to this framework, both physical and social experience are indispensable for mental development. Inhelder and Piaget (1958) put the matter as follows: "The maturation of the nervous system can do no more than determine the totality of possibilities and impossibilities at a given stage. A particular social environment remains indispensable for the realization of these possibilities. It follows that their realization can be accelerated or retarded as a function of cultural and educational conditions" (p. 337).

Elsewhere Piaget said (1966):

The human being is immersed right from birth in a social environment which affects him just as much as his physical environment. Society, even more, in a sense, than the physical environment, changes the very structure of the individual, because it not only compels him to recognize facts, but also provides him with a ready-made system of signs, which modify his thought; it presents him with new values and it imposes on him an infinite series of obligations. (p. 156)

Ginsburg and Opper (1979) summarize the ways in which Piaget felt heredity influenced cognitive development: "(a) Inherited physical structures [e.g., the nervous system] set broad limits on intellectual functioning; (b) Inherited behavioral reactions [e.g., reflexes] have an influence during the first few days of human life but afterward are extensively modified as the infant interacts with his environment; and (c) the maturation of physical structures may have psychological correlates [e.g., when the brain matures to the point where language development is possible]" (p. 17).

And, as we have seen, equilibration, or the tendency to seek a harmony between one's self and the physical environment, is also inherited.

INTO WHAT CAMP DOES PIAGET'S THEORY FALL?

Clearly, Piaget is not an S-R theorist. As we have seen, S-R theorists attempt to determine the relationship between environmental events (S) and responses to those events (R). Most S-R theorists assume a passive organism which builds up response capabilities by accumulating habits. Complex habits, according to this point of view, are merely combinations of simpler habits. Certain S-R relationships are "stamped in" either by reinforcement or by contiguity. Knowledge, according to such a point of view, represents a "copy" of conditions that exist in the physical world. In other words, through learning, relationships that exist in the physical world come to be represented in the organism's brain. Piaget refers to this epistemological position as a copy theory of knowledge.

Piaget's theory is diametrically opposed to the S-R conception of knowledge. As we have seen, Piaget equated knowledge with cognitive structures which provide potential to deal with the environment in certain ways. The cognitive structures provide a framework for experience; that is, they determine what can be responded to and how it can be responded to. In this sense, the cognitive structures are projected onto the physical environment and thus create it. In this way the environment is constructed by the cognitive structures. But it also is correct to say that the environment plays a large part in creating the cognitive structures. As we have seen, the interaction between the environment and the cognitive structures through the processes of assimilation and accommodation is of primary importance in Piaget's theory. Piaget differentiated his views of intelligence and knowledge from those of empiricists as follows (1970b):

In the common view, the external world is entirely separate from the subject, although it encloses the subject's own body. Any objective knowledge, then, appears to be simply the result of a set of perceptive recordings, motor associations, verbal descriptions, and the like, which all participate in producing a sort of figurative copy or "functional copy" (in Hull's terminology) of objects and the connections between them. The only function of intelligence is systematically to file, correct, etc., these various sets of information; in this process, the more faithful the critical copies, the more consistent the final system will be. In such an empiricist prospect, the content of intelligence comes from outside, and the coordinations that organize it are only the consequences of language and symbolic instruments.

But this passive interpretation of the act of knowledge is in fact contradicted at all levels of development and, particularly, at the sensorimotor and prelinguistic levels of cognitive adaptation and intelligence. Actually, in order to know objects, the subject must act upon them, and therefore transform them: he must displace, connect, combine, take apart, and reassemble them.

From the most elementary sensorimotor actions (such as pushing and pulling) to the most sophisticated intellectual operations, which are interiorized actions, carried out mentally (e.g., joining together, putting in order, putting into one-to-one correspondence), knowledge is constantly linked with actions or operations, that is, with *transformations*. (pp. 703–704)

There is both agreement and disagreement between Piaget's theory and Gestalt theory. Both agree that experiences are organized. Both believe that there is an innate need for a psychological balance and that a disbalance has motivational properties. Both believe that prior experience influences present experience. As we noted in the last chapter, the Gestalt theorists contended that as the memory trace becomes more fully established, it has an increasing influence on experience. Thus, when the memory trace of "circleness" is firmly established, an incomplete circle is experienced as a complete circle. The memory trace therefore "constructed" an experience that was not in accordance with physical reality. In a way, we can say that experiences are assimilated into existing memory traces, just as they are assimilated into existing cognitive structures. Just as cognitive structures are slowly changed by cumulative experiences, so are memory traces.

The major source of disagreement between the Gestalt theorists and Piaget is over the developmental nature of one's organizational ability. The Gestalt theorists believe that humans are born with a brain that organizes experiences according to the law of Prägnanz (see previous chapter). They believe that sensory data is experienced in an organized fashion at all stages of development. Piaget, on the other hand, believed that the organizational abilities of the brain develop as the cognitive structures develop. To him, experience is always organized in terms of the cognitive structures, but the cognitive structures are always changing as a function of both biological maturation and sensory experience. Thus, Piaget used the term **progressive equilibrium** to describe the fact that the balance or organization that is sought is optimal under existing circumstances, and that those circumstances are constantly changing.

The difference between Piaget and the Gestalt theorists on the matter of innate organizational abilities would result in a difference in educational practices. Teachers attempting to utilize Gestalt principles in their teaching practices would tend to emphasize the "Gestalt" at all levels of education; seeing the total picture would be all-important. Such teachers would accept group discussions or even the lecture system. Piagetian teachers in attempting to utilize Piaget's theory in their teaching practices, as we mentioned earlier, would be very concerned about the individual student. Such a teacher would first attempt to determine what stage of development a particular student was at before deciding what information to present. She would realize that knowing something about the student's cognitive structures would enable her to present the student with information that he or she would be ready to assimilate. There is considerable difference, then, in assuming that the brain is constantly organizing experiences and in assuming that organizational ability varies at different stages of development.

One can see that Piaget's theory is hard to classify in the traditional categories. It is empirical in the sense that knowledge depends upon experience, but clearly it is not empirical in the same way that an S-R theory is. One is tempted to compare Piaget's theory of knowledge with that of Kant (see chapter 3), but Kant's categories of the mind were innate whereas Piaget's are the result of cumulative experience. Piaget's theory is not entirely empirical, however. The concept of equilibration provides a nativistic component to his theory. It is this innate drive toward harmony between the internal and external environment that provides the basis of all intellectual growth. We see in Piaget's theory, then, a creative mixture of many points of view; for that reason his theory is similar to that of Tolman to which we turn in the next chapter.

SUMMARY OF PIAGET'S THEORY

According to Piaget, children are born with a few sensorimotor schemata which provide the framework for their initial interactions with the environment. The child's early experiences are determined by these sensorimotor schemata. In other words, only those events that can be assimilated into these schemata can be responded to by children, and they therefore set limits on their experience. Through experience, however, these initial schemata are modified. Each experience contains unique elements that the child's cognitive structure must accommodate. Through this interaction with the environment, the child's cognitive structure changes, allowing for an ever growing number of experiences. This is a slow process, however, since new schemata always evolve from those that existed previously. In this way, intellectual growth that starts out with the child's responding reflexively to the environment, develops to the point where the child is able to ponder potential events and to explore mentally probable outcomes.

Interiorization results in the development of operations that free children from needing to deal directly with the environment by allowing them to deal with symbolic manipulations. The development of operations (interiorized actions) provides children with a highly complex means of dealing with the environment and they are, therefore, capable of more complex intellectual actions. Since their cognitive structures are more articulated, so are their physical environments; in fact, their cognitive structures can be said to construct the physical environment. It should be remembered that the term *intelligent* is used by Piaget to describe all adaptive activity. Thus, the behavior of a child grasping a rattle is as intelligent as an older child's solving a complex problem. The difference is in the cognitive structures available to each child. According to Piaget, an intelligent act always tends to create a balance between the organism and its environment under the existing circumstances. The ever present drive toward this balanced state is called equilibration.

Although intellectual development is continuous during childhood, Piaget chose to refer to stages of intellectual development. He described four major stages: (a) sensorimotor, where children deal directly with the environment by utilizing their innate reflexes; (b) preoperational, where children begin rudimentary concept formation; (c) concrete operations, where children use interiorized actions or thought to solve problems in their immediate experience; and (d) formal operations, where children can ponder completely hypothetical situations.

Piaget's theory is currently having a great effect on educational practice in this country. Many educators have attempted to formulate specific policies based on his theory (e.g., Athey & Rubadeau, 1970; Furth, 1970; Ginsburg & Opper, 1979). Others have attempted to develop an intelligence test in accordance with his theory (e.g., Goldschmid & Bentler, 1968).

Clearly Piaget's theory opens new avenues of research that were either unnoticed or ignored by those accepting an associationistic point of view. As we noted in chapter 2, one characteristic of a good scientific theory is that it be heuristic and Piaget's theory is certainly that. We also saw in chapter 2 that scientific revolutions occur when old theories are continuously confronted with data they cannot explain. Under such circumstances, a new theory eventually emerges that explains what the other theories could explain and, in addition, resolves the anomalies that previous theories could not resolve. Piaget's theory offers a promise of revolution that may some day "overthrow" the firmly established doctrine of associationism and resolve some of its many anomalies.

In 1980, the year Piaget died, Jerome Kagan paid him the following tribute:

> Piaget uncovered a host of fascinating, handy phenomena which were under everyone's noses but which few were talented enough to see. The reliability of those discoveries (the eight-month old who is suddenly able to retrieve a hidden toy, . . . and the shift at age 7 from a nonconserving to a conserving reply to the beakers of water) was so consistent across cultures that they resembled demonstrations in a chemistry lecture hall . . . few would question the conclusion that Piaget's writings have been a primary basis for the centrality of the cognitive sciences in contemporary psychology . . . With Freud, Piaget has been a seminal figure in the sciences of human development. (pp. 245–246)

DISCUSSION QUESTIONS

1. How did Piaget's method of studying intelligence differ from the one used at the Binet Laboratory?
2. Explain why Piaget's view of intelligence is called genetic epistemology.
3. Give an example of an experience that involves both assimilation and accommodation.
4. What did Piaget mean by interiorization?
5. Explain how, according to Piaget, heredity and experience both contribute to intellectual growth.
6. Explain what Piaget meant when he said that the cognitive structures "construct" the physical environment.
7. Discuss the nature of knowledge from both the empiricist's point of view and from Piaget's point of view.
8. Discuss Piaget's concept of progressive equilibrium.
9. Describe the educational implications of Piaget's theory.
10. Compare and contrast Piaget's theory of learning with any one of the associationistic theories covered in this text.
11. What do you suppose Piaget's views on the transfer of training would have been? In other words, according to Piaget, what would make it possible to utilize what was learned in one situation in other situations?
12. Outline the major stages of intellectual development as they were viewed by Piaget.

CHAPTER HIGHLIGHTS

Accommodation. The modification of cognitive structures as the result of having an experience that could not be assimilated into existing cognitive structures. Accommodation can be roughly equated with learning.

Assimilation. Responding to the physical environment in accordance with existing cognitive structures. Assimilation refers to a kind of matching between the cognitive structures and the physical environment. Assimilation can be roughly equated with recognition or knowing.

Clinical method. An open-ended form of questioning in which the researcher's questions are guided by the child's answers to previous questions.

Cognitive structure. The schemata that an organism has available at any given time with which to interact with the physical environment. Cognitive structure results from both biological maturation and cumulative experience. The cognitive structure is not only affected by experience but also determines what can be experienced. If a physical event cannot be at least partially assimilated into the organism's cognitive structure, then that physical event cannot constitute a biological stimulus. The dual processes of assimilation and accommodation must always occur with the existing cognitive structure as a point of departure.

Concrete operations. The stage of intellectual development where children can deal logically with only those events that they can experience directly.

Conservation. The realization that number, length, substance, or area has not changed although it may be presented in a number of different ways. The ability to conserve requires the use of reversible operations.

Content. The ingredients that accompany a specific manifestation of a schema.

Epistemology. The study of knowledge.

Equilibration. Piaget's major motivational concept; the innate need for balance between the organism and its environment and within the organism itself. Disbalance has motivational properties that cause the organism to do whatever is necessary to regain a balance. Equilibration is an invariant because it is present at all stages of intellectual development. In fact, it is responsible for continuous intellectual development.

Formal operations. The stage of intellectual development where children can deal logically with hypothetical events in addition to those events that they can experience directly.

Functional invariants. Processes that are not stage specific but are present at all stages of development. Examples would include assimilation, accommodation, and equilibration.

Genetic epistemology. A term often used to describe Piaget's theory. The term *genetic* means *developmental* rather than having anything to do with inheritance. Epistemology refers to the study of knowledge; thus the term *genetic epistemology* is used to describe the study of knowledge as a function of maturation and experience.

Intelligence. Intelligence is a complex term in Piaget's theory, but in general it can be said that an intelligent act always tends to create optimal conditions for an organism's survival under existing circumstances. Intelligence is always related to an organism's adaptation to its environment.

Interiorization. The increased tendency to rely more and more on mental operations in adjusting to the environment as the cognitive structure becomes more articulated. An operation is referred to as an "interiorized" action since it is an adaptive response that occurs mentally rather than overtly.

Learning dilemma. Dollard and Miller's contention that in order for learning to occur, previously learned behavior and innate behavior patterns must be ineffective in solving a problem. In this sense failure is a prerequisite for learning.

Operation. Cognitive action. As a sensorimotor schema manifests itself in overt behavior, an operation manifests itself in covert behavior or thinking. An operation can be thought of as interiorized action.

Preoperational thinking. The stage of intellectual development where children begin to classify objects and events into crude categories.

Progressive equilibrium. Living organisms constantly seek a balance between themselves and their environment. But, according to Piaget, the cognitive structures of an organism are always changing as the result of maturation and experience. Therefore, a balance can never be absolute but must rather be a progressive equilibrium which is a balance that is the best under the prevailing circumstances. As circumstances change, what an optimal balance would consist of must change accordingly.

Reversibility. An important characteristic of mental operations that refers to the process of reversing a thought. For example, one can mentally pour liquid from one container into another, and then reverse the process by mentally pouring the liquid back into the original container. Reversibility of mental operations is a necessary condition for *conservation* (see above) to occur.

Schema. The general potential to engage in a class of overt or covert actions. A schema can also be thought of as an element in an organism's cognitive structure.

Sensorimotor stage. The initial stage of intellectual development where children respond directly to events as they occur in the environment. During this stage of development, children adjust to the environment in terms of their schemata such as grasping, looking, sucking, and reaching.

12

Edward Chace Tolman

Field Expectancies

Field-Cognition Modes

Drive Discriminations

Motor Patterns

Tolman's Attitude Toward His Own Theory

BOLLES'S THEORY OF LEARNING

Tolman (1886–1959) was born in Newton, Massachusetts, and received his BS degree from the Massachusetts Institute of Technology in electrochemistry in 1911. His MA (1912) and PhD (1915) degrees were earned at Harvard University in psychology. He taught at Northwestern University from 1915 to 1918, at which time he was released for "lack of teaching success"; but, more likely it was because of his pacifism during wartime. From Northwestern, he went to the University of California where he remained until his retirement. His stay at the University of California was interrupted, however, when he was dismissed for refusing to sign a loyalty oath. He led a fight against the loyalty oath as an infringement on academic freedom, and was reinstated at the University of California when the professors won their case.

Tolman was raised in a Quaker home and his pacifism was a constant theme running through his career. In 1942, he wrote *Drives Toward War* in which he suggested several changes in our political, educational, and economic systems that would increase the probability of world peace. In the preface of that book, he stated his reasons for writing it: "As an American, a college professor, and one brought up in the pacifist tradition, I am intensely biased against war. It is for me stupid, interrupting, unnecessary, and unimaginably horrible. I write this essay within that frame of reference. In short, I am driven to discuss the psychology of war and its possible abolition because I want intensely to get rid of it" (p. xi).

Tolman spent much of his life being a rebel. Above, we saw that he opposed war when the war was an extremely popular cause, and below, we shall see that he opposed Watsonian behaviorism when behaviorism was an extremely popular school of psychology.

As we mentioned at the conclusion of chapter 10, Tolman's theory of learning can be looked upon as a blending of Gestalt theory and behaviorism. While still a graduate student at Harvard, Tolman traveled to Germany and worked for a short time with Koffka. The influence of Gestalt theory on his own theorizing had a profound and lasting effect. His favorable attitude toward Gestalt theory did not, however, preclude a favorable attitude toward behaviorism. Like the behaviorists, Tolman saw little value in the introspective approach, and he felt psychology had to

Edward Chace Tolman. (From *A History of Psychology in Autobiography*, Vol. 4, p. xii, by C. Murchison, ed., 1952, Worcester, MA: Clark University Press.)

become completely objective. His main disagreement with the behaviorists was over the unit of behavior to be studied. Behaviorists such as Pavlov, Guthrie, Hull, Watson, and Skinner represented, according to Tolman, the psychology of "twitchism," because they felt that large segments of behavior could be divided into smaller segments, such as reflexes, for further analysis. Tolman felt that, by being elementistic, the behaviorists were throwing away the baby with the bathwater. He believed that it was possible to be objective while studying molar behavior (large, intact, meaningful behavior patterns). Unlike the other behaviorists, Tolman chose to systematically study molar behavior. It can be said that Tolman was methodologically a behaviorist, but metaphysically a cognitive theorist. In other words, he studied behavior in order to discover cognitive processes.

Molar Behavior

The chief characteristic of **molar behavior** is that it is purposive; that is, it is always directed toward some goal. Perhaps now the reader can better understand the title of Tolman's major work, *Purposive Behavior in Animals and Men* (1932). Tolman never contended that behavior could not be divided into smaller units for the purposes of study; rather, he felt that whole behavior patterns had a meaning that would be lost if studied from an elementistic viewpoint. Thus, for Tolman, molar behavior constituted a Gestalt that was more than the individual "twitches" that made it up. In other words, purposive behavior patterns can be looked upon as behavioral Gestalten. He said (1932):

> It will be contended by us (if not by Watson) that "behavior-acts," though no doubt in complete one-to-one correspondence with the underlying molecular facts of physics and physiology, have, as "molar" wholes, certain emergent properties of their own. And it is these, the molar properties of behavior-acts, which are of prime interest to us as psychologists. Further, these molar properties of behavior-acts cannot in the present state of our knowledge, i.e., prior to the working-out of many empirical correlations between behavior and its physiological correlates, be known even inferentially from a mere knowledge of the underlying, molecular facts of physics and physiology. For, just as the properties of a beaker of water are not, prior to experience, in any way envisageable from the properties of individual water molecules, so neither are the properties of a "behavior-act" deducible directly from the properties of the underlying physical and physiological processes which make it up. Behavior as such cannot, at any rate at present, be deduced from a mere enumeration of the muscle twitches, the mere motions *qua* motions, which make it up. It must as yet be studied first hand and for its own sake. (pp. 7–8)

The type of behavior that Tolman labels as molar is exemplified in the following passage (1932):

> A rat running a maze; a cat getting out of a puzzle box; a man driving home to dinner; a child hiding from a stranger; a woman doing her washing or gossiping over the telephone; a pupil marking a mental-test sheet; a psychologist reciting a list of nonsense syllables; my friend and I telling one another our thoughts and feelings—*these are behaviors (qua molar)*. And it must be noted that in mentioning no one of them have we referred to, or, we blush to confess it, for the most part even known, what were the exact muscles and glands, sensory nerves, and motor nerves involved. For these responses somehow had other sufficiently identifying properties of their own. (p. 8)

Purposive Behaviorism

Tolman's theory has been referred to as a **purposive behaviorism** because it attempts to explain goal directed behavior. It must be emphasized that Tolman used the term *purpose* as a purely descriptive term. He noted, for example, the searching behavior of a rat in a maze will persist until food is found; therefore it looks "as if" its behavior is goal directed or purposive. For Tolman, the term *purposive* was used to describe behavior just as the terms slow, fast, correct, incorrect, or right turn might be used to describe behavior. There is some similarity between Guthrie and Tolman on this point. For Guthrie, behavior persisted as long as maintaining stimuli were being provided by some need state. For Tolman, behavior will look "as if" it is goal directed as long as the organism is seeking something in the environment. In both cases, the behavior will look purposive. Tolman (1932) said:

it must . . . be emphasized that purposes and cognitions which are thus imme-diately, immanently, in behavior are wholly objective as to definition. They are defined by characters and relationships which we observe out there in the behavior. We, the observers, watch the behavior of the rat, the cat, or the man, and note its character as a getting to such and such by means of such and such a selected pattern of commerces-with. It is we, the independent neutral observers, who note these perfectly objective characters as immanent in the behavior and have happened to choose the terms *purpose* and *cognition* as gener-ic names for such characters. (pp. 12–13)

Although Tolman was a little freer with the terms he was willing to employ in his theory than most behaviorists, he remained a behaviorist, and an objective one. As we shall see below, Tolman developed a cognitive theory of learning, but in the final analysis, he was dealing with what every other behaviorist deals with—observ-able stimuli and overt responses. Tolman (1932) said: "For a Purposive Behav-iorism, behavior, as we have seen, is purposive, cognitive, and molar, i.e., "Ge-stalted." Purposive Behaviorism is a molar, not a molecular, behaviorism, but it is none the less a behaviorism. Stimuli and responses and the behavior-determinants of responses are all that it finds to study" (p. 418).

The Use of Rats

Some may think it strange for a cognitive theorist to use rats as experimental subjects, but Tolman had a special fondness for them. He stimulated the use of rats in psychological experiments at the University of California, and he dedicated his 1932 book to the white rat. Throughout Tolman's writings, one finds humor and wit, as exemplified by his following thoughts on the use of rats as experimental subjects (1945): "Let it be noted that rats live in cages; they do not go on binges the night before one has planned an experiment; they do not kill each other off in wars; they do not invent engines of destruction, and if they did, they would not be so inept about controlling such engines; they do not go in for either class conflicts or race conflicts; they avoid politics, economics, and papers on psychology. They are mar-velous, pure, and delightful" (p. 166).

Elsewhere (1938) Tolman said: "I believe that everything important in psy-chology (except perhaps such matters as the building up of a super-ego, that is, everything save such matters as involve society and words) can be investigated in essence through the continued experimental and theoretical analysis of the determin-ers of rat behavior at a choice-point in a maze. Herein I believe I agree with Professor Hull and also with Professor Thorndike" (p. 34).

MAJOR THEORETICAL CONCEPTS

Tolman introduced the use of intervening variables into psychological research and Hull borrowed the idea from Tolman. Both Hull and Tolman used intervening variables in a similar way in their work. Hull, however, developed a much more comprehensive and elaborate theory of learning than did Tolman. We will consider the formal aspects of Tolman's theory later in this chapter, but first we will turn to a few of his general assumptions about the learning process.

What Is Learned?

In answering the question, the behaviorists, such as Pavlov, Watson, Guthrie, and Hull, would say that stimulus-response associations are learned and that complex learning involves complex S-R relationships. Tolman, however, taking his lead from the Gestalt theorists, said that learning is essentially a process of discovering what leads to what in the environment. The organism, through exploration, discovers that certain events lead to certain other events, or that one sign leads to another sign. For example, we learn that when it's 5 o'clock (S_1), dinner (S_2) will soon follow. For that reason, Tolman was called an S-S rather than an S-R theorist. Learning, for Tolman, was an ongoing process that required no motivation. On this matter Tolman is in agreement with Guthrie and in opposition to Thorndike, Skinner, and Hull.

It should be pointed out, however, that motivation was important in Tolman's theory because it determined which aspects of the environment would be attended to by the organism. For example, the hungry organism would attend to food-related events in the environment, and the sexually deprived organism would attend to sex-related events. In general, an organism's drive state determines which aspects of the environment will be emphasized in its perceptual field. Thus, for Tolman, motivation acted as a perceptual "emphasizer."

According to Tolman, what is learned is "the lay of the land"; the organism learns what is there. It learns that if it turns to the left, it will find one thing, and if it turns to the right, it will find another thing. Gradually it develops a picture of the environment that it can use to get around in it. Tolman called this picture a **cognitive map.** On this point, Tolman was diametrically opposed to the other behaviorists. According to him, it is meaningless to look at individual responses or even individual routes to a goal. Once the organism has developed a cognitive map, it can reach a particular goal from any number of directions. If one commonly used route is blocked, the animal simply takes an alternate route, just as the human takes a detour on the way home from work if the route usually taken is not available. The organism will, however, always choose the shortest route or the one requiring the least amount of work. This is referred to as the **principle of least effort.**

There is a great deal of similarity between Tolman's principle of least effort and Hull's notion of the habit family hierarchy. Both theorists concluded that, after training, an organism can reach a goal using alternate routes. Tolman said that the organism's first choice is the route requiring the least amount of effort. Hull said that the organism prefers the shortest route because it has the shortest delay of reinforcement (J) and therefore, the greatest amount of $_sE_R$ associated with it. Furthermore, the response that has the greatest amount of $_sE_R$ associated with it will tend to occur in any given situation.

Later in this chapter, we shall see some of Tolman's ingenious experimentation designed to show that animals respond according to cognitive maps, rather than according to simple S-R processes.

Confirmation Versus Reinforcement

As with Guthrie, the concept of reinforcement was unimportant to Tolman as a learning variable, but there is some similarity between what Tolman called confirmation and what the other behaviorists call reinforcement. During the development of a cognitive map, expectations are utilized by the organism. Expectations are hunches concerning what leads to what. Early tentative expectations are called **hypotheses** and they are either confirmed by experience or not. Hypotheses that are confirmed are retained and those that are not are abandoned. Through this process, the cognitive map develops.

An expectancy that is consistently confirmed develops into what Tolman referred to as a **means-end readiness,** or what is commonly referred to as a belief. When an expectation is consistently confirmed, the organism ends up "believing" that if it acts in a certain way, a certain result will follow, or if it sees a certain sign (stimulus), another sign will follow. Thus, the confirmation of expectancies in the development of a cognitive map is similar to the notion of reinforcement, as other behaviorists may use the term. It should be noted, however, that the production, acceptance, or rejection of hypotheses is a cognitive process that need not involve overt behavior. Also, the hypotheses-testing process, so important to the development of a cognitive map, does not depend on any physiological need state of the organism. As mentioned above, learning is taking place constantly and does not depend on any motivational state of the organism.

Vicarious Trial and Error

Tolman noted a characteristic of rats learning a maze that he took as support for his cognitive interpretation of learning. He noted that very often a rat would pause at a choice-point and look around as if it were thinking about the various alternatives available to it. This pausing and looking around at the choice-point Tolman called **vicarious trial and error.** Instead of behavioral trial and error, where first one response is tried and then another until a solution to a problem is reached, with vicarious trial and error the testing of different approaches is done cognitively rather than behaviorally.

Learning Versus Performance

We saw in chapter 6 that Hull distinguished between learning and performance. In Hull's final theory, the number of reinforced trials was the only learning variable; the other variables in his system were performance variables. Generally speaking, performance can be thought of as the translation of learning into behavior. Although the distinction between learning and performance was important for Hull, it was even more important for Tolman.

According to Tolman, we know many things about our environment but only act upon this information when we need to do so. As mentioned above, this knowledge, which comes about through reality testing, lies dormant until a need arises. In a state of need, the organism utilizes what it has learned through reality testing to bring it into proximity to those things that will alleviate the need. For example, there may be two drinking fountains in your building and you may have passed them both many times without having paused for a drink; but if you became thirsty, you would merely walk over to one of them and take a drink. You knew for some time how to find a drinking fountain, but you did not need to translate that knowledge into behavior until you became thirsty. We will discuss the learning-performance distinction in more detail when we consider latent learning below.

The points that we have made so far can be summarized as follows:

1. The organism brings to a problem-solving situation various hypotheses that it may utilize in attempting to solve the problem. These hypotheses are based largely on prior experience, but, as we shall see later, Tolman believed that some problem solving strategies may be innate.

2. The hypotheses which survive are those that correspond best with reality; that is, those that result in goal achievement.

3. After awhile a clearly established cognitive map develops which can be used under altered conditions. For instance, when an organism's preferred path is blocked, it simply chooses, in accordance with the principle of least effort, an alternative path from its cognitive map.

4. When there is some sort of demand or motive to be satisfied, the organism will make use of the information in its cognitive map. The fact that information can exist but only be utilized under certain conditions is the basis for the very important distinction between learning and performance.

Latent Learning

Generally speaking, **latent learning** can be thought of as learning that is not translated into performance. In other words, it is possible to have learning remain dormant for a considerable length of time before it is manifested in behavior. The concept of latent learning was very important to Tolman and he felt he succeeded in demonstrating its existence. The now famous experiment that Tolman and Honzik (1930) ran involved three groups of rats learning to solve a maze. One group was never reinforced for correctly traversing the maze, one group was always reinforced, and one group was not reinforced until the eleventh day of the experiment. It was the last group that was of greatest interest to Tolman. His theory of latent learning predicted that this group would be learning the maze just as much as the group that was being regularly reinforced, and that when reinforcement is introduced on the eleventh day, this group should soon perform as well as the group that had been continually reinforced. The results of the experiment are shown in Figure 12-1.

By examining Figure 12-1, three things become apparent: (a) there is slight improvement in performance even in the group never receiving reinforcement; (b)

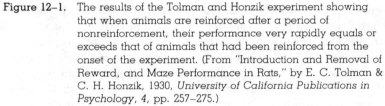

Figure 12-1. The results of the Tolman and Honzik experiment showing that when animals are reinforced after a period of nonreinforcement, their performance very rapidly equals or exceeds that of animals that had been reinforced from the onset of the experiment. (From "Introduction and Removal of Reward, and Maze Performance in Rats," by E. C. Tolman & C. H. Honzik, 1930, *University of California Publications in Psychology, 4,* pp. 257–275.)

the reinforced group showed steady improvement throughout the seventeen days of the experiment; and (c) when reinforcement was introduced on the eleventh day to the group not previously receiving reinforcement, their performance vastly improved. In fact, the latter group performed even better than the group that was reinforced throughout the experiment. Tolman took the results to support his contention that reinforcement was a performance variable and not a learning variable.

The S-R theorists insisted that reinforcement was, in fact, not removed from the situation; why, they asked, would the group never receiving food show slight improvement? They pointed out that simply being removed from the apparatus after reaching the goal box could act as a reinforcer for reaching the goal box. Another S-R interpretation of latent learning, one based on the concept of incentive motivation, will be presented after our discussion of latent extinction.

Latent Extinction. It may be remembered that reinforcement theorists such as Pavlov, Hull, and Skinner viewed extinction as an active process. For them, in order for extinction to occur, a previously reinforced response must be made but not reinforced. Under these circumstances, the rate or magnitude of the previously reinforced response will go back to the level that it was at before reinforcement was introduced. But what does Tolman say? According to Tolman, learning occurs through observation and independent of reinforcement. What an animal learns is to expect reinforcement if a certain response is made because it is this expectation that is confirmed during the acquisition phase of a learning experiment. Tolman's theory predicts that if an animal who has learned an R–S expectancy (e.g., that a certain response will lead to the presence of food) is given the opportunity to *observe* that that response will no longer lead to food, such observation will itself produce extinction. For example, if a rat that had previously learned to traverse a maze or a runway in order to obtain food is placed directly into a now empty goal box, it will stop traversing the maze or runway on subsequent trials. Extinction that occurs under these circumstances is called **latent extinction** because it does not involve the nonreinforced performance of the previously reinforced response. Evidence for latent extinction has been found by many researchers, for example, Deese, 1951; Moltz, 1957; and Seward and Levy, 1949. Bower and Hilgard (1981) summarize these findings:

> These . . . results . . . imply that the strength of an instrumental response sequence can be altered without *that response* occurring and receiving the altered conditions of reinforcement . . . Such results create difficulties for an S–R reinforcement theory which supposes that responses can have their habit strengths altered only when they occur and are then explicitly punished or nonrewarded. The results seem to call for two assumptions; that at the start of a behavior sequence, organisms have available some representation of what goal they expect to achieve at the end of the response sequence; and that that goal expectation can be altered by direct experience with the goal situation without execution of the prior response sequence leading up to it. These, of course, are exactly the assumptions made in Tolman's theory. (pp. 340–341)

S–R theorists, such as Spence, explain latent extinction in terms of motivational factors. It may be remembered from chapter 6 that Spence believed response learning occurred because of contiguity. That is, a goal response is learned simply because it is made. What reinforcement does, according to Spence, is provide an incentive for performing a response that had been learned independent of reinforcement. Furthermore, stimuli that occur prior to primary reinforcement take on secondary reinforcing properties, and it is these secondary reinforcers that provide the incentive for the animal to traverse a maze or runway. According to Spence, what happens in the latent extinction situation is that the animal experiences these stimuli without primary reinforcement and therefore their secondary reinforcing properties extinguish. Thereafter, when the animal is placed in the experimental apparatus, it has less incentive to perform the learned response. This is essentially the same explanation Spence would offer for latent learning. That is, animals learn a variety of responses in a maze or a runway simply by making those responses. When at some point reinforcement is introduced, it provides the animal with incentive to perform a response that it had previously learned via the law of contiguity.

The question as to whether latent learning and latent extinction are explained best in terms of expectancies or in terms of incentive motivation is yet unanswered.

Place Learning Versus Response Learning

Tolman maintained that animals learn where things are, while the S–R theorists maintained that specific responses are learned to specific stimuli. Tolman and his collaborators performed a series of experiments designed to determine whether animals were place learners, as Tolman suggested, or response learners as S–R theory suggested. A typical experiment in this area was done by Tolman, Ritchie, and Kalish (1946b). The apparatus they used is diagrammed in Figure 12-2.

Two groups of rats were utilized. Members of one group were sometimes started at S_1 and sometimes at S_2, but no matter where they started from, they always had to turn in the same direction to be reinforced. For example, if the group was learning to turn right, it was fed at F_1 if they started at S_1, and were fed at F_2 if they started at S_2. This was the **response learning** group. Members of the other group were always fed at the same place (e.g., F_2). If a member of this group started at S_1, it had to turn left to be reinforced. If it started at S_2, it had to turn right. This was the **place learning** group.

The animals were given 6 trials a day for 12 days, or 72 trials. The criterion for learning was 10 successive errorless trials. At the end of the experiment, only three of the eight rats in the response learning group had reached criterion, whereas all eight rats in the place learning group reached criterion. In fact, the mean trials to criterion for the latter group was only 3.5 whereas it was 17.33 for the three response learners that reached criterion. The place learners solved their problem much faster than the response learners solved theirs. It appeared, therefore, that it was more "natural" for animals to learn places than specific responses and this was taken as support for Tolman's theory. The results of the experiment are shown in Figure 12-3.

In another study by Tolman, Ritchie, and Kalish (1946a), animals were first

Figure 12–2.   Apparatus used in the Tolman, Ritchie, and Kalish experiment on place vs. response learning. S_1 and S_2 are starting points, F_1 and F_2 are food boxes, and C is the center point of the maze. (From "Studies in Spatial Learning," by E. C. Tolman, B. F. Ritchie, & D. Kalish, 1946b, *Journal of Experimental Psychology, 36*, p. 223.)

Figure 12–3. The average number of errors made on successive trials by place learning and response learning groups of rats. (From "Studies in Spatial Learning," by E. C. Tolman, B. F. Ritchie, & D. Kalish, 1946b, *Journal of Experimental Psychology*, *36*, p. 226.)

trained in the apparatus shown in Figure 12-4. The animals had to learn to follow the route *A*, *B*, *C*, *D*, *E*, *F*, and *G*. *H* indicates the place where a 5-watt bulb was located, the only illumination in the room during the experiment. After preliminary training, the apparatus shown in Figure 12-4 was removed and was replaced with the apparatus shown in Figure 12-5.

The path the animals were trained to take in the first phase of the experiment was now blocked, but the animals could choose among 18 alternative paths. On the basis of S-R theory, one might expect that when the original path was blocked, the animals would choose the unblocked path closest to the original. This, however, was not the case. The most frequently picked was alley number 6, the one pointing directly to where the goal was during the first phase of the experiment. In fact, the

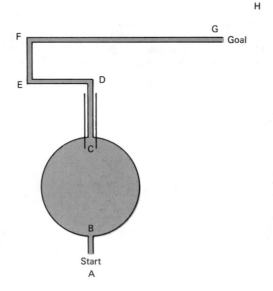

Figure 12–4. Apparatus used for preliminary training in the experiment by Tolman, Ritchie, and Kalish on place vs. response learning. (From "Studies in Spatial Learning," by E. C. Tolman, B. F. Ritchie, & D. Kalish, 1946b, *Journal of Experimental Psychology*, *36*.)

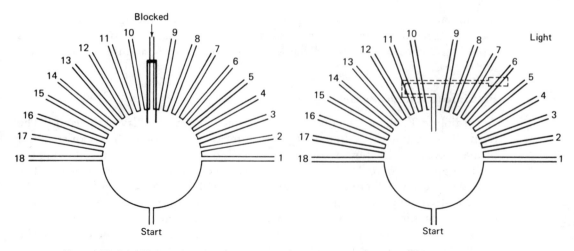

Figure 12–5.   After preliminary training on the apparatus shown in Figure 12–4, the animals were allowed to choose 1 of the 18 alleys shown in the figure to the left. The figure to the right shows the apparatus used for preliminary training superimposed over the test apparatus so that the relationship between the two can be seen. (After Tolman, Ritchie, & Kalish, 1946b)

alleys closest to the original alley were only infrequently chosen (alley 9 by 2% of the rats and alley 10 by 7½%). Tolman, Ritchie, and Kalish reported that the first pathway, the one chosen with the second greatest frequency, was the alley pointing to the place in the room where the animals had been fed in their home cages. The results of the experiment are shown in Figure 12-6.

Once again it looked as if the animals were responding in terms of where something was, rather than in terms of specific responses. The S-R theorists felt that such experiments did not support place learning, since it was entirely possible that

Figure 12–6. The results of the experiment diagrammed in Figures 12–4 and 12–5. It can be seen that the most frequently chosen path on the test trial was the one pointing directly to the goal. Tolman, Ritchie, and Kalish also pointed out that the second most frequently chosen path was the one that pointed to the animals' home cages where they were fed. (After Tolman, Ritchie, & Kalish, 1946a)

the animals simply learned the response of running toward the light. The cognitive theorists refuted this interpretation by saying that if that were true, the animals would have chosen alleys 5 and 7 at least as often as alley 6, and this of course was not the case.

Reinforcement Expectancy

According to Tolman, when we learn, we come to know the "lay of the land." The term "understanding" is not foreign to him as it is to other behaviorists. In a problem-solving situation, we learn where the goal is and we get to it following the shortest possible route. We learn to expect certain events to follow other events. The animal expects that if it goes to a certain place, it will find a certain reinforcer. The S–R theorist would expect that changing reinforcers in a learning situation would not disrupt behavior as long as the quantity of reinforcement was not changed drastically. Tolman, however, predicted that if reinforcers are changed, behavior will be disrupted, since a particular reinforcer becomes a part of what is expected.

Tolman reported an experiment by Elliott (Tolman, 1932, p. 44), who trained one group of rats to run a maze for bran mash and another group to run a maze for sunflower seeds. On the tenth day of training, the group that had been trained on bran mash was switched to sunflower seeds. The results of Elliott's experiment are shown in Figure 12-7.

We see that switching reinforcement considerably disrupted performance, thus supporting Tolman's prediction. It should be noted, however, that the group trained on bran mash performed consistently better than the group trained on sun-

Figure 12–7. The results of an experiment by Elliott (reported by Tolman, 1932, p. 44) showing the disruption in behavior that occurs when a reinforcer other than the one which is expected is experienced. (Reprinted by permission.)

flower seeds before the switch. The Hullians could say that because the bran mash had a larger incentive value (K) than did the sunflower seeds, reaction potential would be greater. After the switch to sunflower seeds, K would go down according- ly. The Hullian explanation can only partially account for the results, however, since the group that switched to sunflower seeds performed much worse than the group consistently trained on sunflower seeds. Even correcting for the differences in incen- tive value, there still seems to be considerable disruption of performance that can be explained by the departure from what was expected.

The reader can certainly recall situations where there has been a discrepancy between what was expected and what was experienced. Examples might include a good friend or relative's acting "totally unlike himself," a familiar house torn down while you've been on vacation, or receiving a raise in pay either larger or smaller than what you expected. In each case, the expected events were not the ones that actually occurred. If a person has important expectations, their failure in being realized could be traumatic. Leon Festinger (1957) constructed a theory of person- ality around this notion. According to Festinger, when a person's beliefs do not conform to what actually occurs, the person experiences a psychological state called **cognitive dissonance.** Cognitive dissonance is a negative drive state and the person experiencing it seeks ways to reduce it, just as the person experiencing hunger seeks to reduce the hunger drive.

THE FORMAL ASPECTS OF TOLMAN'S THEORY

As an example of Tolman's more abstract theorizing, we will summarize his article "The Determiners of Behavior at a Choice Point" (1938). In this example, the choice point is where the rat decides to turn either right or left in a T-maze. Some of the symbols we will be using are seen in the diagram of the T-maze shown in Figure 12-8.

In an experiment where a rat was being trained to turn left in a T-maze, Tolman's dependent variable was a behavior ratio defined as follows:

$$\frac{B_L}{B_L + B_R}$$

This gives the percentage tendency to turn left at any stage of learning. If, for example, an animal turned left 6 out of 10 times, we would have:

$$\frac{6}{6 + 4} = 60\%$$

Tolman felt that the behavior ratio was determined by the collective experi- ences that come from the animal's having turned both ways at the choice point on various trials. This allows the animal to learn what leads to what. The cumulative

$$\Sigma OBO \longrightarrow \frac{B_L}{B_L + B_R}$$

O_c = the choice point
O_R = the complex of stimulus objects that are met after making a right turn
O_L = the complex of stimulus objects that are met after making a left turn
B_R = the behavior of turning right at the choice point
B_L = the behavior of turning left at the choice point
O_{GR} = the goal on the right
O_{GL} = the goal on the left

Figure 12–8. A diagram of a T-maze. (From "The Determiners of Behavior at a Choice Point," by E. C. Tolman, 1938, *Psychological Review, 45,* p. 1. Copyright © 1938 by the American Psychological Association. Reprinted by permission.)

nature of these experiences was diagrammed by Tolman as follows:

$$\Sigma \ (O_c \overset{\displaystyle B_L \nearrow (O_L:O_{GL})}{\underset{\displaystyle B_R \searrow (O_R:O_{GR})}{}} \Bigg\} \rightarrow \frac{B_L}{B_L + B_R}$$

Rather than repeating this cumbersome diagram, Tolman abbreviated it ΣOBO, which stands for the accumulated knowledge that comes from making both B_L and B_R responses and seeing what they lead to. The events involved in T–maze learning are diagrammed in Figure 12–8.

Environmental Variables

Unfortunately, the situation is not as simple as suggested above. Tolman thought of ΣOBO as an independent variable since it directly influenced the dependent variable (i.e., the behavior ratio), and it was under the control of the experimenter who determined the number of training trials. In addition to ΣOBO a number of other independent variables could have an effect on performance. Tolman suggested the following list:

M = maintenance schedule. This refers to the animal's deprivation schedule; for example, the number of hours since it has eaten.

G = appropriateness of goal object. The reinforcer must be related to the animal's current drive state. For example, one does not reinforce a thirsty animal with food.

S = types and modes of stimuli provided. This refers to the vividness of the cues or signals available to the animal in the learning situation.

R = types of motor responses required in the learning situation; for example, running, sharp turns, and so on.

P = pattern of succeeding and preceding maze units. The pattern of turns that need to be made to solve a maze as determined by the experimenter.

ΣOBO = the number of trials and their cumulative nature (see above).

It should be clear that Tolman was no longer talking only about the learning of T-mazes but about the learning of more complex mazes as well.

Individual Difference Variables

In addition to the independent variables described above, there are the variables that the individual subjects bring into the experiment with them. The list of individual difference variables suggested by Tolman is as follows (note their initials create the acronym HATE, a somewhat strange word for Tolman to use):

H = Heredity

A = Age

T = Previous training

E = Special endocrine, drug, or vitamin conditions

Each of the individual difference variables interacts with each of the independent variables, and a combination of all these variables working together is what produces behavior. This can be seen in Figure 12-9.

Intervening Variables

Up to this point, we have been discussing the effects of observed stimulus variables (independent variables) on observed behavior (dependent variables). It would be possible, as Skinner suggests, to conduct thousands of experiments showing how those variables are related to each other in various combinations. The functional analysis suggested by Skinner, however, was not appealing to Tolman, who wanted to move beyond the facts. He said (1938):

But why, you may ask, can we not be satisfied with just experiments and the "facts" resulting from them? I find that there are two reasons. In the first place, an entirely factual empirical establishment of the complete functional

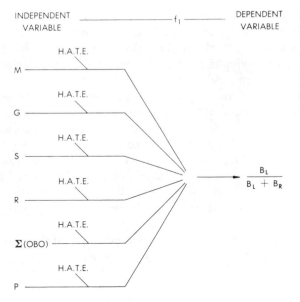

Figure 12–9. Illustration of the relationship between the independent variables, the individual difference variables, and behavior. (From "The Determiners of Behavior at a Choice Point," by E. C. Tolman, 1938, *Psychological Review, 45,* p. 8. Copyright © 1938 by the American Psychological Association. Reprinted by permission.)

relation, f_1, to cover the effects on ($(B_L/B_L + B_R)$) of all the permutations and combinations of M, G, S, etc., etc., would be a humanly endless task. We have time in this brief mortal span to test only a relatively limited number of such permutations and combinations. So, in the first place, we are forced to propose theories in order to use such theories to extrapolate for all these combinations for which we have not time to test.

But I suspect that there is another reason for theories. Some of us, psychologically, just demand theories. Even if we had all the million and one concrete facts, we would still want theories to, as we would say, "explain" those facts. Theories just seem to be necessary to some of us to relieve our inner tensions. (pp. 8–9)

Tolman defined a theory as a set of intervening variables. An intervening variable is a construct created by the theorist to aid in explaining the relationship between an independent variable and a dependent variable. The example given in chapter 2 was that of hunger. It has been found that performance on a learning task varies with hours of food deprivation, and that is an empirical relationship. If one says, however, that *hunger* varies with hours of deprivation and in turn influences learning, the concept of hunger is being used as an intervening variable. As Tolman said, such a concept is used to fill in the blanks in a research program.

For similar reasons, Tolman created an intervening variable to go along with each of his independent variables. In each case, the intervening variable was systematically tied to both an independent variable and a dependent variable. In other words, each of Tolman's intervening variables was operationally defined. **Maintenance schedule,** for example, creates a **demand** which in turn is related to performance. Appropriateness of the goal object is related to *appetite,* which in turn is

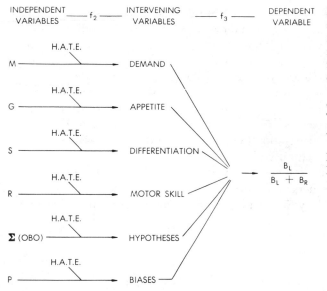

INDEPENDENT VARIABLES —— f_2 —— INTERVENING VARIABLES —— f_3 —— DEPENDENT VARIABLE

H.A.T.E.

M ———— DEMAND

H.A.T.E.

G ———— APPETITE

H.A.T.E.

S ———— DIFFERENTIATION

H.A.T.E.

R ———— MOTOR SKILL

H.A.T.E.

Σ (OBO) ———— HYPOTHESES

H.A.T.E.

P ———— BIASES

$\dfrac{B_L}{B_L + B_R}$

Figure 12–10. The relationship suggested by Tolman between independent variables, individual difference variables, intervening variables, and the dependent variable. (From "The Determiners of Behavior at a Choice Point," by E. C. Tolman, 1938, *Psychological Review, 45,* p. 16. Copyright © 1938 by the American Psychological Association. Reprinted by permission.)

related to performance. Types of stimuli provided are related to the animal's capacity for *differentiation,* and so on. A summary of Tolman's system showing his use of intervening variables is shown in Figure 12-10.

One can now see the similarity between Tolman and Hull in the use of intervening variables. Hull, as we have mentioned, borrowed the approach from Tolman, who introduced the use of intervening variables into psychology. The part of the system shown in Figure 12-10 that relates most closely to the main theme in Tolman's theory is the intervening variable of "hypotheses." As the result of previous experience (ΣOBO) hypotheses are developed which affect behavior ($B_L/B_L + B_R$). As these hypotheses are confirmed by experience, they become means-end readinesses, or beliefs. The function of an intervening variable is seen clearly at this point. It is an empirical fact that performance improves as a function of the number of learning trials, but the intervening variables are created in an effort to explain why this is the case. According to those who use intervening variables, the facts would be the same without their use, but our understanding of the facts would be severely limited.

MacCORQUODALE AND MEEHL'S FORMALIZATION OF TOLMAN'S THEORY

MacCorquodale and Meehl (1953) attempted to do for Tolman's theory what Voeks attempted to do for Guthrie's theory. That is, they attempted to make Tolman's terms more precise and his concepts more easily tested. Most of MacCorquodale and Meehl's restatement of Tolman's theory is beyond the scope of this book, but the brief sample of their work offered below nicely summarizes a few of Tolman's more important concepts.

MacCorquodale and Meehl (1953) describe Tolman's theory as an S_1-R_1-S_2 theory, where S_1 elicits an expectancy of some kind, R_1 indicates the manner in which the expectancy is acted upon, and S_2 indicates what the organism thinks will happen as a result of its actions under the circumstances. In other words, the organism seems to think "under these circumstances (S_1), if I do this (R_1), I will have a certain experience (S_2)." An example would be seeing a friend (S_1) and believing that saying "hello" (R_1) will result in a warm greeting from the friend (S_2). Or, seeing a certain intersection (S_1) and believing that turning to the right (R_1) will result in finding a service station (S_2). The more often the S_1-R_1-S_2 sequence occurs the stronger the expectation will become. Likewise, if S_1 and R_1 occur and S_2 does not follow, the expectation becomes weaker. MacCorquodale and Meehl handle the concept of stimulus generalization within Tolman's theory by saying that if an expectancy is elicited by S_1 it will also be elicited by stimuli similar to S_1.

SIX KINDS OF LEARNING

In his 1949 article, "There Is More Than One Kind of Learning," Tolman proposed six kinds of learning. Each is briefly summarized below.

Cathexes

Cathexis (plural, cathexes) refers to the learned tendency to associate certain objects with certain drive states. For example, certain foods might be available to satisfy the hunger drive of individuals who live in a particular country. Persons who live in a country where fish is usually eaten will tend to seek fish to satisfy their hunger. The same individuals may avoid beef or spaghetti because, for them, those foods have not been associated with the satisfaction of the hunger drive. Since certain stimuli have been associated with the satisfaction of a certain drive those stimuli will tend to be sought out when the drive recurs. Tolman (1949) said: "when a type of goal has been positively cathected it means that when the given drive is in force the organism will tend to apprehend, to approach, and to perform the consummatory reaction upon any instance of this type of goal which is presented by the immediate environment" (p. 146). When the organism has learned to avoid certain objects while in a certain drive state, a negative cathexis is said to have occurred. There is little difference between Tolman and the S-R theorists concerning this kind of learning.

Equivalence Beliefs

When a "subgoal" has the same effect as the goal itself, the subgoal is said to constitute an **equivalence belief.** Although this is extremely close to what the S-R theorists call secondary reinforcement, Tolman felt that this kind of learning more typically involved the "social drives" rather than the physiological drives. He gave the following example (1949): "Insofar as it can be demonstrated that with the reception of the high grades there is some temporary reduction in this student's need for love and approbation even without his going on to tell others about his grade, then we would have evidence for an equivalence belief. The A's would then be accepted by him as equivalent to the love or approbation to which they were originally a mere means" (p. 148).

Here again, there is little difference between Tolman and the S-R theorists, except for the fact that Tolman talked about "love reduction" as the reinforcement, and the S-R theorists would prefer to remain with the reduction of drives such as hunger or thirst.

Field Expectancies

Field expectancies are developed in the same way a cognitive map is developed: the organism learns what leads to what. Upon seeing a certain sign, for instance, it expects that a certain other sign will follow. This general knowledge of the environment is used to explain latent learning, latent extinction, place learning, and the use of shortcuts. This is not S-R learning but rather, S-S or sign-sign learning, that is, when the animal sees one sign, it learns to expect another to follow. The only "reinforcement" necessary for this kind of learning to take place is the confirmation of an hypothesis. His belief in this kind of learning places Tolman in the cognitive camp.

Field-Cognition Modes

This is the kind of learning about which Tolman was least confident. A **field-cognition mode** is a strategy, or a way of approaching a problem-solving situation. It is a tendency to arrange the perceptual field in certain configurations. Tolman suspected that these tendencies were innate but could be modified by experience. In fact, the most important thing about a strategy that works in solving a problem is that it will be tried in similar situations in the future. Thus, effective field-cognition modes, or problem-solving strategies, transfer to related problems. In that way they are similar to means–end readinesses (beliefs) which also transfer to similar situations. Tolman summarized his thinking about this kind of learning as follows (1949): "In a word, I am trying to summarize under this fourth category all those principles as to the structure of environmental fields which are relevant to all environmental fields, and which (whether innate or learned) are carried around by the individual and applied to each new field with which he is presented" (p. 153).

Drive Discriminations

This simply refers to the fact that organisms can determine their own drive state and therefore can respond appropriately. It has been found, for example, that animals can be trained to turn one way in a T-maze when they are hungry, and the other way when they are thirsty (Hull, 1933a; Leeper, 1935). Since Tolman implied a belief in social as well as physiological drives, **drive discrimination** was an important concept to him. Unless an organism can clearly determine its own drive state, it will not know how to read its cognitive map. If an organism's needs are not clear, its goals are not clear and therefore its behavior may be inappropriate. How people will act when they need love, for example, will be different from how they will act when they need water.

Motor Patterns

Tolman pointed out that his theory is mainly concerned with the association of ideas and is not overly concerned with the manner in which those ideas become associated with behavior. **Motor pattern** learning is an attempt to resolve this difficulty. Of all people, Tolman accepted Guthrie's interpretation of how responses become associated with stimuli. He did accept Guthrie reluctantly, however, which is exemplified by the following quotation (1949): "In default of other experimental theories about the learning of motor patterns I am willing to take a chance and to agree with Guthrie that the conditions under which a motor pattern gets acquired may well be those in which the given movement gets the animal away from the stimuli which were present when the movement was initiated" (p. 153).

Tolman was truly an eclectic. Somewhere among the six kinds of learning he described, there is agreement with almost every other major theory of learning. Combining the ideas of Hull, Gestalt theory, and Guthrie in one system would have confused a lesser mind. As for his reason for postulating many kinds of learning rather than one or two kinds, Tolman said the following (1949):

> Why do I want thus to complicate things; why do I not want one simple set of laws for all learning? I do not know. But I suppose it must be due to some funny erroneous equivalence belief on my part to the effect that being sweeping and comprehensive though vague, is equivalent to more love from others than being narrow and precise. No doubt, any good clinician would be able to trace this back to some sort of nasty traumatic experience in my early childhood. (p. 155)

Tolman's Attitude Toward His Own Theory

Tolman presented the final version of his theory in *Psychology: A Study of a Science,* edited by Sigmund Koch, which appeared in 1959, the year Tolman died. There is probably no better indication of how Tolman felt toward his own theory and toward science in general than the first and last paragraphs of his chapter in that volume. They are presented below. First, Tolman's opening statement (1959):

> I would like to begin by letting off steam. If in what follows I have not done a very clear or useful job, I would plead some half-dozen reasons. First, I think the days of such grandiose, all-covering systems in psychology as mine attempted to be are, at least for the present, pretty much passé. I feel therefore, that it might have been more decent and more dignified to let such an instance of the relatively immediate dead past bury its dead. Secondly, I don't enjoy trying to use my mind in too analytical a way. Hence, I have found it frustrating and difficult to try to subject my system to the required sorts of analyses. Thirdly, I suppose I am personally antipathetic to the notion that science

progresses through intense, self-conscious analysis of where one has got and where one is going. Such analyses are obviously a proper function for the philosopher of science and they may be valuable for many individual scientists. But I myself become frightened and restricted when I begin to worry too much as to what particular logical and methodological canons I should or should not obey. It seems to me that very often major new scientific insights have come when the scientist, like the ape, has been shaken out of his up-until-then approved scientific rules such as that food can be reached only by the hand and discovers "out of the blue," and perhaps purely by analogy, . . . the new rule of using a stick (or a sign-Gestalt). Fourthly, I have an inveterate tendency to make my ideas too complicated and too high-flown so that they become less and less susceptible to empirical tests. Fifthly, because of increasing laziness, I have not of late kept up, as I should have, with the more recent theoretical and empirical discussions which bear upon my argument. If I had, the argument would have been different and better and also I would have given more credit to those to whom credit is due. Finally, to talk about one's own ideas and to resort frequently to the use of the first person singular, as one tends to do in such an analysis, bring about a conflict, at least in me, between enjoying my exhibitionism and being made to feel guilty by my superego. (pp. 93–94)

And Tolman's last statement about his theory was as follows (1959):

I started out, as I indicated in the introduction, with considerable uneasiness. I felt that my so-called system was outdated and that it was a waste of time to try to rehash it and that it would be pretentious now to seek to make it fit any accepted set of prescriptions laid down by the philosophy of science. I have to confess, however, that as I have gone along I have become again more and more involved in it, though I still realize its many weak points. The system may well not stand up to any final canons of scientific procedure. But I do not much care. I have liked to think about psychology in ways that have proved congenial to me. Since all the sciences, and especially psychology, are still immersed in such tremendous realms of the uncertain and the unknown, the best that any individual scientist, especially any psychologist, can do seems to be to follow his own gleam and his own bent, however inadequate they may be. In fact, I suppose that actually this is what we all do. In the end, the only sure criterion is to have fun. And I have had fun. (p. 152)

BOLLES'S THEORY OF LEARNING

We have already seen in chapter 7 that Bolles explains classical conditioning as the development of expectancies. That is, upon seeing one stimulus (CS) the organism expects that another stimulus (UCS) will follow. In everyday life, seeing lightning and expecting thunder would exemplify an S-S expectancy. Whereas classical conditioning involves the development of S-S expectancies, operant and instrumental conditioning involve the development of R-S expectancies (Bolles, 1972). For example, the rat learns to expect that if it presses the bar in a Skinner box, food will follow. In everyday life, expecting to hear the sound of a bell when a doorbell is pressed exemplifies an R-S expectancy. In discussing R-S expectancies, it helps to think of the S as an *outcome* produced by the response.

Whereas Tolman concentrated almost exclusively on *learned* S-S and R-S expectancies, Bolles emphasizes *innate* S-S and R-S expectancies in his analysis of behavior. An example of an innate S-S relationship is when a young infant displays fear of a loud noise, suggesting that the infant expects a dangerous event will follow. Innate R-S expectancies are exemplified by the stereotyped behavior that many species of animals engage in in the presence of food, water, danger, and other biologically significant objects or situations.

As evidence for the importance of innate R-S expectancies, Bolles (1970, 1972) notes how animals typically respond to pain. Bolles says that animals respond to pain with a series of **species-specific defensive reactions** (SSDRs). For the rat, such reactions include freezing, fleeing, screaming, leaping-up and aggressing toward some object. In the natural environment, one or more of these innate reactions may lead to safety, and if so, the problem is solved. Also, in a laboratory situation, if one of these innate reactions to pain allows the animal to escape pain, the escape response will be learned rapidly. In fact, under the circumstances just described, the animal really learned nothing; the aversive stimulation simply caused the animal to engage in SSDRs. Avoidance conditioning is a bit more complicated. According to Bolles, avoidance conditioning involves both S-S and R-S expectancies. Since in

Robert C. Bolles. (Courtesy of Robert C. Bolles)

avoidance conditioning a signal precedes an aversive event (e.g., shock), the animal learns to expect pain when, say, a tone is sounded. Since the tone signals danger, it comes to elicit the same SSDRs that are elicited by the aversive stimulus itself. Thus, according to Bolles, either warnings of pain or pain itself evoke SSDRs.

An obvious prediction from Bolles's analysis is that the closer the response required of an animal in an experiment is to what that animal would do naturally in that situation, the more readily the response will be learned. If the required response is not part of the animal's innate response repertoire, it will be learned with great difficulty, or perhaps not at all. An example is the fact that pigeons can easily be taught to fly from one perch to another to avoid shock, but it is practically impossible to teach pigeons to peck a key to avoid shock (Bolles, 1979, p. 185).

Thus, according to Bolles, the choice of the response required of an animal in a learning experiment is a major factor in determining the results of the experiment.

> Even a casual look at rats in different avoidance learning situations reveals that what response we require of them is a tremendously important consideration; it can make the difference between some learning in one trial and no learning in 1000 trials. It is vastly more important than the reinforcement contingencies, various experimental parameters, the animal's prior experience, or different kinds of physiological interventions that might be made. The choice of what the response shall be is clearly not an arbitrary matter, or just a question of convenience, it is the governing factor in whether or how rapidly learning will occur. It is a serious indictment of our classical learning theories that they provide no hint that the choice of the response is so important. (Bolles, 1979, p. 185)

Just as Bolles believes that innate responses play a major role in escape and avoidance learning, so too does he believe that innate responses play a major role in appetitive learning. Not only are there innate reactions to pain, there are also innate reactions to food and water. For example, many species have stereotyped ways of taking and eating food, such as grasping, tearing, chewing, washing, or rooting. According to Bolles, the extent to which such responses are called for in an experiment where food is a reinforcer will determine how easily learning will occur. As with the case of learning to escape or avoid an aversive stimulus, the more unnatural the response that the animal is required to make is, the more difficult it will be for the animal to learn it.

By noting the importance of innate R-S expectancies, Bolles is essentially in agreement with Seligman's contention that how easily an association is learned depends on where that association falls on the preparedness-contrapreparedness continuum. Associations for which an animal is biologically prepared are learned easiest. Also, Bolles agrees with the explanation of instinctual drift offered by the Brelands (see chapter 5). That is, the natural responses associated with eating are more powerful than the responses that the animals had learned in order to obtain food. Therefore, the unnatural learned responses were gradually displaced by the stronger natural responses. Finally, as we saw in chapter 5, Bolles said that autoshaping could be explained as the triggering of innate responses that are appropriate to the situation. Therefore, for Bolles, autoshaping is not shaping at all. Because of the importance that Bolles places on innate behavior tendencies, he joins the growing number of modern psychologists who find it necessary to consider the biological boundaries of learning.

Tolman may have lost many skirmishes with the S-R behaviorists, but with the current emphasis in psychology on the study of cognitive processes, his theory may end up winning the war. The many current theories that emphasize the learning of expectancies and claim that the function of reinforcement is to provide information rather than to strengthen behavior, owe a great debt to Tolman's theory. As we have seen, Bolles's is one such theory. In the next chapter we shall see that the theory proposed by Albert Bandura is another.

DISCUSSION QUESTIONS

1. Why can Tolman's theory be considered a combination of Gestalt psychology and behaviorism?
2. What is purposive behaviorism?
3. Why is Tolman's theory called an S-S theory rather than an S-R theory?
4. Describe a situation that would allow you to determine whether or not an animal is utilizing a cognitive map to solve a problem. Do not use any of the specific studies discussed in this chapter.
5. For Tolman, is reinforcement a learning or a performance variable? Explain.
6. Describe briefly the six kinds of learning proposed by Tolman.
7. Summarize the study performed by Tolman and Honzik on latent learning. What conclusions can be drawn from the results of their study?
8. Describe a typical latent extinction experiment and explain why the phenomenon of latent extinction was thought to support Tolman's theory.
9. Describe, according to Tolman, what events take place as an animal is learning to solve a maze. Incorporate as many of Tolman's theoretical terms into your answer as possible.
10. What would characterize classroom procedures designed in accordance with Tolman's theory?
11. Give instances from your own personal life that would either support or refute Tolman's theory of learning.
12. Summarize MacCorquodale and Meehl's restatement of Tolman's theory.
13. Explain the importance of species-specific defensive reactions (SSDRs) in Bolles's analysis of escape and avoidance learning.
14. According to Bolles, what determines the ease with which a response required in a learning experiment is learned?

CHAPTER HIGHLIGHTS

Cathexis. The formation of an association between a certain drive state, such as hunger, and certain stimuli, such as the foods one is accustomed to eating. When a drive occurs, one actively seeks out the stimuli that have been previously associated with its satisfaction. Cathexis is one of Tolman's six proposed kinds of learning.

Cognitive dissonance. A psychological state experienced when there is a discrepancy between what is expected and what actually occurs.

Cognitive map. A mental picture of the environment.

Confirmation of an expectancy. When the prediction made about some future event is found to be accurate.

Demand. The intervening variable that corresponds to maintenance schedule. As number of hours without eating goes up, for example, demand is thought to increase.

Drive discriminations. The fact that organisms can discriminate between various drive states and can therefore adjust their behavior so that appropriate goal objects can be experienced. Drive discrimination is one of Tolman's six proposed kinds of learning.

Emphasizer. A role that motivation played in Tolman's theory. The motivational state of an organism determines which environmental events will be emphasized in that organism's perceptual field.

Equivalence beliefs. Similar to the notion of secondary reinforcement in that a previously neutral event develops the capability of satisfying a need. One of Tolman's six proposed kinds of learning.

Expectancy. A belief or hypothesis about the occurrence of a future event.

Field-cognition modes. Learned or inherited strategies that are utilized while attempting to solve problems. Field-cognition modes are one of Tolman's six proposed kinds of learning.

Field expectancies. Similar to a cognitive map in that the organism comes to know which events in a given environment lead to other events. Field expectancies is one of Tolman's six proposed kinds of learning.

Hypotheses. Expectancies that occur in the early stages of learning.

Latent extinction. Extinction that occurs simply because an animal is allowed to observe that a reinforcer is no longer available. Such extinction does not depend on the animal performing any nonreinforced responses.

Latent learning. Learning that occurs but is not translated immediately into performance. Rather, it is learning that remains dormant until there is some reason for utilizing it, at which time it is translated into behavior.

Maintenance schedule. The feeding schedule arranged by the experimenter for an organism during a learning experiment.

Means-end readiness. An expectancy that is consistently confirmed; sometimes referred to as a belief.

Molar behavior. See Chapter Highlights for chapter 10.

Motor patterns. The learning of the overt behavior that the organism must utilize in reaching a desired goal. Motor pattern is one of Tolman's six proposed kinds of learning.

Place learning. Learning where an object is located. According to Tolman, once the location of an object is known, it can be reached by any number of alternate routes.

Principle of least effort. The contention that a task will always be done in a manner that requires the least amount of effort or work.

Purposive behavior. Behavior directed toward some goal, such as going to the store, cooking a meal, or solving a maze.

Purposive behaviorism. A behavioristic approach that studies purposive behavior as such and does not attempt to reduce such behavior into smaller elements for further analysis.

Reinforcement expectancy. The fact that an organism learns to expect a certain reinforcer if it engages in certain behaviors. It has been found that performance is disrupted when the original reinforcer used in a learning situation is replaced with a different reinforcer.

Response learning. The learning of specific responses that are effective in solving a problem and thereby providing reinforcement.

Species-specific defensive reactions (SSDRs). According to Bolles, the innate responses that are triggered by an aversive situation and that, under ordinary circumstances, would allow the animal to escape or avoid the aversive situation.

Vicarious trial and error. The hesitation at a choice point in a learning situation where it looks "as if" the animal is weighing the alternatives before it decides what to do.

13

Albert Bandura

SOCIAL LEARNING THEORY

SUMMARY

Albert Bandura was born on December 4, 1925 in Mundare, a small town in Alberta, Canada. He obtained his BA from the University of British Columbia, and his MA in 1951 and his PhD in 1952, both from the University of Iowa. He did a postdoctoral internship at the Wichita Guidance Center in 1953 and then joined the faculty at Stanford University where he has been ever since, except for the 1969–1970 year when he was a fellow at the Center for the Advanced Study in the Behavioral Sciences. Bandura is currently the David Starr Jordan Professor of Social Science in Psychology at Stanford University.

Among Bandura's many honors are included a Guggenheim Fellowship, 1972; a Distinguished Scientist Award from Division 12 of the American Psychological Association, 1972; a Distinguished Scientific Achievement Award from the California Psychological Association, 1973; Presidency of the American Psychological Association, 1974; and the James McKeen Cattell Award, 1977. In addition, Bandura

Albert Bandura. (Courtesy of Albert Bandura)

holds office in several scientific societies and is a member of the editorial boards of 17 scholarly journals.

While at the University of Iowa, Bandura was influenced by Kenneth Spence, a prominent Hullian learning theorist, but Bandura's major interest was in clinical psychology. At this time, Bandura was interested in clarifying the notions thought to be involved in effective psychotherapy and then empirically testing and refining them. It was also during this time that Bandura read Miller and Dollard's book *Social Learning and Imitation* (1941) which greatly influenced him. Miller and Dollard used Hullian Learning Theory (see chapter 6) as the basis of their explanation of social and imitative behavior. As we shall see later on in this chapter, Miller and Dollard's explanation of imitative learning dominated the psychological literature for over two decades. It was not until the early 1960s that Bandura began a series of articles and books that were to challenge the older explanations of imitative learning and expand the topic into what is now referred to as observational learning. There is little doubt that Bandura is now looked upon as the leading researcher and theorist in the area of observational learning, a topic which is currently extremely popular and is growing more popular every day.

EARLIER EXPLANATIONS OF OBSERVATIONAL LEARNING

The belief that humans learn by observing other humans goes back at least to such early Greeks as Plato and Aristotle. For them education was, to a large extent, selecting the best models for presentation to students so that the model's qualities may be observed and emulated. Through the centuries **observational learning** was taken for granted and was usually explained by postulating a natural tendency for humans to imitate what they see others do. As long as this nativist explanation prevailed, little was done to either verify the fact that the tendency to learn by observation was innate or, indeed, to determine whether observational learning occurred at all.

It was Edward L. Thorndike who first attempted to study observational learning experimentally. In 1898, he placed one cat in a puzzle box and placed another cat in an adjoining cage. The cat in the puzzle box had already learned how to escape so the second cat had only to observe the first cat in order to learn the escape response. However, when Thorndike placed the second cat in the puzzle box it did not perform the escape response. The second cat had to go through the same trial-and-error process that the first cat went through before it also learned the escape response. Thorndike ran the same type of experiment with chicks and dogs with the same results. No matter how long a naive animal watched a sophisticated one, the naive animal seemed to learn nothing. In 1901, Thorndike ran similar experiments with monkeys but contrary to the popular belief that "monkey see, monkey do," no observational learning took place. Thorndike concluded, "Nothing in my experience with these animals . . . favors the hypothesis that they have any general ability to learn to do things from seeing others do them" (1901, p. 42).

In 1908, J. B. Watson replicated Thorndike's research using monkeys; he too found no evidence for observational learning. Both Thorndike and Watson concluded that learning can only result from **direct experience** and not from indirect or **vicarious experience.** In other words, they felt that learning occurred as a result of one's personal interactions with the environment and not as a result of observing someone else's interactions.

With only a few exceptions the work of Thorndike and Watson discouraged further research on observational learning. It was not until the publication of Miller and Dollard's book *Social Learning and Imitation* (1941) that interest in observational learning was again stimulated.

Miller and Dollard's Explanation of Observational Learning

Like Thorndike and Watson, Miller and Dollard sought to challenge the nativistic explanation of observational learning. However, unlike Thorndike and Watson, Miller and Dollard did not deny the fact that an organism could learn by observing the activities of another organism. They felt that such learning was rather widespread, but that it could be explained objectively within the framework of Hullian learning theory. That is, if imitative behavior is reinforced it will be strengthened like any other kind of behavior. Thus, according to Miller and Dollard, imitative learning was simply a special case of instrumental conditioning.

Miller and Dollard divided imitative behavior into three categories: (a) **same behavior** such as when two or more individuals respond to the same situation in the same way. For example, most people stop at a red light, applaud when a play or concert is over, and laugh when others laugh. With same behavior, all the individuals involved have learned independently to respond in a particular way to a particular stimulus and their behavior is triggered simultaneously when that stimulus, or one like it, occurs in the environment; (b) **copying behavior** which involves the guiding of one person's behavior by another person, such as when an art instructor gives guidance and corrective feedback to an art student who is attempting to draw a picture. With copying behavior, the final "copied" response is reinforced and thereby strengthened; (c) **matched-dependent behavior** where an observer is reinforced for blindly repeating the actions of a model. As an example of matched-dependent behavior, Miller and Dollard describe a situation where an older child had learned to run to the front door upon hearing his father's footsteps as the father approached the house and the father reinforced the child's efforts with candy. A younger child found that if he happened to be running behind his brother when he ran to the door, he (the younger child) would also receive candy from the father. Soon the younger child learned to run to the door whenever he saw his older brother doing so. At this point the behavior of both children was being maintained by reinforcement but each boy associated reinforcement with different cues. For the older child, the sound of the father's approaching footsteps triggered the running response which was reinforced by candy. For the younger child the sight of his brother running toward the door triggered running on his part which was also reinforced by candy.

Matched-dependent behavior also seems to characterize the behavior of adults who are in an unfamiliar situation. When one is in a foreign country, for example, one may avoid many problems by observing how the natives respond to various situations and then responding as they do, even if the rationale for the behavior is not clearly understood. Perhaps this is the rationale behind the old saying "When in Rome, do as the Romans do."

Miller and Dollard also pointed out that imitation itself could become a habit. In the situation described previously, the younger child could have learned that imitating the behavior of his older brother often had led to reinforcement and therefore the probability of his acting like his older brother in a wide variety of situations would have increased. Miller and Dollard referred to this learned tendency to imitate the behavior of one or more individuals as **generalized imitation.**

Miller and Dollard saw nothing unusual or special about imitative learning. For them the role of the model was to guide the observer's responses until the appropriate one had been made or to demonstrate to an observer which response would be reinforced in a given situation. According to Miller and Dollard, if imitative responses were not made and reinforced, no learning would take place. For them, imitative learning was the result of observation, overt responding, and reinforcement. There is nothing in these conclusions that disagrees with the conclusions reached by Thorndike and Watson. Like their predecessors, Miller and Dollard found that organisms do not learn from observation alone. Perhaps, Miller and Dollard might say that the only mistake that Thorndike and Watson made was not placing the naive animal *inside* the puzzle box with the sophisticated animal. This would have allowed the naive animal to observe, to respond, and to be reinforced, and therefore imitative learning probably would have occurred.

Unlike the nativistic explanations of imitative learning that prevailed for many centuries, Miller and Dollard's explanation offered the first empiricistic explanation of the phenomenon. Their explanation was in accordance with a widely accepted theory of learning and was firmly supported by rigorous experimental research.

As we saw earlier, the work of Thorndike and Watson had laid interest in imitative learning to rest for over three decades. Miller and Dollard's work had the same effect for over two decades. It was not until the early 1960s that the topic was again scrutinized. It was at this time that Bandura challenged earlier explanations of imitative learning and began to formulate his own theory which broke away from the behavioristic mold of the preceding theories. As we shall see, Bandura views observational learning as primarily a cognitive process which involves a number of attributes thought of as distinctly human, such as language, morality, thinking, and the self-regulation of one's behavior.

BANDURA'S ACCOUNT OF OBSERVATIONAL LEARNING

Up to this point we have been using the terms imitation and observational learning interchangeably; however, for Bandura a major distinction must be made between the two concepts. According to Bandura, observational learning may or may not involve imitation. For example, while driving down the street you may see the car in front of you hit a pothole and based on this observation you may swerve in order to miss the hole and avoid damage to your car. In this case, you learned from your observation, but you did not imitate what you had observed. What you learned, according to Bandura, was *information* which was processed cognitively and acted upon in a way that was advantageous. Observational learning, therefore, is much more complex than simple imitation which usually involves mimicking another person's actions.

If one has to choose a theory of learning that is closest to Bandura's, it would be Tolman's theory. Although Tolman was a behaviorist he used mentalistic concepts to explain behavioral phenomena (see chapter 12), and Bandura does the same thing. Also, Tolman looked upon learning as a constant process which does not require reinforcement, and Bandura believes the same thing. Both Tolman's theory and Bandura's theory are cognitive in nature and neither are reinforcement theories. A final point of agreement between Tolman and Bandura concerns the concept of motivation. Although Tolman believed that learning was constant, he believed further that the information gained through learning was only acted upon when there was reason for doing so, such as when a need arose. For example, one may know full well where a drinking fountain is but will only act upon that information when one is thirsty. For Tolman, this distinction between learning and performance was extremely important, and it is also important in Bandura's theory.

The learning-performance distinction is nicely demonstrated in a study performed by Bandura (1965). In this experiment, children observed a film in which a **model** was shown hitting and kicking a large doll. In Bandura's theory a model can be anything that conveys information, such as a person, a film, television, a demonstration, a picture, or instructions. In this case, a film showed an adult modeling aggressiveness. One group of children saw the model being reinforced for his aggressiveness. A second group of children saw the model punished for his aggressiveness. For a third group the consequences of the model's aggressiveness were neutral, that is, the model was neither reinforced nor punished. Later, children in all three groups were exposed to the doll and their aggressiveness toward it was measured. As might be expected, the children who saw the model reinforced for aggressiveness were most aggressive; the children who saw the model punished for aggressiveness were least aggressive; and the children who saw the model experience neutral consequences were between the two other groups in their aggressiveness. This much of the study is interesting because it demonstrates that the children's behavior was influenced by indirect or vicarious experience. In other words, what they observed another person experiencing had an impact on their own behavior. The children in the first group observed **vicarious reinforcement** and it facilitated their aggressiveness; children in the second group observed **vicarious punishment** and it inhibited their aggressiveness. Although the children did not experience reinforcement or punishment directly, it modified their behavior just the same. This is contrary to Miller and Dollard's contention that observational learning will occur only if the organism's *overt* behavior is followed by reinforcement.

The second phase of the study described above was designed to shed light on the learning-performance distinction. In this phase, *all* the children were offered an attractive incentive for reproducing the behavior of the model *and they all did so.* In other words, all the children had *learned* the model's aggressive responses but they had *performed* differentially depending on whether they had observed the model being reinforced, punished, or experiencing neutral consequences. The results of this study are summarized in Figure 13-1.

Note the similarity between the Bandura (1965) experiment and the one run by Tolman and Honzik (1930). In the latter study it was found that if a rat that had run a maze without **reinforcement** was suddenly given reinforcement for making the correct goal response, its **performance** rapidly equaled that of a rat that had been reinforced on every trial. Tolman's explanation for this was that even the nonreinforced rats were learning the maze, and inserting reinforcement into the situation merely caused them to demonstrate the information that they had been accumulating all along. Thus, the purpose of Bandura's experiment (1965) was similar to that of Tolman and Honzik's (1930), and the findings and conclusions about the distinc-

Figure 13–1. The influence of a positive incentive on the manifestation of responses learned by observation. (From "Influence of a Model's Reinforcement Contingencies on the Acquisition of Imitative Responses," by A. Bandura, 1965, *Journal of Personality and Social Psychology, 11,* p. 592. Copyright 1965 by the American Psychological Association. Reprinted by permission of the author.)

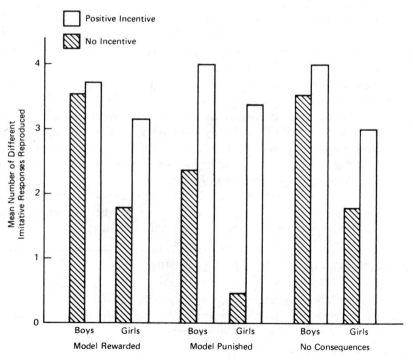

tion between learning and performance were also similar. The major finding from both experiments was that reinforcement is a performance variable and not a learning variable. This, of course, is exactly opposite to the conclusion Hull reached about reinforcement. For him, reinforcement was a learning variable, not a performance variable.

Thus, Bandura disagrees sharply with Miller and Dollard's account of observational learning. For Bandura, observational learning occurs all the time. "After the capacity for observational learning has fully developed, one cannot keep people from learning what they have seen" (1977, p. 38). Also for Bandura, contrary to Miller and Dollard's contention, observational learning requires neither overt responding nor reinforcement.

The Skinnerian Analysis of Observational Learning

The Skinnerian explanation of observational learning is very similar to that of Miller and Dollard's. First, a model's behavior is observed, next the observer matches the response of the model, and, finally, the matching response is reinforced. Furthermore, once learning has occurred in this fashion it is maintained by some kind of schedule of reinforcement in the natural environment. Thus, according to the operant analysis of observational learning, the model's behavior acts as a discriminative stimulus indicating which actions will result in reinforcement. Imitation, then, is nothing more than a discriminative operant (see chapter 5).

Bandura finds several things incorrect about Skinner's and Miller's and Dollard's explanation of observational learning. First, they do not explain how learning can occur when neither the model nor the observer are reinforced for their actions, which research has indicated is the case. Second, they do not explain **delayed modeling** where an observer exhibits learning that occurred from observations made at a much earlier time. Furthermore, it has been found that the observer need not be reinforced for exhibiting this prior learning. Third, unlike Miller and Dollard and Skinner, who believe that reinforcement serves to automatically and mechanically strengthen behavior, Bandura believes that an observer must be aware of the reinforcement contingencies before they can have any effect. Bandura (1977) says: "Because learning by response consequences is largely a cognitive process, consequences generally produce little change in complex behavior when there is no awareness of what is being reinforced" (p. 18).

In short, Bandura maintains that all of the ingredients essential for an operant analysis of observational learning are missing. That is, there is often no discriminative stimulus, no overt responding, and no reinforcement.

VARIABLES AFFECTING OBSERVATIONAL LEARNING

To say that observational learning occurs independent of reinforcement is not to say that other variables do not affect it. Bandura (1977) lists four processes that influence observational learning and they are summarized below.

Attentional Processes

Before something can be learned from a model, the model must be attended to. As was noted above, Bandura thought learning to be an ongoing process, but he points out that only what is observed can be learned. Craighead, Kazdin, and Mahoney (1976) make this point in a rather humorous way:

> Suppose that you are holding a 4-year-old child on your lap while two other 4-year-olds play on separate areas of your living room floor and that, as child A gently pets your English sheepdog, child B inserts a butter knife into an electrical outlet. Everyone would learn something from this incident. Because it was directly associated with severe, unexpected pain and accompanying autonomic arousal, child B would learn to avoid using wall sockets as knife holders, and possibly, to stay away from electrical outlets altogether. Child A might learn, or at least begin to learn, to avoid the sheepdog, or dogs in general. When child B suddenly screamed and cried, it startled child A, and since the occurrence of any strong, sudden, unexpected, and novel stimulus produces autonomic arousal, the harmless dog was associated with a strong, unconditioned response to a stressful stimulus. Depending upon the focus of his or her attention at the time, the child on your lap might later display avoidance of wall sockets (if he/she was watching child B), of dogs (if he/she was watching child A), or of you. Incidentally, since many of the principles of learning apply to both humans and animals, it is also possible that this sheepdog may subsequently try to avoid children. (p. 188)

So the question arises, what determines what is noticed? First, a person's sensory capacities will influence what can be attended to. Obviously, the modeling stimuli used to teach a blind or deaf person will need to be different from those used to teach a person with normal sight or hearing.

An observer's selective attention can be influenced by past reinforcements. For example, if prior activities learned through observation have proved functional in obtaining reinforcement, similar behaviors will be attended to in subsequent modeling situations. In other words, prior reinforcement can create a perceptual set in the observer that will influence future observations.

Various characteristics of models will also affect the extent to which they are attended to. Research has demonstrated that models will be attended to more often if they are similar to the observer (i.e., same sex, age, etc.), are respected, have high status, have demonstrated high competence, are thought of as powerful, and are attractive.

In general, Bandura (1986) says: "[People] pay attention to models reputed to be effective and ignore those who, by appearance or reputation, are presumed to be ineffectual . . . Given the choice, people are more likely to select models who are proficient at producing good outcomes than those who repeatedly get punished" (p. 54).

Retentional Processes

In order for information gained from observation to be useful, it must be retained. It is Bandura's contention that information is stored symbolically in two ways, imaginally and verbally. The imaginally stored symbols are actual stored pictures of the modeled experience which can be retrieved and acted upon long after the observational learning has taken place. Here we have another point of agreement between Bandura's theory and Tolman's theory. Bandura says that behavior is at least partially determined by mental images of past experiences; Tolman said that much behavior is governed by a "cognitive map" which consists of the mental representations of our prior experiences in a given situation.

The second, and for Bandura the more important, kind of symbolization is verbal. Bandura says:

> Most of the cognitive processes that regulate behavior are primarily verbal rather than visual. Details of the route traveled by a model, for example, can be acquired, retained, and later reproduced more accurately by converting the visual information into a verbal code describing a series of right and left turns (e.g., RLRRL) than by reliance upon visual imagery of the route. Observational learning and retention are facilitated by such symbolic codes because they carry a great deal of information in an easily stored form. (1977, p. 26)

Although it is possible to discuss imaginal and verbal symbols separately, they are often inseparable when events are represented in memory. Bandura (1986) says: "Although verbal symbols embody a major share of knowledge acquired by modeling, it is often difficult to separate representation modes. Representational activities usually involve both systems to some degree . . . Words tend to evoke corresponding imagery, and images of events are often verbally cognized as well. When visual and verbal stimuli convey similar meanings, people integrate the information presented by these different modalities into a common conceptual representation" (p. 58).

Once information is stored cognitively, it can be retrieved covertly, rehearsed, and strengthened long after the observational learning has taken place. According to Bandura, "It is the advanced capacity for symbolization that enables humans to learn much of their behavior by observation" (1977, p. 25). It is these stored symbols that make delayed modeling possible—that is, the ability to utilize information long after it has been observed.

Behavioral Production Processes

These processes determine the extent to which that which has been learned is translated into performance. It is clear that one may learn, by observing monkeys, how to swing from tree to tree utilizing a tail, but one would be at a loss to replicate those behaviors if one does not possess a tail. In other words, one may learn a great deal cognitively but be unable to translate that information into behavior for a variety of reasons, such as the motor apparatus necessary to make certain responses may not be available because of one's maturational level, injury, or illness.

Bandura maintains that even if one is equipped with all of the physical apparatus to make appropriate responses, a period of cognitive rehearsal is necessary before an observer's behavior can match that of a model. According to Bandura, the symbols retained from a modeling experience act as a template with which one's actions are compared. During this rehearsal process individuals observe their own behavior and compare it to their cognitive representation of the modeled experience. Any observed discrepancies between one's own behavior and the memory of the model's behavior trigger corrective action. This process continues until there is an acceptable match between the observer's and the model's behavior. Thus, the symbolic retention of a modeling experience creates a "feedback" loop which can be used to gradually match one's behavior with that of a model's by utilizing self-observation and self-correction.

Motivational Processes

In Bandura's theory, reinforcement has two major functions. First, it creates an *expectation* in observers that if they act like a model, who has been seen being reinforced for certain activities, they will be reinforced also. Second, it acts as an *incentive* for translating learning into performance. As we have seen, what has been learned observationally remains dormant until the observer has a reason to use the information. For example, individuals may know where a restaurant is but only visit it when they are hungry. Both functions of reinforcement are *informational,* one function creates an expectancy in observers that if they act in a certain way in a certain situation, they are likely to be reinforced. The other function provides a motive for utilizing what has been learned.

This is a major departure from traditional reinforcement theories that claim only those responses that are overtly made and reinforced in a given situation are strengthened. According to Bandura, not only is reinforcement not necessary for learning to take place but neither is direct experience. An observer can learn simply by observing the consequences of the behavior of others, storing that information symbolically and utilizing it when it is advantageous to do so. Thus, for Bandura, *vicarious* reinforcement or punishment is as informative as direct reinforcement or punishment. In Bandura's theory then, reinforcement and punishment are important but for much different reasons than they are for most reinforcement theorists. Most reinforcement theorists assume that reinforcement or punishment operate gradually, automatically, and usually without the awareness of the organism, to strengthen or weaken an association between a stimulus and a response. For Bandura, however, learners gain information by observing either the consequences of their own behavior or of the behavior of others. The information gained by these observations can then be utilized in a variety of situations when a need to use it arises. Since actions, either one's own or someone else's, that bring about reinforcement and/or avoid punishment are especially functional, it is those actions that individuals will tend to observe and encode into memory for future use. Armed with information gained by prior observations, individuals anticipate that if they act in certain ways in certain situations certain consequences will follow. In this way,

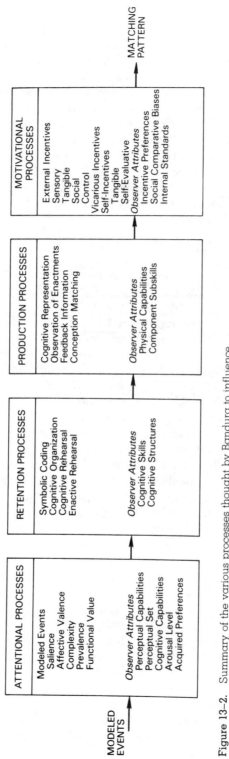

Figure 13–2. Summary of the various processes thought by Bandura to influence observational learning. (From *Social Foundations of Thought & Action*, p. 52, by A. Bandura, © 1986. Reprinted by permission of Prentice-Hall, Inc., Englewood Cliffs, New Jersey.)

anticipated consequences at least partially determine behavior in any given situation. It is important to note, however, that anticipated *environmental* consequences are not the only determiners of behavior. Behavior is also partially influenced by anticipated *self-reactions* which are determined by one's internalized standards of performance and conduct and by one's perceived self-efficacy. We will have more to say about self-regulated behavior later in this chapter.

To summarize this section we can say that observational learning involves attention, retention, behavioral abilities, and incentives. Therefore, if observational learning fails to occur, it could be that the observer did not observe the relevant activities of the model, did not retain them, was physically incapable of performing them, or did not have the proper incentive to perform them. Figure 13-2 summarizes the variables that Bandura feels influence observational learning.

RECIPROCAL DETERMINISM

Perhaps the most basic question in all of psychology is, "Why do people act as they do?" and depending upon one's answer to this question, one can be classified as an environmentalist (empiricist), a nativist, an existentialist, or something else. Environmentalists (e.g., Skinner) would say that behavior is a function of reinforcement contingencies in the environment and therefore if you change reinforcement contingencies you change behavior. Extreme nativists (if you can find one) would emphasize inherited dispositions, traits, or even ideas, in their answer to the question. Existentialists would emphasize free choice in their answer, that is, people do more or less what they choose to do. Thus most of the traditional answers to the question, "Why do people act as they do?" claim that behavior is either a function of the environment, of certain traits or dispositions, or of the freedom that humans possess.

Bandura's answer to the question falls into the "something else" category. His answer is that the person, the environment, and the person's behavior itself all interact to produce the person's subsequent behavior. In other words, none of the three components can be understood in isolation of the others as a determiner of human behavior. Bandura (1986, p. 24) summarizes this three-way interaction as follows:

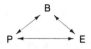

where P is the person, E is the environment and B is the person's behavior.

This position is referred to as **reciprocal determinism.** One deduction from this concept is that it is as valid to say that behavior influences the person and the environment as it is to say that the environment or the person influences behavior.

As an example of behavior influencing the environment, Bandura (1977, p. 196) describes a rat experiment on defensive learning in which a shock is scheduled to be delivered every minute unless a bar press is made, in which case the shock is delayed for 30 sec. Those rats learning to press the bar with a certain frequency can avoid shock completely; those rats who fail to learn the bar press response must go on experiencing periodic shocks. Bandura (1977) concludes: "Though the **potential environment** is identical for all animals, the **actual environment** depends upon their behavior. Is the animal controlling the environment or is the environment controlling the animal? What we have here is a two-way regulatory system in which the organism appears either as an object or an agent of control, depending upon which side of the reciprocal process one chooses to examine" (p. 196).

Bandura maintains that reinforcements, like punishments, exist only potentially in the environment and are only actualized by certain behavior patterns. Therefore, which aspects of an environment influence us are determined by how we act upon that environment. Bandura goes further by saying that behavior can also *create* environments: "We are all acquainted with problem-prone individuals who, through their obnoxious conduct, predictably breed negative social climates wherever they go. Others are equally skilled at bringing out the best in those with whom they interact" (1977, p. 197).

Thus, according to Bandura, people can influence the environment by acting in certain ways and the changed environment will, in turn, influence their subsequent behavior. But, Bandura points out that even though there is an interaction among people, the environment, and behavior, any of these components may be more influential than the others at any given time. For example, a loud noise in the environment may momentarily have more of an influence on a person's behavior than anything else. At other times, one's beliefs may be the most influential determiner of one's actions. In fact, many studies have shown that the behavior of humans is governed more by what they believe is going on than by what is really going on. For example, Kaufman, Baron, and Kopp (1966) ran a study in which all subjects were reinforced about once every minute (variable-interval schedule) for performing a manual response. Although all the subjects were *actually* on the *same* schedule of reinforcement, some were misled about the schedule that they were on. One group was told the truth about the schedule, another group was told that their behavior would be reinforced every minute (fixed-interval schedule), and a third group was told that they would be reinforced after they had made on the average of 150 responses (variable-ratio schedule). It was found that those subjects who believed they were on a fixed-interval schedule responded very slowly, those believing they were on a variable-ratio schedule responded very rapidly, and those that were told the truth about being on a variable-interval schedule responded with a rate in between the other two groups. On the basis of this and similar studies Bandura concludes, "Beliefs about the prevailing conditions of reinforcement outweighed the influence of experienced consequences" (1977, p. 166).

Undoubtedly it is best to have one's beliefs correspond to reality. In the experiment just summarized the participants were misinformed, and they believed and acted upon the misinformation. There are many factors in everyday life that can create nonadapative beliefs in individuals which can lead to ineffective or even bizarre actions. We will consider these factors when we consider faulty cognitive processes later in the chapter.

To summarize, Bandura's concept of reciprocal determinism states that behavior, the environment, and people (and their beliefs) all interact and that this three-way interaction must be understood before an understanding of human psychological functioning and behavior can occur.

SELF-REGULATION OF BEHAVIOR

According to Bandura, "If actions were determined solely by external rewards and punishments, people would behave like weathervanes, constantly shifting in different directions to conform to the momentary influences impinging upon them. They would act corruptly with unprincipled individuals and honorably with righteous ones, and liberally with libertarians and dogmatically with authoritarians" (1977, p. 128). The situation described in this quotation is obviously not the case, but if external reinforcers and punishers do not control behavior, what does? Bandura's answer is that human behavior is largely **self-regulated.** Among the things that humans learn from direct or vicarious experience are performance standards and once these standards are learned, they become the basis of self-evaluation. If a person's performance in a given situation meets or exceeds one's standards, it is evaluated positively; if it falls short of one's standards it is evaluated negatively.

One's standards can arise from one's direct experience with reinforcement by placing a high value on behaviors that have been effective in bringing praise from the relevant individuals in one's life, such as one's parents. Personal standards can also develop vicariously by observing those behaviors for which others have been reinforced. For example, Bandura and Kupers (1964) found that children who were exposed to models who set high performance standards reinforced themselves only for superior performance, and children who were exposed to models who reinforced themselves for minimal performances reinforced themselves for minimal performances.

Bandura believes that the intrinsic reinforcement that comes from self-evaluation is much more influential than the extrinsic reinforcement dispensed by others. In fact, he gives several examples of cases where extrinsic reinforcement for engaging in activities has *reduced* the motivation to engage in them (1977, p. 107). After reviewing a great deal of research on the relative effectiveness of extrinsic (externally administered) versus intrinsic (self-administered) reinforcement Bandura concludes that ". . . self-rewarded behavior tends to be maintained more effectively than if it has been externally reinforced" (1977, p. 144).

Unfortunately, if one's standards of performance are too high, they can be a source of personal distress. Bandura (1977) says: "In its more extreme forms, harsh standards for self-evaluation give rise to depressive reactions, chronic discouragement, feelings of worthlessness, and lack of purposefulness" (p. 141). According to Bandura, working at goals that are too distant or too difficult can be disappointing. "Subgoals of moderate difficulty are therefore likely to be most motivating and satisfying" (1977, p. 162).

Like internalized performance standards, perceived **self-efficacy** plays a major role in self-regulated behavior. Perceived self-efficacy refers to one's impression of what one is capable of doing. Perceived self-efficacy comes from a variety of sources including personal accomplishments and failures, seeing others who are seen as similar to oneself succeed or fail at various tasks, and verbal persuasion. Verbal persuasion may temporarily convince people that they should try or avoid some task but in the final analysis it is one's direct or vicarious experience with success and failure that will most strongly influence one's perceived self-efficacy. For example, a football coach may "fire up" his team before a game by telling its members how great they are, but the enthusiasm will be short-lived if the opposing team is clearly superior.

Persons with high perceived self-efficacy try more, accomplish more, and persist longer at a task than persons with low perceived self-efficacy. People with high perceived self-efficacy also tend to experience less fear than people with low perceived self-efficacy. Bandura (1980b) speculates that this is because people with high perceived self-efficacy tend to have more control over the events in their environment and therefore experience less uncertainty. Since individuals tend to fear events over which they have no control, and therefore are uncertain of, those individuals with high perceived self-efficacy tend to experience less fear.

One's *perceived* self-efficacy may or may not correspond to one's *real* self-efficacy. People may believe their self-efficacy is low when in reality it is high and vice versa. The situation is best when one's aspirations are in line with one's capabilities. If, for example, people continually attempt to do things beyond their capabilities, they experience frustration and despair and may eventually "give up" on most everything. On the other hand, if people with high self-efficacy do not adequately challenge themselves, their personal growth may be inhibited. The development of perceived self-efficacy and its impact on self-regulated behavior are topics about which Bandura is currently writing extensively (see, e.g., Bandura 1980a and 1980b).

Moral Conduct

Like one's performance standards and one's perceived self-efficacy, one's **moral code** develops through interactions with models. In the case of morality, the parents usually model the moral rules and regulations that are ultimately internalized by the child. Once internalized, one's moral code determines which behaviors (or thoughts) are sanctioned and which are not. Departure from one's moral code brings **self-contempt,** which is not a pleasant experience, and thus one typically acts in accordance with one's moral code. Bandura (1977) says: "The anticipation of self-reproach for conduct that violates one's standards provides a source of motivation to keep behavior in line with standards in the face of opposing inducements. There is no more devastating punishment than self-contempt" (p. 154).

Bandura states his opposition to stage theories (e.g., Piaget and Kohlberg) and trait theories (e.g., Allport) rather forcefully. His primary reason for this opposition is that such theories predict a stability in human behavior that Bandura feels does not exist. Stage theories, for example, predict that a person's intellectual or moral capabilities are set by maturation and therefore those intellectual or moral judgments one can make are set by one's age. The same is true for type or trait theories which say that people will act consistently in a wide range of situations because they are certain types of people or because they possess certain traits. Bandura maintains that human behavior is not all that consistent. Rather, he says, it is more circumstantial. In other words, Bandura believes that human behavior is determined more by the situation one is in, and by one's interpretation of that situation, than it is by one's stage of development, by one's traits, or by the type of person one is.

There is no better example of the situational nature of behavior than the topic of morality. Even though one has firm moral principles, there are several mechanisms that can be used to dissociate reprehensible acts from self-sanctions. These mechanisms make it possible for people to radically depart from their moral principles without experiencing self-contempt. These self-exonerating mechanisms are (from Bandura, 1986, pp. 375–385):

1. Moral Justification. One's otherwise reprehensible behavior becomes a means to a higher purpose and therefore is justifiable. "I committed the crime so that I could provide food for my family." Bandura (1986) gives another example:

> Radical shifts in destructive behavior through moral justification are most strikingly revealed in military training. People who have been taught to deplore killing as morally condemnable can be transformed rapidly into skilled combatants, who feel little compunction and even a sense of pride in taking human life . . . In justifying warfare, one sees oneself fighting ruthless oppressors who have an unquenchable appetite for conquest, protecting one's way of life, preserving world peace, saving humanity from being subjugated to an evil ideology, and honoring the country's international commitments. Such restructuring of circumstances is designed to get even considerate people to regard violent means as morally justifiable to achieve humane ends. (p. 376)

2. Euphemistic Labeling. By calling an otherwise reprehensible act something other than what it really is, one can engage in an act without self-contempt. For example, nonaggressive individuals are far more likely to aggress toward another person when doing so is called a game. Bandura (1986) gives other examples of how euphemistic labeling is used to make the reprehensible respectable: "Through the power of hygienic words, even killing a human being loses much of its repugnancy. Soldiers 'waste' people rather than kill them . . . When mercenaries speak of 'fulfilling a contract,' murder is transformed by admirable words into the honorable discharge of duty" (p. 378).

3. Advantageous Comparison. By comparing one's self-deplored acts with even more heinous acts, it makes one's own reprehensible acts look trifling by comparison. "Sure I did that, but look at what he did." Bandura (1986) offers examples:

> Promoters of the Vietnamese War and their supporters, . . . minimized the slaying of countless people as a way of checking massive communist enslave-

ment. Given the trifling comparison, perpetrators of warfare remained unperturbed by the fact that the intended beneficiaries were being killed at an alarming rate. Domestic protesters, on the other hand, characterized their own violence against educational and political institutions as trifling, or even laudable, by comparing it with the carnage perpetuated by their country's military forces in foreign lands. (p. 379)

4. Displacement of Responsibility. Some people can readily depart from their moral principles if they feel a recognized authority sanctions their behavior and takes responsibility for it. "I did it, because I was ordered to do so." Bandura (1986) says: "Nazi prison commandants and their staffs felt little personal responsibility for their unprecedented inhumanities. They were simply carrying out orders. Impersonal obedience to horrific orders was similarly evident in military atrocities, such as the My Lai massacre" (p. 379).

5. Diffusion of Responsibility. A decision to act in an otherwise reprehensible manner which is made by a group is easier to live with than an individual decision. Where everyone is responsible, no single individual feels responsible.

6. Disregard or Distortion of Consequences. Here people ignore or distort the harm caused by their conduct and therefore there is no need to experience self-contempt. The farther people remove themselves from the ill effects of their immoral behavior the less pressure there is to censure it. "I just let the bombs go and they disappeared in the clouds."

7. Dehumanization. If some individuals are looked upon as subhuman, they can be treated inhumanly without experiencing self-contempt. Once a person or a group has been dehumanized, they no longer possess feelings, hopes, and concerns, they can be mistreated without risking self-condemnation. "Why not take their land, they are nothing but savages without souls."

8. Attribution of Blame. One can always choose something that a victim said or did and claim that it caused one to act in a reprehensible way. Bandura (1986) gives an example: "Rapists and males who acknowledge a proclivity to rape subscribe to myths about rape embodying the various mechanisms by which moral self-censure can be disengaged . . . These beliefs hold rape victims responsible for their own victimization because they have supposedly invited rape by sexually provocative appearance and behavior and by resisting sexual assault weakly" (pp. 384–385).

Bandura (1977) attributes most misconduct to these dissociative mechanisms rather than to faulty moral codes: "Because internalized controls are subject to dissociative operations, marked changes in people's moral conduct can be achieved without altering their personality structures, moral principles, or self-evaluative systems. It is self-exonerative processes rather than character flaws that account for most inhumanities" (p. 158).

Determinism Versus Freedom

Does the fact that much behavior is self-regulated mean that humans are free to do whatever they choose? Bandura defines **freedom** in terms of the number of options available to people and their opportunities to exercise them (1986, p. 42). According to Bandura, constraints to personal freedom include incompetence, unwarranted fears, excessive self-censure, and social inhibitors such as discrimination and prejudice.

Thus, in the same physical environment some individuals are freer than others. As we shall see in the next section, another constraint on personal freedom could be faulty cognitive processes which may prevent people from interacting effectively with their environment.

FAULTY COGNITIVE PROCESSES

Bandura places great importance in cognitive processes in the determination of human behavior. We have seen how one's internalized performance standards, perceived self-efficacy, and moral codes play a major role in the self-regulation of behavior. Further evidence for the influence of cognitive processes on one's behavior comes from the fact that we can *imagine* ourselves into almost any emotional state we wish to. We can make ourselves nauseated, angry, peaceful, or sexually aroused simply by conjuring up appropriate thoughts. Thus, according to Bandura, behavior can be strongly influenced by one's own imagination.

Since one's behavior is at least partially determined by one's cognitive processes, it follows that if these processes do not accurately reflect reality, maladaptive behavior can result. Bandura describes several reasons why individuals may develop **faulty cognitive processes.** First, children may develop false beliefs because they tend to evaluate things on the basis of appearance; thus, they conclude that a tall, narrow beaker contains more water than a short, wider beaker because for them "taller" means "bigger." Piaget would say that a child reaching this conclusion has not learned the principle of conservation. Secondly, errors in thought can occur when information is derived from insufficient evidence. Bandura (1977) gives the following example: "Learning from the images conveyed by the mass media is a good case in point. People partly form impressions of the social realities with which they have little or no contact from televised representations of society. Because the world of television is heavily populated with villainous and unscrupulous characters it can distort knowledge about the real world" (p. 184).

According to Bandura, the distorted view of reality can sometimes result in criminal behavior: "Children have been apprehended for writing bad checks to obtain money for candy, for sniping at strangers with BB guns, for sending threatening letters to teachers and for injurious switchblade fights after witnessing similar performances on television. . . ." (1973, pp. 101–102).

Bandura says that once false beliefs are established, they become self-perpetuating, because those holding them seek out individuals or groups who share the same false beliefs. "The various cults and messianic groups that emerge from time to time typify this process" (Bandura, 1977, p. 185). Furthermore, once false beliefs are established, they can be self-fulfilling prophecies. For example, if people believe that they are stupid they will seek experiences and engage in activities that support their belief.

Thirdly, fallacies in thinking can arise from the faulty processing of information. For example, if people believe that all farmers lack intelligence, they would necessarily conclude that any particular farmer lacks intelligence. This deduction is false because the premise (belief) is false, but Bandura points out that one can also make erroneous deductions from correct information. In other words, even if people possess accurate information their deductions may be faulty. An example would be correctly observing that unemployment is higher among black individuals than it is among white individuals, but erroneously concluding from this fact that black individuals are less motivated than white individuals.

In some cases, faulty beliefs can cause bizarre behavior such as when one's life is directed by the belief that he is "God." Also phobias can trigger extreme defensive behaviors such as when people refuse to leave their houses because they are too frightened of dogs. In this case, the fact that most dogs do not bite can never be realized because the people never encounter dogs. What these phobics need, according to Bandura, is "powerful disconfirming experiences" which will force them to change their expectations of how dogs behave. How observational learning is used to treat phobics will be covered in the next section.

PRACTICAL APPLICATIONS OF OBSERVATIONAL LEARNING

What Modeling Can Accomplish

Modeling has been found to have several kinds of effects on observers. New responses may be acquired by watching a model being reinforced for certain actions. Thus, the **acquisition** of behavior results from vicarious reinforcement. A response that otherwise might be readily made in a situation is inhibited when a model is seen being punished for making that response. Thus response **inhibition** results from vicarious punishment. Also seeing a model engage in a feared activity without the model experiencing any ill effects can reduce inhibitions in the observer. The reduction of fear which results from observing a model's unpunished participation in the feared activity is called **disinhibition.** A model may also elicit from an observer a response that has already been learned and for which there is no inhibition. In this case, by performing a response, the model simply increases the likelihood of the observer making a similar response. This is called response **facilitation.** Modeling can also stimulate **creativity.** This can be accomplished by exposing observers to a variety of models that causes the observer to adopt combinations of characteristics or styles. Bandura (1977) says:

> The progression of creative careers through distinct periods provides notable examples of this process. In his earliest works, Beethoven adopted the classical forms of Haydn and Mozart . . . Wagner fused Beethoven's symphonic mode

with Weber's naturalistic enchantment and Meyerbeer's dramatic virtuosity to evolve a new operatic form. Innovators in other endeavors in the same manner initially draw upon the contributions of others and build from their experiences something new. (p. 48)

Innovation can also be stimulated more directly by modeling unconventional responses to common situations. In this case, observers may already possess strategies that are effective in solving a problem but the model teaches bolder, more unconventional problem-solving strategies.

With the possible exception of modeled creativity, the use of modeling to convey information has been criticized for stimulating only response mimicry or imitation. That this is not the case is clearly demonstrated by **abstract modeling.** In abstract modeling people observe models performing various responses that have a common rule or principle running through them. For example, the models could solve problems using a certain strategy or generate sentences that embody a certain grammatical style. It is found, under these circumstances, that observers typically learn whatever rule or principle is being exemplified in the diverse modeling experiences. Furthermore it is found that after the rule or principle is learned by the observer, it can be applied to situations unlike any involved during the modeling. For example, once a problem-solving strategy is extracted from a number of modeling experiences, it can be used effectively to solve problems that are unlike any experienced before. Thus abstract modeling has three components: (a) observing a wide variety of situations that have a common rule or principle in common; (b) extracting the rule or principle from the diverse experiences; and (c) utilizing the rule or principle in new situations.

Since humans constantly encounter a wide variety of modeling experiences, it seems safe to conclude that most of the principles and rules that govern human behavior are derived from something like abstract modeling. Bandura (1977) says: "On the basis of observationally derived rules, people learn, among other things, judgmental orientations, linguistic styles, conceptual schemes, information-processing strategies, cognitive operations, and standards of conduct" (p. 42).

It should be noted that inhibition, disinhibition, and facilitation all increase or decrease the probability of making a response that has already been learned. Acquisition, creativity, and rule or principle extraction involve the development of new learning through modeling.

In addition to acquisition, inhibition, disinhibition, facilitation, rule or principle extraction, and creativity, modeling has also been used to influence observers' moral judgments and their emotional responses. In fact, according to Bandura, *anything that can be learned from direct experience can also be learned by indirect or vicarious experience* (1977, p. 12). Furthermore, it can be learned more efficiently through modeling since much of the trial-and-error process involved in learning by direct experience is eliminated. Bandura (1977) wrote, "observational learning is vital for both development and survival. Because mistakes can produce costly, or even fatal consequences, the prospects for survival would be slim indeed if one could learn only by suffering the consequences of trial and error. . . . The more costly and hazardous the possible mistakes, the heavier is the reliance on observational learning from competent examples" (p. 12).

Modeling in the Clinical Setting

According to Bandura, psychopathology results from dysfunctional learning which results in incorrect anticipations about the world. The job of the psychotherapist is to provide experiences that will disconfirm erroneous expectations and replace them with more accurate and less disabling ones. Bandura has little patience with those psychotherapists who look for "insights" or "unconscious motivations" in their clients. In fact, Bandura feels that the clients of these therapists are used to confirm the therapists' own belief systems.

> Advocates of different theoretical orientations repeatedly discover their chosen motivators at work but rarely find evidence for the motivators emphasized by the proponents of competing views. In fact, if one wanted to predict the types of insights and unconscious motivators that persons are apt to discover in themselves in the course of such analyses, it would be more helpful to know the therapists' conceptual belief system than the clients' actual psychological status. (Bandura, 1977, p. 5)

Bandura and his colleagues have run a number of studies to test the effectiveness of modeling in treating several psychological disorders. For example, Bandura, Grusec, and Menlove (1967) showed children who had a strong fear of dogs a peer interacting fearlessly with a dog. The fear-provoking character of the model's behavior was gradually increased from session to session by relaxing the physical constraints on the dog and by varying the directness of the model's interactions with the dog. A control group also consisting of phobic children did not have the modeling experience. The approach behavior of all the children was measured for both the dog actually involved in the experiment and for an unfamiliar dog. Measures were taken immediately after treatment and one month later. Approach scores were determined by a graded sequence of interactions with the dogs, that is, children were asked to approach and pet the dogs, release them from their pen, take their leashes off and finally, to spend time with the dogs in their pen. It was found that the children who had seen a peer model interact fearlessly with a dog were capable of significantly more approach responses than children in the control group. In fact, two-thirds of the children in the treatment group were able to remain alone with the dog in its pen, while none of the children in the control group could do so. It was also found that the effects of treatment generalized to the unfamiliar dog and the effects were still present one month after the experiment.

It can be seen from the study described above that not only can new responses be learned by observing the consequences of the behavior of models, but responses can also be extinguished in the same way. Thus, not only is vicarious reinforcement important in Bandura's theory, but **vicarious extinction** is equally important. In this study, vicarious extinction was used to reduce or eliminate the avoidance response to dogs and thereby disinhibit the approach response to dogs.

In another study, Bandura and Menlove (1968) had three groups of children with dog phobias watch a series of films under three different conditions: **single-modeling,** where children saw a model interact with increased intimacy with a single dog; **multiple-modeling,** where children saw a variety of models interacting fearlessly with a number of dogs; and a *control condition* where children saw movies involving no dogs. Again, as in the 1967 study, the willingness of the children to approach the dog was measured. It was found that both single- and multiple-modeling significantly reduced the children's fear of dogs, as compared to children in the control group, but only the children in the multiple-modeling group had their fear reduced to the point where they were able to be left alone with the dog in its pen. Again it was found that the effects of treatment generalized to other dogs and endured one month after the experiment. Comparing the results of this study with those of the 1967 study described above, Bandura concluded that, although both **direct modeling** (seeing a live model) and **symbolic modeling** (seeing a model in a film) are both effective in reducing fears, direct modeling appeared to be more effective. However, the apparent reduced effectiveness of symbolic modeling was overcome by showing a variety of models instead of just one.

In the final study to be considered, Bandura, Blanchard, and Ritter (1969) compared the effectiveness of symbolic modeling, modeling with participation, and desensitization as techniques in treating a phobia. In this study, adults and adolescents with a snake phobia were subjects and they were divided into four groups. Group 1 (*symbolic modeling*) was exposed to a film showing children, adolescents, and adults interacting with a large snake. The scenes were graduated showing increased interaction with the snake. Subjects in this group were trained in relaxation techniques and could stop the film whenever they became too anxious. When relaxed enough they started the film again. Each subject continued in this manner until he or she could watch the film without experiencing anxiety. Group 2 (**modeling-participation**) watched a model handle a snake and then were helped by the model to actually come in contact with the snake. The model would first touch the snake and help the observer to do so also, then the model would stroke the snake and encourage the observer to do likewise. This process continued until the observer could hold the snake in his or her lap without assistance. Group 3 received **desensitization therapy** which consisted of asking subjects to imagine anxiety-provoking scenes with snakes, starting with imaginary scenes which caused little anxiety and slowly progressing to imaginary scenes that caused great anxiety. Subjects were asked to continue imagining each scene until it no longer made them anxious. Group 4 received no treatment of any kind. The results of the study indicated that all three treatment conditions were effective in reducing fear of snakes, but that the modeling-participation method was by far the most effective. This can be seen in Figure 13-3.

In fact, Bandura, Blanchard, and Ritter isolated all of the subjects who were unable to achieve the ability to hold the snake in their lap (including the control subjects) and used the modeling-participation method on them. In just a few sessions each subject was able to hold the snake in his or her lap. Follow-up research indicated that not only did the effects of treatment endure, they also generalized to other areas in which fear had existed prior to the experiment. Bandura and his

Figure 13–3. The tendency to approach a snake before and after various kinds of therapeutic treatments. (From "Relative Efficacy of Modeling Therapeutic Changes," by A. Bandura, E. B. Blanchard, & B. J. Ritter, 1969, *Journal of Personality and Social Psychology, 13,* p. 183. Copyright 1969 by the American Psychological Association. Reprinted by permission of the publisher and author.)

associates used a questionnaire to measure the magnitude of various fears before and after the experiment. The change in the magnitude of these fears as a function of the various treatment conditions is shown in Figure 13–4.

THE INFLUENCE OF THE NEWS AND ENTERTAINMENT MEDIA

As we have seen, Bandura believes that we can learn as much from vicarious experiences as from observing the consequences of our own behavior. We have also seen that Bandura defines a model as anything that conveys information. It follows, then, that newspapers, television, and motion pictures act as models from which we can learn a great deal. Of course, not everything learned from the news and entertainment media is negative, but sometimes it can be. We have already seen that television can cause the development of faulty cognitive processes which, in turn, can lead to criminal behavior. Bandura (1986) gives another example of how television programming can stimulate antisocial behavior:

> Sometimes it is the fictional media that furnishes the salient example for the spread of an aggressive style of conduct. The television program *Doomsday Flight* provides an excellent illustration because of its novel modeled strategy.

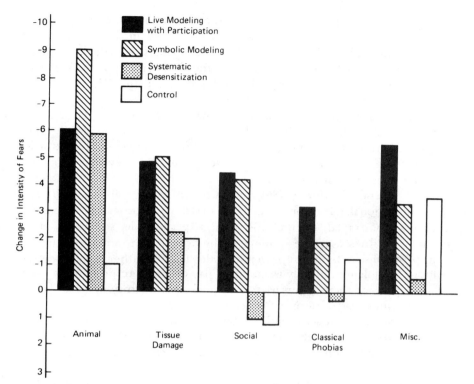

Figure 13–4.   The generalized effects of various kinds of therapeutic
treatments on the intensity of fears other than the one
specifically treated. The higher the minus score, the greater
the difference in the intensity of fear before and after
treatment. (From "Relative Efficacy of Modeling Therapeutic
Changes," by A. Bandura, E. B. Blanchard, & B. J. Ritter,
1969, *Journal of Personality and Social Psychology, 13,* p.
186. Copyright 1969 by the American Psychological
Association. Reprinted by permission of the publisher and
author.)

In this plot, an extortionist threatens airline officials that an altitude-sensitive
bomb will be exploded on a transcontinental airliner in flight as it descends
below 5,000 feet for its landing. In the end, the pilot outwits the extortionist
by selecting an airport located at an elevation above the critical altitude. Extortion attempts using the same barometric-bomb plot rose sharply for two
months following the telecast . . . Moreover, a day or two after the program
was rerun in different cities in the United States and abroad, airlines were
subjected to further extortion demands of money to get the extortionists to
reveal the placement of altitude-sensitive bombs allegedly planted in airliners
in flight. Planes were rerouted to airports at high elevations, and some extortion demands were paid by airline officials, only to learn that the airliner con-

tained no bomb. A rebroadcast of the program in Anchorage made an Alaskan viewer $25,000 richer, and a rerun in Sydney made an Australian instantly wealthy, after collecting $560,000 from Qantas. He added considerable force to his threat by directing Qantas officials to an airport locker where he had placed a sample barometric bomb he had built. (p. 173)

Bandura dismisses the suggestion that all of the above episodes were mere coincidence and, therefore, had nothing to do with the television program *Doomsday Flight*. According to Bandura, the novelty of the strategy used for extortion and the fact that the episodes followed so closely after the television program seem to preclude chance as an explanation.

In general, Bandura (1986) reaches the following conclusion concerning violence in fictional television: "Analyses of televised programs reveal that violent conduct is portrayed, for the most part, as permissible, successful, and relatively clean . . . Witnesses to the violence in the dramatic presentations are more likely to approve of such behavior or to join in the assaults rather than to seek alternative solutions. Violence not only is shown to pay off but is readily used by superheroes, who dispose of their adversaries in a quick, perfunctory way as though slaying human beings was of no great concern" (p. 292).

As we have just seen, violence portrayed on fictional television can encourage violence in some viewers, but what about nonfictional television? According to Bandura (1986) nonfictional television, too, can encourage violence:

> There are several ways in which newscasts of violence can serve as an instrument of influence . . . If televised reports convey detailed information about acts and strategies of aggression, they can contribute to the spread of the very methods they report through the instruction they provide. In addition, media reports of violent episodes can influence restraints over aggression by how the consequences are portrayed. Because each point in audience ratings means millions of dollars in advertising revenue, the visual displays accompanying news reports are selected to attract and hold viewers, as well as to inform. The outcomes of aggression, especially collective actions, are easily misrepresented when dramatic pictorials are favored over less interesting but important consequences. Thus, showing people running off with appliances and liquor from looted stores during an urban riot is more likely to promote aggression in viewers living under similar circumstances than showing the terror and suffering caused by the massive destruction of one's neighborhood. (p. 292)

Pornographic Movies. Clearly not everyone exposed to violence on television or in the newspapers becomes violent. Similarly, not everyone exposed to sexually explicit literature or movies becomes a sexual deviant. In fact, erotic material has been used to successfully treat individuals with sexual problems. Bandura (1986) says: "Sexual modeling has been shown to have long-term effects when used for therapeutic purposes with persons suffering from sexual anxieties and dysfunctions . . . modeling of mutual pleasure alleviates sex anxieties, creates more favorable attitudes toward sex, and sparks inactive sex lives" (p. 294).

In the case of pornography, however, sexual aggression toward women is often modeled, and such modeling can stimulate similar behavior in some viewers. Bandura (1986) explains:

> Content analyses reveal an increase in abusive behavior toward women in pornographic depictions . . . Research has added to our understanding of how violent erotica affects viewers. Males exposed to modeled sexual assault behave more punitively toward women than if exposed to modeled sexual intimacy devoid of aggression . . . Violent erotica often depicts women initially resisting but eventually relishing being raped. Such portrayals reinforce rape myths and weaken restraints over harshness toward women by indicating they enjoy being manhandled. Depictions of rape as pleasurable to women heighten punitiveness toward women regardless of whether males are angry or not. (pp. 294–295)

Although "humane living requires reducing social influences that promote cruelty and destructiveness" and "Society has the right to regulate obscene materials that can cause harm" (Bandura, 1986, p. 296), the recognition and control of such influences and materials are complex matters. First, there is widespread disagreement over what is harmful and what is not. Second, there is concern that suppression of one form of expression (e.g., sexual expression) may threaten other forms of expression. Obviously, this is not a matter that will be resolved soon.

SOCIAL LEARNING THEORY

It is clear that Bandura's theory is a cognitive theory and that it emphasizes the role of vicarious experience (observation) in learning. These facts could also be used to describe Tolman's theory, but Tolman's theory was not referred to as a **social learning theory.** Why is it that Bandura's theory is so often described in that way? The major reason is that Bandura emphasizes the impact of people on people. Whether we learn from direct experience or from vicarious experience, most of our learning usually involves other people in a social setting. It is on the basis of our observations and interactions with other people that our cognitions, including our standards for performance and for moral judgment, are developed. In addition, Bandura's research typically reflects real-life situations and problems. His subjects are humans interacting with other humans, not humans learning lists of nonsense syllables or rats running mazes or pressing a lever in a Skinner box. According to Bandura, it is the human capacity to symbolize that "enables them to represent events, to analyze their conscious experience, to communicate with others at any distance in time and space, to plan, to create, to imagine, and to engage in foresightful action" [1977, p. vii]. These activities are all social in nature and thus we refer to Bandura's theory as a social learning theory.

Currently, Bandura's theory is very popular and it promises to be for a long time. In a way it assimilates many of the traditional theories of learning and in so doing provides a framework for research which is in accordance with many of the concerns within psychology today, such as language and memory. The following quotation from Bower and Hilgard (1981) summarizes Bandura's theory very well:

> In broad outline, social learning theory provides the best integrative summary of what modern learning theory has to contribute to the solution of practical problems. It also provides a compatible framework within which to place information-processing theories of language comprehension, memory, imagery, and problem-solving. These theories, for their part, fill in the details of the "representational systems" and "symbolic processes" that are referred to in applications of social learning theory. For these reasons, social learning theory may provide a basis of consensus for much of the learning research in the next decade.

SUMMARY

The long avoidance of research on observational learning was ended by Bandura's research which first appeared in the literature of the early 1960s. Bandura disagreed with Miller and Dollard's earlier account of observational learning that described it as a special case of instrumental conditioning. Bandura's explanation of learning is close to Tolman's in that learning is assumed to be continuous and not dependent on reinforcement. For Bandura, as for Tolman, reinforcement is a performance variable, not a learning variable. Either direct or vicarious reinforcement provides information as to what behaviors lead to reinforcement in various situations; when a need arises, this information is translated into behavior. Thus, reinforcement provides information that allows observers to anticipate reinforcement if they behave in certain ways. Reinforcement, according to Bandura, does not act to directly strengthen the responses which produce it. In fact, much, if not most, human learning occurs in the absence of direct reinforcement. Rather, human learning typically occurs by observing the consequences of the behavior of models. Such vicarious learning is made possible by the human capacity to symbolize and store information and then to act upon that information at a later time.

Four major processes are thought to influence the course of observational learning: attentional processes, which determine which aspects of a modeling situation are attended to; retentional processes, which involve the imaginal and verbal coding of information so that it may be stored and utilized in the future; behavioral production processes, which involve the ability to make the responses necessary to translate that which had been learned from observation into behavior; and motivational processes, which, since learning occurs continuously, determine which aspects of previously learned responses are translated into action. Reinforcement is the major motivational process since it not only causes an observer to focus on the functional aspects of a model's behavior, but it also provides an incentive for acting upon the information gained by such observation. The information gained by observing reinforcement contingencies can come from either one's direct experience with reinforcement or by vicariously observing the consequences of a model's behavior.

One of Bandura's major concepts is reciprocal determinism which states that there is a constant interaction among the environment, behavior, and the person. According to Bandura, it makes as much sense to say that behavior influences the environment as it makes to say that the environment influences behavior. In addition, the person influences both behavior and the environment.

Unlike traditional learning theorists, Bandura believes that much human behavior is self-regulated. Through direct and observational learning, performance standards develop that act as guides in evaluating one's own behavior. If one's behavior meets or exceeds one's performance standards, it is evaluated positively; if it falls short of one's standards, it is evaluated negatively. Likewise, one's perceived self-efficacy develops from one's direct and vicarious experiences with success and failure. Perceived self-efficacy influences self-regulated behavior in several ways, such as, it determines what is attempted, how long one persists at a task, and what is hoped for. Intrinsic reinforcement (self-reinforcement) has been found to influence one's behavior more than extrinsic, or externally administered, reinforcement. One's moral behavior is governed by internalized moral codes. If one acts contrary to one's moral code, one experiences self-contempt, which acts as a severe punishment. However, Bandura describes a number of mechanisms that allow people to disengage themselves from their moral principles and thereby escape self-contempt for immoral behavior. These disengagement mechanisms include: moral justification, euphemistic labeling, advantageous comparison, displacement of responsibility, diffusion of responsibility, disregard or distortion of consequences, dehumanization, and attribution of blame.

Faulty cognitive processes can develop from inaccurate perceptions, overgeneralization or from incomplete or erroneous information. Most phobias probably result from the overgeneralization from one or more direct or vicarious painful experiences. One way to correct faulty cognitive processes, including phobias, is to provide powerful disconfirming experiences which eventually reduce or eliminate one's inhibitions or fears. In addition to reducing or eliminating inhibitions, modeling can also be used to teach new skills, inhibit responses, facilitate responses, teach creativity, and teach general rules and principles.

Symbolic, live, and participant modeling in the clinical setting have been found effective in treating phobias. However, of all the methods tried, participant-modeling has been found to be the most effective. The process of reducing one's fears by observing another person interacting fearlessly with a feared object is called vicarious extinction. Bandura provides evidence that news and entertainment media act as powerful models and can sometimes encourage aggressive, violent, and criminal behavior.

Bandura's theory is called a social learning theory because it emphasizes the fact that most of the information we gain comes from our interactions with other people. Because of its emphasis on such cognitive processes as language and memory, its effectiveness as a guide in psychotherapeutic practices, its implications for child-rearing and educational practices, and its ability to stimulate new lines of research, Bandura's theory is very popular today and promises to become even more popular in the future.

DISCUSSION QUESTIONS

1. What conclusions did Thorndike and Watson reach about observational learning and why did they reach them?

2. Describe Miller and Dollard's research on observational learning and their explanation for what they found.

3. Defend the statement "Bandura's theory of learning is not a reinforcement theory."

4. Describe the role of reinforcement in Bandura's theory. Include in your answer the ways that Bandura's view of reinforcement differs from the views of traditional reinforcement theorists.

5. Define the terms vicarious reinforcement and vicarious punishment and explain their importance to Bandura's theory.

6. Compare Bandura's theory to Tolman's theory.

7. Briefly describe attentional, retentional, behavioral production, and motivational processes and describe their influence on observational learning.

8. Define and give examples of Bandura's concept of reciprocal determinism.

9. How, according to Bandura, is behavior self-regulated?

10. List several mechanisms that allow a person to act immorally without experiencing self-contempt.

11. Describe several ways that faulty cognitive processes can develop. Give examples of the kinds of behavior that faulty cognitive processes can generate.

12. Describe how modeling can be used to produce each of the following: acquisition, inhibition, disinhibition, facilitation, creativity, and rule-governed behavior. Begin your answer by defining each of the terms.

13. Define each of the following terms: symbolic modeling, live modeling, multiple-modeling, participant modeling, desensitization therapy, and vicarious extinction.

14. Describe, in general, how modeling is used to reduce or eliminate a phobia. Which procedure did Bandura find most effective in treating phobias?

15. Why is Bandura's theory called a social learning theory?

16. Explain why someone who accepts Bandura's theory would be very concerned about the content of children's TV programs.

17. Give a few examples of how Bandura's theory might be used in education and in child rearing.

18. Summarize Bandura's opposition to stage, type, and trait theories.

19. Based on Bandura's theory, do you feel a person would be more likely to respond to the cries of help from an acquaintance or from a stranger? Explain.

20. Attempt to account for those occasions where a person does not learn from observation. For example, if you watched a brain surgeon performing an operation, would you be capable of performing such an operation? Why or why not?

21. Answer the following question from Bandura's point of view. "Why do children imitate some behaviors that they observe and not others?"

22. According to Bandura, what is probably learned by a child who is spanked by a parent for misbehaving?

23. In attempting to explain why people learn vicariously, it has been suggested that answering the question, "What makes a horror movie horrifying to the observer?" would shed some light on the matter. Attempt to answer the question about horror movies and then generalize your answer to the area of observational learning.

CHAPTER HIGHLIGHTS

Abstract modeling. The situation where observers are presented with a variety of modeling experiences from which they extract a common rule or principle. Once extracted, the rule or principle can be applied to new situations.

Acquisition. The gaining of new information from one's observations.

Actual environment. That proportion of a potential environment which is actualized by an organism's behavior.

Advantageous comparison. An attempt to escape from self-contempt by comparing one's immoral actions to another person's even more immoral actions.

Attentional processes. Those variables that determine what is attended to during observational learning.

Attribution of blame. An attempt to escape self-contempt by saying the victim of your immoral actions caused you to act as you did.

Behavioral production processes. Those variables that determine which aspects of what has been learned and retained cognitively can be produced behaviorally.

Cognitive theory. Any theory, such as Bandura's, that assigns a prominent role to mental events.

Copying behavior. A kind of imitative behavior studied by Miller and Dollard where a sophisticated individual guides the behavior of a naive individual until an appropriate response is made.

Creativity. The innovation that results from either synthesizing the influences of several models or from observing a single model demonstrate unconventional problem-solving strategies.

Dehumanization. An attempt to escape self-contempt by making the victim of one's immoral actions appear to be less human.

Delayed modeling. The case where an observer does not display what has been learned from a modeling experience until sometime after the modeling experience has been terminated.

Desensitization therapy. The procedure whereby clients are asked to imagine an anxiety-provoking thought until they are able to ponder the thought without experiencing anxiety.

Diffusion of responsibility. An attempt to escape self-contempt by saying that the decision to engage in an immoral act has been made by a group.

Direct experience. The events that one experiences as a result of his or her own personal interactions with the environment.

Direct modeling. The observation of a live model.

Disinhibition. The removal or reduction of an inhibition to perform a certain response that results from either performing the response without experiencing negative consequences or from seeing a model perform the response without the model experiencing negative consequences.

Displacement of responsibility. An attempt to escape self-contempt by claiming that a person in a position of authority caused you to act immorally.

Disregard or distortion of consequences. An attempt to escape self-contempt by minimizing the harm caused by one's immoral actions.

Euphemistic labeling. An attempt to escape from self-contempt by calling an immoral act something other than what it really is.

Facilitation. The increased probability of making an already learned response which results from observing another person making the response.

Faulty cognitive processes. Those cognitive processes that prevent or inhibit effective and efficient interactions with the social and/or physical environment.

Freedom. According to Bandura, the number of options available to a person and her or his opportunity to exercise them.

Generalized imitation. The learned tendency to imitate the behavior of others in order to be reinforced.

Imaginal symbols. Mental images that represent what has been observed.

Imitative behavior. The learned tendency to mimic the behavior of a model whose behavior has been seen being reinforced. According to Bandura, imitative behavior is only one of many possible results of observational learning.

Inhibition. The reduced probability of performing a previously learned response which results from either direct or vicarious punishment of that response.

Learning. According to Bandura, learning is the acquisition of information that results from observation.

Matched-dependent behavior. A kind of imitative behavior studied by Miller and Dollard where the behavior of one person acts as a cue for another person to behave in a similar way. In operant terms, the first person's behavior acts as a discriminative stimulus for the second person which triggers a response which leads to reinforcement. According to the operant analysis, matched-dependent behavior is a kind of discriminative operant.

Model. Anything that conveys information to an observer. In Bandura's theory, a model can be such things as a person, a film, a picture, instructions, a description, an animal, television, or a newspaper.

Modeling–participation. The situation in which a live model guides the behavior of an observer until an appropriate response is made. This is much like the copying behavior studied by Miller and Dollard.

Moral codes. The internalized criteria that come either from direct or vicarious experience which are used to monitor and evaluate one's own ethical behavior. If one's behavior violates an internalized moral code he or she experiences self-contempt.

Moral justification. An attempt to escape from self-contempt by attributing one's immoral behavior to a higher cause.

Motivational processes. Those variables that provide incentives for translating what has been learned and stored cognitively into behavior.

Multiple–modeling. The observation of two or more models.

Observational learning. The process whereby information is acquired by attending to events in the environment.

Performance. The translation of what has been learned into behavior.

Performance standards. The internalized criteria that come from either direct or vicarious experiences which are used to monitor, evaluate, and reinforce or punish one's own behavior.

Potential environment. The environmental events available to an organism if it acts in ways that actualize them.

Reciprocal determinism. Bandura's contention that the environment, the person, and the person's behavior all interact to produce behavior.

Reinforcement. According to Bandura, reinforcement gives the observer information concerning what leads to what in the environment, so that she or he can anticipate certain outcomes if certain behaviors are engaged in. Because reinforcement creates expectations, it is said (by Bandura) to work forward in time, rather than backward to strengthen the response that produced it, as the traditional reinforcement theorists had assumed.

Reinforcement theory. Any theory that claims learning cannot occur without reinforcement. Bandura's is not a reinforcement theory.

Retentional processes. The variables involved in encoding certain observations for memory. Bandura believes that observations are stored in memory via imaginal and verbal symbols.

Same behavior. A kind of imitative behavior studied by Miller and Dollard where two or more individuals respond in the same way to the same stimulus.

Self-contempt. The self-imposed punishment that is administered when an individual's internalized moral code is violated.

Self-efficacy. One's ability to perform various tasks. One's perceived self-efficacy may or may not correspond to one's actual self-efficacy. Perceived self-efficacy plays a major role in self-regulated behavior.

Self-regulated behavior. Behavior that is regulated by one's own performance standards, moral codes, or imagination.

Single-modeling. The observation of a single model.

Social learning theory. A term often used to describe Bandura's theory since it emphasizes interactions among humans as the major source of information about ourselves and/or the physical world.

Symbolic modeling. The observation of something other than a live model, such as a film or television.

Symbolization. The process that allows humans to store and rehearse information and to act upon it at a future time.

Verbal symbols. The conversion into words of what has been observed. This is to facilitate the storage, rehearsal, and retrieval of information.

Vicarious experience. The impact on one's own learning or behavior that comes from observing the consequences of another person's behavior.

Vicarious extinction. The extinction of a response that comes from observing the fact that a model's performance of that response is not reinforced.

Vicarious punishment. The process by which observing another person's behavior being punished decreases the probability of the observer acting in a similar way.

Vicarious reinforcement. The process by which observing another person's behavior being reinforced increases the probability of the observer acting in a similar way.

14

Donald A. Norman

In this chapter we will review the information-processing approach to psychology. In general, the information-processing approach views humans as receiving information from the environment, processing that information in one or more ways, and then acting upon that information. Before discussing Donald Norman's contributions to the information-processing approach, we will first discuss some antecedents to that approach.

ANTECEDENTS TO THE INFORMATION-PROCESSING APPROACH TO PSYCHOLOGY

S-R Psychology

Associationistic theorists such as I. Pavlov, J. B. Watson, and E. Guthrie viewed living organisms as automatons whose responses to environmental stimuli were governed by the organism's sensory system, response system, and central nervous system consisting of innate circuitry and memories of prior experiences. In other words, Pavlov, Watson, and Guthrie explained the behavior of organisms in terms of environmental stimuli, innate and acquired neural circuitry, and response capabilities.

With slight changes in terminology we see a great deal of similarity between the approach taken by the associationistic theorists and that taken by psychologists stressing information processing. All that needs to be done is replace the term "stimuli" with **input,** replace the term "response" with **output,** and replace the "neural mechanisms" that mediate the relationship between the S and the R with *information-processing mechanisms*. Some information-processing psychologists view their approach as very much in this associationistic tradition.

Cognitive Psychology

Most information-processing psychologists equate input with information. That is, what comes into the system from the environment is information. Through experience, we learn what events have in common, how some events are related to other events, what events are to be approached, what events are to be avoided, what activities work in solving problems and, in general, what to expect in a given situation. According to the information-processing psychologist, the output (behavior) in a given situation is determined by the input provided by the situation and by the evaluation of the situation based, in part, upon the memories of what had resulted in similar situations.

Again with slight changes in terminology we can see a great deal of similarity between the information-processing approach and cognitive theories such as those of Tolman, Piaget, and Bandura. For Tolman it was precisely information that was learned and stored by the organism. It was expectancies, or the anticipation of what leads to what, that were learned and utilized by the organism. These learned expectancies were ultimately reflected in the organism's cognitive map. In Tolman's approach to learning theory, independent variables can be equated with what the information-processing psychologist calls input, his intervening variables can be equated with information-processing mechanisms, and his dependent variables can be equated with output. Bandura's theory also stresses the learning of information which takes the form of expectancies. We concluded chapter 13 by noting the similarity between Bandura's theory and the information-processing approach.

Even though there may be conceptual similarities between the kinds of cognitive psychology just described and information-processing psychology, Norman insists that there is an important difference between the two:

> The important point about information-processing psychology is that it attempts to understand and specify the internal mechanism . . . It is not simply a matter of "expectancies." It is not simply a matter of "processing." The whole point is that one tries to be very specific about the exact stages of processing that take place and to spell out the properties of the internal mechanisms. This is the major difference between information-processing approaches to psychology and other approaches . . . Hence, the detailed analysis and specification of the operation of such things as short-term memory (personal communication, September 19, 1986).

Of all the approaches to cognitive psychology, Piaget's approach seems to have influenced **information-processing psychology** the most. Piaget's concept of schema has been widely adapted by information-processing psychologists and is viewed as an information-processing mechanism. Norman, for example, whose work we will feature in this chapter, relies very heavily on Piaget in his discussion of learning in his influential book *Human Information Processing: An Introduction To Psychology* (coauthored with Lindsay) in 1977. Both Piaget and those following the information-processing approach assume that information from the environment is acted upon (organized, simplified, transformed, selected for further analysis, or ignored) by cognitive structures before it is translated into behavior. In other words, both stress the importance of cognitive structures (schemata) in the processing of information.

Cybernetics

In 1948, Norbert Wiener (1894–1964) defined **cybernetics** as the study of the structure and function of information-processing systems. Wiener was concerned with how various mechanical and biological systems record, process, and transmit information. Of particular interest to Wiener were the automatic control systems called *servomechanisms*. A servomechanism is a system that compares input with some standard or desired state, and if there is a discrepancy between the two, activates mechanisms which attempt to alleviate the discrepancy. The results of corrective action are fed back into the system and another comparison is made. If there is still a mismatch between the input and the desired state, further corrective action is triggered. The process continues until there is an acceptable match between input and the desirable state. The automatic pilot of an airplane and a thermostat are examples of servomechanisms. Another example is shown in Figure 14-1.

In the language of cybernetics, humans can be described as servomechanisms that compare information coming from the environment with what is optimal under the circumstances. If there is a discrepancy humans act upon their environments in such ways as to make input match what is considered optimal (or at least acceptable). The results of various activities provide **feedback** as to the effectiveness of those activities in reducing or eliminating the discrepancy between input and what is considered optimal.

A great deal of what is now called information-processing psychology came directly from Norbert Wiener's notion of cybernetics.

Figure 14–1.   A person adjusting the sound level of a radio exemplifies a
servomechanism.

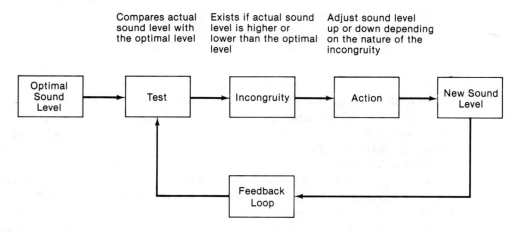

Robotology

Robotology consists of designing a machine that is capable of performing some human function. In 1952, W. R. Ashby created the *Homeostat* which was a machine capable of regulating its own internal environment. In 1953, W. G. Walter designed a machine that mimicked the behavior of an organism in search of food or shelter. In 1954, J. A. Deutsch developed a machine that imitated the maze learning in rats, and in 1962, H. S. Hoffman devised a machine that displayed a number of classical conditioning phenomena. Why is it important to build such machines and what do they say about human behavior? According to Bower and Hilgard (1981), building such devices allows us to test theories of human behavior.

> The prevailing consensus is that a machine which accurately simulates relevant aspects of some organism's behavior indeed constitutes a genuine explanation of that behavior. The idea is that the abstract principles involved in designing the machine—its functional components and their organization—could in fact be the same as those describing the design and functioning of the living organism . . . it is claimed that we have a fairly complete understanding of a piece of behavior when we know how to build a machine that would behave in just that way. (p. 354)

The similarities between robots and living organisms are that both have: (a) mechanisms for receiving information from their external environments; (b) mechanisms for receiving information from their internal environments; (c) mechanisms for learning, processing, and storing information; (d) mechanisms for converting processed information into some form of output or behavior; and (e) mechanisms by which the results of the output or behavior are fed back into the systems. We shall see below that computers possess all of these characteristics, and therefore they, too, can be considered robots that mimic certain aspects of human intellectual functioning.

Information Theory

In 1949, Claude E. Shannon, working for the Bell Telephone Laboratories, and Warren Weaver, working for the Rockefeller Foundation, were seeking ways of improving the purity of a message between the time it is sent to the time that it is received. Their work is taken as the founding of **information theory** (Shannon & Weaver, 1949). The steps involved in sending and receiving a message is referred to as a *communication system* which involves the following:

1. The information source which selects the message to be sent out of many possible messages.
2. The transmitter which encodes the message into a signal which is sent out over the communication channel from the transmitter to the receiver.
3. The receiver which reconstructs (decodes) the signal into the original message.

In order to determine whether or not various procedures enhance communication, Shannon and Weaver needed a precise way of measuring information. The unit of measure that they utilized was the *binary digit* or *bit*. A bit is defined as the amount of information that distinguishes between two likely alternatives. In order to determine whether the number that I jotted down was a 1 or a 2, you would need 1 bit of information. You could ask either if the number was 1 or 2 and regardless of the answer you would learn which number I wrote down. That is, if you asked if the number was 1 and I said yes, you know that number. Likewise, if you asked if the number was 2 and I said no, you would know that it was 1. Now suppose that I jotted down a number from 1 through 4. How many bits would you need in order to discover the correct number? The answer is 2. You could ask, for example, whether the number was 3 or higher (first bit) and if so your next question could be "is the number 3?" (second bit). Again, no matter what the answer is you have all of the information you need in order to discover the correct number. Three bits of information would allow you to decide among 8 equally likely alternatives, 4 among 16, and 5 among 32. The general rule is that every time the number of possible alternatives is increased by a factor of two we need an additional bit of information in order to make the correct decision. This general rule can be summarized as follows:

Alternatives	Bits Needed
2	1
4	2
8	3
16	4
32	5
64	6 etc.

Not only did information theory provide an objective way of measuring information, it also demonstrated the many ways that information could be recoded. For example, a telephone transmitter transforms (recodes) the sound of the human voice into electrical signals which are then reconstructed into the human voice by the receiver. Both computers and humans can be viewed as information systems that recode input in a variety of ways and then translate that recoded input into a desired outcome (output). Most information-processing psychologists believe that humans process information on several levels. For example, information is processed on the sensory level, then on the perceptual level, and then in terms of the memories of prior experience. At each level, information is recoded and, in the process, some information is lost or distorted. Information-processing psychology, like information theory, attempts to discover those processes, structures, and mechanisms that determine what happens to information from the time that it is sent to the time that it is received and acted upon. It is believed that as the operation of these processes, structures, and mechanisms become known, information processing can be enhanced and communication facilitated.

Computers

For most psychologists using the information-processing approach, the computer provides an analogy for how humans process information. Loftus and Loftus (1976) describe this analogy:

> Both computers and humans take in information from the environment. Computers do this using card readers, tape drives, etc., whereas humans do it using their sense organs. Inside a computer, the information from the environment is manipulated, recoded, and combined with other information already there. This is done via activation of electronic registers. Inside a person, information is manipulated, recoded, and combined with other information already there. This is done via activation of neurons. Finally, a computer outputs information to the environment via output devices, such as teletypes and line printers. Likewise, humans output information to the environment via such output devices as mouths and hands.

Loftus and Loftus (1976) extend the analogy by noting that both computers and humans have **hardware.** For the computer, hardware consists of such things as a metal frame, transistors, resistors, and electronic circuitry. For the human, hardware consists of such things as muscles, bones, skin, and neural circuitry. Also, both computers and humans possess **software.** For a computer, software consists of programs that allow it to perform various operations. A computer program is a set of instructions which tells the computer what operations to perform on the information presented to it. For humans, software consists of operations typically learned from experience, for example, how to add and subtract, how to speak and write, how to drive a car, how to recognize and classify objects, how to read, etc. It is these learned programs that allow humans to perform the actions that are appropriate in various situations. When a human performs apparently complex operations while processing information, we refer to such operations as intelligence. When a computer engages in such operations, it is said to exemplify **artificial intelligence.** For example, a computer programmed to play chess demonstrates artificial intelligence.

Extending the analogy between humans and computers still further, Loftus and Loftus (1976) say that the behavior of both may only appear to be too complicated to understand.

> To extend and use the analogy as a basis for theorizing about human behavior, we note that computers (as do humans) exhibit, on the face of things, very complicated behavior. However, we know that the complicated behavior exhibited by computers is interpretable in terms of relatively simple, understandable computer programs. Now we speculate that the complicated behavior of humans may also be generated by relatively simple, understandable programs. The task of the information-processing oriented psychologist then becomes one of deducing (from experimental data) what these programs may look like. (p. 7)

The similarity between computers and humans as processors of information is depicted in Figure 14-2.

It is widely believed that computers provide an excellent way of testing our theories concerning various human processes. Bower and Hilgard (1981) say, "Any theory that is sufficiently well specified can be realized as a computer program" (p. 355). A computer then, can be used to test the accuracy of theories of learning, intelligence, memory, concept formation, and problem solving. Once programmed, we can put the theories into action via the computer. Hill (1985) says:

> What do computer programs tell us about the actual processes of learning and thinking in living organisms? Nothing directly . . . the fact that a computer can be programmed to learn or think by certain processes does not demonstrate that either humans or rats learn or think by the same processes. What these programs can show are the implications of certain assumptions about how organisms learn. A theorist can write a computer program to follow the laws of learning that he thinks organisms follow, then run the program to see what happens. If what happens is similar to the outcome of human or animal learning, this finding makes it more plausible that humans or animals do in fact follow those hypothetical processes when they learn. If what happens is quite different from the outcome of "real" learning, the theorist's assumptions are probably false. Thus the computers provide a more precise way of doing what Hull wanted to do; if he had made use of computers he might have avoided some of the contradictions in his system. The role of the computer program is much like that of mathematical analysis—not to change the logic of theory

Figure 14–2. Similarity of computers and humans as processors of information (from Loftus & Loftus, 1976, p. 6).

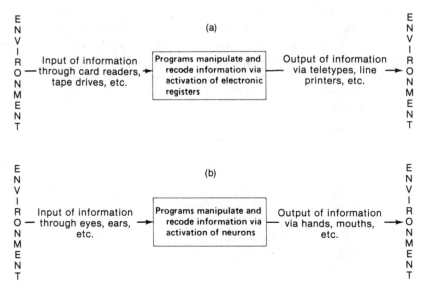

construction, but to carry out that logic more precisely and more thoroughly. (p. 128)

Although the computer is used by a number of information-processing psychologists as a model for how humans process information, there are some who warn that the analogy can be carried too far. In fact, Donald Norman, whose work will be featured next, insists that humans often process and act upon information in ways that are quite different from the ways that computers process and act upon information. Norman (1981) gives the following example:

> An important aspect of everyday behavior is that we do several different activities at the same time, oftentimes for simultaneous (and possibly conflicting) purposes. Even when we do not attempt simultaneous actions, we still might be planning or reviewing one set of things while performing or accomplishing another. We delay and defer goals or actions as needed, waiting for appropriate times for them to be accomplished. This occurs for several reasons. Some biological goals do not need to be satisfied at any particular instant, but within reason, can be executed at convenience (e.g., such things as eating, sleeping, or toilet activities). Some daily tasks have similar characteristics (e.g., going to the bank or post office, purchasing some needed item). Some tasks have to be deferred because there is not sufficient time or information to complete them during one session of work (e.g., writing a scientific paper, reading a book, learning a complex task). Finally, even for tasks that are continually active from start to completion, they may span such a long duration that other things are also done along the way, and the individual components of the major task may have to wait for minutes or even hours before being executed. (p. 1)

Because of observations such as those described in the preceding quotation, Norman (1981) says, "I argue that analyses of human performance imply a class of processing structures quite different than is commonly envisioned within Artificial Intelligence. . . . the human is a special kind of biological processor, and I suspect that surprisingly little of what we know of . . . computers applies to the human" (p. 1).

We next turn to Donald Norman's specific contributions to information-processing psychology.

DONALD A. NORMAN

We chose Donald Norman as our representative of information-processing psychology because of his special interest in learning and because his concerns have been much more comprehensive than most others working in the area.

Donald A. Norman (1935–) is professor of psychology at the University of California, San Diego, where he is director of the Institute for Cognitive Science and chair of the Interdisciplinary PhD Program in Cognitive Science. Norman received

Donald A. Norman. (Courtesy of Donald A. Norman)

his BS degree from the Massachusetts Institute of Technology in electrical engineering in 1957. He received his MA from the University of Pennsylvania in electrical engineering in 1959 and his PhD from the same institution in mathematical psychology in 1962. He was lecturer and research fellow at Harvard University from 1963 until he joined the faculty at the University of California, San Diego, where he has been ever since. Norman has written many articles and several influential books including *Human Information Processing: An Introduction to Psychology* (2nd ed.), which he coauthored with Peter H. Lindsay. Norman is as much interested in application as he is in theory. His applied work focuses on what he calls "cognitive engineering," which can be used to develop human-machine interactive systems that will reduce the incidence of human error. Norman's research includes topics ranging from memory, attention, and learning to the role of conscious and subconscious mechanisms in the control of human behavior. Norman's emphasis is always on how all cognitive and bodily systems *interact* and never on isolated systems.

THE DEFINITION AND THE LAWS OF LEARNING

For Norman, learning and remembering are closely related but learning is more than simply remembering. Learning involves the ability to perform a task with skill. In his book *Learning and Memory* (1982), Norman says: "I use the term 'learning' to refer to the act of deliberate study of a specific body of material, so that the material can be retrieved at will and used with skill. Learning involves purposeful remembering and skillful performance" (p. 3).

With this definition, Norman disagrees with those theorists who view learning as an automatic process. For example, Thorndike's law of effect states that learning will occur automatically when a response is followed by a desirable outcome. Lindsay and Norman (1977) say the following about the law of effect:

> For our purposes, the law of effect is not a sufficient explanation of learning. In our opinion, it suffers the problem of attempting to describe the phenomena of learning by simple description of the events and responses of the organism, without any consideration of the internal information processing that must also be taking place. As a result, the law gets into serious difficulties in attempting to explain the real behavior of complex organisms. The problems result from several sources. First, the law of effect is vague about the temporal conditions that are involved. Second, it ignores the necessity for causal relationships between the actions and the outcome. Finally, the law of effect emphasizes the desirability of the outcome, known as its *reinforcing* value. We believe that the important part of an outcome is its *information*. The outcome serves as a signal to the organism about the result of its acts. (p. 501)

By emphasizing the importance of the information gained from experience, Norman aligns himself with the theories of Tolman and Bandura. In further elaborating what is learned, however, Norman closely follows Piaget.

> In the language of one of the foremost investigators of cognitive development, Jean Piaget, the organism learns by constructing sensorimotor schemas [in our chapter on Piaget we chose schemata as the plural of schema]. It extracts the relationship between the information picked up by its sensory system and its actions (motor activities). A *sensorimotor schema* is a plan (a scheme) for performing an organized sequence of actions to perform some specific act, coordinating the information picked up by the sensory system with the necessary motor (muscle) movements. The acts of eating, walking, or riding a bicycle require their own well-developed sensorimotor schemas. In order to construct these schemas the organism must be particularly sensitive to certain kinds of consequences, such as those associated with a desirable and necessary outcome, like food. (Lindsay & Norman, 1977, p. 500)

Norman continues to follow Piaget closely by assuming that when something is learned and/or remembered it is added to what has already been learned and/or remembered: "Our view of learning is the same as our view of memory: when new information is learned, it is added to preexisting meaning structures within the memory system. The problem facing the learner is to determine the conditions that are relevant to the situation, to determine what the appropriate actions are, and to record that information properly" (Lindsay & Norman, 1977, p. 500).

The Laws of Learning

Norman summarizes his thoughts on learning in three laws, all of which emphasize the *causal* relationship between actions and outcomes.

a. The Law of Causal Relationship

For an organism to learn the relationship between a specific action and an outcome, there must be an apparent causal relation between them.

b. The Law of Causal Learning

For desirable outcomes: The organism attempts to repeat those particular actions that have an apparent causal relationship to the desired outcome.

For undesirable outcomes: The organism attempts to avoid those actions that have an apparent causal relation to the undesirable outcome.

c. The Law of Information Feedback

The outcome of an event serves as information about that event. (Lindsay & Norman, 1977, pp. 501–502)

Norman uses the term "apparent" causal relationship because humans typically are not in a position to know if there is a true causal relationship between their actions and various outcomes.

> The apparent causality may not reflect the real causality that operates in the world. Sometimes real and apparent causality will be the same. Sometimes humans will infer causal relations where there are none. Sometimes, they will not notice causal relations that actually do exist. Unless humans are capable of performing scientific experiments that can reveal the actual causal relationships, they must deal with inferred or apparent causal relationships between their actions and the outcomes. (Lindsay & Norman, 1977, p. 502)

It may be remembered that in chapter 5 on Skinner's theory, we noted that superstitious behavior resulted from noncontingent reinforcement. Under such reinforcement, the organism acts "as if" there is a causal relationship between its actions and a reinforcing outcome, but in reality there is no such relationship. That is, the causal relationship is apparent but not real.

In his book *Social Foundations of Thought and Action* (1986), Bandura points out that apparent but not real relationships are often dysfunctional; that is, they produce undesirable or inappropriate behavior. In a section of the aforementioned book entitled "On Misreading Events," Bandura describes three ways that dysfunctional beliefs can develop. One way is through **coincidental association.** Outcomes are typically preceded by numerous events, and therefore it is always possible to select as a predictor of an outcome the wrong events. Bandura gives as an example a woman who had a negative relationship with a man who wore a bow tie. Afterwards, all her experiences with men that wore bow ties were negative, and she reached the conclusion that all men who wore bow ties were undesirable. According to Bandura (1986), this woman's belief became a self-fulfilling prophecy:

Misbeliefs would not last long were it not for the fact that they influence selection and production of experiences. Coincidental association is often converted through misbeliefs into a genuine correlation. To the extent that anticipatory distrust evokes negative counterreactions from bow-tied men, defensive behavior is perpetuated by the unpleasant experiences it creates. In this process, the inappropriate belief and its accompanying defensiveness are maintained by self-produced reality, rather than by conditions that have existed in the past but are no longer in effect. (p. 219)

According to Bandura, a second way that faulty beliefs can develop is through **inappropriate generalization,** such as when an attack by one dog generalizes into the erroneous belief that all dogs are dangerous, or the crash of one airplane generalizes into the belief that all airplanes are dangerous.

A third kind of dysfunctional belief discussed by Bandura is **perceived self-inefficacy.** Bandura (1986) says:

Persons who judge themselves as lacking coping capabilities, whether the self-appraisal is objectively warranted or not, will perceive all kinds of dangers in situations and exaggerate their potential harmfulness . . . When a few mishaps are read as signs of basic coping inefficacy, all kinds of situations become fraught with danger. To understand people's judgments of external threats it is, therefore, necessary to analyze their judgments of their own coping capabilities which, in large part, determine the subjective perilousness of environmental events. (p. 220)

Learned Helplessness. As we saw in chapter 7, if a person believes that there is nothing that he or she can do to terminate an unpleasant situation, the phenomenon called **learned helplessness** can result. It may be that a person in fact was in a situation in which no action would terminate an unpleasant situation, and if so, it would make sense to give up trying and to develop the belief that "Nothing that I can do will make a difference." This belief becomes faulty, however, if conditions change so that a behavioral solution is now possible or if it generalized into the belief that "I am just not capable of dealing with life's problems." If the person does generalize and concludes that he or she does not possess the skills necessary for solving life's problems, *depression* may result. Believing that one is helpless, when in fact one is not, exemplifies what Norman calls an apparent but not real relationship and what Bandura calls perceived self-inefficacy.

SKILLED PERFORMANCE

Throughout his writings, Norman emphasizes the interrelatedness of learning, memory, and performance. The study of memory attempts to determine how information is stored and retrieved. The study of performance attempts to determine how information is utilized. The study of learning attempts to determine how an organism acquires new information, that is, how it profits from experience. In Norman's view, learning is closely related to understanding.

> You have learned to play chess when you understand the moves, the purpose and the basic strategy of the game. When you learn to drive or to sail, you learn something of the mechanics of the situation, something of the rules of the road, and most important, something of the relationship between your actions and the response of the car or boat. From the outsider's point of view, learning is closely related to performance. You may think you understand chess, but if you cannot play a challenging game, I would say you have not really learned it. (1982, p. 66)

But what is **skilled performance?** Norman is interested in understanding the difference between the skilled performance of experts such as tennis champions and veteran airplane pilots and that of less skilled individuals or amateurs. He lists five variables that differentiate the two.

1. **Smoothness.** Professionals do their job with ease, grace, smoothness, and with less effort than amateurs.

2. **Automaticity.** Most experts perform their task without an awareness of exactly what they are doing. "Ask skilled typists how they type a space. Do they always use the same thumb or do they alternate thumbs according to the particular words they are typing? Many typists do not know what they do" (Norman, 1982, p. 72).

3. **Mental Effort.** "As skill increases, mental effort decreases. The task appears easier, there is less mental fatigue, less need to monitor each action with care. Skilled performers can hold conversations with others, even while performing intricate tasks with their bodies" (1982, pp. 72–73).

4. **Stress.** Performance of amateurs tends to deteriorate under stress, whereas the performance of experts tends not to.

5. **Point of View.** When first learning a skill, one must attend to a wide variety of activities. In learning to drive a car, one needs to learn how to steer, back up, apply the brakes, park, accelerate, decelerate, etc. As an amateur driver, all of these things are attended to. As an expert driver, however, one just drives. Norman (1980a) put it as follows:

> Consider what happens when you first learn to drive an automobile. The instructions you receive emphasize the actions and mechanics: hold the steering wheel this way, synchronize foot (for clutch) and hand (for gearshift) that

---

Figure 14–3 (facing page).   The missionaries and cannibals problem. (From *Learning and Memory,* pp. 76–77, by D. A. Norman, 1982, New York: W. H. Freeman and Company. Copyright © 1982 W. H. Freeman and Company. Reprinted with permission.)

The Missionaries and Cannibals Problem

Three missionaries were lost, exploring the jungles of the planet Aurilion. Separated from their companions, without food or radio, they knew only that their destination was ahead. They stood at a river that blocked their path, wondering what to do. All at once, three cannibals appeared, carrying with them a boat. They too were about to cross the river. Groups of cannibals and missionaries had met before. Each was respectful of the other, but not fully trusting; missionaries took advantage of cannibals whenever they outnumbered them, and the unwitting cannibals were baptized before they could escape.

The three cannibals were willing to help the missionaries cross the river, but their boat could hold only two people at a time, and the cannibals would not let themselves ever be outnumbered by the missionaries. How can the problem be solved?

The Task

Your task is to manipulate the paper clips back and forth across the river: let large clips represent missionaires and small ones cannibals. You must imagine the boat. Remember that the boat holds a maximum of two people at a time. If on one side of the river there are ever more missionaries than cannibals, you have failed and must start over. Remember to count whoever is in the boat, so that one missionary and one cannibal on the river bank plus one or two missionaries in the boat at the same side of the river spells trouble.

Try it. Move the paper clips back and forth. Expect to take as long as 10 minutes to solve it the first time.

Time each attack on the problem. If you err in any manner (dropping a paper clip, moving the wrong clip by mistake, or finding a baptized cannibal), you must start the problem over but without stopping the timing. The time for the task must include all your actions from the start to a successful completion.

Write down the time for each trial on a piece of paper. Keep at the task until you can do it twice in a row in less than 10 seconds each time.

Figure 14–3.

way. As you progress, the point of view changes. Now you are turning the wheel, not moving your hands clockwise. Then you are turning the car, later you are entering that driveway. Eventually, when a truly expert driver, you drive to the bank, go shopping. The differences in the qualitative feeling of the performance are great. At the expert level, you may no longer be aware of all the subsidiary operations that you perform: you look at the driveway, form the intention to enter, and the car obediently follows suit. Driving the car becomes as natural as walking, the car becoming as much a part of the body's controlled appendages as the limbs. (p. 25)

Missionaries and Cannibals. In his book *Learning and Memory* (1982), Norman beckons his readers to experience what it feels like to go from being an amateur to being a skilled performer. As a vehicle for this transition he uses the missionaries and cannibals problem. The problem, as presented by Norman, is found in Figure 14-3.

During the early attempts to solve the problem, one is an amateur and performance is slow, deliberate, and often incorrect. As one continues, however, performance becomes smooth, automatic, and requires less mental effort. Although the early stages of solving this problem involve learning the correct strategy, Norman maintains that the conversion from amateur to expert is not so much a matter of learning how to solve the problem as it is learning how to *perform,* or how to effectively translate what has been learned into behavior. The typical solution to the problem is diagrammed in Figure 14-4(A). After presenting this problem to his classes for many years, Norman himself has reached the point where he can leave out many of the steps typically involved in the solution. Norman's expert method of solution is shown in Figure 14-4(B).

Norman follows Woodworth (1938) in his description of the sequence of experiences that characterize the learning of a complex task such as the solution to the missionaries and cannibals problem. That sequence is: chaos, analysis, synthesis, and automatization.

The sequence proceeds from whole to part and back to whole again. At first the task is chaotic-unorganized. Not enough is known even to perceive the situation easily. Then, with more experience, some of the units emerge. Systematic analysis reveals the component parts, which can then be learned separately, interrelated, and combined. Larger organizational units emerge; the topic takes on some structure and finally seems to be manageable. With further experience, the use of the knowledge becomes automatic, the skilled performance becomes subconscious. (Norman, 1982, pp. 78, 80)

MODES OF LEARNING

In their discussion of the modes of learning, Rumelhart and Norman (1981) display the close relationship between their information-processing approach and Piaget's view of developmental knowledge.

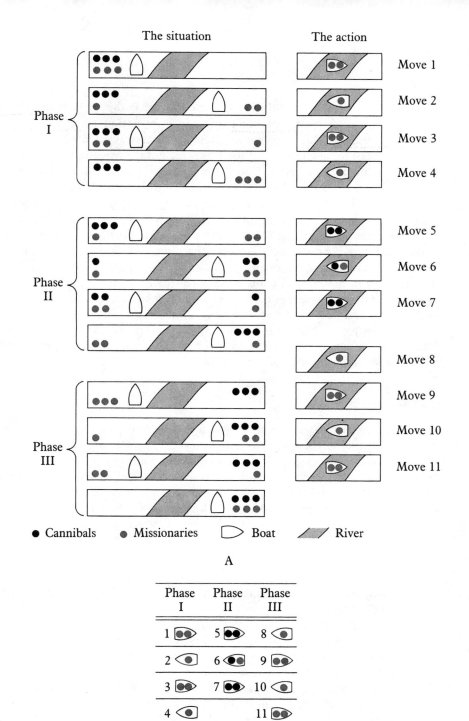

The situation   The action

Phase I

Move 1
Move 2
Move 3
Move 4

Phase II

Move 5
Move 6
Move 7
Move 8

Phase III

Move 9
Move 10
Move 11

● Cannibals   ● Missionaries   ▢ Boat   ▨ River

A

Phase I	Phase II	Phase III
1	5	8
2	6	9
3	7	10
4		11

B

Figure 14–4. Solution to the missionaries and cannibals problem. The upper portion of the figure (A) shows how the amateur typically solves the problem; the lower portion (B) shows how the expert solves it. (From *Learning and Memory*, p. 79, by D. A. Norman, 1982, New York: W. H. Freeman and Company. Copyright © 1982 W. H. Freeman and Company. Reprinted with permission.)

Accretion

According to Rumelhart and Norman, **accretion** is the most common mode of learning and involves the encoding of new information in terms of preexisting memory schemata. Thus, new information is processed in terms of old information. The very act of processing the information changes the existing schemata, however, and the resultant schemata are used to interpret similar future experiences. An example is when you need to learn to drive a car that you have not driven before. Norman (1982) writes, "Presumably you already have a good framework of knowledge for the structure of automobiles and for the mechanics of driving. Still, you must learn the specific details of a new car—where the horn and the emergency brake are located, how much free play the steering wheel has, and how tight the brakes are. Basically, as you come across each new aspect of the car, you are able to tuck it away in memory in some well-established manner" (p. 82).

Using Piaget's terminology, when an experience can be effectively recognized, understood, and dealt with by a schema, assimilation occurs. When a schema must change in order to effectively deal with an experience, accommodation occurs. Norman's concept of accretion involves a large amount of assimilation and only a relatively small amount of accommodation.

Structuring

When existing schemata do not allow effective negotiations with the environment, new ones must be formed. Norman refers to the learning of new schemata as **structuring** and says that it is the most difficult kind of learning. Using the above example, when one first learned how to drive one had to learn a driving schema; once this difficult task was accomplished, it could be applied to almost any automobile with relative ease. Norman's discussion of schema development parallels Piaget's quite closely.

Tuning

It is **tuning** that transforms an amateur into a skilled performer. According to Norman (1982):

> Tuning is the fine adjustment of knowledge to a task. The proper schemas exist and appropriate knowledge is within them. But they are inefficient for the purpose, either because they are too general or because they are mismatched to the particular use that is required of them, so the knowledge must be tuned, continually adjusted to the task. Practice is one way of accomplishing tuning. It may take thousands of hours of practice to reach the stage of tuning that characterizes an expert. Tuning is perhaps the slowest of the modes of learning, but it is what changes mere knowledge of a topic into expert performance. (pp. 81–82)

Tuning, then, consists of a long series of accretions. That is, tuning involves the large number of slight accommodations that are required when adjusting to the unique aspects of experiences that otherwise would not be completely assimilated into a schema.

Learning by Analogy

Norman equates accretion with memory since with both an experience is interpreted and acted upon in terms of existing schemata. Since each experience is unique, such learning does result in slight modifications of existing schemata (i.e., it results in slight accommodation), but it is mainly a matter of what Piaget called assimilation. As mentioned above, tuning involves a series of slight modifications and eventually allows for expertise or skilled performance.

If all learning involved only accretion or tuning, no new schemata would ever be required and, therefore, would not develop. Since new schemata (programs for interpreting and acting upon environmental experience) do develop, the question is by what mechanism are new schemata acquired? Norman's answer is that they develop by analogy to existing schemata.

> We have proposed that complex new procedures can be readily created by modeling them on existing schemas and modifying them slightly. We believe that the typical course of such a learning process consists of an initial creation of a new schema by modeling it on an existing schema. This new schema, however, is not perfect. It may occasionally mispredict events and otherwise be inadequate. We then believe that the newly acquired schema undergoes a process of refinement that we have dubbed *tuning* . . . we believe that this modeling process is properly called **learning by analogy.** [emphasis added] (Rumelhart & Norman, 1981, p. 357)

Complex learning, then, involves finding the most relevant existing schema and applying it to the new situation. This process, according to Norman, will allow at least a partial understanding of the new situation.

> Consider, for example, how we teach children the concept of a fraction. Most curricula use the pie analogy. One-half corresponds to one piece of a pie that has been cut down the middle. One-fourth corresponds to one piece of a pie cut into four equal pieces, etc. Here, the teacher is taking advantage of the child's spatial intuitions to teach the abstract notions of a fraction. This analogy is very useful: upon learning it, the reasoning and problem-solving strategies implicit in his knowledge of pies, operations that can be performed on them, etc., can be carried over into this abstract domain. The child can see that two-quarters make a half, that if you have a whole and take away one-quarter, you have three-quarters remaining, etc. The child needn't know *how* he knows this. These inferences are simply implicit in the analogy. (Rumelhart & Norman, 1981, p. 340)

It is seldom the case, however, that an existing schema is a perfect analogy for another. In other words, learning by analogy is almost always less than perfect.

> Sometimes operations are required in the target domain (in this case with learning fractions) that are difficult or unnatural within the domain of the analogical source. Thus, whereas addition and subtraction of fractions is natural within the pie analogy, multiplication and division of fractions is unnatural and difficult to conceptualize. How do you take one piece of pie times another or, worse yet, how do you divide one piece of pie *into* another (Rumelhart & Norman, 1981, p. 340)

In order to remedy the shortcomings of a particular analogy, Norman suggests that several analogies might be necessary in order to teach a complex topic. If the schemata for multiplication and division have been learned, they could be applied to the above situation to alleviate the inadequacies of the pie analogy.

What Goes on in the Mind of the Learner? In his article "What Goes on in the Mind of the Learner," Norman (1980b) reflects on some of the mistakes that he has made as a teacher and what he has done to correct them. Originally Norman assumed that:

> In order to teach, one must have knowledge of the topic that is to be taught, plus an understanding of the knowledge that the student already possesses. Then, one simply teaches the differences between them . . . Learning is really very simple, according to this point of view. Teaching is relatively simple, also. All one has to worry about is a proper understanding of the knowledge and of the student, and proper selection of the order of presentation.
> Unfortunately, it does not work that way. (1980b, p. 39)

According to Norman, his problem was in accepting the epistemology of the associationists.

> What was wrong was the simple theory of learning. Essentially, I had assumed that students were passive receptacles and that an ideal teaching situation would be one where the students would come into the classroom, unscrew the top of their skulls, and the instructor could walk around the class, peer intently into the brain of each student, and say something like, "Hmmm, you seem to have this connection missing," and then proceed to add the necessary connections. What a lovely vision!
> But students are not passive receptors of knowledge. (1980b, p. 42)

Instead, Norman discovered that students will always respond to what is presented to them in terms of their preexisting ideas or schemata. Students always interpret and understand new material in terms of material that they have already learned.

The student comes to the learning situation with a large set of preexisting ideas, and the material that is presented is interpreted according to these ideas. You cannot prevent it: I have tried. I have tried to present material in a neutral fashion. I have tried methods of discovery learning, in which the student interacts with the task, discovering the important principles of the day. I have carefully worked to set up the task so that the "discovery" leaps out and waves itself in the student's face. Well, sure the student will interact, and sure the student will discover things. But what is discovered and how it is interpreted is up to the student, and sometimes I feel I have remarkably little control over the process. (1980b, p. 42)

So, in answer to the question "What Goes on in the Mind of the Learner?" Norman says, a lot! Although humans have a strong desire to understand new experiences, they always do so in terms of what they already understand. Norman likens learning to theory building. This is both good and bad. As a theorist, the learner will attempt to explain his or her experiences, to give them meaning. That's the good part. "But, like a theorist, a learner builds on incomplete evidence, tends to ignore information that does not fit, and will grasp at any evidence that can serve as confirmation" (1980b, p. 42).

Norman is saying what Piaget had said: If an experience cannot be at least partially assimilated into existing schemata, it cannot exist for the learner. It is inevitable, then, that much of what is presented to students will not register. What, if anything, does register will always depend on how the learner's previous experiences were encoded into memory in the form of schemata. Norman refers to this as the **iceberg model of learning.** From the point of view of the learner, the small visible part of the iceberg represents the facts being presented by the teacher. Based on these facts, the learner must determine the larger structure of knowledge they represent. From the point of view of the teacher, the tip of the iceberg is the behavior of the student. To be effective the teacher must realize that this behavior reflects the much larger, submerged part of the iceberg which consists of the schemata in terms of which the facts are understood (or misunderstood) by the learner. Norman (1980b) says: "The student has erected a huge structure, and if the teacher is to understand the difficulties eventually faced by the student, this structure must somehow be uncovered" (p. 44).

We see that, according to Norman, all important learning is learning by analogy. It is on the basis of preexisting models (ideas, structures, schemata) that new experiences are evaluated, interpreted, understood, misunderstood, learned, or not learned.

MEMORY

If an experience can be assimilated to a large extent, into an existing schema, then memory can adequately deal with it. According to Norman, "To remember is to have managed three things successfully: the acquisition, retention, and retrieval of information" (1982, p. 2). Recall that in chapter 10 we discussed the Gestalt view of memory. According to the Gestalt theorists, each experience we have leaves a memory trace which, as one has more and more related experiences, becomes increasingly strong. Each new experience changes the trace slightly and, in turn, the experience is changed by the trace. Thus, according to the Gestalt theorists, memory is an active process that is transformed by experience and, in turn, modifies subsequent experiences. Since each new experience slightly changes a trace, it can be viewed as a learning experience. This is essentially what Norman means when he discusses accretion as both a form of learning and a model of memory.

However, accretion is the simplest kind of learning. How does memory relate to the kind of learning Norman calls "structuring"? In other words, how does memory come into play when we learn by analogy? To answer this question we must trace what happens to information from the time it enters the organism through various sense receptors, is transformed by various information-processing mechanisms, and is finally translated into some form of behavior.

Sensory Memory

When environmental stimuli impinge upon a sense receptor they are converted into neural impulses, and the information contained in the stimuli remains available for about one second after the stimuli are terminated. The fact that receptor systems retain environmental information for a brief period of time is called **sensory memory** or *sensory store,* and it is with sensory store that Norman begins his analysis of learning and memory. Sensory store is the first stage of information processing, and it is the stage upon which all higher, more complex stages of processing depend. Although each sensory system has the ability to store information for a short time, the visual and auditory systems have been given the most attention because they are the sense modalities through which most of our knowledge of the environment come. The sensory memory corresponding to the visual sense is called **iconic store.** The sensory memory corresponding to the auditory sense is called **echoic store.** Norman (1982) gives the following examples of sensory memory:

> Wave your hand in front of your face. The faint trace that remains after your hand is gone, a remnant of the event just past, is visible evidence of a sensory memory system. Close your hand into a fist, rapidly extend two fingers, then as quickly as possible form a fist again. If you watch closely, you will see a trace of your fingers that lasts long enough for you to count them. Move your hands parallel to each other but in opposite directions. Quickly wave them once before your eyes. Notice the subtle, indescribable feeling of motion associated with each faint trace. The feeling is real. Suppose there is flashed before you a complex image consisting of many objects, some moving clockwise in small circles, others moving counterclockwise. The image vanishes and an arrow points somewhere within the former area of the image. You will be able to report the direction in which the object in that particular place moved. The trace lasts for a few hundred milliseconds after the physical image is gone. (p. 5)

Although there is a vast amount of information in sensory store at any given moment, only a fraction of it is attended to, and thus made available for the next stage of information processing.

Short-Term Memory

Sensory memory has a large capacity. For example, if you were to look up an address in a telephone book, essentially all of the names and addresses on a page will be in sensory memory for about 1 sec. Only the address of interest will be attended to, however, and thus enters **short-term memory** (also called short-term store and primary memory) which lasts about 15 sec; long enough to get a piece of paper and a pencil and jot it down. Unless information in short-term memory is selected for further processing, it, too, will be forgotten in a very short period of time.

Long-Term Memory

Let us say that you wanted to remember the address that you just looked up for a long time. In that case, you would rehearse it over and over enough times to record it in **long-term memory** (also called long-term store and secondary memory). Most

Figure 14–5.   The relationships among environmental information, sensory memory, short-term memory, and long-term memory. Depending on the needs of the organism, certain information from sensory memory is selected for further processing in short-term memory. Again, depending on the organism's needs, certain information is selected from short-term memory to be rehearsed and thereby transferred into long-term memory. At any given moment, then, an organism's behavior is determined by the interaction between stimulating conditions and the long-term memories that those conditions elicit.

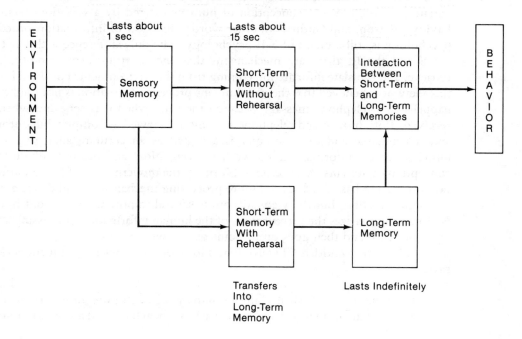

significant, recurring events in our lives are transferred into long-term memory and thus can be used to interpret, categorize, and respond to our everyday experiences. It is in long-term memory that the schemata that have been learned are stored. As we have seen, Norman believes that the most significant kind of learning occurs by analogy, and analogy (comparison) would be impossible if previously learned schemata were not stored in long-term memory. Loftus and Loftus (1976) stress the importance of long-term memory: "We are all aware that humans are able to store vast amounts of information—words, names, faces, places—permanently or semipermanently in long-term store. Without long-term store there would be nothing: no books, no television, no learning, no communication—for it is our ability to recall the past that allows us to interact with our environment in a dynamic way" (p. 56).

Once long-term memories are established, new experiences are processed and acted upon in accordance with them. Again, the schemata (programs) which we have learned are stored in long-term memory, and it is from long-term memory that information appropriate to a situation is retrieved and utilized.

The relationships among the environment, sensory memory, short-term memory, long-term memory, and behavior are depicted in Figure 14-5.

TWELVE ISSUES FOR COGNITIVE SCIENCE

There is a tendency on the part of those using the computer as a model for studying human thought processes, to view the human as a rational, logical information-processing system. For them, there is information from the environment (input), the processing of that information by various programs (e.g., memory and schemata), and output in the form of behavior. This view of humans can be viewed as a variation of the old S-R conception of humans offered by associationists such as Pavlov, Watson, and Guthrie. In other words, this view of information-processing psychology is still a brand of S-R psychology. The only difference is that between the S and the R, there are mechanisms that encode, transform, modify, store, retrieve, and translate information coming from the environment. For those holding this view, it is believed that the way humans process information is not unlike what happens to a telephone message between the time when it is sent and when it is received. Both human and telephone systems are viewed as complex but automatic and machinelike and the computer is accepted as an accurate analogy for how humans process information. As we have seen, Norman does not adhere to this conception of humans. According to Norman, the modern view of human information processing has added several more processing mechanisms, and this is a step in the right direction, but the view still omits several important facts about humans. Norman summarizes the present view of the human information-processing system in Figure 14-6 and then goes on to point out its weaknesses.

In his article entitled "Twelve Issues for Cognitive Science," Norman (1980a) says:

The human is a physical symbol system, yes, . . . But the human is more: The human is an animate organism, with a biological basis and an evolutionary and cultural history. Moreover, the human is a social animal, interacting with others, with the environment, and with itself. The core disciplines of cognitive science have tended to ignore these aspects of behavior. The results have been considerable progress on some fronts, but sterility overall, for the organism we are analyzing is conceived as pure intellect, communicating with one another in logical dialogue, perceiving, remembering, thinking where appropriate, reasoning its way through the well-formed problems that are encountered in the day. Alas, that description does not fit actual behavior. . . . I conclude that there is more to human intelligence than the pure cognitive system, and

Figure 14–6. Norman's summary of the modern view of the human information-processing system (from Norman, 1980a, p. 3). Norman feels that such a view is inadequate for reasons found in the text.

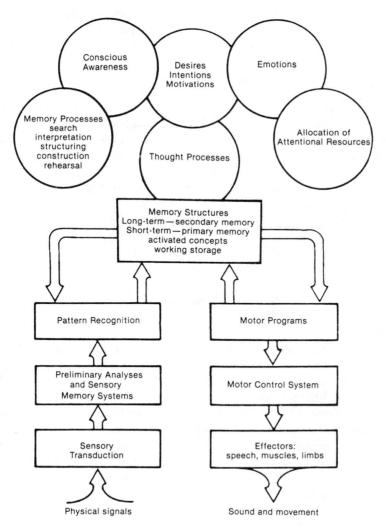

that a science of Cognition cannot afford to ignore these other aspects. (pp. 2–4)

And now the 12 issues that Norman believes cognitive science should address.

1. Belief Systems. According to Norman, what we believe to be true about the world and ourselves (whether those beliefs are correct or not) influences memory, perception, problem solving, and the interpretation of experience in general. It is essential, then, that we know how belief systems are formed, how they operate and how they change. Norman (1980a) has personally experienced the importance of belief systems: "My brief excursions into this area have left me impressed with how much my own hidden belief structures influence my 'pure' logical inference, memory processes, and social interactions. I suspect that we will find that more of our behavior is thus determined, not less" (p. 16).

Insofar as beliefs can be equated with expectancies, researchers such as Bandura have already made substantial gains in determining the importance of beliefs in the living of one's life, but, as Norman suggests, much remains to be done.

2. Consciousness. According to Norman (1980a):

Consciousness, under which I include the issues of conscious and subconscious thought, the problem of self-awareness, attention, the control structures of cognition, the formation of intentions. Here too are such issues as the phenomenological states of awareness, states of consciousness. Hypnosis: a powerful force, potentially a powerful tool for the investigation of consciousness, but little understood, not sufficiently well explored. (p. 16)

Even attention, the aspect of consciousness that has been studied the most, is still little understood. In 1890, William James described attention as follows: "It is the taking possession of the mind, in clear and vivid form, of one out of what seems several simultaneously possible objects or trains of thought. Focalization, concentration of consciousness are of its essence. It implies withdrawal from some things in order to deal effectively with others" (James, 1890, Vol. 1, pp. 403–404).

But, says Norman (1980a):

It is exactly the description given in the quote from James that we do not understand, cannot understand until we come to a better appreciation of the working of the mind, of the several simultaneous trains of thought that can occur, of the differences between conscious and subconscious processing, and of what it means to focus upon one train of thought to the exclusion of others. What—who—does the focussing, what happens to those other trains of thought as they are excluded? (Some, I am certain continue silently, unheeded, as subconscious processes that may later interrupt to again force conscious attention to themselves.) And what does it mean to have *conscious attention*? Can there be attention that is not conscious? What—who—experiences the result of conscious attentional processes? (pp. 16–17)

3. Development. Like Piaget, Norman believes that children and adults process information differently because they have different schemata available to them. Unfortunately, many researchers overlook this fact.

> In the study of adult cognition there seems to be the implicit assumption that once we come to understand adults, children will simply be seen to be at various stages along the pathway towards the adult. Perhaps. But perhaps also that the complexity and experience of the adult will forever mask some properties. Automatic behavior masks the underlying structure, pushing things beneath the conscious surface to the inaccessibility of subconscious processes. Well established belief and knowledge systems mask their content.
> Much of cognitive behavior could be studied best through the developmental cycle, with the history of the development leading to better understanding of the adult. Animate organisms take very long times to reach adulthood: the human is learning new concepts throughout the entire life span. Language learning goes on through the late teenage years, and vocabulary learning never ceases. We are fundamentally organisms that learn, that develop over time. By ignoring this aspect of behavior and concentrating on the static phases we may miss the keys to understanding. (Norman, 1980a, p. 18)

4. Emotion. Many believe that human emotions are an evolutionary carryover from an earlier time when emotional behavior was related to survival and that for modern humans, emotions are irrelevant or even a nuisance. Norman does not believe this. Rather, he believes that emotions play an important part in our commerce with the environment. In Figure 14-7 it can be seen that Norman believes that emotions are placed between the regulatory system and the cognitive system.

This model would explain why when we have experiences or thoughts conducive to survival, we experience positive emotions such as joy, happiness, pleasure,

Figure 14-7. Norman's contention that emotions intercede between an organism's regulatory system (the system related to the organism's survival) and its cognitive system. (Adapted from "Twelve Issues for Cognitive Science," by D. A. Norman, 1980, *Cognitive Science, 4,* 1–32.)

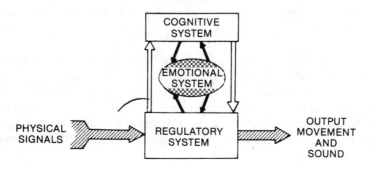

or love. When we have experiences or thoughts that are not conducive to survival, we experience negative emotions such as anger, anxiety, depression, or hate.

For Norman (1980a), it is essential to learn how our cognitive experiences are painted by the brush of emotions: "And what is the role of emotion in the study of cognition? We leave it to the poet, the playwright, the novelist. As people, we delight in art and in music. We fight, get angered, have joy, grief, happiness. But as students of mental events, we are ignorant of why, how" (p. 18).

5. Interaction. Humans are social organisms and yet:

Much of the study of cognitive processes has been the study of the isolated person. Much of the study of interactive groups has been of the dynamics of the situation, or of the behavioral aspects of the group. To my knowledge, little has been done to combine these efforts, to examine the individual cognitive processes as they are used within interactive settings. But, because the normal mode for the human is to interact, the studies of memory and language and problem solving and decision making in isolation address only one part of the mechanisms of human cognition. (Norman, 1980a, p. 19)

6. Language and 7. Perception. Here the problem, according to Norman, is that language and perception receive too much attention. In fact, there is a tendency to equate cognitive science with the study of these two topics. Norman feels that this is a mistake because a complete understanding of human cognition will come only when the nature and influence of such factors as beliefs, consciousness, social interactions, culture, emotions, learning, and memory are understood. According to Norman, these and other factors all interact as the human processes information. Again, to overemphasize a few at the expense of the others is a mistake.

8. Learning. Norman does not think kindly of most of the other theories of learning covered in this text. "Psychologists developed global theories of human and animal behavior, often built around such fundamental learning principles as 'the law of effect' or 'associative properties of learning and memory.' It all has come to nought" (1980a, p. 20).

Earlier in this chapter we reviewed Norman's views of the learning process, especially his emphasis of the importance of learning by analogy. He believes his efforts are just a first step toward understanding the nature of learning, however. In the meantime, little has been done and is being done to understand the nature of complex learning. Norman says (1980a):

There has been remarkably little study of learning—real learning, the learning of complex topics, the learning that takes months, even years to accomplish. Elsewhere I have estimated that experts at a task may spend 5,000 hours acquiring their skills: that is not such a long time; it is 2½ years of full-time study, 40 hours a week, 50 weeks a year. Not much time to become a professional tennis player, or computer programmer, or linguist. What goes on during that time? Whatever it is, it is slow, continuous. No magic dose of knowledge in the form of pill or lecture. Just a lot of slow, continual exposure to the topic, probably accompanied by several bouts of restructuring of the underlying mental representations, reconceptualizations of the concepts, plus many hours of accumulation of large quantities of facts. (p. 20)

9. Memory. Norman (1980a) warns us:

Do not be impressed by all that is presumably known about the psychology of memory. Less is known than you might think . . . How does one find the information required to answer a question when the form of the question was not anticipated at the time of acquiring the information? Not possible with artificial systems today, a commonplace occurrence with people. And how is the desired information recognized once it is found if it wasn't known in the first place? If I seek the name of a long-lost colleague and retrieve the name Isaac Newton, how do I reject that as the name I seek when I do not know the sought-for name? . . . How do we remember stories, events, experiences? More to the point, how do we retrieve them when least we expect them?

Memory has some other puzzles. We recognize the meanings of words in tenths of seconds (as in reading), yet may take hours or days to retrieve one of those words when we seek it for use in a sentence. And what is it that keeps the memory search going for those hours or days, while conscious thought proceeds in other directions, when the need for the word may have long passed? Current events bring to mind previous experiences, not always in any obvious fashion. It is a well accepted statement that memory is associative, that memory structures are organized into some form: networks, concepts, prototypes, basic levels, schemas, frames, units, scripts. How? We need to understand the representation of knowledge, including the process that operates upon the representation. (1980a, pp. 21–22)

10. Performance. Norman marvels at the motor performance of, say, expert typists and indicates that such performance is little understood.

The problems of performance are real, they require understanding of computational issues of considerable sophistication, and they interact with perceptual and thought processes in fundamental ways. It is possible to argue that much of our knowledge of the world resides in our knowledge of the procedures that interact with the world, that the perceptual-cognitive-motor schemas are unitary memory constructs, and the separation of one from the others destroys the whole. (1980a, p. 24)

11. Skill. As we have seen earlier in this chapter, Norman believes that there is both a quantitative and a qualitative difference between someone who is merely competent at a task and someone who is an expert. The expert performs with ease, automatically and without awareness of the many activities involved in performance of the task. The major differences between skilled and unskilled individuals are just now being noted and studied.

12. Thought. Norman believes that too much time and energy has been spent studying pure, abstract thought processes. For example, some information-processing psychologists view humans as general purpose computational devices. This view stresses general problem-solving skills and minimizes the problem-solving strategies that come from specific environmental experiences. Norman says "I believe that too much emphasis has been given to possible formal properties of human reasoning, not enough to informal, experiential based models of reasoning" (1980a, p. 25).

Norman's list of 12 issues for cognitive science suggests that such a science is in its infancy. Although it is true there is much remaining to be understood, Norman (1980a) is pleased that we at least know enough to raise the issues: "The fact that I can write such a paper, ask such questions, complain with some reasonable specificity, is a positive sign about the emergence of a new discipline. It is a sign of progress that things are sufficiently well understood that the list of non-understood topics can be prepared" (p. 28).

It should now be clear that Norman argues that no aspect of cognition can be, nor should be, studied in isolation. Norman (1980a) concludes his article by saying: "I wish Cognitive Science to be recognized as a complex interaction among different issues of concern, an interaction that will not be properly understood until all the parts are understood, with no part independent of the others, the whole requiring the parts, and the parts the whole" (p. 29).

COGNITIVE ENGINEERING

Norman has studied human errors for many years. He has studied errors ranging from turning off an automobile engine while attempting to turn off the windshield wipers, to accidents in nuclear power plants and airplane disasters. In almost all cases, Norman finds fault not with the persons involved but in the design of the equipment that they were operating. "I claim that such errors are not the fault of the operators; they are system induced errors" (Norman, 1982, p. 114).

It is surprising how badly technology matches human capabilities. People are flexible, amazingly so. The range of our abilities is immense. We manage and cope with a wide variety of circumstances. Those who design and construct the tools of modern society, however, seem to have little understanding of our capabilities. As a result, we are slaves to technology. We make errors [and] we assume it is natural and proper to do so. If we get upset about the errors, we are upset at ourselves for being so stupid or forgetful. Nonsense. (Norman, 1982, p. 113)

To solve the problem, everything that we know about cognition must be utilized in designing the machines with which we interact.

> The human is a system of interacting components. Within each of us there are many cognitive mechanisms interacting with one another, interacting with emotions and motivations, with intentions and goals, and with the biological systems and physical parts of the body. Each person also interacts with a complex sociocultural setting. Anyone who attempts to design devices that take into account human functioning must consider all aspects, from the details of short-term memory and attentional limitations to the interactions of human, machine, and society. It will not suffice simply to design a knob to match human requirements; the whole system must be designed to take into account the whole human being. . . Once I argued that it was time for a new discipline: **cognitive engineering** [emphasis added]. At that time I was thinking of education, of the problems of teaching and tutoring, of automated instructional systems. Now, with a wider perception of the need to make technology our friend and ally, not our enemy, I think the time for such a discipline has more than come. (Norman, 1982, pp. 116–117)

EVALUATION

The information-processing approach to psychology is extremely popular today, and it promises to remain so in the future. Some go so far as to say that the information-processing approach represents a new paradigm in psychology. For example, Lachman, Lachman, and Butterfield (1979, p. 113) claim that information-processing psychology has finished its revolution and has now entered a period of normal science. Also, in the preface of their book *Human Information Processing: An Introduction to Psychology* (2nd ed., 1977), Lindsay and Norman express their belief that the information-processing model can be used to study all aspects of human existence: "We believe our extensions of the area of information processing research show how the scientific analyses of this book can help illuminate many if not all human phenomena" (p. v).

We believe, however, that it is premature to conclude that the information-processing approach to psychology represents a new paradigm, and we will list the reasons for reaching this conclusion under "Criticisms" below. Whether or not the information-processing approach can be given the status of paradigm, it is clear that it is extremely useful, effective, and popular, and we next list some reasons why it is.

Contributions

1. The information-processing approach provides a framework within which complex cognitive processes can be studied objectively. For years it was believed that cognitive processes were too mysterious or inaccessible to be studied scientifically. The information-processing approach suggests that this belief is false.

2. The information-processing approach, especially as presented by Norman, encourages the synthesis of many human attributes. For example, Norman stresses the fact that human behavior results from the interaction of current stimulating conditions, memories of past experiences, emotions, beliefs, attitudes, cultural and societal influences, and the presence of fellow humans. According to Norman, to truly understand why humans act as they do, we must understand how these and other variables interact with one another. This approach discourages the study of isolated human attributes such as intelligence, memory, concept formation, or problem solving. Thus the richness and complexity of humans are recognized.

3. The information-processing approach offers a new and exciting way of studying human attributes. Newell (1970), a major contributor to information-processing psychology says: "[I]f one looks at where the excitement has been over the last ten years in psychology—the places where rapid growth is taking place and what people talk about when asked 'what's new'—a substantial fraction of these turn out to be connected to this shift towards information-processing models" (p. 378).

4. The information-processing approach is compatible with the computer. In fact, as we have seen, many information-processing psychologists view humans and computers as functionally very similar. Even if the analogy between computers and humans is not accepted entirely, the information-processing psychologist, like no other psychologist, is in a position to utilize computers to test his or her assumptions about how humans process information. The computer is both a powerful research tool and an intriguing model of human cognitive functioning, and many information-processing psychologists use the computer in both ways.

5. The information-processing approach has caused psychologists to be more precise with their concepts and theories. As we have noted, before a theory can be converted into a computer program, it must be stated clearly and precisely, and it must be logically consistent. If an unclear program is fed into a computer, the computer will either not work or it will produce meaningless results. Thus the information-processing approach to psychology provides the same service as did mathematical models of learning. That is, they both cause researchers to clarify the definition of their terms and to be precise in the formulation of their theories.

Criticisms

1. Other than providing a cleaning-up operation for some concepts and theories, information-processing psychology does not really add anything new to psychology. We have seen in this chapter, for example, that Norman's views on learning are, to a large extent, a refinement of Piaget's views. Similar criticisms have been made concerning the treatment of intelligence, memory, and perception by the information-processing psychologists. Even the informa-

tion-processing approach itself has been found to be nothing new. Leahey (1980) says, for example: "The most modern psychology, information processing cognitive psychology, is remarkably similar to Aristotle's account of mind. Both view the acquisition of knowledge as the internalization and processing of information about the environment which is then stored in some form of memory" (p. 385).

2. The information-processing approach ignores or minimizes important areas of psychology. Most obvious are the areas of abnormal behavior and psychotherapy. Even though Lindsay and Norman's book *Human Information Processing: An Introduction To Psychology* is billed as an introduction to psychology, it excludes the sections on abnormal behavior and psychotherapy typically found in introductory texts. An effort to explain individual differences typically included in a section covering theories of personality is also missing. Norman and others working within information-processing psychology recognize these weaknesses and are beginning to correct them. Norman's stressing of the importance of emotions in human behavior exemplifies his effort to make the information-processing approach more comprehensive.

3. Although the computer is a useful analogy for several human attributes, humans are not computers. Although both humans and computers perform complex operations and retain information, only humans struggle to survive, interact with other humans, and have feelings. The computer, then, has only limited value as a model for studying humans. Norman realizes this perhaps more than anyone else working within information-processing psychology.

4. Behaviorists, such as Skinner, still claim that it is not necessary to know what goes on between a stimulus and a response in order to understand behavior. These radical behaviorists maintain that the information-processing psychologists make the same mistake that the mental philosophers had made, and that was believing that cognitive events are causally related to behavior. Since these behaviorists believe that the causes of behavior are found in the environment, everything between the environment and behavior can be, and should be, ignored. For these behaviorists, information-processing psychology is just one more example of the kind of mentalistic psychology that has done nothing to enhance our understanding of human behavior.

SUMMARY

Antecedents to information-processing psychology include: (a) S-R psychology which viewed humans as interacting with the environment in an automatic, machinelike way; (b) the kinds of cognitive psychology suggested by Tolman, Bandura, and Piaget which stressed the importance of information, expectancies, beliefs, and schemata; (c) cybernetics, which viewed humans as constantly testing sensory input against some standard and then, if there is a discrepancy between the two, engaging in appropriate behavior until the discrepancy is eliminated; (d) robotology, which was successful at creating a variety of machines and devices which successfully mimicked certain activities of living organisms; (e) information theory, which conceptualized the bit as an objective way of measuring information and showed how information is lost as it is encoded and decoded within a communication system; and (f) the computer which acted as a powerful model with which to study human cognitive processes.

For Norman, the concepts of learning and understanding are closely linked. To learn a task is to come to understand the task well enough so that it can be performed with skill. Norman criticizes the law of effect mainly because it ignores the fact that in order for learning to occur, there must be an apparent relationship between an action and an outcome. Sometimes organisms will reach erroneous conclusions about the causal relationships between actions and outcomes, and these faulty conclusions can be dysfunctional. If individuals develop the belief that nothing they can do will produce a favorable outcome or eliminate a negative one, the phenomenon of learned helplessness may result. Since learned helplessness results in a feeling that one is totally ineffective in dealing with life's problems, it often results in the feeling of depression. Norman is very interested in skilled performance and lists five facts that differentiate skilled from amateur performance: smoothness, automaticity, mental effort, the effects of stress, and point of view.

Norman discusses three modes of learning. Accretion, the most common mode, involves the application of an existing schema to a new situation. This results in a slight modification of the schema. Structuring, the most difficult kind of learning, involves the formation of new schemata. Tuning, the slowest kind of learning, involves the application of a schema to a large number and wide variety of related experiences. In his explanation of how new schemata are formed, Norman stresses learning by analogy. New schemata always result from extensions, generalizations, or modifications of existing schemata. Effective teaching, then, must always use a student's existing schemata as a frame of reference in deciding what can be taught and how it can be taught. All humans interact with the world and interpret their experiences in terms of the schemata available to them.

There are three kinds of memory. Sensory memory has enormous capacity but only lasts about one second. Short-term memory consists of those events from sensory memory selected for further processing. Short-term memory lasts for about 15 seconds. That information from short-term memory that is attended to and rehearsed becomes part of long-term memory. Long-term memory lasts indefinitely. The schemata that we have learned from past experience are stored in long-term memory. It is the interaction between present stimulating conditions and the retrieval of relevant information from long-term memory that determines how we respond to a situation.

Norman lists 12 issues that he feels must be addressed in order to improve cognitive science. He says cognitive scientists must recognize the importance of belief systems; understand more fully the nature of conscious and subconscious thought, including selective attention; study the ways children process information to better understand how adults do; recognize the influence of emotions on human information processing; learn how all of the influences on humans interact among themselves; stop equating cognitive science with the study of language and perception; study in more depth the nature of complex learning; continue their efforts to unravel the mysteries of memory; put forth greater effort to understand the nature of skilled performance; and determine how our reasoning abilities are derived from experience.

Norman believes that if what is now known in cognitive science were applied to the design of the tools of modern society, errors could be greatly reduced. He calls the marriage between cognitive science and technology, cognitive engineering.

DISCUSSION QUESTIONS

1. In what way(s) is information-processing psychology compatible with the associationistic views of such individuals as Pavlov, Watson, and Guthrie?

2. Discuss the similarity between information-processing psychology and the views of Tolman, Bandura, and Piaget.

3. First define cybernetics and then describe how it influenced information-processing psychology.

4. First define robotology and then describe how it influenced information-processing psychology.

5. Summarize the accomplishments of information theory and show how they influenced information-processing psychology.

6. In what ways are humans and computers similar? In what ways are they dissimilar?

7. Discuss the various ways in which information-processing psychologists use computers.

8. Summarize Norman's criticisms of Thorndike's law of effect.

9. What does Norman mean by his contention that in order for learning to occur there must be an apparent causal relationship between action and outcome?

10. Describe the negative consequences that can result when apparent causes of outcomes are not real causes.

11. What kinds of experiences result in the phenomenon of learned helplessness?

12. What, according to Norman, distinguishes skilled performance from unskilled, or amateur, performance?

13. Discuss and give an example of accretion, structuring, and tuning.

14. What does Norman mean when he says that most complex learning occurs by analogy? Give an example of such learning.

15. Define sensory, short-term, and long-term memories and describe how they interact.

16. List and briefly describe the 12 issues that Norman feels cognitive science should address.

17. What is cognitive engineering and why does Norman feel that there is a need for it?

CHAPTER HIGHLIGHTS

Accretion. The addition of knowledge to existing schemata, without changing their structure in any fundamental way. Accretion is the most common kind of learning.

Artificial intelligence. A scientific discipline usually part of a computer science or cognitive science department. A person who studies artificial intelligence attempts to build machines that exhibit the same intelligence as humans. Although most work on artificial intelligence is done on the digital computer, it is not necessary that a computer be utilized.

Cognitive engineering. The field that would take the facts from cognitive science and apply them to modern technology.

Coincidental association. According to Bandura, a process by which an event that is present but not causally related to an outcome erroneously becomes associated with that outcome.

Cybernetics. Studies systems which act upon feedback from the environment in such a way as to optimize the relationship between their external and internal environments.

Echoic store. Sensory memory corresponding to the auditory sense modality.

Feedback. Information provided by the outcome of actions which becomes the basis for further actions.

Hardware. The physical properties of an information-processing system.

Iceberg model of learning. From the learner's point of view the facts being presented by the teacher are the tip of the iceberg, and the structure of knowledge that those facts represent is the larger, submerged part of the iceberg. From the teacher's point of view the student's behavior is the tip of the iceberg, and the student's structure of knowledge is the larger, submerged part of the iceberg.

Iconic store. Sensory memory corresponding to the visual sense modality.

Inappropriate generalization. According to Bandura, the process by which outcomes that are causally related to one event become expected when similar events are encountered.

Information-processing psychology. The kind of psychology that views humans as receiving input from the environment in the form of information; encoding, transforming and modifying that information; and then responding to that information in some way. The emphasis is on the determination of the properties of the internal mechanisms that encode, transform, and store information.

Information theory. Devised the bit in order to objectively measure information. The goal of information theory was to increase the accuracy with which a message is transmitted from its source over a transmitting channel to a receiver.

Input. The information entering an information-processing system.

Law of causal learning. An organism learns to repeat those actions that have an apparent causal relationship to desirable outcomes and to avoid those actions that have an apparent causal relationship to undesirable outcomes.

Law of causal relationship. In order for an organism to learn, there must be an apparent causal relationship between its actions and the outcomes of those actions.

Law of information feedback. The outcomes of various actions provide information as to the effectiveness of those actions.

Learned helplessness. The general feeling of helplessness that results when it seems that there is nothing that one can do to terminate an unpleasant situation. In extreme cases, learned helplessness causes a person to give up trying anything and to become depressed.

Learning by analogy. Norman's contention that the learning of new schemata is always relative to existing schemata.

Long-term memory (also called long-term store and secondary memory). If material in short-term memory is rehearsed long enough, it becomes part of long-term memory. It is in long-term memory that schemata are stored. Such memory lasts indefinitely.

Output. The response made by an information-processing system after information has been processed.

Perceived self-inefficacy. According to Bandura, the belief that one is incapable of performing certain actions even if, in reality, one is capable of performing them.

Robotology. The building of machines or devices that mimic certain aspects of the behavior of living organisms.

Sensory memory (also called sensory store). Begins when sense receptors are activated and lasts for about a second. Such memory stores a great deal of information but that information is available for only a very short period of time.

Short-term memory (also called short-term store and primary memory). Memory of material selected from sensory memory for further processing. Such memory lasts for about 15 seconds.

Skilled performance. Performance that is differentiated from amateur performance by its smoothness, automaticity, small amount of mental effort required, resistance to deterioration under stress, and the point of view that one has while performing.

Software. The programs that allow information-processing systems to process information.

Structuring. The creation of new schemata. Structuring is the most difficult kind of learning.

Tuning. The adjustment of a schema to a wide variety of related situations. Tuning is what converts amateur into skilled performance and represents the slowest kind of learning.

15

Donald Olding Hebb

Donald Olding Hebb was born on July 22, 1904 in Chester, Nova Scotia. Both his parents were medical doctors. His mother obtained her medical degree from Dalhousie University in Halifax, Nova Scotia in 1896, making her only the third female to become a physician in the province of Nova Scotia at that time.

In 1925 Hebb received his BA from Dalhousie University with the lowest course average a person could have without actually failing. Since Hebb is one of psychology's most creative researchers and theorists, undergraduate grade point average, in his case, had no predictive value. After graduation, Hebb taught school in the village where he grew up. At the age of 23 he read Freud and decided psychology had a lot of room for improvement. Since the chairman of the psychology department at McGill University in Montreal was a friend of his mother's, he was admitted as a part-time graduate psychology student in spite of his poor undergraduate record. Hebb continued to teach elementary school while he was a graduate student, however, and had a compulsion to reform educational practices. He tried several experiments with various degrees of success. In one experiment he decided that extra schoolwork should not be used as a punishment because doing so would create a negative attitude toward schoolwork. Since he felt some form of punishment was necessary to maintain order, he reverted to mildly slapping the student's hand with a strap for a wrongdoing. Hebb (1980) described an occasion when this disciplinary technique backfired: "One day I set out to strap a boy who flinched so that the end of the strap went by his hand and hit my trousers at the level of the glans penis. It hurt like the devil, and I said to the boy, 'This hurts me more than it does you.' But I don't think he understood the joke" (p. 282).

In addition to wanting to become an educational reformer, another of Hebb's early passions was to write novels for a living, but, like Skinner, his efforts failed.

During his years at McGill, Hebb was trained in the Pavlovian tradition and after writing a thesis compatible with this tradition, he obtained his MA in 1932. In spite of his training Hebb saw restrictions in Pavlovian theory and doubted its importance. While at McGill, Hebb read Köhler's *Gestalt Psychology* and Lashley's work on brain physiology (which we will consider briefly below), and found them both to his liking. In 1934, Hebb decided to continue his education at the University of Chicago where he worked with Lashley and took a seminar from Köhler. Lashley's work cast doubt on the prevailing belief that the brain was a complex switchboard. This **switchboard** (or relay station) **concept** of the brain was held mainly by the behaviorists, for example, Thorndike, Hull, and Watson and by the associationists, for example, Pavlov and Guthrie. It was assumed by those holding this view that certain sensory events stimulate certain areas of the brain, causing specific reactions. Learning, according to this point of view, causes a change in neural circuitry so that sensory events come to stimulate responses other than those they originally stimulated. Lashley's research, which used rats as subjects, raised serious questions about this conception of the brain. The most startling outcome of Lashley's research was his finding that the *location* of the destroyed portion of the brain was not as important as the *amount* of destruction. This consistent finding became Lashley's principle of **mass action,** which stated that the disruption of learning and retention goes up as the amount of cortical destruction goes up, re-

Donald O. Hebb. (Photograph by Chris Payne)

gardless of the location of the destruction. Lashley concluded that the cortex func-tioned as a whole during learning, and if one part of the cortex was destroyed, other parts of the cortex could take over the destroyed portion's function. This ability of one portion of the cortex to take over the function of another was referred to by Lashley as **equipotentiality.** Thus, mass action indicated that the amount of learn-ing and memory disruption is a function of the amount of the cortical area de-stroyed, and equipotentiality indicated that the location of the cortical ablation was unimportant.

Clearly, these findings were not in accordance with Hebb's early training at McGill University and his opposition to Pavlov, which was at first tenuous, now became outright disagreement. "I had all the fervor of the reformed drunk at a temperance meeting; having been a fully convinced Pavlovian, I was now a fully convinced Gestalter-*cum*-Lashleyan" (Hebb, 1959, p. 625). Once again, we are re-minded of an important characteristic of good scientists; they are willing to change their minds.

In 1935, Lashley accepted a professorship at Harvard and he invited Hebb to go with him. In 1936, Hebb obtained his PhD from Harvard and remained there an additional year as a teaching and research assistant.

In 1937, Hebb went to the Montreal Neurological Institute to work with the famous brain surgeon Wilder Penfield. Hebb's job was to study the psychological status of Penfield's patients after brain surgery. Much to Hebb's amazement, he found that even after substantial loss of tissue from the frontal lobes of the brain there was no loss in intelligence and, in some cases, he even detected a gain in intelligence. In some cases, the tissue loss was as much as 20%. These observations cast further doubt on the switchboard concept of the brain and supported the con-tention that somehow the brain functioned as a whole. According to Hebb (1980), it was the questions raised by these observations that acted as a stimulus for his subsequent work: "I could find no sign of loss after large amounts of brain tissue were removed from the frontal lobe . . . . It was this problem that set the main course for all my subsequent work . . ." (p. 290).

After studying Penfield's patients for five years (1937–1942), Hebb reached a conclusion about intelligence that was later to become an important part of his theory: "Experience in childhood normally develops concepts, modes of thought, and ways of perceiving that constitute intelligence. Injury to the infant brain interferes with that process, but the same injury at maturity does not reverse it" (1980, p. 292).

By now Hebb had made three observations that his later theory would attempt to explain: (a) The brain does not act as a simple switchboard as the behaviorists and associationists had assumed. If it did, destroying large amounts of brain tissue from the frontal lobes would have been more disruptive; (b) intelligence comes from experience and, therefore, is not genetically determined; and (c) childhood experiences are more important in determining intelligence than adult experiences.

In 1942, Lashley accepted an appointment as director of the Yerkes Laboratories of Primate Biology in Orange Park, Florida, and again, asked Hebb to join him. While at the Yerkes Laboratories (1942–1947), Hebb studied the emotions and personalities of chimpanzees. Hebb made several observations that further stimulated his own neurophysiological theory of learning and perception. Among them were the following: "[Chimpanzees] were frightened—or better perhaps, horrified—at the sight of a clay model of a chimpanzee head or . . . any recognizable part of either a chimpanzee or a human body (e.g., a head or a hand from a display mannequin)" (1980, p. 294). Based on these and other observations, Hebb devel-

Karl Lashley. (From *Great Experiments in Psychology*, 3rd ed., p. 22, by H. E. Garrett, 1951, New York: Appleton-Century-Crofts.)

oped his own unique explanation of fear which we will review in a later section of this chapter.

In 1948, after five years at the Yerkes Laboratories, Hebb accepted an appointment as professor of psychology at McGill University where he remained until his retirement. At the time of this appointment, physiological psychology was not very popular and Hebb felt very fortunate to get the job. Hebb believed that there were two major reasons why neurophysiological explanations of learning were avoided at this time. First, as the philosophy of science developed and as more was learned about the logic of science, many researchers felt that explaining observable behavior in terms of physiological events was like mixing apples and oranges. Using physiological mechanisms to explain overt behavior involved a change in the level of discourse, and drawing conclusions from one level to the other violated the canons of scientific logic. In other words, it was believed that physiological events, like overt behavior, constitute a self-contained system, and the relationship between the two systems remained indeterminate.

A second reason that physiological explanations were not very popular involved the very nature of the behavioristic movement, which was mainly a reaction against introspection. To the behaviorist, the only legitimate subject matter for psychology was something tangible that everyone could see and investigate. This was not true for the experiences reported on introspectively, and it was not true for physiological events. In concentrating on overt, measurable behavior the behaviorists excluded neurophysiology.

To a large extent it was Hebb that made neurophysiological explanations of learning respectable. Hebb (1960) suggests that the behavioristic movement was only the first stage of a revolution within psychology, a revolution against the older subjective, philosophic schools of psychology. According to Hebb, behaviorism insisted upon the objective study of overt behavior and that was good, but by insisting on *only* the study of behavior, the behaviorists threw out the baby with the bath water. Now, says Hebb, we are ready for the second phase of the revolution— that is, to study cognitive processes objectively. Hebb, as we shall see, has taken the neurophysiological approach to studying cognitive processes, but his is only one approach. The important thing, to Hebb, is that the study of cognitive processes no longer be avoided.

> How are we to learn more about these ideational or mediating processes, and the limits of their role in behavior, except by forming hypotheses (as explicit as we can reasonably make them) and then seeing what implications they have for behavior, and whether these implications are borne out in experiment? By all means, if you will, call these central events mediating processes instead of ideas or cell assemblies, but let us get busy and investigate them. (1959, p. 630)

It is fortunate for psychology that many investigators are currently following Hebb's suggestion. The Gestalt psychologists, Piaget, Tolman, Bandura, and the information-processing psychologists exemplify theorists emphasizing the study of cognitive processes, but unlike Hebb's approach, they do not emphasize neurophysiological concepts.

Among Hebb's many honors are included eight honorary doctorates; the presidency of the Canadian Psychological Association (1952); the presidency of the American Psychological Association (1959); winner of the Warren Medal (1958) and recipient of the distinguished scientific contribution award of the American Psychological Association (1961).

Once converted from the kind of behaviorism derived from Pavlov's theory, Hebb launched an attack on behaviorism that continued all of his life. His first major book was *The Organization of Behavior* (1949). The initials of that book, OOB, bore a strange resemblance to the initials of Skinner's major book *The Behavior of Organisms* (1938), which was affectionately known as BOO. A later publication, "Drives and the C.N.S. (Conceptual Nervous System)" (1955) showed Hebb's willingness to "physiologize" about psychological processes. His very readable *Textbook of Psychology* (1972) provides an excellent overview of his theory. A more technical account of his theory appears in Koch's *Psychology: A Study of a Science* (1959). Hebb's approach is diametrically opposed to Skinner's method of functional analysis, where relationships between stimuli and responses are determined without any reference to internal events.

After his retirement from McGill University in 1974, Hebb moved back to a small farm near Chester, Nova Scotia, where he was born. He remained psychologically and physically active until he died on August 20, 1985 while in the hospital for what was thought to be routine hip surgery (Beach, 1987, p. 187). Some of Hebb's more important theoretical concepts are reviewed below.

CELL ASSEMBLIES
AND PHASE SEQUENCES

We have seen that while working with Penfield, Hebb had reached the conclusion that childhood experience was more important for intellectual development than adult experience. Several other sources also confirmed the importance of early experience. The German ophthalmologist von Senden (1932) had studied adults who had been blind since birth and then were suddenly able to see after an operation such as removal of cataracts. It was found that these individuals could immediately detect the presence of an object but they could not tell what the object was. These findings suggested that some kind of figure-ground perception is innate, but visual experience with various objects is necessary before objects can be differentiated from one another. Gradually, these previously blind individuals learned to identify objects in the environment and their perceptions approached normality.

Austin Riesen (1947) reared infant chimpanzees in total darkness until they were about 2 years old. When they were finally taken from the darkness they acted as if they were completely blind. Within a few weeks, however, they began to see and eventually they behaved like other chimpanzees that had been reared normally. Hebb concluded that the adults that von Senden studied and the chimpanzees that Riesen studied had to *learn* to see.

Numerous other studies supported the conclusion that by restricting early experience, one interferes with normal intellectual and perceptual development. In a study run in Hebb's laboratory (Melzack & Thompson, 1956), it was even shown that Scottish terriers reared in partial isolation were oblivious to pain, in addition to being less aggressive than their normally reared littermates.

All these observations strengthened Hebb's empiricistic position. Intelligence, perception, and even emotions are learned from experience and therefore are not inherited as the nativist claims. Hebb developed a theory which assumed that infants are born with a neural network with random interconnections. It is, according to Hebb, sensory experience that causes this neural network to become organized and to provide a means of interacting effectively with the environment. The two key concepts in Hebb's theory are cell assembly and phase sequence.

Cell Assemblies

According to Hebb, each environmental object we experience fires a complex package of neurons called a **cell assembly.** For example, as we look at a pencil, we will shift our attention from the point to the eraser, to the wooden shaft. As our attention shifts, different neurons are stimulated. However, the entire package of neurons stimulated at the time corresponds to one environmental object—a pencil. All aspects of this complex neural package will, at first, be independent. For example, as one looks at the point of a pencil, a certain group of neurons will fire. They will not, however, initially influence the neurons that fire while one is looking at the eraser or the wooden shaft. Eventually, however, because of the closeness in time between the firing of the neurons corresponding to the point and those corresponding to other parts of the pencil, the various parts of the neurological package become interrelated. Hebb puts the matter as follows (1959):

> If a neuron, *A,* is near enough to another, *B,* to have any possibility of firing it, and if it does take part in firing it on one occasion (it often requires two or more neurons working together to trigger the response in another), the probability is increased that when *A* fires next *B* will fire as a result. In other words, "synaptic resistance" is decreased, by a microscopic growth at the synapse or some chemical change in one of the two cells. The assembly might be made up of perhaps 25, 50, or 100 neurons, and building it up in the first place would be a very slow process, requiring many repetitions of the stimulating conditions. (p. 628)

A cell assembly can be large or small, depending upon the environmental object or event it represents. For example, the cell assembly associated with *door knob* would consist of a relatively small number of neurons, but the cell assembly for *house* would consist of a relatively large number of neurons. The entire cell assembly is an interrelated neurological package that can be fired by either external stimulation, internal stimulation, or by a combination of the two. When a cell assembly fires, we experience the thought of the event the assembly represents. To Hebb, the cell assembly is the neurological basis of an idea or thought. In this way, Hebb explains why a house, or a cow, or a loved one need not be present for us to think of them.

Phase Sequences

Just as different aspects of the same object become neurologically interrelated to form cell assemblies, so do cell assemblies become neurologically interrelated to form phase sequences. A **phase sequence** is "a temporally integrated series of assembly activities; it amounts to one current in the stream of thought" (Hebb, 1959, p. 629). Once developed, a phase sequence, like a cell assembly, can be fired internally, externally, or by a combination of internal and external stimulation. When any single cell assembly or combination of assemblies in a phase sequence is fired, the entire phase sequence tends to fire. When a phase sequence fires, we experience a stream of thought, that is, a series of ideas arranged in some logical order. This explains how a whiff of perfume, or a few strains from a favorite song may trigger memories of a loved one.

Hebb has the following to say about the development of phase sequences (1972):

> cell-assemblies that are active at the same time become interconnected. Common events in the child's environment establish assemblies, and then when these events occur together the assemblies become connected (because they are active together). When the baby hears footsteps, let us say, an assembly is excited; while this is still active he sees a face and feels hands picking him up, which excites other assemblies—so the "footsteps assembly" becomes connected with the "face assembly" and the "being-picked-up assembly." After this has happened, when the baby hears footsteps only, *all three* assemblies are excited; the baby then has something like a perception of the mother's face and the contact of her hands before she has come in sight—but since the sensory stimulations have not yet taken place, this is ideation or imagery, not perception. (p. 67)

For Hebb, there are two kinds of learning. One involves the slow buildup of cell assemblies early in life. The buildup of cell assemblies can probably be explained by one of the S-R theories of learning, such as Guthrie's. This kind of learning is straight associationism. Likewise, the development of phase sequences can be explained using associationistic terminology. That is, objects and events that are related in the environment come to be related on the neurological level. After cell assemblies and phase sequences are developed, however, subsequent learning is more cognitive. Adult learning, for example, often characterized by insight and creativity, probably involves the rearrangement of phase sequences. Thus, Hebb maintains that the variables influencing childhood learning and those influencing adult learning are not the same. Childhood learning provides the framework for later learning. For example, learning a language is a slow, cumbersome process which probably involves the building up of millions of cell assemblies and phase sequences. However, once a language has been learned, an individual can rearrange it in any number of creative ways, perhaps in the form of poetry or a novel. But, says Hebb, first come the building blocks and then comes the insight and creativity which characterize adult learning.

SENSORY DEPRIVATION

We have already seen that restricting the early sensory experience of an organism severely retards its perceptual, intellectual, and emotional development. Hebb's explanation for this is that curtailed sensory experience limits the organism's capacity to develop cell assemblies and phase sequences which are the building blocks of all cognitive activity.

It has been well established that restricted sensory experience inhibits the development of neurophysiological networks which represent objects and events in the environment. But what happens if sensory experience is restricted *after* normal neurophysiological development has already taken place? A series of experiments were run at McGill University under Hebb's supervision to answer this question. In one of these experiments (Heron, 1957) a group of college students were paid 20 dollars a day *to do nothing*. They had only to lie on a comfortable bed with their eyes covered by translucent plastic which permitted them to see diffuse light but not to recognize objects. A constant buzzing sound was transmitted to the subjects through earphones. To further inhibit auditory perception, air-conditioning equipment hummed monotonously in the background. The subjects wore cotton gloves and cardboard cuffs, which extended over their fingertips, to minimize tactile stimulation. These conditions prevailed for almost 24 hours a day and were interrupted only when the subject ate or needed to go to the washroom. This experimental arrangement is shown in Figure 15–1.

Figure 15–1.   An experimental participant in Heron's sensory deprivation experiment. (From "The Pathology of Boredom," by W. Heron, 1957, January, *Scientific American*, p. 53. Copyright © 1957 by Scientific American, Inc. All rights reserved.)

Most subjects could stand the conditions for only two or three days (the longest was six). The subjects typically became irritable and almost childlike in their limited interactions with the experimenter. Much to the surprise of Hebb and his co-workers, **sensory deprivation** produced an effect far beyond simple boredom. Hebb and Donderi (1987) summarize the results of the Heron experiment as follows:

> The experiment showed that humans can be bored, which we knew, but it showed too that boredom is too mild a word for some of the effects of sensory deprivation. The need for the normal stimulation of a varied environment is fundamental. Without it, mental functioning and personality deteriorate. The subjects in isolation complained of being unable to think coherently, they became less able to solve simple problems, and they began to have hallucinations. Some of them saw such things as rows of little men wearing black caps, squirrels marching with sacks over their shoulders, or prehistoric animals in the jungle. These scenes were described as being like animated cartoons. More fundamentally disturbing were somesthetic hallucinations, when a subject perceived two bodies somesthetically or felt as if his head were detached from his body . . . The subjects' very identity had begun to disintegrate.

Later studies have shown that when the conditions of sensory deprivation are made even more severe, subjects can stand them for only a very short period of time. For example, when subjects are immersed in water (breathing through a snorkle tube) in complete darkness, they typically can last no more than a few hours before terminating their involvement in the experiment (see Zubek, 1969).

Hebb concludes from this research that not only is sensory experience necessary for proper neurophysiological development, but it is also necessary for the maintenance of normal functioning. In other words, once the consistent events in one's life are represented neurophysiologically in the form of cell assemblies and phase sequences, they must go on being coordinated with environmental events. If the sensory events that ordinarily occur in one's life do not occur, one experiences stress, fear, or disorientation. So, not only do consistent environmental events give rise to certain neurological circuits, but those same events must go on supporting those circuits. Thus, to the various needs that organisms have, such as the need for food, water, sex, and oxygen, Hebb adds the need for stimulation. As this section indicates, even if all of one's other needs are satisfied, if one does not experience normal stimulation, severe cognitive disorientation results.

ENRICHED ENVIRONMENTS

If sensory deprivation causes a disruption either in development or in normal functioning, is it possible that a rich sensory environment could enhance development? The answer to this question seems to be yes.

Hebb (1949, pp. 298–299) ran what was probably the first experiment designed to investigate the effects of different kinds of rearing conditions on intellectual development. Two groups of rats were involved, one was reared in cages in Hebb's laboratory, the other was reared in Hebb's home by his two daughters. Rats in the latter group spent considerable time roaming around the house, presumably playing with Hebb's children. After several weeks, the "pet" rats were returned to the laboratory and compared to the cage-reared rats. It was found that the performance of the "pet" rats on a series of detour/maze problems was consistently superior to that of the rats reared in the laboratory.

Numerous studies have supported Hebb's early research. For example, a series of experiments run at the University of California by Rosenzweig, Krech, Bennett, and their colleagues have confirmed the fact that rats reared in an **enriched environment** are faster learners than their littermates raised in relative isolation. In this research, the enriched environment consisted of a large cage containing other rats and numerous toy-like objects (see Figure 15-2). Control animals were reared alone in cages which contained no objects.

Hebb's explanation of these findings is straightforward. The greater sensory diversity provided by the enriched environment allowed the animals to build up a larger number of cell assemblies and more complex phase sequences. Once developed, these neural circuits could be utilized in new learning. Because of their more

Figure 15–2. Animals being reared in an enriched environment. (From "Chemical and Anatomical Plasticity of the Brain," by E. L. Bennett, M. C. Diamond, D. Krech, & M. R. Rosenzweig, 1964, *Science, 146,* p. 611. Copyright © 1964 by the American Association for the Advancement of Science.)

austere sensory experiences, control animals had less complex neural circuitry and were therefore inferior problem solvers. The implications of this research for education and child-rearing seem rather clear; the more complex the early sensory environment, the better are the later problem-solving skills.

Are the effects of an impoverished early environment permanent? According to the research of Rosenzweig and his colleagues, apparently not. It was found that the effects of an impoverished sensory environment could be reversed with relative ease by merely placing the animals reared in an impoverished environment in an enriched environment for only a few hours a day. Thus, the damage done by a restricted early environment can be undone if conditions change for the better. In other words, there does not appear to be a critical developmental stage beyond which the damage caused by a restricted sensory environment early in life cannot be remedied.

THE NATURE OF FEAR

While at the Yerkes Laboratories of Primate Biology, Hebb investigated the sources of **fear** in chimpanzees. He exposed his subjects to a wide variety of test objects, for example, a plaster cast of a chimpanzee's head, a doll representing a human infant, a lifelike full-sized human head from a window-display dummy, and an anesthetized infant chimpanzee.

Hebb observed that chimpanzees showed no sign of fear until they were about four months old. After that age, his subjects showed no fear of objects that were completely familiar or completely unfamiliar to them. *It was only when familiar objects were shown in unfamiliar ways that fear was expressed.* For example, whole chimpanzee or human bodies elicited no fear, whereas models of parts of chimpanzee or human bodies did so. Two examples of fear-producing objects are shown in Figure 15-3.

Hebb felt the spontaneity of the fear he observed ruled out an explanation in terms of conditioned responses. Such an explanation would stress repeated pairings of neural objects (e.g., a model of a chimpanzee's head) with an aversive stimulus. Fear developed in this way would develop slowly from experience. This was not the case in the fear that Hebb observed. Rather, the fear response was exhibited at full strength the first time an object was shown to a subject. Hebb's explanation was in terms of cell assemblies and phase sequences. If a completely unfamiliar object is shown to an organism, no cell assembly would have been developed corresponding to that object. With repeated exposures such an assembly would gradually develop. No fear is involved. Likewise, if a familiar object is shown to an organism, the neural circuits that developed from prior experience with that object would be activated and there would be no disruption in behavior. It is only when an object triggers an existing cell assembly or phase sequence and is subsequently not followed by the events that normally accompany the object that fear is elicited. An anesthetized chimpanzee, for example, will trigger the phase sequence associated with the sight of a chimpanzee, but the events that ordinarily follow such a perception do not follow. Instead of the typical responses and sounds made by a chim-

Figure 15–3. Objects that were found to cause fear in chimpanzees. (From *Textbook of Psychology*, 4th ed., p. 246, by D. O. Hebb & D. C. Donderi, 1987, Philadelphia, PA: W. B. Saunders. Copyright © 1958, 1966, 1972 by W. B. Saunders Company. Reprinted by permission of Holt, Rinehart & Winston.)

panzee, there is no movement and there is silence. Thus, a phase sequence was triggered but was not supported by the sensory events that caused the development of the phase sequence to begin with. It is this lack of sensory support that, according to Hebb, causes fear. Hebb explains the human reaction to dead or mutilated bodies in the same way.

Hebb (1946) reached the following conclusion about fear: "Fear occurs when an object is seen which is like familiar objects in enough respects to arouse habitual processes of perception, but in other respects arouses incompatible processes" (p. 268).

Hebb's explanation of fear helps to explain the traumatic nature of sensory deprivation. When adult humans are placed in a sensory deprivation situation, they are well endowed with cell assemblies and phase sequences which may be triggered by internal stimulation, external stimulation, or a combination of the two. In the sensory deprivation situation, however, no sensory support for any neural activity is available. Thus, various neural circuits are triggered but are not followed by the sensory events which normally accompany them. Under these circumstances, it is not surprising to find the subjects experiencing a feeling of disorientation and fear.

It is interesting to speculate on the relationship between incompatible neural activities and humor. One longstanding theory of humor says that for something to be funny it must cause anxiety. For example, there is nothing funny about a man in a tuxedo, nor is there anything funny about a swimming pool, but Hollywood has known for years that a man clad in a tuxedo falling into a swimming pool is funny. Apparently the scene is anxiety-provoking enough to be humorous, but why? It seems that Hebb's incompatibility of neural circuits explanation of fear would also apply to this situation. The man wearing the tuxedo triggers one group of cells and the swimming pool another, but the two groups firing together causes conflict, and therefore, fear or anxiety. Perhaps it is the recognition that the situation is a safe one that allows the mild fear to be expressed in laughter.

AROUSAL THEORY

We have seen that when normal humans experience sensory deprivation their cognitive functioning is disrupted, but what about *too much* sensory stimulation? We have all been in situations where, because of too much noise or commotion, we have not been able to think clearly. This suggests that a level of stimulation that is not too low nor too high would result in optimal cognitive functioning. Hebb explores this relationship between level of stimulation and cognitive functioning within the context of **arousal theory.**

Arousal theory involves the functioning of the **reticular activating system (RAS),** an area about the size of a finger which is located in the brain stem just above the spinal cord and just below the thalamus and hypothalamus. The RAS has been found to be involved in the processes of sleep, attention, and emotional behavior.

According to Hebb (1955), a neural impulse generated by the stimulation of a sense receptor has two functions. One function is referred to as the **cue function.** The sensory stimulus causes an impulse to travel from the sense receptor, up the sensory tract of the spinal cord, to various projection areas, and finally to some area of the cortex. This function of a stimulus allows the organism to gain information about the environment.

The second function of a sensory impulse is its **arousal function.** It has been found that there are collaterals that spill off the sensory track of the spinal cord into the RAS. As sensory information is on its way to the cortex, it influences the RAS through these collaterals and causes it to increase its activity. This tendency for sensory impulses to increase activity in the RAS is referred to as the arousal function of a stimulus.

Amount of activity in the RAS is used as an index of arousal; the greater the amount of RAS activity, the higher the level of arousal. The **electroencephalogram (EEG)** is generally accepted as a measure of arousal and is therefore thought to reflect RAS activity. A very slow EEG pattern indicates sleep. This also indicates a period of relative inactivity in the RAS. The EEG pattern of a very relaxed person is characterized by rhythmic waves of about 8 to 10 cycles per second, and the excited person shows very fast brain wave activity, or relatively high arousal.

It is generally believed that the RAS stimulates the cortex and thus creates a background of electrical activity without which the cue function of an incoming sensory impulse would be lost. For a number of years, it was believed that the arousal function of a stimulus caused the RAS to bombard the entire cortex with nonspecific electrical activity. Now, however, it is believed that certain stimuli stimulate certain parts of the RAS to stimulate certain parts of the cortex. A visual stimulus, for instance, may cause the RAS to increase the electrical activity only in the occipital lobe of the brain. In general, what seems to happen is that the RAS prepares higher centers of the brain to receive and act upon information from the environment.

Hebb (1955) theorized about the relationship between arousal level and performance. He felt that for the cue function of a stimulus to have its full effect, there must be an **optimal level of arousal** provided by the RAS. When arousal level is too low, such as when the organism is asleep, sensory information transmitted to the brain cannot be utilized. Likewise, when arousal is too high, too much information is being analyzed by the cortex and often conflicting responses or irrelevant behavior results. This suggests that a level of arousal that is neither too high nor too low is necessary for optimal cortical functioning and therefore optimal performance. The proposed relationship between arousal level and performance is shown in Figure 15-4.

Hebb speculated that different tasks have different levels of arousal associated with their optimal performance. For example, a simple, well-practiced habit may be performed optimally across a wide range of arousal levels, whereas a highly skilled task may be performed optimally only within a minimal range of arousal levels. Gross behavioral skills may be performed best under extremely high arousal. The proposed relationship between optimal performance on various tasks and arousal level is seen in Figure 15-5.

Relationship Between Arousal Theory and Reinforcement Theory

According to Hebb, if arousal level is too high for the organism to attend to existing conditions optimally, it will operate on the environment in such a way as to reduce

Figure 15–4.   The relationship suggested by Hebb between arousal level and performance. (From *Textbook of Psychology*, 4th ed., p. 237, by D. O. Hebb & D. C. Donderi, 1987, Philadelphia, PA: W. B. Saunders. Reprinted by permission of Holt, Rinehart & Winston.)

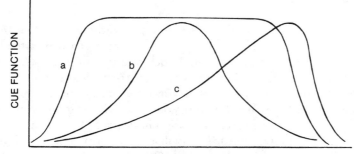

Figure 15–5. The relationship suggested by Hebb between arousal level and performance on three different kinds of tasks. Task a is a well-practiced habit such as giving one's name. Such a task is performed optimally over a wide range of arousal levels. Task b is a complex skill such as typing. Such a task is performed optimally only when arousal is neither too high nor too low. Task c is the kind of task that is relatively uncomplicated but requires the expenditure of a great deal of energy, such as weight-lifting or running a race. Such a task is performed optimally when arousal level is high. (From *Textbook of Psychology*, 4th ed., p. 237, by D. O. Hebb & D. C. Donderi, 1987, Philadelphia, PA: W. B. Saunders. Reprinted by permission of Holt, Rinehart & Winston.)

the arousal level. For example, if students are trying to study while people are talking and the television is on, they may have to tell the people to keep quiet and turn off the TV, or they will simply have to find an environment more compatible with studying. On the other hand, if it is too quiet and there is not enough sensory input to maintain an optimal level of arousal, the students may turn on the radio, talk out loud, or perform some kind of motor task such as fidgeting or rubbing their feet together. Generally speaking, when arousal level is too high, decreasing it is reinforcing, and when the arousal level is too low, increasing it is reinforcing. Unlike Hull's theory, which equates drive reduction with reinforcement, Hebb's theory equates reinforcement with either an increase or decrease in drive, depending on the circumstances. According to Hebb, seeking excitement is a significant motive in human behavior. He says (1955):

> When you stop to think of it, it is nothing short of extraordinary what trouble people will go to in order to get into more trouble at the bridge table, or on the golf course; and the fascination of the murder story, or thriller, and the newspaper accounts of real-life adventure or tragedy, is no less extraordinary. This taste for excitement *must* not be forgotten when we are dealing with human motivation. It appears that, up to a certain point, threat and puzzle have positive motivating value, beyond that point negative value. (p. 250)

LONG-TERM AND SHORT-TERM MEMORY

Although Müller and Pilzecker originally suggested as early as 1900 that there are two distinct kinds of memory, the idea has just recently received wide attention. As we saw in the last chapter, it is now generally believed that there are two kinds of memory: **long-term memory** and **short-term memory.** (Short-term memory is also called either *immediate memory* or *primary memory;* long-term memory is also called *secondary memory*.) Short-term memory is triggered by sensory stimulation and continues for some time after the stimulation has ceased. Exactly how long the activity continues is not known, but it seems that the information stored in short-term memory is available for less than a minute. For example, Peterson and Peterson (1959) read their subjects a consonant trigram (e.g., *QHJ*) and then instructed them to immediately start counting backward by 3s or 4s from a 3-digit number they were given. Different subjects had their counting interrupted at different times and were asked to repeat the consonant trigram that was read to them. The recall intervals were 3, 6, 9, 12, 15, and 18 sec. It was found that the best retention was at a recall interval of 3 sec, with 6 sec next best, etc. The worst recall occurred after 18 sec. Thus, short-term memory seems to decay as a function of time, but its decay is much faster than that of long-term memory.

It is generally believed that sensory experience sets up neural activity that outlasts the stimulation that caused it. Hebb (1949) referred to this as **reverberating neural activity.** It appears that as long as the reverberating neural activity continues after an experience, the memory of that experience can be retrieved.

It is obvious that we retain some information much longer than a few seconds, so there must be some relationship between short-term memory and long-term memory. It is believed that long-term memories develop from short-term memories. Somehow, during the neural activity following an experience, long-term memories consolidate, or become fixed. The short-term memory, which involves continuous neural activity, somehow causes a structural change in the nervous system, which corresponds to the long-term or secondary memory. The contention that short-term memory is somehow translated into long-term memory is referred to as **consolidation theory.** Through the years, Hebb has been a major proponent of the consolidation theory of memory.

Since long-term memory is thought to depend on short-term memory, it follows that anything that disrupts short-term memory should also disrupt long-term memory. Based on this contention, Duncan (1949) trained rats to jump a barrier to avoid an electric shock. If they jumped from one side of an experimental chamber to the other side within 10 sec after they were placed in the apparatus, they could avoid being shocked. If they did not cross over to the "safe" side, they were shocked until they did. The animals were given one learning trial per day. Following each trial, each animal was given an **electroconvulsive shock** (ECS) through two electrodes clipped to the rat's ears. The ECS causes convulsions much like those of an epileptic seizure. Depending on what group the animal was in, the shock occurred 20 sec, 40 sec, 60 sec, 4 min, 15 min, 1 hr, 4 hr, or 14 hr after its learning trial. A control group received no ECS after learning. Training continued for 18 days.

Figure 15–6. The results of Duncan's study showing that as the delay between learning experience and an electroconvulsive shock becomes longer, the disruptive effect of the shock on the retention of the learning experience goes down. (From "The Retroactive Effect of Electroshock on Learning," by C. P. Duncan, 1949, *Journal of Comparative and Physiological Psychology, 42,* p. 35. Copyright © 1949 by the American Psychological Association. Reprinted by permission.)

Figure 15-6 shows the mean number of correct anticipations of the shock for all groups, that is, jumping to the safe side upon being placed in the apparatus.

It can be seen that the more closely the ECS followed a learning trial, the more it tended to disrupt the memory of the learning experience. For example, animals receiving ECS 20 sec after a learning trial continued being shocked—they never learned the avoidance response. When the ECS was administered within an hour of the learning trial, it interfered with memory. After an hour, ECS apparently had no effect on memory. The animals receiving ECS an hour or more after their learning trial performed as well as the control group that received no ECS. The results of Duncan's experiment lent support to consolidation theory and suggests that the consolidation period lasts about an hour. However, the moments immediately following a learning experience seem to be more important for consolidation than those after about the first minute.

Further evidence is provided for consolidation theory by the phenomenon called **retrograde amnesia.** Retrograde amnesia refers to the loss of memory for those events just prior to a traumatic experience, such as an automobile accident or a combat injury. This memory loss for events prior to a traumatic event may involve hours, days, or even months. Usually the memory of such events will slowly return except for those immediately prior to the traumatic event. It is assumed that the traumatic event had the same effect as Duncan's ECS; that is, it interfered with the reverberating neural activity that is necessary for consolidation to take place, thereby making long-term memory impossible.

Consolidation and the Brain

A number of interrelated brain structures, collectively referred to as the **limbic system,** are believed to be important for the experience of various emotions. One of these limbic structures is the **hippocampus.** Peter Milner, one of Hebb's students at McGill University, found that patients with their hippocampus destroyed have no trouble recalling events that took place before the destruction of their hippocampus, but it is impossible for them to form new long-term memories (B. Milner, 1965). Such patients perform well on intelligence tests and do very well on motor skills that were acquired before the damage to their hippocampus. Also, Milner reports no apparent personality change resulting from the brain damage. The remarkable thing about such patients is that they simply cannot retain any new information. As soon as their attention is distracted from an experience, the memory of it is lost. Such individuals look as if their short-term memory is functioning normally but their long-term memory is not.

Milner speculates that in the early stages of learning, there is an interplay between the sensory input, the hippocampus, and the cortex. Through this interrelated activity, the information finally comes to be stored in the cortex as long-term memory. The hippocampus is thus believed to be responsible for consolidation.

Our overview of Hebb's theoretical contributions is now complete. Hopefully, the reader has recognized the fact that Hebb has opened lines of investigation in psychology that were previously ignored or did not exist. We agree with Bugelski's evaluation of Hebb's influence on psychology:

> Hebb's book, *The Organization of Behavior* (1949), marked a revolution in psychology. Psychologists began to learn about the reticular formation and its controlling operations; they began to appreciate the constant activity of the brain with or without external stimulus inputs; they were forced to recognize what Hebb described as "spontaneous neural firing" in his description of the nature of neuronal activity. It became possible for psychologists to entertain the notion that someone might do something or think of something without an external energy activating a chain of neural discharges. Psychologists, at least some of them, took a "new look" at the nervous system. What they saw was that there was not only a switchboard but an exchange center, where operators took time off on occasion, went "on strike," made wrong connections, frequently had busy lines, overloaded lines, or no lines at all for some calls, and where, on occasion, calls went out that nobody made. (1979, p. 59)

Hebb was one of the first to search for the neurophysiological correlates of psychological phenomena, such as learning. Due to a large extent to Hebb's efforts, physiological psychology is very popular today and has expanded into many areas beyond those studied by Hebb and his students. It would not be appropriate in a book such as this one to review the many fruitful lines of inquiry currently occurring within the neurophysiological paradigm. What follows, however, represents a sample of such research. The first topic, "Reinforcement Centers in the Brain," is indirectly related to Hebb's theory since it grew out of an accidental discovery made in Hebb's laboratory while the reticular activating system was being studied. The next three topics, "Research on the Split Brain," "Left–Brain, Right-Brain Learning and Information Processing," and "Visceral Conditioning" are not related to Hebb's theory but are offered as further examples of research taking place within the neurophysiological paradigm on the learning process.

FURTHER EXAMPLES OF NEUROPHYSIOLOGICAL RESEARCH ON LEARNING

Reinforcement Centers in the Brain

In the chapter on Pavlov, we noted that his discovery of the conditioned reflex was quite accidental. **Serendipity,** the finding of one thing while looking for another, has led to the discovery of important phenomena whose investigations sometimes resulted in scientific breakthroughs. Another example of serendipity in science is the discovery of **reinforcement centers in the brain** by Olds and P. Milner (1954). Olds, who was working in Hebb's laboratory at McGill University, describes how the discovery was made (1955):

> In the fall of 1953, we were looking for more information about the reticular activating system. We used electrodes permanently implanted in the brain of a healthy behaving rat. . . . Quite by accident, an electrode was implanted in the region of the anterior commissure.
> The result was quite amazing. When the animal was stimulated at a

James Olds. (Courtesy of James Olds)

specific place in an open field, he sometimes moved away but he returned and sniffed around that area. More stimulations at that place caused him to spend more of his time there.

Later we found that this same animal could be "pulled" to any spot in the maze by giving a small electrical stimulus *after* each response in the right direction. This was akin to playing the "hot" and "cold" game with a child. Each correct response brought electrical pulses which seemed to indicate to the animal that it was on the right track. (pp. 83–84)

Since Olds and P. Milner's accidental discovery of reinforcement centers in rats, reinforcement centers have been found in cats, dogs, goldfish, monkeys, porpoises, pigeons, and humans. When a human being's reinforcement center is stimulated, the person sometimes reports erotic sensations and thoughts, or simply a feeling of pleasure.

Olds and Milner originally felt that the septal region of the brain housed most of the reinforcement centers. Since then, however, such centers have been found scattered throughout the limbic system of the brain. The limbic system, which is involved in motivated and emotional behavior, contains part of the lower cortex, the hippocampus, the amygdala, the septum, and parts of the thalamus and hypothalamus.

These brain areas are called reinforcement centers because when they are stimulated, the animal tends to repeat what it was doing before the stimulation. Because of this, an animal with an electrode implanted in a reinforcement center can be trained to run a maze or to press a bar in a Skinner box simply by stimulating that area of the brain with a mild electrical current when the animal performs the appropriate response.

Reinforcement by direct brain stimulation, however, has been found to have some unusual characteristics and is therefore thought to operate differently from the more traditional reinforcers such as food or water. The unusual characteristics of reinforcement by direct brain stimulation are summarized below:

1. **No Deprivation Needed Before Training.** Unlike training involving the use of food or water as a reinforcer, generally no deprivation schedule is needed when direct brain stimulation is used as a reinforcer. The animal does not need to be in a "drive state." There are exceptions to this, however, and occasionally reinforcement centers are found that do seem to be dependent on the drive state of the organism. For example, it has been found that the stimulation of some brain sites is reinforcing only if the animal is hungry; stimulation of other sites is reinforcing only if the animal is thirsty, and still others if it is sexually aroused.

2. **Satiation Does Not Occur.** When food or water is used as a reinforcer, the animal will eventually satiate; that is, its need for food or water will be satisfied and it will stop responding. With direct brain stimulation, however, the animal will go on responding at an extraordinarily high rate (for example, bar-press rates as high as 7000 per hr have been reported) until it becomes physically exhausted.

3. **Takes Priority Over Other Drives.** Animals continue to press a bar for direct brain stimulation even when food is available and they have not eaten for a considerable length of time. Also, animals will often withstand a greater shock in order to obtain brain stimulation to a reinforcement center than to obtain food even if they have not eaten for 24 hr.

4. **Rapid Extinction.** Although rate of responding is extremely high, as long as the animal is being reinforced by brain stimulation, it stops responding very rapidly when the brain stimulation stops. In other words, rather than the gradual extinction process observed when food or water are the reinforcers, extinction takes place almost immediately when direct brain stimulation reinforcement is terminated. Although extinction is rapid, response rate reoccurs at full strength when the animal is again reinforced.

5. **Most Schedules of Reinforcement Do Not Work.** Since extinction occurs very rapidly when brain stimulation is terminated, any schedule of reinforcement that produces some amount of delay between responding and reinforcement will cause the animal to stop responding. Cats, for example, will stop responding if the delay between a response and a reinforcer is longer than about 15 sec. Therefore, only schedules of reinforcement that provide frequent reinforcement can be used with direct brain stimulation.

As yet, these observations about the reinforcing effects of direct brain stimulation have not been explained in a way that is widely accepted by researchers in the field. The situation is complicated further by the fact that **punishment areas** are often found only millimeters away from a reinforcement area. An animal will quickly learn to perform a response that terminates stimulation to such an area, or will learn a response that prevents it from occurring. Humans receiving stimulation in a punishment area report feelings of anxiety or panic.

RESEARCH ON THE SPLIT BRAIN

The **corpus callosum** is a large mass of fibers that connects the two halves of the cortex. For years, the function of the corpus callosum was unknown, but recently it has been found to be instrumental in transferring information from one side of the cortex to the other. In a series of experiments, Sperry (1961) attempted to determine under what circumstances information is transferred from one side of the cortex to the other. He noted that there were two possible routes for such transfer—the corpus callosum and the optic chiasm. The optic chiasm is the point in the optic nerve where information coming from one eye is projected to the side of the cortex opposite to that eye. Realizing this, Sperry taught intact cats to make a visual discrimination with a patch over one eye. Following discrimination training, he tested for transfer by switching the patch from one eye to the other, and found that the animal was able to perform just as well with either eye. In other words, complete interocular transfer was found.

Now Sperry began a search for the mechanism by which information was transferred from one side of the brain to the other. His first step was to ablate (cut)

Roger W. Sperry. (Photo by Ronald Meyer)

the optic chiasm, both before and after training, and again he found complete transfer of training from one eye to the other. Next, in addition to ablating the optic chiasm, he ablated the corpus callosum *after* the discrimination training, and again he found no interference with the transfer of information from one eye to the other. His next step was to ablate *both* the optic chiasm and the corpus callosum *before* training and he found that such a preparation prevented transfer from one eye to the other. Cutting both the optic chiasm and the corpus callosum created two separate brains with one eye going to each, and with no exchange of information between them. Sperry's split-brain preparation is seen in Figure 15-7.

When the cat's brain was split, as shown in Figure 15-7, and the cat was taught to make a visual discrimination with a patch over one eye, it had no recollection of that learning when tested with the other eye. The two halves of the split brain appeared to learn independently. In fact, with a patch over one eye, the animal could be taught to do one thing, such as approach a door with a cross on it, and with a patch over the other eye, it could be taught to approach the adjoining door with a circle on it; thus the two brains in the same skull have learned contradictory habits. It is also possible to teach an animal to approach a stimulus (e.g., a circle) with a patch over one eye, and to avoid the same stimulus with a patch over the other eye.

For various medical reasons, Sperry's split-brain procedure has been used on humans. In addition to being effective in treating brain abnormalities, the procedure has been instrumental in providing information about how the left and right hemispheres differ in the way they process information. It is to the differences between left and right brain functioning that we turn next.

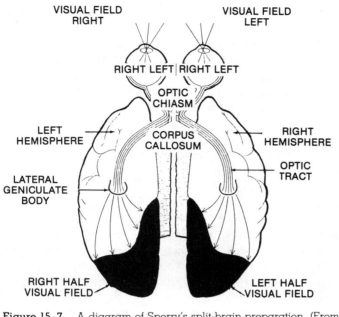

Figure 15–7. A diagram of Sperry's split-brain preparation. (From "The Great Cerebral Commissure," by R. W. Sperry, 1964, January, *Scientific American*, p. 46. Copyright © 1964 by Scientific American, Inc. All rights reserved.)

LEFT-BRAIN, RIGHT-BRAIN LEARNING AND INFORMATION PROCESSING

Anatomically the cerebral cortex is bilaterally symmetrical. That is, one hemisphere appears to be physically the same as the other. Furthermore, control over the body's movement and sensation is divided evenly between the two cerebral hemispheres, but this is done in a crossed fashion. That is, the left hemisphere controls the right side of the body and the right hemisphere controls the left side. Anatomically, then, it appears that we actually have two brains just as we have two eyes, two ears, two kidneys, two nostrils, and so forth. It is tempting to conclude that because the two hemispheres are physically similar that they are also similar in function. But is this the case? The question as to whether or not the two hemispheres are functionally symmetrical was not easy to answer.

Among the first to find evidence that the two hemispheres were not functionally symmetrical was a little known medical doctor named Marc Dax. In 1836, Dax reported that loss of speech resulted from damage to the left cerebral hemisphere but not to the right. Dax's observation was essentially ignored until, 25 years later, the prominent physician Paul Broca made the same observation. In 1861, Broca did an autopsy on a man whose only disorder, before he died, was that he was unable to speak. Upon examining the man's cortex, the only damage Broca could find was a lesion in the left hemisphere. Broca correctly assumed that the lesion was responsible for the man's inability to speak and, thereafter, the cortical area in which the lesion was found was referred to as *Broca's Area*. The finding that a speech area exists on the left hemisphere but not on the right provided the first scientific evidence that the two cerebral hemispheres were asymmetrical in function.

It was now clear that the left cerebral hemisphere was involved with speech, but what was the function of the right hemisphere? Since nothing as dramatic as the loss of speech resulted from damage to the right hemisphere, it was assumed for many years that the right hemisphere was inferior to the left. The left hemisphere, therefore, was called the dominant or superior hemisphere. It was not until recently that evidence was provided that necessitated a radical change in beliefs concerning the function of the right cerebral hemisphere. In 1962, a series of reports by such individuals as Mountcastle, Geschwind, Kaplan, Sperry, and Gazzaniga, showed that the right hemisphere was not only equal in importance to the left hemisphere, but for certain nonverbal functions it was actually superior. Evidence that the two cerebral hemispheres are asymmetrical in their functioning has been provided by individuals with brain damage, individuals who for medical reasons have had their cortex surgically divided and, by using ingenious experimental apparatus, from individuals with normal, intact brains.

It has been found that individuals with damage to their right hemispheres are likely to display difficulties related to attention or perception. For example, individuals with right-brain damage are likely to be disoriented in even familiar surroundings and have difficulty recognizing familiar faces and objects. Also, unlike individuals with left-brain damage, individuals with right-brain damage are likely to display the **neglect syndrome.** The neglect syndrome involves either not seeing or not paying attention to the left visual field or even to the left side of the body. Individuals displaying the neglect syndrome have been known to shave only the right half of their face or eat food only off of the right side of a plate. When patients with right hemisphere damage are asked to reproduce pictures placed in front of them, the results are often like those shown in Figure 15-8.

The fact that the neglect syndrome results from damage to the right hemisphere but not to the left was taken as further evidence that the two cerebral hemispheres function differently.

Recent interest in how the two cortical hemispheres function has been stimulated by the existence of patients who for medical reasons have had the cortical pathways connecting the two hemispheres severed. For example, it has been found that severing the corpus callosum of patients suffering otherwise intractable epilepsy confines abnormal electrical discharge to only one cerebral hemisphere and thereby reduces the frequency and severity of seizures. Except for periodic seizures these split-brain patients function normally. It is possible, however, to use such patients to study how the cerebral hemispheres function separately. There are now several techniques that can be used to present sensory information to just one hemisphere at a time. No matter which technique is used, however, the findings are rather consistent. Springer and Deutsch (1985) summarize these findings: "The left hemisphere has been found to be predominantly involved with analytic processes, es-

Model   **Patient's Copy**

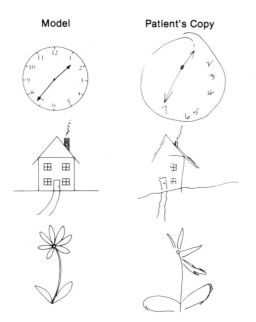

Figure 15–8. Attempts of a patient with right-brain damage to copy drawings of various objects. The incomplete copies exemplify the neglect syndrome. (From *Left Brain, Right Brain*, rev. ed., p. 160, by S. P. Springer & G. Deutsch, 1985, San Francisco: W. H. Freeman and Company. Copyright © 1981, 1985. Reprinted with the permission of W. H. Freeman and Company.)

pecially the production and understanding of language, and it appears to process input in a sequential manner. The right hemisphere appears to be responsible for certain spatial skills and musical abilities and to process information simultaneously and holistically" (pp. 4–5).

Hemispheric Functioning in Normal Brains

On the basis of the study of brain-damaged individuals and those that had their brains surgically split for medical reasons, it was clear that each hemisphere of the brain could perceive, learn, remember, and feel independently of the other hemisphere. The question next became whether or not findings from research on damaged or surgically prepared brains could be generalized to the functioning of normal brains. To answer the question a number of techniques have been developed that allow hemispheric functioning to be investigated using normal, intact brains. For example, EEG recordings can be taken from each cerebral hemisphere separately. When the brain is resting, it is characterized by a slow EEG pattern called alpha rhythms. When the brain is active, the alpha rhythms are blocked and are replaced by much faster EEG patterns. Using EEG recordings, Ornstein (1978) found that the alpha rhythms of the left hemisphere are blocked when a subject is presented problems that require verbal, mathematical, or analytic solutions. The alpha rhythms of the right hemisphere are blocked when the subject is presented with spatial, perceptual, and other nonverbal problems.

Another method used to determine how the two cerebral hemispheres function in individuals with normal, intact brains is **dichotic listening.** Although dichotic listening was used earlier by Broadbent to study selective attention, it was

Doreen Kimura (1961, 1967) who used it as a safe and reliable method of studying cerebral asymmetry in normal subjects. The dichotic listening technique involves sending competing information, such as pairs of syllables or digits, to the left and right ears simultaneously through stereo headphones. For example, the syllable "ba" might be presented to the subject's left ear and the syllable "ga" might be presented to his or her right ear at the same time. Keeping in mind that information presented to the left ear is projected mainly onto the right hemisphere and information presented to the right ear is projected mainly onto the left hemisphere, the question is which of the two simultaneously presented syllables or digits will be reported accurately. Under the circumstances just described, nearly all right-handers and most left-handers accurately report the digits or syllables presented to their right ears more often than those presented to their left ears. Thus, the contention that, in most humans, it is the left hemisphere that is responsible for processing verbal information was again confirmed.

Some have argued that instead of concluding from dichotic listening research that the left hemisphere is specialized for speech perception, it is more accurate to conclude that it is specialized for auditory perception in general or for general attention. However, the fact that most normal right-handers perceive melodies (Kimura, 1964) and environmental sounds such as dogs barking and automobile engines (Curry, 1967) better with their left ears (right hemispheres) does not support such an argument.

Considering the evidence gathered from all available sources, the views of hemispheric functioning that we are left with is as follows:

Left Hemisphere	**Right Hemisphere**
Verbal	Nonverbal
Logical, analytical	Synthetic
Rational	Intuitive
Objective	Subjective

Speculations

Once the functioning of the two hemispheres was established, a great deal of speculation began concerning what cerebral asymmetry means in everyday life. Springer and Deutsch (1985) describe some of these speculations:

> It has been claimed that these differences clearly show the traditional dualisms of intellect versus intuition, science versus art, and the logical versus the mysterious. . . . It has also been suggested that lawyers and artists use different halves of the brain in their work and that the differences between the halves show up in activities not related to their work. Others have extended this idea further and have claimed that everyone may be classified as a right-hemisphere person or a left-hemisphere person, depending on which hemisphere guides the bulk of an individual's behavior. (p. 6)

Bogen (1977) suggests that the dichotomous ways in which the world or thought processes are often described reflect the two kinds of hemispheric intelligence. According to Bogen, dichotomies such as those listed below are but manifestations of how the left and right brains process information (from Bogen, 1977, p. 135):

Left Hemisphere	Right Hemisphere
Intellect	Intuition
Convergent	Divergent
Realistic	Impulsive
Intellectual	Sensuous
Discrete	Continuous
Directed	Free
Rational	Intuitive
Historical	Timeless
Analytic	Holistic
Successive	Simultaneous
Objective	Subjective
Atomistic	Gross

Currently, there is lively debate over whether such dichotomies are simply convenient verbal labels that describe extremes of continuous phenomena or reflections of the ways that the two hemispheres process information.

The attempt to find dichotomies such as those listed above and then to explain their existence in terms of the ways the cerebral hemispheres process information has been called **dichotomania.** After reviewing the research on laterality, Beaton (1985) concluded that it is inappropriate to describe hemispheric functioning in terms of *any* dichotomies:

There are certain problems in attempting to encapsulate some "fundamental" hemispheric difference in terms of . . . dichotomies. In the first place, virtually all investigators are agreed that cerebral asymmetry is not absolute but a matter of degree. It has not been shown, for example, that one hemisphere is totally incapable of carrying out the functions normally ascribed to its partner. Even with regard to language, the area in which left-right asymmetry is most unequivocal, it is evident that the right hemisphere possesses considerable powers of comprehension and can, under certain circumstances, demonstrate some expressive ability . . . While it is a truism that the term "language" does not refer to a single function, it is also true that attempts to dichotomize left and right hemisphere functions presuppose some single organising principle. With regard to the verbal/non-verbal distinction this principle is clearly breached.

Other dichotomies are even less securely founded . . . Perhaps [then] the search for a dichotomy of function between the left and right hemispheres is bound to fail. There is, after all, no reason *why* the brain should have evolved so conveniently. Certainly, many of the phenomena of everyday life cannot be described as *either* analytic *or* holistic, temporal *or* spatial or whatever . . . Perhaps then, a single dichotomy of brain function is inherently improbable . . . It may, therefore, be profoundly misleading to assume that the relationship between the hemispheres as a whole can be described in terms of any single principle. (pp. 285–288)

Jerre Levy, a longtime researcher of left-brain, right-brain functioning, believes that although it is possible, under special circumstances, to demonstrate that the two hemispheres function differently, it is impossible to separate those functions in a normal, intact brain. In her article "Right Brain, Left Brain: Fact and Fiction" (1985), Levy says:

The two-brain myth was founded on an erroneous premise: that since each hemisphere was specialized, each must function as an independent brain. But, in fact, just the opposite is true. To the extent that regions are differentiated in the brain, they must integrate their activities. Indeed, it is precisely that integration that gives rise to behavior and mental processes greater than and different from each region's special contribution. Thus, since the central premise of the mythmakers is wrong, so are all the inferences derived from it . . . The popular myths are misinterpretations and wishes, not the observations of scientists. Normal people have not half a brain nor two brains but one gloriously differentiated brain, with each hemisphere contributing its specialized abilities . . . We have a single brain that generates a single mental self. (pp. 43–44)

Dichotomania persists, however, and it has spilled over into the realm of education. It is now widely believed that education in the Western world encourages left-brain functions and education in the Eastern world encourages right-brain functions. For example, Robert Ornstein (1978) says that because of the emphasis in our schools on left-brain functions:

Our intellectual training unduly emphasizes the analytic, with the result that we have learned to look at unconnected fragments instead of an entire solution. Perhaps when the history of the 20th century is written, it will be said that the overriding belief of its dominant cultures was an entity referred to as The Facts. All questions seemed to be resolved by an appeal to them.

As a result of this preoccupation with isolated facts, it is not surprising that we face so many simultaneous problems whose solutions depend upon our ability to grasp the relationship of parts to wholes. . . .

Split- and whole-brain studies have led to a new conception of human knowledge, consciousness, and intelligence. All knowledge cannot be expressed in words, yet our education is based almost exclusively on its written or spoken forms . . . Our schools offer an education for half our minds, and it is time to reinstate a balance. (pp. 82–83)

We will have more to say about the implications of left-brain, right-brain research for education in the next chapter.

There is no doubt that research on cerebral laterality has led to exciting discoveries and it will continue to do so. However, since such discoveries tend to stimulate the imagination, it is important to concentrate on the actual research data so that the distinction between fact and fantasy will not be blurred.

VISCERAL CONDITIONING

Current research has indicated that individuals can control their own internal environment. For example, it has been found that individuals can control their own heart rate, blood pressure, and skin temperature. Until recently, it was believed that operant conditioning was possible only for responses that involve the skeletal or striped muscles and that responses involving the smooth muscles and glands could not be operantly conditioned. The smooth muscles and glands are controlled by the autonomic nervous system and, generally, it was believed that responses mediated by the autonomic nervous system could not be operantly conditioned.

To demonstrate that autonomic responses could be operantly conditioned, Miller and Carmona (1967) gave one group of thirsty dogs water whenever they salivated spontaneously. Another group of thirsty dogs was given water for going for long intervals of time without salivating. The rate of salivation went up for the former group and down for the latter group. Thus, it was demonstrated that sali-

Neal E. Miller. (Courtesy of Neal Miller)

vation, which is governed by the autonomic nervous system, was modifiable through operant conditioning procedures.

In other studies, Miller has taught curarized rats to raise or lower their heart rate, to raise or lower their blood pressure, to modify the functioning of their kidneys, and even to vary the amount of blood in their left and right ears. Curare is a drug that paralyzes the skeletal muscles so their involvement could not have been a factor in this research. Miller used direct stimulation of the reinforcement areas of the brain as reinforcement for his curarized animals.

Shapiro, Tursky, Gerson, and Stern (1969) taught 20 male college students to raise or lower their blood pressure by showing them a picture of a nude female from *Playboy* magazine whenever the student's blood pressure was altered in the direction desired by the experimenter. At the conclusion of the experiment, the students, with only two exceptions, were unaware of the fact that their blood pressure had been systematically altered by the experimenter.

In other studies, heart patients have been taught to control their cardiac abnormalities, epileptics have learned to suppress abnormal brain activity, and individuals suffering from migraine headaches have learned to avoid them by controlling the degree of dilatation of blood vessels surrounding the brain. In cases such as these, a device is used to display to the patients the changes in the internal events that they are trying to control, for example, high blood pressure or irregular heart activity. Such a display is called **biofeedback** because it provides the patient with information about some internal biological event. Usually after monitoring the biofeedback for a period of time, the patients become aware of their internal state and can respond accordingly—either raise or lower their blood pressure—without the aid of biofeedback. Obviously, this whole area of research, sometimes called **visceral conditioning,** has vast implications for the practice of medicine in the future. For a more detailed review of visceral conditioning research see DiCara, 1970; Jonas, 1973; Kimmel, 1974; and Miller, 1969.

SUMMARY

After a shaky academic start, Hebb entered graduate school at McGill University where he was trained in the Pavlovian tradition. He became disenchanted with Pavlov when he read about Gestalt psychology and Lashley's work on the brain. At the University of Chicago, while working with Lashley, Hebb was convinced that the brain did not work as a complex switchboard, as the behaviorists and associationists maintained; rather, it worked as an interrelated whole. This Gestalt conception of the brain was further reinforced when Hebb, while working with Wilder Penfield, observed that large areas of the human brain could be removed without any apparent loss in intellectual functioning.

Hebb's major theoretical terms are cell assembly and phase sequence. A cell assembly is the neural package that is associated with an environmental object. If this neural package is stimulated in the absence of the object with which it is associated, an idea of the object is experienced. A phase sequence is a series of interrelated cell assemblies. If a series of events typically occur together in the environment, they become represented on the neural level as a phase sequence. The stimulation of phase sequence causes a flow of related ideas. For Hebb there are two kinds of learning. First, there is the slow buildup of cell assemblies and phase sequences early in life. Second, there is the more insightful kind of learning that characterizes adult life. Adult learning involves the rearrangement of cell assemblies and phase sequences rather than their development.

Sensory deprivation disrupts normal cognitive functioning because it interferes with the relationship between neural circuits and environmental events. Results of sensory deprivation studies show that organisms need normal stimulation just as they need food, water, and oxygen. Research indicates that animals reared in enriched sensory environments are subsequently better learners than animals reared in relatively simple sensory environments. Hebb's explanation for this is that animals reared in enriched environments develop more complex neural circuitry which, later, can be applied to new learning.

While studying fear, Hebb discovered that chimpanzees were not frightened of either completely familiar or completely unfamiliar objects. What did frighten the chimpanzees was presenting a familiar object in an unfamiliar way. Hebb's explanation for this was that a familiar object triggered the neural circuits associated with it, but then subsequent events did not support or confirm those neural circuits, thus a conflict occurred which stimulated fear. This could also explain why sensory deprivation is so disabling.

Arousal theory states that an environmental cue has two functions: (a) a cue function which conveys information about the environment; and (b) an arousal function which stimulates the reticular activating system (RAS). To allow optimal intellectual functioning, arousal must be neither too high nor too low. If arousal is too low for the optimal performance of a given task, anything that increases it is reinforcing; if arousal is too high for the optimal performance of a certain task, anything that decreases it is reinforcing.

Hebb believes that there are two kinds of memory—short-term memory and long-term memory. Short-term memory lasts less than a minute and is associated with the reverberating neural activity caused by an environmental event. If an experience is repeated often enough, it is stored in the long-term memory. The process whereby a short-term memory is converted into long-term memory is called consolidation. If a traumatic experience occurs during the consolidation period, short-term memory is prevented from being transferred into long-term memory. Research indicates that the entire consolidation period lasts about an hour. A brain structure that appears vital for consolidation is the hippocampus.

While Olds and P. Milner were doing research in Hebb's laboratory on the arousal system, they accidentally discovered reinforcement centers in the brain. By stimulating these centers they were able to shape a variety of behavioral patterns. Reinforcement via brain stimulation was found to have several unusual characteristics: (a) no deprivation is needed for it to be effective; (b) the animal does not seem to be able to get enough of it; (c) it takes priority over other drives; (d) behavior maintained by it extinguishes very rapidly; and (e) most schedules of reinforcement do not work with its use.

Sperry found that by ablating both the optic chiasm and the corpus callosum, he could create two independent brains in one skull. Such brains could be taught opposing habits and one could be active while the other is relaxing. Further work on the brain has indicated that, although the left and right cerebral hemispheres are alike anatomically, they perform different functions. The left hemisphere is associated with verbal and mathematical skills and the right hemisphere with perceptual, attentional, and artistic skills. It is inappropriate to dichotomize hemispheric functions completely, however, since most human activities and thought processes involve both hemispheres and, at least to some extent, functions performed by one hemisphere can be performed by the other.

Until recently it had been assumed that only responses controlled by the skeletal muscles were conditionable, but current research has indicated that individuals can exercise considerable control over their own internal environments. By using biofeedback to display the status of internal events, individuals can learn to control such things as their heart rate, blood pressure, and skin temperature. Such internal control has vast implications for the practice of medicine.

Although, with the exception of Hebb's work, research using the neurophysiological paradigm is often diffuse and unrelated, it is beginning to contribute to our further understanding of the learning process. In chapter 3, it was said that our understanding of the learning process is enhanced when viewed from different angles. The neurophysiological paradigm provides us with one additional viewing angle.

DISCUSSION QUESTIONS

1. Discuss several observations that Hebb made during his early years as a psychologist that he later attempted to account for with his neurophysiological theory.

2. Discuss Lashley's concepts of mass action and equipotentiality.

3. Describe the switchboard conception of the brain. What was Hebb's opposition to such a conception and what did he offer as an alternative conception?

4. Why, according to Hebb, were neurophysiological explanations of learning so unpopular at the time that he accepted his professorship at McGill?

5. Discuss the concepts of cell assembly and phase sequence.

6. What, according to Hebb, is the difference between childhood learning and adult learning?

7. Describe the effects of sensory deprivation and Hebb's explanation of these effects.

8. How might Hebb explain dreams? For example, why might a backfiring car cause a person to have a crime-related dream?

9. How might Hebb explain the Gestalt principle of closure?

10. Summarize the results of research on the effects of enriched environments on subsequent functioning.

11. Summarize Hebb's research on fear. What did he find and how did he explain what he found?

12. What does Hebb mean by an optimal level of stimulation?

13. Differentiate between the cue function and the arousal function of a stimulus.

14. Why, according to Hebb, do people sometimes go out of their way to get into trouble?

15. Describe the relationship between arousal theory and reinforcement theory.

16. Differentiate between short-term and long-term memory. In your answer include an explanation of consolidation and those things that interfere with consolidation.

17. Describe the unique characteristics of reinforcement by direct brain stimulation.

18. Summarize Sperry's research on the split brain.

19. Summarize the functions that appear to be associated with the left and right cerebral hemispheres.

20. Describe how Kimura used dichotic listening to study cerebral asymmetry.

21. What is the reason that it may be inappropriate to describe hemispheric functioning in terms of dichotomies?

22. Discuss the implications of visceral conditioning for the practice of medicine.

CHAPTER HIGHLIGHTS

Arousal function of a stimulus. That function of a stimulus that increases the activity of the reticular activating system, thereby increasing the electrical activity in certain higher centers of the brain.

Arousal theory. The contention that brain wave activity ranges from very fast to very slow with a rate in between that allows for the optimal performance of certain tasks.

Biofeedback. The information provided to individuals by some mechanical device concerning the status of one or more of their internal biological events. For example, a flashing light can be set to reflect heart rate or an auditory signal can be triggered when blood pressure goes beyond a certain level.

Cell assembly. The pattern of neural activity that is caused when an environmental object or event is experienced. When the cell assembly is well developed, the person is able to think of the entire event following the stimulation of the assembly, even if the object itself or the event is physically absent.

Consolidation period. The period of time when the short-term memory of an experience is converted into long-term memory.

Corpus callosum. A massive bundle of fibers that connects the two hemispheres of the cortex.

Cue function of a stimulus. That function of a stimulus that provides us with information about the environment.

Dichotic listening. The technique whereby conflicting information is simultaneously presented to the two ears of a subject.

Dichotomania. The tendency to explain the functioning of the left and right cerebral hemispheres in terms of two clearly delineated sets of functions.

Electroconvulsive shock. A severe shock that causes convulsions, thereby preventing the electrical activity that appears to be necessary for consolidation to take place.

Electroencephalogram (EEG). A recording of the electrical activity in the brain usually taken by placing electrodes on the scalp of the subject. (Also called electroencephalograph.)

Enriched environment. An environment that contains many objects and events which, according to Hebb, stimulates the development of complex neural circuitry.

Equipotentiality. The finding that the cortex functions as a whole and that if one part of the cortex is destroyed, any one of a number of cortical areas can take over its function.

Fear. According to Hebb, the emotion experienced when there is an incompatibility between ongoing neural activity and the environmental events that accompany that activity.

Hippocampus. A brain structure within the limbic system thought to be involved in the conversion of short-term memory into long-term memory.

Limbic system. A number of interrelated brain areas believed to be related to emotional experience.

Long-term memory. Also called secondary memory. The memory of an experience that lasts for a considerable length of time after the experience. Whereas short-term memory is usually measured in terms of seconds, long-term memory can be measured in terms of years.

Mass action. The finding that disruption of learning and memory is a function of the amount of cortical tissue destroyed.

Neglect syndrome. The tendency for patients with damage to the right cerebral hemispheres to ignore or neglect the left side of their bodies or perceptual fields.

Optimal level of arousal. The level of brain activity that is most conducive to the performance of a certain task.

Phase sequence. A sequence of temporarily related cell assemblies. Cell assemblies that consistently follow one another in time form a unit or a phase sequence.

Punishment centers in the brain. Areas of the brain that, when stimulated, cause the organism to refrain from whatever behavior preceded their stimulation.

Reinforcement centers in the brain. Areas of the brain which, when stimulated, cause the organism to repeat whatever behavior preceded their stimulation.

Reticular activating system (RAS). A structure located in the brain stem that appears to be responsible for regulating the electrical activity in the higher centers of the brain.

Retrograde amnesia. The inability to remember the events that took place just prior to a traumatic experience, such as an automobile accident.

Reverberating neural activity. A system of self-perpetuating neural activity that lasts for a few seconds after the source of stimulation has been removed. Reverberating neural activity is thought by some to be the basis of short-term memory.

Sensory deprivation. The condition where an organism's sensory stimulation is drastically reduced.

Serendipity. Finding one thing while looking for something else.

Short-term memory. Also called immediate memory and primary memory. The memory of an experience that persists for only a short period of time after the experience.

Split-brain preparation. The arrangement where both the optic chiasm and the corpus callosum are severed, thereby causing the two halves of the cortex to function independently.

Switchboard conception of the brain. The view that the brain acts only as a relay station between sensory events and responses.

Visceral conditioning. The conditioning of internal organs under the control of the autonomic nervous system, such as the stomach, intestines, heart, bladder, or arteries.

16

Implications for Education

We begin this chapter with an attempt to relate the major theories of learning covered in the preceding chapters to educational practices. The specification of this relationship is easier for some theories than with others. Theorists such as Thorndike, Skinner, Guthrie, and the Gestalt theorists have written extensively about how their views on learning relate to teaching practices. For them, therefore, what follows is mainly a review of the material that was covered earlier in this text. Theorists like Pavlov and Hull, however, never made an effort to extend their theory to the realm of education. Tolman's theory of learning is especially difficult to relate to education since he postulated six different kinds of learning. In our treatment of his theory below, we emphasize only the kind of learning that he called "cognitive."

After discussing what each of the major theorists says, or seems to say, about education, we will turn to some of the more general differences between cognitive and behavioristic theories as they apply to the classroom.

APPLICATION OF SPECIFIC THEORIES OF LEARNING TO THE CLASSROOM

Thorndike

Thorndike would have an orderly classroom with the objectives clearly defined. These educational objectives must be within the learner's response capabilities and they must be divided into manageable units so that the teacher can apply "a satisfying state of affairs" when the learner makes an appropriate response. Learning proceeds from the simple to the complex.

Motivation is relatively unimportant, except in determining what will constitute a "satisfying state of affairs" for the learner. The learner's behavior is determined primarily by external reinforcers and not by intrinsic motivation. Emphasis is on bringing about correct responses to certain stimuli. Incorrect responses are to be corrected rapidly so that they are not practiced. Therefore, examinations are important: they provide the learner and the teacher with feedback concerning the learning process. If students learn their lesson well, they are to be reinforced quickly. If students have learned something incorrectly, their mistakes must be corrected quickly; thus examinations must be taken regularly.

The learning situation must be made to resemble the "real world" as much as possible. As we have seen, Thorndike believed that learning will transfer from the classroom to the environment outside only insofar as the two situations are similar. Teaching children to solve difficult problems does not enhance their reasoning capacity. Therefore, teaching Latin, mathematics, or logic is only justified when students will be solving problems involving Latin, mathematics, or logic when they leave school. With his identical elements theory of transfer of training, Thorndike opposed the traditional formal discipline or "mental muscle" approach to explaining transfer.

The Thorndikian teacher would use positive control in the classroom, since satisfiers strengthen connections but annoyers do not weaken them. The Thorndikian teacher would also avoid lecturing, preferring to deal with students on a one-to-one basis.

Guthrie

Like Thorndike, Guthrie would begin the educational process by stating objectives, that is, stating what responses are to be made to what stimuli. Then he would have the learning environment arranged so that the desired responses are elicited in the presence of the stimuli that they are supposed to be attached to.

Motivation was even less important for Guthrie than it was for Thorndike. All that is necessary for Guthrie is that the student respond appropriately in the presence of certain stimuli.

Practice is important in that it causes more and more stimuli to elicit desired behavior. Since each experience is unique, one must "relearn" things over and over again. Guthrie would say that learning to add two and two at the blackboard is no guarantee that students will add two and two at their seats. Students must not only learn that two red blocks plus two more equals four red blocks, but they must make new two-plus-two-equals-four associations with apples, dogs, books, and so on.

Although learning constantly takes place, classroom education is an attempt to purposefully associate certain stimuli and responses. Learning, however, can be easily interfered with outside the classroom if new responses are made in the presence of stimuli similar to the ones the student experienced in school. It is also possible that a student will learn to attach responses to the stimuli in the classroom and another set of responses to similar stimuli outside the classroom. For example, seeing an elderly person in school may tend to elicit "respectful" behavior, whereas an elderly person experienced outside of school may elicit "disrespectful" behavior.

Like Thorndike, Guthrie believed that formal education should resemble real-life situations as much as possible. In other words, the Guthrian teacher would have students do in school what they are expected to do when they leave school.

Guthrian teachers may sometimes use a form of punishment in dealing with disruptive behavior, but they would realize that to be effective, punishment must be used as the disruptive behavior is occurring. Furthermore, the punishment must cause behavior that is incompatible with the disruptive behavior. If, for example, students are being too noisy and punishment (such as yelling at them) causes them to become noisier, the punishment will strengthen the very behavior that the teacher is attempting to eliminate.

Hull

The major differences among Hull, Thorndike, and Guthrie concerned their emphasis on motivation. You will recall that Hull's was a drive reduction, or a drive-stimulus reduction, theory of learning. As for the issues of specifiability of objectives, orderliness of the classrooms, and proceeding from the simple to the complex, Hull would be in agreement with Thorndike and Guthrie. Learning for him, however, must involve a reducible drive. It is hard to imagine how the reduction of a primary drive can play a part in classroom learning; however, some of Hull's followers (e.g., Janet Taylor Spence) have emphasized anxiety as a drive in human learning. From this line of reasoning, it would follow that encouraging some anxiety in students that would subsequently be reduced by success would be a necessary condition for classroom learning. Too little anxiety would result in no learning (because there is no drive to be reduced) and too much anxiety would be disruptive. Therefore, students who are mildly anxious are in the best position to learn and are therefore easiest to teach.

Practice would be carefully distributed so that inhibition would not be built up. The Hullian teacher would intersperse the topics to be taught so that the learner would not build up fatigue that would interfere with learning. Likewise, topics would be arranged so that those that are maximally dissimilar would follow each other. For example, one reasonable sequence of subjects may be math, physical education, English, art, and history. This, of course, would reduce fatigue and facilitate attention span.

Miller and Dollard (1941) have summarized Hull's theory as it applies to education:

Drive: The learner must want something.
Cue: The learner must attend to something.
Response: The learner must do something.
Reinforcement: The learner's response must get him or her something he or she wants.

Spence's revision of Hull's theory suggested that students learn what they do. Thus, Spence was a contiguity theorist as Guthrie was. For Spence, however, incentives were important since they motivated students to translate what had been learned into behavior. By relating incentives (reinforcers) to performance instead of to learning, Spence's position was close to the positions of Tolman and Bandura.

Skinner

Skinner, of course, has much in common with the theorists mentioned so far. For example, he would insist that the course objectives be completely specified before teaching commences. Further, he would insist that the objectives be defined *behaviorally*. If a unit is designed to teach creativity, he would ask, "What are students *doing* when they are being creative?" If a unit is designed to teach the understanding of history, he would ask, "What are students *doing* when they are understanding history?" If educational objectives cannot be specified behaviorally, instructors have no way of knowing whether or not they have accomplished what they had set out to do. Likewise, if objectives are specified in terms not easily transformed into behavioral terms, it is next to impossible to determine to what extent the course objectives have been met. We will have more to say about behavioral objectives later in this chapter.

The stimuli associated with certain responses are not as important for Skinner as they are for Thorndike, Guthrie, or Hull. Skinner is more interested in starting with the responses as they occur "naturally," or, if they do not occur naturally, *shaping* them into existence. As with most behaviorists, he would start with the simple and proceed to the complex. Complex behavior is thought to consist of simpler forms of behavior. Skinner's approach to presenting material to be learned is best exemplified by programmed learning, to which we will turn in a later section of this chapter.

As with Thorndike, motivation to Skinner is only important in determining what will act as a reinforcer for a given student. Secondary reinforcers are very important, too, since these are normally utilized in the classroom. Examples of secondary reinforcers would include verbal praise, positive facial expressions, gold stars, feelings of success, points, grades, and the opportunity to work on what one wants to. Like Thorndike and Hull, Skinner stresses the use of extrinsic reinforcers in education. In fact, for the Skinnerian teacher, the main function of education is to arrange reinforcement contingencies so that the behavior that has been deemed important is encouraged. Intrinsic reinforcement is thought to be of minimal importance.

It is also important for the Skinnerian teacher to move from a 100% reinforcement schedule to a partial reinforcement schedule. During the early stages of training, a correct response is reinforced each time it occurs. Later, however, it is only reinforced periodically. This, of course, makes the response more resistant to extinction.

All the S-R behaviorists would prescribe a learning environment that allows for individual differences in learning rate. They would either want to deal with students individually, or provide a group of students with material that allows for individual self-pacing, such as teaching machines or specially constructed workbooks. The behaviorists would tend to avoid the lecture technique since there is no way of knowing when learning is taking place and therefore when to administer reinforcers. We will have more to say about both individualized courses and the lecture technique later in this chapter.

Skinnerian teachers would avoid the use of punishment. They would reinforce appropriate behavior and ignore inappropriate behavior. Since the learning environment is designed so that students experience maximal success, they usually attend to the material to be learned. According to the Skinnerians, behavior problems in school are the result of poor educational planning, such as failure to provide self-pacing, failure to use reinforcers appropriately, offering the material in chunks too large to be easily comprehended, using discipline to control behavior, having rigid plans that all students must follow, or making unreasonable demands on students (such as not moving or not making noise).

In his recent article "The Shame of American Education" (1984), Skinner insists that the greater use of programmed instruction in our schools would not only facilitate student learning but would also increase respect for teachers:

> Success and progress are the very stuff on which programmed instruction feeds. They should also be the stuff that makes teaching worthwhile as a profession. Just as students must not only learn but know that they are learning, so teachers must not only teach but know that they are teaching. Burnout is usually regarded as the result of abusive treatment by students, but it can be as much the result of looking back upon a day in the classroom and wondering what one has accomplished. Along with a sense of satisfaction goes a place in the community. One proposed remedy for American education is to give teachers greater respect, but that is putting it the wrong way around. Let them teach twice as much in the same time and with the same effort, and they will be held in greater respect. (p. 952)

Gestalt Theory

The Gestalt-oriented teacher would stress meaningfulness and understanding. Parts must always be related to a whole so that they have meaning to the student. Historical names or dates will have little meaning unless they are related to current events or to something personally important to the student. An understanding of history is the important thing and it is gained by studying individual events. But the understanding of history is always greater than the sum of individual events.

As we have seen, the Gestaltists view unsolved problems as creating ambiguity or an organizational disbalance in the student's mind, a condition that is undesirable. In fact, ambiguity is looked upon as a negative state that persists until a problem is solved. Students confronted with a problem will either seek new information or will rearrange old information until they gain insight into the solution of the problem. The solution is as satisfying to the problem-solver as a hamburger is to a hungry person. In a sense, the reduction of ambiguity can be seen as the Gestalt equivalent to the behaviorist's notion of reinforcement. However, the reduction of ambiguity can be thought of as an "intrinsic" reinforcer, while the behaviorists usually stress external, or "extrinsic," reinforcers.

Jerome Bruner, while discussing curiosity as an innate human motive, comes close to what the Gestaltists refer to as a need to reduce ambiguity. Bruner says (1966):

> Curiosity is almost a prototype of the intrinsic motive. Our attention is attracted to something that is unclear, unfinished, or uncertain. We sustain our attention until the matter on hand becomes clear, finished, or certain. The achievement of clarity or merely the search for it is what satisfies. We would think it preposterous if somebody thought to reward us with praise or profit for having satisfied our curiosity. (p. 114)

John Holt makes a similar point in his book *How Children Learn* (1967):

> What we want to know, we want to know for a reason. The reason is that there is a hole, a gap, an empty space in our understanding of things, our mental model of the world. We feel that gap like a hole in a tooth and want to fill it up. It makes us ask How? When? Why? While the gap is there, we are in tension, in suspense. Listen to the anxiety in a person's voice when he says, "This doesn't make sense!" When the gap in our understanding is filled, we feel pleasure, satisfaction, relief. Things make sense again—or at any rate, they make more sense than they did. When we learn this way, for these reasons, we learn both rapidly and permanently. The person who really needs to know something, does not need to be told many times, drilled, tested. Once is enough. The new piece of knowledge fits into the gap ready for it, like a missing piece in a jigsaw puzzle. Once in place, it is held in, it can't fall out. (pp. 187–188)

Bruner and Holt share the Gestalt notion that learning is personally satisfying and that it need not be prodded by external reinforcement. Holt (1967) concludes his book with the following statement:

> Birds fly, fish swim; man thinks and learns. Therefore, we do not need to "motivate" children into learning, by wheedling, bribing, or bullying. We do not need to keep picking away at their minds to make sure they are learning. What we need to do, is bring as much of the world as we can into the school and the classroom; give children as much help and guidance as they need and ask for; listen respectfully when they feel like talking; and then get out of the way. We can trust them to do the rest. (p. 189)

The Gestalt-oriented classroom would be characterized by a give-and-take relationship between students and teacher. The teacher helps students see relations and to organize their experiences into meaningful patterns. Planning a Gestalt learning experience includes starting with something familiar and basing each step in the educational process on those already taken. All aspects of the course are divided into meaningful units and the units themselves must relate to an overall concept or experience. The Gestalt-oriented teacher might use the lecture technique but would insist that it allow for student-teacher interactions. Above all, rote memorization of facts and/or rules should be avoided. It is only when students grasp the principles involved in a learning experience that they truly understand them. When what is learned is understood instead of memorized, it can easily be applied to new situations and it is retained for a very long time.

Piaget

Clearly, according to Piaget, educational experiences must be built around the learner's cognitive structure. Children of the same age and from the same culture tend to have similar cognitive structures, but it is entirely possible for them to have different cognitive structures and therefore require different kinds of learning material. Educational material that cannot be assimilated into a child's cognitive structure cannot have any meaning to the child. If, on the other hand, the material can be completely assimilated, no learning will take place. In order for learning to take place, the material needs to be partially known and partially unknown. The part that is known will be assimilated and the part that is unknown will necessitate a slight modification in the child's cognitive structure. Such modification is referred to as accommodation, which can be roughly equated with learning.

Thus, for Piaget, optimal education involves mildly challenging experiences for the learner so that the dual processes of assimilation and accommodation can provide for intellectual growth. In order to create that kind of experience, the teacher must know the level of functioning of each student's cognitive structure. We find, then, that both Piaget (a representative of the cognitive paradigm) and most of the behaviorists have reached the same conclusion about education; namely, that it must be *individualized.* Piaget reached this conclusion by realizing that the ability to assimilate varies from child to child and that educational material must be tailored to each child's cognitive structure. The behaviorists reached the conclusion through their recognition that reinforcement must be contingent upon appropriate behavior and the proper dispensing of reinforcers requires a one-to-one relationship between the student and the teacher, or between the student and programmed educational material.

Tolman

In many respects, Tolman and the Gestaltists agree about educational practices: both would emphasize the importance of thinking and understanding. For Tolman, it would be important to have the student test hypotheses in a problem situation. On this matter, Tolman is in close agreement with Harlow's error factor theory, which states that learning is not so much a matter of building up correct responses or strategies as it is a matter of eliminating incorrect responses or strategies. Both Tolman and the Gestalt theorist would encourage small groups for classroom discussions. The important thing is for students to have the opportunity, individually or as part of a group, to test the adequacy of their ideas. Hypotheses or strategies effective in solving a problem are those that are maintained by the student. The teacher, then, acts as a consultant to assist students in clarifying and then confirming or disconfirming hypotheses.

Like the Gestalt theorist, Tolman would also suggest that the student be exposed to a topic from different viewpoints. This would allow the student to develop a "cognitive map" that could be utilized to answer questions about that particular topic and related topics.

Finally, like the Gestalt theorists, Tolman would say that extrinsic reinforcement is unnecessary for learning to take place. Learning, according to Tolman, occurs constantly. Students, like everyone else, are attempting to develop expectancies or beliefs that reliably conform to reality. The Tolmanian teacher aids students in formulating the testing hypotheses and provides confirming experiences when hypotheses are accurate. In this way students develop complex cognitive maps that guide their activities.

Popper

In chapter 2 we encountered Karl Popper's influential views of science. In their recent book *Learning from Error: Karl Popper's Psychology of Learning* (1984), Berkson and Wettersten have attempted to distill Popper's views of the learning process from his writings on the philosophy of science. We include Popper's views on learning here because they seem especially applicable to education.

Like Tolman, Harlow, and the Gestalt theorists, Popper sees learning as problem solving. As was mentioned in chapter 2, Popper sees science as a means of effectively solving problems. For Popper, a problem exists when an observation is contrary to what was expected. This discrepancy between observation and expectancy stimulates efforts to correct expectancies so that they are compatible with the previously surprising observation. The newly formulated expectancies remain intact until observations are made that are incompatible with them at which point they are revised again. This process of adjusting and readjusting one's expectations so that they agree with observation is an unending process. However, it is a process that, hopefully, makes expectancies and reality increasingly compatible. According to Popper, this process of adjusting one's expectations so that they agree with actual experience is motivated by an innate **cognitive hunger,** which refers to the fact that "we have been born with the task of developing a realistic set of expectations about the world" (Berkson & Wettersten, 1984, p. 16).

According to Popper, both scientific knowledge and personal knowledge grow in the same way and for the same reason. First, as we have seen, there is a problem (a discrepancy between what is observed and what is expected). Next, possible solutions to the problem are conjectured and, if possible, the proposed solutions are refuted. Solutions that survive serious attempts at *refutation* are retained until they, too, are contradicted by observation, at which point the process starts over. In the process of problem solving, Popper believes that conjectures should be bold and creative and attempts at refutation severe. Berkson and Wettersten (1984) summarize Popper's beliefs concerning how both scientific and personal knowledge grows and improves: "Because we do in fact learn by conjectures and refutations in an effort to solve problems, the best way to make progress in the growth of knowledge is to focus on and articulate problems, to conjecture solutions boldly and imaginatively, and to assess the proposed solutions critically" (p. 27).

The implications of Popper's theory of learning for education seem clear. A problem is presented to the class, and students propose solutions to the problem. Each proposed solution is critically analyzed and those found ineffective are rejected. The process continues until the best possible solution is arrived at. Problems could be scientific, sociological, ethical, philosophical, or even personal. The classroom atmosphere should be informal and relaxed enough to encourage bold conjecture, but at the same time, the participants should be encouraged to offer objective criticism when it is called for. "What is wrong with that proposed solution?" would be a reoccurring question. With appropriate adjustments for age levels, there is no reason why this classroom procedure could not be used from primary to graduate school. Hopefully, students involved in such exercises would be better able to articulate problems, be more creative in seeking solutions to problems, and be better able to distinguish between effective and ineffective solutions to problems.

Pavlov

Pavlovian principles are difficult to apply to classroom education, although they are no doubt operating all the time. In general, we can say that every time a neutral event is paired with a meaningful event, classical conditioning occurs; obviously, pairings of that kind take place all the time. When a cologne that was consistently worn by a favorite teacher is experienced later in life, it will tend to elicit favorable memories of school; learning math in a rigid authoritarian atmosphere may create a negative attitude toward math; being made to write something over and over again as a disciplinary action may create a negative attitude toward writing; having difficult subjects in the morning may create at least a mild dislike for mornings; and a likable, knowledgeable teacher may inspire certain students to consider a teaching career. The feelings of anxiety associated with failure in school may create an aversion to problem-solving situations outside of school. You may remember that the "Garcia effect" showed that strong aversions to a situation can develop if a negative experience is associated with that situation. Thus, animals that eat a certain food and become ill develop a strong aversion to that food. It is possible that if classroom experiences are negative enough, students may develop lifelong aversions to education. In addition, students with this negative attitude toward education may be the ones who attack either teachers or school property in order to vent their frustrations.

Although the influence of classical conditioning in the classroom is strong, it is usually incidental. The principles of classical conditioning, however, can be purposively utilized in an education program, as they were in the case of Albert (see chapter 7). When Pavlovian techniques are used to modify behavior, the situation appears to resemble brainwashing more than education. To find examples of Pavlovian principles used to modify attitudes, one only needs to carefully observe television commercials. The advertiser's procedure involves pairing a neutral object (the product) with something someone likes (e.g., wealth, health, youth, sex, prestige). Gradually, the product will cause viewers to have the same feeling that they used to get only from the object or event it was paired with. Next, it is assumed that the viewer will feel successful smoking Brand X cigarettes, be sexier driving a certain kind of car, or be more youthful using a certain hair preparation.

Again, these "incidental" aspects of education are no doubt occurring all the time that a child is in school. The modification of attitudes and emotions involved in learning based on classical conditioning must be taken into consideration in designing any truly effective educational program.

Bandura

Bandura's theory has many implications for education. You may recall that Bandura believes that anything that can be learned by direct experience can also be learned from observation. Bandura also believes that models are most effective if they are seen as having respect, competence, high status and/or power. This means that, in most cases, teachers can be highly influential models. Through careful planning of what is presented, teachers can teach not only routine information and skills, but also problem-solving strategies, moral codes, performance standards, general rules and principles, and creativity. Teachers can model conduct which is then internalized by students and thus becomes the standard for self-evaluation. For example, internalized standards become the basis for self-criticism or self-praise. When students act in accordance with their own standards, the experience is reinforcing. When the actions of students fall short of their standards, the experience is punishing. Thus, for Bandura, like for the Gestalt theorists and Tolman, intrinsic reinforcement is far more important than extrinsic reinforcement. In fact, says Bandura, extrinsic reinforcement can actually reduce a student's motivation to learn. Reaching a personal goal is also reinforcing, and, realizing this, teachers should help students formulate goals that are neither too easy nor too difficult to achieve. This, of course, needs to be done individually for each student.

To say that students learn what they observe is an oversimplification, since observational learning is governed by four variables that must be taken into consideration by the teacher. *Attentional processes* will determine what is observed by the student and such processes will vary as a function of both maturation and the student's previous learning experiences. Even if something is attended to and learned, it must be retained if it is to be of any value; thus *retention processes* are important. According to Bandura, retention is largely determined by one's verbal ability. A teacher must, therefore, take the verbal ability of the students into consideration when planning a modeling experience. Even if something is attended to and retained, the student may not have the motor skills necessary to reproduce a skill even if it has been learned. Thus, a teacher must be aware of a student's *behavioral production processes*. Lastly, even if students attend to and retain what has been observed and are capable of behaviorally producing their observations, they must have an incentive for doing so. Thus the teacher must be aware of *motivational processes*. At this point extrinsic reinforcement may be useful. For example, students may be willing to demonstrate what they have learned if they are offered points, stars, grades, and/or the admiration of the teacher. Note, however, that extrinsic reinforcement is being used to influence *performance* rather than learning.

We see then that observational learning has many educational implications, but to use it effectively in the classroom the teacher must take into consideration the attentional, retentional, motor, and motivational processes of each student. With these things in mind, films, television, lectures, slides, tapes, demonstrations, and displays can all be used to effectively model a wide variety of educational experiences.

Norman

In chapter 15, we noted that Norman feels that most complex learning occurs by analogy. That is, new material is learned by relating it to material already known. Effective teaching, then, requires that the teacher know something about the student's cognitive structure or, using Norman's iceberg analogy, the submerged portion of the student's iceberg. Understanding the nature of a student's cognitive structure is not an easy matter, but Norman suggests that one important source for such understanding is the number of questions a student asks. Miyake and Norman (1979) tested the hypothesis that frequency of question asking in class is a function of the amount of knowledge that a student possesses and task complexity. To test their hypothesis, Miyake and Norman taught a class on computer programming. Half of the students were given pretraining on the material (trained) and half were not (novices). Also, half the students used a difficult training manual and half used an easy training manual. Thus, the four following groups participated in the experiment:

Pretraining—easy material
No pretraining—easy material
Pretraining—difficult material
No pretraining—difficult material

It was found that for easy material, students with no pretraining asked more questions than students with pretraining, and that for difficult material the students with pretraining asked more questions than students with no pretraining. Thus, the hypothesis was supported. The results were interpreted as indicating that for difficult material, untrained students did not know enough to formulate meaningful questions; that is, they did not have an appropriate cognitive structure available to them. Trained students did have such a structure and, therefore, were able to ask questions that allowed refining and expansion of their cognitive structure. With easy material, untrained students could use previous knowledge to at least partially understand the material and, therefore, formulate questions. The trained students knew the easy material so well that there was no need to ask questions. Thus, according to Miyake and Norman (1979), both knowing too little and knowing too much inhibits question asking. The highest frequency of question asking occurs when there is a reasonable match between a student's cognitive structure and the material being presented. On this matter, Norman and Piaget are in close agreement.

Hebb

For Hebb, there are two kinds of learning. The first involves the gradual buildup of cell assemblies and phase sequences during infancy and early childhood. This early learning results in the objects and events in the environment having neurological representation. When this neural development has taken place, the child can *think* of an object or events, or a series of objects and events, when they are not physically present. In a sense, copies of those environmental objects now exist in the child's nervous system. During this early learning it would be important for the child to experience an enriched environment. An enriched environment consists of a wide variety of sights, sounds, textures, shapes, objects, and so on. The more complex the environment, the more there is to be represented on the neurological level. The more there is that is represented on the neural level, the more the child can think about. Thus, the Hebbian teacher dealing with young children would create an educational environment with great variety. According to Hebb, it is during early learning that certain associationistic principles may be operating. The associationistic principles that seem most important for the development of cell assemblies and phase sequences are the principles of contiguity and frequency. For example, if a series of environmental events occurs often enough it becomes represented neurologically as a phase sequence. Reinforcement appears to have nothing to do with it.

The second kind of learning, according to Hebb, is explained more by Gestalt principles than by associationistic ones. Once cell assemblies and phase sequences have been developed early in life, subsequent learning typically involves their rearrangement. In other words, once the building blocks have been established, they can be rearranged in almost an infinite number of configurations. Later learning then is perceptual, rapid, and insightful. The job of the teacher dealing with older children is to help them see what they have already learned in new, creative ways.

Hebb also says that the physical characteristics of the learning environment are very important. For any given task and for any given student there is an optimal level of arousal that will allow for most efficient learning. Since arousal level is controlled primarily by external stimulation, the level of stimulation in the learning environment will determine, to a large extent, how much learning takes place. If there is too much stimulation (e.g., commotion in the classroom) learning will be difficult. Likewise, if there is not enough stimulation (e.g., a deadly quiet classroom) learning will also be difficult. What is needed is an optimal level of stimulation for both the task and the student at hand.

Left-Brain, Right-Brain Learning

We learned in the last chapter that there is considerable evidence that the two cerebral hemispheres process information differently. It appears that the left hemisphere is best suited for the processing of verbal, mathematical, and sequential information, and the right hemisphere is best suited for processing perceptual, attentional, global, and simultaneous information. The apparent asymmetry of hemispheric functioning has led some researchers to conclude that there are two different kinds of intelligence. We have already seen that Ornstein (1979) believes that the Western world emphasizes the kind of intelligence associated with the left hemisphere and minimizes the kind associated with the right hemisphere.

Bogen (1977) also believes that there are two kinds of intelligence and different students possess them to varying degrees. According to Bogen, frustration occurs when there is a mismatch between what a student is asked to learn and the kind of intelligence that he or she possesses:

> When a child's talents lie in visual-spatial relations and he or she is being forced into a curriculum that emphasizes the verbal articulatory modes of solving a conceptual problem, this child will encounter enormous frustration and difficulty which may well result in hostility toward the teacher and, worse, toward the learning process itself. If the teacher were to be made aware that the child is specialized in visual-spatial skills and the same conceptual problem is introduced, both the discouragement and the subsequent hostility might be avoided if the child is allowed to use his special talents. Conversely, the child with high verbal skills may quite frequently be unable to visualize the spatial aspect of an assigned task; in this case also, far better results could be obtained if he is not forced into academic areas for which he is not naturally equipped. (pp. 94–95)

If current speculations about hemispheric functioning prove correct, they would go a long way in explaining individual differences in student performance. Perhaps in the future, different yardsticks will need to be used to measure the potential and accomplishments of different students. There is good reason to be cautious about these generalizations, however. A number of researchers of hemispheric functioning insist that although special experimental procedures can be employed to show that the two cerebral hemispheres function differently in isolation, they never function in isolation in the normal, intact brain. That is, because of such structures as the corpus callosum, what happens to the left hemisphere influences the right hemisphere and vice versa. Since the normal brain functions as an interrelated whole, it is impossible, say these researchers, to arrange an educational experience exclusively for one hemisphere. Levy (1985) makes this point: "Since the two hemispheres do not function independently, and since each hemisphere contributes its special capacities to all cognitive activities, it is quite impossible to educate one hemisphere at a time in a normal brain. The right hemisphere is educated as much as the left in a literature class, and the left hemisphere is educated as much as the right in music and painting classes" (p. 44).

Although it may be possible to criticize school curricula and teaching methodologies for many reasons, it may be premature, if not incorrect, to worry too much about matching learning experiences with the hemispheric dominance of students.

GENERAL DIFFERENCES BETWEEN COGNITIVE AND BEHAVIORISTIC THEORIES

What Is Learned?

In describing what is learned, behaviorists use terms like S-R associations, habits, and contingencies. Cognitive theorists describe what is learned in terms of information, expectancies, schemata, principles, and insights.

What Is the Function of Reinforcement?

For most behaviorists, reinforcement is a necessary condition for learning. For them, it is reinforcement that causes S-R associations to form, contingencies to be learned, or the rate or probability of responding to change. On the other hand, most cognitive theorists believe that learning occurs independent of reinforcement. For them, what reinforcement does is provide the organism with information that can act as an incentive to translate what has already been learned into behavior.

How Are Problems Solved?

Most behaviorists claim a problem is approached in accordance with its similarity to other problems individuals have experienced in the past. If the attempted solutions fail, or if learners have never confronted such a problem, they resort to trial-and-error behavior until they hit upon a solution. The cognitive theorist maintains that learners "think" about the problem until they gain an insight into its solution. The behaviorist would emphasize *behavioral* trial and error; the cognitivist would emphasize *cognitive,* or vicarious, trial and error, that is, thinking.

What Assumptions Are Made About the Learner?

Certainly what teachers believe to be the nature of the human mind will influence what they believe would be effective teaching practices. We have already seen two examples of this. The behaviorists, who tend to accept Aristotle's and Locke's position that the mind begins as a *tabula rasa* (blank slate), emphasize the importance of sensory experience in formulating the content of the mind. Teachers accepting this position would specify educational objectives in behavioral terms, and then define the kinds of experiences that would bring about the desired behavior. Behavioristically oriented teachers would be more educational arrangers than anything else. Their most important task would be to arrange an environment that is responsive to the behaviors deemed important by the school; that is, they must create an environment that allows the student to be reinforced for behaving in accordance with various course objectives.

The cognitive theorists believe that the mind is not a blank slate at birth and that the mind is active, not passive. The mind is capable of weighing alternatives (thinking) and has the built-in need to reduce ambiguity and to make everything as simple as possible. Teachers accepting this Gestalt point of view are not mere arrangers of the learning environment; rather, they are active participants in the learner-teacher relationship. Teachers must help the students to see that facts and ideas are part of a larger concept. That the students are able to recite numerous facts without seeing their interrelationship is meaningless to such teachers. If one took an automobile completely apart and threw all the parts on a pile, it would not be what we ordinarily call an automobile, although all the parts are there. *How* the parts are arranged is at least as important as *what* the parts are. As we have seen, the Gestalt point of view always emphasizes that the whole is more than the sum of its parts.

The cognitively oriented teacher's job consists of two things: (a) to induce ambiguity, and (b) help the student clarify the ambiguity. The teacher induces ambiguity by introducing problems and then helps clarify the ambiguity by suggesting strategies for solving the problems. As stated earlier, classroom practices based on Gestalt principles would involve a give-and-take between the teacher and the students. Unlike the behavioristically oriented teachers, they would not strongly emphasize working with individual students, and they would be perfectly content to work with small groups. Self-pacing and small-step learning procedures may or may not be important to the Gestalt-oriented teacher; their suitability must be determined for each student. A Gestalt-oriented teacher attempts to determine for each student the best strategy for learning; that is, such a teacher must know the conceptual basis from where each student is starting before he or she can help the student continue toward understanding the concept being taught. This, of course, is another reason why there must be close contact between the student and the teacher.

How Is the Transfer of Training Explained?

The behaviorist tends to accept Thorndike's identical elements theory of transfer: as the number of common elements in two situations goes up, the tendency to make similar responses in both situations goes up. According to the behaviorist, if you want to enhance transfer of training from classroom education to experiences outside the classroom, you are obliged to increase the similarity between the two situations. For example, if one purpose in teaching mathematics is to provide students with the information necessary for filling out tax forms, the behavioristically oriented teacher would have students work on tax forms.

The cognitive theorist would tend to emphasize the transfer of principles. Using the tax form example, the cognitively oriented teacher might claim that the learning of mathematical skills will transfer readily to filling out tax forms and grocery shopping, even if tax forms and shopping had not been experienced in the classroom. This is because the *principles* involved in both situations are believed to be the same.

The issue of transfer of training, clearly one of the most important problems in education, is still highly controversial. In fact, it appears that the notion of formal discipline, based on faculty psychology, is still alive and well in the American school system. For example, the prominence given the teaching of mathematics in our schools seems to reflect the belief that studying mathematics creates a stronger "reasoning faculty," especially since most Americans require less than a fifth-grade level of proficiency in mathematics for the needs of their daily life. For a discussion of the reappearance of formal discipline in American schools see Kolesnik (1958) or Symonds (1960).

PROGRAMMED LEARNING

Programmed learning is a technique that is much more likely to be used by a behavioristically oriented teacher than a cognitively oriented one. Programmed learning incorporates many of the principles of reinforcement theory, although the technique was not invented by a reinforcement theorist. The technique was originally developed by Sidney L. Pressey (1926, 1927). Pressey's "testing machine" was effective, but it did not become popular. Thus, we have an example of *Zeitgeist* (spirit of the times). Although Pressey's idea was good, it was not appropriate to the spirit of the time he proposed it. It was left to Skinner to rediscover programmed learning and make it popular. Skinner's detailed account of the rationale behind programmed learning can be found in chapter 5.

Skinner's approach to programming has been called *linear* and involves the following features derived from his theory of learning:

1. **Small steps.** Learners are exposed to small amounts of information and proceed from one frame, or one item of information, to the next in an orderly fashion. This is what is meant by a **linear program.**

2. **Overt responding.** Students are required to respond overtly so that their correct responses can be reinforced and their incorrect responses can be corrected.

3. **Immediate feedback.** Immediately after making responses, students are informed as to whether or not they are correct. This feedback acts as a reinforcer if the answers were correct and as a corrective measure if the answers were wrong.

4. **Self-pacing.** Students proceed through the program at their own pace.

Figure 16-1 provides an example of a Skinnerian linear program.

There are a number of variations of the linear program. For example, some provide students with the opportunity to skip information that they are already familiar with. This procedure usually involves giving students a pre-test on a certain section of the program, and if they perform adequately they are instructed to advance to the next section.

Another kind of programming that allows for even more flexibility is the **branching program.** The branching program is much more complicated than the linear program, since it attempts to *diagnose* the student's responses. The branching program usually involves a multiple choice format. After students have been presented a certain amount of information, they are given a multiple choice question. If they answer correctly, they advance to the next body of information. If they answer incorrectly, they are directed to additional information, depending on the mistake that was made. For example, the program may say "If you picked *B* as your answer, go back and review the material on page 24; if you picked *D* as your answer, repeat Section 3; if you chose *A,* you are correct; please proceed to the next section." Diagrams of various programming techniques are shown in Figure 16-2.

The generalizations from reinforcement theory upon which programmed learning is based can be summarized as follows:

1. Individuals must have feedback in order to learn. That is, they must have the opportunity to determine whether or not their actions or thoughts were correct. Ordinarily, reinforcement acts as feedback in a learning situation.

1. A mass of data, by itself, would be of little use to a researcher unless he had certain procedures for describing or analyzing it.

2. Procedures used to analyze data are called *statistics*. One important function of statistics is to provide information concerning a distribution of individual datum, or *scores*.

3. Procedures used to "make sense" out of a large number of scores are called

   _____ .   statistics

4. The most common questions researchers ask about scores concern *measures of central tendency* and *measures of variability*.

5. Measures of central tendency provide information about the *typical* or *average* score.

6. Measures of variability provide information about how the scores are spread out—that is, how dispersed they are.

7. Measures of central tendency and measures of variability are both procedures used to "make sense" out of a distribution of scores. They are therefore both called

   _____ .   statistics

8. Measures of central tendency are used to find the _____ score.   typical/average/
                                                                                                          representative

9. In order to find information about the dispersion of scores we use measures of

   _____ .   variability

10. There is no one measure of central tendency; there are many. Which one is used depends on the situation. Three of the most commonly used are the *mode*, the *mean*, and the *median*.

11. The average score in a distribution is found by using a measure of _____   central

    _____ .   tendency

12. The mode is merely the score that occurs most frequently in a distribution of scores.

13. The score occurring most frequently in a distribution is called the _____ .   mode

14. What is the mode of this distribution?

20	
18	
18	
18	_____
17	
17	
13	
12	

    18

15. Is 18 the *average* score of the above distribution? _____   yes

16. Is 18 the *typical* score of the above distribution? _____   yes

17. The *mean*, like the mode, is a measure of _____ .   central
                                                                                                          tendency

18. The mean is found by first adding up all the scores in the distribution and then dividing the sum by the number of scores in the distribution. This can be summarized as follows:

    $$\frac{\Sigma X}{N}$$

    Where: Σ = add everything that follows
    X = a score in the distribution
    N = the total number of scores

19. The mean is found by first adding up all the _____ in the   scores
                                                                                                          distribution
    _____ and then _____ the sum by the _____ of   dividing
                                                                                                          number
    scores in the distribution.

Figure 16–1. An example of a linear program where all students cover the same information in the same order. (From *A Self-Directing Introduction to Psychological Experimentation*, p. 13, by B. R. Hergenhahn, 1974, Monterey, CA: Brooks/Cole.)

Linear Programming

Modified Linear Programs

1. Linear program where information can be skipped if it is too easy or already known:

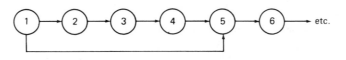

2. Conversational chaining where the answer to a question asked in a previous frame is answered somewhere in the next frame:

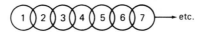

Branching Program

With the branching program, the student's response is used more as a diagnostic tool than a learning device. Typically with this kind of program, students are instructed to move forward in the program if they answer questions correctly. If they answer incorrectly, however, they are instructed to different parts of the program *depending on what kind of mistakes the students make.* Students may, for example, be instructed to repeat an entire section of the program or they may be directed to other information which attempts to clarify their particular type of misunderstanding. In either case the students are again tested and thereafter proceed through the program in a manner dictated by their performances on the test.

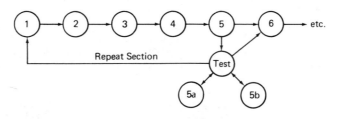

Figure 16–2. Diagrams of various programming techniques.

2. The more quickly a reinforcer follows a desired act, the greater is the likelihood that the act will be repeated. Absence or delay of reinforcement following an act reduces the likelihood that the act will be repeated.

3. The more often an act is reinforced, the more likely the act will be repeated.

4. Through the process of differential reinforcement and successive approximation, students' behavior can be shaped toward a desired goal.

5. Students' behavior can be developed into a complex pattern by first shaping the basic elements of the pattern and then combining the elements into a chainlike sequence.

Is Programmed Learning Effective?

Schramm (1964) reviewed 165 studies of programmed learning. Of the 36 studies that compared programmed instruction with the more traditional kinds of instruction, 17 found programmed instruction to be more effective than traditional instruction; 18 found both kinds of instruction to be equally effective, and only 1 found traditional techniques to be more effective than programmed ones. Therefore, the answer seems to be that programmed learning *is* effective, at least in the areas where it has been tried thus far.

The question as to *why* it is effective is not so easily answered. At present, there is widespread disagreement concerning which aspect of programmed learning results in its effectiveness. For example, the Guthrians maintain that programming is effective because it assures that an appropriate response terminates each frame. It is this event, and not the reinforcing of overt responses, as the Skinnerians would claim, that makes for effective learning (see, e.g., Lumsdaine, 1964). Controversy also exists over the importance of all other aspects of programmed learning, for instance, the nature and importance of knowledge of results, what constitutes a "small step," and the importance of self-pacing. At this time it can be concluded that programmed learning is an effective teaching device, but the essential ingredients that make it effective are still a matter of speculation.

COMPUTER-ASSISTED INSTRUCTION (CAI)

Programmed instructional material can be presented in book form, by teaching machine (see chapter 5), or by computer. When a computer is used to present programmed, or other kinds of instructional material, the process is called **computer-assisted instruction** (CAI). We will discuss several advantages that CAI has over other ways of presenting instructional material.

Using CAI, student-computer interactions can be personalized by giving each student an identification number which when typed into the computer causes the computer to greet the individual student. For example, the computer can print, or vocalize, "Good morning, Linda. You did a fine job yesterday. Let's see how you do today. Are you ready?"

The computer can present complex branching programs that, depending on a student's response, can provide the student with various kinds of corrective information, or can send the student on to the next segment of the program. In this regard, some computers are programmed so that they are capable of carrying on a kind of dialogue with the student by providing various kinds of feedback. For example, if a student responds correctly to a question, the computer may print, or vocalize, "That's correct. Good job! Please continue." If a student responds incorrectly, the computer may respond, "That is incorrect. Please press A, read the material carefully, and try again. Good luck!"

Not only can the computer be used to present instructional material, it can also evaluate how well that material has been learned. After a segment of a program has been completed, the computer can give an achievement test, grade it, and compare the score with the scores of others taking the program. Thus, the computer not only provides immediate feedback during the learning process, it can also provide immediate results of achievement tests for both the students and the teacher. Depending on how students perform, the teacher can determine how well the instructional material is working and take whatever corrective measures that may be necessary. This cannot be done as easily when a textbook and lectures are used to present the material and a midterm and final examination are used to evaluate student learning.

CAI, by providing immediate feedback, personal attention, exciting visual displays, and a gamelike atmosphere, motivates students to learn in ways that traditional instruction may not. In fact, students are often so motivated by CAI that depriving them of their turn with the computer acts as a punishment, and giving them additional time with the computer acts as a reinforcer (Hess & Tenezakis, 1970).

There is considerable evidence that students learn more from CAI than from traditional instruction, and they do so in a shorter period of time. Linskie (1977), for example, reports that third-grade students learning math via CAI achieved much more than students taking traditional classes, and they did so with much greater enthusiasm. Linskie (1977) describes her experience with CAI:

> The students watched the clock to get down to the computer center on time. Once there, seated before the keyboard, the degree of concentration was almost unbelievable. No matter that the nine other students were typing away and that the nine other computers were typing back: nothing seemed to distract the students. The math period became almost like a daily relay race with students waiting impatiently for their own ten minutes with the machine. And there was no paper work to take home, no dirty smudges to displease the teacher, and no plague of broken pencils. . . At the end of the year, the third-graders using the computer-assisted instruction showed a gain of just under two years in achievement while the third-graders taught by conventional methods progressed just over one year. When the experiment was tried in other schools, similar results were achieved through grade six. (p. 210)

Although CAI has been widely used to present various kinds of linear and branching programs, it can do much more. Programs have been written that allow the implications of different kinds of political and sociological systems to be studied, simulate a variety of psychological experiments, perform chemistry experiments without the need to handle equipment or chemicals (Bunderson, 1967) and teach problem-solving skills to engineers (Brown & Burton, 1975). Indeed, CAI is becoming so sophisticated that there are many who believe that it can be used to teach anything that a good teacher is capable of teaching. It is claimed that even such topics as philosophy, religion, art appreciation, and creativity could be taught by CAI, if instructional goals could be clearly specified. If we can get teachers to clearly describe what a student is doing when he or she is being creative or appreciating art, say CAI enthusiasts, we can write a program that will teach those behaviors. There is a relationship, then, among programmed learning, CAI, and the topic to which we turn next, behaviorally defined educational objectives.

EDUCATIONAL OBJECTIVES STATED IN BEHAVIORAL TERMS

Clearly, the best teaching technique is the one that allows teachers to most effectively and efficiently meet their course objectives. Any teaching method must be evaluated in terms of course objectives. This means that instructors must be able to determine whether or not, and to what extent, the objectives of their course have been met. In other words, performance on each course objective must be measurable, and unless the objectives manifest themselves in behavior, they cannot be measured. The course objectives should tell the students what the instructor hopes they will learn in the course, and the evaluative devices, such as examinations, should allow both the instructor and the student to determine to what extent the objectives have been met.

In *Preparing Instructional Objectives* (1961) Mager puts the matter as follows:

> Suppose I offered to teach your children to be logical thinkers for $1,000. Now, if I could do it, you would be getting a real bargain. But would you agree to such a bargain unless I told you beforehand more explicitly what I intended to accomplish and how we would measure my success? I hope not. In a sense, a teacher makes a contract with his students. The students agree to pay a certain sum in return for certain skills and knowledge. But most of the time, they are expected to pay for something that is never carefully defined or described. They are asked to buy (with effort) a product that they are not allowed to see and that is only vaguely described. The teacher, who does not describe to the best of his ability how he intends the learner to be different after his instruction, is certainly taking unfair advantage of his students. (p. 16a)

Preparing measurable educational objectives is difficult, since educational goals have traditionally been stated in subjective terms. Mager (1972, p. vi) calls these subjective goals "Fuzzies" because "There is no way of telling when you have one." In order to "unfuzzify" an abstract concept or goal, Mager suggests a **goal analysis** involving the following steps (1972):

Robert F. Mager. (Courtesy of R. F. Mager)

1. Write down the goal.

2. Jot down, in words or phrases, the performances that, if achieved, would cause you to agree the goal is achieved.

3. Sort out the jottings. Delete duplications and unwanted items. Repeat steps one and two for any unwanted abstractions (Fuzzies) considered important.

4. Write a complete statement for each performance, describing the nature, quality, or amount you will consider acceptable.

5. Test the statements with the question. If someone achieved or demonstrated each of these performances, would I be willing to say he has achieved the goal? When you can answer yes, the analysis is finished. (p. 72)

Elsewhere, Mager (1961, p. 11) offers a comparison between some words used in defining educational objectives that are easily translated into behavior and some that are not (that is, Fuzzies):

Words Open to Many Interpretations

To know   To grasp the significance of

To understand   To enjoy

To **really** understand   To believe

To appreciate   To have faith in

To **fully** appreciate

Words Open to Fewer Interpretations

To write	To construct
To recite	To list
To identify	To compare
To differentiate	To contrast
To solve	

It should be noted that what applies to defining course objectives also applies to defining institutional objectives. For example, the extent to which institutional objectives—such as "to realize the interrelatedness of knowledge" or "to fully appreciate the impact of one's values on one's behavior"—have been met would be very difficult to determine.

Once they are clearly stated, measurable course objectives create a situation where students may meet those objectives in a variety of ways. Some students may wish to take the class as a traditional lecture class. Other students, however, may meet the course objectives by independent reading, related employment or travel, interviewing certain individuals, or writing a research paper. Once course objectives are stated in measurable terms, it is possible to determine the extent to which anyone has met them. It should not matter where or how the necessary information was gathered. If students can demonstrate that they have met the course objectives, they can be given credit in the course.

Although a number of alternative educational formats are currently being explored, the structured course with scheduled lectures and examinations is still very popular among both instructors and students. As popular as the lecture format is, however, in some cases it may not be the most effective teaching technique.

THE LECTURE AS A TEACHING TECHNIQUE

There are a number of instructors who, for one reason or another, question the effectiveness of the lecture as a teaching technique and, as we have seen, a number of learning theorists also have reservations about lecturing. One concern about lecturing is the fact that it typically moves along at a certain pace although there are vast individual differences among the students listening in terms of their ability to keep up and understand what is being presented. Another concern with the lecture is over its usefulness in teaching factual information. For example, Bugelski (1979, p. 379) reports a study in which 30 facts were presented to college students in a short lecture. After one presentation of the material the average number of facts remembered was only seven.

Obviously, one alternative to lecturing is to simply have students read the material they are to learn. Printed material can be read at the student's own pace, and if something is missed, the student can go back over the material as many times as is necessary. The idea that reading may be a more efficient way of learning than attending a lecture is not new. Samuel Johnson had the following to say in 1766: "People have nowadays . . . got a strange opinion that everything should be taught by lectures. Now, I cannot see that lectures can do so much good as reading the books from which the lectures are taken" (Boswell, 1952, p. 144). And in 1781, he said: "Lectures were once useful; but now, when all can read, the books are so numerous, lectures are unnecessary. If your attention fails and you miss a part of a lecture, it is lost; you cannot go back as you do upon a book" (Boswell, 1952, p. 471).

Even with the possible shortcomings of the lecture, there appears to be at least three conditions under which its use is clearly justified. First, it may be the best way to share new ideas that are not yet available in print. Second, most of us enjoy listening to a prominent individual present his or her ideas to an audience. For example, the major addresses given by prominent psychologists at conventions are almost always well attended. Third, a good lecturer can instill interest in a topic because of his or her enthusiasm and manner of presentation. Thus, a good lecturer can sometimes motivate students to learn in a way that printed material cannot.

What about the situation where a great person is not available, lectures are less than enthusiastic, and where the information lectured on is readily available in other forms, such as books, articles, handouts, films, tapes, and so on? Under these circumstances, many instructors seek an alternative to lecturing, and of course, there are many. Some instructors restrict the size of their classes so that active discussion is possible. Some have students do independent study which is then discussed either with the instructor alone or with a small group. Others use programmed material extensively. Still others turn to PSI or personalized systems of instruction. It is this latter form of instruction to which we turn next.

PERSONALIZED SYSTEMS OF INSTRUCTION

What is now called **"a personalized system of instruction"** or **PSI** was originally called the "Keller Plan" after Fred Keller who developed it (Keller, 1968). Keller argues that calling this approach to education the Keller Plan is unfortunate since (a) he was not alone in developing it; (b) someone may try it and fail, in which case he would not want his name associated with it; and (c) he may come up with an even better plan in the future. So, although Keller can be looked upon as responsible for the development of personalized instruction, we now refer to such instruction as PSI rather than the Keller Plan.

At the present time there is a trend in this country toward individualized instruction. Offering an individualized course usually involves four steps that can be summarized as follows:

1. Determine the material to be covered in the course.
2. Divide the material into self-contained segments.
3. Create methods of evaluating the degree to which the student has conquered the material in a given segment.
4. Allow students to move from segment to segment at their own pace.

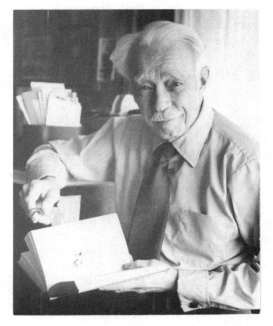

Fred S. Keller. (Courtesy of F. S. Keller)

These are the main ingredients in most individualized courses; but even after one has decided upon individualized instruction, there are a number of decisions yet to be made. For example:

1. What material should be included in the course?

2. How many individual segments should the course contain?

3. What should a segment consist of? (For example, reading assignments, films, audio tapes, field trips, a programmed unit, travel, attending a play or concert or speech, conducting an interview with a politician or an author, conducting an experiment, and so on.)

4. How is performance on a given segment to be evaluated? (For example, essay exam, multiple choice exam, oral exam, a research project, a written report, and so on.)

5. What degree of proficiency will be required? (For example, an instructor may demand complete mastery in one segment of the course before the student is permitted to commence with the next segment.)

6. Should any time limit be imposed on the students as to when they must finish individual segments or the entire course? (For example, the instructor may say that all students must finish the course no later than the end of the academic term; however, within that period, students can move from segment to segment at whatever pace they feel is best for them.)

7. Should optional discussion sessions be scheduled so that students can discuss course material with the instructor and other interested students?

8. Should students be given the opportunity to retake examinations on which they did poorly? Some instructors allow students to take segment tests more than once in which case the highest score is retained and the other score or scores is discarded.

9. Should bonus points be given to students who progress through the course in accordance with a certain schedule? The biggest problem in a PSI course is procrastination. That is, when students can take tests whenever they choose to do so, many of them delay taking tests too long and fall behind. Many students who procrastinate too long end up needing to take a large number of tests at the end of the term and their grades suffer. One way to solve this problem is to add bonus points to the test scores of students who take tests at a reasonable rate, for example, once a week.

What does individualizing a course do to test score distributions? The answer to this question depends on how the instructor deals with item 5 above, degree of proficiency required. For example, if the instructor demands complete mastery of each segment, there will be no distribution of scores. Each student finishing the course will receive the same grade, presumably an A. But the instructor may not demand complete mastery on one segment before the student is allowed to proceed to the next. The instructor may just test over the material in a segment and how well students do on the test will determine what grade they receive on that segment. Because students in an individualized course decide for themselves when they are ready to take a test, the latter procedure also results in a very restricted distribution of test scores.

Even when complete mastery is not required, students in an individualized course will generally obtain As or Bs as a final grade. This is because, within an individualized course, many personal factors that cause test score distributions are eliminated. If students are ill, emotionally disturbed, overloaded with other work, in need of additional information, or for whatever reason are not ready to be tested, they simply postpone taking the test. What usually happens in a self-paced course is that there are periods when students will go through two or three segments very rapidly, and then may not take another segment test for a considerable length of time. Presumably personal events in their lives are constantly changing, and therefore, one time is better for taking a test than another time.

Are PSI Courses Effective?

Ryan (1974) reviewed a large number of studies where student performance in PSI courses was compared with student performance in lecture courses and reached the following conclusion: "Without exception, these studies have shown that students learning under the personalized system achieve at superior levels compared to students learning under the lecture format" (p. 16). Kulik, Kulik, and Carmichael (1974) reached a similar conclusion after reviewing college science courses where either a PSI or a lecture format was employed.

What do students think of the PSI format? Ryan (1974) summarized student reactions to PSI courses as follows: "If student reactions were the only criterion to be considered when contemplating a shift from lecture-discussion teaching to a personalized course, it is easy to get the impression that there would be little defense for remaining committed to a conventional mode. The students sampled in the studies reviewed here were overwhelmingly in favor of personalized courses" (p. 20). Ryan (1974) warns, however, that PSI is based on sound learning principles, and if these principles are either not understood or ignored, the PSI format could be ineffective.

People involved in the frustrating job of teaching are always looking for something that works. There is a danger that people not as knowledgeable about behavior theory principles as they should be will adopt the method wholesale and proceed to implement the technique's prescription regardless of the situational appropriateness. The eventual result is another heavy-handed, mechanical-educational practice that relentlessly satisfies its own needs rather than those of the students. (p. 22)

Criticisms of PSI. PSI has been criticized for many of the same reasons that programmed learning and CAI have been criticized. Many feel that none of these techniques exemplify "true" teaching because they minimize the role of the teacher. Critics say that all three approaches create an instructional situation that is cold, mechanical, and dehumanizing. That is, the important, spontaneous interactions between teacher and students, and among students themselves, is absent from programmed learning, CAI, and PSI. Some critics also say that the most important kind of educational material cannot be specified to the point where it can be programmed or arranged in segments. A related criticism concerns the usual demand on the part of those using programmed learning, CAI, or PSI that course objectives be specified in behavioral terms. Many critics insist that the loftiest and most desirable educational objectives cannot be easily measured and perhaps never fully reached. For example, Meek (1977) maintains that, because those teaching PSI courses usually insist on having course objectives that are clearly specified and measurable, PSI courses generally do not have very important objectives. Meek offers the following suggestions as to what the goals of a PSI or any kind of course, should be: "The primary goals of such courses should involve an attempt to develop the ability of the student to think critically, to sort, to order, to choose among, to evaluate, and to interrelate competing ideals and ideas. The student must learn how to learn, how to evaluate ideas and data, and how to relate information acquired to her or his own values and those that are present in the larger society . . . It is basic nonsense to talk about the degree of 'mastery' of such goals" (pp. 115–116).

In spite of criticisms such as those described above, many instructors and administrators, once skeptical of PSI, are now arguing for its expanded utilization. Entire departments, and in some cases, entire colleges, use PSI exclusively. Although this approach to education started in psychology, it is now being utilized to teach such topics as mathematics, language, statistics, English, philosophy, engineering, and political science.

In his now famous article "Good-Bye Teacher" (1968), Fred Keller described his individualized approach to education that we summarized above. Upon noting the superiority of this technique over the more traditional lecture technique of teaching, Keller concluded the following about the teacher of tomorrow (1968):

> He becomes an educational engineer, a contingency manager, with the responsibility of serving the great majority, rather than the small minority, of young men and women who come to him for schooling in the area of his competence. The teacher of tomorrow will not, I think, continue to be satisfied with a 10 per cent efficiency (at best) which makes him an object of contempt by some, commiseration by others, indifference by many, and love by a few. No longer will he need to hold his position by the exercise of functions that neither transmit culture, dignify his status, nor encourage respect for learning in others. No longer will he need to live, like Ichabod Crane, in a world that increasingly begrudges providing him room and lodging for a doubtful service to its young. A new kind of teacher is in the making. To the old kind, I, for one, will be glad to say, "Good-Bye." (p. 89)

Keller's point, of course, is that instructors will need to become more concerned with how their students learn. The time is near when an instructor no longer will be able to merely dispense information and leave it up to the students to learn it. Tomorrow's instructor, whether cognitively or behavioristically oriented, will need to ponder various classroom formats in order to discover which one is optimally conducive to learning. Such an individual will need to be converted from the traditional college professor to what Carl Rogers calls a "facilitator of learning" or what Keller calls either an "educational engineer" or a "contingency manager."

Although Keller is now well into his eighties, he still believes that widespread utilization of the PSI format would cure many of the ills that characterize our educational system. Following is part of a conversation that Keller had with Paul Chance. The entire conversation is published in the September 1984 issue of *Psychology Today*.

> *Keller* . . . . We've got to make fundamental changes in the educational system. I keep thinking, where is the soft, round belly of the beast? How can we get into this structure and change it? Ah, it isn't easy.
>
> *Chance*. You sound very pessimistic.
>
> *Keller*. Well, it's time for pessimism. Look at what the recent reports on education have recommended: Lengthen the school day and the school year.
>
> *Chance*. Yes. What we're doing now isn't working, so let's do more of it.
>
> *Keller*. It's sad, isn't it? Or they say, "Crack the whip."
>
> *Chance*. Make it even more unpleasant than it is now.

Keller. Amazing. But what do they recommend to improve teaching? What do they say about making learning more interesting, more effective, less fraught with failure? Very little. We have an alternative. We know it will work, and that it will avoid many of the problems associated with group instruction. But we aren't willing to make the necessary changes in the educational institution.

Chance. You used to be more optimistic. In 1974 you wrote, "The days of traditional group education may be numbered."

Keller. Oh, God. I was so naive. Well, by 1974 we had 10 years of research showing that PSI was better than the traditional approach. The evidence was so clear. I thought, "Well, we have got a better mousetrap and the world will beat a path to our door." It didn't happen. I had no idea how immovable the educational establishment was.

Chance. Do you think it's possible that things are finally so bad that the traditional system will collapse?

Keller. That would be wonderful. I would like to believe that. But I really don't hold out much hope for it happening in this century.

Chance. It's a possibility, isn't it? I'm trying to find a way to end this conversation on an optimistic note.

Keller. Well, every once in awhile I read about somebody who has come out in favor of self-pacing or mastery of small units. I see things like that, and I think, "Well, we haven't been entirely without effect." But is anybody ever going to say, "Let's swallow the whole damn pill"? No, I don't look for it. I wish I could.

Chance. Does that mean you've given up?

Keller. No, I haven't given up. This is something positive I can work for, something I can put my heart into. I'll keep at it. And I'll probably be at it the day I die. (p. 48)

In summary, many believe that modern teachers will have an attitude of openness, a willingness to try a variety of approaches to teaching, and a receptivity for new information about learning and about the learner. They will have a dedication to task analysis in order to determine what a learning experience consists of. They will have a greater realization that there may be other people or events that can do a far better job of teaching than they can. Teachers will be more willing to delegate responsibility for teaching to individuals or events in a better position to teach than they are. Such teachers will be transformed from knowledge dispensers to arrangers of optimal learning experiences. This will be true at all educational levels. The school will become a place where learning experiences are evaluated and strategies for optimal learning for the student are formulated.

The answer to the question, "How best to teach?" is unfolding rapidly these days. The real problem in the future will be to determine what is worth knowing.

DISCUSSION QUESTIONS

1. What would be the basic differences between the behavioristically oriented teacher and the cognitively oriented teacher in their approach to teaching?

2. Why, according to Skinner, do teachers get so little respect and what does Skinner say they could do to get more respect?

3. Summarize Popper's theory of learning and show how it might be applied in the classroom.

4. What, according to Norman, can the frequency with which questions are asked in the classroom tell the teacher about the students' cognitive structures?

5. Discuss what implications the findings from research on hemispheric functioning may have for educational practices.

6. Contrast the view of reinforcement of the behaviorist with that of the cognitive theorist.

7. Why, according to Mager, is it important to avoid terms such as "to know," "to understand," "to appreciate," and "to grasp the significance of" while specifying course objectives?

8. Describe how, according to Mager, an abstract concept or goal can be "unfuzzified."

9. What is meant by the statement, "Different assumptions about human nature suggest different approaches to education"? Give a few examples of how an assumption about human nature might affect one's approach to teaching.

10. Do you feel that it is important that teachers be familiar with various theories of learning? Defend your answer.

11. What theory of transfer of training do you feel public school curriculum is based upon? Do you see any remnants of formal discipline in American education? Explain.

12. Describe the advantages and disadvantages of programmed learning.

13 Discuss the advantages of CAI over other methods of presenting educational material. Also, describe any disadvantages you feel CAI has.

14. Summarize the steps involved in creating a PSI course.

15. Discuss the pros and cons of lecturing as a teaching technique.

16. For what has the PSI format been criticized? Do you agree or disagree with these criticisms? Explain.

17. React to the statement: "Either students meet the objectives of a course or they do not. If they do, they should be given credit for taking the course. If they do not, no credit should be given. In other words, students are either given credit or not, with no shades in between."

18. What, according to Keller, would revolutionize American education? Do you agree or disagree with Keller? Explain.

CHAPTER HIGHLIGHTS

Behaviorally defined objectives. Course, or institutional, objectives that are defined in terms of the behavior that is exhibited when a student meets a specified objective.

Branching program. A type of programmed learning that directs learners to different parts of the program, depending upon their performance at any particular point of the program. For example, if they make a serious mistake, they may be directed to repeat a previous section of the program.

Cognitive hunger. Popper's term for the innate desire to continuously revise expectancies so that they are increasingly accurate in reflecting reality.

Computer-assisted instruction (CAI). The utilization of computers to present and evaluate a wide variety of educational materials.

Contingency management. Arranging an environment so that certain responses are reinforced and others are not.

Facilitator of learning. Someone who, according to Carl Rogers, attempts to discover what a student is interested in knowing, and then determines the best way to make that information available to the student.

Formal discipline (also called mental discipline). See Chapter Highlights for chapter 3.

Frame. A term used in programmed learning to describe the small amount of information presented to the learner. In a linear program, the learner proceeds through the program frame by frame until a body of information is mastered.

Goal analysis. A procedure that converts a subjective goal into examples of the kinds of behavior that will be engaged in when the goal is reached.

Immediate feedback (also called immediate knowledge of results). The arrangement whereby learners are informed about the accuracy of their answers immediately following a learning or testing experience.

Linear program. A type of program that requires each student to go through the same sequence of information in the same order.

Overt responding. A response that can be observed by others, as opposed to a covert response, which is not publicly observable.

Performance-based course. Any course that is arranged so that progress through it, or completion of it, is contingent upon the performance of the student.

Personalized System of Instruction (PSI). A teaching technique developed by Keller that involves dividing course material into segments, evaluating student performance on each segment, and allowing students to move from segment to segment at their own pace.

Programmed learning. See Chapter Highlights for chapter 5.

Self-paced course. A course arranged so that students can determine for themselves the best pace with which to proceed through the course.

Transfer of training. See Chapter Highlights for chapter 3.

17

A Final Word

In chapter 1, an effort was made to define learning and to differentiate it from other processes such as habituation, sensitization, and instinct. In chapter 2, the characteristics of science were discussed as they apply to the study of learning. Chapter 3 outlined the historical antecedents of learning theory. Subsequent chapters provided detailed accounts of the major theories that grew out of this rich philosophical heritage. Each of the major theories was listed under one of four paradigms, depending upon which historical theme it followed. The theories that were strongly influenced by Darwin were listed under the functionalistic paradigm. Those theories following in the tradition of Aristotle and Locke were listed under the associationistic paradigm. The theories following in the tradition of Plato, Descartes, Kant, and the faculty psychologists were listed under the cognitive paradigm. Hebb's theory was offered as an example of the neurophysiological paradigm which also has its historical roots in the work of Descartes.

In this final chapter, we will discuss what the trends seem to be within current learning theory. Our discussion of current trends in no way implies that the information presented in the preceding chapters is obsolete. Almost everything occurring in learning theory today is, in some way, an extension of one of the major theories of learning presented in this book. In order to truly understand such an extension it is necessary to understand the theory from which it is derived.

Thus, we have explored learning theory's past and present. In this chapter, we will attempt to indicate where learning theory seems to be heading and ponder a few questions that it will need to address in the future.

CURRENT TRENDS IN LEARNING THEORY

At least four major trends can be seen in today's approach to the study of learning. First, today's learning theory is more humble in scope. Instead of attempting to explain all aspects of learning, today's theorist is content to investigate some aspect of the learning process. The theories of Estes in chapter 9 offer examples of the reduced domain of contemporary learning theories.

A second major trend in current research on learning is the increased emphasis on neurophysiological techniques. As we saw in chapter 15, neurophysiological explanations of learning have come from a position of obscurity during the peak of the behavioristic movement to one of the most popular approaches to the study of learning today.

Third, cognitive processes such as concept formation, risk taking, and problem solving are again a respectable and popular topic of study. Cognitive processes, because of their apparent close relationship to introspection, were largely ignored during the dominance of behaviorism. It should be clear that in turning again to cognitive processes, psychology is broadening its base, but it is not becoming unscientific. Behaviorism was an extreme reaction to the method of introspection and was an attempt to make psychology a science by giving it a reliable, observable subject matter—behavior. There are those who maintain that behaviorism threw out the baby with the bath water by defining behavior in such a way as to exclude "higher mental processes," such as concept formation and problem solving, or thinking in general. Currently, these areas are of vital interest to psychologists and they are being explored scientifically. As with any other scientific research, the ultimate authority in research on cognitive processes is empirical observation. Theories are devised, hypotheses are generated, experiments are run, and as the result of their outcome, theories are strengthened or weakened. The method is the same as that of the traditional behaviorist; what has changed is the behavior that is being studied. Saltz says (1971):

> After many years of very self-conscious empiricism, the psychology of human learning has begun to show signs of a vigorous interest in new (and often dramatic!) theoretical approaches. We find the postulations of multiple storage systems for memory; the distinction between learning systems and retrieval systems; the attempt to analyze "what is learned" into a complex system of interacting variables.
>
> Further, there is evidence to suggest that psychologists in the area of human learning may have lost some of their fear of studying complex processes. There has developed a lively new interest in such issues as the nature of concept acquisition; the role of strategies in learning; and the more general question of the nature and function of variables like intention, meaning, and imagery. In short, there is a new interest in the role of the *cognitive,* information-processing variables in human learning. (p. vii)

The trend toward cognitive theory by no means indicates that behaviorism is dead. Behaviorism remains a powerful force in psychology and will no doubt remain so for a considerable time. Skinner (1974) says that true behaviorism has never really been tried. If it had, he maintains, it would be possible to solve many human problems. Skinner pleads for the development of a technology of human behavior based on behavioristic notions. He claims older strategies for solving major human problems based on mentalistic or cognitive theories of behavior have been totally ineffective, and unless a more effective means of dealing with these problems is found, they will persist. Skinner put the matter as follows (1974):

> I contend that behavioral science has not made a greater contribution just because it is not very behavioristic. It has recently been pointed out that an International Congress on Peace was composed of statesmen, political scientists, historians, economists, physicists, biologists—and not a single behaviorist in the strict sense. Evidently behaviorism was regarded as useless. But we must ask what the conference achieved. It was composed of specialists from many different fields, who probably spoke the commonsense lingua franca of the layman, with its heavy load of references to inner causation. What might the conference have achieved if it could have abandoned this false scent? The currency of mentalism in discussions of human affairs may explain why conferences on peace are held with such monotonous regularity year after year. (p. 250)

Skinner has never waivered in his attack on cognitive psychology. At best, he says, cognitive psychology is simply old wine in new bottles: "Cognitive psychology is certainly in the ascendant. The word *cognitive* is sprinkled through the psychological literature like salt—and, like salt, not so much for any flavor of its own but to bring out the flavor of other things, things which a quarter of a century ago would have been called by other names" (Skinner, 1984, p. 949).

At worst, cognitive psychology makes flagrant mistakes that retard our understanding of human behavior. Skinner (1987) lists the many mistakes he feels cognitive psychology is making in the form of accusations:

> I *accuse* cognitive scientists of misusing the metaphor of storage. The brain is not an encyclopedia, library, or museum. People are changed by their experiences; they do not store copies of them as representations or rules.
>
> I *accuse* cognitive scientists of speculating about internal processes which they have no appropriate means of observing. Cognitive science is premature neurology.
>
> I *accuse* cognitive scientists of emasculating laboratory research by substituting descriptions of settings for the settings themselves and reports of intentions and expectations for action.
>
> I *accuse* cognitive scientists of reviving a theory in which feelings and states of mind observed through introspection are taken as the causes of behavior rather than as collateral effects of the causes.
>
> I *accuse* cognitive scientists, as I would accuse psychoanalysts, of claiming to explore the depths of human behavior, of inventing explanatory systems that are admired for a profundity more properly called inaccessibility.
>
> I *accuse* cognitive scientists of speculation characteristic of metaphysics, literature, and daily intercourse, speculation perhaps suitable enough in such arenas but inimical to science.
>
> Let us bring behaviorism back from the Devil's Island to which it was transported for a crime it never committed, and let psychology become once again a behavioral science. (p. 111)

At the moment, it appears that Skinner's brand of behaviorism is losing ground to cognitive psychology, but the battle is far from over.

A fourth major trend in learning theory today is the increased concern with the application of learning principles to the solution of practical problems. Recently, there have been many attempts to show how learning principles can be used to improve teaching and child rearing. Learning is currently being emphasized in the explanation of personality development. Some of the more effective psychotherapeutic techniques of today are based on learning principles. Learning principles are being used as a basis for redesigning mental and penal institutions. Learning principles are currently being investigated in their relationship to warfare, international relations, legal and judicial procedures, and public health. Learning is being explored as a means of modifying national attitudes toward pollution and population control. And, related to the last point, learning is being studied as a means of instituting cultural change in general. Also, as we saw in chapter 14, Norman is calling for the development of a field called cognitive engineering, which would wed technology with the principles of cognitive science. Such a marriage, Norman believes, would reduce errors that result from human-machine interactions and also would increase productivity. No doubt the next decade will see an ever-growing concern with the application of learning principles to the solution of many human problems.

SOME UNANSWERED QUESTIONS ABOUT LEARNING

How Does Learning Vary as a Function of Maturation?

Many investigators have found that the learning that occurs at one maturational stage is not the same as that which occurs at another maturational stage (Piaget and Hebb). Instead of thinking of learning as a unitary process that either occurs or not, we need to explore further how the learning process may change as a function of maturation. Indeed, such information will be vital in the areas of education and child rearing.

Does Learning Depend on Reinforcement?

Many learning theorists would answer this question in the affirmative, but their opinions would vary when it came time to describe the nature of reinforcement. Thorndike's concept of reinforcement would be "a satisfying state of affairs." Pavlov equates reinforcement with an unconditioned stimulus. For Guthrie, it is anything that causes an abrupt change in stimulating conditions. For Skinner, it is anything that increases the rate of responding. For Hull, it is anything that causes drive stimulus reduction. For Tolman, it would be the confirmation of an expectancy. The Gestaltists would liken reinforcement to the reduction of ambiguity. For Bandura, intrinsic reinforcement is the feeling one has when one's performance matches or exceeds one's internalized standards or when a personal goal is attained. Also for Bandura, as for Tolman, Norman, and Spence, extrinsic reinforcers can be used to cause an organism to convert what had previously been learned into behavior. Thus for Bandura, Norman, Spence, and Tolman, extrinsic reinforcers influence performance, not learning. Although these definitions of reinforcement, in some cases, are substantially different, they all point out that some of our innumerable daily experiences "stick" and others do not. The process that causes some experiences to be retained can be loosely referred to as reinforcement. What, if anything, all these versions of reinforcement have in common has not yet been determined.

How Does Learning Vary as a Function of Species?

Animals higher on the phylogenetic scale have more highly developed brains and a more complex central nervous system in general. Can we, therefore, expect to find a difference in learning ability among different species of animals? Bitterman (1960) has found that some species of animals cannot learn at all what another species can learn with ease. To what extent can we generalize what we learn about learning from one animal species to another? What, for example, can studying the learning process in the rat tell us about the learning process in humans? The problem of the generalizability of research findings in learning is currently receiving wide attention.

How Does Learned Behavior Interact with Instinctive Behavior?

We noted in chapter 5, that the Brelands (1961) observed that animals that were conditioned to perform various tricks, such as placing coins in a bank, would eventually revert back to behaviors that they would normally engage in under the circumstances. For example, raccoons that were reinforced with food for dropping coins in a bank eventually refused to give up the coins. Instead they would hold the coins and rub them together. In other words, they treated the coins as if they were food. This phenomenon was referred to as instinctual drift, because it seemed that the organism's learned behavior gradually gave way to its instinctive behavior. Such observations have led many psychologists to conclude that an organism's innate response tendencies may place limits on the extent to which its behavior can be modified through learning. The extent of these limits, and whether such limits exist on the human level, remain unanswered questions.

Can Some Associations Be Learned More Easily Than Others?

In chapter 7, we saw that Seligman (1970) concluded that organisms are biologically prepared to form some associations, biologically contraprepared to form others, and are biologically neutral in terms of forming still other associations. As evidence for his contention, Seligman offered the work of Garcia and his colleagues who found that taste aversions are formed rapidly (sometimes in just one trial) and last for a very long period of time. Furthermore, Garcia and his colleagues found that other associations that were less natural were difficult to form. This suggests that those associations that are directly related to an organism's survival are easiest for the organism to form. Thus, we have another example of how an organism's genetic endowment interacts with the learning process. Which associations are easiest to learn for various species and why some are easier to learn than others are questions that are currently receiving considerable attention.

How Does Learning Vary as a Function of Personality Characteristics?

After operationally defining such traits as introversion or extroversion using existing paper and pencil tests, is it possible that learning ability may be found to differ as a function of such traits? Research has shown, for example, that high-anxious subjects are conditioned more rapidly than low-anxious subjects (Taylor, 1951). In Taylor's research, high- and low-anxious subjects were distinguished by using the Taylor Manifest Anxiety Scale. How many other personality traits can be operationally defined and found to interact with learning rate? The answer to this question will be especially important in the realm of education. Since personality is currently thought of as the product of early learning, the question here is really how learning early in life affects later learning, or how the development of a cluster of strong habits influences the development of subsequent habits.

To What Extent Is Learning a Function of the Total Environment?

How does what children learn in school relate to what they learn from their parents, from television, from books, from toys and games, or from their peers? What happens when teachers encourage behavior that is not supported by anyone else in the children's lives? What happens if parents are encouraging certain behavior patterns in their children, but their peer groups encourage other, and perhaps incompatible, forms of behavior? Of concern here is how the many learning experiences a person has in a short period of time are related to each other.

How Do All of the Preceding Questions Interact with Type of Learning?

The term *interaction* is one of the most important terms in science. In general, two variables are said to interact when the effect of one variable is different at different levels of the second variable. Aspirin, for example, has different effects on people, depending on whether or not they consumed alcohol before taking it. Aspirin and alcohol, then, are said to interact. Lack of sleep may have no effect on weightlifting, but it may have a deleterious effect on typewriting. In this case, the effects of sleep loss on performance are said to interact with task complexity. That is, at one level of task complexity—weightlifting—loss of sleep has little or no effect, whereas at another—typing—it has a considerable effect.

Assuming that there is more than one kind of learning, it is possible that motivation (e.g., drive) may be important for one kind of learning but not for another. Drive may be important for instrumental conditioning, but not for what Tolman called sign-learning. It may be that the laws of classical and instrumental conditioning are the same for all species of animals, but other forms of learning are only found in animals high on the phylogenetic scale. It could be that some learning occurs in an all-or-none fashion, while other kinds of learning may be incremental. It may be that personality type also interacts with type of learning. For example, there may be a difference in learning rate between high- and low-anxious subjects in a classical conditioning situation, but not in a problem-solving situation. A crisscross interaction is even possible in some cases. For example, high- and low-anxious subjects may perform in an opposite manner when the type of learning required of them is changed. This theoretical possibility is shown in Figure 17-1.

Obviously, it is possible that mediational processes are very important for concept formation and problem solving, but may not be at all important for classical or operant conditioning. Thus, Thorndike's contention that learning is direct and independent of mediational processes would be true of only some kinds of learning. Likewise, the Gestalt contention that learning involves the conscious reduction of ambiguity would also be only partially true. Whether or not "thinking" is important may depend entirely on what kind of learning one is talking about.

Figure 17–1. A theoretical interaction showing how anxiety level has a different effect on learning rate depending on what kind of learning is involved. In this case, low-anxious subjects learn to solve a problem much faster than high-anxious subjects. When classical conditioning is examined, however, it is seen that low-anxious subjects take much longer to condition than high-anxious subjects.

Also, it could turn out that everyone's notion of reinforcement is correct. Classical conditioning could, indeed, depend upon the presentation of an unconditioned stimulus. Instrumental conditioning may depend on drive stimulus reduction as described by Hull, or on a "satisfying state of affairs" as described by Thorndike. Other kinds of learning may be more conveniently explained by using the concept of reinforcement suggested by Guthrie, Skinner, Premack, Tolman, or the Gestaltists. The current belief that there are a number of different kinds of learning, rather than one or two, makes all these positions plausible. This, of course, is the approach that Tolman was suggesting in his 1949 article "There Is More Than One Kind of Learning," and more recently by Gagné (1970).

As we have seen, learned behavior appears to interact with instinctive behavior. It is possible that when certain lower animals are in certain situations where instinctive behavior is appropriate, learned behavior cannot compete. This may be true for only certain organisms and certain situations. Furthermore, it may not be at all true at the human level. Also, we have seen that for certain organisms, learning principles can be used to readily form some associations, but other associations are formed with great difficulty. Thus, we see that genetic endowment, the nature of the learning task, and learning principles all seem to interact in a complex way.

It seems that as more is known about any area, it is easier to make finer distinctions within it. As more is known about the area of learning, it becomes more differentiated. The area of learning has become very heterogeneous, compared to the rather undifferentiated field it was not too many years ago. Like most subjects that we come to know more about, learning has become more complicated instead of less complicated. As it stands today, the field of learning can justify a number of different approaches to its study and a variety of explanations of its facts. As each of the new subdivisions of learning is studied more extensively, we will see more spinoffs from the general field of learning into separate autonomous fields, such as the neurophysiology of learning, cognitive learning, and mathematical models of learning. As these areas themselves become more differentiated, we will begin to see spinoffs from them, for example, "Markov models of learning," "learning and the single cell," and "the effects of early experience on learning." And on it goes. One can see this process of differentiation in the evolution of any science.

NO FINAL ANSWERS ABOUT THE LEARNING PROCESS

There are no final answers concerning the nature of the learning process found in this book. But that fact should not bother the student, since in science there are never any final answers. In science, knowledge evolves and evolution depends upon variety. Clearly, most of what is now known about learning came out of the great debates among learning theorists that took place in the 1930s and 1940s. Healthy criticism and defense of one's position seem to provide an atmosphere conducive to the growth of a young science. Fortunately, such an atmosphere still exists in psychology, but the debate among theorists is not as intense as it once was.

Where does this leave the student who is interested in learning about learning? The student has a smorgasbord of approaches to the study of learning before her or him. He or she can either choose the one that best satisfies the appetite and concentrate exclusively on it, or the student can sample from all of them. While building a house, sometimes a hammer is the most effective tool, sometimes a screwdriver, and at still other times, a saw. The student who decides to sample from the smorgasbord is like the house builder who selects different tools as different problems emerge. A third approach may result if a student cannot develop an appetite for any of the theories developed thus far. Such a student may someday develop his or her own theory. After all, this is what Thorndike, Pavlov, Skinner, Hull, Guthrie, Piaget, Tolman, Bandura, Norman, Hebb, and the Gestalt psychologists did. At this stage of knowledge concerning the nature of learning, all three approaches are necessary.

In the determination of man's behavior, there is no process more important than learning, and if that be so, one of the most worthwhile enterprises a person could engage in is to help unravel the mysteries of that process.

DISCUSSION QUESTIONS

1. Define the term interaction. Give a few examples of interactions not described in this chapter.
2. Discuss four major trends in learning theory today.
3. Summarize Skinner's opposition to cognitive psychology.

4. What is meant by the statement, "The field of learning is becoming increasingly differentiated"?

5. List and briefly discuss the unanswered questions about learning.

6. Why, in your opinion, are there no final answers in science? Relate your answers to the study of the learning process.

7. In outline form, respond to the question, "What is the nature of the learning process?"

8. Write what you feel is an acceptable definition of learning.

References

ALLPORT, G.W. (1961). *Pattern and growth in personality.* New York: Holt, Rinehart & Winston.

AMSEL, A. (1958). The role of frustrative nonreward in noncontinuous reward situations. *Psychological Bulletin, 55,* 102–119.

AMSEL, A. (1962). Frustrative nonreward in partial reinforcement and discrimination learning: Some recent history and a theoretical extension. *Psychological Review, 69,* 306–328.

AMSEL, A., & ROUSSEL, J. (1952). Motivational properties of frustration: I. Effect on a running response of the addition of frustration to the motivational complex. *Journal of Experimental Psychology, 43,* 363–368.

ANDERSON, B.F. (1971). *The psychology experiment.* Belmont, CA: Brooks/Cole.

ASHBY, W.R. (1952). *Design for a brain.* New York: Wiley.

ATHEY, I.J., & RUBADEAU, D.O. (Eds.). (1970). *Educational implications of Piaget's theory.* Waltham, MA: Ginn-Blaisdell.

BABKIN, B.P. (1949). *Pavlov: A biography.* Chicago: University of Chicago Press.

BAKER, A.G., & MACKINTOSH, N.J. (1977). Excitatory and inhibitory conditioning following uncorrelated presentations of CS and US. *Animal Learning and Behavior, 5,* 315–319.

BANDURA, A. (1965). Influence of a model's reinforcement contingencies on the acquisition of imitative responses. *Journal of Personality and Social Psychology, 11,* 589–595.

BANDURA, A. (1973). *Aggression: A social learning analysis.* Englewood Cliffs, NJ: Prentice-Hall.

BANDURA, A. (1977). *Social learning theory.* Englewood Cliffs, NJ: Prentice-Hall.

BANDURA, A. (1980a). The self and mechanisms of agency. In J. Suls (Ed.), *Social psychological perspectives on the self.* Hillsdale, NJ: Erlbaum.

BANDURA, A. (1980b). Self-referent thought: The development of self-efficacy. In J. Flavell

& L.D. Ross (Eds.), *Cognitive social development: Frontiers and possible futures.* New York: Cambridge University Press.

BANDURA, A. (1986). *Social foundations of thought and action: A social cognitive theory.* Englewood Cliffs, NJ: Prentice-Hall.

BANDURA, A., BLANCHARD, E.B., & RITTER, B.J. (1969). Relative efficacy of modeling therapeutic changes for inducing behavioral, attitudinal and affective changes. *Journal of Personality and Social Psychology, 13,* 173–199.

BANDURA, A., GRUSEC, J.E., & MENLOVE, F.L. (1967). Vicarious extinction of avoidance behavior. *Journal of Personality and Social Behavior, 5,* 16–23.

BANDURA, A., & KUPERS, C.J. (1964). The transmission of patterns of self-reinforcement through modeling. *Journal of Abnormal and Social Psychology, 69,* 1–9.

BANDURA, A., & MENLOVE, F.L. (1968). Factors determining vicarious extinction of avoidance behavior through symbolic modeling. *Journal of Personality and Social Psychology, 8,* 99–108.

BEACH, F.A. (1987). Donald Olding Hebb (1904–1985). *American Psychologist, 42,* 186–187.

BEARD, R.M. (1969). *An outline of Piaget's developmental psychology for students and teachers.* New York: Mentor.

BEATON, A. (1985). *Left side, right side: A review of laterality research.* New Haven, CT: Yale University Press.

BENNETT, E.L., DIAMOND, M.C., KRECH, D., & ROSENZWEIG, M.R. (1964). Chemical and anatomical plasticity of brain. *Science, 146,* 610–619.

BERKSON, W., & WETTERSTEN, J. (1984). *Learning from error: Karl Popper's psychology of learning.* LaSalle, IL: Open Court.

BEST, M.R., & GEMBERLING, G.A. (1977). Role of short-term processes in the conditioned stimulus preexposure effect and the delay of reinforcement gradient in long-delay taste-aversion learning. *Journal of Experimental Psychology: Animal Behavior Processes, 3,* 253–263.

BIJOU, S.W., & BAER, D.M. (1961). Child development (Vol. 1). *A systematic and empirical theory.* Englewood Cliffs, NJ: Prentice-Hall.

BIJOU, S.W., & BAER, D.M. (1965). Child development (Vol. 2). *The universal stage of infancy.* Englewood Cliffs, NJ: Prentice-Hall.

BITTERMAN, M.E. (1960). Toward a comparative psychology of learning. *American Psychologist, 15,* 704–712.

BOGEN, J.E. (1977). In M.C. Wittrock (Ed.), *The human brain.* Englewood Cliffs, NJ: Prentice-Hall.

BOLLES, R.C. (1970). Species-specific defense reactions and avoidance learning. *Psychological Review, 77,* 32–48.

BOLLES, R.C. (1972). Reinforcement, expectancy, and learning. *Psychological Review, 79,* 394–409.

BOLLES, R.C. (1975). *Theory of motivation* (2nd ed.). New York: Harper & Row.

BOLLES, R.C. (1979). *Learning theory* (2nd ed.). New York: Holt, Rinehart & Winston.

BOSWELL, J. (1952). *Life of Samuel Johnson LL.D.* Chicago: Encyclopedia Britannica.

BOWER, G.H. (1962). The influence of graded reductions in reward and prior frustrating events upon the magnitude of the frustration effect. *Journal of Comparative and Physiological Psychology, 55,* 582–587.

BOWER, G.H., & HILGARD, E.R. (1981). *Theories of learning* (5th ed.). Englewood Cliffs, NJ: Prentice-Hall.

BREGMAN, E.O. (1934). An attempt to modify the emotional attitudes of infants by the conditioned response technique. *Journal of Genetic Psychology, 45,* 169–198.

BRELAND, K., & BRELAND, M. (1961). The misbehavior of organisms. *American Psychologist, 16,* 681–684.

BROWN, J.S., & BURTON, R. (1975). Multiple representations of knowledge for tutorial reasoning. In D.G. Bobrow & A. Collins (Eds.), *Representation and understanding: Studies in cognitive science.* New York: Academic Press.

BROWN, P.L., & JENKINS, H.M. (1968). Auto-shaping of the pigeon's key-peck. *Journal of the Experimental Analysis of Behavior, 11,* 1–8.

BROWN, R. (1965). *Social psychology.* New York: Free Press.

BRUNER, J.S. (1966). *Toward a theory of instruction.* Cambridge, MA: Harvard University Press.

BUGELSKI, B.R. (1979). *Principles of learning and memory.* New York: Praeger.

BUNDERSON, V. (1967). The role of computer-assisted instruction in university education. *Progress Report to the Coordination Board of the Texas College and University System.* Austin: University of Texas Press.

CARLSON, J.G. (1980). Guthrie's theory of learning. In G.M. Gazda & R.J. Corsini (Eds.), *Theories of learning: A comparative approach.* Itasca, IL: Peacock.

CHANCE, P. (1984, September). The revolutionary gentleman. *Psychology Today,* pp. 44–48.

CHOMSKY, N. (1959). [Review of *Verbal Behavior* by B.F. Skinner]. *Language, 35,* 26–58.

CRAIGHEAD, W.E., KAZDIN, A.E., & MAHONEY, M.J. (1976.) *Behavior modification: Principles, issues, and applications.* Boston: Houghton Mifflin.

CRESPI, L. (1942). Quantitative variation of incentive and performance in the white rat. *American Journal of Psychology, 55,* 467–517.

CRESPI, L. (1944). Amount of reinforcement and level of performance. *Psychological Review, 51,* 341–357.

CURRY, F.K.W. (1967). A comparison of left-handed and right-handed subjects on verbal and non-verbal dichotic listening tasks. *Cortex, 3,* 343–352.

DALY, H.B. (1969). Learning of a hurdle-jump response to escape cues paired with reduced reward or frustrative nonreward. *Journal of Experimental Psychology, 79,* 146–157.

DARWIN, C. (1872). *The expression of emotions in man and animals.* London: John Murray.

DEESE, J. (1951). Extinction of a discrimination without performance of the choice response. *Journal of Comparative and Physiological Psychology, 44,* 362–366.

DEUTSCH, J.A. (1954). A machine with insight. *Quarterly Journal of Experimental Psychology, 6,* 6–11.

DEWEY, J. (1896). The reflex arc concept in psychology. *Psychological Review, 3,* 357–370.

DiCARA, L.V. (1970). Learning in the autonomic nervous system. *Scientific American, 222,* 30–39.

DOLLARD, J.C., & MILLER, N.E. (1950). *Personality and psychotherapy.* New York: McGraw-Hill.

DUNCAN, C.P. (1949). The retroactive effect of electroshock on learning. *Journal of Comparative and Physiological Psychology, 42,* 34–44.

EBBINGHAUS, H. (1913). *On memory* (H.A. Ruger & C. Bossinger, Trans.). New York: Teachers College Press. (Original work published 1885)

EGGER, M.D., & MILLER, N.E. (1962). Secondary reinforcement in rats as a function of information value and reliability of the stimulus. *Journal of Experimental Psychology, 64,* 97–104.

EGGER, M.D., & MILLER, N.E. (1963). When is a reward reinforcing?: An experimental study of the information hypothesis. *Journal of Comparative and Physiological Psychology, 56,* 132–137.

ESTES, W.K. (1944). An experimental study of punishment. *Psychological Monographs, 57* (Whole No. 263).

ESTES, W.K. (1950). Toward a statistical theory of learning. *Psychological Review, 57,* 94–107.

ESTES, W.K. (1960). Learning theory and the new "mental chemistry." *Psychological Review, 67,* 207–223.

ESTES, W.K. (1964a). All-or-none processes in learning and retention. *American Psychologist, 19,* 16–25.

ESTES, W.K. (1964b). Probability learning. In A.W. Melton (Ed.), *Categories of human learning.* New York: Academic Press.

ESTES, W.K. (1969a). Reinforcement in human learning. In J. Tapp (Ed.), *Reinforcement and behavior.* New York: Academic Press.

ESTES, W.K. (1969b). New perspectives on some old issues in association theory. In N.J. MacKintosh & W.K. Honig (Eds.), *Fundamental issues in association learning.* Halifax, Nova Scotia: Dalhousie University Press.

ESTES, W.K. (1971). Reward in human learning: Theoretical issues and strategic choice points. In R. Glaser (Ed.), *The nature of reinforcement.* New York: Academic Press.

ESTES, W.K. (1972). An associative basis for coding and organization in memory. In A.W. Melton & E. Martin (Eds.), *Coding processes in human memory.* New York: Halstead.

ESTES, W.K. (1973). Memory and conditioning. In F.J. McGuigan & D.B. Lumsden (Eds.), *Contemporary approaches to conditioning and learning.* Washington, DC: Winston & Sons.

ESTES, W.K. (1976). The cognitive side of probability matching. *Psychological Review, 83,* 37–64.

ESTES, W.K. (1978). On the organization and core concepts of learning theory and cognitive psychology. In W.K. Estes (Ed.), *Handbook of learning and cognitive processes* (Vol. 6). Hillsdale, NJ: Erlbaum.

ESTES, W.K., HOPKINS, B.L., & CROTHERS, E.J. (1960). All-or-none and conservation effects in the learning and retention of paired associates. *Journal of Experimental Psychology, 60,* 329–339.

ESTES, W.K., & SKINNER, B.F. (1941). Some quantitative properties of anxiety. *Journal of Experimental Psychology, 29,* 390–400.

ESTES, W.K., & STRAUGHAN, J.H. (1954). Analysis of a verbal conditioning situation in terms of statistical learning theory. *Journal of Experimental Psychology, 47,* 225–234.

FENWICK, S., MIKULKA, P.J., & KLEIN, S.B. (1975). The effect of different levels of preexposure to sucrose on acquisition and extinction of conditioned aversion. *Behavioral Biology, 14,* 231–235.

FERSTER, C.B., & SKINNER, B.F. (1957). *Schedules of reinforcement*. Englewood Cliffs, NJ: Prentice-Hall.

FESTINGER, L. (1957). *A theory of cognitive dissonance*. Stanford, CA: Stanford University Press.

FLAVELL, J.H. (1963). *The developmental psychology of Jean Piaget*. New York: Van Nostrand Reinhold.

FOWLER, H., & MILLER, N.E. (1963). Facilitation and inhibition of runway performance by hind- and forepaw shock of various intensities. *Journal of Comparative and Physiological Psychology, 56,* 801–805.

FURTH, H.G. (1969). *Piaget and knowledge: Theoretical foundations*. Englewood Cliffs, NJ: Prentice-Hall.

FURTH, H.G. (1970). *Piaget for teachers*. Englewood Cliffs, NJ: Prentice-Hall.

GAGNÉ, R.M. (1970). *The conditions of learning* (2nd ed.). New York: Holt, Rinehart & Winston.

GARCIA, J., & KOELLING, R.A. (1966). Relation of cue to consequence in avoidance learning. *Psychonomic Science, 4,* 123–124.

GINSBURG, H., & OPPER, S. (1979). *Piaget's theory of intellectual development* (2nd ed.). Englewood Cliffs, NJ: Prentice-Hall.

GOLDSCHMID, M.L., & BENTLER, P.M. (1968). *Conservation concept diagnostic kit: Manual and keys*. San Diego, CA: Educational and Industrial Testing Service.

GUSTAVSON, G.R., GARCIA, J., HANKINS, W.G., & RUSINIAK, K.W. (1974). Coyote predation control by aversive conditioning. *Science, 1843,* 581–583.

GUTHRIE, E.R. (1935). *The psychology of learning*. New York: Harper & Row.

GUTHRIE, E.R. (1938). *The psychology of human conflict*. New York: Harper & Row.

GUTHRIE, E.R. (1940). Association and the law of effect. *Psychological Review, 47,* 127–148.

GUTHRIE, E.R. (1942). Conditioning: A theory of learning in terms of stimulus, response, and association. In N.B. Henry (Ed.), *The forty-first yearbook of the national society for the study of education: Pt. II. The psychology of learning*. Chicago: University of Chicago Press.

GUTHRIE, E.R. (1952). *The psychology of learning* (rev. ed.). New York: Harper & Row.

GUTHRIE, E.R. (1959). Association by contiguity. In S. Koch (Ed.), *Psychology: A study of a science* (Vol. 2). New York: McGraw-Hill.

GUTHRIE, E.R., & HORTON, G.P. (1946). *Cats in a puzzle box*. New York: Rinehart.

GUTHRIE, E.R., & POWERS, F.F. (1950). *Educational psychology*. New York: Ronald Press.

HARLOW, H.F. (1949). The formation of learning sets. *Psychological Review, 56,* 51–65.

HARLOW, H.F. (1950). Analysis of discrimination learning by monkeys. *Journal of Experimental Psychology, 40,* 26–39.

HARLOW, H.F. (1959). Learning set and error factor theory. In S. Koch (Ed.), *Psychology: A study of a science* (Vol. 2). New York: McGraw-Hill.

HARRIS, B. (1979). Whatever happened to little Albert? *American Psychologist, 34,* 151–160.

HEBB, D.O. (1946). On the nature of fear. *Psychological Review, 53,* 259–276.

HEBB, D.O. (1949). *The organization of behavior*. New York: Wiley.

HEBB, D.O. (1955). Drives and the C.N.S. (Conceptual nervous system). *Psychological Review, 62,* 243–254.

HEBB, D.O. (1959). A neuropsychological theory. In S. Koch (Ed.), *Psychology: A study of a science* (Vol. 1). New York: McGraw-Hill.

HEBB, D.O. *Textbook of psychology* (3rd ed.). Philadelphia, PA: W.B. Saunders.

HEBB, D.O. (1980). [Autobiography]. In G. Lindzey (Ed.), *A history of psychology in autobiography* (Vol. VII). San Francisco: Freeman.

HEBB, D.O., & DONDERI, D.C. (1987). *Textbook of psychology* (4th ed.) Hillsdale, NJ: Erlbaum.

HERGENHAHN, B.R. (1972). *Shaping your child's personality.* Englewood Cliffs, NJ: Prentice-Hall.

HERGENHAHN, B.R. (1974). *A self-directing introduction to psychological experimentation* (2nd ed.). Monterey, CA: Brooks/Cole.

HERGENHAHN, B.R. (1986). *An introduction to the history of psychology.* Belmont, CA: Wadsworth.

HERON, W. (1957, January). The pathology of boredom. *Scientific American,* pp. 52–56.

HERRNSTEIN, R.J. (1961). Relative and absolute strength of response as a function of frequency of reinforcement. *Journal of the Experimental Analysis of Behavior, 4,* 267–272.

HESS, E.H. (1958). "Imprinting" in animals. *Scientific American, 198,* 81–90.

HESS, R.D., & TENEZAKIS, M.D. (1970). *The computer as a socializing agent: Some socio-affective outcomes of CAI.* Stanford: Stanford Center for Research and Development in Teaching.

HILGARD, E.R., & BOWER, G.H. (1975). *Theories of learning* (4th ed.). Englewood Cliffs, NJ: Prentice-Hall.

HILGARD, E.R., & MARQUIS, D.G. (1940). *Conditioning and learning.* Englewood Cliffs, NJ: Prentice-Hall.

HILL, W.F. (1985). *Learning: A survey of psychological interpretations* (4th ed.). New York: Harper & Row.

HINDE, R.A., & TINBERGEN, N. (1958). The comparative study of species-specific behavior. In A. Roe & G.G. Simpson (Eds.), *Behavior and evolution.* New Haven, CT: Yale University Press.

HOFFMAN, H.S. (1962). The analogue lab: A new kind of teaching device. *American Psychologist, 17,* 684–694.

HOLLAND, J.G., & SKINNER, B.F. (1961). *The analysis of behavior: A program for self-instruction.* New York: McGraw-Hill.

HOLLAND, P.C. (1977). Conditioned stimulus as a determinant of the form for the Pavlovian conditioned response. *Journal of Experimental Psychology: Animal Processes, 3,* 77–104.

HOLLIS, K. (1982). Pavlovian conditioning of signal-centered action patterns and autonomic behavior: A biological analysis of function. In J.S. Tosenblatt, R.A. Hinde, C. Beer, & M. Busnel (Eds.), *Advances in the study of behavior* (Vol. 12). New York: Academic Press.

HOLT, J. (1967). *How children learn.* New York: Pitman.

HOMME, L., CSANYI, A.P., GONZALES, M.A., & RECHS, J.R. (1970). *How to use contingency contracting in the classroom.* Champaign, IL: Research Press.

HOMME, L.E., DE BACA, P., DIVINE, J.V., STEINHORST, R., & RICKERT, E.J. (1963). Use of the Premack principle in controlling the behavior of school children. *Journal of the Experimental Analysis of Behavior, 6,* 544.

HULL, C.L. (1928). *Aptitude testing.* Yonkers-on-Hudson, NY: World Book.

HULL, C.L. (1933a). Differential habituation to internal stimuli in the albino rat. *Journal of Comparative Psychology, 16,* 255–273.

HULL, C.L. (1933b). *Hypnosis and suggestibility: An experimental approach.* New York: Naiburg.

HULL, C.L. (1943). *Principles of behavior.* Englewood Cliffs, NJ: Prentice-Hall.

HULL, C.L. (1952). *A behavior system: An introduction to behavior theory concerning the individual organism.* New Haven, CT: Yale University Press.

HULSE, S.H. (1958). Amount and percentage of reinforcement and duration of goal confinement in conditioning and extinction. *Journal of Experimental Psychology, 56,* 48–57.

HULSE, S.H., EGETH, H., & DEESE, J. (1980). *The psychology of learning* (5th ed.). New York: McGraw-Hill.

HUMPHREYS, L.G. (1939a). Acquisition and extinction of verbal expectations in a situation analogous to conditioning. *Journal of Experimental Psychology, 25,* 294–301.

HUMPHREYS, L.G. (1939b). The effect of random alternation of reinforcement on the acquisition and extinction of conditioned eyelid reactions. *Journal of Experimental Psychology, 25,* 141–158.

INHELDER, B., & PIAGET, J. (1958). *The growth of logical thinking from childhood to adolescence* (A. Parson & S. Milgram, Trans.). New York: Basic Books.

JAMES, W. (1890). *The principles of psychology* (2 vols.). New York: Henry Holt.

JAMES, W. (1892). *Psychology: Briefer course.* New York: Henry Holt.

JENKINS, H.M., & MOORE, B.R. (1973). The form of the autoshaped response with food or water reinforcers. *Journal of the Experimental Analysis of Behavior, 20,* 163–181.

JONAS, G. (1973). *Visceral learning: Toward a science of self-control.* New York: Viking Press.

JONCICH, G. (1968). *The sane positivist: A biography of Edward L. Thorndike.* Middletown, CT: Wesleyan University Press.

JONES, M.C. (1924). A laboratory study of fear: The case of Peter. *Pedagogical Seminary, 31,* 308–315.

JONES, M.C. (1974). Albert, Peter, and John B. Watson. *American Psychologist, 29,* 581–583.

KAGAN, J. (1980, September). Jean Piaget's contributions. *Phi Delta Kappan,* pp. 245–246.

KAMIN, L.J. (1969). Predictability, surprise, attention, and conditioning. In B.A. Campbell & R.M. Church (Eds.), *Punishment and aversive behavior.* Englewood Cliffs, NJ: Prentice-Hall.

KAUFMAN, A., BARON, A., & KOPP, R.E. (1966). Some effects of instructions on human operant behavior. *Psychonomic Monograph Supplements, 1,* 243–250.

KELLER, F.S. (1968). Good-bye teacher. *Journal of Applied Behavior Analysis, 1,* 69–89.

KELLER, F.S., & SCHOENFELD, W.N. (1950). *Principles of psychology.* New York: Appleton-Century-Crofts.

KIMBLE, G.A. (1961). *Hilgard and Marquis' conditioning and learning* (2nd ed.). Englewood Cliffs, NJ: Prentice-Hall.

KIMBLE, G.A., & GARMEZY, N. (1968). *Principles of general psychology* (3rd ed.). New York: Ronald Press.

KIMMEL, H.D. (1974). Instrumental conditioning of autonomically mediated responses in human beings. *American Psychologist, 29,* 325–335.

KIMURA, D. (1961). Cerebral dominance and the perception of verbal stimuli. *Canadian Journal of Psychology, 15,* 166–171.

KIMURA, D. (1964). Left-right differences in the perception of melodies. *Quarterly Journal of Experimental Psychology, 16,* 355–358.

KIMURA, D. (1967). Functional asymmetry of the brain in dichotic listening. *Cortex, 3,* 163–178.

KOFFKA, K. (1963). *Principles of Gestalt psychology.* New York: Harcourt, Brace, and World. (Original work published 1935)

KÖHLER, W. (1925). *The mentality of apes.* London: Routledge and Kegan Paul Ltd.

KÖHLER, W. (1929). *Gestalt psychology.* New York: Liveright.

KÖHLER, W. (1947). *Gestalt psychology: An introduction to new concepts in modern psychology* (rev. ed.). New York: Liveright.

KOLESNIK, W.B. (1958). *Mental discipline in modern education.* Madison: University of Wisconsin Press.

KUHN, T.S. (1973). *The structure of scientific revolutions* (3rd ed.). Chicago: University of Chicago Press.

KULIK, J.A., KULIK, CHEN-LIN, & CARMICHAEL, K. (1974). The Keller plan in science teaching. *Science, 183,* 379–383.

LACHMAN, R., LACHMAN, J.L., & BUTTERFIELD, E.C. (1979). *Cognitive psychology and information processing.* Hillsdale, NJ: Erlbaum.

LASHLEY, K.S. (1929). *Brain mechanisms and intelligence.* Chicago: University of Chicago Press.

LEAHEY, T.H. (1980). *A history of psychology.* Englewood Cliffs, NJ: Prentice-Hall.

LEEPER, R. (1935a). The role of motivation in learning: A study of the phenomenon of differential motivational control of the utilization of habits. *Journal of Genetic Psychology, 46,* 3–40.

LEFRANÇOIS, G.R. (1968). A treatment for the acceleration of conservation of substance. *Canadian Journal of Psychology, 22,* 277–284.

LEHRER, K., & BEANBLOSSOM, R. (Eds.). (1975). *Thomas Reid's inquiry and essays.* Indianapolis, IN: Bobbs-Merrill.

LEVY, J. (1985, May). Right brain, left brain: Fact and fiction. *Psychology Today,* pp. 38–39, 42–44.

LINDSAY, P.H., & NORMAN, D.A. (1977). *Human information processing: An introduction to psychology* (2nd ed.). New York: Academic Press.

LINSKIE, R. (1977). *The learning process: Theory and practice.* New York: D. Van Nostrand.

LOFTUS, G.R., & LOFTUS, E.F. (1976). *Human memory: The processing of information.* Hillsdale, NJ: Erlbaum.

LORENZ, K. (1952). *King Solomon's ring.* New York: Crowell.

LORENZ, K. (1965). *Evolution and modification of behavior.* Chicago: University of Chicago Press.

LORENZ, K. (1970). *Studies in animal and human behavior* (Vol. 1). Cambridge, MA: Harvard University Press.

LUMSDAINE, A.A. (1964). Educational technology, programmed learning, and instructional sciences. In E.R. Hilgard (Ed.), *Theories of learning and instruction.* Chicago: University of Chicago Press.

LUNDIN, R.W. (1974). *Personality: A behavioral analysis* (2nd ed.). New York: Macmillan.

MacCORQUODALE, K., & MEEHL, P.E. (1953). Preliminary suggestions as to a formalization of expectancy theory. *Psychological Review, 60,* 55–63.

MACKINTOSH, N.J. (1975). A theory of attention: Variations in the associability of stimuli with reinforcement. *Psychological Review, 82,* 276–298.

MAGER, R.F. (1961). *Preparing instructional objectives.* Palo Alto, CA: Fearon.

MAGER, R.F. (1972). *Goal analysis.* Belmont, CA: Fearon.

MAIER, S.F., SELIGMAN, M.E.P., & SOLOMON, R.L. (1969). Pavlovian fear conditioning and learned helplessness: Effects on escape and avoidance behavior of (a) the CS-US contingency, and (b) the independence of the US and voluntary responding. In B.A. Campbell & R.M. Church (Eds.), *Punishment and Aversive Behavior.* New York: Appleton-Century-Crofts.

MARX, M.H., & CRONAN-HILLIX, W.A. (1987). *Systems and theories in psychology* (4th ed.). New York: McGraw-Hill.

MEEHL, P.E. (1950). On the circularity of the law of effect, *Psychological Bulletin, 47,* 52–75.

MEEK, R.L. (1977). The traditional in non-traditional learning methods. *Journal of Personalized Instruction, 2,* 114–119.

MELZACK, R., & THOMPSON, W.R. (1956). Effects of early experience on social behavior. *Canadian Journal of Psychology, 10,* 82–90.

MILLER, G.A. (1965). Some preliminaries to psycholinguistics. *American Psychologist, 20,* 15–20.

MILLER, N.E. (1969). Learning of visceral and glandular responses. *Science, 163,* 434–445.

MILLER, N.E., & CARMONA, A. (1967). Modification of a visceral response, salivation in thirsty dogs, by instrumental training with water reward. *Journal of Comparative and Physiological Psychology, 63,* 1–6.

MILLER, N.E., & DOLLARD, J.C. (1941). *Social learning and imitation.* New Haven, CT: Yale University Press.

MILNER, B. (1965). Memory disturbance after bilateral hippocampal lesions. In P. Milner & S. Glickman (Eds.). *Cognitive processes and the brain.* Princeton, NJ: Van Nostrand.

MIYAKE, N., & NORMAN, D.A. (1979). To ask a question, one must know enough to know what is not known. *Journal of Verbal Learning and Verbal Behavior, 18,* 357–364.

MOLTZ, H. (1957). Latent extinction and the fractional anticipatory response mechanism. *Psychological Review, 64,* 229–241.

MORGAN, C.L. (1891). *An introduction to comparative psychology.* London: W. Scott.

MOUNT, G.R., PAYTON, T., ELLIS, J., & BARNES, P. (1976). A multimodal behavioral approach to the treatment of alcoholism. *Behavioral Engineering, 33,* 61–66.

MOWRER, O.H. (1956). Two-factor learning theory reconsidered, with special reference to secondary reinforcement and the concept of habit. *Psychological Review, 63,* 114–128.

MOWRER, O.H. (1960). *Learning theory and behavior.* New York: Wiley.

MÜLLER, G.E., & PILZECKER, A. (1900). *Experimentelle Beiträge Zur Lehre Vom Gedachtniss.* Leipzig.

MUNN, N.L., FERNALD, D.L., JR., & FERNALD, P.S. (1972). *Introduction to psychology.* Boston: Houghton Mifflin.

MURDOCK, B.B., JR. (1961). The retention of individual items. *Journal of Experimental Psychology, 62,* 618–625.

NEWELL, A. (1970). Remarks on the relationship between artificial intelligence and cognitive psychology. In R. Banerji & M.D. Mesarovic (Eds.), *Theoretical approaches to nonnumerical problem solving.* New York: Springer-Verlag.

NORMAN, D.A. (1980a). Twelve issues for cognitive science. *Cognitive Science, 4,* 1–32.

NORMAN, D.A. (1980b). What goes on in the mind of the learner? *New Directions for Teaching and Learning, 2,* 37–49.

NORMAN, D.A. (1981). A psychologist views human processing: Human error and other phenomena suggest processing mechanisms. *Proceedings of the International Joint Conference on Artificial Intelligence.* Vancouver, British Columbia.

NORMAN, D.A. (1982). *Learning and memory.* New York: Freeman.

OBRIST, P.A., SUTTERER, J.R., & HOWARD, J.L. (1972). Preparatory cardiac changes: A psychobiological approach. In A.H. Black & W.F. Prokasy (Eds.), *Classical conditioning II.* Englewood Cliffs, NJ: Prentice-Hall.

OLDS, J. (1955). Physiological mechanisms of reward. In M.R. Jones (Ed.), *Nebraska Symposium on Motivation.* Lincoln: University of Nebraska Press.

OLDS, J., & MILNER, P. (1954). Positive reinforcement produced by electrical stimulation of septal area and other regions of rat brain. *Journal of Comparative and Physiological Psychology, 47,* 419–427.

ORNSTEIN, R.E. (1978). The split and whole brain. *Human Nature, 1,* 76–83.

PAVLOV, I.P. (1927). *Conditioned reflexes.* London: Oxford University Press.

PAVLOV, I.P. (1928). *Lectures on conditioned reflexes.* New York: Liveright.

PAVLOV, I.P. (1941). *Conditioned reflexes and psychiatry.* New York: International.

PAVLOV, I.P. (1955). *Selected works.* Moscow: Foreign Languages Publishing House.

PETERSON, L.R., & PETERSON, M.J. (1959). Short term retention of individual verbal items. *Journal of Experimental Psychology, 58,* 193–198.

PHILLIPS, J.L., JR. (1975). *The origins of intellect: Piaget's theory* (2nd ed.). San Francisco: Freeman.

PHILLIPS, J.L., JR. (1981). *Piaget's theory: A primer.* San Francisco: Freeman.

PIAGET, J. (1966). *Psychology of intelligence.* Totowa, NJ: Littlefield, Adams.

PIAGET, J. (1970a). *Genetic epistemology* (E. Duckworth, Trans.). New York: Columbia University Press.

PIAGET, J. (1970b). Piaget's theory. In P.H. Mussen (Ed.), *Carmichael's manual of child psychology* (Vol. 1). New York: Wiley.

Piaget, J., & Inhelder, B. (1969). *The psychology of the child* (H. Weaver, Trans.). New York: Basic Books.

Plato. (1928). *The republic.* New York: Scribner.

Popper, K. (1963). *Conjectures and refutations.* New York: Basic Books.

Premack, D. (1959). Toward empirical behavior laws: Vol. I. Positive reinforcement. *Psychological Review, 66,* 219–233.

Premack, D. (1962). Reversibility of the reinforcement relation. *Science, 136,* 255–257.

Pressey, S.L. (1926). A simple apparatus which gives tests and scores—and teaches. *School and Society, 23,* 373–376.

Pressey, S.L. (1927). A machine for automatic teaching of drill material. *School and Society, 25,* 549–552.

Rachlin, H. (1976). *Behavior and learning.* San Francisco: Freeman.

Rachlin, H. (1976). *Introduction to modern behaviorism* (2nd ed.). San Francisco: Freeman.

Rachlin, H., & Green, L. (1972). Commitment, choice and self-control. *Journal of the Experimental Analysis of Behavior, 17,* 15–22.

Random House dictionary of the English language. (1968). New York: Random House.

Razran, G. (1961). The observable unconscious and the inferable conscious in current Soviet psychophysiology. *Psychological Review, 68,* 81–147.

Reiss, B.F. (1946). Genetic changes in semantic conditioning. *Journal of Experimental Psychology, 36,* 143–152.

Rescorla, R.A. (1966). Predictability and number of pairings in Pavlovian fear conditioning. *Psychonomic Science, 4,* 383–384.

Rescorla, R.A. (1967). Pavlovian conditioning and its proper control procedures. *Psychological Review, 74,* 72–80.

Rescorla, R.A., & Wagner, A.R. (1972). A theory of Pavlovian conditioning: Variations in the effectiveness of reinforcement and non-reinforcement. In A.H. Black & W.F. Prokasy (Eds.), *Classical conditioning II.* Englewood Cliffs, NJ: Prentice-Hall.

Riesen, A.H. (1947). The development of visual perception in man and chimpanzee. *Science, 106,* 107–108.

Rimm, D.C., & Masters, J.C. (1979). *Behavior therapy.* New York: Academic Press.

Robinson, D.N. (1981). *An intellectual history of psychology* (rev. ed.). New York: Macmillan.

Romanes, G.J. (1882). *Animal intelligence.* London: Kegan Paul, Trench.

Romanes, G.J. (1884). *Mental evolution in animals.* New York: Appleton-Century-Crofts.

Romanes, G.J. (1885). *Mental evolution in man.* London: Kegan Paul.

Ruja, H. (1956). Productive psychologists. *American Psychologist, 11,* 148–149.

Rumelhart, D.E., & Norman, D.A. (1981). Analogical processes in learning. In J.R. Anderson (Ed.), *Cognitive skills and their acquisition.* Hillsdale, NJ: Erlbaum.

Ryan, B.A. (1974). *PSI: Keller's personalized system of instruction: An appraisal.* Washington, DC: American Psychological Association.

Saltz, E. (1971). *The cognitive bases of human learning.* Homewood, IL: Dorsey Press.

Sargent, S.S., & Stafford, K.R. (1965). *Basic teachings of the great psychologists.* Garden City, NY: Doubleday.

SARTAIN, Q.A., NORTH, J.A., STRANGE, R.J., & CHAPMAN, M.H. (1973). *Psychology: Understanding human behavior* (4th ed.). New York: McGraw-Hill.

SCHRAMM, W. (1964). *The research on programmed instruction: An annotated bibliography.* Washington, DC: U.S. Office of Education (OE-34034).

SCHWARTZ, B. (1984). *Psychology of learning and behavior* (2nd ed.). New York: Norton.

SEARS, R.R. (1944). Experimental analysis of psychoanalytic phenomena. In J. McV. Hunt (Ed.), *Personality and the behavior disorders.* New York: Ronald Press.

SEARS, R.R., MACCOBY, E.E., & LEVIN, H. (1957). *Patterns of child rearing.* New York: Harper & Row.

SEARS, R.R., WHITING, J.W.M., NOWLIS, V., & SEARS, P.S. (1953). Some child-rearing antecedents of aggression and dependency in young children. *Genetic Psychology Monographs, 47,* 135–236.

SELIGMAN, M.E.P. (1969). Control group and conditioning: A comment on operationism. *Psychological Review, 76,* 484–491.

SELIGMAN, M.E.P. (1970). On the generality of the laws of learning. *Psychological Review, 77,* 406–418.

SELIGMAN, M.E.P. (1972). Phobias and preparedness. In M.E.P. Seligman & J.L. Hager (Eds.), *Biological boundaries of learning.* New York: Appleton-Century-Crofts.

SELIGMAN, M.E.P. (1975). *Helplessness.* San Francisco: Freeman.

SELIGMAN, M.E.P., & HAGER, J.L. (Eds.). (1972). *Biological boundaries of learning.* New York: Appleton-Century-Crofts.

SELIGMAN, M.E.P., & MAIER, S.F. (1967). Failure to escape traumatic shock. *Journal of Experimental Psychology, 74,* 1–9.

SENDEN, M.V. (1932). *Raum-und gestaltauffassung bei operierten blindgeborenen vor und nach der operation.* Leipzig: Barth.

SEWARD, J.P., & LEVY, N.J. (1949). Sign learning as a factor in extinction. *Journal of Experimental Psychology, 39,* 660–668.

SHANNON, C.E., & WEAVER, W. (1949). *The mathematical theory of communication.* Urbana: University of Illinois Press.

SHAPIRO, D., TURSKY, B., GERSON, E., & STERN, M. (1969). Effects of feedback and reinforcement on the control of human systolic blood pressure. *Science, 163,* 588–589.

SHARPLESS, S., & JASPER, H. (1956). Habituation of the arousal reaction. *Brain, 79,* 655–680.

SHEFFIELD, F.D., & ROBY, T.B. (1950). Reward value of a non-nutritive sweet taste. *Journal of Comparative and Physiological Psychology, 43,* 471–481.

SIEGEL, S. (1979). The role of conditioning in drug tolerance and addiction. In J.D. Keehn (Ed.), *Psychopathology in animals: Research and clinical implications.* New York: Academic Press.

SKINNER, B.F. (1938). *The behavior of organisms: An experimental analysis.* Englewood Cliffs, NJ: Prentice-Hall.

SKINNER, B.F. (1948). *Walden Two.* New York: Macmillan.

SKINNER, B.F. (1950). Are theories of learning necessary? *Psychological Review, 57,* 193–216.

SKINNER, B.F. (1951). How to teach animals. *Scientific American, 185,* 26–29.

SKINNER, B.F. (1953). *Science and human behavior.* New York: Macmillan.

SKINNER, B.F. (1954). The science of learning and the art of teaching. *Harvard Educational Review, 24,* 86–97.

SKINNER, B.F. (1956). A case history in scientific method. *American Psychologist, 11,* 221–233.

SKINNER, B.F. (1957). *Verbal behavior.* Englewood Cliffs, NJ: Prentice-Hall.

SKINNER, B.F. (1958). Teaching machines. *Science, 128,* 969–977.

SKINNER, B.F. (1960). Pigeons in a pelican. *American Psychologist, 15,* 28–37.

SKINNER, B.F. (1967). In E.G. Boring & G. Lindzey (Eds.), *A history of psychology in autobiography.* New York: Naiburg.

SKINNER, B.F. (1971). *Beyond freedom and dignity.* New York: Knopf.

SKINNER, B.F. (1974). *About behaviorism.* New York: Knopf.

SKINNER, B.F. (1984). The shame of American education. *American Psychologist, 39,* 947–954.

SKINNER, B.F. (1986). What is wrong with daily life in the Western world? *American Psychologist, 41,* 568–574.

SKINNER, B.F. (1987). *Upon further reflection.* Englewood Cliffs, NJ: Prentice-Hall.

SMEDSLUND, J. (1961). The acquisition of conservation of substance and weight in children: I. Introduction. *Scandinavian Journal of Psychology, 2,* 11–20.

SPENCE, K.W. (1936). The nature of discrimination in animals. *Psychological Review, 43,* 427–449.

SPENCE, K.W. (1937). The differential response in animals to stimuli varying within a single dimension. *Psychological Review, 44,* 430–444.

SPENCE, K.W. (1942). The basis of solution by chimpanzees of the intermediate size problem. *Journal of Experimental Psychology, 31,* 257–271.

SPENCE, K.W. (1952). Clark Leonard Hull: 1884–1952. *American Journal of Psychology, 65,* 639–646.

SPENCE, K.W. (1956). *Behavior theory and conditioning.* New Haven, CT: Yale University Press.

SPENCE, K.W. (1960). *Behavior theory and learning: Selected papers.* Englewood Cliffs, NJ: Prentice-Hall.

SPENCE, K.W., & LIPPITT, R. (1940). "Latent" learning of a simple maze problem with relevant needs satiated. *Psychological Bulletin, 37,* 429.

SPERRY, R.W. (1961). Cerebral organization and behavior. *Science, 133,* 1749–1757.

SPERRY, R.W. (1964). The great cerebral commissure. *Scientific American, 210,* 42–52.

SPRINGER, S.P., & DEUTSCH, G. (1985). *Left brain, right brain* (rev. ed.). San Francisco: Freeman.

STEVENS, S.S. (1951). Psychology and the science of science. In M.H. Marx, *Psychological theory: Contemporary readings.* New York: Macmillan.

SYMONDS, P.M. (1960). What education has to learn from psychology: VII. Transfer and formal discipline. *Teachers College Record, 61,* 30–45.

TAYLOR, J.A. (1951). The relationship of anxiety to the conditioned eyelid response. *Journal of Experimental Psychology, 41,* 81–92.

TERRACE, H.S. (1963). Errorless transfer of a discrimination across two continua. *Journal of the Experimental Analysis of Behavior, 6,* 223–232.

THORNDIKE, E.L. (1898). Animal intelligence: An experimental study of the associative processes in animals. *Psychological Review* [Monograph Suppl., 2, No. 8].

THORNDIKE, E.L. (1901). The mental life of the monkeys. *Psychological Review Monograph, 3*(15).

THORNDIKE, E.L. (1905). *The elements of psychology* (2nd ed.). New York: Seiler.

THORNDIKE, E.L. (1906). *The principles of teaching: Based on psychology.* New York: Seiler.

THORNDIKE, E.L. (1911). *Animal intelligence.* New York: Macmillan.

THORNDIKE, E.L. (1912). *Education, a first book.* New York: Macmillan.

THORNDIKE, E.L. (1913a). *Educational psychology: Vol. 2. The original nature of man.* New York: Teachers College Press.

THORNDIKE, E.L. (1913b). *Educational psychology: Vol. 1. The psychology of learning.* New York: Teachers College Press.

THORNDIKE, E.L. (1922). *The psychology of arithmetic.* New York: Crowell-Collier and Macmillan.

THORNDIKE, E.L. (1924). Mental discipline in high school studies. *Journal of Educational Psychology, 15,* 1–22, 83–98.

THORNDIKE, E.L. (1932). *The fundamentals of learning.* New York: Teachers College Press.

THORDIKE, E.L. (1940). *Human nature and the social order.* New York: Macmillan.

THORNDIKE, E.L. (1949). *Selected writings from a connectionist's psychology.* New York: Appleton-Century-Crofts.

THORNDIKE, E.L., & WOODWORTH, R.S. (1901). The influence of improvement in one mental function upon the efficiency of other functions. *Psychological Review, 8,* 247–261, 384–395, 553–564.

THORPE, W.H. (1963). *Learning and instinct in animals* (2nd ed.). Cambridge, MA: Harvard University Press.

TOLMAN, E.C. (1932). *Purposive behavior in animals and men.* New York: Naiburg.

TOLMAN, E.C. (1938). The determiners of behavior at a choice point. *Psychological Review, 45,* 1–41.

TOLMAN, E.C. (1942). *Drives toward war.* New York: Appleton-Century-Crofts.

TOLMAN, E.C. (1945). A stimulus-expectancy need-cathexis psychology. *Science, 101,* 160–166.

TOLMAN, E.C. (1949). There is more than one kind of learning. *Psychological Review, 56,* 144–155.

TOLMAN, E.C. (1959). Principles of purposive behavior. In S. Koch (Ed.), *Psychology: A study of a science* (Vol. 2). New York: McGraw-Hill.

TOLMAN, E.C., & HONZIK, C.H. (1930). Introduction and removal of reward, and maze performance in rats. *University of California Publications in Psychology, 4,* 257–275.

TOLMAN, E.C., RITCHIE, B.F., & KALISH, D. (1946a). Studies in spatial learning. I. Orientation and the short-cut. *Journal of Experimental Psychology, 36,* 13–24.

TOLMAN, E.C., RITCHIE, B.F., & KALISH, D. (1946b). Studies in spatial learning. II. Place learning versus response learning. *Journal of Experimental Psychology, 36,* 221–229.

UNDERWOOD, B.J., & KEPPEL, G. (1962). One-trial learning? *Journal of Verbal Learning and Verbal Behavior, 1,* 1–13.

VOEKS, V.W. (1950). Formalization and clarification of a theory of learning. *Journal of Psychology, 30,* 341–363.

WAGNER, A.R. (1961). Effects of amount and percentage of reinforcement and number of acquisition trials on conditioning and extinction. *Journal of Experimental Psychology, 32,* 234–242.

WAGNER, A.R. (1963). Conditioned frustration as a learned drive. *Journal of Experimental Psychology, 64,* 142–148.

WAGNER, A.R. (1969). Stimulus selection and a "modified continuity theory." In G.H. Bower & J.T. Spence (Eds.), *The psychology of learning and motivation* (Vol. 3). New York: Academic Press.

WAGNER, A.R. (1971). Elementary associations. In H.H. Kendler & J.T. Spence (Eds.), *Essays in neobehaviorism: A memorial volume to Kenneth W. Spence.* Englewood Cliffs, NJ: Prentice-Hall.

WAGNER, A.R. (1978). Expectancies and the priming of STM. In S.H. Hulse, H. Fowler, & W.K. Honig (Eds.), *Cognitive processes in animal behavior.* Hillsdale, NJ: Erlbaum.

WAGNER, A.R., & RESCORLA, R.A. (1972). Inhibition in Pavlovian conditioning: Application of a theory. In R.A. Boakes & M.S. Halliday (Eds.), *Inhibition and learning.* New York: Academic Press.

WALTER, W.G. (1953). *The living brain.* New York: Norton.

WALTERS, G.C., & GRUSEC, J.E. (1977). *Punishment.* San Francisco: Freeman.

WATSON, J.B. (1908). Imitation in monkeys. *Psychological Bulletin, 5,* 169–178.

WATSON, J.B. (1913). Psychology as the behaviorist views it. *Psychological Review, 20,* 158–177.

WATSON, J.B. (1925). *Behaviorism.* New York: Norton.

WATSON, J.B. (1926). Experimental studies on the growth of the emotions. In C. Murchison (Ed.), *Psychologies of 1925.* Worcester, MA: Clark University Press.

WATSON, J.B. (1936). John B. Watson. In C. Murchison (Ed.), *History of psychology in autobiography* (Vol. 3). Worcester, MA: Clark University Press.

WATSON, J.B., & McDOUGALL, W. (1929). *The battle of behaviorism.* New York: Norton.

WATSON, J.B., & RAYNER, R. (1920). Conditioned emotional reactions. *Journal of Experimental Psychology, 3,* 1–14.

WEIMER, W.B. (1973). Psycholinguistics and Plato's paradoxes of the Meno. *American Psychologist, 28,* 15–33.

WERTHEIMER, M. (1912). Experimentelle studien über das sehen von bewegung. *Zeitschrift Für Psychologie, 61,* 161–265.

WERTHEIMER, M. (1959). *Productive thinking,* enlarged ed. by Max Wertheimer, edited by Michael Wertheimer. New York: Harper & Row. (Original work published 1945)

WERTHEIMER, MICHAEL. (1980). Gestalt theory of learning. In G.M. Gazda & R. J. Corsini (Eds.), *Theories of learning: A comparative approach.* Ithasca, IL: Peacock.

WIENER, N. (1948). *Cybernetics.* New York: Wiley.

WILCOXON, H.C., DRAGOIN, W.B., & KRAL, P.A. (1971). Illness-induced aversions in rat and quail: Relative salience of visual and gustatory cues. *Science, 171,* 826–828.

WILLIAMS, D.R., & WILLIAMS, H. (1969). Auto-maintenance in the pigeon: Sustained pecking despite contingent non-reinforcement. *Journal of the Experimental Analysis of Behavior, 12,* 511–520.

WOLPE, J. (1958). *Psychotherapy by reciprocal inhibition.* Stanford, CA: Stanford University Press.

WOODWORTH, R.S. (1938). *Experimental psychology.* New York: Henry Holt.

ZEAMAN, D. (1949). Response latency as a function of the amount of reinforcement. *Journal of Experimental Psychology, 39,* 466–483.

ZENER, K. (1937). The significance of behavior accompanying conditioned salivary secretion for theories of the conditioned response. *American Journal of Psychology, 50,* 384–403.

ZUBEK, J.P. (1969). *Sensory deprivation: Fifteen years of research.* New York: Appleton-Century-Crofts.

AUTHOR INDEX

Socrates, 31
Solomon, R.L., 181, 474
Spence, J.T., 427, 480
Spence, K.W., 124, 138, 141, 145-151, 154, 204, 259-260, 298, 319, 427-428, 460, 478
Sperry, R., 409-410, 411, 412, 420, 478, 479
Springer, S.P., 412-413, 414, 479
Stafford, K.R., 57, 477
Steinhorst, R., 113, 472
Stern, M., 418, 477
Stevens, S.S., 15, 479
Strange, R.J., 248, 477
Straughan, J.H., 229, 469
Suls, J., 466
Sutterer, J.R., 175, 475
Symonds, P.M., 439, 479

Tapp, J., 469
Taylor, J.A., 461, 479
Tenezakis, M.D., 444, 471
Terrace, H.S., 68, 69, 479
Thompson, W.R., 394, 474
Thoreau, H.D., 80
Thorndike, E.L., 41, 50, 54-76, 80, 82, 90, 95, 107, 114, 127, 128, 160,

161, 162, 166, 170, 173, 174, 192, 201, 202, 205-206, 209, 213, 218, 226, 229-230, 252, 256, 319, 320, 321, 361, 389, 425, 426, 427, 428, 439, 460, 462, 463, 464, 479
Thorpe, W.H., 5, 479
Tinbergen, N., 5, 471
Titchener, E., 44, 48
Tolman, E.C., 49, 50, 56, 145, 147, 186, 236, 246, 252, 268, 284, 289-311, 314, 323, 326, 344, 353, 361, 383, 392, 428, 431-432, 434, 460, 463, 464, 479, 480
Tosenblatt, J.S., 471
Tursky, B., 418, 477

Underwood, B.J., 233-234, 480

Voeks, V.W., 219-220, 480

Wagner, A.R., 151, 178-179, 181, 183, 184, 185, 476, 480
Walter, W.G., 355, 480
Walters, G.C., 216, 480
Watson, J.B., 46-48, 53, 138, 189-190,

191, 199, 209, 243, 290, 291, 292, 294, 319, 320, 321, 352, 374, 389, 480, 481
Weaver, W., 355, 356, 477
Weimer, W.B., 35, 481
Wertheimer, Max, 243-244, 260-265, 481
Wertheimer, Michael, 260, 264, 481
Wettersten, J., 27, 432, 467
Whiting, J.W.M., 141, 477
Wiener, N., 354, 481
Wilcoxon, H.C., 187, 481
Williams, D.R., 117, 481
Williams, H., 117, 481
Wittrock, M.C., 467
Wolpe, J., 193-194, 481
Woodworth, R.S., 66, 366, 479, 481
Wundt, W., 44, 45, 53

Yerkes, R.M., 391, 392, 399, 481

Zeigarnik, B., 252
Zener, K., 175, 481
Zigler, E., 160
Zubek, J.P., 397, 481

SUBJECT INDEX